Signaling System No. 7 (SS7/C7):
Protocol, Architecture, and Services

Lee Dryburgh
Jeff Hewett

Cisco Press

800 East 96th Street
Indianapolis, IN 46240 USA

Signaling System No. 7 (SS7/C7):
Protocol, Architectures, and Services

Lee Dryburgh

Jeff Hewett

Copyright © 2005 Cisco Systems, Inc.

Published by:
Cisco Press
800 East 96th Street
Indianapolis, Indiana 46240 USA

Printed in the United States of America   2 3 4 5 6 7 8 9 0

Second Printing, February 2006

Library of Congress Cataloging-in-Publication Number: 2001090446

ISBN: 1-58705-040-4

Trademark Acknowledgments

Warning and Disclaimer

Corporate and Government Sales

Cisco Press offers excellent discounts on this book when ordered in quantity for bulk purchases or special sales. For more information, please contact:

U.S. Corporate and Government Sales: 1-800-382-3419   corpsales@pearsontechgroup.com

For sales outside of the U.S. please contact: international@pearsoned.com

Feedback Information

At Cisco Press, our goal is to create in-depth technical books of the highest quality and value. Each book is crafted with care and precision, undergoing rigorous development that involves the unique expertise of members of the professional technical community.

Reader feedback is a natural continuation of this process. If you have any comments about how we could improve the quality of this book or otherwise alter it to better suit your needs, you can contact us through e-mail at feedback@ciscopress.com. Please be sure to include the book title and ISBN in your message.

We greatly appreciate your assistance.

Publisher	John Wait
Editor-in-Chief	John Kane
Cisco Press Program Manager	Nanette M. Noble
Cisco Marketing Program Manager	Edie Quiroz
Acquisitions Editor	Amy Moss
Managing Editor	Patrick Kanouse
Development Editor	Jennifer Foster
Technical Editors	Franck Noel, Brad Dunsmore, Trevor Graham, Andreas Nikas, Jan Van Geel, Murry Gavin
Project Editor	Marc Fowler
Copy Editors	Bridget Collins, Gayle Johnson
Team Coordinator	Tammi Barnett
Book and Cover Designer	Louisa Adair
Production Team	Octal Publishing, Inc.
Indexers	Larry Sweazy
	Tim Wright

CISCO SYSTEMS

Corporate Headquarters
Cisco Systems, Inc.
170 West Tasman Drive
San Jose, CA 95134-1706
USA
www.cisco.com
Tel: 408 526-4000
     800 553-NETS (6387)
Fax: 408 526-4100

European Headquarters
Cisco Systems International BV
Haarlerbergpark
Haarlerbergweg 13-19
1101 CH Amsterdam
The Netherlands
www-europe.cisco.com
Tel: 31 0 20 357 1000
Fax: 31 0 20 357 1100

Americas Headquarters
Cisco Systems, Inc.
170 West Tasman Drive
San Jose, CA 95134-1706
USA
www.cisco.com
Tel: 408 526-7660
Fax: 408 527-0883

Asia Pacific Headquarters
Cisco Systems, Inc.
Capital Tower
168 Robinson Road
#22-01 to #29-01
Singapore 068912
www.cisco.com
Tel: +65 6317 7777
Fax: +65 6317 7799

Cisco Systems has more than 200 offices in the following countries and regions. Addresses, phone numbers, and fax numbers are listed on the
Cisco.com Web site at www.cisco.com/go/offices.

Argentina • Australia • Austria • Belgium • Brazil • Bulgaria • Canada • Chile • China PRC • Colombia • Costa Rica • Croatia • Czech Republic
Denmark • Dubai, UAE • Finland • France • Germany • Greece • Hong Kong SAR • Hungary • India • Indonesia • Ireland • Israel • Italy
Japan • Korea • Luxembourg • Malaysia • Mexico • The Netherlands • New Zealand • Norway • Peru • Philippines • Poland • Portugal
Puerto Rico • Romania • Russia • Saudi Arabia • Scotland • Singapore • Slovakia • Slovenia • South Africa • Spain • Sweden
Switzerland • Taiwan • Thailand • Turkey • Ukraine • United Kingdom • United States • Venezuela • Vietnam • Zimbabwe

About the Authors

Lee Dryburgh, BSc MIEE, is a specialist in SS7/C7 and the services it empowers. He provides training and consulting through his company, Bit Tech Limited. His entire career has focused on SS7/C7. He has uniquely tackled the subject from many career positions, including software engineering, testing, training, security auditing, and architectural design, in both fixed-line and cellular networks. He is a member of several professional telecommunications bodies and holds a degree in computer science. He is currently studying for an engineering doctorate at the University College of London. He can be reached at lsd@bittech.co.uk. He very much welcomes specific feedback about this book. Such comments can be addressed to him at book@c7.com.

Jeff Hewett is a technical leader at Cisco Systems and is currently working in Voice over IP software development for the Government Systems Business Unit. Having been involved with SS7 for more than 16 years, he has worked in SS7 software development, testing, and training. He is a patent holder in SS7-related software development and has written about SS7 in popular journals. He has provided a broad range of SS7 training for Regional Bell Operating Companies, independent operators, and telecommunications vendors dating back to the initial rollout of SS7 in the U.S. network. In recent years, Jeff has been involved with Operating System development and Voice over Packet solutions as an engineer in the Cisco Networked Solutions Integration Test Engineering (NSITE) lab. Prior to joining Cisco, he worked in SS7 and AIN software development for a major switching vendor. He holds degrees in science and engineering and computer information systems. You can contact him at jhewett@cisco.com.

About the Technical Reviewers

Franck Noel, CCNA, CCNP, CCIP, is a consulting systems engineer with Cisco Systems, Inc. He has been in the telecommunications industry for 13 years. Most recently he has focused on designing and deploying end-to-end packet-based integrated voice and data solutions for service provider customers. Before coming to Cisco, he was on the technical staff at AT&T Bell Labs, where he worked on switching and signaling and participated in the ITU/ANSI SS7 standards. He holds a master's degree in electrical engineering.

Brad Dunsmore is a new-product instructor in advanced services at Cisco Systems. He is responsible for designing and deploying new networks for his group. Currently he specializes in SS7 offload solutions, WAN communication, and network security. He holds a B.S. in management of information systems, and he has obtained industry certifications in MCSE+Internet, MCDBA, CCNP, CCDP, CCSP, INFOSEC, and CCSI. He recently passed his written exam for the R/S CCIE and is now working on his lab.

Trevor Graham is a seasoned professional with more than 10 years of experience in the telecommunications industry. During the last four years, he has been an interconnection consultant for Cisco Systems, focusing on the Cisco voice switching products. He is responsible for defining many of the signaling and functional requirements for the switching products that Cisco will introduce into new countries, regions, and operators. Before joining Cisco, he was European switching operations manager for a large, multinational telecommunications operator. He also owned an interconnect consultancy company that provided technical interconnection consultancy and SS7 testing services to telecom operators and vendors throughout Europe.

Andreas Nikas works for the Multiservice Voice Solutions team at Cisco Systems. He has held positions in Advanced Engineering Services (AES) and Solutions Support, all with Cisco Systems. He worked for more than four years with various signaling and switching platforms related to both voice and SS7, such as the SC 2200/PGW 2200. Previously he worked for Tekelec in the Network Switching Division as a First Office Application (FOA) and Technical Assistance Center (TAC) engineer for five years in support of the Eagle Signaling Transfer Point (STP). He also worked for the U.S. Air Force and the Department of Defense for eight years in the telecommunications field.

Murry Gavin graduated from West Liberty State College in 1971 with a bachelor's degree in electrical engineering. In the past, he has worked for Stomberg-Carlson during the development and deployment of it's first electronic common control central office; Nortel and Bell Northern Research in a variety of different positions during the development and deployment of their SP-1, DMS-10, and DMS-100 family of products; and Sprint PCS Technology and Integration Center during their nation-wide deployment of services. Murry currently works at NSITE (a Cisco affiliate) and is involved with building its VoIP lab. He has also been involved in Lawful Intercept and Land Mobile Radio projects. His hobbies include amateur radio, target shooting, and sailing.

Dedications

Lee Dryburgh: To Rhoda.

"If I have any beliefs about immortality, it is that certain dogs I have known will go to heaven, and very, very few persons." *James Thurber*

Jeff Hewett: To Janet, who is always there to encourage me.

Acknowledgments

Lee Dryburgh: Thanks to all of those at Cisco Press for their great support—in particular, John Kane, Amy Moss, and Dayna Isley. A big hello to all of those nice people at Cisco Systems who made me most welcome during my time there, especially Nigel Townley. A big thank you to the technical reviewers for their valuable input and enthusiasm. A big thank you to Ken Morneault of Cisco Systems for his valuable contribution toward the book, especially considering the circumstances. And finally, a big thank you to Tektronix for its products and support, and in particular, to Wayne Newitts, who has the unique ability to inject humor into any situation over any medium, not to mention a strange obsession with *Star Wars* and the battle between good and evil.

Jeff Hewett: As anyone who has undertaken the task knows, writing technical books is a difficult and time-consuming effort. My first acknowledgment must be to my wife Janet, who spent many evenings alone and never complained while I worked on writing material for this book. Many thanks to the people at Cisco Press for their patience and support throughout this endeavor. Also, thanks to Ken Morneault for his contribution on SIGTRAN, given such a tight schedule. I am also grateful for all of the valuable input from our technical reviewers. And finally, I'd like to say that it has been a great experience to work with the NSITE engineering group here at Cisco, with whom I shared my SS7 knowledge and from whom I gained knowledge about data networks from the best in the business.

Contents at a Glance

Table of Contents

Icons Used in This Book

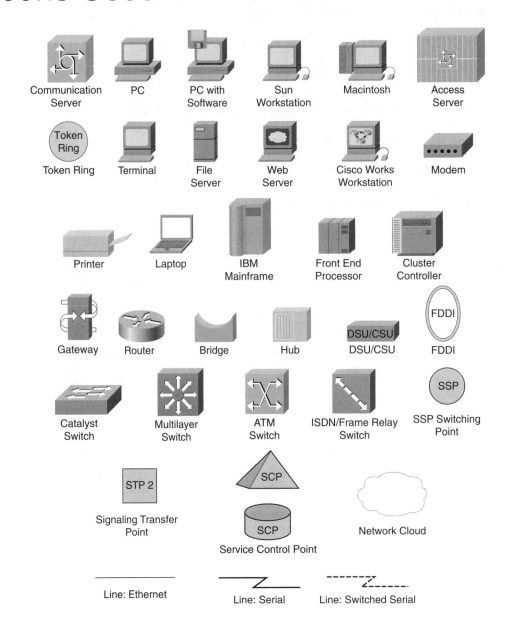

Communication Server

PC

PC with Software

Sun Workstation

Macintosh

Access Server

Token Ring

Terminal

File Server

Web Server

Cisco Works Workstation

Modem

Printer

Laptop

IBM Mainframe

Front End Processor

Cluster Controller

Gateway

Router

Bridge

Hub

DSU/CSU

FDDI

Catalyst Switch

Multilayer Switch

ATM Switch

ISDN/Frame Relay Switch

SSP Switching Point

Signaling Transfer Point

SCP

Service Control Point

Network Cloud

Line: Ethernet

Line: Serial

Line: Switched Serial

Command Syntax Conventions

The conventions used to present command syntax in this book are the same as the conventions used in the IOS Command Reference. The Command Reference describes these conventions as follows:

- Vertical bars (|) separate alternative, mutually exclusive elements.

- Square brackets ([ ]) indicate an optional element.

- Braces ({ }) indicate a required choice.

- Braces within brackets ([{ }]) indicate a required choice within an optional element.

- **Bold** indicates commands and keywords that are entered literally as shown. In actual configuration examples and output (not general command syntax), bold indicates commands that are manually input by the user (such as a **show** command).

- *Italic* indicates arguments for which you supply actual values.

Reference Information

The chapters in this book include references to a variety of supporting documents, such as ITU-T and ANSI standards. These supporting documents are listed in the "References" section at the end of the book. Each document in this section is numbered. The corresponding number appears in the chapter text.

Introduction

SS7/C7 is a signaling network and protocol that is used worldwide to bring telecommunications networks, both fixed-line and cellular, to life. Setting up phone calls, providing cellular roaming and messaging, and converged voice/data services, such as Internet Call Waiting, are only a few of the vast number of ways that SS7/C7 is used in the communications network. SS7/C7 is at the very heart of telecommunications, and as voice networks and data networks converge, SS7/C7 will provide the technology to bridge the gap between the two worlds. Anyone who is interested in telecommunications should have a solid understanding of SS7/C7. The convergence of voice and data has extended the need to understand this technology into the realm of those working with data networks.

Who Should Read This Book?

This book was written in such a way that those who have a general interest in communications and those who are heavily involved in SS7/C7 can benefit. Although many of the earlier chapters are interesting to those who require only introductory knowledge, many of the later chapters are more interesting to those who have a deeper interest and are already involved in telecommunications.

How This Book Is Organized

Those who are new to the world of telecommunications signaling should read Chapters 1 to 5 first, in sequence. Those who are already comfortable with telecommunications and signaling concepts can read particular chapters of interest. This book should prove the most valuable for those who already consider themselves experts in SS7/C7; in particular, attention should be given to the extensive appendixes.

Part I: Introductions and Overviews

Chapter 1: The Evolution of Signaling

This chapter introduces the concept of signaling. It is a great starting point for those who are unfamiliar with signaling or telecommunications in general. It introduces concepts and terminology that are used throughout the book.

Chapter 2: Standards

This chapter introduces the relevant standards and the bodies that are involved in creating them. It also provides some background on both the history of the standards and the bodies themselves. In addition, it introduces the concept of standards on different planes—national, regional, and international.

Chapter 3: The Role of SS7

This chapter is an excellent introduction to SS7/C7 and its relevance. Any reader can read it, regardless of background. Hopefully even those who are very knowledgeable in SS7/C7 will find this chapter interesting, because it lists the functions and services offered by SS7/C7 and explains its relevance in the daily lives of people across the globe.

Chapter 4: SS7 Network Architecture and Protocols Introduction

This chapter provides a technical overview of the SS7 protocol and network architecture. Those who are new to the subject will find it particularly interesting. It provides an introductory technical overview of SS7 in such a way that newcomers can assimilate subsequent chapters more effectively.

Chapter 5: The Public Switched Telephone Network (PSTN)

This chapter provides a brief overview of the Public Switched Telephone Network. It helps you understand SS7 in its native environment as the primary form of interoffice signaling in the PSTN. It also briefly introduces the PSTN's transition to the next-generation Voice Over Packet architecture.

Part II: Protocols Found in the Traditional SS7/C7 Stack

Chapter 6: Message Transfer Part 2 (MTP2)

This chapter examines the first protocol on top of the physical layer. It covers frame format, functions, and procedures—packet delineation, error correction, error detection, alignment, managing the signaling link, procedures for establishing a signaling link, flow control, and link error monitoring.

Chapter 7: Message Transfer Part 3 (MTP3)

This chapter covers the core concepts of how SS7 network nodes communicate with each other. It discusses network addressing and routing in detail, along with examples of how messages flow through an SS7 node. It also explains the numerous messages and procedures that MTP3 uses to maintain a healthy network.

Chapter 8: ISDN User Part (ISUP)

This chapter explains how the ISUP portion of the protocol is used to set up and tear down calls, provide trunk maintenance functions, and deliver supplementary services. It defines ISUP message structure as well as the most commonly used messages and parameters. The association between call processing at an SSP and the ISUP protocol is described, thereby helping you understand how an SS7-signaled call is processed at an SSP.

Chapter 9: Signaling Connection Control Part (SCCP)

This chapter looks at the enhanced functionality that the addition of this protocol brings—namely, application management, more flexible and powerful routing through the use of global titles, and mechanisms for transferring application data over the signaling network.

Chapter 10: Transaction Capabilities Application Part (TCAP)

This chapter describes the role of TCAP in providing a generic protocol mechanism for transferring information components between applications across the network. It helps you understand the key role TCAP plays in communication between SSP and SCP nodes. TCAP message formats and component definitions, including ITU and ANSI formats, are explained.

Part III: Service-Oriented Protocols

Chapter 11: Intelligent Networks (IN)

This chapter explains the concept of the Intelligent Network, how it has evolved, and how it is used to implement telecommunications services. It provides a detailed explanation of the IN call model and explains the parallels and differences between the ITU CS model and the North American AIN model. Several examples of IN services, such as toll-free calling and local number portability, are included to show how IN services are used.

Chapter 12: Cellular Networks

This chapter introduces GSM public land mobile networks (PLMNs) so that the following chapter can cover additional SS7 protocols used in cellular networks. It introduces cellular network entities, addressing, terminology, and concepts.

Chapter 13: GSM and ANSI-41 Mobile Application Part (MAP)

This chapter explains the operations and associated procedures that allow cellular subscribers to have mobility; this is the key functionality expected of a cellular network. Subscriber authentication, operations and maintenance, supplementary service, unstructured supplementary service (USS), and short message service (SMS) operations and procedures are also detailed.

Part IV: SS7/C7 Over IP

Chapter 14: SS7 in the Converged World

This chapter introduces the next-generation network architecture using media gateway controllers, media gateways, and signaling gateways. Its primary purpose is to provide an in-depth look at the Signaling Transport protocol (Sigtran), used between the media gateway controller and the signaling gateway. Sigtran is particularly interesting to those who are learning about SS7, because it provides a common signaling protocol interface between legacy SS7 networks and voice over IP networks.

Part V: Supplementary Topics

Chapter 15: SS7 Security and Monitoring

This chapter explains the need for SS7/C7 security practices. It describes the current means of providing security: traffic screening and monitoring. Details of providing traffic screening are supplied. Monitoring functionality and what should be monitored also are covered.

Chapter 16: SS7 Testing

This chapter explains the tools used for SS7/C7 protocol verification and how to create appropriate test specifications. It also outlines sample test cases for each protocol layer.

Part VI: Appendixes

Appendix A: MTP Messages (ANSI/ETSI/ITU)

This appendix lists all of the messages used by MTP3 for ANSI- and ITU-based networks. It also lists the message codes.

Appendix B: ISUP Messages (ANSI/UK/ETSI/ITU-T)

This appendix lists all of the messages used by ISUP for ANSI- and ITU-based networks. It also lists the message codes.

Appendix C: SCCP Messages (ANSI/ETSI/ITU-T)

This appendix lists all of the messages used by SCCP for ANSI- and ITU-based networks. It also lists the message codes.

Appendix D: TCAP Messages and Components

This appendix lists all of the messages and components used by MTP3 for ANSI- and ITU-based networks. It also lists the message codes.

Appendix E: ITU-T Q.931 Messages

Q.931 is the Layer 3 protocol of the subscriber signaling system that is used for ISDN, known as Digital Subscriber Signaling System No. 1 (DSS 1). It employs a message set that is made for interworking with SS7's ISUP. This appendix lists and describes the purpose of the Q.931 message set.

Appendix F: GSM and ANSI MAP Operations

This appendix lists the operations found in GSM MAP and their respective codes.

Appendix G: MTP Timers in ITU-T/ETSI/ANSI Applications

This appendix lists ANSI- and ITU-specified MTP timers.

Appendix H: ISUP Timers for ANSI/ETSI/ITU-T Applications

This appendix lists ANSI- and ITU-specified ISUP timers.

Appendix I: GSM Mobile Country Codes (MCC) and Mobile Network Codes (MNC)

This appendix lists all of the MCC codes and the respective MNCs found against the MCC.

Appendix J: ITU and ANSI Protocol Comparison

This appendix covers some of the main differences between ANSI and ITU (international).

Appendix K: SS7 Standards

This appendix presents the main SS7 standards alongside the respective standards body.

Appendix L: Tektronix Supporting Traffic

This appendix contains reference traffic caught on a Tektronix K1297 protocol analyzer.

Appendix M: Cause Values

Cause values, which are included as a field in each ISUP REL message, indicate why a call was released. This appendix lists and defines the ITU-T and ANSI cause values.

Introductions and Overviews

CHAPTER 1

The Evolution of Signaling

This chapter is intended to provide a sound introduction to the world of telecommunications signaling. It is particularly written for those readers who have little or no signaling knowledge. It provides a solid foundation to help you grasp signaling ideas, concepts, terminology, and methods. A strong foundation will provide the novice reader with a better understanding of the book's main topic: Signaling System No. 7. Today, Signaling System No. 7 is the most advanced and widely used signaling system for both cellular and fixed-line telecommunications networks.

This chapter covers the following topics:

- What signaling is and why it is relevant

- Overview of subscriber and network signaling

- The history of signaling and the development of the Public Switched Telephone Network (PSTN)

- Overview of the Channel Associated Signaling (CAS) method of signaling and its common implementations

- Overview of the Common Channel Signaling (CCS) method of signaling and its operational modes

- The limitations of CAS and CCS

Signaling System No. 7, known more commonly in North America as SS7 and elsewhere as C7, is both a network architecture and a series of protocols that provide telecommunications signaling. In order to begin studying SS7, you must first learn what telecommunications signaling is by studying its origins and purpose.

The ITU-T defines signaling as, [47] "The exchange of information (other than by speech) specifically concerned with the establishment, release and other control of calls, and network management, in automatic telecommunications operation."

In telecommunications, the network's components must indicate (that is, signal) certain information to each other to coordinate themselves for providing services. As such, the signaling network can be considered the telecommunications network's nervous system. It breathes life into the infrastructure. Richard Manterfield, author of *Telecommunications Signaling*, has stated this poetically [103]:

"Without signaling, networks would be inert and passive aggregates of components. Signaling is the bond that provides dynamism and animation, transforming inert components into a living, cohesive and powerful medium."

For example, if a subscriber wishes to place a call, the call must be signaled to the subscriber's local switch. The initial signal in this process is the off-hook condition the subscriber causes by lifting the handset. The action of lifting the handset signals to the network that the subscriber wishes to engage telephony services. The local switch should then acknowledge the request for telephony services by sending back a dial tone, which informs the subscriber that he can proceed to dial the called party number. The subscriber has a certain amount of time to respond to the dial tone by using the telephone keypad to signal the digits that comprise the called party number. The network signals that it is receiving the dialed digits with silence (as opposed to a dial tone).

Up to this point, the signaling is known as *subscriber signaling* and takes place between the subscriber and the local switch. Subscriber signaling is also known as *access signaling*. The "Subscriber Signaling" section of this chapter further describes subscriber signaling.

NOTE   The calling party is often referred to as the A party. Similarly, the called party is referred to as the B party.

When a complete called party number is received or enough digits are collected to allow the routing process to proceed, the calling party's local switch begins signaling to the other nodes that form part of the core network.

The signaling that takes place between core network nodes (and switches and, over the past two decades, databases) is known as network signaling.

NOTE   Switches are also known as exchanges; within the United States, the term exchange is used interchangeably with Central Office (CO) or End Office (EO).

Network signaling is also known as inter-switch signaling, network-network signaling, or trunk signaling.

The purpose of network signaling is to set up a circuit between the calling and called parties so that user traffic (voice, fax, and analog dial-up modem, for example) can be transported bi-directionally. When a circuit is reserved between both parties, the destination local switch places a ringing signal to alert the called party about the incoming call. This signal is classified as subscriber signaling because it travels between a switch (the called party's local switch) and a subscriber (the called party). A ringing indication tone is sent to the calling party telephone to signal that the telephone is ringing. If the called party wishes to engage the call, the subscriber lifts the handset into the off-hook condition. This moves the call from the set-up phase to the call phase.

At some point in the call phase, one of the parties will wish to terminate the call, thereby ending the call phase. The calling party typically initiates this final phase, which is known as the clear-down or release phase. The subscriber signals the network of the wish to terminate a call by placing the telephone back in the on-hook condition; hence, subscriber signaling. The local switch proceeds with network signaling to clear the call down. This places an expensive resource (the circuit) back to an idle condition, where it can be reserved for another call.

The previous high-level example relates to a basic telephone service call; that is, simple call setup and clear down. As you will discover, the signaling network can do far more than carry the digits you dial, release calls, notify the network that you went on or off-hook, and so forth. The signaling network can also translate toll-free numbers into "routable" numbers, validate credit and calling cards, provide billing information, remove faulty trunks from service, provide the support for supplementary services (such as caller ID), allow you to roam with your cellular telephone, and makes *local number portability (LNP)* possible. This list is by no means exhaustive; see Chapters 3, "The Role of SS7," and 11, "Intelligent Networks (IN)," for more example services.

The main function of signaling is still that of circuit supervision: setting up and clearing down circuits (that is, trunks). Traditionally, once a circuit was set up, no other signaling was performed apart from releasing the call; therefore, all calls were simple, basic telephone service calls. However, modern telephone networks can perform signaling while a call is in progress, especially for supplementary services—for example, to introduce another called party into the call, or to signal the arrival of another incoming call (call waiting) to one of the parties. In fact, since the 1980s, signaling can take place even when there is not a call in place. This is known as *non-circuit related signaling* and is simply used to transfer data between networks nodes. It is primarily used for query and response with telecommunications databases to support cellular networks, intelligent networks, and supplementary services. For example, in Public Land Mobile Networks (PLMNs), the visitor location register (VLR) that is in charge of the area into which the subscriber has roamed updates the home location register (HLR) of the subscriber's location. PLMNs make much use of non-circuit-related signaling, particularly to keep track of roaming subscribers. Chapter 13, "GSM and ANSI-41 Mobile Application Part (MAP)," covers this topic in more detail.

Network signaling is further described in the "Network Signaling" section of this chapter.

The History of Signaling

To appreciate signaling in today's network and its role in future networks, let's examine the history of signaling. The history of signaling has been inextricably linked to the history of telecommunications and, in particular, switching. As telecommunications advances, so do the signaling systems that support it.

1889–1976

The earliest telephone switches were manual; operators used a switchboard and wire cords to connect and disconnect all calls. The first manual exchange occurred in 1878 in New Haven, Connecticut. It was introduced to avoid the imminent problem of running wires from each telephone to every other telephone (a fully meshed topology). The first manual switch appeared in Great Britain in 1879. It was also within this same year that subscribers came to be called by numbers rather than by names. Within a decade of introducing the manual switch, the United States had 140,000 subscribers and a staggering 8000 exchanges— that is, a switch for every 17.5 subscribers!

A subscriber who was connected to a manual switch would crank a lever to electronically send an alerting signal that lit up a bulb on the operator's switchboard. The operator would then connect her telephone to the calling line, and ask for the called number. Next the operator would connect her telephone to the called line, where she would place a ringing signal. If the called party answered the call, the operator would establish the connection by plugging in a cord between the two terminal jacks on the switchboard. Figure 1-1 shows this process; on the switchboard, each terminal jack represents a subscriber.

Figure 1-1   *Simple Call Setup Via a Manual Operator with Automatic Equivalent*

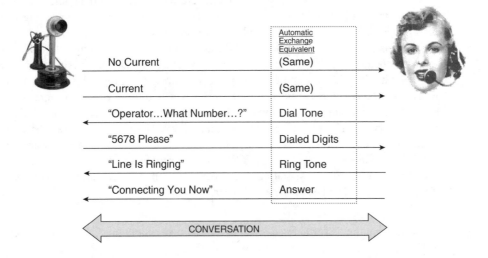

	Automatic Exchange Equivalent
No Current	(Same)
Current	(Same)
"Operator...What Number...?"	Dial Tone
"5678 Please"	Dialed Digits
"Line Is Ringing"	Ring Tone
"Connecting You Now"	Answer

CONVERSATION

Signaling, as we know it today, began around 1889 with the invention of the Strowger exchange (which was patented 1891). The Strowger exchange was an electromechanical device that provided automatic switching using the simple idea of two-motion selectors for establishing calls between two subscribers. It was also known as a step-by-step switch because it followed pre-wired switching stages from start to finish.

Inventing the Strowger Exchange

Almon B. Strowger was a schoolteacher and part-time undertaker. His reportedly constant feuds with manual switchboard operators inspired him to develop an automatic switching system and the dial telephone so he could bypass manual switchboard operators [102]. One reported feud concerned an alleged business loss resulting from the complete lack of privacy offered by a manual exchange. Strowger claimed that an operator at the new manual exchange in Connecticut had intentionally directed a call to a competitor—an allegation that gave rise to tales that the operator was either married to or was the daughter of a competing under- taker. Strowger moved from Topeka to Kansas City, where he hoped his new, larger funeral home would earn him his fortune. However, he suffered a similar fate there; he believed that the manual operators there were intentionally giving his customers a busy signal. Strowger therefore decided to do away with operators; he hired several electromechanical technicians, who created the first automatic exchange within a year. As a result, the telephone became faster, easier to use, and more private for everyone.

The first Strowger exchange in the United States opened in La Porte, Indiana in 1892 and had the switching capacity for ninety-nine lines. Lobby groups protested at the automatic exchange, and one lobby group championed the personalized service afforded by manual exchanges. The lobby group did not have much success, however; manual switchboards could not service the dramatic increase in telephone subscribers. By 1900 there were 1.4 million telephones in the United States.

In Great Britain, the first Strowger exchange opened at Epsom in Surrey in 1912. The last Strowger switch was not removed from the British Telecom (BT) service network until June 23, 1995, when it was removed from Crawford, Scotland.

Strowger sold his patents to his associates for $1,800 in 1896 and sold his share in the company for $10,000 in 1898. He died in 1902. In 1916, his patents were sold to Bell Systems for $2.5 million dollars.

Strowgers' dial telephone is considered the precursor of today's touch-tone phone. It had three buttons: one for hundreds, one for tens, and one for units. To call the number 322, the caller had to push the hundreds button three times, the tens button two times, and the units button two times.

In 1896 the Automatic Electric Company developed a rotary dial to generate the pulses. This method of transmitting the dialed digits became known as *pulse dialing* and was commonplace until the latter half of the twentieth century, when *tone dialing* became available. See "Address Signals" in the "Subscriber Signaling" section of this chapter for a discussion of pulse and touch-tone dialing. It is interesting to note that early users did not like the dial pulse handset because they felt they were doing the "telephone company's job."

Even in Great Britain in 1930, the majority of all local and long distance calls were still connected manually through an operator. But gradually, calls placed between subscribers served by the same local switch could be dialed without the help of an operator. Therefore, only subscriber signaling was required because an operator would perform any inter-switch signaling manually. In the decades that followed, it became possible to dial calls between subscribers who were served by nearby switches. Thus the requirement for network signaling was born. Most large U.S. cities had automatic exchanges by 1940.

Direct Distance Dialing (*DDD*) was introduced in the United States in the 1950s. DDD allowed national long distance calls to be placed without operator assistance, meaning that any switch in the United States could route signaling to any other switch in the country. *International Direct Distance Dialing* (IDDD) became possible in the 1960s, thus creating the requirement for signaling between international switches.

From 1889 to 1976, signaling had three main characteristics, which resulted because only basic telephone services were available [102]:

- Signaling was fairly simple. All that was required of the signaling system was the setting-up and releasing of circuits between two subscribers.

- Signaling was always circuit-related; that is, all signals related directly to the setting-up or clearing of circuits.

- There was a deterministic relationship, known as *Channel Associated Signaling (CAS)*, between the signaling and the voice traffic it controlled. The "Channel Associated Signaling" section of this chapter discusses CAS.

1976 to Present Day

Another form of signaling was introduced in 1976: *Common Channel Signaling* (CCS). The "Common Channel Signaling" section of this chapter further explains CSS.

CCS has been used to implement applications beyond the scope of basic telephone service, including Intelligent Networks (INs), supplementary services, and signaling in cellular mobile networks. As you will learn, SS7 is the modern day CCS system that is used for network signaling. As with any technical subject, signaling can be split into a number of classifications. The broadest classification is whether the signaling is subscriber or networked signaling. The following sections discuss these types of signaling.

Subscriber Signaling

Subscriber signaling takes place on the line between the subscribers and their local switch. Most subscribers are connected to their local switch by analog subscriber lines as opposed to a digital connection provided by an Integrated Services Digital Network (ISDN). As a result, subscriber signaling has evolved less rapidly than network signaling.

Subscriber signals can be broken down into the following four categories:

- Address Signals
- Supervisory Signals
- Tones and Announcements
- Ringing

Address Signals

Address signals represent the called party number's dialed digits. Address signaling occurs when the telephone is off-hook. For analog lines, address signaling is either conveyed by the dial pulse or Dual-Tone Multiple Frequency (DTMF) methods. Local switches can typically handle both types of address signaling, but the vast majority of subscribers now use Dual-Tone Multi Frequency (DTMF), also known as touch-tone.

The precursor to (DTMF) was dial pulse, which is also known as rotary dialing. In rotary dialing, the address signals are generated by a dial that interrupts the steady DC current at a sequence determined by the selected digit. The dial is rotated clockwise, according to the digit selected by the user. A spring is wound as the dial is turned; when the dial is subsequently released, the spring causes the dial to rotate back to its original resting position. Inside the dial, a governor device ensures a constant rate of return rotation, and a shaft on the governor turns a cam that opens and closes switch contact. The current flowing into the telephone handset is stopped when the switch contact is open, thereby creating a dial pulse. As the dial rotates, it opens and closes an electrical circuit.

The number of breaks in the string represents the digits: one break for value 1, two breaks for value 2, and so on (except for the value of 0, which is signaled using ten breaks). The nominal value for a break is 60 ms. The breaks are spaced with make intervals of nominally 40 ms. As shown in Figure 1-2, consecutive digits are separated by an inter-digit interval of a value greater than 300 ms.

Figure 1-2   *Dial Pulse Address Signals*

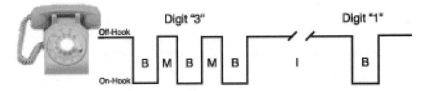

The rotary dial was designed for operating an electromechanical switching system; the speed of the dial's operation was approximately to match the switches' operating speed.

DTMF is a modern improvement on pulse dialing that first appeared during the 1960s and is now widespread. A DTMF signal is created using a pair of tones, each with a different frequency. It is much faster than the previous pulse method and can be used for signaling after call completion (for example, to operate electronic menu systems or activate supplementary services, such as a three-way call). The standard DTMF has two more buttons than dial pulse systems: the star (*) and the pound, or hash (#) buttons. These buttons are typically used in data services and customer-controlled features. The CCITT has standardized the DTMF frequency combinations, as shown in Table 1-1. For additional information regarding the CCITT, see Chapter 2, "Standards."

Table 1-1   *Tones Used to Create DTMF Signals*

	1209 Hz	1336 Hz	1477 Hz	1633 Hz
697 Hz	1	2	3	A
770 Hz	4	5	6	B
852 Hz	7	8	9	C
941 Hz	*	0	#	D

The fourth column (1633 Hz) has several special uses that are not found on regular telephones. The four extra digits were used on special handsets to designate the priority of calls on the Automatic Voice Network (AUTOVON), the U.S. military phone network that has since been replaced with the Defense Switched Network (DSN). In AUTOVON, the keys were called Flash, Immediate, Priority, and Routine (with variations) instead of ABCD. Telephone companies still use the extra keys on test handsets for specific testing purposes.

All modern telephone handsets support both DTMF and dial pulse. Because an electronic handset has buttons rather than a rotary dial, the numbers are temporally stored in the telephone memory to generate pulse dialing. The handset then transmits the dial pulses. This arrangement is sometimes known as *digipulse*.

Supervisory Signals

A telephone has two possible supervision states: *on-hook* or *off-hook*. On-hook is the condition in which the telephone is not in use, which is signaled when the telephone handset depresses the cradle switch. The term on-hook comes from the days when the receiver part of the telephone rested on a hook. The telephone enters the off-hook condition when the handset is lifted from its cradle, thereby releasing the cradle switch and signaling to the exchange that the subscriber wishes to place an outgoing call.

Residential systems worldwide use a change in electrical conditions, known as *loop start signaling*, to indicate supervision signals. The local switch provides a nominal –48 V direct current (DC) battery, which has the potential to flow through the subscriber line (between the local switch and the subscriber). When a telephone is off-hook, DC can flow in the subscriber line; when a telephone is on-hook a capacitor blocks the DC. The presence or absence of direct current in the subscriber's local switch line determines the telephone's supervision state. Loop start systems are adequate for residential use, but a problem known as *glare* makes loop start unacceptable in typical business applications in which private exchanges (PBXs) are used. PBXs use a system known as *ground start signaling*, particularly in North America.

Ground start systems combat glare by allowing the network to indicate off-hook (seizure) for incoming calls, regardless of the ringing signal. This reduces the probability of simultaneous seizure, or glare, from both ends. Ground start requires both ground and current detectors in customer premise equipment (CPE).

Tones and Announcements

Tones and announcements are audible backward signals, such as dial tone, ring back, and busy-tone, that are sent by a switch to the calling party to indicate a call's progress. Table 1-2 shows the call progress tones that are used in North America.

Table 1-2   *Call Progress Tones Used in North America*

Tone	Frequency (Hz)	On Time (Sec)	Off Time (Sec)
Dial	350+440	Continuous	
Busy	480+620	0.5	0.5
Ring back, Normal	440+480	2	4
Ring back, PBX	440+488	1	3
Congestion (Local)	480+620	0.3	0.2
Congestion (Toll)	480+620	0.2	0.3
Howler (Receiver wrongly off-hook)	1400+2060+2450+2600	0.1	0.1

Forward signals refer to signals that transfer in the direction of call establishment, or from the calling party to the called party. Backward signals refer to signals that transfer in the reverse direction.

Ringing

Ringing is a forward signal sent by the switch to the called subscriber to indicate the arrival of a call. It is known more specifically as power ringing to distinguish it from audible ringing, which is played to the calling party to alert him that the called party phone is ringing. Each country has a ringing pattern, which is known as the *cadence*. In North America the pattern is two seconds on, four seconds off.

Note that audible and power ringing are not synchronized. This is why, on a rare occasion, a caller is already on the line when you lift the handset. This situation generally causes confusion because the calling party, who has heard audible ringing, is unaware of the problem since the problem occurs because the caller's switch does not generate an independent ringing signal for each line. Instead, it generates one signal that is applied to whichever lines are to be played audible ringing. Therefore, if you have an incoming call, the switch must wait until the next on-cycle to ring your telephone. If you happen to pick up the telephone during the few off-cycle seconds and a call has just come in, you have answered a call before the exchange has had the opportunity to alert you of the incoming call. In North America, the silent period during which inbound calls cannot be announced is 3.9 seconds. Countries that use a short period of silence in the ringing cadence are less susceptible to this problem.

NOTE   If you are one of those people who say that you will call home and let the telephone ring twice when you get to your destination safely, note that you have no guarantee that the telephone will actually ring twice—or even ring at all. You might hear two rings, but that does not mean the called party will hear two, or even any, rings because their power ringing pattern might be in an off period.

The problems associated with the lack of synchronization between the calling and called party is typically addressed in North American non-residential systems (PBX systems) by using ground start rather than loop start. Other countries often employ a simple technique known as *ring splash*. With ring splash, a PBX issues a brief ringing tone within a few hundred milliseconds of the trunk being seized (the incoming call), after which normal ringing cadence resumes. The downside to this solution is that the ringing cadence sounds strange because it is not synchronized with the initial ring.

Network Signaling

As previously described, network signaling takes place between nodes in the core network. This is generally from the local switch, through the core network, and to the destination local switch—in other words, between the calling and the called party switch.

Figure 1-3 shows where subscriber and network signaling occur in the PSTN.

Figure 1-3   *Subscriber and Network Signaling*

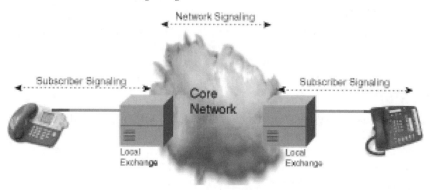

For obvious reasons, the signaling system employed on the local loop (between the subscriber and the local switch) differs from that which is used in the core network. The subscriber must only generate a limited number of signals: on or off hook, called party digits, and possibly a few commands for supplementary services. In comparison, a modern core network must perform very complex signaling, such as those to support database driven services like Local Number Portability (LNP), credit or calling card validation, and cellular roaming. Therefore, subscriber signaling systems are simple compared to modern network signaling systems.

Network signaling was previously implemented using *Channel Associated Signaling (CAS)* techniques and systems. However, for the past two decades, it has been replaced with *Common Channel Signaling (CCS)* systems. Apart from a rare trace of Signaling System No. 6 (SS6) signaling, System No. 7 (SS7) is almost the exclusive CSS system; thus, CCS can almost be taken to refer exclusively to the use of SS7. The remaining sections of this chapter discuss CAS and CCS methods.

Channel Associated Signaling

The key feature that distinguishes Channel Associated Signaling (CAS) from CCS is the deterministic relationship between the call-control signals and the bearers (voice circuits) they control in CAS systems. In other words, a dedicated fixed signaling capacity is set aside for each and every trunk in a fixed, pre-determined way.

Channel Associated Signaling (CAS) is often still used for international signaling; national systems in richer nations almost exclusively use Common Channel Signaling (CCS). CCS is replacing CAS on international interfaces.

CAS can be implemented using the following related systems:

- Bell Systems MF, R2, R1, and C5.
- Single-frequency (SF) in-band and out-of-band signaling
- Robbed bit signaling

The following sections discuss these methods in context with the type of signal, either address or supervisory.

Address Signals

Multifrequency systems, such as the Bell System MF, R2, R1, and C5, are all types of address signals used by CAS.

Multifrequency

The CAS system can be used on either analog Frequency Division Multiplexed (FDM) or digital Time Division Multiplexed (TDM) trunks. MF is used to signal the address digits between the switches.

Multifrequency (MF) signaling can still be found in traces within the United States, and it is still often found on international interfaces. On international interfaces outside of North America, MF is still used via the CCITT System 5 (C5) implementation. C5 is quite similar to Bell MF and was developed jointly by Bell Laboratories and the British Post Office [102]. R2 is the MF system that was deployed outside North America and is still used in less developed nations. R2 was developed by CEPT (which later became ETSI; see Chapter 2) and was previously known as Multifrequency Compelled (MFC) signaling. The CCITT later defined an international version; see Chapter 2 for additional information regarding the international version [102].

MF simultaneously sends two frequencies, from a choice of six, to convey an address signal. The switch indicates to the switch on the other end of a trunk that it wishes to transmit address digits by sending the KP (start pulsing) signal, and indicates the end of address digits by sending the ST (end pulsing) signal. The timing of MF signals is a nominal 60 ms, except for KP, which has a nominal duration of 100 ms. A nominal 60 ms should be between digits.

Table 1-3 shows the tone combinations for Bell System MF, R1, and C5. R2 tone combinations are not shown.

Table 1-3   *Tones Used to Create MF Signals*

Digit	Frequencies					
	700	**900**	**1100**	**1300**	**1500**	**1700**
1	+	+				
2	+		+			
3		+	+			
4	+			+		
5		+		+		
6			+	+		
7	+				+	
8		+			+	
9			+		+	
0				+	+	
KP			+			+
ST					+	+
11 (*)	+					+
12 (*)		+				+
KP2 (*)				+		+

* = Used only on CCITT System 5 (C5) for international calling.

As stated, many international trunks still use C5. Signal KP2 indicates that the number is an international number; by inference, KP indicates that the number is a national number. International operators also use codes 11 and 12. More details on C5 are available in ITU-T Q.152. Supervision signals for MF systems are performed on FDM trunks by the use of Single Frequency (SF), which we describe in the following section.

For circuit supervision, both Bell System MF and R1 use Single Frequency (SF) on FDM trunks and employ robbed bit signaling on TDM controlled trunks. C5 uses a different set of MF tones for supervisory signaling.

Supervisory Signals

Single frequency systems, robbed bit signaling, and digital signaling are all types of *supervisory signals* used by CAS.

Single Frequency(SF)

Single Frequency (SF) was used for supervisory signaling in analog CAS-based systems. North America used a frequency of 2600 Hz (1600 Hz was previously used), and Great Britain used 2280 Hz (as defined in British Telecom's SSAC15 signaling specification). When in an on-hook state, the tone is present; when in an off-hook state, the tone is dropped.

NOTE   Supervisory signals operate similarly to those used in access signaling; however, they signal the trunk state between two switches rather than the intention to place or terminate a call. Supervisory signals are also known as line signals.

Table 1-4 details the tone transitions Bell System MF and R1 use to indicate the supervision signals. C5 uses a combination of both one and two in-band signaling tones, which are not presented here.

Table 1-4   *Bell System MF and R1 Supervision Signaling*

Direction	Signal Type	Transition
Forward	Seizure	On-hook to off-hook
Forward	Clear-forward	Off-hook to on-hook
Backward	Answer	On-hook to off-hook
Backward	Clear-back	Off-hook to on-hook
Backward	Proceed-to-send (wink)	Off-hook pulse, 120–290 ms

As with the MF address signaling, SF is sent switch to switch. A trunk is initially on-hook at both ends. One of the switches sends a forward off-hook (seizure) to reserve a trunk. The receiving switch indicates that it is ready to receive address digits, (after connecting a digit received by the line by sending a wink signal. When the originating switch receives the wink signal, it transmits the digits of the called party number. When a call is answered, the called parties switch sends an off-hook signal (answer). During the conversation phase, both ends at each trunk are off-hook. If the calling a party clears the call, it sends a clear-forward signal; likewise, when the called party hangs up, it sends a clear-backward signal.

SF uses an *in-band* tone. In-band systems send the signaling information within the user's voice frequency range (300 Hz to 3400 Hz). A major problem with in-band supervisory signaling, however, is its susceptibility to fraud. The hacker quarterly magazine "2600" was named for the infamous 2600 Hz tone, which could be used by the public to trick the phone system into giving out free calls. The subscriber could send supervisory tone sequences down his telephone's mouthpiece using a handheld tone generator. This enabled the subscriber to instruct switches and, in doing so, illegally place free telephone calls.

The other major problem with in-band signaling is its contention with user traffic (speech). Because they share the same frequency bandwidth, only signaling or user traffic can be present at any one time. Therefore, in-band signaling is restricted to setting up and clearing calls down only because signaling is not possible once a call is in progress.

Subscriber Line Signaling

A regular subscriber line (that is analog) still uses in-band access signaling. For example, DTMF is used to signal the dialed digits and the frequencies used are within the voice band (see Table 1-1). You can prove that DTMF uses in-band signaling by using a device, such as a computer, to generate the tones for each digit (with correct pauses). Simply play the tones from the computer speaker down the mouthpiece of a touch-tone telephone. This allows you to dial a number without using the telephone keypad. Because the signaling is sent down the mouthpiece, you can be certain that it traveled within the user's voice frequency range.

FDM analog systems nearly always reserve up to 4000 Hz for each circuit, but only use 300–3400 Hz for speech; therefore, signaling is sent above the 3400 Hz (and below 4000 Hz). This is known as out-of-band signaling and is used in R2 for supervisory signaling. Unlike with in-band signaling, no contention exists between user traffic and signaling. North America uses a frequency of 3700 Hz, and CCITT (international) uses 3825 Hz. Table 1-5 details the tone transitions that indicate the supervision signals used in R2 and R1.

Table 1-5   *R2 Supervision Signaling*

Direction	Signal Type	Transition
Forward	Seizure	Tone-on to tone-off
Forward	Clear-forward	Tone-off to tone-on
Backward	Answer	Tone-on to tone-off
Backward	Clear-back	Tone-off to tone-on
Backward	Release-guard	450 ms tone-off pulse
Backward	Blocking	Tone-on to tone-off

R2 does not use a proceed-to-send signal; instead, it includes a blocking signal to stop the circuit that is being seized while maintenance work is performed on the trunk. The release guard signal indicates that the trunk has been released after a clear-forward signaling, thereby indicating that the trunk can be used for another call.

Digital

Supervisory signaling can be performed for R2 on digital TDM trunks. On an E1 facility, timeslot 16 is set aside for supervisory signaling bits (TS16). These bits are arranged in a multiframe structure so that specific bits in the multiframe's specific frames represent the signaling information for a given TDM audio channel. See Chapter 5, "The Public Switched Telephone Network (PSTN)," for explanation of facilities and timeslots.

Limitations of CAS

We discuss the general disadvantages of CAS for the purpose of reinforcing the concepts and principles we have introduced thus far. CAS has a number of limitations, including:

- Susceptibility to fraud
- Limited signaling states
- Poor resource usage/allocation

The following sections discuss these limitations in more detail.

Susceptibility to Fraud

CAS employing in-band supervisory signaling is extremely susceptible to fraud because the subscriber can generate these signals by simply using a tone generator down a handset mouthpiece. This type of device is known as a *blue box*; from the beginning of the 1970s, it could be purchased as a small, handheld keypad. Blue box software was available for the personal computer by the beginning of the 1980s.

Limited Signaling Information

CAS is limited by the amount of information that can be signaled using the voice channel. Because only a small portion of the voice band is used for signaling, often CAS cannot meet the requirements of today's modern networks, which require much higher bandwidth signaling.

Inefficient Use of Resources

CAS systems are inefficient because they require either continuous signaling or, in the case of digital CAS, at regular intervals even without new signals.

In addition, there is contention between voice and signaling with in-band CAS. As a result, signaling is limited to call set-up and release phases only. This means that signaling cannot take place during the call connection phase, severely imposing technological limits on the system's complexity and usefulness.

Common Channel Signaling (CCS)

CCS refers to the situation in which the signaling capacity is provided in a common pool, with the capacity being used as and when necessary. The signaling channel can usually carry signaling information for thousands of traffic circuits.

In North America, signaling can be placed on its own T1 carrier even though it only takes up one timeslot. This means that two physical networks, "speech" and "signaling," can have different routings. (Please refer to Chapter 5 for a description of carriers and timeslots.) Alternatively, the signaling might exist on a carrier with other user traffic, depending on the network operator.

Outside of North America, the signaling is placed in its own timeslot on an E1 (that is, logically rather than physically separated). The other timeslots on E1 are for user traffic—apart from TS0, which is used for synchronization. E1 systems tend to use the TS16 timeslot for signaling; some core network equipment ignores TS16, expecting it to be used for signaling traffic because it has historically been the timeslot for digital CAS signaling.

The only CCS systems that have been implemented to date are Signaling Systems No. 6 and No. 7 (SS6 and SS7). The ITU for the international network originally standardized SS6, but they saw limited deployment. AT&T nationalized SS6 for the North American network and called it Common Channel Interoffice Signaling (CCIS) No. 6. SS6 saw a limited deployment after the mid-1970s because it had far less bandwidth and a much smaller packet size than SS7. In addition, its evolutionary potential was severely limited because it was not a layered protocol architecture.

CCS systems are packet-based, transferring over 200 bytes in a single SS7 packet, as opposed to a few bits allocated to act as indicators in digital CAS. The signaling information is transferred by means of *messages*, which is a block of information that is divided into fields that define a certain parameter or further sub-field. The signaling system's specifications (Recommendations and Standards) define the structure of a message, including its fields and parameters.

Because CCS is packet-based and there is not a rigid tie between the signaling and the circuits it controls, it can operate in two distinct ways. These two distinct ways are circuit-related signaling and non-circuit-related signaling.

Circuit-Related Signaling

Circuit-related signaling refers to the original functionality of signaling, which is to establish, supervise, and release trunks. In other words, it is used to set up, manage, and clear down basic telephone service calls. Circuit-related signaling remains the most common mode of signaling. As it is with CAS, signaling capacity is not pre-allocated for each traffic circuit. Rather, it is allocated as it is required. Each signaling message is related to a traffic circuit. Because no dedicated relationship exists between the circuits and the signaling, it is necessary to identify the traffic circuit to which a particular signal message refers. This is achieved by including a circuit reference field in each signaling message.

Non-Circuit-Related Signaling

Non-circuit-related signaling refers to signaling that is not related to the establishment, supervision, and release of trunks. Due to the advent of supplementary services and the need for database communication in cellular networks and Intelligent Networks, for example, signaling is no longer exclusively for simply setting up, managing, and clearing down traffic circuits. Non-circuit-related signaling allows the transfer of information that is not related to a particular circuit, typically for the purpose of transmitting both the query and response to and from telecommunication databases. Non-circuit-related signaling provides a means for transferring data freely between network entities without the constraint of being related to the control of traffic circuits.

Common Channel Signaling Modes

A signaling mode refers to the relationship between the traffic and the signaling path. Because CCS does not employ a fixed, deterministic relationship between the traffic circuits and the signaling, there is a great deal of scope for the two to have differing relationships to each other. These differing relationships are known as *signaling modes*.

There are three types of CCS signaling modes:

- Associated
- Quasi-associated
- Non-associated

SS7 runs in associated or quasi-associated mode, but not in non-associated mode. Associated and quasi-associated signaling modes ensure sequential delivery, while non-associated does not. SS7 does not run in non-associated mode because it does not have procedures for reordering out-of-sequence messages.

Associated Signaling

In *associated* mode, both the signaling and the corresponding user traffic take the same route through the network. Networks that employ only associated mode are easier to design and maintain; however, they are less economic, except in small-sized networks. Associated mode requires every network switch to have signaling links to every other interconnected switch (this is known as a fully meshed network design). Usually a minimum of two signaling links are employed for redundancy, even though the switched traffic between two interconnected switches might not justify such expensive provisioning. Associated signaling mode is the common means of implementation outside of North America. Figure 1-4 illustrates the associated concept.

Figure 1-4   *Associated Mode*

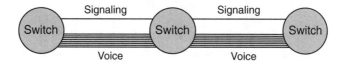

Quasi-Associated Signaling

In *quasi-associated* mode, signaling follows a different route than the switched traffic to which it refers, requiring the signaling to traverse at least one intermediate node. Quasi-associated networks tend to make better use of the signaling links; however, it also tends to create a more complex network in which failures have more potential to be catastrophic.

Quasi-associated signaling can be the most economical way of signaling for lightly loaded routes because it avoids the need for direct links. The signaling is routed through one or more intermediate nodes. Signaling packets arrive in sequence using quasi-associated signaling because the path is fixed for a given call (or database transaction) at the start of a call (or transaction). Figure 1-5 shows the quasi-associated signaling mode, which is the common means of implementation within North America.

Figure 1-5   *Quasi-Associated Mode*

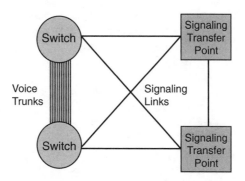

Non-Associated Signaling

Because the path is not fixed at a given point in time in *non-associated* mode, the signaling has many possible routes through the network for a given call or transaction. Therefore, the packets might arrive out of sequence because different routes might have been traversed.

SS7 does not run in non-associated mode because no procedures exist for reordering out-of-sequence messages. Associated and quasi-associated signaling modes assure sequential delivery, while non-associated signaling does not. Quasi-associated mode is a limited case of non-associated mode, in which the relative path is fixed.

Summary

CCS has evolved to address the limitations of the CAS signaling method. CCS has the following advantages over CAS:

- Much faster call set-up time
- Greater flexibility
- Capacity to evolve
- More cost effective than CAS
- Greater call control

Most CCS calls can be set up in half the time it takes to set up CAS calls. CCS achieves greater call control because no contention exists between signaling and user traffic as it does with in-band CAS. Because the subscriber cannot generate particular signals intended for inter-switch (core network) signaling, CCS offers a greater degree of protection against fraud than analog CAS methods.

CCS has the following disadvantages in comparison to CAS:

- CCS links can be a single point of failure—a single link can control thousands of voice circuits, so if a link fails and no alternative routes are found, thousands of calls could be lost.
- There is no inherent testing of speech path by call set-up signaling, so elaborate Continuity Test procedures are required.

CHAPTER 2

Standards

Standards are documents containing agreements reached by standards bodies responsible for that particular area of telecommunications. They are the result of study, discussion, and analysis. Standards may be endorsed at different levels—company, national, regional, and international—as appropriate. This chapter provides an overview of the organizations that set Signaling System No. 7 (SS7) standards at the national, regional, and international levels.

The standards process works through agreement among relevant experts from across a spectrum of private and public sectors. These experts debate, contribute views, and investigate, often with a multitiered political backdrop, to arrive at an agreed-upon specification. The process of getting a consensus from different experts after working through the technical issues almost always leads to a better specification in comparison to one developed by a single vendor or government department. A consensus-based specification takes longer to produce than a single-party specification approach because of the time-consuming nature of multiparty discussions. Although the process might be somewhat slower, it leads to a superior specification that will be supported by a wide base of manufacturers—bringing with it interoperability.

The fact that Internet, wireless, and fixed-line standards are all being addressed by the SS7/C7 standards bodies is a sign of the central role that SS7/C7 plays in the convergence of today's voice and data networks. Until the early 1990s, largely separate worlds existed for telecommunications standards and for Internet standards. These two worlds are now intersecting, creating the need for additional standards to address new architectures, protocols, and features.

Test specifications are used to facilitate the standards process by helping validate that equipment conforms to the documented standard(s). Testing is normally performed by an independent organization. Quite often this happens to be a department of an incumbent or private company that has been spun off. C7/SS7 testing is discussed in Chapter 16, "SS7 Testing."

This chapter begins with a historical outline of the development of international telephony standards. It then details the standards bodies, beginning at the international level, moving into the regional level, and finishing at the national level.

History of International Telephony Standards

Electric telegraphy became available to the general public in the late 1850s. But messages could not electrically cross national borders because each country used different coding systems. Messages had to be handed over at frontiers after someone transcribed and translated them. The messages then had to be retransmitted in the telegraph network of the neighboring country. Because of the overhead and the bottleneck created by this cumbersome way of working, many countries decided to make arrangements to aid the interconnection of their national networks. These arrangements were managed on a national level, meaning that countries often ended up having a huge number of separate agreements, depending on how many frontier localities they had on their borders. Because of the complexity of these arrangements, countries began making bilateral or regional agreements to simplify matters. But again, because of rapid expansion, a large number of bilateral or regional agreements had come into existence by 1864.

For the first time, 20 European countries were forced to develop a framework for international interconnection. This framework entailed uniform operating instructions, tariff and accounting rules, and common rules to standardize equipment to facilitate an international interconnection. It was published in 1865 and was known as the International Telegraph Convention. The International Telegraph Union (ITU) was established to facilitate subsequent amendments to this initial agreement. Ten years later, because of the invention and rapid deployment of telephony services, the ITU began recommending legislation governing the use of telephony.

By 1927 there were subcommittees known as the Consultative Committee for International Radio (CCIR), the Consultative Committee for International Telephone (CCIF), and the Consultative Committee for International Telegraph (CCIT).

In 1934 the International Telegraph Union changed its name to the present-day meaning— the ITU. By this time the ITU covered all forms of wireline and wireless communication.

In 1947 the ITU became a United Nations (UN) specialized agency. It has always operated from Geneva, Switzerland. The UN is responsible for worldwide telecommunications standardization. The ITU functions to this day under the auspices of the UN. Historically, nearly all national networks have been run by government-operated agencies (the "incumbents")—hence, the placement of the ITU within the UN.

In 1956 the CCIF and CCIT were combined and became the CCITT—the Consultative Committee for International Telegraph and Telephone.

When telecommunication networks were government monopolies, the ITU could have been considered the Parliament of monopoly telecommunications carriers. But during the 1980s, competition began to be seen in some countries following market deregulation. This is still putting pressure on the ITU to change and adapt.

In 1992 the ITU was dramatically remodeled with the aim of giving it greater flexibility to adapt to today's increasingly complex, interactive, and competitive environment. It was split into three sectors corresponding to its three main areas of activity: telecommunication standardization (ITU-T), radio communication (ITU-R), and telecommunication development (ITU-D). The CCITT that had been established in 1956 as part of the ITU ceased to exist and became the ITU-T.

The ITU-T continues to refine and develop international standards for SS7 protocols, intelligent networks, and bearer/signaling transport over IP.

ITU-T (Formerly CCITT) International Standards

The ITU has been creating worldwide telephony standards since the invention of the telephone network. It is the international standards body for the telecom industry worldwide. The ITU first appeared in 1865 when it produced the first cross-country telegraphy standards. Membership in the ITU is open to all governments that belong to the UN; these are called *member states*. Equipment vendors, telecommunication research institutions, and regional telecommunication organizations can now also hold membership; they are called *sector members*. For example, Cisco Systems and the European Telecommunications Standards Institute (ETSI) are vendor and regional organization sector members. Members are required to pay a membership fee.

The CCITT had a fixed four-year study period in which to publish standards, which it called *recommendations*. The term *recommendation* reflects the fact that member states do not have to adopt them, although they are proposed as an international standard. The industry, however, views them as standards. With the role of government diminishing, it makes even greater sense as time goes by to view the recommendations as standards. Recommendations are available for a fee.

If a recommendation was ready before the end of the four-year period, it could not be endorsed until it was approved by the CCITT at the end of the four-year period at a formal meeting (plenary assembly meeting). After being endorsed, the recommendations were published en bloc in sets. The covers were a different color for every study period. For example, Blue Book refers to the 1988 recommendations, and Red Book refers to the 1984 recommendations.

A fresh set of standards every four years did not fare well in the accelerating telecommunications industry. When the CCITT was rebranded the International Telecommunication Union Telecommunication Standardization Sector (ITU-T) in 1992, the notion of a fixed four-year period was dropped. Instead, the study groups were given greater autonomy so that they could approve their recommendations themselves without having to wait for a full ITU meeting at the end of every four years. The last issue of the "CCITT colored books" was the Blue Book (1988). From 1992 onward, the recommendations were published in separate booklets and weren't grouped for publishing en bloc every four years (at the end of every study period). Because the ITU-T recommendations had no cover color as they had under the CCITT, people have referred to them as "White Book" editions. Therefore, references to White Books implies separate booklets and not grouped books.

This book is primarily focused on ITU-T international standards and the North American American National Standards Institute (ANSI) regional standards. The C7 protocols are covered in the ITU Q series of recommendations, switching and signaling—specifically, the Q.7xx series—because these specifications are concerned with what we may now, in hindsight, call the core/traditional C7 protocols. Table 2-1 lists the ITU Q.7xx series.

Table 2-1   *ITU Core/Traditional C7 Recommendations*

Recommendation	Title
Q.700	Introduction to CCITT SS7
Q.701	Functional description of the message transfer part (MTP) of SS7
Q.702	Signaling data link
Q.703	Signaling link
Q.704	Signaling network functions and messages
Q.705	Signaling network structure
Q.706	Message transfer part signaling performance
Q.707	Testing and maintenance
Q.708	Assignment procedures for international signaling point codes
Q.709	Hypothetical signaling reference connection
Q.710	Simplified MTP version for small systems
Q.711	Functional description of the signaling connection control part
Q.712	Definition and function of signaling connection control part messages
Q.713	Signaling connection control part formats and codes
Q.714	Signaling connection control part procedures
Q.715	Signaling connection control part user guide
Q.716	SS7—Signaling connection control part (SCCP) performance
Q.721	Functional description of the SS7 Telephone User Part (TUP)
Q.722	General function of telephone messages and signals
Q.723	Telephone user part formats and codes
Q.724	Telephone user part signaling procedures
Q.725	Signaling performance in the telephone application
Q.730	ISDN user part supplementary services
Q.731.1	Direct dialing in (DDI)

Table 2-1   *ITU Core/Traditional C7 Recommendations (Continued)*

Recommendation	Title
Q.731.3	Calling line identification presentation (CLIP)
Q.731.4	Calling line identification restriction (CLIR)
Q.731.5	Connected line identification presentation (COLP)
Q.731.6	Connected line identification restriction (COLR)
Q.731.7	Malicious call identification (MCID)
Q.731.8	Subaddressing (SUB)
Q.732.2	Call diversion services
Q.732.7	Explicit Call Transfer
Q.733.1	Call waiting (CW)
Q.733.2	Call hold (HOLD)
Q.733.3	Completion of calls to busy subscriber (CCBS)
Q.733.4	Terminal portability (TP)
Q.733.5	Completion of calls on no reply
Q.734.1	Conference calling
Q.734.2	Three-party service
Q.735.1	Closed user group (CUG)
Q.735.3	Multilevel precedence and preemption
Q.735.6	Global Virtual Network Service (GVNS)
Q.736.1	International Telecommunication Charge Card (ITCC)
Q.736.3	Reverse charging (REV)
Q.737.1	User-to-user signaling (UUS)
Q.741	SS7—Data user part
Q.750	Overview of SS7 management
Q.751.1	Network element management information model for the Message Transfer Part (MTP)
Q.751.2	Network element management information model for the Signaling Connection Control Part
Q.751.3	Network element information model for MTP accounting
Q.751.4	Network element information model for SCCP accounting and accounting verification

continues

Table 2-1   *ITU Core/Traditional C7 Recommendations (Continued)*

Recommendation	Title
Q.752	Monitoring and measurements for SS7 networks
Q.753	SS7 management functions MRVT, SRVT, CVT, and definition of the OMASE-user
Q.754	SS7 management Application Service Element (ASE) definitions
Q.755	SS7 protocol tests
Q.755.1	MTP Protocol Tester
Q.755.2	Transaction capabilities test responder
Q.756	Guidebook to Operations, Maintenance, and Administration Part (OMAP)
Q.761	SS7—ISDN User Part functional description
Q.762	SS7—ISDN User Part general functions of messages and signals
Q.763	SS7—ISDN User Part formats and codes
Q.764	SS7—ISDN User Part signaling procedures
Q.765	SS7—Application transport mechanism
Q.765bis	SS7—Application Transport Mechanism: Test Suite Structure and Test Purposes (TSS & TP)
Q.765.1bis	Abstract test suite for the APM support of VPN applications
Q.765.1	SS7—Application transport mechanism: Support of VPN applications with PSS1 information flows
Q.765.4	SS7—Application transport mechanism: Support of the generic addressing and transport protocol
Q.765.5	SS7—Application transport mechanism: Bearer Independent Call Control (BICC)
Q.766	Performance objectives in the integrated services digital network application
Q.767	Application of the ISDN user part of CCITT SS7 for international ISDN interconnections
Q.768	Signaling interface between an international switching center and an ISDN satellite subnetwork
Q.769.1	SS7—ISDN user part enhancements for the support of number portability
Q.771	Functional description of transaction capabilities
Q.772	Transaction capabilities information element definitions
Q.773	Transaction capabilities formats and encoding
Q.774	Transaction capabilities procedures

Table 2-1   *ITU Core/Traditional C7 Recommendations (Continued)*

Recommendation	Title
Q.775	Guidelines for using transaction capabilities
Q.780	SS7 test specification—General description
Q.781	MTP level 2 test specification
Q.782	MTP level 3 test specification
Q.783	TUP test specification
Q.784	TTCN version of Recommendation Q.784
Q.784.1	Validation and compatibility for ISUP '92 and Q.767 protocols
Q.784.2	Abstract test suite for ISUP '92 basic call control procedures
Q.784.3	ISUP '97 basic call control procedures—TSS & TP
Q.785	ISUP protocol test specification for supplementary services
Q.785.2	ISUP '97 supplementary services—TSS & TP
Q.786	SCCP test specification
Q.787	Transaction Capabilities (TC) test specification
Q.788	User network interface-to-user network interface compatibility test specifications for ISDN, non-ISDN, and undetermined accesses interworking over international ISUP
Q.795	OMAP

Within the ITU-T, Study Group 11 (SG11) is responsible for signaling recommendations. The output from SG11 (recommendations), in addition to setting a standard for the global level, also serves as the basis for study at regional, national, and industry levels. SG11 is also responsible for signaling protocols for ISDN (narrowband and broadband), network intelligence, mobility, and signaling transport mechanisms.

NOTE   ITU-T specifies C7 protocol recommendations for use at two levels—international and national. There is a lot of confusion surrounding this point in many published texts and other sources such as websites.

The recommendations to be used on the international level must be implemented without adaptation on the international interface in every country that wants to connect internationally using C7. For example, one of the call control protocols used on the international level is ISDN User Part (ISUP), as specified in Q.767 [81]. Each country that wants to connect to the international level using ISUP must conform to this specification.

However, ITU-T recommendations to be used at the national level have nationalization options and coding space that can be tailored to each country's needs. As such, each country follows the ITU-T recommendations by selecting the options it requires and by using the coding space to code additional messages or parameters that are required (if any). The hundreds of names of protocols simply reflect the name given to each nationalized ITU-T recommendation. For example, UK ISUP, Finnish ISUP, Swedish ISUP, and the other hundred or so ISUPs all relate to documents specifying the nationalization of the ITU-T ISUP recommendations (Q.761 through Q.764 [75–78]) for each of these countries.

This means that each country runs two sets of protocols—one for international signaling, implemented at each country's international node, and one implemented at a national node. It should be clear that an international node requires both protocol implementations—one to speak intercountry using the international signaling standard (for example, international ISUP Q.767), and one to speak intracountry using the nationalized protocol following the ITU-T recommendations to be used on a national level (for example, ISUP Q.761 through Q.764). This is shown in Figure 2-1.

Figure 2-1   *National and International Signaling Networks Exist at Different Hierarchical Levels*

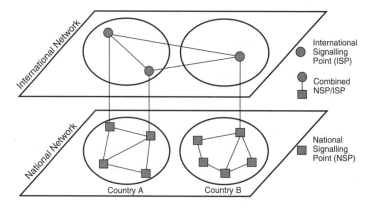

For example, in Great Britain, UK ISUP [41] may be used for call-control signaling. But if an international call is placed, and C7 is to be used for international signaling (as opposed to C5, for example), the international component of the call uses international ISUP (ITU-T Q.767 [81]) for signaling. If the called country is Sweden, for example, Sweden's international switch converts the incoming international signaling into its national signaling standard, Swedish ISUP.

The ITU-T creates a recommendation with coding space and options for countries to select from. National standards are then formulated from these recommendations with the options and extensions deemed necessary by each country. Some countries—namely, Japan, China, and North America—use national standards that extend beyond the ITU national framework in certain areas, such as node address ranges (point codes). This does not cause a problem for international interoperability, because ITU international signaling is used on the international side, and national signaling (such as ANSI in North America) is used on the national side.

Confusion surrounding ITU-T standards sometimes arises because of the two meanings of "international" in relation to ITU-T C7 standards. "International" is used in the context of ITU-T C7 standards to mean unmodified over international interfaces (international gateways, such as international switches). "International" is also used to express the fact that there are ITU-T C7 standards to be implemented worldwide on a national level. When "nationalized," they are renamed, such as UK ISUP.

This process of "nationalizing" ITU-T standards is carried out by each country's national standards body or by the national operator where telecommunications is a government monopoly. For example, in the UK, the British Standards Institute (BSI) is responsible for the ongoing revision of the UK's C7 implementation. In North America, ANSI has the same responsibility. "Nationalization" is the process of specifying a profile that makes choices from the many offered by the ITU-T recommendation based on national preferences, government regulations, and so on. However, Japan, China, and North America have extended the ITU-T recommendations beyond a simple profile (delta document) to meet the needs of their national networks.

Apart from the core C7 protocols to be used at the international and national levels, the ITU-T has also had the role of developing other recommendations relating to signaling. This includes the international Intelligent Network (IN) standards, international ISDN standards, and third-generation (3G) technologies.

It should be clear that the ITU definition of C7 allows for national variants, such as those already mentioned as well as regional standards, such as the ETSI standard used in Europe. The regional standards used in North America produced by ANSI and Telcordia (formerly Bellcore) are within the basic framework of the ITU-T recommendations, but they have adaptations outside the nationalization framework.

Regional Standards

North America, Europe, and Japan play a major role in the ITU-T and also set their own regional standards based on the ITU-T recommendations.

ETSI

ETSI is a nonprofit organization responsible for setting standards for telecommunications systems in Europe. ETSI was set up by the CEC (Commission of the European Communities). ETSI is an open forum that unites 728 members from 51 countries, representing administrations, network operators, manufacturers, service providers, and users. Any European organization proving an interest in promoting European telecommunications standards has the right to represent that interest in ETSI and, thus, to directly influence the standards-making process.

The purpose of ETSI was to create something in between the international level and the national level for pan-European use so that EU member countries could have cross-border signaling that was not as restricted as that found on the international level.

3rd Generation Partnership Project

When the ITU solicited solutions to meet the requirements laid down for IMT-2000 (3G cellular), various standards groups proposed varying technologies. ETSI proposed a Wideband Code Division Multiple Access (WCDMA) solution using FDD. Japan proposed a WCDMA solution using both TDD and FDD. The Koreans proposed two types of CDMA solutions—one similar to the ETSI solution and one more in line with the North American solution (CDMA 2000).

Instead of having different regions working alone, it was decided that it would be better to pool resources. To this end, the 3rd Generation Partnership Project (3GPP) was created to work on WCDMA, and 3GPP2 was formed to work on CDMA-2000.

3GPP is a collaboration agreement that was established in December 1998. It brings together a number of telecommunications standards bodies called organization partners. The current organization partners are Association of Radio Industries and Businesses (ARIB—Japan), China Wireless Telecommunication Standards group (CWTS—China), European Telecommunications Standards Institute (ETSI—Europe), Committee T1 (North America), Telecommunications Technology Association (TTA—Korea), and Telecommunication Technology Committee (TTC—Japan). The Telecommunications Industry Association (TIA—North America) is an observer to 3GPP.

The scope of 3GPP was subsequently amended to include the maintenance and development of the Global System for Mobile communication (GSM), General Packet Radio Service (GPRS), and Enhanced Data rates for GSM Evolution (EDGE). Previously, it focused only on developing standards for third-generation mobile systems. The GSM standard has been transferred to 3GPP from ETSI, although the vast majority of individual member organizations in 3GPP come from the ETSI membership list.

3GPP's third-generation systems operate in at least the five regions of the partner standards bodies—this is a big improvement over the GSM situation, which is incompatible with the Japanese second-generation system and, in terms of frequency band employed, even the GSM implementations in the U.S. The advantages of this multiregional approach are no doubt why 3GPP was formed.

3rd Generation Partnership Project 2

3GPP2 is to CDMA-2000 what 3GPP is to W-CDMA. Furthermore, 3GPP2 was created in the image of 3GPP. They develop 3G standards for carriers that currently have CDMA systems (such as IS-95 or TIA/EIA-95) installed. This group works closely with TIA/EIA TR-45.5, which originally was responsible for CDMA standards, as well as other TR-45 subcommittees—TR-45.2 (network), TR-45.4 ("A" interface), and TR-45.6 (packet data).

ETSI is not involved in any way with 3GPP2, and it does not publish the output of 3GPP2. Although 3GPP and 3GPP2 are separate organizations, they cooperate when it comes to specifying services that ideally should be the same (from the users' perspective), regardless of infrastructure and access technology. It should also be noted that quite a few equipment manufacturers need to keep their fingers in all pies and consequently are members of both projects. The five officially recognized standards-developing organizations that form the 3GPP2 collaborative effort (organization partners) are ARIB, CWTS, TIA/EIA, TTA, and TTC. In addition, market representation partners are organizations that can offer market advice to 3GPP2. They bring to 3GPP2 a consensus view of market requirements (for example, services, features, and functionality) falling within the 3GPP2 scope. These organizations are the CDMA develop group (CDG), the Mobile Wireless Internet Forum (MWIF), and the IPv6 forum.

3GPP2 is the culmination of efforts led by ANSI, TIA/EIA, and TIA/EIA TR-45. TIA/EIA has been chosen to be secretariat to 3GPP2. Observers from ETSI, Telecommunications Standards Advisory Council of Canada (TSACC), and China participate in 3GPP2.

National and Industry Standards

National standards are based on either ITU-T standards for nationalization or regional standards that are ITU-T standards that have been regionalized in much the same way that national standards are produced.

ANSI

ANSI was founded in 1918 by five engineering societies and three government agencies. The Institute remains a private, nonprofit membership organization supported by a diverse constituency of private-sector and public organizations. ANSI's T1 committee is involved in the standardization of SS7. These standards are developed in close coordination with the ITU-T.

ANSI is responsible for accrediting other North American standards organizations, including the Alliance for Telecommunications Industry Solutions (ATIS), EIA, and TIA.

ANSI has more than 1000 company, organization, government agency, institutional, and international members. ANSI defines protocol standards at the national level. It works by accrediting qualified organizations to develop standards in the technical area in which they have expertise. ANSI's role is to administer the voluntary consensus standards system. It provides a neutral forum to develop policies on standards issues and to serve as an oversight body to the standards development and conformity assessment programs and processes.

T1 Committee

The T1 Committee is sponsored by ATIS. It is accredited by ANSI to create network interconnections and interoperability standards for the U.S.

Telcordia (Formerly Bellcore)

Before its divestiture in 1984, the Bell System was a dominant telecom service provider and equipment manufacturer. It provided most of the service across the U.S. and set the de facto standards for the North American telecommunications network.

Bell Communications Research (Bellcore) was formed at divestiture in 1984 to provide centralized services to the seven regional Bell holding companies and their operating company subsidiaries, known as Regional Bell Operating Companies (RBOCs). Bellcore was the research and development arm of the former Bell System (the "baby Bells") operating companies. It defined requirements for these companies. These were documented in its Technical Advisories (TA series), Technical References (TR series), and Generic Requirements (GR series).

Although Bellcore specifications are somewhat prevalent in the telecommunications industry, they are not prescribed standards, although they had often become the de facto standards. This is because they were originally created in a closed-forum fashion for use by the RBOCs. Even post-divestiture, the specifications remain focused on the interests of the RBOCs. As such, they are industry standards but are not national standards.

Bellcore was acquired by Science Applications International Corporation (SAIC) in 1997 and was renamed Telcordia Technologies in 1999. Although Telcordia was previously funded by the RBOCs, it now operates as a regular business, providing consulting and other services. The Telcordia specifications are derived from the ANSI specifications, but it should be noted that Telcordia has often been a driver for the ANSI standards body.

The core ANSI standards [1-4] and the Bellcore standards [113] for SS7 are nearly identical. However, Bellcore has added a number of SS7 specifications beyond the core GR-246 specifications for RBOCs and Bellcore clients.

TIA/EIA

TIA is a nonprofit organization. It is a U.S. national trade organization with a membership of 1000 large and small companies that manufacture or supply the products and services used in global communications. All forms of membership within the organization, including participation on engineering committees, require corporate membership. Engineering committee participation is open to nonmembers also. Dues are based on company revenue.

TIA represents the communications sector of EIA. TIA/EIA's focus is the formation of new public land mobile network (PLMN) standards. It is an ANSI-accredited standards-making body and has created most of the PLMN standards used in the U.S. One very well-known standard is IS-41, which is used as the Mobile Application Part (MAP) in CDMA networks in the U.S. to enable cellular roaming, authentication, and so on. IS-41 is described in Chapter 13, "GSM MAP and ANSI-41 MAP." TIA/EIA develops ISs. Following the publication of an IS, one of three actions must be taken—reaffirmation, revision, or rescission. Reaffirmation is simply a review that concludes that the standard is still valid and does not require changes. Revision is exactly that—incorporating additional material and/or changes to technical meaning. Rescission is the result of a review that concludes that the standard is no longer of any value.

If the majority of ANSI members agree on the TIA/EIA interim standard, it becomes a full ANSI national standard. It is for this reason that IS-41 is now called ANSI-41. IS-41 was revised a number of times and then became a national standard. It progressed to Revision 0, then Revision A, then Revision B, then Revision C, and then it became a nationalized standard—ANSI-41 on Revision D. Currently it is on Revision E, and Revision F is planned.

In addition to ISs, TIA/EIA also publishes Telecommunications Systems Bulletins (TSBs). These provide information on existing standards and other information of importance to the industry.

TIA/EIA is composed of a number of committees that develop telecommunications standards. The TR committees are concerned with PLMN standards. Nine TR committees currently exist, as shown in Table 2-2.

Table 2-2   *TIA/EIA TR Committees*

TIA/EIA TR Committee Number	TIA/EIA TR Committee Name
TR-8	Mobile and Personal/Private Radio Standards
TR-14	Point-to-Point Communications
TR-29	Facsimile Systems and Point-to-Multipoint
TR-30	Data Transmission Systems and Equipment
TR-32	Personal Communications Equipment
TR-34	Satellite Equipment and Systems
TR-41	User Premises Telecommunications Requirements
TR-45	Mobile and Personal Communications Systems Standards
TR-46	Mobile & Personal Communications 1800 Standards

ATIS

ATIS is the major U.S. telecom standards organization besides TIA/EIA. Most notably, it is responsible for ANSI SS7 standards. This organization was previously called Exchange Carriers Standards Association (ECSA).

BSI

The BSI was formed in 1901 and was incorporated under the Royal Charter in 1929. BSI is the oldest national standards-making body in the world. Independent of government, industry, and trade associations, BSI is an impartial body serving both the private and public sectors. It works with manufacturing and service industries, businesses, and governments to facilitate the production of British, European, and international standards. As well as facilitating the writing of British standards, it represents UK interests across the full scope of European and international standards committees.

NICC

The Network Interoperability Consultative Committee (NICC) is a UK telecommunications industry committee that acts as an industry consensus group in which specifications and technical issues associated with network competition can be discussed. It also is a source of advice to the Director General of Telecommunications for the Office of Telecommunications (OFTEL) on the harmonization of interconnection arrangements.

NICC deals with particular issues via its interest groups, which aim to represent particular sectors of the industry. They include representatives of network operators, public exchange manufacturers, terminal equipment suppliers, and service providers. There is also a separate users' panel that works electronically to provide a user's perspective on NICC activities.

At the NICC's top level is the NICC Board, which is composed mainly of representatives of the interest groups that form the whole NICC. PNO is the Public Network Operators interest group. Company representatives can join the appropriate interest groups directly, but the board members are elected from the interest group participants.

Technical issues addressed so far by the NICC include the further development of interconnect signaling standards, methods of achieving geographic and nongeographic number portability, and defining interfaces for service providers. NICC has defined UK C7 (IUP) [40] signaling independent of British Telecom Network Requirements (BTNR) and has developed intelligent network and database solutions for number portability.

IETF

The Internet Engineering Task Force (IETF) is a nonprofit organization that is composed of a vast number of volunteers who cooperate to develop Internet standards. These volunteers come from equipment manufacturers, research institutions, and network operators.

The process of developing an Internet standard is documented in RFC 2026. A brief overview is provided here. An Internet standard begins life as an Internet Draft (ID), which is just an early specification. The draft can be revised, replaced, or made obsolete at any time. The draft is placed in the IETF's IDs directory, where anyone can view it. If the draft is not revised within 6 months or has not been recommended for publication as an RFC, it is removed from the directory and ceases to exist.

If the Internet Draft is sufficiently complete, it is published as an RFC and is given an RFC number. However, this does not mean that it is already a standard. Before a RFC becomes a proposed standard, it must have generated significant interest in the Internet community and must be stable and complete. The RFC does not have to be implemented before becoming a proposed standard.

The next step is that the RFC changes status from a proposal to a draft standard. For this to happen, there must have been at least two successful implementations of the specification, and interoperability must have been demonstrated.

The final step to turn the RFC into a standard is to satisfy the Internet Engineering Steering Group (IESG). The IESG needs to be satisfied that the specification is both stable and mature and that it can be successfully deployed on a large scale. When the RFC becomes a standard, it is given a standard (STD) number, but it retains its previous RFC number. STD 1 lists the various RFCs and is updated periodically.

One working group within the IETF that is of particular interest in relation to SS7 is Sigtran. Sigtran is concerned with the transport of signaling within IP-based networks including ISDN, SS7/C7, and V5. It is described in Chapter 14, "SS7 in the Converged World." The Sigtran architecture is defined in RFC 2719, *Framework Architecture for Signalling Transport*. Other RFCs and IDs relate to Sigtran. See Appendix J, "ITU and ANSI Protocol Comparison."

CHAPTER 3

The Role of SS7

The purpose of this chapter is to introduce Signaling System No. 7 (SS7/C7) and give the reader an indication of how it affects the lives of nearly two billion people globally. The chapter begins by providing a brief introduction to the major services that SS7/C7 provides and explains how the protocol has been and will continue to be a key enabler of new telecommunication services. It concludes with an explanation of why SS7/C7 is a cornerstone of convergence.

SS7/C7 is the protocol suite that is employed globally, across telecommunications networks, to provide signaling; it is also a private, "behind the scenes," packet-switched network, as well as a service platform. Being a signaling protocol, it provides the mechanisms to allow the telecommunication network elements to exchange control information.

AT&T developed SS7/C7 in 1975, and the *International Telegraph and Telephone Consultative Committee* (CCITT) [109] adopted it in 1980 as a worldwide standard. For more information on the standards bodies, see Chapter 2, "Standards." Over the past quarter of a century, SS7 has undergone a number of revisions and has been continually enhanced to support services that are taken for granted on a daily basis.

SS7/C7 is the key enabler of the public switched telephone network (PSTN), the integrated services digital network (ISDN), intelligent networks (INs), and public land mobile networks (PLMNs).

Each time you place and release a telephone call that extends beyond the local exchange, SS7/C7 signaling takes place to set up and reserve the dedicated network resources (trunk) for the call. At the end of the call, SS7/C7 takes action to return the resources to the network for future allocation.

TIP Calls placed between subscribers who are connected to the same switch do not require the use of SS7/C7. These are known as intraoffice, intraexchange, or line-to-line calls.

Each time a cellular phone is powered up, SS7/C7-based transactions identify, authenticate, and register the subscriber. Before a cellular call can be made, further transactions check that the cellular phone is not stolen (network dependent option) and qualify permission to place the call (for example, the subscriber may be barred from International usage). In addition, the SS7/C7 network tracks the cellular subscriber to allow call delivery, as well as to allow a call that is already in progress to remain connected, even when the subscriber is mobile.

Although the average person typically uses SS7/C7 several times a day, it is largely unheard of by the general public because it is a "behind the scenes" private network—in stark contrast to IP. Another reason for its great transparency is its extreme reliability and resilience. For example, SS7/C7 equipment must make carrier grade quality standards—that is, 99.999 percent availability. The three prime ways it achieves an industry renowned robustness is by having a protocol that ensures reliable message delivery, self-healing capabilities, and an over-engineered physical network.

Typically, the links that comprise the network operate with a 20–40 percent loading and have full redundancy of network elements. SS7/C7 might well be the most robust and reliable network in existence.

SS7/C7 is possibly the most important element from a *quality of service* (QoS) perspective, as perceived by the subscriber.

NOTE   Here QoS refers to the quality of services as perceived by the subscriber. It should not be confused with QoS as it relates specifically to packet networks.

QoS is quickly becoming a key in differentiating between service providers. Customers are changing service providers at an increasing pace for QoS reasons, such as poor coverage, delays, dropped calls, incorrect billing, and other service-related impairments and faults. SS7/C7 impairments nearly always impact a subscriber's QoS directly. A complete loss of signaling means a complete network outage, be it a cellular or fixed-line network. Even a wrongly-provisioned screening rule at a SS7/C7 node in a cellular network can prohibit subscribers from roaming internationally or sending text messages. A loss of one signaling link could potentially bring down thousands of calls. For this reason, the SS7/C7 network has been designed to be extremely robust and resilient.

Impact of SS7 Network Failure

The critical nature of the SS7 network and the potential impact of failures was demonstrated in January 1990 when a failure in the SS7 software of an AT&T switching node rippled through over 100 switching nodes. The failure caused a nine-hour outage, affecting an estimated 60,000 people and costing in excess of 60 million dollars in lost revenue as estimated by AT&T.

Signaling System No. 7-Based Services

In addition to setting up and releasing calls, SS7/C7 is the workhorse behind a number of telecommunication services, including:

- Telephone-marketing numbers such as toll-free and freephone
- Televoting (mass calling)
- Single Directory Number
- *Enhanced 911* (E911)—used in the United States
- Supplementary services
- Custom local area signaling services (CLASS)
- Calling name (CNAM)
- Line information database (LIDB)
- Local number portability (LNP)
- Cellular network mobility management and roaming
    - Short Message Service (SMS)
    - *Enhanced Messaging Service* (EMS)—Ringtone, logo, and cellular game delivery
- Local exchange carrier (LEC) provisioned private virtual networks (PVNs)
- Do-not-call enforcement

The following sections describe these telecommunications services.

Telephone-Marketing Numbers

The most commonly used telephone-marketing numbers are *toll-free* calling numbers (800 calling), known as *freephone* (0800) in the United Kingdom. Because the call is free for the caller, these numbers can be used to win more business by increasing customer response. Telephone-marketing numbers also provide premium rate lines in which the subscriber is charged at a premium in exchange for desired content. Examples of such services include adult services and accurate road reports.

Another popular telephone-marketing number is *local call*, with which a call is charged as a local call even though the distance might be national. In recent years in the United Kingdom, marketing numbers that scarcely alter the call cost have been a popular means of masking geographical location. These numbers allow for a separation between the actual number and the advertised number.

Televoting

Televoting is a mass calling service that provides an easy method of surveying the public on any imaginable subject. The host (for example, a deejay at a radio station) presents specific questions and the caller uses a telephone keypad to select a choice; the caller's action adds to the vote for that particular choice. The conversation phase is usually limited to a simple, automated "thank you for…" phrase. Televoting can also be used in many other areas, such as responding to fundraising pleas and telephone-based competitions. A single night of televoting might result in 15 million calls [110]. Televoting services represent some of the most demanding—as well as lucrative—call scenarios in today's telephone networks. Revenue generation in this area is likely to grow as customers shift more toward an "interactive" experience, on par with convergence.

Single Directory Number

Another service that uses SS7/C7 and has been deployed in recent years is the single directory number, which allows a company with multiple offices or store locations to have a single directory number. After analyzing the calling party's number, the switch directs the call to a local branch or store.

Enhanced 911

E911, which is being deployed across some states in the United States, utilizes SS7 to transmit the number of the calling party, look up the corresponding address of the subscriber in a database, and transmit the information to the emergency dispatch operator to enable a faster response to emergencies. E911 might also provide other significant location information, such as the location of the nearest fire hydrant, and potentially the caller's key medical details. The *Federal Communications Commission* (FCC) also has a cellular 911 program in progress; in addition to providing the caller's telephone number, this program sends the geographical location of the antenna to which the caller is connected. Enhancement proposals are already underway to obtain more precise location information.

Supplementary Services

Supplementary services provide the subscribers with more than *plain old telephony service* (POTS), without requiring them to change their telephone handsets or access technology. Well-known supplementary services include three-way calling, *calling number display* (CND), call-waiting, and call forwarding. Note that the exact names of these services might differ, depending on the country and the operator.

Recently, supplementary services have been helpful in increasing operators' revenues since revenues against call minutes have been on the decline. Usually the subscriber must pay a fixed monthly or quarterly fee for a supplementary service.

Custom Local Area Signaling Services (CLASS)

Custom local area signaling services (CLASS) are an extension of supplementary services that employ the use of SS7 signaling between exchanges within a local geographical area. Information provided over SS7 links, such as the calling party number or the state of a subscriber line, enable more advanced services to be offered by service providers. A few examples of CLASS services include:

- **Call block**—Stops pre-specified calling party numbers from calling.

- **Distinctive ringing**—Provides a distinct ringing signal when an incoming call originates from a number on a predefined list. This feature is particularly beneficial to households with teenagers.

- **Priority ringing**—Provides a distinct ring when a call originates from a pre-specified numbers. If the called subscriber is busy and has *call waiting,* the subscriber receives a special tone indicating that a number on the priority list is calling.

- **Call completion to busy subscriber (CCBS)**—If a subscriber who has CCBS calls a party who is engaged in another call, the subscriber can activate CCBS with a single key or sequence. When activated, CCBS causes the calling party's phone to ring when the called party becomes available; when the calling party answers, the called party's phone automatically rings again. This feature saves the calling party from continuously attempting to place a call to a party is still unavailable.

Note that the exact names of these services might differ, depending on the country and the operator. In addition, the term "CLASS" is not used outside of North America.

Calling Name (CNAM)

Calling name (CNAM) is an increasingly popular database-driven service that is only available in the United States at this time. With this service, the called party receives the name of the person calling in addition to their number. The called party must have a compatible display box or telephone handset to use this service. The CNAM information is typically stored in regional telecommunications databases. SS7/C7 queries the database for the name based on the number and delivers the information to the called party's local switch.

Line Information Database (LIDB)

Line information database (LIDB) is a multipurpose database that stores valuable information about individual subscribers to provide feature-based services (it is only available in the United States at this time). Such information might include the subscriber's profile, name and address, and billing validation data. The name and address information can be used to power CNAM, for example. The billing validation data is used to support alternate billing services such as calling card, collect, and third number billing. Alternate billing services allow subscribers to bill calls to an account that is not necessarily associated with the originating line. For example, it can be used to validate a subscriber's calling card number that is stored in the LIDB, designating this as the means of payment. SS7/C7 is responsible for the real-time database query/response that is necessary to validate the calling card before progressing to the call setup phase.

Local Number Portability (LNP)

Local number portability (LNP) provides the option for subscribers to retain their telephone number when changing their telephone service. There are three phases of number portability:

- Service Provider Portability
- Service Portability
- Location Portability

The various phases of LNP are discussed in more detail in Chapter 11, "Intelligent Networks."

The FCC mandated this feature for fixed-line carriers in the United States as part of the Telecommunications Act of 1996; later that same year, the act was also clarified to cover cellular carriers.

LNP is primarily aimed at stimulating competition among providers by removing the personal inconvenience of changing phone numbers when changing service providers. For example, many businesses and individuals spend relatively large sums of money to print their phone numbers on business cards, letterheads, and other correspondence items. Without LNP, people would have to reprint and redistribute these materials more often. This contributes to the inconvenience and detracts from the profitability of changing the telephone number, thereby making changing providers far more prohibitive.

Since telephone networks route calls based on service provider and geographic numbering plan information, SS7/C7 must figure out where the ported number's new terminating switch is by performing additional signaling before setting the call up. This step should add only a second to the call overhead setup; however, it is a technically challenging network change because it complicates the process by which SS7/C7 establishes a call behind the scenes. This process is further discussed in Chapter 8, "ISDN User Part (ISUP)."

2nd and 3rd Generation Cellular Networks

Cellular networks use SS7/C7 for the same reasons they use fixed line networks, but they place much higher signaling demands on the network because of subscriber mobility. All cellular networks, from 2G (GSM, ANSI-41, and even PDC, which is used in Japan) to 3G (UMTS and cdma2000), use SS7/C7 for call delivery, supplementary services, roaming, mobility management, prepaid, and subscriber authentication. For more information, see Chapter 13, "GSM and ANSI-41 Mobile Application Part (MAP)."

Short Message Service (SMS)

Short Message Service (SMS) forms part of the GSM specifications and allows two-way transmission of alphanumeric text between GSM subscribers. Although it is just now catching on in North America, SMS has been an unexpected and huge revenue source for operators around the world. Originally, SMS messages could be no longer than 160 alphanumeric characters. Many handsets now offer concatenated SMS, which allows users to send and receive messages up to 459 characters (this uses EMS described below). Cellular operators usually use SMS to alert the subscribers that they have voice mail, or to educate them on how to use network services when they have roamed onto another network. Third party companies offer the additional delivery services of sending SMS-to-fax, fax-to-SMS, SMS-to-e-mail, e-mail-to-SMS, SMS-to-web, web-to-SMS, and SMS notifications of the arrival of new e-mail.

Some European (Spain, Ireland, and Germany, for example) and Asian countries (the Philippines, for example) are rolling out fixed-line SMS, which allows users to send SMS through their fixed phone line to cell phones and vice versa, as well as to other fixed-line SMS-enabled phones, fax machines, e-mail, and specialized web pages. Thus far, each European rollout has also offered SMS-to-voice mail. If a caller sends a text message to a subscriber without fixed-line SMS facility, the SMS is speech-synthesized to the subscriber's and their voice mailbox. Fixed-line SMS requires compatible phones, which are becoming readily available.

SMS is carried on the SS7/C7 network, and it makes use of SS7/C7 for the required signaling procedures. For more information, see Chapter 13, "GSM and ANSI-41 Mobile Application Part (MAP)."

Enhanced Messaging Service (EMS)

Enhanced Messaging Service (*EMS*) adds new functionality to the SMS service in the form of pictures, animations, sound, and formatted text. EMS uses existing SMS infrastructure and consists largely of header changes made to a standard SMS message. Since EMS is simply an enhanced SMS service, it uses the SS7/C7 network in the same way; the SS7/C7 network carries it, and it uses SS7/C7 for the required signaling procedures.

EMS allows users to obtain new ring tones, screensavers, pictures, and animations for their cell phones either by swapping with friends or purchasing them online.

Operators have recently begun using EMS for downloading games (from classics like Asteroids, to newer games like Prince of Persia), which can be purchased from operator web sites.

Private Virtual Networks

Although the *private virtual networks* concept is not new, SS7/C7 makes it possible for a *Local exchange carrier* (LEC) to offer the service. The customer receives PVNs, which are exactly like leased (private) lines except that the network does not allocate dedicated physical resources. Instead, SS7/C7 signaling (and a connected database) monitors the "private customer" line. The customer has all the features of a leased-line service as well as additional features, such as the ability to request extra services ad hoc and to tailor the service to choose the cheapest *inter-exchange carrier* (IC), depending on the time of day, day or week, or distance between the two parties.

Do-Not-Call Enforcement

In the United States, federal and state laws have already mandated do-not-call lists [108] in over half the states, and all states are expected to follow suit. These laws restrict organizations (typically telemarketers) from cold-calling individuals. To comply with these laws, SS7 can be used to query state and federal do-not-call lists (which are stored on a database) each time a telemarketer makes an outbound call. If the number is on a do-not-call list, the call is automatically blocked and an appropriate announcement is played to the marketer.

Signaling System No. 7: The Key to Convergence

Telecommunications network operators can realize increased investment returns by marrying existing SS7/C7 and intelligent networking infrastructures with Internet and other data-centric technologies. SS7/C7 is a key protocol for bridging the telecom and datacom worlds.

The following sections describe the exemplar hybrid network services that SS7/C7 enable:

- Internet Call Waiting
- Internet Calling Name Services
- Click-to-Dial Applications
- Web-Browser-Based Telecommunication Services
- WLAN "Hotspot" Billing
- Location-Based Games

Internet Call Waiting and Internet Calling Name Services

Internet call waiting is a software solution that alerts online Internet users with a call-waiting message on their computer screens when a telephone call enters the same phone line they use for their Internet service. The user can then send the call to voice mail, accept the call, or reject it.

Some providers linking it to CNAM, as mentioned in Calling Name (CNAM), have enhanced the Internet call-waiting service. This service is known as Internet calling name service, and it provides the calling party's name and number.

Click-to-Dial Applications

Click-to-dial applications are another SS7-IP growth area. An example of a click-to-dial application is the ability to click a person's telephone number in an email signature to place a call. These types of services are particularly beneficial to subscribers because they do not require them to change their equipment or access technologies; a POTS and a traditional handset are the only requirements.

Web-Browser-Based of Telecommunication Services

Over the coming decade, we are likely to witness an increase in web based telecommunications services. An example is customer self-provisioning via the Internet, a practice that has been in the marketplace for some time and is likely to increase in both complexity and usage. A customer can already assign himself a premium or toll-free "number for life" via the Internet. The customer can subsequently use a Web interface to change the destination number it points to at will, so that during the day it points to the customer's office phone, and in the evening it points to the customer's cell phone, and so forth.

Another example is the "call me" service, which allows a customer to navigate a Web page to arrange a callback from a department, rather than navigating interactive voice response (IVR) systems through the use of voice prompts and a touch-tone phone.

The potential extends far beyond traditional telecommunications services, to the point where the distinction between Web and telecommunications services is blurred. An example of such an enabling technology is Voice Extensible Markup Language (VoiceXML), which extends Web applications to telephones and shields application authors from low-level, platform-specific *interactive voice response* (IVR) and call control details.

The marriage is not only between SS7/C7, the Internet, and fixed-line networks—it also extends to cellular networks. Plans are underway to put the location-based information and signaling found in cellular networks into hybrid use. For example, Web-based messenger services could access cellular network *home location registers* (HLRs) to enable a user to locate a friend or relative in terms of real-time geographic location.

WLAN "Hotspot" Billing

SS7/C7 has recently begun playing a role in the marriage of wireless (WLANs) and cellular networks. A subscriber can use a cellular subscriber identity module (SIM) card for authentication and billing purposes from a WLAN hotspot. For example, if a subscriber is at a café with WLAN facilities (typically wi-fi), the subscriber can request permission to use the service via a laptop screen. This request triggers a short cellular call to authenticate the subscriber (using SS7/C7 signaling). The usage is then conveniently billed to the subscriber's cellular phone bill.

NOTE   A SIM is used in 2nd generation cellular networks based on GSM, and on 2.5/3G networks as defined by 3GPP. A SIM contains the subscriber's identity so that the subscriber can change cellular equipment freely by simply changing the SIM card over to the new device. This means that the subscriber can plug the SIM into a new cellular handset and the number "transfers" to that handset, along with the billing.

Location-Based Games

SS7/C7 is not only used to deliver games to cell phones, but it also plays a role in the creation of a new genre of location-based games and entertainment. Cellular games incorporate the player's location using SS7/C7 to provide mobility information a dedicated web site as a central point. Some of the games that are emerging at the time of this writing are using global positioning system (GPS), WLAN support, and built-in instant messaging capabilities (to help tease your opponents) to blend higher location accuracy.

Summary

This chapter has shown that, although it is transparent, SS7/C7 plays a role in the lives of virtually every individual in developed countries. It is also the key to new, revenue-generating services and is crucial to the QoS as perceived by subscribers—both of which lie at the very heart of success in a fiercely competitive telecommunications market. Furthermore SS7/C7 is a common thread that ties fixed-line, cellular, and IP networks together, and it is a key enabler for the convergence of the telecommunications and data communications industries.

CHAPTER 4

SS7 Network Architecture and Protocols Introduction

The *International Telecommunication Union (ITU)* is the international governing body for Signaling System No. 7. More specifically, it is governed by the Telecommunication Standardization Sector of the ITU (ITU-TS or ITU-T for short). Formerly it was governed by the ITU's Consultative Committee for International Telegraph and Telephone (CCITT) subcommittee until that was disbanded in 1992 as part of a process to speed up the production of recommendations (as well as other organization changes). See Chapter 2, "Standards," for more information on standards-making bodies.

Signaling System No. 7 is more commonly known by the acronyms SS7 and C7. Strictly speaking, the term C7 (or, less commonly, CCS7) refers to the international Signaling System No. 7 network protocols specified by the ITU-T recommendations as well as national or regional variants defined within the framework provided by the ITU-T. The term C7 originates from the former title found on the specifications—CCITT Signaling System No. 7. The term SS7 tends to specifically refer to the North American regional standards produced by Telcordia (formerly known as Bell Communications Research or Bellcore) and the American National Standards Institute (ANSI). The North American standards themselves are based on the ITU-T recommendations but have been tailored outside the provided framework. The differences between ITU and Telcordia/ANSI are largely subtle at the lower layers. Interaction between ANSI and ITU-T networks is made challenging by different implementations of higher-layer protocols and procedures.

For the purpose of this book, we will use the term SS7 to refer generically to any Signaling System No. 7 protocol, regardless of its origin or demographics. An overview of SS7 by the ITU-T can be found in recommendation Q.700 [111], and a similar overview of SS7 by ANSI can be found in T1.110 [112].

Chapter 3, "The Role of SS7," provides a comprehensive list of the functions and services afforded by SS7. These can be summarized as follows:

- Setting up and tearing down circuit-switched connections, such as telephone calls made over both cellular and fixed-line.

- Advanced network features such as those offered by supplementary services (calling name/number presentation, Automatic Callback, and so on).

- Mobility management in cellular networks, which permits subscribers to move geographically while remaining attached to the network, even while an active call is in place. This is the central function of a cellular network.

- *Short Message Service (SMS)* and *Enhanced Messaging Service (EMS)*, where SS7 is used not only for signaling but also for content transport of alphanumeric text.

- Support for *Intelligent Network (IN)* services such as toll-free (800) calling.

- Support for ISDN.

- *Local Number Portability (LNP)* to allow subscribers to change their service, service provider, and location without needing to change their telephone number.

After reading the preceding chapters, you know that signaling serves the requirements of the telecommunications service being delivered; it is not an end in itself. Signaling enables services within the network.

This chapter makes you familiar with the SS7 network, protocols, fundamental concepts, and terminology so that the topics covered in the rest of the book will be more accessible if you're unfamiliar with the subject. This chapter begins with a brief description of pre-SS7 systems and SS7 history. The chapter then presents the protocol stack, showing how SS7 protocols fit together. It concludes with a discussion of the relevant protocols.

Pre-SS7 Systems

The following are the main systems that preceded SS7:

- CCITT R1 (regional 1) was deployed only on a national level. R1 is a *Channel Associated Signaling (CAS)* system that was employed in the U.S. and Japan. It uses multifrequency (MF) tones for signaling. It is no longer in general operation, although some remnants might remain in the network.

- CCITT R2 (regional 2) was deployed only on a national level. R2 is a CAS system that was employed in Europe and most other countries. It used *Multifrequency Compelled (MFC)* for signaling; it compelled the receiver to acknowledge a pair of tones before sending the next pair. It is no longer in general operation, although some remnants might remain in the network.

- Signaling systems that have been deployed for both national and international (between international switches) signaling have progressed from CCITT #5 (C5) to CCITT #6 (C6) and finally to CCITT #7 (C7):

  — C5 (CCITT Signaling System No. 5) is a CAS system standardized in 1964 that has found widespread use in international signaling. It is still in use today on a number of international interfaces. National implementations are now scarce, except in less-developed regions of the world, such as Africa, which makes extensive use of the protocol. C5 can be used in both analog and digital environments. In an analog setting, it uses tones for signaling. In a digital setting, a digital representation of the tone is sent instead (a pulse code modulation [PCM] sample).

  — C6 (CCITT Signaling System No. 6), also called SS6, was the first system to employ *Common Channel Signaling* (CCS). It was standardized in 1972. (CAS and CCS are explained in Chapter 1, "The Evolution of Signaling.") C6 was a pre-OSI model and as such had a monolithic structure as opposed to a layered one. C6 was a precursor to C7 and included the use of data links to carry signaling in the form of packets. It had error correction/detection mechanisms. It employed a common signaling channel to control a large number of speech circuits, and it had self-governing network management procedures. C6 had a number of advantages over C5, including improvements in post-dial delay and the ability to reject calls with a cause code. The use of locally mapped cause codes allowed international callers to hear announcements in their own language. Although C6 was designed for the international network, it was not as widely deployed as C5. However, it was nationalized for the U.S. network and was deployed quite extensively under the name *Common Channel Interoffice Signaling System* 6 *(CCIS6)* in the AT&T network. C6 was introduced into the Bell system in the U.S. in 1976, and soon after, Canada. All deployments have now been replaced by SS7.

The next section provides a brief history of SS7.

History of SS7

The first specification (called a *recommendation* by the CCITT/ITU-T) of CCITT Signaling System No. 7 was published in 1980 in the form of the CCITT *yellow book* recommendations. After the yellow book recommendations, CCITT recommendations were approved at the end of a four-year study period. They were published in a colored book representing that study period.

Table 4-1 provides an evolutionary time line of CCITT/ITU-T SS7.

Table 4-1   *CCITT/ITU-T SS7 Timeline*

Year	Publication	Protocols Revised or Added
1980	CCITT Yellow Book	MTP2, MTP3, and TUP, first publication.
1984	CCITT Red Book	MTP2, MTP3, and TUP revised. SCCP and ISUP added.
1988	CCITT Blue Book	MTP2, MTP3, TUP, and ISUP revised. ISUP supplementary services and TCAP added.
1992	ITU-T Q.767	International ISUP, first publication.
1993	ITU-T "White Book 93"	ISUP revised.
1996	ITU-T "White Book 96"	MTP3 revised.
1997	ITU-T "White Book 97"	ISUP revised.
1999	ITU-T "White Book 99"	ISUP revised.

Under the CCITT publishing mechanism, the color referred to a published set of recommendations—that is, all protocols were published at the same time. The printed matter had the appropriate colored cover, and the published title contained the color name. When the ITU-T took over from the CCITT, it produced single booklets for each protocol instead of producing en bloc publications as had been the case under the supervision of the CCITT. Under the new mechanism, the color scheme was dropped. As a result, the ITU-T publications came to be known as "White Book" editions, because no color was specified, and the resulting publications had white covers. Because these publications do not refer to a color, you have to qualify the term "White Book" with the year of publication.

As Table 4-1 shows, when SS7 was first published, the protocol stack consisted of only the Message Transfer Part 2 (MTP2), Message Transfer Part 3 (MTP3), and Telephony User Part (TUP) protocols. On first publication, these were still somewhat immature. It was not until the later Red and Blue book editions that the protocol was considered mature. Since then, the SS7 protocols have been enhanced, and new protocols have been added as required.

Figure 4-1 shows how many pages the ITU-T SS7 specifications contained in each year. In 1980, there were a total of 320 pages, in 1984 a total of 641 pages, in 1988 a total of 1900 pages, and in 1999 approximately 9000 pages.

Figure 4-1   *How Many Pages the ITU C7 Specifications Covered Based on Year (Source: ITU [Modified])*

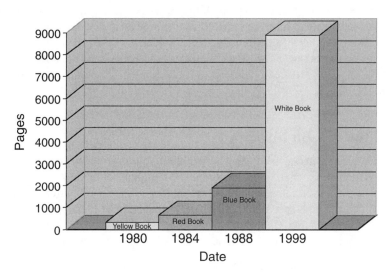

The following section introduces the SS7 network architecture.

SS7 Network Architecture

SS7 can employ different types of signaling network structures. The choice between these different structures can be influenced by factors such as administrative aspects and the structure of the telecommunication network to be served by the signaling system.

The worldwide signaling network has two functionally independent levels:

- International
- National

This structure makes possible a clear division of responsibility for signaling network management. It also lets numbering plans of SS7 nodes belonging to the international network and the different national networks be independent of one another.

SS7 network nodes are called signaling points (SPs). Each SP is addressed by an integer called a point code (PC). The international network uses a 14-bit PC. The national networks also use a 14-bit PC—except North America and China, which use an incompatible 24-bit PC, and Japan, which uses a 16-bit PC. The national PC is unique only within a particular operator's national network. International PCs are unique only within the international network. Other operator networks (if they exist) within a country also could have the same PC and also might share the same PC as that used on the international network. Therefore, additional routing information is provided so that the PC can be interpreted correctly—that is, as an international network, as its own national network, or as another operator's national network. The structure of point codes is described in Chapter 7, "Message Transfer Part 3 (MTP3)."

Signaling Links and Linksets

SPs are connected to each other by signaling links over which signaling takes place. The bandwidth of a signaling link is normally 64 kilobits per second (kbps). Because of legacy reasons, however, some links in North America might have an effective rate of 56 kbps. In recent years, high-speed links have been introduced that use an entire 1.544 Mbps T1 carrier for signaling. Links are typically engineered to carry only 25 to 40 percent of their capacity so that in case of a failure, one link can carry the load of two.

To provide more bandwidth and/or for redundancy, up to 16 links between two SPs can be used. Links between two SPs are logically grouped for administrative and load-sharing reasons. A logical group of links between two SP is called a *linkset*. Figure 4-2 shows four links in a linkset.

Figure 4-2   *Four Links in a Linkset Between SPs*

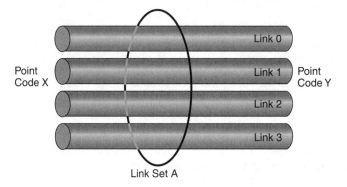

A number of linksets that may be used to reach a particular destination can be grouped logically to form a *combined linkset*. For each combined linkset that an individual linkset is a member of, it may be assigned different priority levels relative to other linksets in each combined linkset.

A group of links within a linkset that have the same characteristics (data rate, terrestrial/ satellite, and so on) are called a *link group*. Normally the links in a linkset have the same characteristics, so the term *link group* can be synonymous with *linkset*.

Routes and Routesets

SS7 routes are statically provisioned at each SP. There are no mechanisms for route discovery. A *route* is defined as a preprovisioned path between source and destination for a particular relation. Figure 4-3 shows a route from SP A to SP C.

Figure 4-3   *Route from SP A to SP C*

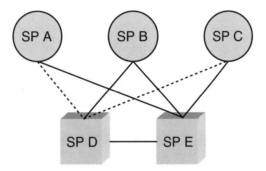

All the preprovisioned routes to a particular SP destination are called the *routeset*. Figure 4-4 shows a routeset for SSP C consisting of two routes.

Figure 4-4   *Routeset from SP A to SP C*

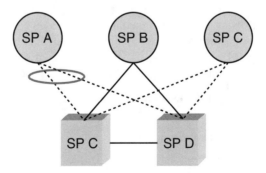

The following section discusses the SP types.

Node Types

There are three different types of SP (that is, SS7 node):

- Signal Transfer Point
- Service Switching Point
- Service Control Point

Figure 4-5 graphically represents these nodes.

Figure 4-5   *SS7 Node Types*

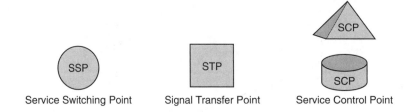

Service Switching Point   Signal Transfer Point   Service Control Point

The SPs differ in the functions that they perform, as described in the following sections.

Signal Transfer Point

A Signal Transfer Point (STP) is responsible for the transfer of SS7 messages between other SS7 nodes, acting somewhat like a router in an IP network.

An STP is neither the ultimate source nor the destination for most signaling messages. Generally, messages are received on one signaling link and are transferred out another. The only messages that are not simply transferred are related to network management and global title translation. These two functions are discussed more in Chapters 7 and 9. STPs route each incoming message to an outgoing signaling link based on routing information contained in the SS7 message. Specifically, this is the information found in the MTP3 routing label, as described in Chapter 7.

Additionally, standalone STPs often can screen SS7 messages, acting as a firewall. Such usage is described in Chapter 15, "SS7/C7 Security and Monitoring."

An STP can exist in one of two forms:

- Standalone STP
- Integrated STP (SP with STP)

Standalone STPs are normally deployed in "mated" pairs for the purposes of redundancy. Under normal operation, the mated pair shares the load. If one of the STPs fails or isolation occurs because of signaling link failure, the other STP takes the full load until the problem with its mate has been rectified.

Integrated STPs combine the functionality of an SSP and an STP. They are both the source and destination for MTP user traffic. They also can transfer incoming messages to other nodes.

Service Switching Point

A Service Switching Point (SSP) is a voice switch that incorporates SS7 functionality. It processes voice-band traffic (voice, fax, modem, and so forth) and performs SS7 signaling. All switches with SS7 functionality are considered SSPs regardless of whether they are local switches (known in North America as an end office) or tandem switches.

An SSP can originate and terminate messages, but it cannot transfer them. If a message is received with a point code that does not match the point code of the receiving SSP, the message is discarded.

Service Control Point

A Service Control Point (SCP) acts as an interface between telecommunications databases and the SS7 network. Telephone companies and other telecommunication service providers employ a number of databases that can be queried for service data for the provision of services. Typically the request (commonly called a query) originates at an SSP. A popular example is freephone calling (known as toll-free in North America). The SCP provides the routing number (translates the toll-free number to a routable number) to the SSP to allow the call to be completed. For more information, see Chapter 11, "Intelligent Networks (IN)."

SCPs form the means to provide the core functionality of cellular networks, which is subscriber mobility. Certain cellular databases (called registers) are used to keep track of the subscriber's location so that incoming calls may be delivered. Other telecommunication databases include those used for calling card validation (access card, credit card), calling name display (CNAM), and LNP.

SCPs used for large revenue-generating services are usually deployed in pairs and are geographically separated for redundancy. Unless there is a failure, the load is typically shared between two *mated* SCPs. If failure occurs in one of the SCPs, the other one should be able to take the load of both until normal operation resumes.

Queries/responses are normally routed through the mated pair of STPs that services that particular SCP, particularly in North America.

See Chapters 10, "Transaction Capabilities Application Part (TCAP)," and 11, "Intelligent Networks (IN)," for more information on the use of SCPs within both fixed-line and cellular networks. See Chapters 12, "Cellular Networks," and 13, "GSM and ANSI-41 Mobile Application Part (MAP)," for specific information on the use of SCPs within cellular networks.

The following section introduces the concept of link types.

Link Types

Signaling links can be referenced differently depending on where they are in the network. Although different references can be used, you should understand that the link's physical characteristics remain the same. The references to link types A through E are applicable only where standalone STPs are present, so the references are more applicable to the North American market.

Six different link references exist:

- Access links (A links)
- Crossover links (C links)
- Bridge links (B links)
- Diagonal links (D links)
- Extended links (E links)
- Fully associated links (F links)

The following sections cover each link reference in more detail.

NOTE   In the figures in the sections covering the different link references, dotted lines represent the actual link being discussed, and solid lines add network infrastructure to provide necessary context for the discussion.

Access Links (A Links)

Access links (A links), shown in Figure 4-6, provide access to the network. They connect "outer" SPs (SSPs or SCPs) to the STP backbone. A links connect SSPs and SCPs to their serving STP or STP mated pair.

Figure 4-6   *A Links*

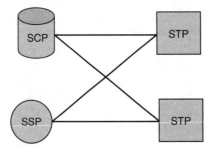

Cross Links (C Links)

Cross links (C links), shown in Figure 4-7, are used to connect two STPs to form a mated pair — that is, a pair linked such that if one fails, the other takes the load of both.

Figure 4-7   *C Links*

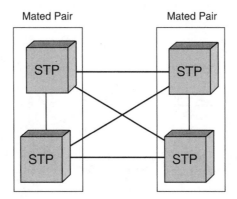

Mated Pair   Mated Pair

C links are used to carry MTP user traffic only when no other route is available to reach an intended destination. Under normal conditions, they are used only to carry network management messages.

Bridge Links (B Links)

Bridge links (B links) are used to connect mated pairs of STPs to each other across different regions within a network at the same hierarchical level. These links help form the backbone of the SS7 network. B links are normally deployed in link quad configuration between mated pairs for redundancy.

Figure 4-8 shows two sets of mated pairs of B links.

Figure 4-8   *B Links*

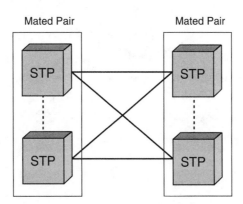

Mated Pair   Mated Pair

Diagonal Links (D Links)

Diagonal links (D links), shown in Figure 4-9, are the same as B links in that they connect mated STP pairs.

Figure 4-9 *D Links*

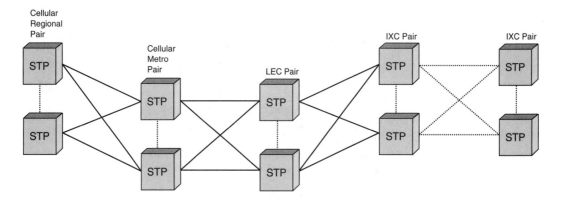

The difference is that they connect mated STP pairs that belong to different hierarchical levels or to different networks altogether. For example, they may connect an interexchange carrier (IXC) STP pair to a local exchange carrier (LEC) STP pair or a cellular regional STP pair to a cellular metro STP pair.

As mentioned, B and D links differ in that D links refer specifically to links that are used either between different networks and/or hierarchical levels, as shown in Figure 4-10.

Figure 4-10 *Existence of an STP Backbone and STP Hierarchy*

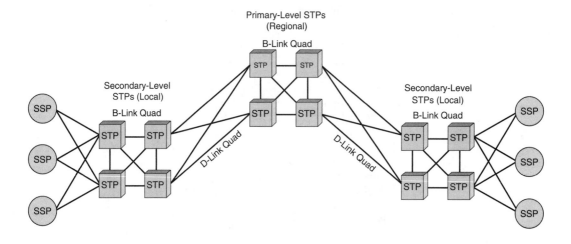

Extended Links (E Links)

Extended links (E links), shown in Figure 4-11, connect SSPs and SCPs to an STP pair, as with A links, except that the pair they connect to is not the normal home pair. Instead, E links connect to a nonhome STP pair. They are also called alternate access (AA) links. E links are used to provide additional reliability or, in some cases, to offload signaling traffic from the home STP pair in high-traffic corridors. For example, an SSP serving national government agencies or emergency services might use E links to provide additional alternate routing because of the criticality of service.

Figure 4-11 *E Links*

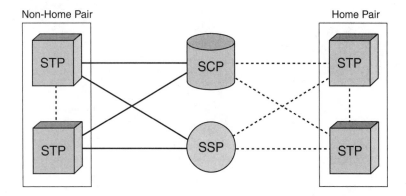

Fully-Associated Links (F Links)

Fully-associated links (F links), shown in Figure 4-12, are used to connect network SSPs and/or SCPs directly to each other without using STPs. The most common application of this type of link is in metropolitan areas. F links can establish direct connectivity between all switches in the area for trunk signaling and Custom Local Area Signaling Service (CLASS), or to their corresponding SCPs.

Figure 4-13 shows an SS7 network segment. In reality, there would be several factors more SSPs than STPs.

Figure 4-12 *F Links*

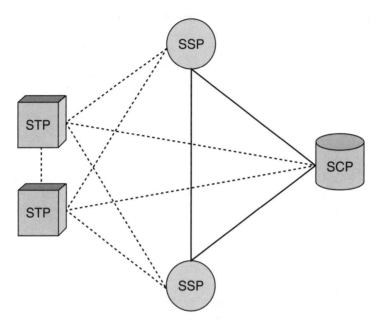

Signaling Modes

The signaling relationship that exists between two communicating SS7 nodes is called the signaling mode. The two modes of signaling are associated signaling and quasi-associated signaling. When the destination of an SS7 message is directly connected by a linkset, the *associated* signaling mode is being used. In other words, the source and destination nodes are directly connected by a single linkset. When the message must pass over two or more linksets and through an intermediate node, the *quasi-associated* mode of signaling is being used.

It's easier to understand the signaling mode if you examine the relationship of the point codes between the source and destination node. When using the associated mode of signaling, the Destination Point Code (DPC) of a message being sent matches the PC of the node at the far end of the linkset, usually referred to as the far-end PC or adjacent PC. When quasi-associated signaling is used, the DPC does not match the PC at the far end of the connected linkset. Quasi-associated signaling requires the use of an STP as the intermediate node because an SSP cannot transfer messages.

Figure 4-13 *SS7 Network Segment*

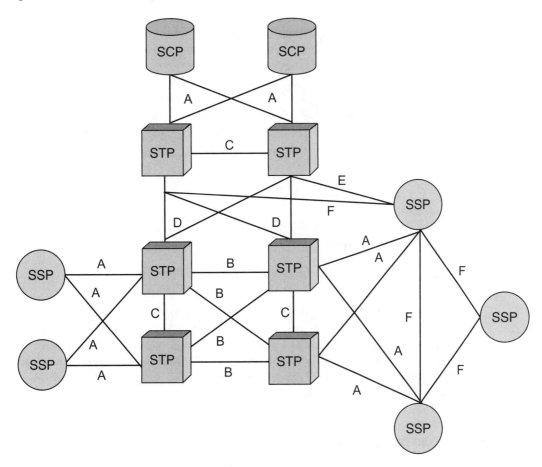

In Figure 4-14, the signaling relationships between each of the nodes are as follows:

- SSP A to SSP B uses quasi-associated signaling.
- SSP B to SSP C uses associated signaling.
- STP 1 and STP 2 use associated signaling to SSP A, SSP B, and each other.

As you can see from Figure 4-14, associated signaling is used between nodes that are directly connected by a single linkset, and quasi-associated signaling is used when an intermediate node is used. Notice that SSP C is only connected to SSP B using an F link. It is not connected to any other SS7 nodes in the figure.

Figure 4-14 *SS7 Signaling Modes*

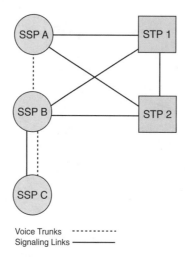

When discussing the signaling mode in relation to the voice trunks shown between the SSPs, the signaling and voice trunks follow the same path when associated signaling is used. They take separate paths when quasi-associated signaling is used. You can see from Figure 4-14 that the signaling between SSP B and SSP C follows the same path (associated mode) as the voice trunks, while the signaling between SSP A and SSP B does not follow the same path as the voice trunks.

Signaling Network Structure

Standalone STPs are prevalent in North America because they are used in this region to form the backbone of the SS7 network. Attached to this backbone are the SSPs and SCPs. Each SSP and SCP is assigned a "home pair" of STPs that it is directly connected to. The network of STPs can be considered an overlay onto the telecommunications network—a packet-switched data communications network that acts as the nervous system of the telecommunications network. Figure 4-15 shows a typical example of how SSPs are interconnected with the STP network in North America.

STPs are not as common outside North America. Standalone STPs typically are used only between network operators and/or for applications involving the transfer of noncircuit-related signaling. In these regions, most SSPs have direct signaling link connections to other SSPs to which they have direct trunk connections. Figure 4-16 shows an example of this type of network with most SSPs directly connected by signaling links.

Figure 4-15 *Typical Example of North American SSP Interconnections*

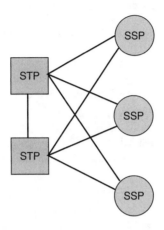

Figure 4-16 *Typical Example of SSP Interconnections in Most Areas Outside North America*

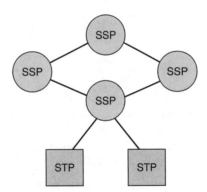

SSPs often have indirect physical connections to STPs, made through other SSPs in the network. These are usually implemented as nailed-up connections, such as through a Digital Access Cross-Connect System or other means of establishing a semipermanent connection. Logically, these SSPs are directly connected to the STP. The signaling link occupies a digital time slot on the same physical medium as the circuit-switched traffic. The SSPs that provide physical interconnection between other SSPs and an STP do not "transfer" messages as an STP function. They only provide physical connectivity of the signaling links between T1/E1 carriers to reach the STP. Figure 4-17 shows an example of a network with no STP connection, direct connections, and nondirect connections. SSP 1 is directly connected to an STP pair. SSP 4 uses direct signaling links to SSP 2 and SSP 3, where it also has direct trunks. It has no STP connection at all. SSP 2 and SSP 3 are connected to the STP pair via nailed-up connections at SSP 1.

Figure 4-17 *Example of Direct and Indirect SSP Interconnections to STPs*

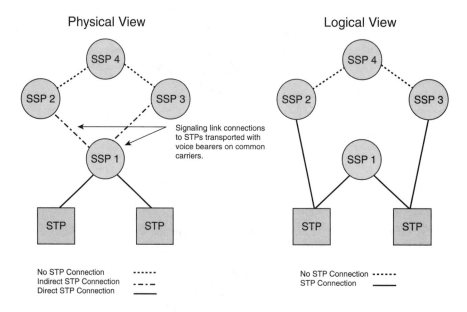

Normally within networks that do not use STPs, circuit-related (call-related) signaling takes the same path through the network as user traffic because there is no physical need to take a different route. This mode of operation is called *associated signaling* and is prevalent outside North America. Referring back to Figure 4-14, both the user traffic and the signaling take the same path between SSP B and SSP C.

Because standalone STPs are used to form the SS7 backbone within North America, and standalone STPs do not support user traffic switching, the SSP's signaling mode is usually quasi-associated, as illustrated between SSP A and SSP B in Figure 4-14.

In certain circumstances, the SSP uses associated signaling within North America. A great deal of signaling traffic might exist between two SSPs, so it might make more sense to place a signaling link directly between them rather than to force all signaling through an STP.

SS7 Protocol Overview

The number of possible protocol stack combinations is growing. It depends on whether SS7 is used for cellular-specific services or intelligent network services, whether transportation is over IP or is controlling broadband ATM networks instead of time-division multiplexing

(TDM) networks, and so forth. This requires coining a new term—traditional SS7—to refer to a stack consisting of the protocols widely deployed from the 1980s to the present:

- Message Transfer Parts (MTP 1, 2, and 3)
- Signaling Connection Control Part (SCCP)
- Transaction Capabilities Application Part (TCAP)
- Telephony User Part (TUP)
- ISDN User Part (ISUP)

Figure 4-18 shows a common introductory SS7 stack.

Figure 4-18 *Introductory SS7 Protocol Stack*

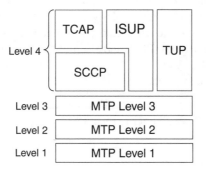

Such a stack uses TDM for transport. This book focuses on traditional SS7 because that is what is implemented. Newer implementations are beginning to appear that use different transport means such as IP and that have associated new protocols to deal with the revised transport.

The SS7 physical layer is called MTP level 1 (MTP1), the data link layer is called MTP level 2 (MTP2), and the network layer is called MTP level 3 (MTP3). Collectively they are called the *Message Transfer Part (MTP)*. The MTP protocol is SS7's native means of packet transport. In recent years there has been an interest in the facility to transport SS7 signaling over IP instead of using SS7's native MTP. This effort has largely been carried out by the Internet Engineering Task Force (IETF) SigTran (Signaling Transport) working group. The protocols derived by the SigTran working group so far are outside the scope of this introductory chapter on SS7. However, full details of SigTran can be found in Chapter 14, "SS7 in the Converged World."

TUP and ISUP both perform the signaling required to set up and tear down telephone calls. As such, both are circuit-related signaling protocols. TUP was the first call control protocol specified. It could support only plain old telephone service (POTS) calls. Most countries are replacing TUP with ISUP. Both North America and Japan bypassed TUP and went straight from earlier signaling systems to ISUP. ISUP supports both POTS and ISDN calls. It also has more flexibility and features than TUP.

With reference to the Open System Interconnection (OSI) seven-layer reference model, SS7 uses a four-level protocol stack. OSI Layer 1 through 3 services are provided by the MTP together with the SCCP. The SS7 architecture currently has no protocols that map into OSI Layers 4 through 6. TUP, ISUP, and TCAP are considered as corresponding to OSI Layer 7 [111]. SS7 and the OSI model were created at about the same time. For this reason, they use some differing terminology.

SS7 uses the term *levels* when referring to its architecture. The term *levels* should not be confused with OSI layers, because they do not directly correspond to each other. *Levels* was a term introduced to help in the discussion and presentation of the SS7 protocol stack. Levels 1, 2, and 3 correspond to MTP 1, 2, and 3, respectively. Level 4 refers to an MTP *user*. The term *user* refers to any protocol that directly uses the transport capability provided by the MTP—namely, TUP, ISUP, and SCCP in traditional SS7. The four-level terminology originated back when SS7 had only a call control protocol (TUP) and the MTP, before SCCP and TCAP were added.

The following sections provide a brief outline of protocols found in the introductory SS7 protocol stack, as illustrated in Figure 4-18.

MTP

MTP levels 1 through 3 are collectively referred to as the MTP. The MTP comprises the functions to transport information from one SP to another.

The MTP transfers the signaling message, in the correct sequence, without loss or duplication, between the SPs that make up the SS7 network. The MTP provides reliable transfer and delivery of signaling messages. The MTP was originally designed to transfer circuit-related signaling because no noncircuit-related protocol was defined at the time.

The recommendations refer to MTP1, MTP2, and MTP3 as the physical layer, data link layer, and network layer, respectively. The following sections discuss MTP2 and MTP3. (MTP1 isn't discussed because it refers to the physical network.) For information on the physical aspects of the Public Switched Telephone Network (PSTN), see Chapter 5, "The Public Switched Telephone Network (PSTN)."

MTP2

Signaling links are provided by the combination of MTP1 and MTP2. MTP2 ensures reliable transfer of signaling messages. It encapsulates signaling messages into variable-length SS7 packets. SS7 packets are called signal units (SUs). MTP2 provides delineation of SUs, alignment of SUs, signaling link error monitoring, error correction by retransmission, and flow control. The MTP2 protocol is specific to narrowband links (56 or 64 kbps).

MTP3

MTP3 performs two functions:

- **Signaling Message Handling (SMH)** — Delivers incoming messages to their intended User Part and routes outgoing messages toward their destination. MTP3 uses the PC to identify the correct node for message delivery. Each message has both an Origination Point Code (OPC) and a DPC. The OPC is inserted into messages at the MTP3 level to identify the SP that originated the message. The DPC is inserted to identify the address of the destination SP. Routing tables within an SS7 node are used to route messages.

- **Signaling Network Management (SNM)** — Monitors linksets and routesets, providing status to network nodes so that traffic can be rerouted when necessary. SNM also provides procedures to take corrective action when failures occur, providing a self-healing mechanism for the SS7 network.

Figure 4-19 shows the relationship between levels 1, 2, and 3.

Figure 4-19 *A Single MTP3 Controls Many MTP2s, Each of Which Is Connected to a Single MTP1*

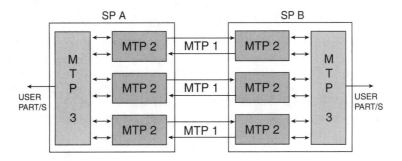

TUP and ISUP

TUP and ISUP sit on top of MTP to provide circuit-related signaling to set up, maintain, and tear down calls. TUP has been replaced in most countries because it supports only POTS calls. Its successor, ISUP, supports both POTS and ISDN calls as well as a host of other features and added flexibility. Both TUP and ISUP are used to perform interswitch call signaling. ISUP also has inherent support for supplementary services, such as automatic callback, calling line identification, and so on.

SCCP

The combination of the MTP and the SCCP is called the *Network Service Part (NSP)* in the specifications (but outside the specifications, this term is seldom used).

The addition of the SCCP provides a more flexible means of routing and provides mechanisms to transfer data over the SS7 network. Such additional features are used to support noncircuit-related signaling, which is mostly used to interact with databases (SCPs). It is also used to connect the radio-related components in cellular networks and for inter-SSP communication supporting CLASS services. SCCP also provides application management functions. Applications are mostly SCP database driven and are called subsystems. For example, in cellular networks, SCCP transfers queries and responses between the Visitor Location Register (VLR) and Home Location Register (HLR) databases. Such transfers take place for a number of reasons. The primary reason is to update the subscriber's HLR with the current VLR serving area so that incoming calls can be delivered.

Enhanced routing is called global title (GT) routing. It keeps SPs from having overly large routing tables that would be difficult to provision and maintain. A GT is a directory number that serves as an alias for a physical network address. A physical address consists of a point code and an application reference called a subsystem number (SSN). GT routing allows SPs to use alias addressing to save them from having to maintain overly large physical address tables. Centralized STPs are then used to convert the GT address into a physical address; this process is called Global Title Translation (GTT). This provides the mapping of traditional telephony addresses (phone numbers) to SS7 addresses (PC and/or SSN) for enhanced services. GTT is typically performed at STPs.

NOTE   It is important not to confuse the mapping of telephony numbers using GTT with the translation of telephony numbers done during normal call setup. Voice switches internally map telephony addresses to SS7 addresses during normal call processing using number translation tables. This process does not use GTT. GTT is used only for noncircuit-related information, such as network supplementary services (Calling Name Delivery) or database services (toll-free).

In addition to mapping telephony addresses to SS7 addresses, SCCP provides a set of subsystem management functions to monitor and respond to the condition of subsystems. These management functions are discussed further, along with the other aspects of SCCP, in Chapter 9, "Signaling Connection Control Part (SCCP)."

TCAP

TCAP allows applications (called subsystems) to communicate with each other (over the SS7 network) using agreed-upon data elements. These data elements are called *components*. Components can be viewed as instructions sent between applications. For example, when a subscriber changes VLR location in a global system for mobile communication (GSM) cellular network, his or her HLR is updated with the new VLR location by means of an UpdateLocation component. TCAP also provides transaction management, allowing multiple messages to be associated with a particular communications exchange, known as a transaction.

There are a number of subsystems; the most common are

- Toll-free (E800)
- Advanced Intelligent Network (AIN)
- Intelligent Network Application Protocol (INAP)
- Customizable Applications for Mobile Enhanced Logic (CAMEL)
- Mobile Application Part (MAP)

Figure 4-20 illustrates these subsystems as well as another protocol that uses SCCP, the Base Station Subsystem Application Part. It is used to control the radio-related component in cellular networks.

Figure 4-20 *Some Protocols That Might Exist on Top of the SCCP, Depending on the Application*

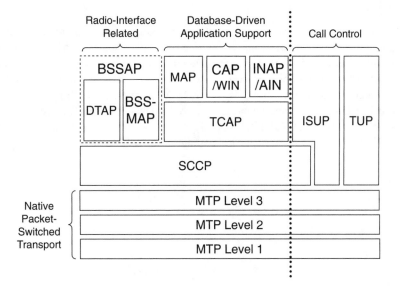

It is highly unlikely that a protocol such as the one shown in Figure 4-20 would exist at any one SP. Instead, protocol stacks vary as required by SP type. For example, because an STP is a routing device, it has only MTP1, MTP2, MTP3, and SCCP. A fixed-line switch without IN support might have only MTP1, MTP2, MTP3, and ISUP, and so forth. A diagram showing how the SS7 protocol stack varies by SP can be found in Chapter 13.

Summary

SS7 is a data communications network that acts as the nervous system to bring the components of telecommunications networks to life. It acts as a platform for various services described throughout this book. SS7 nodes are called signaling points (SPs), of which there are three types:

- Service Switching Point (SSP)
- Service Control Point (SCP)
- Signal Transfer Point (STP)

SSPs provide the SS7 functionality of a switch. STPs may be either standalone or integrated STPs (SSP and STP) and are used to transfer signaling messages. SCPs interface the SS7 network to query telecommunication databases, allowing service logic and additional routing information to be obtained to execute services.

SPs are connected to each other using signaling links. Signaling links are logically grouped into a linkset. Links may be referenced as A through F links, depending on where they are in the network.

Signaling is transferred using the packet-switching facilities afforded by SS7. These packets are called signal units (SUs). The Message Transfer Part (MTP) and the Signaling Connection Control Part (SCCP) provide the transfer protocols. MTP is used to reliably transport messages between nodes, and SCCP is used for noncircuit-related signaling (typically, transactions with SCPs). The ISDN User Part (ISUP) is used to set up and tear down both ordinary (analog subscriber) and ISDN calls. The Transaction Capabilities Application Part (TCAP) allows applications to communicate with each other using agreed-upon data components and manages transactions.

CHAPTER 5

The Public Switched Telephone Network (PSTN)

The term Public Switched Telephone Network (PSTN) describes the various equipment and interconnecting facilities that provide phone service to the public. The network continues to evolve with the introduction of new technologies. The PSTN began in the United States in 1878 with a manual mechanical switchboard that connected different parties and allowed them to carry on a conversation. Today, the PSTN is a network of computers and other electronic equipment that converts speech into digital data and provides a multitude of sophisticated phone features, data services, and mobile wireless access.

TIP   PSTN voice facilities transport speech or voice-band data (such as fax/modems and digital data), which is data that has been modulated to voice frequencies.

At the core of the PSTN are digital switches. The term "switch" describes the ability to cross-connect a phone line with many other phone lines and switching from one connection to another. The PSTN is well known for providing reliable communications to its subscribers. The phrase "five nines reliability," representing network availability of 99.999 percent for PSTN equipment, has become ubiquitous within the telecommunications industry.

This chapter provides a fundamental view of how the PSTN works, particularly in the areas of signaling and digital switching. SS7 provides control signaling for the PSTN, so you should understand the PSTN infrastructure to fully appreciate how it affects signaling and switching. This chapter is divided into the following sections:

- Network Topology
- PSTN Hierarchy
- Access and Transmission Facilities
- Network Timing

- The Central Office
- Integration of SS7 into the PSTN
- Evolving the PSTN to the Next Generation

We conclude with a summary of the PTSN infrastructure and its continuing evolution.

Network Topology

The topology of a network describes the various network nodes and how they interconnect. Regulatory policies play a major role in exactly how voice network topologies are defined in each country, but general similarities exist. While topologies in competitive markets represent an interconnection of networks owned by different service providers, monopolistic markets are generally an interconnection of switches owned by the same operator.

Depending on geographical region, PSTN nodes are sometimes referred to by different names. The three node types we discuss in this chapter include:

- **End Office (EO)**—Also called a Local Exchange. The End Office provides network access for the subscriber. It is located at the bottom of the network hierarchy.

- **Tandem**—Connects EOs together, providing an aggregation point for traffic between them. In some cases, the Tandem node provides the EO access to the next hierarchical level of the network.

- **Transit**—Provides an interface to another hierarchical network level. Transit switches are generally used to aggregate traffic that is carried across long geographical distances.

There are two primary methods of connecting switching nodes. The first approach is a mesh topology, in which all nodes are interconnected. This approach does not scale well when you must connect a large number of nodes. You must connect each new node to every existing node. This approach does have its merits, however; it simplifies routing traffic between nodes and avoids bottlenecks by involving only those switches that are in direct communication with each other. The second approach is a hierarchical tree in which nodes are aggregated as the hierarchy traverses from the subscriber access points to the top of the tree. PSTN networks use a combination of these two methods, which are largely driven by cost and the traffic patterns between exchanges.

Figure 5-1 shows a generic PSTN hierarchy, in which End Offices are connected locally and through tandem switches. Transit switches provide further aggregation points for connecting multiple tandems between different networks. While actual network topologies vary, most follow some variation of this basic pattern.

Figure 5-1   *Generic PSTN Hierarchies*

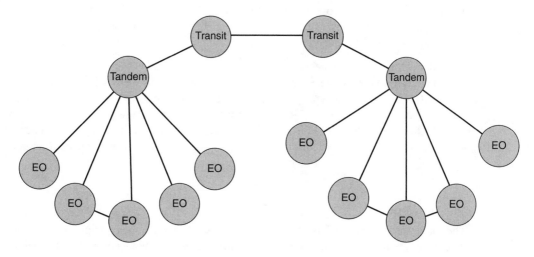

PSTN Hierarchy

The PSTN hierarchy is implemented differently in the United States and the United Kingdom. The following sections provide an overview of the PSTN hierarchy and its related terminology in each of these countries.

PSTN Hierarchy in the United States

In the United States, the PSTN is generally divided into three categories:

- Local Exchange Networks
- InterExchange Networks
- International Networks

Local Exchange Carriers (LECs) operate Local Exchange networks, while InterExchange Carriers (IXCs) operate InterExchange and International networks.

The PSTN hierarchy in the United States is also influenced by market deregulation, which has allowed service providers to compete for business and by the divestiture of Bell.

Local Exchange Network

The Local Exchange network consists of the digital switching nodes (EOs) that provide network access to the subscriber. The Local Exchange terminates both lines and trunks, providing the subscriber access to the PSTN.

A Tandem Office often connects End Offices within a local area, but they can also be connected directly. In the United States, Tandem Offices are usually designated as either Local Tandem (LT) or Access Tandem (AT). The primary purpose of a Local Tandem is to provide interconnection between End Offices in a localized geographic region. An Access Tandem provides interconnection between local End Offices and serves as a primary point of access for IXCs. Trunks are the facilities that connect all of the offices, thereby transporting internodal traffic.

InterExchange Network

The InterExchange network is comprised of digital switching nodes that provide the connection between Local Exchange networks. Because they are points of high traffic aggregation and they cover larger geographical distances, high-speed transports are typically used between transit switches. In the deregulated U.S. market, transit switches are usually referred to as *carrier switches*. In the U.S., IXCs access the Local Exchange network at designated points, referred to as a Point of Presence (POP). POPs can be connections at the Access Tandem, or direct connections to the End Office.

International Network

The International network consists of digital switching nodes, which are located in each country and act as international gateways to destinations outside of their respective countries. These gateways adhere to the ITU international standards to ensure interoperability between national networks. The international switch also performs the protocol conversions between national and international signaling. The gateway also performs PCM conversions between A-law and μ-law to produce compatible speech encoding between networks, when necessary.

Service Providers

Deregulation policies in the United States have allowed network operators to compete for business, first in the long-distance market (InterExchange and International) beginning in the mid 1980s, and later in the local market in the mid 1990s. As previously mentioned, LECs operate Local Exchange networks, while IXCs operate the long-distance networks. Figure 5-2 shows a typical arrangement of LEC-owned EOs and tandems interconnected to

IXC-owned transit switches. The IXC switches provide long-haul transport between Local Exchange networks, and international connections through International gateway switches.

Figure 5-2   *Generic U.S. Hierarchies*

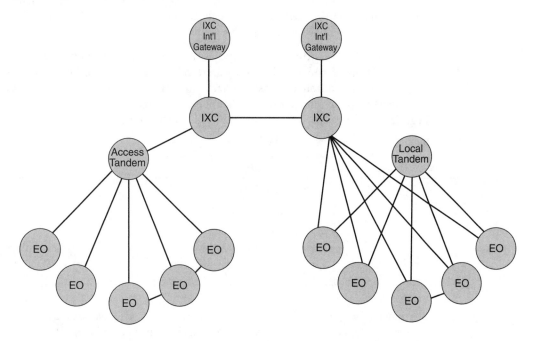

Over the last several years, the terms ILEC and CLEC have emerged within the Local Exchange market to differentiate between the Incumbent LECs (ILECS) and the Competitive LECs (CLECS). ILECs are the incumbents, who own existing access lines to residences and corporate facilities; CLECs are new entrants into the Local Exchange market. Most of the ILECs in the United States came about with the divestiture of AT&T into the seven Regional Bell Operating Companies (RBOC). The remainder belonged to Independent Operating Companies (IOCs). Most of these post-divestiture companies have been significantly transformed today by mergers and acquisitions in the competitive market. New companies have experienced difficulty entering into the Local Exchange market, which is dominated by ILECs. The ILECs own the wire to the subscriber's home, often called the "last mile" wiring. Last mile wiring is expensive to install and gives the ILECs tremendous market leverage. The long-distance market has been easier for new entrants because it does not require an investment in last mile wiring.

Pre-Divestiture Bell System Hierarchy

Vestiges of terminology relating to network topology remain in use today from the North American Bell System's hierarchy, as it existed prior to divestiture in 1984. Telephone switching offices are often still referred to by *class*. For example, an EO is commonly called a class 5 office, and an AT is called a class 4 office. Before divestiture, each layer of the network hierarchy was assigned a class number.

Prior to divestiture, offices were categorized by class number, with class 1 being the highest office category and class 5 being the lowest (nearest to subscriber access). Aggregation of transit phone traffic moved from the class 5 office up through the class 1 office. Each class of traffic aggregation points contained a smaller number of offices. Table 5-1 lists the class categories and office types used in the Bell System Hierarchy.

Table 5-1   *Pre-Divestiture Class Categories and Office Types*

Class	Office Type
1	Regional Center
2	Sectional Center
3	Primary Center
4	Toll Center
5	End Office

Local calls remained within class 5 offices, while a cross-country call traversed the hierarchy up to a regional switching center. This system no longer exists, but we included it to give relevance to the class terminology, which the industry still uses often.

PSTN Hierarchy in the United Kingdom

Figure 5-3 shows the PSTN topology used in the United Kingdom. End Offices are referred to as Digital Local Exchanges (DLE). A fully meshed tandem network of Digital Main Switching Units (DMSU) connects the DLEs. Digital International Switching Centers (DISC) connect the DMSU tandem switches for international call connections.

Figure 5-3   *U.K. PSTN Hierarchy*

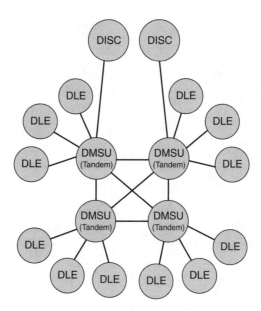

Access and Transmission Facilities

Connections to PSTN switches can be divided into two basic categories: lines and trunks. Individual telephone lines connect subscribers to the Central Office (CO) by wire pairs, while trunks are used to interconnect PSTN switches. Trunks also provide access to corporate phone environments, which often use a Private Branch eXchange (PBX)—or in the case of some very large businesses, their own digital switch. Figure 5-4 illustrates a number of common interfaces to the Central Office.

Figure 5-4   *End Office Facility Interfaces*

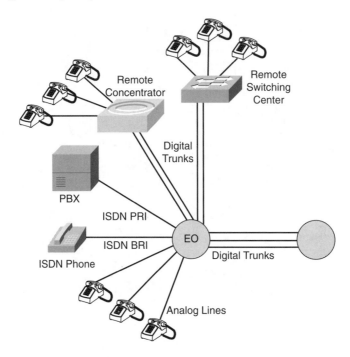

Lines

Lines are used to connect the subscriber to the CO, providing the subscriber access into the PSTN. The following sections describe the facilities used for lines, and the access signaling between the subscriber and the CO.

- The Local Loop
- Analog Line Signaling
- Dialing
- Ringing and Answer
- Voice Encoding
- ISDN BRI

The Local Loop

The local loop consists of a pair of copper wires extending from the CO to a residence or business that connects to the phone, fax, modem, or other telephony device. The wire pair consists of a tip wire and a ring wire. The terms *tip* and *ring* are vestiges of the manual switchboards that were used a number of years ago; they refer to the tip and ring of the actual switchboard plug operators used to connect calls. The local loop allows a subscriber to access the PSTN through its connection to the CO. The local loop terminates on the Main Distribution Frame (MDF) at the CO, or on a remote line concentrator.

Remote line concentrators, also referred to as Subscriber Line Multiplexers or Subscriber Line Concentrators, extend the line interface from the CO toward the subscribers, thereby reducing the amount of wire pairs back to the CO and converting the signal from analog to digital closer to the subscriber access point. In some cases, remote switching centers are used instead of remote concentrators.

Remote switching centers provide local switching between subtending lines without using the resources of the CO. *Remotes,* as they are often generically referred to, are typically used for subscribers who are located far away from the CO. While terminating the physical loop, remotes transport the digitized voice stream back to the CO over a trunk circuit, in digital form.

Analog Line Signaling

Currently, most phone lines are analog phone lines. They are referred to as analog lines because they use an analog signal over the local loop, between the phone and the CO. The analog signal carries two components that comprise the communication between the phone and the CO: the voice component, and the signaling component.

The signaling that takes place between the analog phone and the CO is called in-band signaling. In-band signaling is primitive when compared to the out-of-band signaling used in access methods such as ISDN; see the "ISDN BRI" section in this chapter for more information. DC current from the CO powers the local loop between the phone and the CO. The voltage levels vary between different countries, but an on-hook voltage of –48 to –54 volts is common in North America and a number of other geographic regions, including the United Kingdom.

TIP

The actual line loop voltage varies, based on the distance and the charge level of the batteries connected to the loop at the CO. When the phone receiver is on-hook, the CO sees practically no current over the loop to the phone set. When the phone is off-hook, the resistance level changes, changing the current seen at the CO. The actual amount of loop current that triggers an on/off-hook signal also varies among different countries. In North America, a current flow of greater than 20 milliamps indicates an off-hook condition. When the CO has detected the off-hook condition, it provides a dial tone by connecting a tone generation circuit to the line.

Dialing

When a subscriber dials a number, the number is signaled to the CO as either a series of pulses based on the number dialed, or by Dual Tone Multi-Frequency (DTMF) signals. The DTMF signal is a combination of two tones that are generated at different frequencies. A total of seven frequencies are combined to provide unique DTMF signals for the 12 keys (three columns by four rows) on the standard phone keypad. Usually, the dialing plan of the CO determines when all digits have been collected.

Ringing and Answer

To notify the called party of an incoming call, the CO sends AC ringing voltage over the local loop to the terminating line. The incoming voltage activates the ringing circuit within the phone to generate an audible ring signal. The CO also sends an audible ring-back tone over the originating local loop to indicate that the call is proceeding and the destination phone is ringing. When the destination phone is taken off-hook, the CO detects the change in loop current and stops generating the ringing voltage. This procedure is commonly referred to as *ring trip*. The off-hook signals the CO that the call has been answered; the conversation path is then completed between the two parties and other actions, such as billing, can be initiated, if necessary.

Voice Encoding

An analog voice signal must be encoded into digital information for transmission over the digital switching network. The conversion is completed using a codec (coder/decoder), which converts between analog and digital data. The ITU G.711 standard specifies the Pulse Coded Modulation (PCM) method used throughout most of the PSTN. An analog-to-digital converter samples the analog voice 8000 times per second and then assigns a quantization value based on 256 decision levels. The quantization value is then encoded into a binary number to represent the individual data point of the sample. Figure 5-5 illustrates the process of sampling and encoding the analog voice data.

Figure 5-5   *Voice Encoding Process*

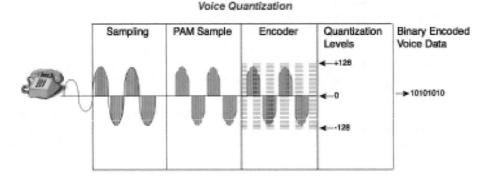

Two variations of encoding schemes are used for the actual quantization values: A-law and μ-Law encoding. North America uses μ-Law encoding, and European countries use A-law encoding. When voice is transmitted from the digital switch over the analog loop, the digital voice data is decoded and converted back into an analog signal before transmitting over the loop.

The emergence of voice over IP (VoIP) has prompted the use of other voice-encoding standards, such as ITU G.723, G.726, and ITU G.729. These encoding methods use algorithms that produce more efficient and compressed data, making them more suitable for use in packet networks. Each encoding method involves trade-offs between bandwidth, processing power required for the encoding/decoding function, and voice quality. For example, G.711 encoding/decoding requires little processing and produces high quality speech, but consumes more bandwidth. In contrast, G.723.1 consumes little bandwidth, but requires more processing power and results in lower quality speech.

ISDN BRI

Although Integrated Services Digital Network (ISDN) deployment began in the 1980s, it has been a relatively slow-moving technology in terms of number of installations. ISDN moves the point of digital encoding to the customer premises. Combining ISDN on the access portion of the network with digital trunks on the core network provides total end-to-end digital connectivity. ISDN also provides out-of-band signaling over the local loop. ISDN access signaling coupled with SS7 signaling in the core network achieves end-to-end out-of-band signaling. ISDN access signaling is designed to complement SS7 signaling in the core network.

There are two ISDN interface types: Basic Rate Interface (BRI) for lines, and Primary Rate Interface (PRI) for trunks. BRI multiplexes two bearer (2B) channels and one signaling (D) channel over the local loop between the subscriber and the CO; this is commonly referred to as 2B+D. The two B channels each operate at 64 kb/s and can be used for voice or data communication. The D channel operates at 16 kb/s and is used for call control signaling for the two B channels. The D channel can also be used for very low speed data transmission. Within the context of ISDN reference points, the local loop is referred to as the U-loop. It uses different electrical characteristics than those of an analog loop.

Voice quantization is performed within the ISDN phone (or a Terminal Adapter, if an analog phone is used) and sent to a local bus: the S/T bus. The S/T bus is a four-wire bus that connects local ISDN devices at the customer premises to a Network Termination 1 (NT1) device. The NT1 provides the interface between the Customer Premises Equipment (CPE) and the U-loop.

TIP   CPE refers to any of the ISDN-capable devices that are attached to the S/T bus.

The NT1 provides the proper termination for the local S/T bus to individual devices and multiplexes the digital information from the devices into the 2B+D format for transmission over the U-loop. Figure 5-6 illustrates the BRI interface to the CO. Only ISDN devices connect directly to the S/T bus. The PC uses an ISDN Terminal Adapter (TA) card to provide the proper interface to the bus.

Figure 5-6   *ISDN Basic Rate Interface*

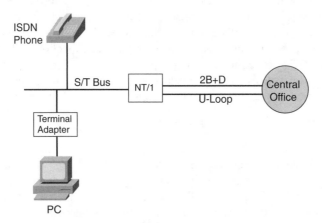

The ISDN U-Loop terminates at the CO on a line card that is specifically designed to handle the 2B+D transmission format. The call control signaling messages from the D channel are designed to map to SS7 messages easily for outbound calls over SS7 signaled trunks.

TIP   For U.S. networks, the Telcordia TR-444 (Generic Switching Systems Requirements Supporting ISDN access using the ISDN User Part) standard specifies the inter-working of ISDN and SS7.

Trunks

Trunks carry traffic between telephony switching nodes. While analog trunks still exist, most trunks in use today are digital trunks, which are the focus of this section. Digital trunks may be either four-wire (twisted pairs) or fiber optic medium for higher capacity. T1 and E1 are the most common trunk types for connecting to End Offices. North American networks use T1, and European networks use E1.

On the T1/E1 facility, voice channels are multiplexed into digital bit streams using Time Division Multiplexing (TDM). TDM allocates one timeslot from each digital data stream's frame to transmit a voice sample from a conversation. Each frame carries a total of 24 multiplexed voice channels for T1 and 30 channels for E1. The T1 frame uses a single bit for framing, while E1 uses a byte. Figure 5-7 shows the formats for T1 and E1 framing.

Figure 5-7   *T1/E1 Framing Formats*

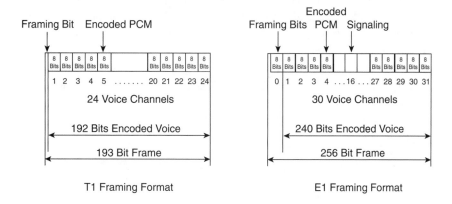

T1 Framing Format   E1 Framing Format

The E1 format also contains a channel dedicated to signaling when using in-band signaling. The T1 format uses "robbed bit" signaling when using in-band signaling. The term "robbed bit" comes from the fact that bits are taken from the PCM data to convey trunk supervisory signals, such as on/off-hook status and winks. This is also referred to as A/B bit signaling. In every sixth frame, the least significant bits from each PCM sample are used as signaling bits. In the case of Extended Superframe trunks (ESF), A/B/C/D bits are used to indicate trunk supervision signals. A/B bit signaling has been widely replaced by SS7 signaling, but it still exists in some areas.

Trunks are multiplexed onto higher capacity transport facilities as traffic is aggregated toward tandems and transit switches. The higher up in the switching hierarchy, the more likely optical fiber will be used for trunk facilities for its increased bandwidth capacity. In North America, Synchronous Optical Network (SONET) is the standard specification for transmission over optical fiber. SONET defines the physical interface, frame format, optical line rates, and an OAM&P protocol. In countries outside of North America, Synchronous Digital Hierarchy (SDH) is the equivalent optical standard. Fiber can accommodate a much higher bandwidth than copper transmission facilities, making it the medium of choice for high-density trunking.

Standard designations describe trunk bandwidth in terms of its capacity in bits/second. The basic unit of transmission is Digital Signal 0 (DS0), representing a single 64 kb/s channel that occupies one timeslot of a Time Division Multiplex (TDM) trunk. Transmission rates are calculated in multiples of DS0 rates. For example, a T1 uses 24 voice channels at 64 kb/s per channel to produce a DS1 transmission rate of 1.544 mb/s, calculated as follows:

24 x 64 kb/s = 1.536 kb/s + 8000 b/s framing bits = 1.544 mb/s

The optical transmission rates in the SONET transport hierarchy are designated in Optical Carrier (OC) units. OC-1 is equivalent to T3. Higher OC units are multiples of OC-1; for example, OC-3 is simply three times the rate of OC-1. In North America, the electrical equivalent signals are designated as Synchronous Transport Signal (STS) levels. The ITU SDH standard uses the STM to designate the hierarchical level of transmission. Table 5-2 summarizes the electrical transmission rates, and Table 5-3 summarizes the SONET/SDH transmission rates.

Table 5-2 *Electrical Transmission Rates*

Designation	Voice Channels	Transmission Rate mb/s
T1 (North America)	24	1.544
E1 (Europe)	30	2.048
E3 (Europe)	480	34.368
T3 (North America)	672	44.736

Table 5-3 *SONET/SDH Transmission Rates*

SONET Optical Level	SONET Electrical Level	SDH Level	Voice Channels	Transmission Rate mb/s
OC-1	STS-1	—	672	51.840
OC-3	STS-3	STM-1	2016	155.520
OC-12	STS-12	STM-4	8064	622.080
OC-48	STS-48	STM-16	32,256	2488.320
OC-96	STS-96	STM-32	64,512	4976.64
OC-192	STS-192	STM-64	129,024	9953.280
OC-768	STS-768	STM-256	516,096	39,813.120

In addition to copper and fiber transmission mediums, microwave stations and satellites are also used to communicate using radio signals between offices. This is particularly useful where it is geographically difficult to install copper and fiber into the ground or across rivers.

ISDN PRI

Primary Rate Interface (PRI) provides ISDN access signaling over trunks and is primarily used to connect PBXs to the CO. As with BRI, PRI converts all data at the customer premises into digital format before transmitting it over the PRI interface. In the United States, PRI uses 23 bearer channels for voice/data and one signaling channel for call control. The single signaling channel handles the signaling for calls on the other 23 channels. This scheme is commonly referred to as 23B+D. Each channel operates at a rate of 64 kb/s. Figure 5-8 illustrates a PBX connected to the CO through a PRI trunk.

Figure 5-8   *ISDN Primary Rate Interface*

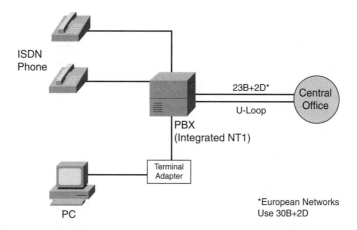

Other variations of this scheme use a single D channel to control more than 23 bearer channels. You can also designate a channel as a backup D channel to provide redundancy in case of a primary D channel failure. In the United States, U-Loop for PRI is a four-wire interface that operates at 1.544 mb/s. The U-Loop terminates to an NT1, which is typically integrated into the PBX at the customer premises.

In Europe, PRI is based on 32 channels at a transmission rate of 2.048 mb/s. There are 30 bearer channels and two signaling channels, which are referred to as 30B+2D.

Network Timing

Digital trunks between two connecting nodes require clock synchronization in order to ensure proper framing of the voice channels. The sending switch clocks the bits in each frame onto the transmission facility. They are clocked into the receiving switch at the other end of the facility. Digital facility interfaces use buffering techniques to store the incoming frame and accommodate slight variation in the timing of the data sent between the two ends. A problem arises if the other digital switch that is connected to the facility has a clock signal that is out of phase with the first switch. The variation in clock signals eventually causes errors in identifying the beginning of a frame. This condition is known as *slip*, and it results in buffer overrun or buffer underrun. Buffer overrun occurs if the frequency of the sending clock is greater than the frequency of the receiving clock, discarding an entire frame of data. Buffer underrun occurs if the frequency of the sending clock is less than the frequency of the receiving clock, repeating a frame of data. Occasional slips do not present a real problem for voice calls, although excessive slips result in degraded speech quality. However, they are more detrimental to the data transfer, in which each bit is important. Therefore, synchronization of time sources between the digital switches is important. Because digital transmission facilities connect switches throughout the network, this requirement escalates to a network level, where the synchronization of many switches is required.

There are various methods of synchronizing nodes. One method involves a single master clock source, from which other nodes derive timing in a master/slave arrangement. Another method uses a plesiochronous arrangement, where each node contains an independent clock whose accuracy is so great that it remains independently synchronized with other nodes. You can also use a combination of the two methods by using highly accurate clocks as a Primary Reference Source (PRS) in a number of nodes, providing timing to subtending nodes in the network.

The clocks' accuracy is rated in terms of stratum levels. Stratums 1 through 4 denote timing sources in order of descending accuracy. A stratum 1 clock provides the most accurate clock source with a free-running accuracy of $\pm1 \times 10^{-11}$, meaning only one error can occur in 10^{11} parts. A stratum 4 clock provides an accuracy of $\pm32 \times 10^{-6}$.

Since the deployment of Global Positioning System (GPS) satellites, each with a number of atomic clocks on-board, GPS clocks have become the preferred method of establishing a clock reference signal. Having a GPS clock receiver at each node that receives a stratum 1-quality timing signal from the GPS satellite flattens the distributed timing hierarchy. If the GPS receiver loses the satellite signal, the receiver typically runs free at stratum 2 or less. By using a flattened hierarchy based on GPS receivers, you remove the need to distribute the clock signal and provide a highly accurate reference source for each node. Figure 5-9 shows an example that uses a stratum 1 clock at a digital switching office to distribute timing to subtending nodes, and also shows an example that uses a GPS satellite clock receiver at each office.

Figure 5-9 *Network Timing for Digital Transmission*

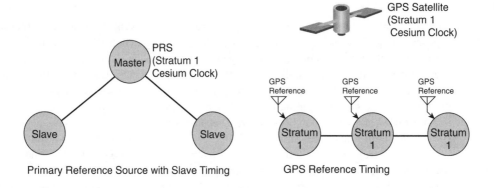

SS7 links are subject to the same timing constraints as the trunk facilities that carry voice/ data information because they use digital trunk transmission facilities for transport. If they produce unrecoverable errors, slips on the transmission facilities might affect SS7 messages. Therefore, you must always consider network timing when establishing SS7 links between nodes in the PSTN.

The Central Office

The Central Office (CO) houses the digital switching equipment that terminates subscribers' lines and trunks and *switch* calls. The term *switch* is a vestige of the switchboard era, when call connections were manually created using cords to connect lines on a plugboard. Electro-mechanical switches replaced manual switchboards, and those eventually evolved into the computer-driven digital switches of today's network. Now switching between calls is done electronically, under software control.

The following section focuses on these areas of the CO:

- The Main Distribution Frame
- The Digital Switch
- The Switching Matrix
- Call Processing

Main Distribution Frame

Incoming lines and trunks are terminated on the Main Distribution Frame (MDF). The MDF provides a junction point where the external facilities connect to the equipment within the CO. Jumpers make the connections between the external facilities and the CO equipment, thereby allowing connections to be changed easily. Line connections from the MDF to the digital switching equipment terminate on line cards that are designed to interface with the particular type of line being connected—such as POTS, ISDN BRI, and Electronic Key Telephone Set (EKTS) phone lines. For analog lines, this is normally the point at which voice encoding takes place. Trunk connections from the MDF are terminated on trunk interface cards, providing the necessary functions for message framing, transmission, and reception.

The Digital Switch

The digital switch provides a software-controlled matrix of interconnections between phone subscribers. A handful of telecommunications vendors produce the digital switches that comprise the majority of the modern PSTN; Nortel, Lucent, Siemens, Alcatel, and Ericsson hold the leading market share. While the digital switch's basic functionality is common across vendors, the actual implementation is vendor dependent. This section provides a general perspective on the functions of the digital switch that are common across different implementations.

All digital switches are designed with some degree of distributed processing. A typical architecture includes a central processing unit that controls peripheral processors interfacing with the voice channels. Redundancy is always employed in the design to provide the high reliability that is expected in the telephony network. For example, the failure of one central processing unit results in the activation of an alternate processing unit.

The line and trunk interface cards, mentioned previously, represent the point of entry into the digital switch. These cards typically reside in peripheral equipment that is ultimately controlled by the central processor. Within the digital switch, all voice streams are digitized data. Some voice streams, such as those from ISDN facilities and digital trunks, enter the switch as digital data. Other voice streams, such as the analog phone, enter as analog data but undergo digital conversion at their point of entry. Analog lines interface with line cards that contain codecs, which perform the PCM processing to provide digital data to the switch and analog data to the line. Using the distributed processing architecture, many functions related to the individual voice channels are delegated to the peripheral interface equipment. This relieves the central processor of CPU intensive, low-level processing functions, such as scanning for on/off hooks on each individual line to determine when a subscriber wants to place a call.

The central processing unit monitors information from peripheral processors on call events— such as origination, digit collection, answer, and termination—and orchestrates the actual call setup and release. Information from these events is also used to perform call accounting, billing, and statistical information such as Operational Measurements (OM).

Although the main purpose of the digital switch is to perform call processing, much of its functionality is dedicated to maintenance, diagnostics, and fault recovery to ensure reliability.

TIP   An OM is a counter that records an event of particular interest, such as the number of call attempts or the number of a particular type of message received, to service providers. OMs can also be used to record usage in terms of how long a resource is used. Modern digital switches usually record hundreds, or even thousands of different types of OMs for various events taking place in the switch.

Switching Matrix

A modern digital switch can process many voice channels. The actual number of channels it processes varies with the switch vendor and particular model of switch, but they often process tens of thousands of voice channels in a single switch. A number of switches have capacities of over 100,000 connections.

The switch is responsible for many tasks, but one of its primary functions is connecting voice channels to create a bi-directional conversation path between two phone subscribers. All digital switches incorporate some form of switching matrix to allow the connection of voice channels to other voice channels. Once a circuit is set up between the two subscribers, the connection remains for the duration of the call. This method of setting up call connections is commonly known as circuit switching.

Figure 5-10 illustrates how a switching matrix demultiplexes individual timeslots from a multiplexed stream of voice channels and inserts them into the appropriate time slot for a connection on another facility, to connect voice channels. For example, in the figure, time slot 4 from the digital stream on the left connects to timeslot 30 of the digital stream on the right. The figure shows thirty channels, but the number of channels depends on the individual implementation of the switching matrix.

Figure 5-10 *TDM Switching Matrix*

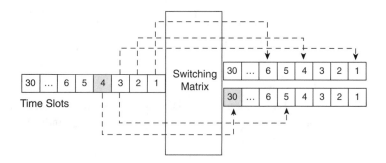

Each timeslot represents a voice connection path. The matrix connects the two paths to provide a conversation path between two parties. For long-distance calls that traverse a number of switches, an individual call goes through multiple switching matrices and is mapped to a new timeslot at each switching point. When the call is set up, it occupies the voice channel that was set up through the network for the duration of the call.

Call Processing

Call processing is associated with the setup, maintenance, and release of calls within the digital switch. The process is driven by software, in response to stimulus from the facilities coming into the switch. Signaling indications, such as on/off-hook, dialing digits, and answer, are all part of the stimuli that drive the processing of calls.

Each call process can be represented as an originating call half and a terminating call half. When combined, the two halves are completely representative of the call. The originating half is created when the switch determines that the originator is attempting a call. The terminating call half is created when the destination has been identified, typically at the translations or routing phase. The Intelligent Network standards have established a standardized call model, which incorporates the half-call concept. A complete discussion of the call model is presented in Chapter 11, "Intelligent Networks (IN)."

Call processing can be broken down in various ways; the following list provides a succinct view of the major stages of establishing and disconnecting a call.

- Origination
- Digit Collection
- Translation (Digit Analysis)
- Routing
- Connection
- Disconnection

Additional functions, such as billing and service interactions, also take place, but are excluded in our simple view of processing.

Origination

For a line, this initial phase of call processing occurs when a subscriber goes off-hook to initiate a call. The actual event provided to the digital switch to indicate a line origination can be a change in loop current for analog lines, or a setup message from an ISDN BRI facility. In-band A/B bit off-hook signaling, an ISDN PRI setup message, or an Initial Address Message from an SS7 signaled trunk can signal a digital trunk's origination. All of these events indicate the origination of a new call. The origination event creates the originating half of the call.

Digit Collection

For analog line originations, the switch collects digits as the caller dials them. Inter-digit timing monitors the amount of time the caller takes to dial each digit so that the line cannot be left in the dialing state for an infinite amount of time. If the caller does not supply the required number of digits for calling within a specified time, the caller is usually connected to a digital announcement to indicate that there is a problem with dialing, a Receiver Off-Hook (ROH) tone, or both. The dialing plan used for the incoming facility usually specifies the number of digits that are required for calling.

For ISDN lines, the dialed digits are sent in an ISDN Setup message.

Translation

Translation, commonly referred to as digit analysis, is the process of analyzing the collected digits and mapping them to a result. The translation process directs calls to their network destination. The dial plan associated with the incoming line, or trunk, is consulted to determine how the digits should be translated. Different dial plans can be associated with different incoming facilities to allow flexibility and customization in the translation of incoming calls. The dial plan specifies such information as the minimum and maximum number of digits to be collected, acceptable number ranges, call type, special billing indicators, and so forth. The translation process can be somewhat complex for calls that involve advanced services like Centrex, which is often associated with business phones.

TIP   Centrex is a set of services provided by the local exchange switch to business subscribers, including features like ring again, call parking, and conferencing. Centrex allows businesses to have many of the services provided by a PBX without the overhead of PBX cost, administration, and maintenance.

The process of digit translation can produce several different results. The most common result is a *route* selection for the call to proceed. Other results include connection to a recorded announcement or tone generator, or the sending of an Intelligent Network Query message for calls involving Intelligent Network services. Network administrators provision dial plan, routing information, and other translation-related information on the switch. However, information returned from IN queries can be used to modify or override statically provisioned information, such as routing.

Routing

The call proceeds to the routing stage after translation processing. Routing is the process of selecting a voice channel (on a facility) over which to send the outbound call toward its intended destination, which the dialed digits identify during translation. Routing typically uses route lists, which contain multiple routes from which to choose. For calls that are destined outside of the switching node, a *trunk group* is selected for the outbound call. A trunk group is a collection of trunk members that are connected to a single destination. After a trunk group is selected, an individual *trunk member* is selected from the group. A trunk member occupies an individual time slot on a digital trunk.

Routing algorithms are generally used for selecting the individual trunk circuit. For example, members of an outgoing trunk group are commonly selected using algorithms such as least idle, most idle, and ascending or descending order (based on the numerical trunk member number).

Connection

Call connection must take place on both the transmit and receive paths for a bi-directional conversation to take place. Each involved switch creates a connection between the originating half of the call and the terminating half of the call. This connection must be made through the switching matrix, and the speech path must be *cut through* between the incoming and outgoing voice channels. Supervision messages or signals sent from the central processor to the peripheral interfaces typically cut through the connection for the speech path. The central processor uses supervision signals to indicate how the peripheral processors should handle lower-level functions. It is typical to cut through the backward speech path (from terminator to originator) before cutting through the forward speech path. This approach allows the terminating switch to send the audible ringback over the voice channel, to the originating switch. When the originating switch receives an answer indication, the call path should be connected in both directions.

Disconnection

A call may be disconnected when it is active, meaning that it has been set up and is in the talking state. Disconnection can be indicated in a several ways. For analog lines, the originating or terminating side of the call can go on-hook, causing a disconnection.

TIP   Actually, the call is not disconnected when the terminating line goes on-hook, in some cases. These cases are examined further in Chapter 8, "ISUP."

ISDN sets send a Disconnect message to disconnect the call. For trunks using in-band signaling, on-hook is signaled using the signaling bits within the voice channel. For SS7 trunks, a Release message is the signal to disconnect a call.

Call Setup

Figure 5-11 shows a typical call setup sequence for a line-to-trunk call. For these calls, the originator dials a number and the digits are collected and processed according to the originating line's dial plan. The dial plan yields a result and points to a list of routes to another switching node. The route list contains a list of trunk groups, from which one group will be selected, usually based on primary and alternate route choices. After the group is selected, an actual trunk member (digital timeslot) is chosen for the outgoing path. The selection of the individual trunk member is typically based on standardized trunk selection algorithms, such as:

- **Most Idle**—The trunk member that has been used the least
- **Least Idle**—The trunk member that has been used the most

- **Ascending**—The next non-busy trunk member, in ascending numerical order
- **Descending**—The next non-busy trunk member, in descending numerical order

Both a call origination endpoint and a call termination endpoint have been established in respect to the digital switch processing the call. The connection can now be made through the switching matrix between the two endpoints. The timing of the actual speech path cut-through between the external interfaces varies based on many factors, but the switch now has the information it needs to complete the full connection path at the appropriate time, as determined by software.

Figure 5-11 *Basic Origination Call Processing*

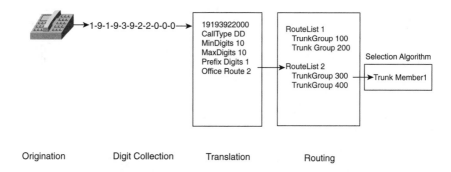

Origination   Digit Collection   Translation   Routing

Integration of SS7 into the PSTN

This section provides a brief overview of how the SS7 architecture is applied to the PSTN. Since SS7 has not been presented in great detail, the examples and information are brief and discussed only in the context of the network nodes presented in this section.

The PSTN existed long before SS7. The network's general structure was already in place, and it represented a substantial investment. The performance requirements mandated by the 800 portability act of 1993 was one of the primary drivers for the initial deployment of SS7 by ILECs in the United States. IXCs embraced SS7 early to cut down on post-dial delay which translated into significant savings on access/egress charges. Federal regulation, cost savings, and the opportunity to provide new revenue generating services created a need to deploy SS7 into the existing PSTN.

SS7 was designed to integrate easily into the existing PSTN, to preserve the investment and provide minimal disruption to the network. During SS7's initial deployment, additional hardware was added and digital switches received software upgrades to add SS7 capability to existing PSTN nodes. In the SS7 network, a digital switch with SS7 capabilities is referred to as a Service Switching Point (SSP). When looking at the SS7 network topologies in later chapters, it is important to realize that the SSP is not a new node in the network.

Instead, it describes an existing switching node, to which SS7 capabilities have been added. Similarly, SS7 did not introduce new facilities for signaling links, but used timeslots on existing trunk facilities. PSTN diagrams containing End Offices and tandems connected by trunks represent the same physical facilities as those of SS7 diagrams that show SSP nodes with interconnecting links. The introduction of SS7 added new nodes, such as the STP and SCP; however, all of the switching nodes and facilities that existed before SS7 was introduced are still in place. Figure 5-12 shows a simple view of the PSTN, overlaid with SS7-associated signaling capabilities.

Figure 5-12 *SS7 Overlaid onto the PSTN*

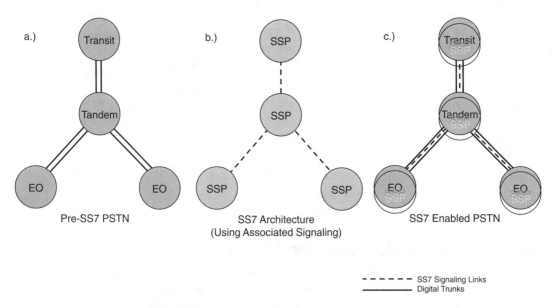

View *a* in the previous figure shows that trunk facilities provide the path for voice and in-band signaling. View *b* shows the SS7 topology using simple associated signaling for all nodes. View *c* shows the actual SS7-enabled PSTN topology. The existing switching nodes and facilities are enhanced to provide basic SS7 call processing functionality. Although this associated signaling architecture is still quite common in Europe, the United States primarily uses a quasi-associated signaling architecture.

SS7 Link Interface

The most common method for deploying SS7 links is for each link to occupy a timeslot, such as a T1 or E1, on a digital trunk. As shown in Figure 5-12, the signaling links actually travel on the digital trunk transmission medium throughout the network. At each node, the

SS7 interface equipment must extract the link timeslot from the digital trunk for processing. This process is typically performed using a channel bank, or a Digital Access and Cross-Connect (DAC), which demultiplexes the TDM timeslot from the digital trunk. The channel bank, or DAC, can extract each of the timeslots from the digital stream, allowing them to be processed individually. The individual SS7 link provides the SS7 messages to the digital switch for processing. While implementations vary, dedicated peripheral processors usually process the lower levels of the SS7 protocol (Level 1, Level 2, and possibly a portion of Level 3); call- and service-related information is passed on to the central processor, or to other peripheral processors that are designed for handling call processing–related messages. Of course, this process varies based on the actual equipment vendor.

Evolving the PSTN to the Next Generation

The expansion of the Internet continues to drive multiple changes in the PSTN environment. First, more network capacity is used to transport data over the PSTN. Dial-up Internet services use data connections that are set up over the PSTN to carry voice-band data over circuit-switched connections. This is a much different situation than sending data over a data network. Data networks use packet switching, in which many data transactions share the same facilities. Circuit-switched connections are dedicated connections, which occupy a circuit for the duration of a call. The phone networks were originally engineered for the three-minute call, which was the average length used for calculations when engineering the voice network. Of course, Internet connections tend to be much more lengthy, meaning that more network capacity is needed. The changes driven by the Internet, however, reach much further than simply an increase in network traffic. Phone traffic is being moved to both private packet-based networks and the public Internet, thereby providing an alternative to sending calls over the PSTN. Several different architectures and protocols are competing in the VoIP market to establish alternatives to the traditional circuit-switched network presented in this chapter. The technologies are not necessarily exclusive; some solutions combine the various technologies. Among the current leading VoIP technologies are:

- Soft switches
- H.323
- Session Initiation Protocol (SIP)

Each of these VoIP architectures use VoIP-PSTN gateways to provide some means of communication between the traditional PSTN networks and VoIP networks. These gateways provide access points for interconnecting the two networks, thereby creating a migration path from PSTN-based phone service to VoIP phone service. The core network interface connections for VoIP into the PSTN are the trunk facilities that carry the voice channels and the signaling links that carry SS7 signaling. PRI is also commonly used for business to network access. Figure 5-13 shows the interconnection of VoIP architectures to the PSTN using signaling gateways and trunking gateways. Chapter 14, "SS7 in the Converged World," discusses these VoIP technologies in more detail.

Figure 5-13 *VoIP Gateways to the PSTN*

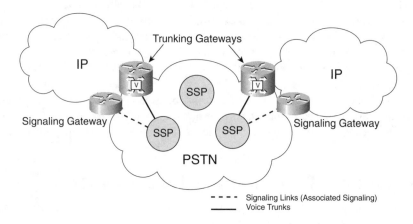

Summary

This chapter provides an overview of the PSTN, as it existed before VoIP technologies emerged. The majority of the PSTN still appears as this chapter presents it. Many of the diagrams in telecommunications literature illustrating *next generation* technologies—such as soft switches, H.323, and Session Initial Protocol (SIP)—show interfaces to the PSTN. The diagrams refer to the PSTN discussed here, dominated by large, digital switches. The technologies introduced often replace some portion of the existing PSTN; however, they must also remain connected to the existing PSTN to communicate with the rest of the world. The VoIP-PSTN gateways provide this transition point, thus enabling a migration path from the traditional PSTN to the next generation architecture.

While the PSTN varies in its implementation from country to country, a number of common denominators exist. The PSTN is a collection of digital switching nodes that are interconnected by trunks. The network topology is usually a hierarchical structure, but it often incorporates some degree of mesh topology. The topology provides network access to residential and business subscribers for voice and data services. VoIP began another evolution of the PSTN architecture. The PSTN is a large infrastructure that will likely take some time to completely migrate to the next generation of technologies; but this migration process is underway.

Protocols Found in the Traditional SS7/C7 Stack

CHAPTER 6

Message Transfer Part 2 (MTP2)

This chapter is the first in a series of chapters that examine a specific SS7/C7 protocol layer. This chapter details the Layer 2 protocol, which is known as *Message Transfer Part 2 (MTP2)*. MTP2 corresponds to OSI Layer 2 (the data link layer) and as such is the lowest protocol in the stack. Sitting on the physical layer, it provides a reliable means of transfer for signaling information between two directly connected signaling points (SPs), ensuring that the signaling information is delivered in sequence and error-free.

MTP2 performs the following functions:

- Delimitation of signal units
- Alignment of signal units
- Signaling link error detection
- Signaling link error correction by retransmission
- Signaling link initial alignment
- Error monitoring and reporting
- Link flow control

The signaling information is transmitted in frames called signal units (SUs). SUs are of variable length, thereby requiring the start and end of each SU to be flagged in the data stream. MTP2 performs this function, which is called signal unit delimitation. The ability to correctly recognize signal units is achieved through signal unit alignment.

Error correction is implemented by retransmitting the signal unit(s) received in error. The link is also continuously monitored to ensure that error rates are within permissible limits. If the error rate becomes greater than predefined limits, MTP2 reports the failure to Message Transfer Part 3 (MTP3), which subsequently orders MTP2 to remove the link from service. Conversely, initial alignment procedures are used to bring links into service.

Link flow control procedures are provided to resolve congestion at the MTP2 layer. Congestion occurs if MTP3 falls behind in processing SUs from the MTP2 buffer.

This chapter describes each of the previously outlined functional areas of MTP2.

It is important to understand that the MTP2 protocol does not work end to end. Rather, it operates on a link-by-link basis (known in datacoms as point to point) between two SPs. Therefore, each signaling data link has an associated MTP2 at each end.

Signal Unit Formats

SUs transfer information, which originates from higher layers (MTP3, ISUP, SCCP, TUP, and so on) in the form of messages, over the signaling link. MTP2 is similar to data network bit-oriented link protocols such as HDLC, SDLC, and LAPB. The primary difference with these protocols comes from the performance requirements in terms of lost and out-of-sequence messages and delay.

There are three types of SUs, each with its own format: the fill-in signal unit (FISU), the link status signal unit (LSSU), and the Message Signal Unit (MSU). An in-service signaling link carries a continuous SU stream in each direction.

FISUs and LSSUs are used only for MTP2 functions. MSUs also contain the same MTP2 fields, but they have two additional fields filled with information from MTP3 and Level 4 users that contain the real signaling content. This chapter describes the MTP2 fields and the functions they perform. It begins by presenting the three SU formats.

NOTE   The formats shown are for 64-kbps links. The formats for high-speed (1.5/2.0 Mbps) signaling links might differ slightly in that the sequence number might be extended to 12 bits. More details are available in Annex A of ITU-T Q.703 [51].

Fill-In Signal Units

FISUs are the most basic SU and carry only MTP2 information. They are sent when there are no LSSUs or MSUs to be sent, when the signaling link would otherwise be idle. Sending FISUs ensures 100 percent link occupancy by SUs at all times. A cyclic redundancy check (CRC) checksum is calculated for each FISU, allowing both signaling points at either end of the link to continuously check signaling link quality. This check allows faulty links to be identified quickly and taken out of service so that traffic can be shifted to alternative links, thereby helping meet the SS7/C7 network's high availability requirement. Because MTP2 is a point-to-point protocol, only the MTP2 level of adjacent signaling points exchanges FISUs.

The seven fields that comprise a FISU, shown in Figure 6-1, are also common to LSSUs and MSUs. MTP2 adds the fields at the originating signaling point and processes and removes them at the destination signaling point (an adjacent node).

Figure 6-1   *FISU Format*

Link Status Signal Units

LSSUs carry one or two octets of link status information between signaling points at either end of a link. The link status controls link alignment, indicates the link's status, and indicates a signaling point's status to the remote signaling point. The presence of LSSUs at any time other than during link alignment indicates a fault—such as a remote processor outage or an unacceptably high bit error rate affecting the ability to carry traffic.

The timers associated with a particular status indication govern the transmission interval. After the fault is cleared, the transmission of LSSUs ceases, and normal traffic flow can continue. As with FISUs, only MTP2 of adjacent signaling points exchanges LSSUs. LSSUs are identical to FISUs, except that they contain an additional field called the *Status field (SF)*. Figure 6-2 shows the eight fields that comprise an LSSU.

Figure 6-2   *LSSU Format*

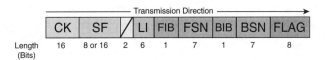

Currently only a single-octet SF is used, even though the specifications allow for a two-octet SF. From the single octet, only the first 3 bits are defined. These bits provide the status indications shown in Table 6-1.

Table 6-1   *Values in the Status Field*

C	B	A	Status Indication	Acronym	Meaning
0	0	0	O: Out of Alignment	SIO	Link not aligned; attempting alignment
0	0	1	N: Normal Alignment	SIN	Link is aligned
0	1	0	E: Emergency Alignment	SIE	Link is aligned
0	1	1	OS: Out of Service	SIOS	Link out of service; alignment failure
1	0	0	PO: Processor Outage	SIPO	MTP2 cannot reach MTP3
1	0	1	B: Busy	SIB	MTP2 congestion

Message Signal Units

As shown in Figure 6-3, MSUs contain the common fields of the FISU and two additional fields: the Signaling Information Field (SIF) and the Service Information Octet (SIO). MSUs carry the signaling information (or messages) between both MTP3 and Level 4 users. The messages include all call control, database query, and response messages. In addition, MSUs carry MTP3 network management messages. All messages are placed in the SIF of the MSU.

Figure 6-3 *MSU Format*

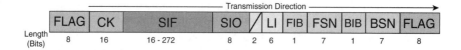

MTP2 Overhead

Figure 6-4 shows an MSU. The MTP2 overhead is exactly the same for both LSSUs and FISUs, except that an LSSU has an SF.

Figure 6-4 *Fields Created and Processed by MTP2*

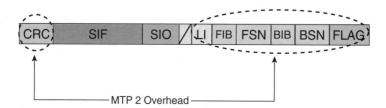

Field Descriptions

Table 6-2 details the fields that are found inside the signal units. MTP2 exclusively processes all fields except the SIO and the SIF.

Table 6-2 *Field Descriptions*

Field	Length in Bits	Description
Flag	8	A pattern of 011111110 to indicate the start and end of an SU.
BSN	7	Backward sequence number. Identifies the last correctly received SU.
BIB	1	Backward indicator bit. Toggled to indicate an error with the received SU.

Table 6-2   *Field Descriptions (Continued)*

Field	Length in Bits	Description
FSN	7	Forward sequence number. Identifies each transmitted SU.
FIB	1	Forward indicator bit. Toggled to indicate the retransmission of an SU that was received in error by the remote SP.
LI	6	Length indicator. Indicates how many octets reside between itself and the CRC field. The LI field also implies the type of signal unit. LI = 0 for FISUs, LI = 1 or 2 for LSSUs, and LI >2 for MSUs.
SF	8 to 16	Status field. Provides status messages in the LSSU only.
CK	16	Check bits. Uses CRC-16 to detect transmission errors.
SIO	8	Service Information Octet. Specifies which MTP3 user has placed a message in the SIF.
SIF	16 to 2176	Signaling Information Field. Contains the "real" signaling content. The SIF is also related to call control, network management, or databases query/response.

Signal Unit Delimitation

A flag octet that is coded as 01111110 separates consecutive signal units on a signaling data link. The flag octet indicates the beginning or end of an SU.

NOTE   It is optional whether a single flag is used to mark both the beginning and end of an SU, or whether a common flag is used for both. The latter is the most common implementation.

Because the 01111110 flag pattern can also occur in an SU, the SU is scanned before a flag is attached, and a 0 is inserted after every sequence of five consecutive 1s. This method is called *bit stuffing* (or *0 bit insertion*). It solves the problem of false flags, because it prevents the pattern 01111110 from occurring inside an SU. The receiving MTP2 carries out the reverse process, which is called *bit removal* (or *0 bit deletion*). After flag detection and removal, each 0 that directly follows a sequence of five consecutive 1s is deleted. Figure 6-5 shows how the sending node adds a 0 following five 1s while the receiving node removes a 0 following five 1s.

As another example, if the pattern 01111100_{LSB} appears in the SU, the pattern is changed to 001111100_{LSB} and then is changed back at the receiving end.

This method continuously processes the stream of data on the link, inserting a 0 after five contiguous 1s without examining the value of the next bit.

Figure 6-5   *Zero Bit Insertion and Deletion*

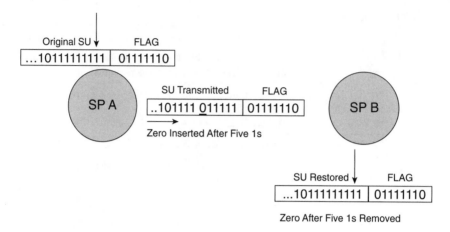

Length Indicator

MTP2 must be able to determine the SU type to process it. The length indicator (LI) provides an easy way for MTP2 to recognize the SU type. The LI indicates the number of octets between the LI and the CRC fields. Using telecommunications conventions, MTP2 measures the size of SUs in octets. An octet is simply another term for a byte; all SUs have an integral number of octets.

The LI field implies the type of signal unit. LI = 0 for FISUs, LI = 1 or 2 for LSSUs, and LI >2 for MSUs. Because MSUs contain the actual signaling content, their size is relatively large compared to the two other types of SUs.

NOTE   Layers above the MTP can handle larger data streams than the MTP; however, these streams must be segmented into MSUs at MTP2 for transmission over the signaling link.

The signaling payload is placed in the SIF, which is found in an MSU. The SIF can be up to 272 octets in size, rendering the maximum length for an MSU as 279 octets. If the MSU size is greater than 62 octets, the LI is set to the value of 63; therefore, an LI of 63 means that the SIF length is between 63 and 272 octets. This situation arises from backward-compatibility issues. The Red Book specified the maximum number of octets in the SIF as 62, and the Blue Book increased it to 272 (which was previously allowed only as a national option). (See the section "ITU-T (Formerly CCITT) International Standards" in Chapter 2, "Standards," for information about the meaning of the Red Book and Blue Book.)

MTP2 uses the LI information to determine the type of SU with minimum processing overhead; therefore, the inaccuracy of the indicator above 62 octets is not an issue. MTP2 adds an overhead of six octets along with one additional octet for the MTP3 SIO when creating each MSU. This brings the total maximum size of a transmitted SU to 279 octets (272 maximum SIF size plus seven for MTP2 overhead and the SIO).

NOTE   In ANSI networks, when 1.536-Mbps links are used, a 9-bit length indicator is used, and the actual SU length is checked against the LI value.

Signal Unit Alignment

Loss of alignment occurs when a nonpermissible bit pattern is received or when an SU greater than the maximum SU size is received.

MTP2 constantly processes the data stream, searching for flags that delineate the SUs. The maximum number of consecutive 1s that should be found in the bit stream is six (as part of the flag), because the transmitting end performs 0 bit insertion. If seven or more consecutive 1s are detected, this signifies a loss of alignment.

The SU length should be in multiples of octets (8 bits). The minimum size of an SU is six octets (FISU), and the maximum size is 279 octets (MSU). If an SU is outside these parameters, this is considered a loss of alignment, and the SU is discarded.

Error Detection

The error detection method is performed by a 16-bit CRC on each signal unit. These 16 bits are called check bits (CK bits).

NOTE   The process uses the Recommendation V.41 [ITU-T Recommendation V.41: CODE-INDEPENDENT ERROR-CONTROL SYSTEM, November 1988] generator polynomial $X^{16} + X^{12} + X^5 + 1$. The transmitter's 16-bit remainder value is initialized to all 1s before a signal unit is transmitted. The transmission's binary value is multiplied by X^{16} and then divided by the generator polynomial. Integer quotient values are ignored, and the transmitter sends the complement of the resulting remainder value, high-order bit first, as the CRC field. At the receiver, the initial remainder is preset to all 1s, and the same process is applied to the serial incoming bits. In the absence of transmission errors, the final remainder is 1111000010111000 ($X^0 + X^{15}$).

The polynomial that is used is optimized to detect error bursts. The check bits are calculated using all fields between the flags and ignoring any inserted 0s. The SP then appends the calculation to the SU before transmission as a two-octet field (CK field). The receiving SP performs the same calculation in an identical manner. Finally, the two results are compared; if an inconsistency exists, the SU is discarded, and the error is noted by adding to the Signal Unit Error Rate Monitor (SUERM). In this case, the error correction procedure is applied.

Error Correction

Two methods of error correction are available: basic error correction (BEC) and preventive cyclic retransmission (PCR) method. The basic method is used for signaling links using nonintercontinental terrestrial transmission and for intercontinental links that have a one-way propagation delay of less than 30 ms. The PCR method is used for all signaling links that have a propagation delay greater than or equal to 125 ms and on all satellite signaling links [115]. Where the one-way propagation delay is between 30 and 125 ms, other criteria must be considered that are outside the scope of this book (see [115]). Depending on other additional criteria, PCR can also be employed on links that have a one-way propagation delay between 30 ms and 125 ms [52].

For cases in which only one link in a linkset uses PCR, the other links should use PCR, regardless of their propagation delays. For example, if a single link in an international linkset is established by satellite, the PCR method should also be used for all other links in that linkset—even if the other links are terrestrial. (For information on linksets, see Chapter 4, "SS7 Network Architecture and Protocols Introduction.") This approach reduces the chances of different methods of error correction being provisioned at either side of the same link.

Neither method tries to repair a corrupt MSU; rather, they both seek correction by MSU retransmission. For this reason, a signaling point has a retransmission buffer (RTB). The RTB stores copies of all the MSUs it has transmitted until the receiving SP positively acknowledges them.

Basic Error Correction

The basic method is a noncompelled, positive/negative acknowledgment, retransmission error correction system [51]. Noncompelled means that messages are sent only once—that is, unless they are corrupted during transfer. Positive/negative acknowledgment means that each message is acknowledged as being received, along with an indicator that the message was received error-free. Retransmission error correction system simply means that no attempt is made to repair the corrupt message; instead, correction is achieved through retransmission.

In normal operation, this method ensures the correct transfer of MSUs—in the correct sequence and without loss or duplication—over a signaling link. Therefore, no resequencing is required at MTP2.

Basic error correction is accomplished using a backwards retransmission mechanism, in which the sender retransmits the corrupt (or missing) MSU and all subsequent MSUs. This method uses both negative and positive acknowledgments. Positive acknowledgments (ACKs) indicate the correct reception of an MSU, and negative acknowledgments (NACKs) are used as explicit requests for retransmission. Only MSUs are acknowledged and resent, if corrupt, to minimize retransmissions. FISUs and LSSUs are neither acknowledged nor resent if corrupt; however, the error occurrences are noted for error rate monitoring purposes.

The basic error correction fields occupy a total of two octets in each SU and consist of an FSN, BSN, FIB, and BIB. The Forward Sequence Number (FSN) and Backward Sequence Number (BSN) are cyclic binary counts in the range 0 to 127. The Forward Indicator Bit (FIB) and Backward Indicator Bit (BIB) are binary flags that are used in conjunction with the FSN and BSN for the basic error correction method only.

NOTE   In ANSI networks, the sequence numbers extend up to 4095 for high-speed links. Links using bit rates of 64 kbps or lower are still limited to a maximum value of 127.

Sequence Numbering

Each SU carries two sequence numbers for the purpose of SU acknowledgment and sequence control. Whereas the FSN is used for the function of SU sequence control, the BSN is used for the function of SU acknowledgment.

Before it is transmitted, each MSU is assigned an FSN. The FSN is increased linearly as MSUs are transmitted. The FSN value uniquely identifies the MSU until the receiving SP accepts its delivery without errors and in the correct sequence. FISUs and LSSUs are not assigned new FSNs; instead, they are sent with an FSN value of the last MSU that was sent. Because the FSN has a range of 127, it has to start from 0 again after it reaches a count of 127. This dictates that the RTB cannot store more than 128 MSUs.

Positive Acknowledgment

When the BIB in the received SU has the same value as the FIB that was sent previously, this indicates a positive acknowledgment.

The receiving SP acknowledges positive acceptance of one or more MSUs by copying the FSN value of the last accepted MSU into the SU's BSN, which it transmits. All subsequent SUs in that direction retain the same BSN value until a further incoming MSU requires acknowledgment. The BIB is set to the same value as the received FIB to indicate positive acknowledgment.

Negative Acknowledgment

When the BIB in the received SU is not the same value as the FIB that was sent previously, this indicates a negative acknowledgment.

The receiving SP generates a negative acknowledgment for one or more MSUs by toggling the BIB's value. It then copies the FSN value of the last accepted MSU into the SU's BSN, which it transmits in the opposite direction.

Response to a Positive Acknowledgment

The transmitting SP examines the BSN of the received SU. Because they have been positively acknowledged, the MSUs in the RTB that have an FSN equal to or less than the BSN are removed.

If an SU is received with a BSN that does not equal the previously sent BSN or one of the FSNs in the RTB, it is discarded. If an incorrect BSN is received three consecutive times, MTP2 informs MTP3 that the link is faulty, therefore resulting in an order for MTP2 to remove the link from service.

The *excessive delay of acknowledgment* (T7) timer ensures that acknowledgments are received in an appropriate amount of time. Because the FSN values cannot be used again until they have been acknowledged, excessive delay would quickly exhaust the available FSNs. For example, if at least one outstanding MSU is in the RTB, and no acknowledgment is received within expiration of T7, a link failure indication is passed to MTP3. A list of MTP2 timers appears in Appendix G, "MTP Timers in ITU-T/ETSI/ANSI Applications."

Response to a Negative Acknowledgment

When the MSU receives a negative acknowledgment, retransmission occurs beginning with the MSU in the RTB having a value of 1 greater than the NACKed MSU. All MSUs that follow in the RTB are retransmitted in the correct sequence. During this period, transmission of new MSUs is halted.

At the start of retransmission, the FIB is inverted so that it equals the BIB again. The new FIB is maintained in subsequently transmitted SUs until a new retransmission is required.

If an SU is received with a toggled FIB (indicating the start of retransmission) when no negative acknowledgment has been sent, the SU is discarded. If this occurs three consecutive times, MTP2 informs MTP3 that the link is faulty, resulting in an order for MTP2 to remove the link from service.

Examples of Error Correction

Figure 6-6 shows the fundamental principles of basic error correction by examining the error correction procedure for one direction of transmission between SP A and SP B. A similar relationship exists between the FSN/FIB from SP B and the BSN/BIB from SP A.

Figure 6-6   *Principles of Basic Error Correction*

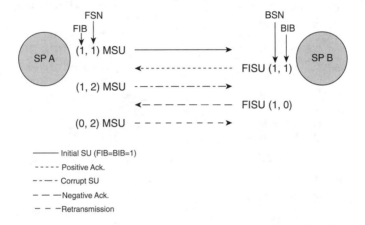

Although the bit rate on the signaling link in either direction is the same, note that the number of SUs transmitted by the two SPs in a time interval is likely to differ because of the MSUs' variable lengths. As a consequence, an SP might receive a number of SUs before it can acknowledge them. Figure 6-7 shows an example of basic error correction with a differing number of SUs sent between two SPs in a given amount of time.

In Figure 6-7, the FIB and BIB are set to 1 for both SPs at the start of the transmissions. The SU (c) acknowledges two MSUs positively (ii and iii). Because the SU (x) is a FISU, it takes on the FSN value of the MSU that was sent last. SP B receives the MSU (vii) sent by SP A in error. SP B in SU (g) sends a negative acknowledgment. BIB is inverted, and BSN contains the FSN of the last correctly received SU. SP A detects negative acknowledgment upon receiving message (g) and, beginning with MSU (xi), resends all MSUs after the last positive acknowledgment in sequence. The SU (I) is the first positive acknowledgment since retransmission began.

The error correction procedure operates independently in both directions. Figure 6-8 shows how the FSNs and FIBs carried by SUs in the direction SP A to SP B, and the BSNs and BIBs carried by SUs in the direction SP B to SP A, act as the error correction and sequencing fields for messages that are sent from SP A to SP B. Independently from the error correction and sequencing being performed in the SP A–to–SP B direction, error correction and sequencing take place in the SP B-to-SP A direction. Figure L-1 in Appendix L, "Tektronix Supporting Traffic," shows a trace file with the FSN/BSN/FIB/BIB fields exchanged between two SPs.

Figure 6-7   *Basic Error Correction*

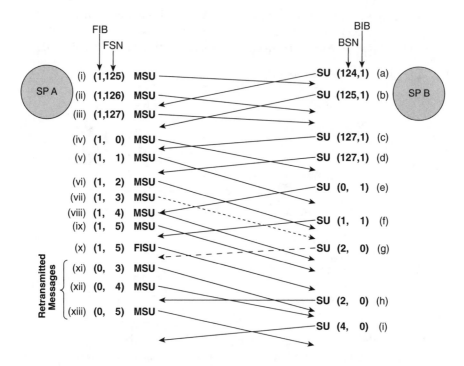

Figure 6-8   *Relevance of Fields Related to the Direction of Transmission*

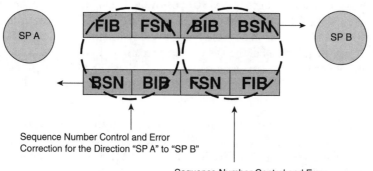

Figure 6-9 shows basic error correction in both directions.

Figure 6-9 *Basic Error Correction in Both Directions*

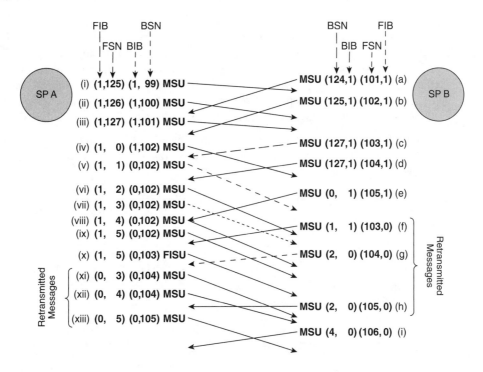

In Figure 6-9, SP A receives in error the MSU (c) sent by SP B. SP A in MSU (v) sends a negative acknowledgment. BIB is inverted, and BSN contains the FSN of the last correctly received SU. SP B detects the negative acknowledgment upon receiving the message (v) and resends all MSUs, beginning with MSU (c), after the last positive acknowledgment in sequence. FISU (x) is the first positive acknowledgment since retransmission began.

Preventive Cyclic Retransmission

The preventive cyclic retransmission (PCR) method is a noncompelled, positive acknowledgment, cyclic retransmission, forward error correction system. This means that no negative acknowledgments are used and that the system relies on the absence of a positive acknowledgment to indicate the corruption of SUs.

As in basic error correction, the FSN identifies the position of an MSU in its original transmission sequence, and the BSN identifies the most recently accepted MSU. Because PCR uses only positive acknowledgments, indicator bits FIB and BIB are ignored (they are permanently set to 1). The receiving SP simply accepts or discards an error-free MSU based on the FSN's value, which must exceed the FSN of the most recently accepted MSU by 1 (modulo 128).

A transmitted SU is retained in the RTB until a positive acknowledgment for that SU is received. When one of the SPs no longer has new LSSUs or MSUs to send, it starts a PRC in which the MSUs in its RTB are retransmitted in sequence, beginning with the oldest one (the lowest FSN). If all MSUs have been acknowledged, resulting in an empty RTB, FISUs are transmitted. Any retransmitted MSUs that have already been accepted by the receiving SP but have not yet been positively acknowledged arrive out-of-sequence and are discarded.

This method ensures that, if any MSUs are not accepted, the receiving SP receives fresh copies periodically until it gives a positive acknowledgment. Figure 6-10 shows a unidirectional example of how PCR works.

Figure 6-10 *PCR*

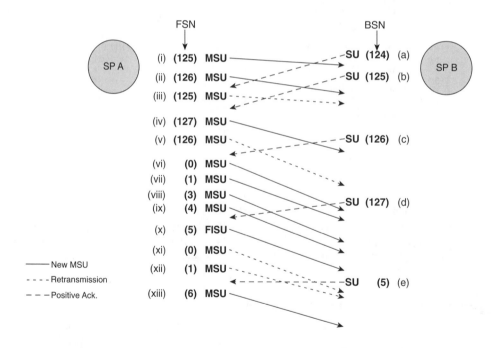

As shown in Figure 6-10, SP A has no more new LSSUs or MSUs to send after it transmits MSU (ii), so it begins a retransmission cycle with MSU (iii). At this point, SP A's RTB has only two MSUs (MSU with FSN = 125 and MSU with FSN = 126). After MSU (iii) has been retransmitted, a new MSU becomes available for transmission. After the new MSU

(iv) has been transmitted, SP A finds itself without a new MSU or LSSU to send; therefore, it begins a retransmission cycle with MSU (v). Again, the retransmission cycle stops after just one MSU is retransmitted, because SP A finds itself with five new MSUs to send (vi to x). After the new MSU (x) has been transmitted, again SP A finds itself without a new MSU or LSSU to send, so it begins a retransmission cycle with MSU (xi). The retransmission cycle stops after just two MSUs have been retransmitted, because SP A finds new MSUs to send (xiii). At this point, SP A has only one MSU in its RTB (MSU with FSN = 6).

This primitive forward error correction, which assumes loss in the absence of an acknowledgment, allows retransmissions to take place much sooner than in basic error correction. This is why PCR is used on signaling data links with propagation times that make basic error correction impractical. As mentioned previously, PCR is used on signaling links that have long propagation times and for all signaling links established via satellite [115], because the basic error correction method would result in MSU queuing delays that are too great for call control applications (such as ISUP).

Forced Retransmission Cycles

Approximately 20 to 30 percent of the traffic load using PCR is new traffic (such as MSUs and LSSUs) [115].

This low utilization gives more-than-adequate capacity to perform enough retransmission cycles. During periods of heavy traffic load (new MSUs), the rate at which retransmission cycles take place can be severely impaired, because new MSUs and LSSUs have priority. Under these conditions, the RTB might become full, because it has limited capacity to store 128 messages; this impairs the error correction method. To overcome this impairment, PCR includes forced retransmission cycles in which MTP2 constantly monitors the number of MSUs and the number of octets in the RTB. If either of these two values exceeds a predetermined value, a forced retransmission cycle occurs. Both values are implementation-dependent. Setting the thresholds too low results in frequent use of the forced transmission procedure, which results in excessive delays for new transmissions. Likewise, setting the thresholds too high causes forced retransmissions to take place too infrequently. Unlike normal retransmission cycles, forced retransmission cycles end only when all MSUs in the RTB have been retransmitted.

Note that LSSUs are always transmitted ahead of MSUs. If a new LSSU is queued for transmission, it is sent—regardless of the RTB's contents.

Comparison with the Basic Error Correction Method

The basic error correction method is preferred on links that have one-way propagation times of less than 30 ms [115], because this allows higher MSU loads than with PCR. PCR achieves lower MSU loads because it expends a relatively large amount of time needlessly retransmitting MSUs that have already been received correctly (even though they have not yet been acknowledged). PCR links are highly underutilized because spare capacity is required to ensure that retransmissions can take place.

Signaling Link Initial Alignment

The purpose of the signaling link alignment procedure is to establish SU timing and alignment so that the SPs on either side of the link know where SUs begin and end. In doing so, you must inherently test a link's quality before putting it into use. Example L-1 in Appendix L shows a trace file of two aligned SPs.

The signaling link alignment procedure ensures that both ends have managed to correctly recognize flags in the data stream.

Initial alignment is performed for both initial activation of the link (power on) to bring it to service and to restore a link following a failure. Alignment is based on the compelled exchange of status information and a proving period to ensure that SUs are framed correctly. MTP3 requests initial alignment, which is performed by MTP2. Because MTP2 operates independently on each link, the initial alignment procedure is performed on a single link without involving other links. There are two forms of alignment procedures: the emergency procedure and the normal alignment procedure. The emergency procedure is used when the link being aligned is the only available link for any of the routes defined within the SSP. Otherwise, the normal alignment procedure is used.

Status Indications

LSSUs are exchanged as part of the alignment procedure. There are six different status indications, as shown earlier in Table 6-1. Only the first four indications are employed during the initial alignment procedure.

The alignment procedure passes through a number of states during the initial alignment:

- Idle
- Not Aligned
- Aligned
- Proving
- Aligned/Ready
- In Service

Idle

When an SP is powered up, the links are initially put in the idle state. The idle state is the first state entered in the alignment procedure; it indicates that the procedure is suspended. If the procedure fails at any time, it returns to the idle state. Timer T17 (MTP3) prevents the rapid oscillation from in service to out of service. Timer T17 is started when the link begins the alignment procedure. No further alignment attempts are accepted from a remote or local SP until T17 has expired. LSSUs of SIOS (out of service) are sent during the idle state. LSSUs of this type are sent continuously until the link is powered down or until an order to begin initial alignment is received from MTP3. The FIB and the BIB of the LSSUs are set to 1, and the FSN and BSN are set to 127.

Not Aligned

When MTP2 receives an order to begin initial alignment, the SP changes the status of the transmitted LSSUs to indication SIO (out of alignment) and starts the timer T2. If T2 expires, the status of the transmitted LSSUs reverts to SIOS.

Aligned

During T2 SIO, if SIN (normal alignment) or SIE (emergency alignment) is received from the remote SP, T2 is stopped, and the transmission of SIO ceases. The SP then transmits SIN or SIE, depending on whether normal or emergency alignment has been selected and timer T3 is started. The link is now aligned, indicating that it can detect flags and signal units without error. If T3 expires, the alignment process begins again, transmitting LSSUs with a status field of SIOS. The aligned state indicates that the link is aligned and can detect flags and signal units without error.

Proving

Timer T4 governs the proving period, and the Alignment Error Rate Monitor (AERM) is used during this period.

The *proving period* is used to test the signaling link's integrity. FISUs are sent and errors (CRC and signaling unit acceptance) are counted during the proving period. LSSUs are also sent, indicating whether this is a SIN or SIE alignment.

The proving period is shorter for emergency alignment and as a result is not as thorough. As previously stated, emergency alignment is selected if only one in service (or none) exists between two SPs. If the local SP detects an emergency alignment situation, emergency alignment is used regardless of whether an SIN or SIE is received from the distant SP. Similarly, emergency alignment is used if an SIE is received from the distant SP, even when the local MTP3 indicates a normal alignment situation (more than one in-service link between the two adjacent nodes).

If four errors are detected during the proving period, the link is returned to state 00 (idle), and the procedure begins again.

Aligned/Ready

When T4 expires, the transmission of SIN/SIE ceases, timer T1 is started, and FISUs are transmitted. If timer T1 expires, the transmission of FISUs ceases, and LSSUs of type SIOS are transmitted.

In Service

Timer T1 stops upon receiving either FISUs or MSUs. When it stops, the SUERM becomes active. Figure 6-11 shows the initial alignment procedure.

Figure 6-11 *Procedure for Signaling Link Alignment*

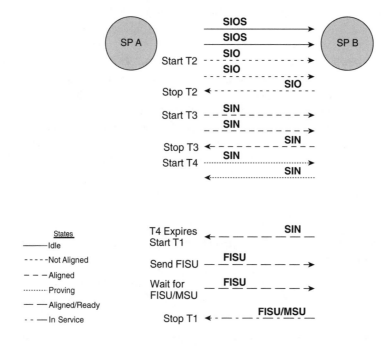

Figure 6-12 is an overview diagram of initial alignment control, taken from ITU-T recommendation Q.703 [51].

Figure 6-12 *Outline of the Initial Alignment Procedure*

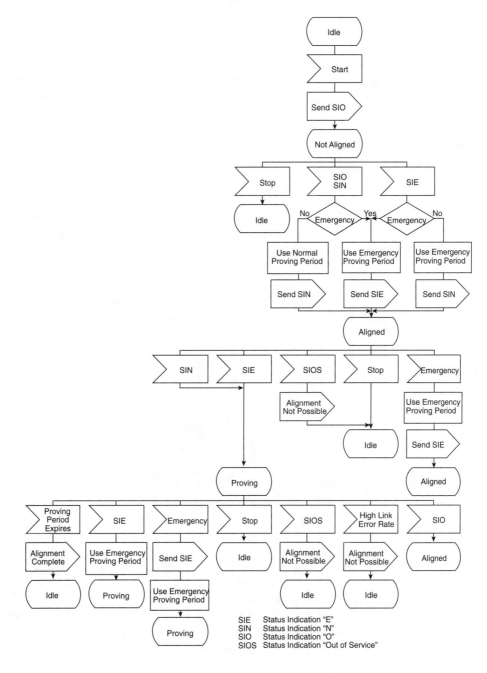

Signaling Link Error Monitoring

Error rate monitoring is performed both for an in-service link and when the initial alignment procedure is performed. Signal Unit Error Rate Monitor (SUERM) and the Alignment Error Rate Monitor (AERM) are the two link error rate monitors that are used [51]. The SUERM performs monitoring when the link is in service, and the AERM performs monitoring when the link is undergoing initial alignment to bring it into service. The following sections describe these two link error rate monitors.

SUERM

The SUERM is active when a link is in service, and it ensures the removal of a link that has excessive errors. It employs a *leaky bucket* counter, which is initially set to 0. The counter is increased by 1 for each SU that is received in error. The counter is decreased by 1 for each block of D consecutive SUs received without error, if it is not at 0. If the link reaches a threshold of T, MTP2 informs MTP3, which removes it from service. For a 64-kbps link, the values of D and T are 256 and 64, respectively.

NOTE   In ANSI networks, high-speed links (1.536 Mbps) use an *errored interval monitor,* which differs in its threshold and counting values from those used by the SUERM on low-speed links (see Figure 6-13). Refer to ANSI T1.111 for more information.

Figure 6-13 *SUERM Counter*

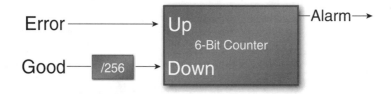

The SUERM enters *octet counting mode* if an SU fails the acceptance procedure (seven or more consecutive 1s, length is not a multiple of 8 bits, or SU length is not between 6 and 279 octets). For every block of *N* octets counted during octet counting mode, the SUERM is increased by 1. If the octet counting mode continues for a significant period of time (meaning that SUs cannot be identified from the received data), the link is removed from service. The SUERM reverts to normal mode if a correctly checked SU is received.

AERM

The AERM is active when the link is in the proving period of the initial alignment procedure. The counter is initialized to 0 at the start of the proving period and is increased for every LSSU that is received in error. If octet counting mode is entered during the proving period, the counter is increased for every block of N octets that is counted. The proving period is aborted if the counter reaches a threshold value of T_i; it is reentered upon receiving a correct LSSU, or upon the expiration of the aborted proving period. Different threshold values T_{in} and T_{ie} are used for the normal and emergency alignment procedures, respectively. If the proving is aborted M times, the link is removed from service and enters the idle state.

The values of the four parameters for 64-kbps and lower bit rates (both for ITU and ANSI) are as follows:

- $T_{in} = 4$
- $T_{ie} = 1$
- $M = 5$
- $N = 16$

Processor Outage

The processor outage condition occurs when SUs cannot be transferred to MTP3 or above. This could be the result of a central processing failure or communication loss between MTP2 and Levels 3/4 when a distributed processing architecture is used. A processor outage condition won't necessarily affect all signaling links in an SP, nor does it exclude the possibility that MTP3 can control the operation of the signaling link. When MTP2 recognizes a local processor outage condition, it transmits LSSUs with the status field set to *status indication processor outage (SIPO)* and discards any MSUs it has received. When the distant SP receives the SIPO status LSSU, it notifies its MTP3 and begins to continuously transmit FISUs. Note that the affected links remain in the aligned state.

Flow Control

Flow control allows incoming traffic to be throttled when the MTP2 receive buffer becomes congested. When an SP detects that the number of received MSUs in its input buffer exceeds a particular value—for example, because MTP3 has fallen behind in processing these MSUs—it begins sending out LSSUs with the status indicator set to *busy* (SIB). These LSSUs are transmitted at an interval set by timer T5, *sending SIB* (80 to 120 ms), until the congestion abates. The congested SP continues sending outgoing MSUs and FISUs but discards incoming MSUs. It also "freezes" the value of BSN and the BIB in the SUs it sends out to the values that were last transmitted in an SU before the congestion was recognized. This acknowledgment delay would normally cause timer T7, *excessive delay of acknowledgment,* at the distant SP to time out; however, timer T7 restarts each time an SIB is received. Therefore, timer T7 does not time out as long as the distant SP receives SIBs.

Timer T6, *remote congestion,* is started when the initial SIB is received. If timer T6 expires, it is considered a fault, and the link is removed from service. Timer T6 ensures that the link does not remain in the congested state for an excessive period of time.

When congestion abates, acknowledgments of all incoming MSUs are resumed, and periodic transmission of the SIB indication is discontinued. When the distant SP receives an SU that contains a negative or positive acknowledgment whose backward sequence number acknowledges an MSU in the RTB, timer T6 is stopped, and normal operation at both ends ensues. Figure 6-14 depicts flow control using LSSUs with status indication busy.

Figure 6-14 *Flow Control Using Status Indication SIB*

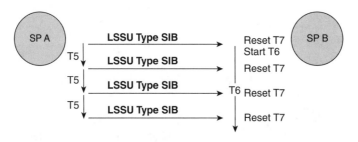

NOTE   The mechanism for detecting the onset of congestion is implementation-specific and should be chosen to minimize the oscillation between the onset and abatement of congestion.

Summary

MTP2 works point to point and "frames" signaling information into packets called *signaling units (SUs).* There are three types of SUs:

- Fill-in Signal Unit (FISU)
- Link Status Signal Unit (LSSU)
- Message Signal Unit (MSU)

MTP2 uses flags (delimitation) to separate SUs.

FISUs are fillers that are sent when no LSSUs or MSUs are to be sent. LSSUs are sent to convey link status information between two adjacent signaling points (SPs). MSUs carry the real signaling content: messages for call control, network management, and TCAP query/response. MTP2 ensures that MSUs are received in sequence and without errors.

MTP2 provides monitoring functions to MTP3 by using error rate counters. If specified thresholds are exceeded, MTP3 asks MTP2 to put the link out of service. If instructed by MTP3 to do so, MTP2 attempts to put specified links in service by following an alignment procedure. MTP2 also provides status indications when it encounters congestion and when layers above MTP2 can no longer process MSUs because of failure.

CHAPTER 7

Message Transfer Part 3 (MTP3)

Level 3 of the Message Transfer Part resides at layer 3 of the OSI model and performs the SS7 protocol's network functions. The primary purpose of this protocol level is to route messages between SS7 network nodes in a reliable manner. This responsibility is divided into two categories:

- Signaling Message Handling (SMH)
- Signaling Network Management (SNM)

Signaling Message Handling is concerned with routing messages to the appropriate network destination. Each node analyzes the incoming message based on its Destination Point Code (DPC) to determine whether the message is destined for that node. If the receiving node is the destination, the incoming message is delivered to the appropriate MTP3 user. If the receiving node is not the destination and the message has routing capability, i.e., is an STP, an attempt is made to route the message.

Signaling Network Management is a set of messages and procedures whose purpose is to handle network failures in a manner that allows messages to continue to reach their destination whenever possible. These procedures work together to coordinate SS7 resources that are becoming available or unavailable with the demands of user traffic. Network nodes communicate with each other to remain aware of which routes are available for sending messages so they can adjust traffic routes appropriately.

This chapter examines network addressing, how messages are routed, and the robust network management procedures instituted by the protocol to ensure successful message delivery with minimal disruption. The following sections address these topics:

- Point Codes
- Message Format
- Signaling Message Handling
- Signaling Network Management
- Summary

Point Codes

As discussed in Chapter 4, "SS7 Network Architecture and Protocols Introduction," each node is uniquely identified by a *Point Code*. A national Point Code identifies a node within a national network, and an *International Signaling Point Code (ISPC)* identifies a node within the international network. An *International Switching Center (ISC)* is identified by both a national and international Point Code. All nodes that are part of the international signaling network use the ITU-T ISPC globally. However, national point codes are based on either the ITU national format or the ANSI format (North America). The structure for international and national Point Codes is discussed in the sections on ITU-T and ANSI, later in this chapter.

Each MSU contains both an *Originating Point Code (OPC)* and a *Destination Point Code (DPC)*. The DPC is used for identifying the message's destination, and the OPC is used for identifying which node originated the message. As mentioned in the previous section and further discussed in the section "Signaling Message Handling," the DPC is the key entity for routing messages within a network. The OPC identifies which node originated the message.

NOTE   While a message's OPC and DPC reflect the MTP3 origination and destination points, they might be altered by *Global Title Translations (GTT)*. GTT, which is covered in Chapter 9, "Signaling Connection Control Part (SCCP)," sets the OPC to the point code of the node performing GTT and, in most cases, changes the DPC to a new destination. From an MTP viewpoint, GTT establishes new origination and destination points (when a new DPC is derived). As a result, the OPC and DPC of a message for which GTT has been performed do not necessarily reflect the ultimate origination and destination points for the MTP user within the network.

The identity of the originator is needed for the message to be processed for the correct node. The received OPC can also be used to determine how to populate the DPC when formulating response messages. Because Point Codes are an integral part of MTP3, this chapter discusses them in various contexts, such as network hierarchy, message format, and Signaling Message Handling.

ITU-T International and National Point Codes

ITU-T defines Point Codes for both national and international networks. The international Point Code is based on a hierarchical structure that contains the following three fields:

- Zone
- Area/Network
- Signaling Point

As shown in Figure 7-1, the ITU-T has defined six major geographical zones that represent the major areas of the world. A Zone number that forms the first part of the Point Code represents each geographical zone.

Figure 7-1   *ITU-T World Zone Map*

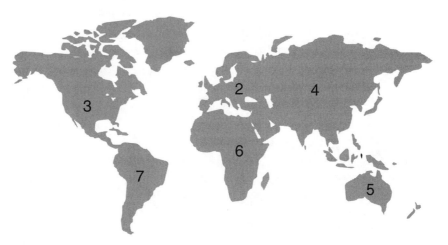

Each zone is further divided into an Area or Network based on a specific geographical area within the zone, or as designated by a particular network within the zone. Together, the Zone and Area/Network form the Signaling Area/Network Code (SANC). ITU-T Q.708 lists the SANC codes for each geographical zone. For example, Figure 7-2 shows the SANC designations for the United Kingdom area. The SANC codes are administered by the ITU. ITU operational bulletins publish updates to the numbering assignments after the publication of Q.708.

The Signaling Point identifies the individual signaling node represented by the Point Code.

ITU-T National Point Codes do not have a standardized scheme for defining hierarchy. Each Point Code is a single identifier that designates a specific node.

ANSI National Point Codes

For national Point Codes, ANSI uses a hierarchical scheme similar to that defined by the ITU-T for international signaling. The ANSI Point Code is comprised of three identifiers:

- Network
- Cluster
- Member

Figure 7-2   *UK Network/Area Point Code Numbers*

The Network identifier represents the highest layer of the SS7 signaling hierarchy and is allocated to telecommunications companies that have large networks.

NOTE   ANSI T1.111.8, Annex A defines a "large" network as one that has a minimum of 75 nodes, including six STPs in the first year of operation and 150 nodes with 12 STPs by the fifth year of operation. Small networks are defined as those that do not meet the criteria for large networks.

For example, each of the major operating companies in the U.S. (Verizon, Southwestern Bell, Bellsouth, and Qwest) is allocated one or more Network identifier codes, which identify all messages associated with their network. Smaller, independent operating companies share Network Identifiers, in which case they must use the remaining octets of the Point Code to discriminate between them. Within a network, the Cluster is used to group nodes in a meaningful way for the network operator. If an operating company owns a Network Identifier, it can administer the Cluster assignments in any manner of its choice. Clusters are often used to identify a geographical region within the operator's network; the Member identifies the individual signaling node within a cluster. Figure 7-3 shows the address hierarchy of ANSI networks.

Figure 7-3   *Address Hierarchy of ANSI Networks*

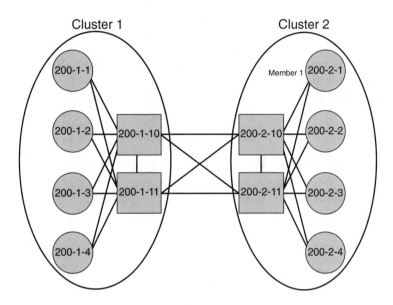

Network 200

For the purpose of Point Code allocation, networks are divided into three categories:

- Large Networks
- Small Networks
- CCS Groups

Assignable Point Code Network IDs are numbered 1–254. Network ID 0 is not used, and Network ID 255 is reserved for future use. Point Codes for large networks are assigned in descending order, beginning with Network ID 254.

Point Codes for small networks are assigned in ascending order from the point codes within the Network ID range of 1–4. Each small network is assigned a cluster ID, along with all of the Point Code members within that cluster. A small network operator may be assigned multiple clusters if the network is large enough to warrant the number of Point Codes.

Network ID 5 is used for CCS groups. These groups are blocks of Point Codes belonging to a set of signaling points that are commonly owned but do not have any STPs in the network. These are the smallest category of networks. Point Codes within a cluster may be shared by several different networks depending on the size of the CCS groups. Telcordia administers ANSI Point Codes.

Network ID 6 is reserved for use in ANSI-41 (Mobile Networks) and CCS groups outside of North America.

Message Format

The MTP3 portion of an SS7 message consists of two fields: the Signaling Information Field (SIF) and the Service Information Octet (SIO). The SIF contains routing information and the actual payload data being transported by the MTP3 service. The SIO contains general message characteristics for identifying the network type, prioritizing messages (ANSI only), and delivering them to the appropriate MTP3 user. When an SS7 node receives messages, Signaling Message Handling (SMH) uses the SIO and the portion of the SIF that contains routing information to perform discrimination, routing, and distribution. SMH functions are discussed in the "Signaling Message Handling" section, later in this chapter.

Service Information Octet

As shown in Figure 7-4, the SIO is a one-octet field composed of the Service Indicator (SI) and the Subservice Field (SSF). While the SI occupies the four least significant bits of the SIO, the SSF occupies the four most significant bits.

Figure 7-4   *SIO Fields*

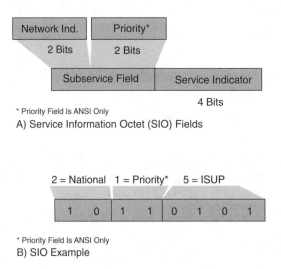

A) Service Information Octet (SIO) Fields

B) SIO Example

The Service Indicator designates the type of MTP payload contained in the Signaling Information Field. MTP3 uses the SI to deliver the message payload to the appropriate MTP3 user, using the message distribution function discussed later in the "Signaling Message Handling" section. The message is delivered to MTP3 for SI values of 0–2; the message is delivered to the appropriate User Part for SI values of 3 and higher. For example, all ISUP messages used in setting up phone calls would use a Service Indicator of 5. Table 7-1 lists the values for the Service Indicator.

Table 7-1   *Service Indicator Values*

Binary Value	Type of Payload
0000	Signaling Network Management Messages
0001	Signaling Network Testing and Maintenance Messages
0010	Signaling Network Testing and Maintenance Special Messages (ANSI) or Spare (ITU-T)
0011	SCCP
0100	Telephone User Part
0101	ISDN User Part
0110	Data User Part (call and circuit-related messages)
0111	Data User Part (facility registration and cancellation messages)
1000	Reserved for MTP Testing User Part
1001	Broadband ISDN User Part
1010	Satellite ISDN User Part
1011 – 1111	Spare[*]

[*]   ANSI reserves values 1101 and 1110 for individual network use.

The SSF consists of two fields: the Network Indicator (NI) and Priority. The priority field is defined for ANSI networks and is an option that may be implemented in ITU-T national networks. The priority bits are spare bits in ITU-T networks when not used for Priority. The NI indicates whether the message is for a national or international network. A national network can also discriminate between different Point Code structures used by different countries and invoke the appropriate version of the message handling functions accordingly. Table 7-2 lists the values for the NI.

Table 7-2   *Network Indicator Values*

Binary Value	Message Type
0000	International
0001	International Spare
0010	National
0011	National Spare

Messages are usually routed using the national or international values. The spare values are often used for testing and for temporary use during Point Code conversions. The national spare value can also be used for creating an additional national network. For example, in some European countries, network operators have used the national spare network indicator for creating a national interconnect network. Using this method, the switches between operator networks have two Point Codes assigned: one for the interconnect network using the national network indicator, and the other for the operator network using the national spare network indicator. This allows the network operator to administer Point Codes as he chooses within his national network, while using the interconnect network to interface with other network operators.

The ITU-T defines the two least significant bits of the SSF as spare bits. These bits are used to define message priority in ANSI networks, but are unused in ITU-T networks. The ANSI message priority values are 0–3 with 3 being the highest priority. The node originating the message assigns the priority to allow message throttling during periods of network congestion. The use of the message priority field is discussed in the section, "Multiple Congestion Levels."

Signaling Information Field (SIF)

The SIF contains the actual user data being transported by MTP, such as telephone numbers, control signals, or maintenance messages. The Service Indicator designates the type of information contained within the SIF user data field. For example, a Service Indicator of 0 indicates that the SIF contains Signaling Network Maintenance data. A Service Indicator of 5 indicates that the SIF contains ISUP information. The beginning portion of the SIF also contains the Routing Label that is used for routing the message within the network. The Routing Label contains the following three components:

- **Originating Point Code (OPC)** — Identifies the node originating the message
- **Destination Point Code (DPC)** — Identifies the destination node
- **Signaling Link Selector (SLS)** — An identifier used for load sharing across linksets and links

Figure 7-5 shows the fields in the routing label.

When a node generates a message, it inserts its own Point Code into the OPC field. This Point Code identifies the node that originated the message to subsequent nodes. As previously discussed, the DPC field is populated based on the internal routing tables. The SLS code is used for load sharing MTP3 User Part messages across links and linksets. The originating node generates a bit pattern and places it in this field. The SLS code maps the message to a particular link among the linksets and links that are available for routing. It is generated in a manner that minimizes mis-sequencing of messages belonging to a particular transaction from the perspective of MTP users, while balancing the load across the links and linksets.

Figure 7-5   *Routing Label Fields*

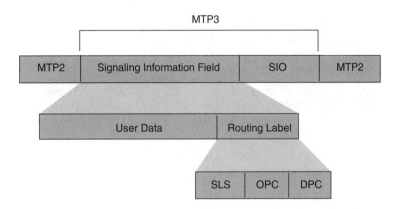

For more information about the use of the SLS code for load sharing, see "Routing" within the "Signaling Message Handling" section. The Signaling Link Code (SLC) for messages generated by MTP3 (e.g., SNM) replaces the SLS field. The "Message Load Sharing" section discusses the SLC code further.

The ITU-T and ANSI Routing Labels are similar in structure, but differ slightly in size and meaning. The following sections detail these differences.

ITU-T Routing Label

The ITU-T routing label consists of the following fields:

- DPC
- OPC
- SLS

The ITU-T point codes are 14 bits in length. For ITU-T national networks, all 14 bits are interpreted as a single identifier that is often referred to as a structureless Point Code. For international networks, an International Signaling Point Code (ISPC) is subdivided into hierarchical fields, shown in Figure 7-6.

The SLS is a four-bit field that identifies the link and/or linkset on which a message is transmitted.

Figure 7-6   *ITU-T Routing Label*

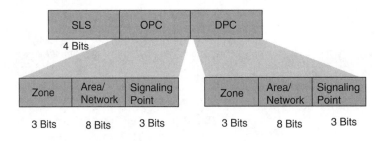

ANSI Routing Label

The ANSI routing label consists of the following fields:

- DPC
- OPC
- SLS

The ANSI Point Code is 24 bits in length and is subdivided into three fields of one octet each, as shown in Figure 7-7. The three octets define the network, cluster, and member that uniquely identify the signaling node within the network hierarchy. The SLS field is an eight-bit field used for selecting the link and/or linkset for message transmission. This field was only five bits in earlier versions of the protocol, but was extended for better load sharing across signaling links in the 1996 version of the ANSI standards.

Figure 7-7   *ANSI Routing Label*

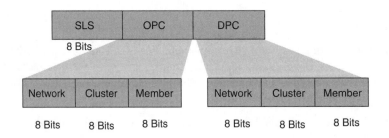

Signaling Message Handling

MTP3 processes all incoming MSUs to determine whether they should be sent to one of the MTP3 users or routed to another destination. The term "MTP3 user" refers to any user of MTP3 services, as indicated by the Service Indicator in the SIO. This includes messages generated by MTP3 itself, such as SNM, or those that are passed down from the User Parts at level 4 of the SS7 protocol, like ISUP and SCCP. The term "MTP User Part" is also used, but more specifically refers to the User Parts at level 4. When a node generates an MSU, MTP3 is responsible for determining how to route the message toward its destination using the DPC in the Routing Label and the Network Indicator in the SIO. Figure 7-8 shows how MTP3 message processing can be divided into three discrete functions: discrimination, distribution, and routing.

Figure 7-8   *Signaling Message Handling*

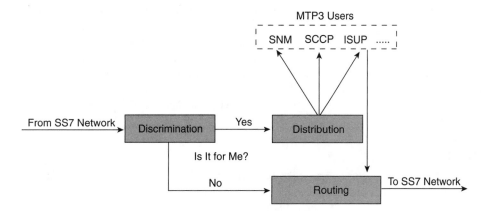

Discrimination

Message *discrimination* is the task of determining whether an incoming message is destined for the node that is currently processing the message. Message discrimination makes this determination using both the NI and the DPC.

Each node's Point Code is defined as belonging to a particular network type. The network types are those that are specified by the NI, discussed earlier in this chapter. An ISC will have both a *National* network and *International* type, with Point Codes in each. Nodes that do not function as an ISC are generally identified as a *National* network with a single Point Code. In some cases, multiple Point Codes can identify a national node; for example, a network operator might use both *National* and *National Spare* network types at a network node, with Point Codes in each network. The NI in an incoming message's SIO is examined to determine the network type for which the message is destined.

Each time a node receives a message, it must ask, "Is it for me?" The node asks the question by comparing the incoming DPC in the Routing Label to its own Point Code. If the Point Codes match, the message is sent to Message Distribution for processing. If the Point Codes do not match, the message is sent to the Routing function if the node is capable of routing. A Signaling End Point (SEP), such as an SSP or SCP, is not capable of routing messages; only an STP or an Integrated Node with transfer functionality (SSP/STP) can forward messages.

Distribution

When the discrimination function has determined that a message is destined for the current node, it performs the d*istribution* process by examining the Service Indicator, which is part of the SIO in the Routing Label. The Service Indicator designates which MTP3 user to send the message to for further processing. For example, MTP3 SNM processes a message with a Service Indicator of 0 (SNM messages), while a message with a Service Indicator of 5 is sent to ISUP for processing. Within SS7 protocol implementations, the Service Indicator is a means of directing the message to the next logical stage of processing.

Routing

Routing takes place when it has been determined that a message is to be sent to another node. There are two circumstances in which this occurs. The first is when a node originates a message to be sent to the network. For example, an MTP3 user (such as ISUP or SCCP) generates a message for MTP3 to send. The second is when an STP has received a message that is destined for another node. The routing function is invoked if the discrimination function has determined that the received message is not destined for the STP. If a Signaling End Point (SSP or SCP) receives a message and the discrimination function determines that the message is not for that node, the message is discarded because these nodes do not have transfer capability. A User Part Unavailable (UPU) is sent to the originating node to indicate that the message could not be delivered. In other words, SEPs can only route the messages they originate. A node examines one or more routing tables to attempt to find a match for the DPC to which the message is to be routed.

In the case where a node transfers the message, the DPC from the incoming message's Routing Label determines the route to the destination. MTP3 uses next-hop routing so the destination can be an adjacent node, or simply the next node en route to the final destination. The implementation of the routing tables is vendor dependent; ultimately, however, the DPC must be associated with a linkset (or combined linkset) for sending the message.

Figure 7-9 shows an example of a routeset table. The routeset table contains routesets for all of the possible destinations that can be reached. The table is searched to find a match for the DPC to be routed. If a match is found in the list of routesets, a linkset is chosen from the available routes associated with the routeset. After choosing a linkset, a link is selected from the linkset over which the message will be transmitted. In the example, the discrimination function has determined that Point Code 200-1-2 does not match the point code of the current STP, and has therefore passed the message to the routing function. The routing table is searched for a match for DPC 200-1-2, and a match is found at the second entry. The routeset contains two routes: LS_1 and LS_3, which represent linkset 1 and linkset 3. In this example, a priority field with the highest priority number is the preferred route, so linkset LS_3 is chosen to send the message to DPC 200-1-2. The priority field used here should not be confused with the message priority field of MTP3. Again, the actual implementation of routing tables is vendor specific, and a vendor might choose to label this field differently.

Figure 7-9   *Routing Table Lookup*

Name	DPC	ROUTE	Priority
RS_SSPA	200-1-1	LS_1	10
		LS_2	20
RS_SSPB	200-1-2	LS_1	10
		LS_3	20
RS_SSPC	200-1-3	Ls_1	10
		LS_4	20
RS_STPB	200-20-10	LS_1	10

200-1-2 ➡

ANSI Network and Cluster Routing

Routing is often performed in a hierarchical fashion. In ANSI networks, messages can be routed by matching only part of the DPC. The match is done on a portion of the Most Significant Bits of the DPC, allowing messages to be routed using fewer entries in the routing tables. This saves on administration overhead and eliminates the need for detailed information about node addresses. It is especially useful when dealing with traffic that is destined for another operator's network. For example, it is quite common to aggregate routes using network or cluster routing. With network routing, a route is selected by matching only the network octet of the DPC; when cluster routing is used, the network and cluster octet of the DPC must be matched to a routing table entry, as shown in Figure 7-10.

Figure 7-10 *Example of ANSI Cluster Routing*

Name	DPC	ROUTE	Priority
RS_SSPA	200-1-1	LS_1	10
		LS_2	20
RS_NETX	240-*-*	LS_1	10
		LS_3	20

Network Route to
Net 240.

Alias Point Code Routing

An alias Point Code is a secondary PC used, in addition to the unique primary Point Code, for identifying a node. Another common name for an alias is a Capability Point Code. Multiple nodes (usually two) share the alias PC; this allows messages to be routed to either node using a common PC. The alias PC is typically used to identify a pair of STPs. Its primary purpose is to allow the load sharing of SCCP traffic across the STP pair. Because SMH discrimination at either STP will accept a message with the alias PC, the message can be delivered to the SCCP User Part, where GTT is performed. Figure 7-11 shows an example using an alias PC. The PC for STP 1 is 200-1-1, and the PC for STP 2 is 200-1-2. The alias PC 200-1-10 is used to identify both STP 1 and STP 2. As a result, SSP A can route messages requiring SCCP GTT to 200-1-10 while load sharing across STP 1 and STP 2. Since STP 1 and STP 2 each must have a unique PC, SSP A cannot perform load sharing of SCCP traffic to the STP pair using the unique PC of either STP. However, the alias PC allows either node to accept and process the message.

Message Load Sharing

A properly designed SS7 network employs alternate message paths to create network redundancy. User traffic is typically load-shared across different paths to maintain a balanced load on network equipment. Load sharing also ensures that problems on each path are detected quickly because they are carrying traffic. There are two types of SS7 load sharing:

- Load-sharing across linksets in a combined linkset
- Load-sharing across links within a linkset

Figure 7-11 *Example of Alias Point Code Routing*

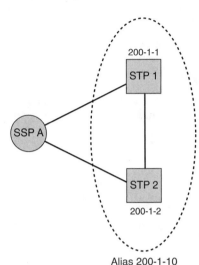

Link selection is done when a node originates messages for normal MTP3 user traffic so that overall traffic distribution is even across the links. The actual algorithm for generating the SLS code is not specified by the SS7 standards, but the result should be as even a traffic distribution as possible. There are times when load sharing is not desired, as outlined later in this section and in the section, "Load sharing and MTP3 User Parts."

When load sharing is used, the SLS field determines the distribution of messages across linksets and links as they traverse the network. The originating node generates an SLS code and places it into the Routing Label. At each node in the message path the SLS is used to map the message to a specific link and, if using a combined linkset, to a specific linkset.

Load Sharing and MTP3 User Parts

As previously mentioned, a general goal of SS7 routing is to attempt to distribute traffic evenly across links as much as possible. However, there are special considerations within the MTP3 user parts when the SLS codes are being generated.

The SLS codes for messages related to a particular communications exchange, such as an ISUP call, are generated with the same value. If different SLS values for messages belonging to the same call were used, there would be an increased chance of out-of-sequence messages because they could take different network routes, affecting the order in which they are received. Figure 7-12 shows a phone call being signaled between SSP A and SSP B using ISUP. SSP A generates the same SLS code 0100 for all messages associated with this particular call. This causes the same linkset and link to be chosen for each of the messages. The same linkset/link selection algorithm is applied at subsequent network nodes, resulting in the same choice of linkset and links each time. This ensures that all messages take the same path through the network and minimizes the chance for messages within a specific communications exchange to be mis-sequenced. Messages from SSP B that are related to the same call use SLS code 0101 for all messages.

Of course, the possibility always exists that network failures can cause alternate paths to be taken; this increases the chance for out-of-sequence delivery.

Figure 7-12 *SLS Generation for In-Sequence Delivery*

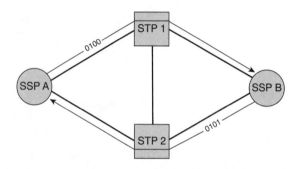

The previous example showed the SLS values for an individual phone call. However, the same principle applies to other User Part communication exchanges, such as SCCP. SCCP generates the same SLS values to be used by MTP when the in-sequence delivery option is set within SCCP.

The least significant bits of the Circuit Identification Code (CIC) are placed in the SLS field when the MTP3 user is the Telephone User Part (TUP). All messages related to a particular call use the same CIC, resulting in the same SLS value in each message. Chapter 8, "ISDN User Part (ISUP)," explains the CIC.

Messages generated by MTP3 (SNM, SNT, and SNTS messages) replace the SLS field with the Signaling Link Code (SLC). No load sharing is performed for these messages. Although there are exceptions, the SLC usually specifies the signaling link to be used when sending a message. The "Signaling Network Management" section discusses the SLC and its specific use.

SLS in ITU-T Networks

ITU-T networks use a four-bit SLS value. The SLS value remains the same as the message travels through the network. If a combined linkset is being used, one bit of the SLS code is used to select the linkset at each node. The remaining bits are used to select the link within the linkset. If a combined linkset is not being used, all bits can be used to select a link within the linkset. The ITU-T standards are not explicit about which bits are used for link and linkset selection.

SLS in ANSI Networks

ANSI networks use an eight-bit SLS code. The SLS code was originally 5 bits, but was later increased to 8 bits to provide better distribution across links.

At a SEP, the least significant bit of the SLS is used for linkset selection and the remaining bits are used for link selection if the message is being routed over a combined linkset. All bits are used to select the link when routing over a single linkset.

The least significant bit is also used for linkset selection at an intermediate node routing over a combined linkset; however, only the three most significant bits and the second through fourth least significant bits are concatenated for link selection. When routing over a single linkset at the intermediate node, the three most significant bits are concatenated with the four least significant bits to form an SLS code for choosing a link.

Using SLS bit rotation is the standard method of load sharing in ANSI networks. The original SLS code is right bit-shifted before the message is transmitted onto the link. The bit rotation occurs at each node, before the message is transmitted. An exception to this scheme is that SLS rotation is not performed for messages transmitted over C-Links. Bit rotation is only done on the five least significant bits to maintain backward compatibility with five-bit SLS codes. Figure 7-13 shows an example of SLS rotation for messages that originate at SSP A. The least significant bit is used to choose the linkset from a combined linkset to STP 1 or STP 2. After linkset and link selection and before message transmission, a right bit rotation is performed on the five least significant bits. At STP 1 and STP 2, a single link-set is used to route the message to SSP B.

Figure 7-13 *SLS Rotation*

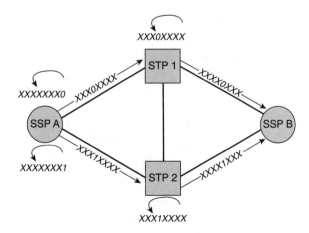

Comparing the IP and MTP3 Protocols

The MTP3 message handling is similar to the Internet Protocol (IP) in some respects. For those who are familiar with IP, a comparison of the two protocols helps to put MTP3 in perspective. This is not intended to suggest an exact comparison; rather, to relate something that is known about one protocol to something similar in the other. The main point is that both protocols are packet based and designed to deliver messages to a higher layer service at a node in the network. It is not surprising that there are a number of commonalities given that the requirements are similar. In fact, studying a number of communications transport protocols shows that many share a common functionality and structure, with each diverging slightly to address its particular requirements. Table 7-3 lists an association of key IP packet fields with their MTP3 counterparts.

Table 7-3   *Comparison of IP and MTP3 Packet Fields*

IP	SS7
Source IP Address	Originating Point Code
Destination IP Address	Destination Point Code
Protocol	Service Indicator
Precedence (part of TOS field)	Priority
Data	User Data

In addition to the similarity in the packet fields, the network nodes and their functions also share common aspects. A typical IP network contains a number of hosts that communicate with other hosts, sometimes in different networks. Routers connect the different networks and allow hosts to communicate with each other. The SS7 network's SSP and SCP nodes can be viewed in much the same way as hosts in the IP network. The STP node in an SS7 network is similar to the IP router. It is used to interconnect various hosts in a hierarchical fashion and to route messages between different networks.

One important distinction in this analogy is that the STP only uses static routes; it has no "routing protocols," such as those used in IP networks.

While network design varies greatly between the two different types of networks, both networks employ a means of hierarchical address structure to allow for layered network design. The IP network uses classes A, B, and C, which are identified by the bit mask structure of the address. The hierarchical structure in SS7 is created by dividing the Point Code bits into identifiers that specify a level within the network. The identifiers are different in ITU-T and ANSI, but they function in the same manner. For example, ANSI creates this hierarchy by dividing the Point Code into network, cluster, and member. Both IP and SS7 have their own uniqueness; no analogy is perfect, but they do share similarities.

MTP3 Message Handling Example

To better understand the entire process of Message Handling, consider the example in Figure 7-14. Here, SP A is a typical SSP with two linksets connecting it to the SS7 network via an STP. Suppose that SSP A sends and receives ISUP traffic with SSP B. There is no need to be concerned with the details of ISUP at the moment—only the fact that an SSP A User Part (ISUP) needs to communicate via MTP3 with an SSP B User Part (ISUP). SSP A is setting up a call to SSP B and needs to send an ISUP message. It requests MTP3 to send a message (routing function). The payload (ISUP information) is placed in the MTP3 SIF User Info field. The destination indicated by the user part is placed in the Routing Label's DPC field. The Point Code of the node sending the message (SSP A) is placed in the OPC field. The SLS is generated and placed in the Routing Label's SLS field. MTP3 attempts to find a routeset for the Destination Point Code in its routing table; it finds a match and determines which route is associated with the routeset. The SLS is examined and a link for transmitting the message is selected. The message arrives at STP 1. Upon receiving the message, the STP examines the DPC and compares it to its own Point Code (discrimination function). The comparison fails because the DPC is the Point Code for SSP B. This causes the STP to attempt to route the message. The STP searches its routing table to find a match for the DPC. It finds a match, selects a linkset to route the message, and puts the SLS code into the message, which is modified using bit rotation, if necessary (ANSI networks). The message arrives at SSP B and is passed to MTP3 Signaling Message Handling. SSP B compares the message's DPC to its own Point Code (discrimination function) and determines that it matches. The SI is then examined to determine which User Part should receive the message (distribution function). An SI of 5 identifies the User Info as ISUP, and the message is passed to the ISUP layer for processing. This completes MTP3 message handling for this message.

Figure 7-14 *Example of Message Handling*

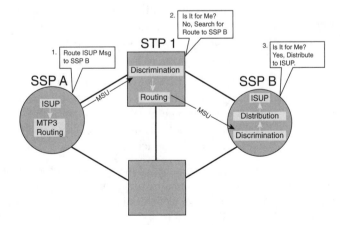

Signaling Network Management

Failures in the SS7 network have potentially devastating effects on the communications infrastructure. The loss of all SS7 signaling capabilities at an SP isolates it from the rest of the network. The SS7 networks in existence today are known for their reliability, primarily due to the robustness of the SS7 protocol in the area of network management. Of course, this reliability must be accompanied by good network design to provide sufficient network capacity and redundancy. MTP3 Network Management is comprised of a set of messages and procedures that are used to ensure a healthy signaling transport infrastructure. This involves automatically invoking actions based on network events, such as link or route failures and reporting network status to other nodes.

Signaling Network Management is divided into three processes:

- Traffic management
- Route management
- Link management

Traffic management is responsible for dealing with signaling traffic, which are the messages generated by MTP3 users, such as ISUP and SCCP. The goal of Traffic management is to keep traffic moving toward its destination, even in the event of network failures and congestion, with as little message loss or mis-sequencing as possible. This movement often involves rerouting traffic onto an alternate network path and, in some situations, might require message retransmission.

Route management exchanges information about routing status between nodes. As events occur that affect route availability, route management sends messages to notify other nodes about the change in routing states. Route management supplies information to traffic management, allowing it to adjust traffic patterns and flow accordingly.

Link management activates, deactivates, and restores signaling links. This involves notifying MTP users of the availability of signaling links and invoking procedures to restore service when a disruption has occurred. This level of network management is most closely associated with the physical hardware.

A number of *timers* are involved in all of these network management procedures. Timers are used to ensure that actions occur when they should. Without timers, network management procedures could halt at certain points and it would take forever for an event to happen. For example, when a message is transmitted, timers are often started to ensure that a response is received within a specified period of time.

The following section discusses a number of the timers used for Signaling Network Management. It enhances the description of the procedure but is not intended to be a complete reference for every timer used. A complete list of timers can be found in Appendix G, "MTP Timers in ITU-T/ETSI/ANSI Applications."

Network Management Messages (H0/H1 Codes)

All network management messages contain a routing label and an identifier known as an H0/H1 code. Additional message fields are often included based on the particular message type. The general format of a Network Management message is shown in Figure 7-15.

Figure 7-15 *Basic Network Management Message*

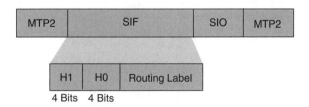

The "H0/H1" codes, or "Heading" codes, are simply the message type identifiers. There are two Heading Codes for each message: H0 for the family of messages, and H1 for the specific message type within the family. Table 7-4 lists the H0/H1 codes for each message type. The family (H0 code) is listed on the left of the chart. All messages in a row belong to the same message family. For example, the H0/H1 code for a COA message is 12 and it belongs to the CHM (Changeover Message) family. Appendix A, "MTP Messages (ANSI/ETSI/ITU)," provides the full message name and description for each message entry in Table 7-4.

Table 7-4 *H0/H1 Codes*

Message Group	H1 H0	0	1	2	3	4	5	6	7	8
	0									
Changeover (CHM)	1		COO	COA			CBD	CBA		
Emergency Changeover (ECM)	2		ECO	ECA						
Flow Control (FCMI	3		RCT	TFC						
Transfer (TFM)	4		TFP	TCP*	TFR	TCR*	TFA	TCA*		
Routeset Test (RSM)	5		RST RSP*	RSR	RCP*	RCR*				
Management Inhibiting (MIM)	6		LIN	LUN	LIA	LUA	LID	LFU	LLT/LLI*	LRT/LRI*

continues

Table 7-4 *H0/H1 Codes (Continued)*

Message Group	H1 H0	0	1	2	3	4	5	6	7	8
Traffic (TRM)	7		TRA	TRW[*]						
Data Link (DLM)	8		DLC	CSS	CNS	CNP				
	9									
User Part Flow Control (UFC)	A		UPU							

* ANSI only.

Link Management

Links are physical entities that are made available to MTP3 users when they have proven worthy of carrying messages. If a link fails, it has a direct impact on the two nodes the link connects. It is link management's responsibility to detect any communication loss and attempt to restore it. Both nodes connected to the link invoke procedures for restoration in an attempt to restore communication. Link management can be divided into three processes:

- Activation
- Deactivation
- Restoration

Activation is the process of making a link available to carry MTP3 user traffic. Maintenance personnel typically perform it by invoking commands from an OAM interface to request that the link be activated for use. When a link is aligned at level 2 and passes the proving period, the link is declared available to traffic management.

Deactivation removes a link from service, making it unavailable for carrying traffic. Like activation, this process is typically initiated by invoking commands from an OAM interface. The link is declared unavailable to traffic management when it is deactivated.

Restoration is an automated attempt to restore the link to service after a failure, making it available for traffic management use. The link alignment procedure is initiated when level 2 has detected a link failure. When the link is aligned and has passed the proving period, a signaling link test is performed. After the signaling link test has successfully completed, traffic management makes the link available for use.

Signaling Link Test Control

When a signaling link is activated, it must undergo initial alignment at MTP2. After a successful initial alignment, the link performs a signaling link test initiated by the *Signaling Link Test Control (SLTC)* function.

SLTC messages are identified by MTP3 with a Service Indicator of 1 or 2. An SI of 1 indicates a Signaling Network Test message and is used for ITU-T networks. An SI of 2 indicates a Signaling Network Test Special message and is used in ANSI networks. SLTC messages follow the same message structure as Signaling Network Management messages; they use a Heading code, which immediately follows the Routing Label. Table 7-5 shows the H0 and H1 field values.

Table 7-5   *H0 and H1 Field Values*

Message Group	H1 H0	0	1	2
	0			
SLT	1		SLTM	SLTA

MTP3 sends an SLTM (Signaling Link Test Message) over the link with the node's DPC at the far end of the linkset. The SLC code in the routing label identifies the link on which the message is sent. The test is performed only if the SLC matches the link on which the message is sent, and if the OPC in the routing label matches the far end Point Code of the receiving node. The message's user data is a simple test pattern of bytes and is typically user configurable. The receiving node responds with a *Signaling Link Test Acknowledgement* (SLTA) containing the test pattern received in the SLTM message. The SLTA test pattern must match what was sent in the SLTM or the test is considered a failure. In addition, the DPC, network indicator, and SLC in the SLTM are checked to ensure that they match the information at the node on the receiving end of the link over which the message was sent. Figure 7-16 shows an example of an SLTM/SLTA exchange with a test pattern.

Figure 7-16   *Signaling Link Test Control*

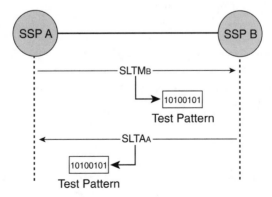

The SLTC ensures that the two connected nodes can communicate at level 3 before placing a link into service for user traffic. At this point the SLTC can detect problems, such as an incorrectly provisioned Point Code or network indicator, in link activation. If alignment or the signaling link test fails, the procedure is restarted after a period of time designated by T17. In ANSI networks, a link failure timer (T19) is used to guard the amount of time the link remains out of service. Upon its expiration, a notification is raised to system maintenance, where the restoration procedure can be restarted or the link can optionally be declared as "failed" until manual intervention occurs.

Automatic Allocation of Signaling Terminals and Links

The SS7 standards provide specifications for the *automatic allocation* of both signaling terminals and signaling links. The automatic allocation of signaling terminals allows a pool of signaling terminals to exist that can be mapped to a signaling link for use. The robustness of electronic circuitry today makes this option of little value for most network operators. Redundancy for signaling terminal hardware can be achieved in parallel with link redundancy using alternate links. Link redundancy is a better choice because links are much more likely to fail than signaling terminal hardware.

Automatic link allocation allows other digital circuits normally used to carry voice to be allocated as signaling links, when needed. Automatic signaling terminal and automatic link allocation are rarely used in networks.

Route Management

Signaling *route management* communicates the availability of routes between SS7 nodes. Failures such as the loss of a linkset affect the ability to route messages to their intended destination. A failure can also affect more than just locally connected nodes. For example, the linkset between STP1 and SSP B has failed in Figure 7-17. As a result, SSP A should only route messages to SSP B through STP1 as a last resort because STP1 no longer has an associated route. Even though none of the links belonging to SSP A have failed, its ability to route messages to SSP B is affected. Signaling route management provides the means to communicate these types of changes in route availability using Signaling Network Management messages.

Figure 7-17 *How Loss of Linkset Affects Routes*

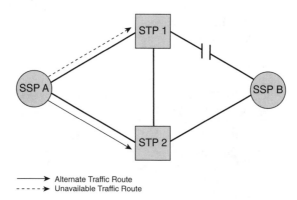

Route management uses the following messages to convey routing status to other network nodes:

- Transfer Prohibited (TFP)
- Transfer Restricted (TFR)
- Transfer Allowed (TFA)
- Transfer Controlled (TFC)

The following additional messages are used for conveying the routing status of clusters. They are only used in ANSI networks:

- Transfer Cluster Prohibited (TCP)
- Transfer Cluster Restricted (TCR)

Each node maintains a state for every destination route. As route management messages are received, the state is updated based on the status conveyed by the message. This allows nodes to make appropriate routing choices when sending messages. Routes can have one of three different states:

- Allowed
- Prohibited
- Restricted

The following sections discuss each of these states and the messages and procedures that are associated with them.

As shown in Figure 7-18, the messages used by route management all have a common format consisting of a standard routing label, an H0/H1 code identifying the type of network management message and a destination. The destination is the Point Code of the node for which routing status is being conveyed.

Figure 7-18 *Route Status Message Format*

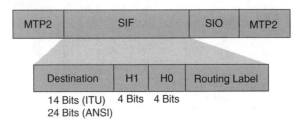

Transfer Restricted

The *restricted* state indicates a limited ability to route messages. This status signifies that the primary route is unavailable and that another route should be chosen, if it exists. If the restricted route is the last available route in a routeset, it is still used for routing.

In Figure 7-19, a linkset failure has occurred between SSP A and STP 2. The loss of the linkset causes STP2 to change its routing status to restricted for SSP A. Note that it can still route messages over the C-Link to STP1, destined for SSP A; this makes the status restricted and not prohibited. In this case, the linkset from STP 2 to SSP A is an associated route and is ordinarily designated as the "primary" route, while the linkset to STP 1 is a quasi-associated route and is therefore designated as an "alternate," or secondary route to SSP A.

Figure 7-19 *Transfer Restricted*

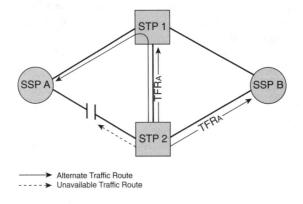

The Transfer Restricted message is sent to adjacent nodes to notify them of the restricted route. TFR is used in ANSI networks and is a national option in ITU networks. As shown in Figure 7-18, the TFR message contains the H0/H1 code, which identifies it as a TFR message and the Point Code of the affected destination.

Upon receiving a Transfer Restricted message, traffic management shifts traffic to another route, provided that another route toward the affected destination is available. In Figure 7-19, when the TFR message is received at SSP B, traffic management performs a controlled reroute is to switch traffic to the linkset between SSP B and STP1. For a description of the controlled reroute procedure, refer to the "Controlled Rerouting" section. After receiving a Transfer Restricted message, a Routeset Restricted message is sent periodically to test the status of the routeset. The Routeset Restricted message asks the question, "Is the route still restricted?" Refer to the "Routeset Test" section for more information on testing the routeset status.

Transfer Prohibited

The *Transfer Prohibited* state indicates a complete inability to route messages to the affected destination. If one exists, another route must be chosen for routing. If no route exists, traffic management is notified that it cannot route messages to the destination.

In Figure 7-20 a linkset failure occurs, causing STP 1 to become isolated from SSP B. Notice that there are no possible routes by which STP1 can reach SSP B. STP1 changes its routing status to "prohibited" concerning SSP B. A TFP message is sent to convey the prohibited status to other nodes. There are two methods of sending the TFP status:

- Broadcast method
- Response method

When the broadcast method is used, all adjacent nodes are immediately notified about the prohibited route status. The response method does not send notification until an attempt is made to reach the affected destination. The choice of which method to use is often implemented as a provisioned option that can be set on the signaling equipment. If the broadcast method is being used but for some reason a node still receives an MSU for a prohibited destination, a TFP is still sent using the response method. Figure 7-20 demonstrates the use of the broadcast method.

Figure 7-20 *Transfer Prohibited*

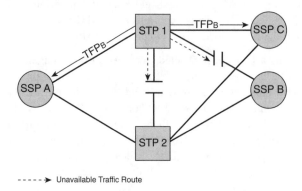

Figure 7-18 shows that the TFP message contains the H0/H1 code, identifying the message as a TFP message and the Point Code of the affected destination.

When a TFP message is received, traffic management performs a forced reroute to immediately route traffic over another route, if another route to the destination is available. Refer to the section on "Forced Rerouting" for a complete description of forced rerouting. If an STP receives a TFP and the route on which it is received is the last available route, the STP sends out TFP messages to its adjacent nodes to indicate that it can no longer route to the affected destination.

Transfer Allowed

The *transfer allowed* state indicates that a route is available for carrying traffic. This is the normal state for in-service routes. When a route has been in the restricted or prohibited state and full routing capability is restored, the route's status is returned to transfer allowed. The transfer allowed message is sent to convey the new routing status to adjacent nodes. Figure 7-21 shows that the linkset between SSP B and STP 1, along with the linkset between STP 1 and STP 2, has been restored to service. STP 1 recognizes that it has regained full routing capability to SSP B and sends a TFA message to its adjacent nodes to update their routing status.

Figure 7-18 shows that the TFA message contains the H0/H1 code, which identifies the message as a TFA message and the Point Code of the affected destination.

Figure 7-21 *Transfer Allowed*

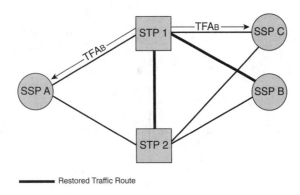

Routeset Test

Routeset Test is part of the Transfer Prohibited and Transfer Restricted procedures. While Transfer Prohibited and Transfer Restricted convey the status of the routeset, Routeset Test checks to ensure that the status is correct.

The Routeset Test message tests the state of a routeset when it is prohibited or restricted. Each time a Routeset Test message is received, the status is compared to the current status of the affected destination. If the states match, the message is discarded and no further action is taken; otherwise, an appropriate message is sent to update the status. The state testing is performed to ensure that both nodes are in sync regarding the routing status. Figure 7-22 shows an example in which the routeset for SSP A is prohibited at STP 1. If, for some reason, the STP sent a Transfer Allowed message to the SSP for a previously prohibited routeset and the SSP failed to receive the message, the STP would have a routeset marked as Transfer Allowed and the SSP would think it was still Transfer Prohibited.

The frequency with which the Routeset Test message is sent is based on timer T10. Each time T10 expires, a Routeset Test message is sent to test the routeset status. In Figure 7-22, STP 1 has sent a TFP message to SSP B. SSP B responds by sending Routeset Prohibited Test messages on a periodic basis.

The Routeset Test procedure is stopped when a TFA for the affected destination is received.

Figure 7-22 *Routeset Test*

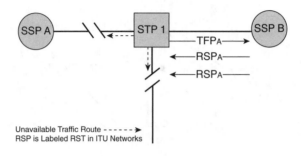

Transfer Controlled

The *Transfer Controlled* message is used to indicate congestion for a route to a particular destination. The TFC message implies "transmit" congestion, in contrast to the "receive" buffer congestion handled by MTP2. Figure 7-23 shows a typical example in which an STP receives messages from a number of nodes for the same destination. This queues a large number of messages in the transmit buffer for the destination, putting the destination route into a congested state. The STP sends a TFC message to the SPs that generate the traffic, informing them that the STP 1 route to the destination is congested.

Figure 7-23 *Transfer Controlled*

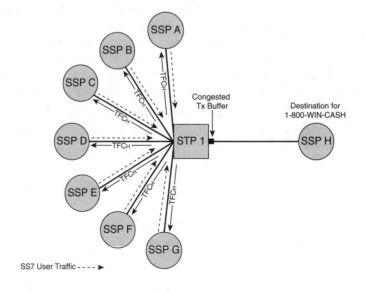

In the international network and ITU-T networks that do not implement the option of multiple congestion levels, the TFC simply indicates that the destination is in a congested state. In ANSI networks, the TFC includes a congestion level to indicate the severity of the congestion. The congestion level is used in conjunction with the message priority level to throttle messages during periods of congestion. The TFC message contains the H0/H1 code that identifies the message as a TFC message, the Point Code of the affected destination, and the congestion status shown in Figure 7-24.

Figure 7-24 *Transfer Controlled Message Format*

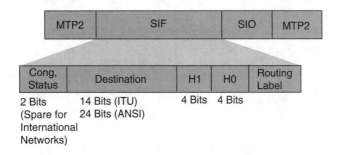

Multiple Congestion Levels

Congestion levels are part of the Transfer Controlled message.

The ITU-T defines an option for national networks to allow the use of multiple congestion levels to throttle traffic during periods of congestion. ANSI networks implement this option. There are three levels of congestion, 1 being the lowest and 3 being the highest. A congestion level of 0 indicates no congestion. The congestion levels represent the level of message queuing for a specific route. Figure 7-25 demonstrates the use of the TFC using multiple congestion levels.

When an STP receives a message for a congested routeset, the priority field in the SIO is compared with the congestion level of the congested routeset. If the priority of the message is lower than the congestion level, a TFC message is sent to the message originator indicating the current congestion level. The originating node updates the congestion status of the routeset and notifies its MTP users with an MTP congestion primitive so they can take the appropriate action to reduce traffic generation. The "MTP3/User Part Communication" section discusses MTP primitives further.

Figure 7-25 *ANSI Routeset Congestion (National Multilevel)*

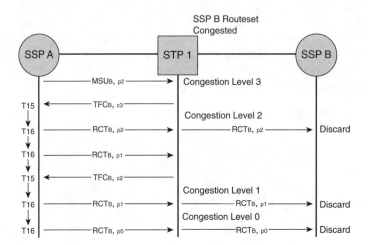

To begin the Routeset Congestion Test procedure, timer T15 is started when the TFC message is received. If timer T15 expires before receiving another TFC message, an RCT message is sent to the congested destination. The RCT message has its priority field set to a value of one less than the routeset's current congestion. If the routeset congestion level at the STP remains the same, another TFC message is sent in response to the RCT. Remember, any message with a lower priority than the current congestion level invokes the TFC to be sent. If, however, the congestion level has lowered, the RCT message is allowed to route to its destination. The RCT message is simply discarded when it arrives at the destination. Its only purpose is to test the path through the network.

Timer T16 is started when the RCT message is sent. If a TFC is not received before the expiration of T16, another RCT message is sent with a message priority one lower than the previous RCT. This cycle is repeated until the congestion level reaches 0.

Routeset Congestion Test

The *Routeset Congestion Test* message tests the congestion level of a network destination. It poses the question, "Is the Routeset still at congestion level x?"

As shown in Figure 7-18, the RCT message contains the H0/H1 code that identifies the message as a RCT message and the Point Code of the affected destination. As discussed in the previous section, the RCT message is sent in response to a TFC. The priority of the RCT message is set to one less than the congestion level identified in the TFC message. The node sending the RCT can determine whether to resume traffic transmission of a given priority based on whether a TFC is received in response to the RCT. As shown in Figure 7-25, if no TFC is received within T16, the sending node marks the routeset with the new congestion level, which is based on the priority of the transmitted RCT message. Refer to section "Multiple Congestion Levels" for a complete discussion of how the RCT message is used in the transfer controlled procedure.

Traffic Management

Traffic management is the nucleus of the MTP network management layer that coordinates between the MTP users' communication needs and the available routing resources. It is somewhat of a traffic cop in stopping, starting, redirecting, and throttling traffic. Traffic is diverted away from unavailable links and linksets, stopped in the case of unavailable routesets, and reduced where congestion exists.

Traffic management depends on the information provided by link management and route management to direct user traffic. For example, when a TFP is received for a destination, traffic management must determine whether an alternate route is available and shift traffic to this alternate route. During this action, it determines what messages the unavailable destination has not acknowledged so those messages can be retransmitted on the alternate route. This section discusses the following procedures that are employed by traffic management to accomplish such tasks:

- Changeover
- Emergency changeover
- Time-controlled changeover
- Changeback
- Time-controlled diversion
- Forced rerouting
- Controlled rerouting
- MTP restart
- Management inhibiting

Changeover

Changeover is the process of diverting traffic to a new link when a link becomes unavailable. When a link becomes unavailable and there are other links in the linkset, traffic is "changed over" to one of the other links. If there are no other available links in the linkset and another linkset is available, traffic is diverted to the alternate linkset. The node at either end of the link can detect the failure, and it is possible that both ends might detect it simultaneously. When the link is determined to be unavailable, a Changeover Order (COO) message is sent to the far end to initiate the changeover. The COO contains the SLC of the failed link and the Forward Sequence Number (FSN) of the last accepted message. Figure 7-26 shows the format of the COO message.

Figure 7-26 *Changeover Message Format*

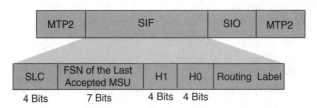

Each link contains a retransmission buffer that holds messages until they are acknowledged. When the COO is received, the FSN is compared to the messages in the retransmission buffer to determine which messages need to be retransmitted because the far end has not received them. All messages received with a sequence number higher than the FSN in the COO are retransmitted. The messages in the transmission and retransmission buffer are diverted to the new signaling link for transmission with the traffic that is normally destined for that link. The correct message sequence for the retransmitted messages is maintained based on the SLS values. The SLS values for new messages are mapped to the remaining available signaling links so the new traffic being transmitted is no longer sent to the unavailable link. A Changeover Acknowledgement (COA) is sent in response to a Changeover order. The COA also contains the SLC of the failed link and the FSN of the last accepted message. This allows the node receiving the COA to determine where to begin retransmission of Signaling Units.

Both nodes connected to the link might receive notification from link management and begin changeover at the same time, sending a COO simultaneously. If a COO has been sent by one node and a COO is received for the same link, the changeover proceeds using the received COO as an acknowledgement. The COA message is still sent to acknowledge the changeover, but the changeover procedure does not wait if it has already received a COO. Figure 7-27 shows SSP A with one link in each linkset to STP 1 and STP 2. When the link to STP 2 fails, SSP A detects the failure and performs a changeover to the STP 1 linkset. The changeover is made to a new linkset because no other links are available in the same linkset. If more links were available in the STP 2 linkset, the changeover would be to a new link in the same linkset.

Figure 7-27 *Changeover to a New Linkset*

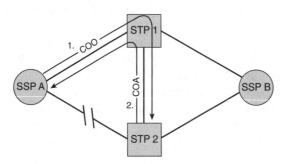

Emergency Changeover

It is possible that a node cannot determine the last acknowledged message when a link fails. An example is the failure of the signaling terminal hardware. Typically, the signaling terminal hardware contains the receive buffers and keeps track of the FSN for incoming signaling units. There is no way to determine where the request for retransmission should start if this information is lost. In this case, an *Emergency Changeover (ECO)* is sent to the far end to initiate a changeover. The ECO does not contain the last accepted FSN field because the last good message cannot be determined. Figure 7-28 shows the format for the ECO message.

Figure 7-28 *Emergency Changeover Message*

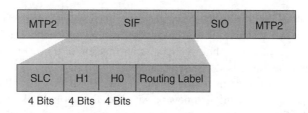

Because there is no FSN to compare with the messages in the retransmission buffer, buffer updating is not performed when the ECO is received. All traffic that has not been transmitted is diverted to the new signaling link to be sent out with the normal traffic for that link. This obviously increases the chances of message loss as compared to a normal changeover; however, this is to be expected because the recovery is from a more catastrophic failure.

Time-Controlled Changeover

There are times when a link might fail and no alternate path exists between the nodes at each end of the link. Because a changeover message cannot be sent to inform the far end, after a certain period of time the traffic is simply diverted over an alternate path to the destination. Figure 7-29 shows an example of a *Time-Controlled Changeover* at SSP A from the STP 2 linkset to the STP 1 linkset.

Figure 7-29 *Time-Controlled Changeover*

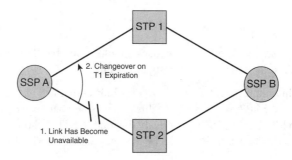

When this situation occurs, a timer (T1) is started and, when the timer expires, traffic is sent on an alternate route. The time-controlled changeover procedure can also be used in two other situations: for a processor outage, and when a link is put into the inhibited state.

The SS7 standards do not fully specify the use of the time-controlled changeover for a processor outage. When used for an inhibited link, traffic is simply diverted to the alternate route at timer expiry, without a link failure.

Changeback

Changeback is the process of diverting traffic from an alternative signaling link back to the link that is usually used.

When a link becomes unavailable, a changeover occurs, diverting traffic to another link. When the link becomes available again, a changeback restores traffic to its normal pattern. When link management declares the link available, transmission of traffic over the alternative link is stopped and the traffic is stored in a changeback buffer. A Changeback Declaration (CBD) message is sent over the alternate signaling link; it indicates that all diverted traffic being sent over the alternate link will now be sent over the normal link. A changeback code is assigned by the SP performing the changeback and is included in the CBD message. This allows a specific changeback to be identified when multiple changebacks are happening in parallel. When the CBD message is received, a Changeback Acknowledgement (CBA) is sent in response. Both the CBD and CBA messages contain the H0/H1 code that identifies the message type and the changeback code, as shown in Figure 7-30.

Figure 7-30 *Changeback Declaration Message*

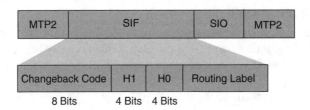

Time-Controlled Diversion

There are situations where a changeback should occur, but there is no way to signal the changeback to the other end of the signaling link.

As shown in Figure 7-31, the SSP A – STP 2 linkset that was unavailable has been restored. Assuming that SSP A set its routing table to load share between STP 1 and STP 2 for traffic destined to SSP B, the MSUs previously diverted to STP 1 should now be sent to STP 2. If a path existed between STP 1 and STP 2, either SSP A or STP 1 normally sends a CBD.

Although the path does not exist in this case, the need to divert the MSUs still exists. After the link to STP 2 completes the MTP restart procedure, timer T3 is started. At the expiration of T3, the normal traffic to STP 2 is restarted.

Figure 7-31 *Time-Controlled Diversion*

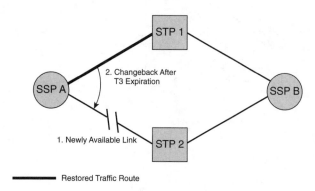

Forced Rerouting

Forced rerouting is used to divert traffic away from an unavailable route immediately. This occurs in response to a TFP message. As previously discussed, the TFP message is used to signal the inability to route to a particular destination.

When a route toward a destination signaling point has become unavailable, traffic for that route is stopped and stored in a forced rerouting buffer. An alternative route is then determined by searching for the route with the next highest priority in the routeset. The diverted traffic is then transmitted over the alternative route, along with the normal traffic flow for that route. The messages from the forced rerouting buffer are sent out before any new traffic is diverted. If no alternative route exists, the internal routeset state for the signaling point is changed to prohibited to indicate that messages can no longer be sent to that destination. If the node is an STP, it sends TFP messages out to its connected nodes to signal its inability to reach the destination.

In Figure 7-32, the route from STP 1 to SSP B has become unavailable, causing STP 1 to send TFP concerning SSP B. SSP A contains two routes in the routeset for SSP B: a route via STP 1, and another via STP 2. Traffic is diverted from the STP 1 route to the STP 2 route. Receiving a TFP message always causes a Forced Reroute, provided that there is another available route to which to shift traffic.

Figure 7-32 *Forced Rerouting*

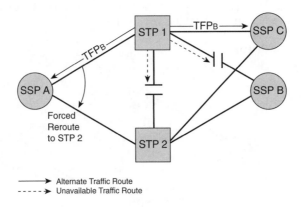

Controlled Rerouting

Controlled rerouting is used in response to TFR and TFA messages. This procedure is more "controlled" than forced rerouting in the sense that traffic is sent over an available route and is shifted to another available route.

Forced rerouting is performed when messages must be shifted away from a route that is no longer available. With controlled rerouting, transmission of traffic over the linkset is stopped and stored in a controlled rerouting buffer, and timer T6 is started. When timer T6 expires, traffic is restarted on the new linkset, beginning with the transmission of messages stored in the controlled rerouting buffer. The use of the timer helps prevent out-of-sequence messages by allowing traffic to complete on the previous route before restarting on the new route.

In Figure 7-33, SSP A receives a TFR from STP 1 for SSP B. SSP A has a routeset for destination SSP B with two routes in the routeset. SSP A performs controlled rerouting of traffic from STP 1 to STP 2. When the route from STP1 to SSP B is restored, STP 1 sends a TFA to indicate that full routing capability toward SSP B has been restored. SSP A performs controlled rerouting again, this time shifting traffic from the STP 2 route to the STP 1 route using the same basic procedure.

Figure 7-33 *Controlled Rerouting*

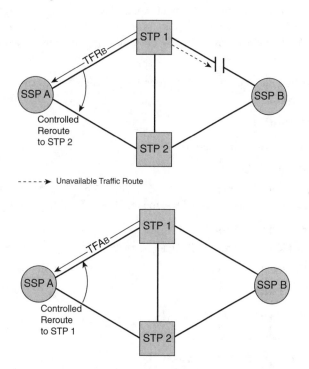

MTP Restart

MTP Restart

The *MTP restart* procedure was not a part of the early SS7 standards; it was added later to address issues with nodes coming into service or recovering from SS7 outages. The newly in-service or recovering node deals with heavy SS7 management traffic and might have limited SS7 resources available initially. The routing information the node maintains might also be stale from lack of communication with the remainder of the network. The restart procedure provides a dampening effect to the network management procedures that take place when a node causes major changes in network status. This allows the node to stabilize and bring sufficient SS7 links into service to handle the impending traffic.

The overall MTP restart procedure is handled using a restart timer (T20). If the restart is occurring at an STP, an additional timer (T18) is used to divide the restart into two phases. The MTP restart procedure begins when the first link of the restarting MTP becomes available. Routing status updates (TFP, TFR) are then received from adjacent nodes, followed by the TRA message that signals the end of the updates. If the node is an STP, it will then broadcast its own routing status updates. The TRA message is unique to the MTP restart procedure and is used to signal that the routing status update is complete and traffic is now allowed. As shown in Figure 7-15, the TRA message contains the H0/H1 code that indicates a TRA message.

The following lists summarize the procedures that take place during the MTP restart for a SSP and a STP:

SSP MTP Restart

- First link comes into service.
- Start Timer T20.
- Update routing tables based on TFP, TFR, and TFA messages from adjacent nodes. Each adjacent node sends TRA to signal the end of the routing update.
- T20 is stopped or expired.
- Send TRA messages to all adjacent nodes.
- Notify local MTP users of the routing status of routesets maintained by the node.

STP MTP Restart

- First link comes into service.
- Start Timer T18 and T20.
- Update routing tables based on TFP, TFR, and TFA messages from adjacent nodes. Each adjacent node sends TRA to signal the end of the routing update.
- T18 is stopped or expires.
- TFP and TFR messages are broadcast to all adjacent nodes for inaccessible destinations.
- T20 is stopped or expires.
- Send TRA messages to all adjacent nodes.
- Notify local MTP users of the routing status of routesets maintained by the node.

Figure 7-34 shows SSP A undergoing an MTP restart. Routing status is received from adjacent nodes, followed by TRA messages. The expiration of timer T20 completes the restart. The SSP sends TRA messages to each of the connected STPs and notifies the user parts of routing status.

Figure 7-34 *MTP Restart*

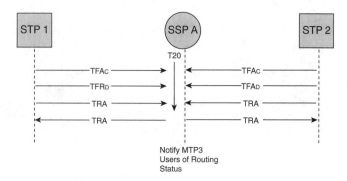

Management Inhibiting

Signaling link *management inhibiting* is used to prevent user traffic on the links while leaving the links themselves in service. This process is useful for isolating links for testing purposes.

Maintenance personnel typically initiate management inhibiting by issuing commands via a maintenance interface to the SS7 equipment. When a link is placed in the "inhibited" traffic state, only MTP3 maintenance and test messages (Service Indicator 0–2) are permitted on the link. The actual state of the link from the perspective of signaling link management does not change. Links can only be inhibited if they do not cause any destinations (routesets) defined at the node to become isolated. The link continues to transmit FISUs, MSUs, and LSSUs as needed. The inhibit procedure uses the Link Inhibit (LIN) and Link Inhibit Acknowledgement (LIA) messages to communicate between the two nodes concerning the linkset being inhibited. These messages use the basic network management format, as shown in Figure 7-15.

Inhibiting

In Figure 7-35, a maintenance engineer at STP 1 must perform testing on a link that has had intermittent problems. The engineer issues the command at a maintenance terminal to place the link in an inhibited state so it is not used by normal user traffic. STP 1 sends a LIN message to SSP A. Because SSP A has other links available for routing, it determines that it can safely remove the link from traffic service and respond with an LIA back to STP 1 in acknowledgement. Because SSP A has only 1 per linkset, it performs a controlled reroute of traffic to STP 2 linkset.

Figure 7-35 *Link Inhibit*

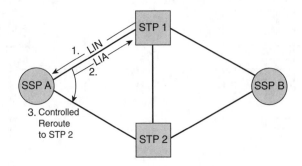

Uninhibiting

When a link is in the inhibited state, an inhibit test message is periodically sent to verify that the link is still in the inhibited state. Since an inhibited link is not available for user traffic, the inhibit test is a safeguard to ensure that the link state is correctly marked as inhibited at the far end of the link. Both the locally inhibited node and the remote node perform the inhibit test. ITU-T and ANSI use the following messages and timers to perform the inhibit test:

ITU-T

- Local Link Inhibit Test message (LLT)—T22
- Remote Link Inhibit Test message (LRT)—T23

ANSI

- Local Link Inhibit Test message (LLI)—T20
- Link Remote Inhibit Test message (LRI)—T21

Although the message acronyms chosen by ITU-T and ANSI are slightly different, both network types use the same respective messages.

The node at which the link is locally inhibited sends a Link Local Inhibit Test message at each Local Inhibit Test timer period (T20 or T22). The remote node receiving the message checks the state at its end to ensure that it is still set as "remotely inhibited." The remote end also sends a LRI message at each LRT timer period (T21 or T23). The node at the locally inhibited link that receives the message checks the state to ensure that it is still set as "locally inhibited." The periodic test continues between the nodes at each end of the link until the link is uninhibited. Figure 7-36 shows an example of the link inhibit test between SSP A and STP 1 where the link has been locally inhibited by SSP A. The example shows an ANSI network; ITU-T and ANSI differ only in the message acronyms and timer labels used.

Figure 7-36 *Link Inhibit Test*

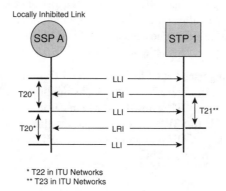

Locally Inhibited Link

The *link uninhibit* procedure does the reverse of the inhibit procedure: it puts the link back into service for user traffic. The uninhibit procedure is invoked by issuing commands at a maintenance interface to the SS7 equipment. The procedure makes use of the LUN message to request that the link be uninhibited, and the LUA message acknowledges the request.

In Figure 7-37, the link from STP 1 to STP A is ready to return to use for user traffic. A command is issued to "uninhibit" it at the maintenance position. The command causes an LUN (Link Uninhibit) message to be sent from STP 1 to SSP A, and SSP A responds with an LUA. Because each linkset contains only one link, a controlled reroute shifts user traffic back to its original route using STP 1.

Figure 7-37 *Link Uninhibit*

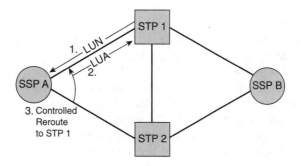

Forced Uninhibiting

In the period during which a link is inhibited, the loss of other links can cause the inhibited link to become a critical resource. The *forced uninhibit* or "Management-initiated" uninhibit is a way for a node to request that an inhibited link be restored to service for user traffic when no other links are available.

Forced uninhibiting uses the LFU (Link Forced Uninhibit) message to request that the link be uninhibited. In Figure 7-38, SSP A has inhibited the link from SSP A to STP 1. The link from STP 1 to STP 2 now fails, which causes STP 1 to be isolated from SSP A. STP 1 sends an LFU to SSP A to request that the link be uninhibited for use by user traffic. SSP A sends an LUN to uninhibit the link. STP 1 now responds with an LUA and user traffic can flow over the link.

Figure 7-38   *Link Forced Uninhibit*

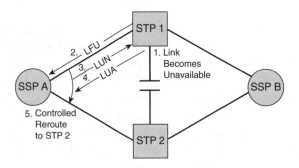

MTP3/User Part Communication

As shown in Figure 7-39, MTP3 uses primitives to communicate with MTP users about its routing status. A *primitive* is simply an indication that is passed between levels of the protocol by the software implementing the SS7 software stack. The primitives indicate the ability or inability of MTP3 to route messages. Primitives are not seen on the network because they are part of the MTP3 implementation at a node; however, as with most of the network management procedures, primitives are related to SS7 Network Management messages. As seen from the description of the primitives, changing network conditions communicated by SNM messages cause different primitives to be sent to the user parts.

- **MTP-Transfer**—Indicates the ability to transfer messages to a destination. The transfer primitive is used to pass signaling message data between the MTP3 users and the MTP3 Signaling Message Handling function. This is the normal state for a destination when the network is healthy.

- **MTP-Pause**—Indicates the complete inability to transfer messages to a particular destination. This primitive informs the MTP user that no messages should be sent to the destination. When the destination is available again, MTP3 sends an MTP-Resume. This indication is sent to the user part when a TFP has been received for a destination.

- **MTP-Resume**—Indicates the ability to transfer messages to a previously unavailable destination. This indication is sent to the user part when a TFA is received and an MTP-Pause had previously been sent to the user part.

- **MTP-Status**—Indicates a partial routing ability. This is used to indicate the congestion level to the user part in the case of multiple-level congestion. The user part uses this information to prevent sending messages that have a priority less than the reported congestion level. It can also be used to indicate that a user part is unavailable.

Figure 7-39 *MTP3/User Part Communication*

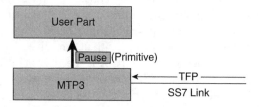

Signaling Network Management Example

As noted throughout this chapter, traffic, route, and link management are coupled in a modular fashion to form a complete network management system for SS7. Here we examine a failure scenario to show how these cooperating components depend on and communicate with each other.

Figure 7-40 shows a typical failure scenario in an SS7 network. SSP A has two linksets connecting it to the network, with one link in each linkset. This is a common configuration for SSPs.

The single link within the linkset connecting SSP A to STP 2 is broken. This type of problem often occurs when aggressive backhoe operators are digging near buried communications spans. From the diagram, you can see all three of the major SNM blocks at work. Link management detects that the link has failed and reports this loss to both traffic management and route management. Next it begins link restoration procedures by attempting to align the link. Recall from the chapter on MTP2 that the alignment procedure sends out an LSSU of type SIOS (Status Indication Out of Service), followed by SIO (Status Indication Out of Alignment). This occurs at both SSP A and STP 2, and link management attempts to restore the link at each node. Of course, with the broken link path, the alignment fails and the process is repeated. Having received link management's notification of the loss of the only direct link to STP 2, traffic management at SSP A performs a changeover to the linkset to STP 1, sending a COO to STP 2. The COO contains the FSN of the last MSU that was acknowledged on the link before it went down. STP 2 uses this information to resend the messages from its retransmit buffer to SSP A via the C-Link to STP 1, beginning with the "FSN + 1" sequence number. STP 2 sends a COA to SSP A to acknowledge the COO message and performs a changeover on its end. The COA contains the FSN of the last MSU acknowledged by STP 2. This allows SSP A to determine the correct point to start retransmission of messages to STP 2.

Both SSP A and STP 2 have now informed each other about where message retransmission should start when traffic restarts on the alternate route. Route management at STP 2 responds to the link management's notification by sending a TFR for SSP A to all of its connected linksets, except for the linkset of its quasi-associated route to SSP A. SSP B and SSP C perform controlled rerouting of traffic destined for SSP A to their STP 1 linkset. They also respond to the TFR by periodically sending RSR based on the routeset test timer (T10). They repeat sending the RSR every T10 until they receive a TFA. Route management at STP 2 sends a TFP message to STP 1 for SSP A. The loss of its direct route to SSP A means that any messages it receives for SSP A must be routed over its quasi-associated route via STP 1. The TFP is sent to STP 1 to prevent it from sending any messages for SSP A; otherwise those messages would have to be sent back to STP 1, causing unnecessary traffic over the C-Links and at STP 2, as well as a potential loop routing.

Figure 7-40   *Signaling Network Management Failure Scenario*

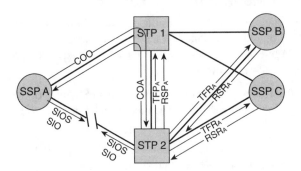

The final result is that the route to SSP A over the STP2 linkset is now marked as "restricted" at SSP B and C. They send all traffic destined for SSP A to STP 1, unless they lose the linkset to STP 1. The loss of the STP1 linkset would leave the restricted route through STP 2 as the only available path to SSP A, resulting in messages being routed over the C-link from STP2 to STP1, and finally to SSP A.

Summary

MTP3 provides reliable message delivery for signaling traffic between SS7 nodes. The network structure provides for a hierarchical design, using the point code to discriminate between hierarchy levels.

Signaling Message Handling uses the Point Code to send messages to the correct destination and discriminate incoming messages to determine whether they have reached their destination. The message handling functions use static routing information maintained at each node to populate the MTP Routing Label and to select the correct link for sending the message.

SS7's Signaling Network Management procedures provide a mechanism to handle network failures and congestion with minimal loss, duplication, or mis-sequencing of messages. Due to the critical nature of SS7 signaling, the procedures for handling failures and congestion are comprehensive. SNM uses the exchange of messages between nodes to communicate failure and recovery events as well as the status of routes. Timers monitor SNM procedures and messages to ensure that appropriate action is taken to maintain network integrity.

Because MTP3 adheres to the modularity of the OSI model, the user parts can depend on the MTP3 transport without being aware of the underlying details. The two levels exchange a simple set of primitives to communicate status.

CHAPTER 8

ISDN User Part (ISUP)

The *ISDN User Part (ISUP)* is responsible for setting up and releasing trunks used for inter-exchange calls. As its name implies, ISUP was created to provide core network signaling that is compatible with ISDN access signaling. The combination of ISDN access signaling and ISUP network signaling provides an end-to-end transport mechanism for signaling data between subscribers. Today, the use of ISUP in the network has far exceeded the use of ISDN on the access side. ISUP provides signaling for both non-ISDN and ISDN traffic; in fact, the majority of ISUP-signaled traffic currently originates from analog access signaling, like that used by basic telephone service phones.

The primary benefits of ISUP are its speed, increased signaling bandwidth, and standardization of message exchange. Providing faster call setup times than Channel Associated Signaling (CAS), it ultimately uses trunk resources more effectively. The difference in post-dial delay for calls using ISUP trunks is quite noticeable to the subscriber who makes a call that traverses several switches.

NOTE Post-dial delay is the time between when the originator dials the last digit and the originating end receives an indication (or audible ringback).

In addition to its speed efficiencies, ISUP enables more call-related information to be exchanged because it uses Common Channel Signaling (CCS). CAS signaling severely limits the amount of information that can be exchanged over trunks because it shares a small amount of space with a call's voice stream. ISUP defines many messages and parameters, therefore, allowing information about a call to be exchanged both within the network and between end-users. Although messages and parameters do vary between different countries, a given variant provides a standard means of exchanging information between vendor equipment within the national network, and to a large degree, at the international level.

For the reader who is unfamiliar with the PSTN and how switching exchanges work, Chapter 5, "The Public Switched Telephone Network (PSTN)," explains the PSTN, describes the basic concepts of call processing at an exchange, and introduces the concepts of trunks, trunkgroups, and routing.

ISUP consists of call processing, supplementary services, and maintenance functions. This chapter is divided into the following sections, which describe the specific components of ISUP:

- Bearers and Signaling
- ISUP and the SS7 Protocol Stack
- ISUP Message Flow
- Message Timers
- Circuit Identification Codes
- Enbloc and Overlap Address Signaling
- Circuit Glare
- Continuity Test
- ISUP Message Format
- Detailed Call Walk-Through
- Circuit Suspend and Resume
- ISUP and Local Number Portability
- ISUP–ISUP Tandem Calls
- Interworking with ISDN
- Supplementary Services
- Additional Call Processing Messages
- Maintenance Messages and Procedures

Bearers and Signaling

ISUP allows the call control signaling to be separated from the circuit that carries the voice stream over interoffice trunks. The circuit that carries the voice portion of the call is known within the telephone industry by many different terms. Voice channel, voice circuit, trunk member, and bearer all refer to the digital time slot that transports the voice (fax, modem, or other voiceband data) part of a call. The term "voice circuit" can be somewhat ambiguous in this context because sometimes it is used to refer to the trunk span that is divided into time slots, or to an individual time slot on a span.

The signaling component of the call is, of course, transported over SS7 signaling links. This creates two independent paths for call information between nodes: the voice path and the signaling path. The signaling mode describes the signaling relation between the two paths. Following is a brief review of the associated and quasi-associated signaling modes as they relate to ISUP, which we discussed in earlier chapters.

If the signaling travels on a single linkset that originates and terminates at the same nodes as the bearer circuit, the signaling mode is associated. If the signaling travels over two or more linksets and at least one intermediate node, the signaling mode is quasi-associated. In Figure 8-1, part A shows quasi-associated signaling between SSP A and SSP B and between SSP B and SSP C. In part B of Figure 8-1, the same SSP nodes are shown using associated signaling. Notice that the signaling links in part B terminate at the same point as the trunks. Also, the signaling link is shown as a separate entity in part B to illustrate the signaling mode; however, it is typically just another time slot that is dedicated for signaling on a trunk span.

Figure 8-1   *Signaling Mode Relating to ISUP Trunks*

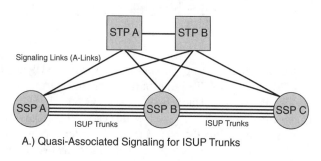

A.) Quasi-Associated Signaling for ISUP Trunks

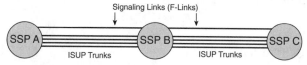

B.) Associated Signaling for ISUP Trunks

The signaling mode used for ISUP depends greatly on what SS7 network architecture is used. For example, North America uses hierarchical STPs for aggregation of signaling traffic. Therefore, most ISUP trunks are signaled using quasi-associated signaling. Using this mode, the signaling is routed through the STP before reaching the destination SSP. In contrast, while the U.K. uses quasi-associated signaling for some SSPs, they also heavily use associated signaling with directly connected signaling links between many SSPs.

ISUP and the SS7 Protocol Stack

As shown in Figure 8-2, ISUP resides at Level 4 of the SS7 stack with its predecessor, the Telephone User Part (TUP). TUP is still used in many countries, but ISUP is supplanting it over time. TUP also provides a call setup and release that is similar to ISUP, but it has only a subset of the capabilities. TUP is not used in North America because its capabilities are not sufficient to support the more complex network requirements.

Figure 8-2   *ISUP at Level 4 of the SS7 Stack*

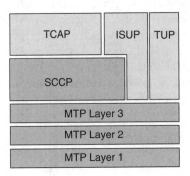

As you can see in Figure 8-2, a connection exists between ISUP and both the SCCP and MTP3 levels. ISUP uses the MTP3 transport services to exchange network messages, such as those used for call setup and clear down. The connection to SCCP is for the transport of end-to-end signaling. While SCCP provides this capability, today ISUP end-to-end signaling is usually transported directly over MTP3. The "Interworking with ISDN" section of this chapter further discusses end-to-end signaling and the two different methods using MTP3 and SCCP for transport.

ISUP Standards and Variants

The ITU-T defines the international ISUP standards in the Q.767 and the national standards in the Q.761–Q.764 series of specifications. The ITU-T standards provide a basis from which countries or geographical regions can define regional or national versions of the protocol, which are often referred to as variants. For the U.S. network, the following standards provide the primary specifications for the ISUP protocol and its use in local and long distance networks:

- ANSI T1.113–ANSI ISUP

- Telcordia GR-246 Telcordia Technologies Specification of Signaling System No. 7, Volume 3. (ISUP)

- Telcordia GR-317 LSSGR—Switching System Generic Requirements for Call Control Using the Integrated Services Digital Network User Part (ISDNUP)

- Telcordia GR-394 LSSGR—Switching System Generic Requirements for Interexchange Carrier Interconnection (ICI) Using the Integrated Services Digital Network User Part (ISDNUP)

In Europe, the following ETSI standards provide the basis for the national ISUP variants:

- ETSI ETS 300-121 Integrated Services Digital Network (ISDN); Application of the ISDN User Part (ISUP) of CCITT Signaling System No. 7 for international ISDN interconnections

- ETSI ETS 300-156-x Integrated Services Digital Network (ISDN); Signaling System No. 7; ISDN User Part (ISUP) for the international interface

The ETS 300-121 is version 1, and the ETS 300-156-x (where x represents an individual document number) is a suite of specifications that covers ETSI ISUP versions 2–4.

A multitude of different country requirements have created many ISUP variants. A few of the several flavors are Swedish ISUP, U.K. ISUP, Japanese ISUP, Turkish ISUP, Korean ISUP. Each variant is tailored to the specific national requirements. Although not certain of the exact number of variants that are in existence today, the author has encountered over a hundred different ISUP variants while developing software for switching platforms.

ISUP Message Flow

This section provides an introduction to the core set of ISUP messages that are used to set up and release a call. The ISUP protocol defines a large set of procedures and messages, many of which are used for supplementary services and maintenance procedures. While the ITU Q.763 ISUP standard defines nearly fifty messages, a core set of five to six messages represent the majority of the ISUP traffic on most SS7 networks. The basic message flow that is presented here provides a foundation for the remainder of the chapter. Additional messages, message content, and the actions taken at an exchange during message processing build upon the foundation presented here.

A basic call can be divided into three distinct phases:

- Setup
- Conversation (or data exchange for voice-band data calls)
- Release

ISUP is primarily involved in the set-up and release phases. Further ISUP signaling can take place if a supplementary service is invoked during the conversation phase.

In Figure 8-3, part A illustrates the ISUP message flow for a basic call. The call is considered basic because no supplementary services or protocol interworking are involved. The next section, "Call Setup," explains the figure's message timer values.

Figure 8-3   *Simple ISUP Message Flow*

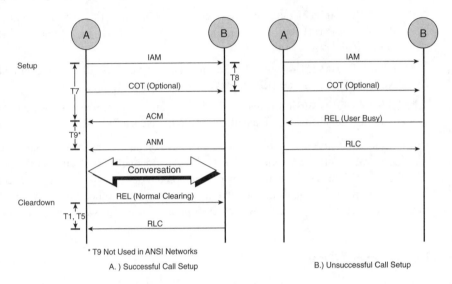

Call Setup

A simple basic telephone service call can be established and released using only five ISUP messages. In Figure 8-3, part A shows a call between SSP A and SSP B. The Initial Address Message (IAM) is the first message sent, which indicates an attempt to set up a call for a particular circuit. The IAM contains information that is necessary to establish the call connection—such as the call type, called party number, and information about the bearer circuit. When SSP B receives the IAM, it responds with an Address Complete Message (ACM). The ACM indicates that the call to the selected destination can be completed. For example, if the destination is a subtending line, the line has been determined to be in service and not busy. The Continuity message (COT), shown in the figure, is an optional message that is used for continuity testing of the voice path before it is cut through to the end users. This chapter's "Continuity Test" section discusses the COT message.

Once the ACM has been sent, ringing is applied to the terminator and ring back is sent to the originator. When the terminating set goes off-hook, an Answer Message (ANM) is sent to the originator. The call is now active and in the talking state. For an ordinary call that does not involve special services, no additional ISUP messages are exchanged until one of the parties signals the end of the call by going on-hook.

Call Release

In Figure 8-3, the call originator at SSP A goes on-hook to end the call. SSP A sends a Release message (REL) to SSP B. The REL message signals the far end to release the bearer channel. SSP B responds with a Release Complete message (RLC) to acknowledge the REL message. The RLC indicates that the circuit has been released.

If the terminating party goes on-hook first, the call might be suspended instead of being released. Suspending a call maintains the bearer connection for a period of time, even though the terminator has disconnected. The terminator can go off-hook to resume the call, providing that he does so before the expiration of the disconnect timer or a disconnect by the originating party. This chapter discusses suspending and resuming a connection in more detail in the section titled "Circuit Suspend and Resume."

NOTE	Several different terms are used to identify the two parties who are involved in a telephone conversation. For example, the originating party is also known as the calling party, or the "A" party. The terminating party, or "B" party, are also synonymous with the called party.

Unsuccessful Call Attempt

In Figure 8-3, part B shows an unsuccessful call attempt between SSP A and SSP B. After receiving the IAM, SSP B checks the status of the destination line and discovers that it is busy. Instead of an ACM, a REL message with a cause value of User Busy is sent to SSP A, indicating that the call cannot be set up. While this example shows a User Busy condition, there are many reasons that a call set-up attempt might be unsuccessful. For example, call screening at the terminating exchange might reject the call and therefore prevent it from being set up. Such a rejection would result in a REL with a cause code of Call Rejected.

NOTE	Call screening compares the called or calling party number against a defined list of numbers to determine whether a call can be set up to its destination.

Message Timers

Like other SS7 protocol levels, ISUP uses timers as a safeguard to ensure that anticipated events occur when they should. All of the timers are associated with ISUP messages and are generally set when a message is sent or received to ensure that the next intended action occurs. For example, when a REL message is sent, Timer T1 is set to ensure that a RLC is received within the T1 time period.

ITU Q.764 defines the ISUP timers and their value ranges. In Figure 8-3, part A includes the timers for the messages that are presented for a basic call. The "Continuity Test" section of this chapter discusses the timers associated with the optional COT message. Following are the definitions of each of the timers in the figure:

- **T7 awaiting address complete timer**—Also known as the network protection timer. T7 is started when an IAM is sent, and is canceled when an ACM is received. If T7 expires, the circuit is released.

- **T8 awaiting continuity timer**—Started when an IAM is received with the Continuity Indicator bit set. The timer is stopped when the Continuity Message is received. If T8 expires, a REL is sent to the originating node.

- **T9 awaiting answer timer**—Not used in ANSI networks. T9 is started when an ACM is received, and is canceled when an ANM is received. If T9 expires, the circuit is released. Although T9 is not specified for ANSI networks, answer timing is usually performed at the originating exchange to prevent circuits from being tied up for an excessive period of time when the destination does not answer.

- **T1 release complete timer**—T1 is started when a REL is sent and canceled when a RLC is received. If T1 expires, REL is retransmitted.

- **T5 initial release complete timer**—T5 is also started when a REL is sent, and is canceled when a RLC is received. T5 is a longer duration timer than T1 and is intended to provide a mechanism to recover a nonresponding circuit for which a release has been initiated. If T5 expires, a RSC is sent and REL is no longer sent for the nonresponding circuit. An indication of the problem is also given to the maintenance system.

We list the timers for the basic call in part A of Figure 8-3 to provide an understanding of how ISUP timers are used. There are several other ISUP timers; a complete list can be found in Appendix H, "ISUP Timers for ANSI/ETSI/ITU-T Applications."

Circuit Identification Codes

One of the effects of moving call signaling from CAS to Common Channel Signaling (CCS) is that the signaling and voice are now traveling on two separate paths through the network. Before the introduction of SS7 signaling, the signaling and voice component of a call were always transported on the same physical facility. In the case of robbed-bit signaling, they are even transported on the same digital time slot of that facility.

The separation of signaling and voice create the need for a means of associating the two entities. ISUP uses a Circuit Identification Code (CIC) to identify each voice circuit. For example, each of the 24 channels of a T1 span (or 30 channels of an E1 span) has a CIC associated with it. When ISUP messages are sent between nodes, they always include the CIC to which they pertain. Otherwise, the receiving end would have no way to determine the circuit to which the incoming message should be applied. Because the CIC identifies a bearer circuit between two nodes, the node at each end of the trunk must define the same CIC for the same physical voice channel.

Not defining CICs so that they match properly at each end of the connection is a common cause of problems that occur when defining and bringing new ISUP trunks into service.

ITU defines a 12-bit CIC, allowing up to 4096 circuits to be defined. ANSI uses a larger CIC value of 14 bits, allowing for up to 16,384 circuits.

Figure 8-4 shows an ISUP message from SSP A that is routed through the STP to SSP B. For simplicity, only one STP is shown. In the message, CIC 100 identifies the physical circuit between SSP A and B to which the message applies. Administrative provisioning at each of the nodes associates each time slot of the digital trunk span with a CIC. As shown in the figure, Trunk 1, time slot (TS) 1 is defined at each SSP as CIC 100. Trunk 1, time slot 2 is defined as CIC 101, and so on.

Figure 8-4   *CIC Identifies the Specific Voice Circuit*

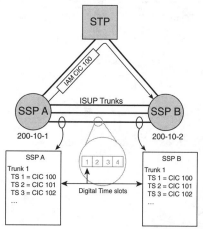

Note: TS = Time Slot of the Trunk Span

DPC to CIC Association

Since each ISUP message is ultimately transported by MTP, an association must be created between the circuit and the SS7 network destination. This association is created through provisioning at the SSP, by linking a trunk group to a routeset or DPC.

The CIC must be unique to each DPC that the SSP defines. A CIC can be used again within the same SSP, as long as it is not duplicated for the same DPC. This means that you might see CIC 0 used many times throughout an SS7 network, and even multiple times at the same

SSP. It is the combination of DPC and CIC that uniquely identifies the circuit. Figure 8-5 shows an example of three SSPs that are interconnected by ISUP trunks. SSP B uses the same CIC numbers for identifying trunks to SSP A and SSP C. For example, notice that it has two trunks using CIC 25 and two trunks using CIC 26. Since SSP A and SSP C are separate destinations, each with their own unique routeset defined at SSP B, the DPC/CIC combination still uniquely identifies each circuit. SSP B can, in fact, have many other duplicate CIC numbers associated with different DPCs.

Figure 8-5 *Combination of DPC/CIC Provide Unique Circuit ID*

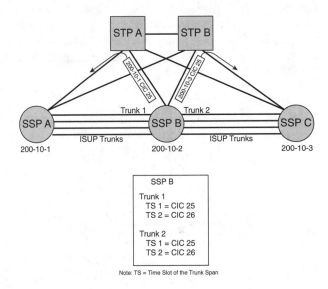

Unidentified Circuit Codes

When a message is received with a CIC that is not defined at the receiving node, an Unequipped Circuit Code (UCIC) message is sent in response. The UCIC message's CIC field contains the unidentified code. The UCIC message is used only in national networks.

Enbloc and Overlap Address Signaling

The Called Party Number (CdPN) is the primary key for routing a call through the network. When using ISUP to set up a call, the CdPN can be sent using either enbloc or overlap signaling. In North America, enbloc signaling is always used; in Europe, overlap signaling is quite common, although both methods are used.

Enbloc Signaling

The enbloc signaling method transmits the number as a complete entity in a single message. When using enbloc signaling, the complete number is sent in the IAM to set up a call. This is much more efficient than overlap signaling, which uses multiple messages to transport the number. Enbloc signaling is better suited for use where fixed-length dialing plans are used, such as in North America. Figure 8-6 illustrates the use of enbloc signaling.

Figure 8-6   *Enbloc Address Signaling*

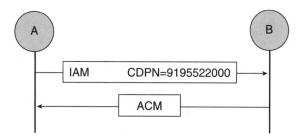

Overlap Signaling

Overlap signaling sends portions of the number in separate messages as digits are collected from the originator. Using overlap signaling, call setup can begin before all the digits have been collected. When using the overlap method, the IAM contains the first set of digits. The Subsequent Address Message (SAM) is used to transport the remaining digits. Figure 8-7 illustrates the use of overlap signaling. Local exchange A collects digits from the user as they are dialed. When enough digits have been collected to identify the next exchange, an IAM is sent to exchange B. When tandem exchange B has collected enough digits to identify the next exchange, it sends an IAM to exchange C; exchange C repeats this process. After the IAM is sent from exchange C to exchange D, the destination exchange is fully resolved. Exchange D receives SAMs containing the remaining digits needed to identify the individual subscriber line.

When using dialing plans that have variable length numbers, overlap signaling is preferable because it decreases post-dial delay. As shown in the preceding example, each succeeding call leg is set up as soon as enough digits have been collected to identify the next exchange.

As discussed in Chapter 5, "The Public Switched Telephone Network (PSTN)," interdigit timing is performed as digits are collected from a subscriber line. When an exchange uses variable length dial plans with enbloc signaling, it must allow interdigit timing to expire before attempting to set up the call. The exchange cannot start routing after a specific number of digits have been collected because that number is variable. By using overlap signaling, the call is set up as far as possible, waiting only for the final digits the subscriber dials. Although overlap signaling is less efficient in terms of signaling bandwidth, in this situation it is more efficient in terms of call set-up time.

Figure 8-7 *Overlap Address Signaling*

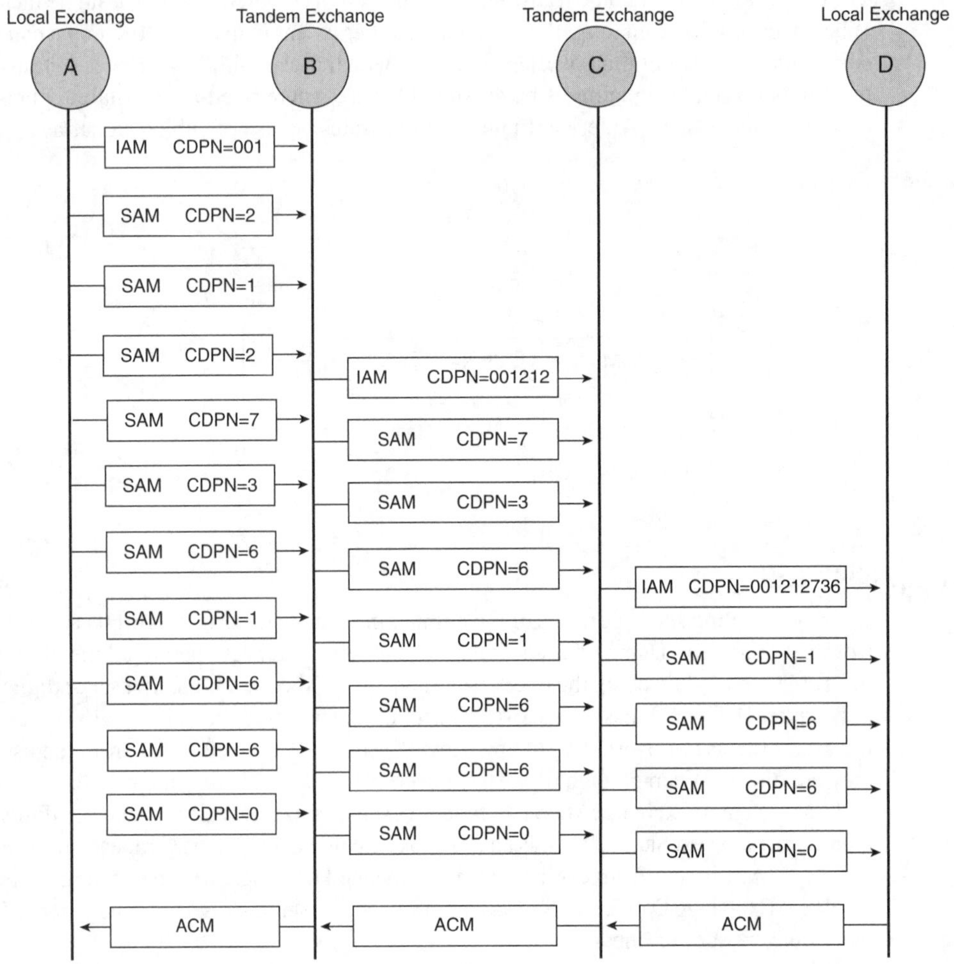

Local Exchange   Tandem Exchange   Tandem Exchange   Local Exchange

A   B   C   D

A → B	B → C	C → D
IAM CDPN=001		
SAM CDPN=2		
SAM CDPN=1		
SAM CDPN=2	IAM CDPN=001212	
SAM CDPN=7	SAM CDPN=7	
SAM CDPN=3	SAM CDPN=3	
SAM CDPN=6	SAM CDPN=6	IAM CDPN=001212736
SAM CDPN=1	SAM CDPN=1	SAM CDPN=1
SAM CDPN=6	SAM CDPN=6	SAM CDPN=6
SAM CDPN=6	SAM CDPN=6	SAM CDPN=6
SAM CDPN=0	SAM CDPN=0	SAM CDPN=0
ACM	ACM	ACM

Circuit Glare (Dual-Seizure)

Circuit glare (also known as dual-seizure) occurs when the node at each end of a two-way trunk attempts to set up a call over the same bearer at the same time. Using ISUP signaling, this occurs when an IAM for the same CIC is simultaneously sent from each end. Each end sends an IAM to set up a call before it receives the IAM from the other end. You will recall from our discussion of the basic ISUP message flow that once an IAM is sent, an ACM is expected. When an IAM is received after sending an IAM for the same CIC, glare has occurred.

Resolving Glare

When glare is detected, one node must back down and give control to the other end. This allows one call to complete, while the other call must be reattempted on another CIC. There are different methods for resolving which end takes control. For normal 64-kb/s connections, two methods are commonly used. With the first method, the point code and CIC numbers are used to determine which end takes control of the circuit. The node with the higher-numbered point code takes control of even number CICs, and the node with the lower-numbered point code takes control of odd numbered CICs. This provides a fair mechanism that allows each node to control approximately half of the calls encountering glare. In the United States, an example of this use would be two peer End Office exchanges. The second method of glare resolution is handled by prior agreement between the two nodes about which end will back down when glare occurs. One node is provisioned to always back down, while the other node is provisioned to take control. A typical example of this arrangement in the U.S. network would be a hand-off between non-peer exchanges, such as an IXC to AT. The method to use for glare resolution can usually be provisioned at the SSP, typically at the granularity level of the trunk group.

Figure 8-8 illustrates a glare condition when SSP A and B have both sent an IAM before receiving the IAM from the other end. Assuming that the point code/CIC method of resolving glare is being used, SSP B takes control of the circuit because the CIC is even numbered and SSP B has a numerically higher point code.

Figure 8-8   *Glare Condition During Call Setup*

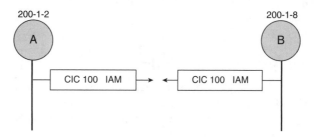

Avoiding Glare

When provisioning trunks, glare conditions can be minimized by properly coordinating the trunk selection algorithms at each end of a trunk group. A common method is to perform trunk selection in ascending order of the trunk member number at one end of the trunk group, and in descending order at the other end. This minimizes contention to the point of selecting the last available resource between the two ends. Another method is to have one end use the "Most Idle" trunk selection while the other end uses the "Least Idle" selection. The idea is to have an SSP select a trunk that is least likely to be selected by the SSP at the other end of the trunk group.

Continuity Test

Continuity testing verifies the physical bearer facility between two SSPs. When CAS signaling is used, a call setup fails if the voice path is faulty. Using ISUP signaling, it is possible to set up a call using the signaling network without knowing that the bearer connection is impaired or completely broken.

The voice and signaling channels are usually on separate physical facilities, so a means of verifying that the voice facility is connected properly between the SSPs is needed. Many digital voice transmission systems provide fault detection on bearer facilities, which are signaled to the connected switching system using alarm indication bits within the digital information frame. However, these bits are not guaranteed to be signaled transparently through interconnecting transmission equipment, such as a Digital Access Cross Connect system (DACS) or digital multiplexers. Some networks require these alarm indications to be passed through without disruption, therefore, reducing the need for continuity testing.

Continuity testing can be considered part of the ISUP maintenance functions. It can be invoked to test trunks manually, as part of routine maintenance and troubleshooting procedures. Continuity testing can also be provisioned to take place during normal call setup and it has an impact on the flow of call processing. During call processing, the originating exchange determines whether a continuity test should be performed. Network guidelines vary concerning whether and how often continuity testing is performed. The determination is typically based on a percentage of call originations. For example, in the United States, the generally accepted practice is to perform continuity testing on 12 percent of ISUP call originations (approximately one out of eight calls). This percentage is based on Telcordia recommendations.

Loopback and Transceiver Methods

The actual circuit testing can be performed using either the loopback or the transceiver method. The loopback method is performed on four-wire circuits using a single tone, and the transceiver method is used for two-wire circuits using two different tones. The primary difference between the two methods is related to the action that takes place at the terminating end. When using either method, a tone generator is connected to the outgoing circuit at the originating exchange. Using the loopback method, the terminating exchange connects the transmit path to the receive path, forming a loopback to the originator. The originator measures the tone coming back to ensure that it is within the specified parameters. When the transceiver method is used, the transmit and receive path are connected to a tone transceiver that measures the tone coming from the originating exchange and sends a different tone back to the originating exchange. The tone frequencies vary between countries. The following tones are used for the continuity test in North America:

- 2010 Hz from the originating exchange
- 1720 Hz from the terminating exchange (transceiver method only)

Another example of the COT tone frequency is 2000 Hz, which is used in the U.K.

Continuity Check Procedure

The Initial Address Message contains a *Continuity Check Indicator* as part of the *Nature of Connection* field. When an ISUP trunk circuit is selected for an outgoing call and the exchange determines that a continuity check should be performed, the Continuity Check Indicator is set to true. A tone generator is connected to the outgoing circuit, and the IAM is sent to the SSP at the far end of the trunk. Timer T25 is started when the tone is applied, to ensure that tone is received back within the T25 time period. When the SSP at the far end receives the IAM with the Continuity Check Indicator set to true, it determines whether to create a loopback of the transmit and receive path, or to connect a transceiver. The transceiver receives the incoming tone and generates another tone on the outgoing circuit. The determination of whether to use a loopback or transceiver is typically based on provisioned data at the receiving exchange. Upon receipt of the IAM, Timer T8 is started at the terminating exchange, awaiting the receipt of a COT message to indicate that the test passed. The terminating exchange does not apply ringing to the called party or send back ACM until the COT message has been received with a continuity indicator of continuity check successful to indicate that the bearer connection is good.

The originating exchange measures the received tone to ensure that it is within an acceptable frequency range and decibel level. Next it sends a COT message to the terminating exchange to indicate the test results. If the test passes, the call proceeds as normal; if the test fails, the CIC is blocked, the circuit connection is cleared, and the originating exchange sends a Continuity Check Request (CCR) message to request a retest of the failed circuit. While ISUP maintenance monitors the failed circuit's retest, ISUP call processing sets the call up on another circuit. Figure 8-9 shows a successful COT check using the loopback method.

Figure 8-9   *Successful COT Check Using the Loopback Method*

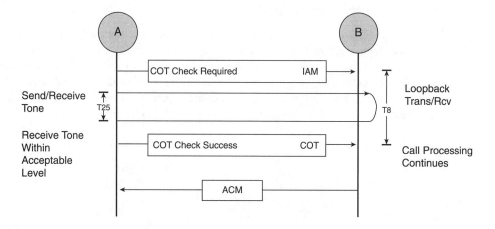

ISUP Message Format

The User Data portion of the MTP3 Signaling Information Field contains the ISUP message, identified by a Service Indicator of 5 in the MTP3 SIO field. Each ISUP message follows a standard format that includes the following information:

- **CIC**—The Circuit Identification Code for the circuit to which the message is related.

- **Message Type**—The ISUP Message Type for the message (for example, an IAM, ACM, and so on).

- **Mandatory Fixed Part**—Required message parameters that are of fixed length.

- **Mandatory Variable Part**—Required message parameters that are of variable length. Each variable parameter has the following form:

  - Length of Parameter

  - Parameter Contents

Because the parameter is not a fixed length, a field is included to specify the actual length.

- **Optional Part**—Optional fields that can be included in the message, but are not mandatory. Each optional parameter has the following form:

  - Parameter Name

  - Length of Parameter

  - Parameter Contents

Figure 8-10 shows the ISUP message structure, as described here. This message structure provides a great deal of flexibility for constructing new messages. Each message type defines the mandatory parameters that are necessary for constructing a message. The mandatory fixed variables do not contain length information because the ISUP standards specify them to be a fixed length. Because the mandatory variable parameters are of variable lengths, pointers immediately follow the mandatory fixed part to point to the beginning of each variable parameter. The pointer value is simply the number of octets from the pointer field to the variable parameter length field.

In addition to the mandatory fields, each message can include optional fields. The last of the pointer fields is a pointer to the optional part. Optional fields allow information to be included or omitted as needed on a per-message basis. The optional fields differ based on variables such as the call type or the supplementary services involved. For example, the Calling Party Number (CgPN) field is an optional parameter of the IAM, but is usually included to provide such services as Caller ID and Call Screening.

Figure 8-10 *ISUP Message Format*

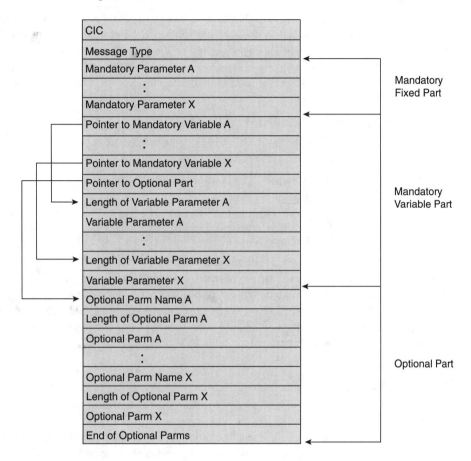

A single message can include many optional parameters. The optional part pointer field only points to the first parameter. Because the message might or might not include the parameters, and because the parameters can appear in any order, the first octet includes the name of each parameter in order to identify it. The parameter length follows the name to indicate how many octets the parameter contents include. When the parameter name is coded as zero, it signals the end of the optional parameters. During parsing of an incoming ISUP message, optional parameters are processed until the *end of optional parameters* marker is reached. If the message does not have any optional parameters, the pointer to the optional part is coded to zero.

Basic Call Message Formats

Here, we examine the six messages shown in the basic call setup because they comprise the core message set for basic call setup and release, and are therefore used frequently. There are slight variations in the messages used based on the individual network. For example, Europe uses the SAM frequently and the COT message more rarely. In North America, SAM is not used at all, but COT is used more often. This section considers the following messages:

- Initial Address Message (IAM)
- Subsequent Address Message (SAM–ITU Networks only)
- Continuity Message (COT)
- Address Complete Message (ACM)
- Answer Message (ANM)
- Release Message (REL)
- Release Complete Message (RLC)

The following sections show only the mandatory fields for each message. Keep in mind that many optional parameters can also be included. In each of the figures, the fixed mandatory fields with sub-fields have been expanded to show what they are. For the sake of brevity in the figures, the variable subfields have not been expanded. All of the ISUP Message formats and parameters are documented in ITU-T Q.763. ANSI T1.113 documents the North American version of the messages.

Initial Address Message (IAM)

The IAM contains the information needed to set up a call. For a basic call, it is the first message sent and is typically the largest message in terms of size. Figure 8-11 shows the mandatory fields that the message includes. In addition to the mandatory fields, the ITU-T Q.764 lists more than 50 optional parameters that can be included in the IAM. The mandatory parameters for ITU and ANSI are the same, with the exception of the Transmission Medium Requirements parameter. In ANSI networks, the User Service Info field is used instead.

As shown in Figure 8-11, the *Nature of Connection Indicators (NOC)* pass information about the bearer circuit connection to the receiving node. The indicators consist of the following subfields:

- **Satellite Indicator**—Specifies whether one or more satellites have been used for the circuit connection that is being set up. This information is useful when setting up calls to prevent an excessive number of satellite hops, which can reduce the quality of calls.
- **Continuity Indicator**—Designates whether to perform a continuity check on the circuit being set up.
- **Echo Control Device Indicator**—Specifies whether echo suppression is used on the circuit. Echo suppression is used to increase the quality of voice calls by reducing echo, but it can damage data and fax calls because it subtracts a portion of the voice-band signal.

Figure 8-11 *IAM Message Format*

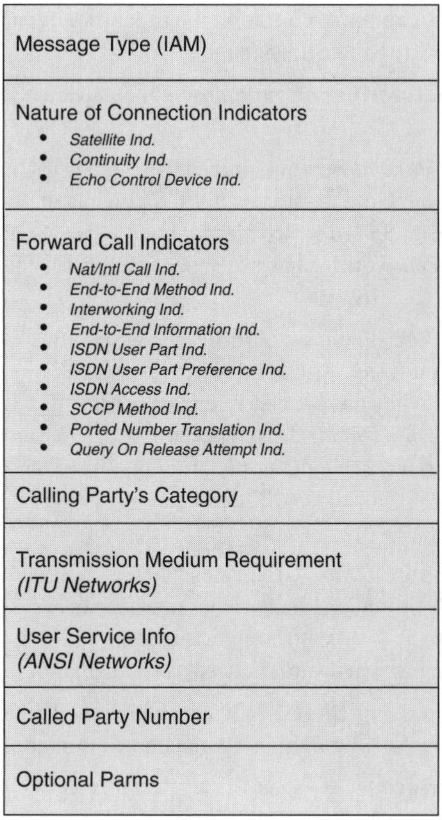

```
┌────────────────────────────────────────┐
│ Message Type (IAM)                       │
├────────────────────────────────────────┤
│ Nature of Connection Indicators          │
│   • Satellite Ind.                       │
│   • Continuity Ind.                      │
│   • Echo Control Device Ind.             │
├────────────────────────────────────────┤
│ Forward Call Indicators                  │
│   • Nat/Intl Call Ind.                   │
│   • End-to-End Method Ind.               │
│   • Interworking Ind.                    │
│   • End-to-End Information Ind.           │
│   • ISDN User Part Ind.                  │
│   • ISDN User Part Preference Ind.        │
│   • ISDN Access Ind.                     │
│   • SCCP Method Ind.                     │
│   • Ported Number Translation Ind.        │
│   • Query On Release Attempt Ind.         │
├────────────────────────────────────────┤
│ Calling Party's Category                 │
├────────────────────────────────────────┤
│ Transmission Medium Requirement          │
│ (ITU Networks)                           │
├────────────────────────────────────────┤
│ User Service Info                        │
│ (ANSI Networks)                          │
├────────────────────────────────────────┤
│ Called Party Number                      │
├────────────────────────────────────────┤
│ Optional Parms                           │
└────────────────────────────────────────┘
```

The *Forward Call Indicators (FCI)* contain information that specifies both the preferences about call setup in the forward direction and the conditions encountered so far in setting up the call. They include the following subfields:

- **National/International Call Indicator**—Indicates whether the call is coming in as National or International. International calls are specified by ITU international procedures, and national calls are processed according to national ISUP variant standards.

- **End-to-End Method Indicator**—Indicates the method used for signaling end-to-end information. SCCP and pass-along are the two end-to-end methods that are used. The pass-along method traverses each node in the connection to deliver information to the correct node. The SCCP method uses connectionless signaling to send information directly to its destination.

- **Interworking Indicator**—Indicates whether the connection has encountered interworking with non-SS7 facilities (for example, MF trunks). Interworking with non-SS7 facilities can limit or prohibit the capability of supplementary services or certain call types that require SS7 signaling.

- **End-to-End Information Indicator**—Indicates whether any end-to-end information is available.

- **ISDN User Part Indicator**—Indicates whether ISUP has been used for every leg of the connection. Note that this is not the same as the Interworking Indicator. It is possible to have an SS7-signaled circuit, but not use ISUP (for example, TUP signaling); however, if interworking has been encountered, this indicator is set to *ISDN User Part not used all the way.*

- **ISDN User Part Preference Indicator**—Specifies whether an ISUP facility is required or preferred when choosing an outgoing circuit. Some supplementary services or call types are not possible over non-ISUP facilities. If ISUP is required but not available, the call is released because the requested facility's preference cannot be met. If the preference indicator is set to *preferred*, an ISUP facility is chosen, if available; however, the call is still set up as long as a facility is available, even if it is not ISUP.

- **ISDN Access Indicator**—Indicates whether the originating access is ISDN or non-ISDN. ISDN provides a much richer interface to services that is not available on plain analog lines. This indicator suggests that the ISDN interface is available so that end-to-end signaling, backward requests for information, and so on can be carried out.

- **SCCP Method Indicator**—Indicates which method, if any, is used for SCCP end-to-end signaling. SCCP might use connection-oriented, connectionless, or both.

The *Calling Party's Category* specifies a general category into which the calling party is classified—such as an ordinary calling subscriber, operator, payphone, or test call.

The *Transmission Medium Requirement* (*TMR*) is not applicable to ANSI networks and is only supported in ITU-T networks. It contains the requirements for the bearer circuit capabilities (speech, 3.1-kHz audio, 64-Kb unrestricted, and so forth) that are needed for the call being set up. For example, a video conference might require a 384-Kbs unrestricted circuit to guarantee an acceptable level of video quality.

User Service Information (*USI*) is used in ANSI networks instead of the ITU-T specified TMR. It contains the requirements for the bearer circuit capabilities (speech, 3.1-kHz audio, and 64-Kbs unrestricted) along with additional information such as layer 1 codec, circuit, or packet transfer mode and other bearer-related specifics.

The *Called Party Number (CdPN)* is the destination number that the calling party dials. The CdPN contains the following fields:

- **Odd/Even Indicator**—Indicates an odd or even number of digits in the CdPN.

- **Nature of Address Indicator**—Indicates the type of number (for example, National Significant Number or International). The receiving switch uses this indicator during translations to apply the number's proper dial plan.

The *Internal Network Number Indicator* (*INN*), which is not used for ANSI, specifies whether routing to an internal network number is permitted. This field is used to block routing to specific numbers that should not be directly accessible from outside of the network. For example, if a premium rate number is translated to an internal number, the subscriber is blocked from dialing the internal number to ensure that the appropriate premium rate charges are collected.

- **Numbering Plan Indicator**—Specifies the type of number plan used. The E.164 ISDN numbering plan is commonly used for voice calls.

- **Address Signals**—The actual digits that comprise the called number. This includes digits 0–9 and the overdecadic digits (A–F), however, the overdecadic digits are not supported in all networks. Each digit is coded as a four-bit field.

Subsequent Address Message (SAM–ITU Networks Only)

Shown in Figure 8-12, the SAM is used to send subsequent address signals (digits) when using overlap signaling for call setup. It has one mandatory variable parameter: the *subsequent number*. One or more SAMs can be sent after an IAM to carry subsequent digits for call setup that are part of a destination's complete telephony number.

Figure 8-12 *SAM Message Format*

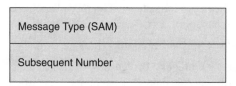

Continuity Message (COT)

As shown in Figure 8-13, the COT message contains the results of a continuity test. It has only one field: the *Continuity Indicators*. This field uses a single bit to indicate whether a continuity test passed or failed. The test's originator sends the message to the far end of the circuit that is being tested.

Figure 8-13 *COT Message Format*

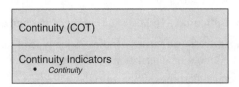

Address Complete Message (ACM)

As shown in Figure 8-14, a destination node sends the ACM to indicate that a complete CdPN has been received. When enbloc signaling is used to set up the call, the ACM is sent after receiving the IAM; when overlap signaling is used, it is sent after the last SAM is received. In addition to indicating the successful reception of the CdPN, the ACM sends Backward Call Indicators (BCI) to signal information about the call setup. It is not mandatory for an ACM to be sent when setting up a call. It is permissible to send an ANM after receiving an IAM; this is sometimes referred to as "fast answer."

Many of the fields contained in the Backward Call Indicators are the same as those in the Forward Call Indicators (FCI), which are contained in the IAM. While the FCI signals the call indicators in the forward direction to provide information on the call setup to the terminating access (and intermediate nodes), the BCI signals similar information in the backward direction to the originator.

Here we discuss only the fields that are unique to the BCI. The remaining fields are the same as those we discussed for the FCI, except that they are representative of the call from the terminating end. For example, the ISDN Access Indicator specifies whether the "terminator" is ISDN.

- **Charge Indicator** — Indicates whether a call should be charged as determined by the charging exchange.
- **Called Party's Status Indicator** — Indicates whether the subscriber is free.
- **Called Party's Category Indicator** — Indicates the general category of the called party, an ordinary subscriber, or payphone.
- **Holding Indicator** — Indicates whether holding is required. This indicator can be used for special services, such as Operator Signaling Services or Malicious Call Tracing, to indicate that the incoming connection should be held. No specification for ANSI networks exists.

Figure 8-14 *ACM Message Format*

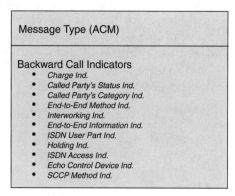

Message Type (ACM)

Backward Call Indicators
- *Charge Ind.*
- *Called Party's Status Ind.*
- *Called Party's Category Ind.*
- *End-to-End Method Ind.*
- *Interworking Ind.*
- *End-to-End Information Ind.*
- *ISDN User Part Ind.*
- *Holding Ind.*
- *ISDN Access Ind.*
- *Echo Control Device Ind.*
- *SCCP Method Ind.*

Answer Message (ANM)

The ANM is sent to the previous exchange when the called party answers (off-hook). Although it might contain many optional parameters, the ANM does not contain any mandatory fields other than the message type.

Release Message (REL)

As shown in Figure 8-15, the REL message indicates that the circuit is being released. When a RLC has been received in response, the circuit can be returned to the idle state for reuse. The REL message can be sent in either direction. It contains a single mandatory *Cause Indicators* field to indicate why the circuit is being released.

Figure 8-15 *REL Message Format*

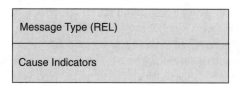

Message Type (REL)

Cause Indicators

Cause Indicators specify the cause information associated with the circuit being released. The Cause Indicators contain the general location in the network (such as local, remote, or transit) in which the circuit was released. The Coding Standard indicates which standard is used for decoding the Cause Value (such as ANSI, ITU). ANSI and ITU define some cause values differently, and ANSI also has additional values the ITU does not include.

The *Cause Value* contains an integer that represents the reason the circuit is being released. This value can be further decomposed into a class and a value. The most significant three bits of the Cause Value field represent the class. Each class is a general category of causes; for example, binary values of 000 and 001 are *normal event* class, and a value of 010 is *resource unavailable*. So, a cause value of 1 (unallocated number) is in the *normal event* class and a cause value of 34 (no circuit available) is in the *resource unavailable* class. Appendix M, "Cause Values," contains a complete list of the ITU and ANSI cause values.

The *Diagnostics* field is only applicable to certain cause values. It provides further information pertaining to the circuit release (for example, Transit Network Identity, Called Party Number [CdPN]) for those cause values.

Release Complete Message (RLC)

The RLC message is sent to acknowledge a REL message. Upon receipt of an RLC, a circuit can return to the idle state.

Detailed Call Walk-Through

Earlier in this chapter, we presented an ISUP message flow in order to illustrate the exchange of messages to establish and release an ISUP call. Now that we have discussed more of the ISUP details, we will build on that illustration. This section provides more detail about the call processing that was driven by the ISUP message events used in the earlier example. Although this chapter's primary focus is the ISUP protocol, it is important to understand how ISUP is applied in its normal domain of trunk call processing.

Call Setup

Refer back to Figure 8-3, where a call originates from a line at SSP A and terminates to a line at SSP B over an interexchange ISUP trunk. When call processing has completed translations of the called number at SSP A, the translations' results indicates that the call requires routing to an interexchange trunk group. The provisioned signaling type for the selected trunk group determines whether ISUP signaling or some other signaling, such as Multifrequency (MF), is used. When the signaling type is determined to be ISUP, the trunk circuit to be used for the outgoing call is reserved for use.

The SSP populates the IAM with information about the call setup, such as the CIC, CdPN, Call Type, CgPN, and PCM Encoding scheme. The IAM information is placed in the User Data field of the MTP3 SIF. The MTP3 information is populated based on the SS7 network information that is associated with the selected trunk group. As previously noted, each switching exchange contains a provisioned association (usually static) between routesets and trunkgroups. The IAM is then transmitted onto a signaling link toward the destination identified in the message by the DPC. If quasi-associated signaling is used, the message's next-hop node is an STP that will route the message to the intended SSP. If associated signaling is used, the IAM is transmitted directly to the SSP that is associated with the trunk being set up. SSP A starts timer T7, which is known as the *network protection timer*, or the *awaiting ACM timer*, to ensure that an ACM is received in response to the IAM.

When SSP B receives the MTP3 message, it recognizes it as an ISUP message by the SIO's Service Indicator bit. Then the message is passed to ISUP for processing, during which it extracts the message information. An IAM indicates a request to set up a call so SSP B enters the call processing phase for a trunk origination. The CdPN and Calling Party Category fields provide key pieces of information from the IAM for SSP B to complete number translations for this simple call.

NOTE   The CdPN is commonly used to enter number translations processing; however, depending on call specifics, other fields can be used for translation. For example, calls involving ported numbers can use the Generic Address Parameter during number translation to determine the outgoing call destination.

In this example, the number translates to a subtending line of SSP B, which checks the line to determine whether it is available. An ACM is built and sent to SSP A, notifying that the call can be completed and is proceeding. At this point, the speech path in the backward direction (from SSP B to SSP A) should be cut through to allow the ring-back tone to be sent over the bearer channel from the terminating exchange to the originating exchange. This indicates that the terminator is being alerted.

NOTE   Note that the terminating office does not always send the ring-back tone. For example, ISDN can use the ACM message to notify the originating phone terminal to provide the ring-back tone.

Ringing is now applied to the terminating set, while ring back occurs at the originating set. Answer timing is usually applied at the originating switch to limit the amount of time an originator waits for answer.

When the terminating subscriber goes off-hook, an ANM is sent back to the originator to indicate that an answer has occurred. By this point, the voice path should be cut through in the forward direction to allow the conversation to take place. Note that the voice path can be cut through before receiving the ANM, but it must be cut through no later than the ANM. The call is now in the active, or talking, state. This is often a point of interest for billing procedures that require capturing the time at which a call conversation begins. For an ordinary call, no further signaling messages are exchanged for the duration of the conversation. When either of the parties goes on-hook, it initiates signaling for the release of the call. The following section discusses Call release.

Call Release

When either the originating or terminating subscriber goes on-hook, it signals an attempt to disconnect the call. In Figure 8-3, the originator at SSP A goes on-hook. SSP A recognizes the signal to disconnect the call and sends a Release message (REL) to SSP B. SSP B responds by sending a Release Complete message (RLC) as an acknowledgement. The trunk member is freed and placed back into its idle queue to be used for another call.

Terminal Portability

The ITU defines terminal portability in Q.733.4 for allowing the called or calling party to hang up a phone and resume a conversation at another phone that is connected to the same line. When the two parties are connected over an inter-exchange ISUP trunk, suspend and resume messages are used to maintain the trunk connection until the on-hook party has gone off-hook. Terminal portability requirements for the called party exist in many countries; however, terminal portability for the calling party is not supported as often. ANSI networks do not support terminal portability for the calling party.

Circuit Suspend and Resume

In Figure 8-3, the originating subscriber goes on-hook first. The originator is normally considered in control of the call, so the circuit is released when the originator goes on-hook. If the terminator goes on-hook while the originator remains off-hook, there are two methods of handling the disconnection.

The first method is for the terminating exchange to release the call by sending a REL message to the originating exchange. This is no different than the scenario presented for a release initiated at the originating exchange; the originating switch responds with an RLC and the circuit is idled at each SSP.

The other method is for the terminating exchange to send a Suspend (SUS) message in the backward direction when it receives a disconnect indication from the terminating line. The SUS message provides notification that the terminating party has disconnected but that the circuit connection is still being maintained. Suspending the call allows the person who receives the call an opportunity to pick up on another phone extension.

When the SUS is received, the originating exchange starts a suspend timer (Timer T6, or Timer T38 in the case of an international exchange). If the terminating party reconnects (off-hook) before the suspend timer expires, a Resume (RES) message is sent in the backward direction, allowing the conversation to continue.

Figure 8-16 shows an example of a Suspend (SUS) and Resume (RES) being sent from the terminating exchange. If the suspend timer expires, a REL is sent in the forward direction. In the event that the originator goes on-hook during the time the circuit is suspended, the originating exchange sends a REL forward and normal call clearing takes place. The terminating exchange responds with a RLC.

Figure 8-16 *ISUP Suspend/Resume*

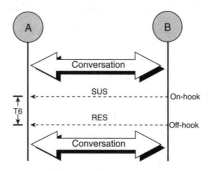

Support for SUS/RES varies, based on factors such as the type of service and the local network policies. For example, in the United States, SUS/RES is only supported for non-ISDN service.

ISUP and Local Number Portability

Local Number Portability (LNP) is the concept of having phone numbers that remain the same for the subscriber, regardless of whether the subscriber changes service providers or geographic location. Historically, phone numbers have been associated with a particular geographic region or a particular service provider. The actual use of LNP in the network exists today, but only to a small degree. It is being expanded in phases and will take some time before it is ubiquitous across all networks and locations. This section examines the different mechanisms used to provide portability services and how these mechanisms relate to setting up calls with ISUP.

Chapter 11, "Intelligent Networks (IN)" provides an overview of the various phases identified under the umbrella of Number Portability (NP), such as service provider portability and location portability. Some of the mechanisms used for NP employ Intelligent Network (IN) databases, so we cover NP in part both in the Chapter 11 and in this chapter.

When NP is implemented, numbers are transitioned from physical addresses that identify an exchange location to virtual addresses that identify a subscriber. A means of mapping must be used to derive a physical address in the network from the called number because the number no longer identifies a physical destination. The network in which the physical number existed before portability was introduced is called a *donor* network. Each time a number is ported and becomes a virtual address, the network has "donated" a number that previously belonged to that network. We use the term "donor" or "donor network" several times during the discussion of NP. The network in which the physical number now resides is called the *recipient* network.

Currently, four mechanisms are defined for implementing NP:

- All Call Query (ACQ)
- Query on Release (QOR)
- Dropback or Release to Pivot (RTP)
- Onward Routing (OR)

Each method has its merits in terms of resource efficiencies, maintainability, and competitive fairness among network operators, but those topics are outside of the scope of the book. The details of how each mechanism is implemented also vary from country to country. The following section provides a general understanding of NP and how it affects the ISUP call flow and messages.

All Call Query (ACQ)

ACQ sends an IN query to a centrally administered database to determine the call's physical address or routing address. Chapter 11 discusses the details of the IN query. The way the routing number returned by the query is used varies based on national standards. The following example illustrates how the routing number is used in North America.

The number returned from the database is a Location Routing Number (LRN) that identifies the exchange serving the called number. Each exchange in the network is assigned an LRN. The IAM sent after the database query is performed contains the LRN in the CdPN field. The call is routed on the CdPN using switching translations to reach the destination exchange. The IAM also includes a Generic Address Parameter (GAP) with the original dialed number (the virtual address). This allows the destination exchange to set up the call to the intended subscriber because the LRN can only identify the exchange. The Forward Call Indicators of the IAM include a Ported Number Translation Indicator (PNTI), which indicates that a query for the ported number has been performed.

Query On Release (QOR)

QOR routes the call from the originator to the donor network's ported number in the same manner used prior to NP. The donor network releases the call back with a cause value of *Number Portability QOR number not found* (ITU causes value 14, ANSI causes value 27 in the REL message). The originating network then performs a query to an NP database to determine what routing number to use in the IAM in order to reach the recipient network.

Dropback (Also Known as Release to Pivot)

Dropback, or *Release to Pivot* (*RTP*), routes the call to the ported number in the donor network, just like QOR. However, instead of having the originating network query for the number, the donor exchange provides the routing number for the ported number when it releases back to the originator.

Onward Routing (OR)

Onward Routing (*OR*) also routes the call to the donor network's ported number. It differs from QOR and RTP in that it does not release the call back to the originating network. Rather, it references an internal database to determine the new routing number that is associated with the ported number and uses the new number to route the call.

Using the QOR and RTP mechanisms, an IAM is sent and an REL received back from the donor network, therefore, requiring a subsequent call attempt. The ACQ and OR do not release back or require subsequent call attempts. The OR mechanism creates additional call legs because the call is being connected through the donor network rather than being directly set up to the recipient network.

ISUP-ISUP Tandem Calls

Previous scenarios have focused on line-ISUP and ISUP-line calls. ISUP processing at a tandem switch occurs in the same sequence as the line to ISUP calls we discussed previously. However, in the case of ISUP-ISUP calls, the trigger for call processing events on the originating and terminating side are incoming ISUP messages.

This section discusses the following three areas that are related to ISUP processing at a tandem node:

- ISUP Message Processing
- Continuity Testing
- Transporting Parameters

ISUP Message Processing at a Tandem

In Figure 8-17, the call origination at SSP B is based on an incoming ISUP origination (IAM) from another exchange. The fields that are necessary for number translation, such as CdPN, are extracted from the IAM and used to process the call at the tandem node to determine the outgoing destination. The translation and routing process results in the selection of an outgoing ISUP trunk. An IAM is sent in the forward direction to SSP C, updating fields in the message as necessary. For example, a new CdPN might be inserted as a result of translations. The NOC field is updated based on information such as whether a satellite is being used for the voice circuit or whether a continuity check is being performed.

Figure 8-17 *ISUP-ISUP Tandem Calls*

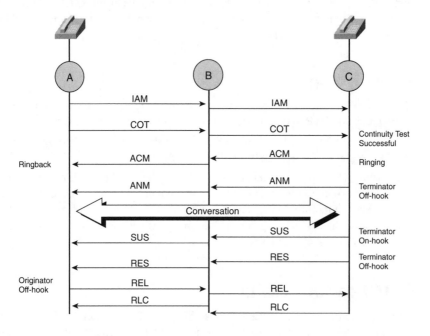

When the ACM and ANM are received at SSP B, they are propagated to SSP A, updating fields such as the BCI as necessary. Each leg of the call cuts through the speech path in the same manner discussed in the "Detailed Call Walk-Through" section of this chapter.

When SSP A sends an REL message, SSP B responds with an RLC. It does not need to wait for the RLC to be sent from SSP C. Next, SSP B sends an REL to SSP C and waits for RLC to complete the release of that leg of the call. Keep in mind that even though some messages in a multi-hop ISUP call are propagated, the entire call actually consists of independent circuit segments. The release procedure is a reminder of this fact because the RLC can be sent immediately after receiving a REL.

Continuity Testing

When a call is set up across multiple exchanges, continuity testing is performed independently on each leg of the call. If a call traverses three trunks across four different exchanges and continuity is done on a statistical basis, it will likely only be performed on some of the trunks involved in the call. While the actual continuity test is performed independently on each call leg, the end-to-end call setup is dependent on each leg passing the test. If a continuity test is successfully performed on the second leg of the call (SSP B to SSP C), the results are not reported until the COT results have been received from the previous leg of the call (SSP A to SSP B). If a previous leg of the call connection cannot be set up successfully, there is no need to continue. For example, if SSP A reports a COT failure, it would attempt to establish a new connection in the forward direction by selecting another circuit to set up the call. There is no need to continue the previous connection from SSP B to SSP C because the new call attempt from SSP A will come in as a new origination to SSP B.

Transporting Parameters

A tandem node can receive ISUP parameters that are only of interest to the destination exchange. This is particularly true of many optional parameters, which are passed transparently in the outgoing messages across tandem nodes. However, the tandem might update some fields during call processing, based on new information encountered while processing. For example, a tandem node that selects an outgoing ISUP facility over a satellite connection would update the NOC *Satellite Indicator* field in the outgoing IAM. This distinction is made because the tandem node might be required to have knowledge of how to process some parameters, but not others. When parameters are passed across a tandem node without processing the information, it is sometimes referred to as "ISUP transparency." Since the parameters do not need to be interpreted by the tandem, they are considered transparent and are simply relayed between the two trunks.

Interworking with ISDN

ISDN uses a common channel (the D channel) for access signaling; this compliments the common channel network signaling ISUP uses and provides a complete digital signaling path between end users when ISDN is used for network access and ISUP is used throughout the core network. The ISUP/ISDN interworking specifications for ITU-T, ETSI, and Telcordia are found in the following standards:

- ITU-T Q.699—Interworking of Signaling Systems—Interworking Between Digital Subscriber Signaling System No. 1 and Signaling System No. 7

- ETSI EN 300-899-1 Integrated Services Digital Network (ISDN); Signaling System No. 7; Interworking Between ISDN User Part (ISUP) Version 2 and Digital Subscriber Signaling System No. one (DSS1); Part 1: Protocol Specification

- Telcordia GR-444 Switching System Generic Requirements Supporting ISDN Access Using the ISDN User Part

A correlation exists between the ISDN messages from the user premises and the ISUP messages on the network side of the call. Figure 8-18 illustrates this correlation using an ISDN-to-ISDN call over an ISUP facility. Table 8-1 lists the message mapping that occurs between the two protocols for the basic call setup shown in the diagram.

Figure 8-18 *ISUP-ISDN Interworking*

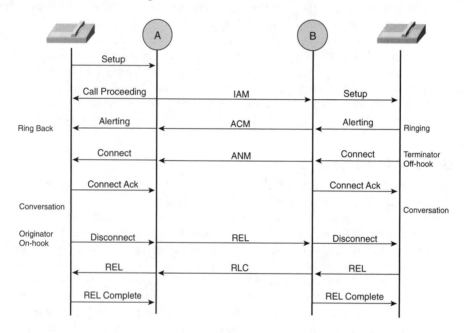

Table 8-1   *Message Mapping Between ISDN and ISUP*

ISDN	ISUP
Setup	IAM
Alerting	ACM (or CPG)
Connect	ANM (or CON)
Disconnect	REL
Release	RLC

Many of the fields within these messages also have direct mappings. For example, the bearer capability field in the ISDN Setup message maps to the ANSI User Service Info or the IAM's ITU Transmission Medium Requirements field. There are fields that have no direct mapping, such as the NOC Indicators and FCIs in the IAM. Many of the fields that do not have direct mapping contain network-specific information that would not be useful for the ISDN signaling endpoint.

End-to-End Signaling

The ability to perform end-to-end signaling is accomplished using ISDN access signaling and ISUP network signaling. End-to-end signaling is the passing of information across the network that is only pertinent to the two communicating endpoints. Generally, this means that the two phone users are connected across the network. The network itself can be viewed as a communications pipe for the user information.

There are two different methods for end-to-end signaling over ISUP: the *Pass Along Method (PAM)* and the *SCCP Method.* As shown in Figure 8-19, PAM exchanges end-to-end signaling by passing along information from one node to the next, based on the physical connection segments. The SCCP method uses a call reference to pass end-to-end data between endpoints without having to pass through each individual hop. PAM is the method that is currently used throughout the network for end-to-end signaling.

Figure 8-19 *ISUP End-to-End Signaling*

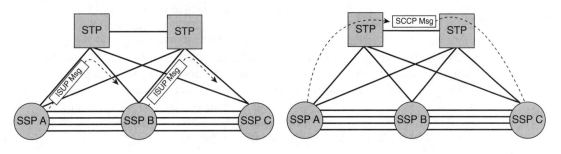

A.) PAM End-to-End Signaling   B.) SCCP End-to-End Signaling

ISDN Signaling Indicators in the IAM

The following set of fields in the IAM *FCI* comprises what is known as the *Protocol Control Indicator (PCI)*:

- End-to-end method indicator
- Interworking indicator
- IAM segmentation indicator
- ISDN User Part indicator

These fields provide information about the protocol communication across the ISUP connection. The Protocol Control Indicator fields are of particular importance to ISDN because they identify whether ISDN signaling can be exchanged across the network. If the Interworking Indicator is set to *interworking encountered*, it indicates that a non-SS7 connection (such as MF signaling) has been used in a circuit connection. It also indicates that SS7 signaling cannot be exchanged across this connection because it would prevent an ISDN terminal from being able to relay signaling across the network that depended on an SS7 connection all the way.

The ISDN User Part indicator field indicates whether ISUP has been used for every call leg up to the current exchange. If this field is set to *ISDN User Part not used all the way*, it might not be possible to pass ISDN information across the network.

The ISDN User Part preference indicator field indicates to the receiving node whether the call needs an outgoing ISUP connection.

The preference field might contain the following values:

* ISDN User Part preferred
* ISDN User Part required
* ISDN User Part not required

For calls originating from an ISDN set, the preference field is set to *ISDN User Part preferred* unless specified otherwise by different services. If it is available during outgoing trunk selection, an ISUP facility is chosen; an ISUP facility is "preferred," but not necessarily required. If an ISUP facility is not available, the call is still set up if a non-ISUP facility is available. If a call is being established that requires the ability to pass service information—such as end-to-end signaling—across the network, the preference field is set to *ISDN User Part required*. A call with a preference of "required" is not set up unless an ISUP facility is available. For example, setting up a multichannel ISDN video connection would not be possible without end-to-end ISUP signaling.

Although the PCI provides information about the connection across the network, it does not specify the actual protocol of the access signaling. The FCI includes the *ISDN access indicator* bit to indicate whether the originating terminal is an ISDN set.

Supplementary Services

Supplementary services are one of the ISUP advantages noted in this chapter's introduction. ISUP provides many messages and parameters that are explicitly created for the support of supplementary services across the network. The introduction of ISUP has helped to greatly standardize widely used services, allowing them to operate across networks and between vendors more easily. Service specifications still vary between different networks based on differences in locales and market needs. ISUP provides the flexibility to accommodate these differences using a rich message set and a large set of optional parameters.

The ITU-T defines a core set of widely used ISDN services in the Q.730–Q.739 series of specifications using ISUP network signaling. The actual specification of these services at the national level can vary. In addition, national networks and private networks offer many services outside of those that are specified by the ITU-T. In the United States, Telcordia has defined a large number of services in various Generic Requirements (GR) specifications for U.S. network operators.

The list of services implemented on modern telephony switches has grown quite long. However, the purpose of this section is not to explore the services themselves, but to provide examples of how ISUP is used to support them. Two examples of common services have been chosen to discuss how ISUP provides support for them: Calling Line Identification and Call Forwarding Unconditional.

Calling Line Identification (CLI) Example

ITU Q.731 specifies Calling Line Identification (CLI). Calling party information can be used at the terminating side of a call in many different ways. Following are a few examples:

- Calling Number Delivery (CND)
- Calling Name Delivery (CNAMD)
- Incoming Call Screening
- Customer Account Information Retrieval (Screen Pops)

Being able to identify the calling party allows the called party to make decisions before answering a call. For example, an end user can use call screening to allow them to choose which calls they wish to accept. A business might use the incoming number to speed the retrieval of customer account information to call centers. If the called party subscribes to Calling Name Delivery, the CgPN is used at the terminating exchange to retrieve the name associated with the number.

CLI is specifically defined by the ITU-T as:

- Calling Line Identification Presentation (CLIP)
- Calling Line Identification Restriction (CLIR)

The ISUP CdPN parameter contains an *Address Presentation Restricted indicator* that specifies whether the calling party identification can be presented to the called party. The Address Presentation Restricted indicator has the following possible values:

- Presentation allowed
- Presentation restricted
- Address not available
- Reserved for restriction by the network

If the terminating party subscribes to the CLI service, the terminating exchange uses this indicator's value to determine whether the number can be delivered. The number is delivered only if the value is set to Presentation allowed. If the connection encounters non-SS7 interworking, the address information might not be available for presentation. In addition, transit network operators might not transport the information in some cases, depending on regulatory policies. While the actual display to the end-user varies depending on location, it is quite common to see restricted addresses displayed as "private" and unavailable addresses displayed as "unknown" or "out of area."

In some networks, if the CLI is not present in the IAM, it might be requested from the calling party using an Information Request (INR) message. The originating exchange delivers the requested CLI using an Information (INF) message.

Call Forwarding Example

Call Forwarding is part of a larger suite of services known as Call Diversion services. There are many variations of Call Forwarding. The ITU-T in the Q.732 specification defines the standard set of Call Forwarding variations as follows:

- Call Forward Unconditional (CFU)
- Call Forward No Reply (CFNR)
- Call Forward Busy (CFB)

Other variations of Call Forwarding exist within localized markets. For example, Call Forwarding Selective is another variation that allows forwarding for calls that originate from selective calling numbers. For this example, we have chosen Call Forward Unconditional to illustrate the use of ISUP signaling.

In Figure 8-20, the ITU-T message flow is shown for CFU at SSP B. The ANSI message flow differs slightly from that shown for ITU. A subscriber at SSP B has forwarded their calls to a number at SSP C. When SSP B attempts to terminate the call and encounters the Call Forward service, a new IAM is sent to SSP C. Keep in mind that a call might be forwarded multiple times before reaching its destination. The additional parameters included in the IAM for Call Forwarding convey information about the first and last instances of forwarding. In our example, the IAM to SSP C contains the following parameters, specific to the call redirection:

- Redirection Information (RI)
- Redirecting Number (RN)
- Original Called Number (OCN)

The inclusion of the RI parameter varies among different networks, so it might or might not be present. The RI parameter contains the following information fields:

- **Redirecting Indicator**—*Not specified for ANSI networks*. This field indicates how the call was forwarded and the presentation restriction indicators regarding the RI and RN.

- **Original Redirecting Reason**—Indicates why the first forwarding station forwarded the call (for example, *no reply* or *unconditional*). This field is set to *unconditional* in the example illustrated in Figure 8-20.

- **Redirection Counter**—Indicates the number of times a call has been forwarded. This counter is used to eliminate forwarding loops where a call ties up network resources because it is forwarded an excessive number of times. The ITU and ANSI standard for maximum redirections is five. In ANSI networks, the Hop Counter parameter provides this counter when RI is not included for forwarded calls. This field is set to 1 in the example illustrated in Figure 8-20.

- **Redirecting Reason**—Indicates the reason the call is being forwarded. In our example using CFU, the reason indicator is set to *unconditional*.

The OCN is the number dialed by the originator at A. The RN is the number of the station that forwarded the call. The RN is usually the same as the OCN, unless the call has been forwarded multiple times. If multiple forwardings have occurred, the RN is the number of the last station that forwarded the call. The CdPN will be set to the "forwarded to" number. Translation and routing using the new CdPN from the forwarding service at SSP B determine that the call should be directed to SSP C.

Figure 8-20 *ISUP Call Forwarding Signaling*

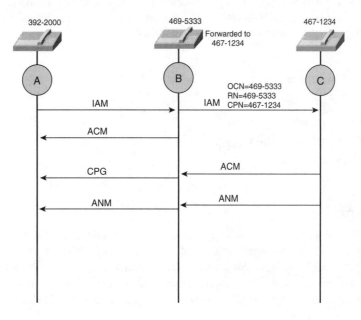

At SSP B, an ACM is returned to the originator and a new call is attempted to the forwarding destination. *Note that for ANSI networks, an ACM is not returned until the ACM is received from the new destination exchange, therefore, eliminating the CPG message.*

Additional Call Processing Messages

In addition to messages presented in the chapter, many other messages are used in various contexts for call processing. Some of the additional messages are used to support supplementary services, while others indicate specific network actions. Appendix B, "ISUP Messages (ANSI/UK/ETSI/ITU-T)," includes a complete list of all ISUP messages, their binary encoding, and a brief description.

Maintenance Messages and Procedures

ISUP provides an entire category of messages that are commonly categorized as "maintenance" messages. Until now, this chapter has focused on the call processing aspect of ISUP. This section discusses those messages that are used for diagnostics, maintenance, and the manipulation of ISUP facilities outside of the normal call processing realm.

The exchange can autonomously generate some maintenance messages, such as blocking (BLO) and Continuity Check Request (CCR), in response to an event or invoked manually by maintenance personnel. The collective set of messages described here helps to maintain trunk facilities and the integrity of user traffic. When necessary, trunks can be blocked from user traffic, tested, and reset to a state of sanity. The following sections illustrate how ISUP maintenance is used to accomplish these tasks:

- Circuit Ranges
- Circuit States
- Circuit Validation
- Continuity
- Blocking and Unblocking Circuits
- Circuit Reset

Circuit Ranges

ISUP maintenance messages apply to the CIC that is designated in the ISUP message. However, many messages can be applied to a range of CICs. These messages are referred to as "group" messages. Since ISUP trunk circuits are usually multiplexed together on digital spans, an action must often be applied to a larger group of circuits, such as the entire span. If a span is removed from service or brought into service, ISUP messages are sent to update the status of each of the span's circuits. If multiple spans are involved and individual messages were sent for each circuit, a flood of messages would occur over the SS7 network. Not only does this consume additional bandwidth on the SS7 links, but it also requires more processing by both the sending and receiving nodes. Using a single message with a CIC range eliminates the need to send a message for each CIC. Blocking messages, which we discuss later in this section, are a good example of where ranges are often used.

It is important to be aware that a message range can only be sent for contiguous CICs. If a span's CIC ranges were numbered using only even numbers such as 0, 2, 4, and 6, a message with a CIC range could not be used; individual messages would have to be sent for each CIC. It is good practice to number a span's CICs contiguously to maximize the efficiency of CIC ranges and effectively minimize message traffic.

Circuit States

An exchange maintains a circuit state for each bearer channel. Maintenance procedures and messages can affect that state. For example, maintenance messages can be sent to make circuits available for call processing, remove them from service, or reset them. A trunk circuit can have one of the following states:

- **Unequipped**—Circuit is not available for call processing.

- **Transient**—Circuit is waiting for an event to occur in order to complete a state transition. For example, an REL message has been sent, but an RLC has not been received.

- **Active**—Circuit is available for call processing. The circuit can have a substate of idle, incoming busy, or outgoing busy.

- **Locally blocked**—The local exchange has initiated the blocking of the circuit.

- **Remotely blocked**—The remote exchange has initiated the blocking of the circuit.

- **Locally and remotely blocked**—Both the local and remote exchanges have initiated blocking.

The following messages are used for querying the state of a group of circuits. These messages are usually sent in response to maintenance commands entered at a maintenance interface, or by automated trunk diagnostics that are performed as part of routine trunk testing.

- **Circuit Query Message (CQM)**—Sent to the far end exchange to query the state of a group of circuits. This allows the states to be compared to ensure that the two nodes agree on the status of the facilities. It provides a safeguard against a state mismatch in the event that a message indicating a change of state is sent, but not received.

- **Circuit Query Response Message (CQR)**—Sent in response to a CQM to report the state of the requested group of circuits.

Circuit Validation (ANSI Only)

Circuit validation determines whether translations data specific to the selection of an ISUP circuit has been set up correctly. The translations data at both ends of a circuit and between two exchanges is verified to ensure that the physical bearer channel can be derived. All switching systems require provisioning data to create the proper associations between trunkgroups, trunk members, CICs, and physical trunk circuits. Circuit Validation testing traverses these associations to ensure that they have been properly created. The Circuit Validation Test is particularly useful when turning up new trunk circuits because there is a greater potential for errors in newly provisioned facilities.

The Circuit Validation Test is typically invoked through a user interface at the switching system. Translations data at the local end is verified before sending a CVT message to the far end. The following messages are exchanged to perform the test:

- **Circuit Validation Test (CVT)**—Sent to the far end exchange to validate circuit-related translations data for an ISUP circuit. *This message is only used in ANSI networks.*

- **Circuit Validation Response (CVR)**—Sent in response to a CVT message to report the results of a Circuit Validation Test. The CVR message reports a success or failure for the Circuit Validation Test, along with characteristics of the circuit group being tested. For example, one reported characteristic is the method of glare handling being used for the circuit group. *This message is only used in ANSI networks.*

Continuity Testing

We have discussed continuity testing in the context of call processing where a circuit is tested before setting up a call. Continuity testing can also be performed manually by maintenance personnel, or by automated facilities testing.

The maintenance test procedure is slightly different than when it is performed as part of call processing. You will recall from the section on continuity testing that an indicator in the IAM is used for signifying that a test is required. When invoked as part of a maintenance procedure, the Continuity Check Request (CCR) message is used to indicate that a continuity test is required. The CCR is sent to the far end, and the continuity test proceeds as we discussed previously. The far end sends back a Loop Back Acknowledgement to acknowledge that a loop back or transceiver circuit has been connected for the test. The results are reported using a COT message by the node that originated the test. For additional information on continuity testing, refer to the "Continuity Test" section of this chapter. The following messages are used during the maintenance initiated continuity test:

- **Continuity Check Request (CCR)**—Sent to the far end to indicate that a continuity test is being performed. The far end connects a loopback or transceiver for the test.

- **Loop Around (LPA)**—Sent in response to a CCR to indicate that a loop back or transceiver has been connected to a circuit for continuity testing.

- **Continuity Test (COT)** — Sent to the far end to report the results of the continuity test. Indicates success if the received COT tones are within the specified guidelines of the country's standards. Otherwise, the message indicates a failure.

Blocking and Unblocking Circuits

ISUP provides blocking to prevent call traffic from being sent over a circuit. Maintenance messages can continue to be sent over the circuit. The two primary reasons for blocking are to remove a circuit from use when a problem has been encountered, or to allow for testing of the circuit. The local software blocks a trunk's local end. A blocking message notifies the trunk's far end about blocking. Unblocking is performed when circuits are ready to be returned to service for call traffic. The exchange unblocks locally and sends an unblocking message to the far end to provide notification of the state change. Both blocking and unblocking messages are acknowledged to ensure that both ends of the circuit remain in sync concerning the state of the trunk. The following messages are used in blocking and unblocking circuits:

- **Blocking (BLO)** — Sent to the far end to indicate the blocking of a circuit.
- **Blocking Acknowledgement (BLA)** — Sent as an acknowledgement in response to a BLO.
- **Circuit Group Blocking (CGB)** — Sent to the far end to indicate blocking for a range of circuits. The CICs must be contiguous for the group of circuits being blocked.
- **Circuit Group Blocking Acknowledgement (CGBA)** — Sent as an acknowledgement in response to a CGB.
- **Unblocking (UBL)** — Sent to the far end to indicate the unblocking of a blocked circuit.
- **Unblocking Acknowledgement (UBA)** — Sent as an acknowledgement in response to a UBL.
- **Circuit Group Unblocking (CGU)** — Sent to the far end to indicate unblocking for a range of blocked circuits.
- **Circuit Group Unblocking Acknowledgment (CGUA)** — Sent as an acknowledgement in response to a CGU.

Circuit Reset

A circuit is reset as an attempt to recover from an error condition or an unknown state. There are several reasons a circuit might need to be reset. Memory corruption or a mismatch of trunk states by the trunk's local and remote ends are examples of the need to reset a circuit. Calls are removed if they are active on the circuit that is being reset. A circuit reset reinitializes the local resources that are associated with the circuit and returns it to an idle state so it can be used again. Note that only group resets receive an acknowledgement from the far end; an individual reset does not. The following messages are associated with circuit resets:

- **Reset Circuit (RSC)**—Sent to the far end to indicate that the circuit is being reset to the idle state.

- **Group Reset Circuit (GRS)**—Sent to the far end to indicate that a contiguous group of CICs are being reset.

- **Group Reset Acknowledgement (GRA)**—Sent as an acknowledgement in response to GRS.

Summary

ISUP provides a rich network interface to call processing at an SSP. The increased bandwidth and protocol standardization allow a greater range of services that are able to interwork both within a network and across network boundaries. ISUP was designed to interface well with ISDN access signaling by providing event mapping and facilitating end-to-end user signaling. The protocol's use of optional message parameters achieves flexibility and extensibility.

ISUP uses a CIC identifier in each message to correlate the signaling with the correct circuit. The CIC is the key to associating signaling with bearer circuits.

ISUP also provides a set of maintenance messages for diagnostics and maintenance of ISUP facilities. These messages allow for blocking, testing, and resetting circuits and inquiring about circuit status.

CHAPTER 9

Signaling Connection Control Part (SCCP)

The Signaling Connection Control Part (SCCP) is defined in ITU-T Recommendations Q.711-Q.716 [58–63] and for North American markets in ANSI T1.112 [2]. SCCP sits on top of Message Transfer Part 3 (MTP3) in the SS7 protocol stack. The SCCP provides additional network layer functions to provide transfer of noncircuit-related (NCR) signaling information, application management procedures and alternative and more flexible methods of routing.

NOTE   Technically, SCCP can also transfer circuit-related signaling information; however, this is an exception.

As shown in Figure 9-1, the combination of the MTP, and the SCCP is termed the Network Service Part (NSP). The NSP follows the principles of the OSI reference model, as defined in Recommendation X.200 [99]; as such, it provides a subset of the Layer 3 services, which are defined in Recommendation X.213 [100].

SCCP was developed after the MTP, and together with the MTP3, it provides the capabilities corresponding to Layer 3 of the OSI reference model.

Because SCCP is OSI Layer 3 compliant, in theory it can be transmitted over any OSI-compliant network.

Because the MTP was originally designed to transfer call-control messages coming from the Telephony User Part (TUP), it was, therefore, designed to transfer only circuit-related signaling. In combination with the MTP, the SCCP can transfer messages that are not circuit-related. These messages are used to support services such as toll-free calling, Local Number Portability (LNP) and Completion of Calls to Busy Subscribers (CCBS) in Intelligent Networks and mobility, roaming, and SMS in cellular networks.

Figure 9-1 *SS7 Stack with the Network Service Part (NSP) Highlighted*

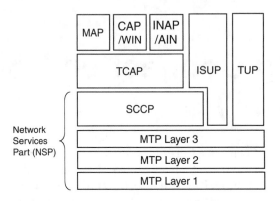

SCCP provides the following additional capabilities over the MTP:

- Enhances MTP to meet OSI Layer 3

- Powerful and flexible routing mechanisms

- Enhanced transfer capability, including segmentation/reassembly when message is too large to fit into one Message Signal Unit (MSU)

- Connectionless and connection-oriented data transfer services

- Management and addressing of subsystems (primarily database-driven applications)

SCCP is used extensively in cellular networks. Base Station Subsystem Mobile Application Part (BSSMAP) and Direct Transfer Application Part (DTAP) use it to transfer radio-related messages in Global System for Mobile communication (GSM). In conjunction with Transfer Capabilities Application Part (TCAP), SCCP is also used throughout the GSM Network Switching Subsystem (NSS) to transport Mobile Application Part (MAP) signaling between the core GSM components to enable subscriber mobility and text messaging (SMS), among other items. For example, when the Visitor Location Register (VLR) queries the Home Location Register (HLR) to obtain the subscriber's profile, SCCP is responsible for transferring both the query and the response back to the VLR. For more information about GSM, see Chapter 13, "GSM and ANSI-41 Mobile Application Part (MAP)."

Cellular intelligent network protocols, Wireless Intelligent Network (WIN), and Customizable Applications for Mobile Enhanced Logic (CAMEL) also use SCCP with TCAP (see Chapter 10, "Transaction Capabilities Application Part [TCAP]") to provide intelligent network functionality in a cellular environment. Figure 9-2 shows a typical cellular protocol stack, as found at a GSM-MSC.

Figure 9-2   *Typical SS7 Stack Used in GSM Networks*

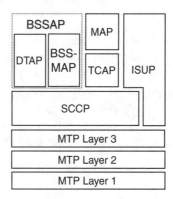

Fixed-line networks primarily use SCCP for intelligent network applications and advanced supplementary services. Fixed-line intelligent networks use Advanced Intelligent Network (AIN) within North America and Intelligent Network Application Protocol (INAP) outside of North America (see Chapter 11, "Intelligent Networks [IN]"). AIN/INAP both use SCCP's transport, application management, and enhanced routing functionalities. Two example supplementary services that require the use of SCCP include CCBS and Completion of Calls on No Reply (CCNR).

This chapter looks at the functions of SCCP in some detail, beginning with an outline of the SCCP architecture and then moving onto protocol classes, connectionless and connection-oriented procedures, SCCP management functions, and most importantly, SCCP routing, including the use of global titles.

SCCP Architecture

As shown in Figure 9-3, SCCP is composed of the following four functional areas:

- **SCCP connection-oriented control (SCOC)**—Responsible for setting up and releasing a virtual connection between two SCCP users. SCOC can offer features including sequencing, flow control, and segmentation and can override congestion procedures by assigning data priority. The section, "SCCP Connection-Oriented Control (SCOC)" describes SCOC in more detail

- **SCCP connectionless control (SCLC)**—Responsible for transferring data between SCCP users without creating a virtual connection. SCLC is described in the "SCCP Connectionless Control (SCLC)" Section. In addition to segmentation, it can perform limited sequencing.

- **SCCP routing control (SCRC)**—Provides additional routing beyond that offered by MTP3, through the use of global titles. The "Global Title Routing" section fully explains global titles.

- **SCCP management (SCMG)**—Responsible for tracking application status and informing SCMG at other SCCP nodes, as necessary. It is described later in this chapter in the section, "SCCP Management (SCMG)."

The term *SCCP Users* refers to the applications that use SCCP's services. These are primarily database-driven applications. Such applications use the services of TCAP described in Chapter 10 for peer application layer communication and the services of SCCP for managing the transport of messages between those applications.

Applications that use the services of SCCP are known as *subsystems*.

Figure 9-3 *The SCCP Architecture*

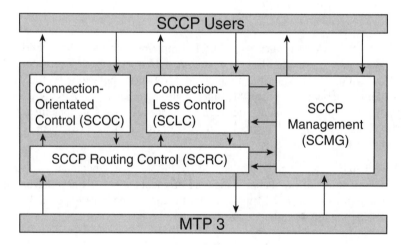

SCCP Message Transfer Services

The SCCP provides two categories of service for data transfer: connection-oriented services and connectionless services. Within each service category, two classes of service are defined as follows:

- **Class 0**—Basic connectionless class
- **Class 1**—In-sequence delivery connectionless class
- **Class 2**—Basic connection-oriented class
- **Class 3**—Flow control connection-oriented class

Connection-oriented Versus Connectionless Services

The analogy of sending letters and postcards best explains the difference between the connection-oriented and the connectionless services. The postal service carries out the physical transfer and is therefore analogous to MTP. Connection-oriented service is much like the exchange of formal letters. When you send a formal letter, you might assign a reference to it—"Our Reference X." When the receiving party responds, they might also assign their own reference to the letter and also copy the sender's reference—"Your Reference X." From that point on, both parties state their own and each other's assigned reference. SCCP connection-oriented service uses the same principles; the "Our Reference" is known as the Source Local Reference (SLR), and the "Your Reference" is known as the Destination Local Reference (DLR). This is similar in principle to Transmission Control Protocol (TCP): data is sent only when a virtual connection has been established through the initial exchange of identifiers. Figure 9-4 illustrates this principle.

Figure 9-4   *Analogy of Connection-oriented Service with Official Mail Correspondence*

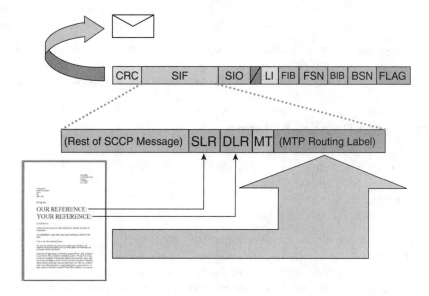

Connectionless service is like sending postcards, where the sender and recipient do not establish references. In principle, it is similar to User Datagram Protocol (UDP): data is sent without first establishing a virtual connection using identifiers.

NOTE   SCCP transfers the data using the signaling network for transport. Trunks are not involved.

User Data and Segmentation

The data (from subsystems) is sent in information elements called Network Service Data Units (NSDUs). SCCP provides the capability to segment or reassemble an NSDU that is too large to fit in a single MTP message (MSU) so that it can be transmitted over a number of MSUs (16 maximum). When using the connectionless classes, if an NSDU is greater than 255 octets when using a UDT message or 254 when using a XUDT message, the originating node splits the NSDU into a number of XUDT messages. For a description of UDT and XUDT messages, see section "Message Types" and refer to Appendix C, "SCCP Messages (ANSI/ETSI/ITU-T)." If an NSDU is greater than 255 octets when using the connection-oriented classes, the originating node splits the NSDU into several DT messages. The receiving node reassembles the NSDU. For a description of the DT message, see the section on "Message Types" and refer to Appendix C. Theoretically, the maximum amount of user data is 3952^1 octets in ITU-T SCCP [58-61] and [2] 3904 octets in ANSI SCCP. This excludes optional parameters and global titles, which will appear to be repeated in each message. The ITU-T recommends using 2560 as the maximum NSDU size as a safe implementation value [16] because it allows for the largest global title and numerous optional parameters. The section on "SCCP Routing Control (SCRC)" covers global titles.

The parameter Protocol Class within each SCCP message specifies the protocol class. Before giving a further explanation of connectionless and connection-orientated procedures the following sections discuss the four classes of data transfer that SCCP provides.

Connectionless Protocol Classes

Class 0 provides a basic connectionless service and has no sequencing control. It does not impose any conditions on the Signaling Link Selection (SLS) values that MTP3 inserts; therefore, SCCP messages can be delivered out of sequence. Class 0 can be considered a pure connectionless service. See Chapter 7, "Message Transfer Part 3 (MTP3)," for information about the SLS field.

Class 1 service adds sequence control to the Class 0 service by requiring the SCCP to insert the same SLS field for all NSDUs that have the same Sequence Control parameter. The higher layers indicate to SCCP whether or not a stream of NSDUs should be delivered in sequence. Therefore Class 1 is an enhanced connectionless service that provides basic in sequence delivery of NSDUs. Failures at the MTP level can still result in messages being delivered out of sequence.

TCAP is the typical user of SCCP connectionless services. The other user is Base Station Subsystem Application Part (BSSAP), which is used solely for GSM cellular radio related signaling. See Chapter 3, "The Role of SS7," for a brief description of BSSAP. Although

---

1. $3952 = (254 - 7) * 16$, where 254 is the user data length fitting in one XUDT, 16 is the maximal number of segments and 7 is the length of the optional parameter: "segmentation" is followed by the end of the optional parameters octet [16].

the applications (subsystems) use TCAP directly, they are considered SCCP users because TCAP is considered transparent. See Chapter 10 for more information about TCAP.

NOTE   Common subsystems include Local Number Portability (LNP), Customizable Application Part (CAP), MAP, INAP, and AIN.

Table 9-1 shows the connectionless service protocol classes and features.

Table 9-1   *Connectionless Service Protocol Classes*

Protocol Class and Name	Features	Example Use
Protocol Class 0: Basic Connectionless	Independent message transport, no sequencing	Some BSSMAP messages (Paging), TCAP
Protocol Class 1: Connectionless Service	Independent message transport, limited sequencing	TCAP

Connection-oriented Protocol Classes

Class 2 provides a basic connection-oriented service by assigning local reference numbers to create a logical connection. Messages that belong to the same connection are assigned the same SLS value to ensure sequencing. Class 2 does not provide flow control, loss, or missequence detection.

Class 3 is an enhanced connection-oriented service that offers detection of both message loss and mis-sequencing (for each connection section). Class 3 also offers flow control using an expedited data transfer function. The ETSI European SCCP standard, ETS 300-009 [10], offers support for Class 3 only from V1.4.2 (November 1999) onwards.

The ITU-T had specified a Class 4, but this was never implemented on live networks and was later removed in White Book editions.

Table 9-2 shows the connection-oriented service protocol classes and features.

Table 9-2   *Connection-oriented Service Protocol Classes*

Protocol Class and Name	Features	Example Use
Protocol Class 2: Basic Connection-oriented Service	Logical signaling connection used for message transport	Some BSSMAP messages (Setup)
Protocol Class 3: Connection-oriented Service	Logical signaling connection used for message transport, and flow control (expedited data transfer)	No known current use

SCCP Connectionless Control (SCLC)

SCLC is used to provide the capabilities that are necessary to transfer one NSDU in the "data" field of a UDT, Long Unit Data (LUDT), and XUDT message. For a description of SCCP messages, see section "Message Types" and Appendix C. The SCLC routes the message without regard to the route that the messages follow through the network. These services are provided without setting up a logical connection.

SCLC formats the user data into a message of the appropriate protocol class (0 or 1 in the case of connectionless) and transfers it to SCRC for routing. The section on "SCCP Routing Control (SCRC)" describes SCRC. On receiving a message, SCLC is responsible for decoding and distributing the message to the appropriate subsystem. Figure 9-5 shows data transfer using SCLC: data is simply sent without the prior establishment of references at each side.

Figure 9-5   *The Transfer of Connectionless Messages from One SCCP User to Another*

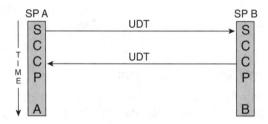

SCCP Connection-Oriented Control (SCOC)

SCOC is used to route messages through a specific, fixed logical network path. To establish a dedicated logical connection between an originating SCCP user (subsystem) and a terminating SCCP user (subsystem), the SCCP users residing at different nodes throughout the network communicate with each other.

A signaling connection between the SCCP users is established, making both SCCP users aware of the transaction by using the DLR and SLR parameters. The signaling connection is released at the end of the transaction (information transfer). This is similar to SS7 protocol TUP/ISUP, which is used to control telephony calls, in that a connection is setup and released at a later time. However, the connection is virtual; there is not a trunk with user traffic being set up and released—rather, there is a virtual connection over the signaling network for the purpose of data transfer between applications (subsystems).

NOTE	SCCP connection-oriented services (Class 2 and Class 3) are virtual connections between users of the signaling system and bear no relation to connections between subscribers (trunks).

Connection-oriented procedures can be split into three phases:

- **Connection Establishment Phase**—The SCCP users set up a logical, fixed path that the data packets will follow. The path might involve only two or three nodes with SCCP capability or, depending on how many intermediate nodes exist between the originator and terminator, it might involve a much larger number.

- **Data Transfer Phase**—After the connection is established, the data that is to be transferred is converted into an NSDU and sent in a DT1 or DT2 message. For a description of SCCP messages, see the section on "Message Types" and Appendix C. Each NSDU is uniquely identified as belonging to a specific signaling connection. In this way, it is possible for the SCCP to simultaneously handle independent signaling connections.

- **Connection Release Phase**—After all NSDUs have been transmitted and confirmed, either or both of the user applications that initiated the process release the logical path. A release can also occur if the connection fails.

An example of a connection-oriented data transfer is carried out in Figure 9-6. At the request of the SCCP user, SCCP A establishes a logical connection by sending a Connection Request (CR) message to SCCP B and assigning a SLR to the request. The remote node confirms the connection by sending a Connection Confirm (CC) message and includes its own SLR and a DLR that is equal to SCCP A's SLR. This gives both sides a reference for the connection.

The CR message contains the address of the destination SCCP node and user. The subsequent data message DT1 only needs to send the DLR because the logical connection has been established through the proceeding exchange of SLR and DLR. The clear-down messages contain both SLR and DLR. If intermediate nodes are involved, they make associations between pairs of SLR/DLRs to establish the logical connection. Upon release, the SLR/DLR references are available for further use on other transactions. SCCP nodes can establish multiple simultaneous logical connections through the use of the SLR and DLR.

In Figure 9-5, if SCCP B received a CR message and either the SCCP B or the SCCP A could not establish the connection, a Connection Refused (CREF) message would have been returned.

Figure 9-6 *The Transfer of Connection-oriented Messages from One SCCP User to Another Using a Temporary Connection*

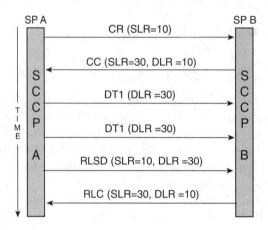

Classes 2 and 3 (discussed previously) can either establish temporary connections (that is, on demand by SCCP user), as shown in Figure 9-5, or permanent signaling connections that are established by management action. Temporary connections are analogous to dialup connections, and permanent connections are analogous to leased lines. The connection establishment and release services are not required on permanent connections.

SCCP Messages and Parameters

A full list and descriptions of ITU-T and ANSI SCCP messages is provided in Appendix C. This section concentrates on the core messages and parameters. Table 9-3 shows the full list of SCCP messages in a chart that shows the protocol class(es) in which the messages operate. Both ANSI [2] and ITU-T [60] have identical SCCP message sets.

Table 9-3 *The SCCP Message Types and Corresponding Protocol Class(es)*

	Protocol Classes			
SCCP Message	**0**	**1**	**2**	**3**
CR (Connection Request)			X	X
CC (Connection Confirm)			X	X
CREF (Connection Refused)			X	X
RLSD (Released)			X	X
RLC (Release Complete)			X	X
DT1 (Data Form 1)			X	

Table 9-3   *The SCCP Message Types and Corresponding Protocol Class(es) (Continued)*

SCCP Message	Protocol Classes			
	0	**1**	**2**	**3**
DT2 (Data Form 2)				X
AK (Data Acknowledgment)				X
UDT (Unitdata)	X	X		
UDTS (Unitdata Service)	X[1]	X[1]		
ED (Expedited Data)				X
EA (Expedited Data Acknowledgment)				X
RSR (Reset Request)				X
RSC (Reset Confirm)				X
ERR (Protocol Data Unit Error)			X	X
IT (Inactivity Test)			X	X
XUDT (Extended Unitdata)	X	X		
XUDTS (Extended Unitdata Service)	X[1]	X[1]		
LUDT (Long Unitdata)	X	X		
LUDTS (Long Unitdata Service)	X[1]	X[1]		

[1]   Type of protocol class is indeterminate (absence of protocol class parameter).

Message Structure

Figure 9-7 shows the format of an SCCP message.

Apart from the absence of a Circuit Identification Code field (CIC) field following the routing label, the basic message format is the same as an ISUP message (see Chapter 8, "ISDN User Part [ISUP]"). As with all other MTP users, SCCP messages are composed of three parts: a mandatory fixed part, mandatory variable part, and an optional part. All SCCP messages contain a mandatory fixed part, but not all of them have parameters to place in the mandatory variable or optional part. The following sections describe these three parts in more detail.

Mandatory Fixed Part (MF)

The *mandatory fixed part* consists of those parameters that must be present in the message and that are of a fixed length. Because the parameters are of a fixed length and are mandatory, no length indicator is required. In addition, because the parameter types and their order is known from the SCCP message type, no parameter names are required for stating the parameter types.

Figure 9-7 *The SCCP Message Structure*

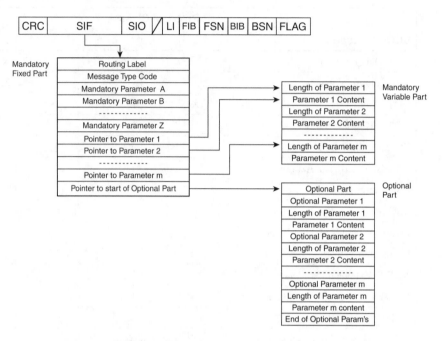

The mandatory fixed part contains pointers to the *mandatory variable part* and the *optional part* of the message. A pointer to the optional part is only included if the message type permits an optional part. If, on the other hand, the message type permits an optional part but no optional part is included for that particular message, then a pointer field that contains all zeros is used.

NOTE   A pointer is simply a single- or double-octet field that contains an offset, that is, a count from the beginning of the pointer to the first octet to which it points.

Mandatory Variable Part (MV)

The *mandatory variable part* consists of those parameters that must be present in the message and that are of a variable length. A pointer is used to indicate the start of each parameter. A length indicator precedes each parameter because the parameters are of a variable length. No parameter tags are required to state the parameter types because the parameter types and their order is explicitly defined by the SCCP message type. The parameters can occur in any order, but the associated pointers must occur in the same order as specified by the particular message type.

NOTE	The length indicator value excludes itself and the parameter name.

Optional Part (O)

The *optional part* consists of those parameters that are not always necessary. Each parameter is preceded by a parameter name and a length indicator. The parameter name is a unique one-octet field pattern that is used to indicate the parameter type. Because the parameter types and their order are unknown, it is required for each parameter type.

A one-octet End of Optional Parameters field is placed at the end of the last optional parameter. It is simply coded as all zeros.

Figure 9-8 illustrates an example message that contains all three parts. The message could contain no optional parameters, or even more optional parameters than in the example shown. Appendix L, "Tektronix Supporting Traffic," includes a trace that shows a CR message decode. The following section details the CR message.

Figure 9-8   *An Example of a Connection Request (CR) Message Structure*

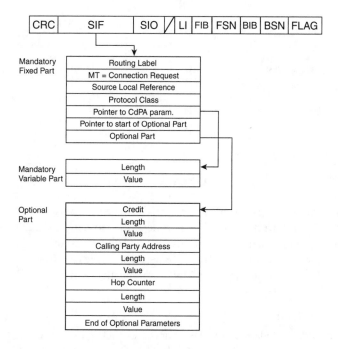

Message Types

This section details example SCCP messages that are used in both connectionless and connection-oriented services. Appendix C presents a full list and description of ITU-T and ANSI SCCP messages.

Connection Request (CR)

Connection-oriented protocol Class 2 or 3 uses a CR message during the connection establish-ment phase. It is sent by an originating SCCP user to a destination SCCP user to set up a sig-naling connection (a virtual connection) between the two signaling points. As shown in Table 9-4, the various parameters that compose the message dictate the connection requirements. After receiving the CR message, SCCP initiates the virtual connection setup, if possible.

Table 9-4   *CR Message Parameters*

Parameter	Type	Length (octets)
Message type code	MF	1
Source local reference	MF	3
Protocol class	MF	1
Called party address	MV	3 minimum
Credit	O	3
Calling party address	O	4 minimum
Data	O	3–130
Hop counter	O	3
Importance[1]	O	3
End of optional parameters	O	1

[1]   This parameter is not present in ANSI SCCP

In GSM cellular networks, a CR message could be used between a Mobile Switching Center (MSC) and a Base Station Controller (BSC) to setup a signaling connection. Its data parameter could contain a BSSAP location update request or a BSSAP handover request, for example. A description of the GSM network entities MSC and BSC can be found in Chapter 13, "GSM and ANSI-41 Mobile Application Part (MAP)."

Connection Confirm (CC)

Connection-oriented protocol Class 2 or 3 uses a CC message during the connection estab-lishment phase. SCCP sends it at the destination node as an acknowledgement to the orig-inating SCCP that it has set up the signaling connection. When the originating SCCP receives the CC message, it completes the setup of the signaling connection. Table 9-5 shows the parameters that comprise a CC message.

Table 9-5   *CC Message Parameters*

Parameter	Type	Length (octets)
Message type code	MF	1
Destination local reference	MF	3
Source local reference	MF	3
Protocol class	MF	1
Credit	O	3
Called party address	O	4 minimum
Data	O	3–130
Importance[1]	O	3
End of optional parameters	O	1

[1]   This parameter is not present in ANSI SCCP [2]

Connection Refused (CREF)

The connection-oriented protocol Class 2 or 3 can use a CREF message during the connection establishment phase. The destination SCCP or an intermediate node sends it to indicate to the originating SCCP that the signaling connection setup has been refused. As such, it is a negative response to a CR message. The refusal cause value is supplied to the originating SCCP. Table 9-6 shows the parameters of a CREF message.

Table 9-6   *Connection Refused (CREF) Message Parameters*

Parameter	Type	Length (octets)
Message type code	MF	1
Destination local reference	MF	3
Refusal cause	MF	1
Called party address	O	4 minimum
Data	O	3–130
Importance[1]	O	3
End of optional parameters	O	1

[1]   This parameter is not present in ANSI SCCP [2]

In GSM cellular networks, a CREF message can be sent from an MSC to a BSC (or vice versa) to refuse the requested signaling connection because the SCCP of the signaling point (MSC or BSC) cannot provide the connection.

Released (RLSD)

The connection-oriented protocol Class 2 or Class 3 uses a RLSD message during the release phase. It is sent in the forward or backward direction to indicate that the sending SCCP wants to release the signaling connection. Table 9-7 shows the parameters of a RLSD message.

Table 9-7   *RLSD Message Parameters*

Parameter	Type	Length (octets)
Message type code	MF	1
Destination local reference	MF	3
Source local reference	MF	3
Release cause	MF	1
Data	O	3–130
Importance[1]	O	3
End of optional parameters	O	1

[1]   This parameter is not present in ANSI SCCP [2]

In GSM cellular networks, a RLSD message is always sent from the MSC to the BSC (or vice versa) to release the SCCP connection and the resources that are associated with it.

Release Complete (RLC)

The connection-oriented protocol Class 2 or 3 uses a RLC message during the release phase. It is sent in the forward or backward direction as a response to the RLSD message to indicate the receipt of the RLSD and the execution of the appropriate actions for releasing the connection. Table 9-8 shows the parameters of an RLC message.

Table 9-8   *RLC Message Parameters*

Parameter	Type	Length (octets)
Message type code	MF	1
Destination local reference	MF	3
Source local references	MF	3

NOTE   Do not confuse a SSCP RLC message with an ISUP RLC message. The former has nothing to do with clearing voice circuits, while the latter does. They belong to different user parts and are distinguished as such by the Service Indicator Octet (SIO) described in Chapter 7.

Data Form 1 (DT1)

Only connection-oriented protocol Class 2 uses a DT1 message during the data transfer phase. Either end of a signaling connection sends it to transparently pass SCCP user data between two SCCP nodes. Table 9-9 shows the parameters of a DT1 message.

Table 9-9   *DT1 Message Parameters*

Parameter	Type	Length (octets)
Message type code	MF	1
Destination local reference	MF	3
Segmenting/reassembling	MF	1
Data	MV	2–256

DT1 messages are used in cellular networks to transfer data between the BSC and MSC after CR and CC messages have established the connection. All data transfer between BSC and MSC is performed using DT1 messages. DT2 messages (used for protocol Class 3) are not used in GSM (or DCS1800).

Unitdata (UDT)

A UDT message is used to send data in connectionless mode using connectionless protocol Class 0 and Class 1. Table 9-10 shows the parameters of a UDT message.

Table 9-10   *Unitdata Message (UDT) Parameters*

Parameter	Type	Length (octets)
Message type code	MF	1
Protocol class	MF	1
Called party address	MV	3 minimum
Calling party address	MV	2 minimum[1]
Data	MV	2-X^2

[1] ITU-T states a minimum length of 3, and a minimum length of 2 only in a special case. ANSI specifies a minimum length of 2.

[2] ITU-T states that the maximum length is for further study. ITU-T further notes that the transfer of up to 255 octets of user data is allowed when the SCCP called and calling party address do not include a global title. ANSI states that the maximum length is 252 octets.

UDT messages are commonly used for TCAP communication within IN services. In GSM cellular networks, UDT messages are used by the MAP protocol to send its messages. For a description of the MAP protocol see Chapter 13, "GSM and ANSI-41 Mobile Application Part (MAP)." SCCP management messages are transmitted using also the UDT message. SCCP management message are described in Section SCCP Management (SCMG) and in Appendices C, "SCCP Messages (ANSI/ETSI/ITU-T)."

Unitdata Service (UDTS)

A UDTS message is used in connectionless protocol Class 0 and 1. It indicates to the originating SCCP that a UDT message that is sent cannot be delivered to its destination. A UDTS message is only sent if the option field in the received UDT was set to return an error. Table 9-11 shows the parameters of a UDTS message.

NOTE   UDTS, LUDTS, and XUDTS indicate that the corresponding message (UDT, LUDT, and XUDT respectively) could not be delivered to the destination.

Table 9-11   *UDTS Message Parameters*

Parameter	Type	Length (octets)
Message type code	MF	1
Return cause	MF	1
Called party address	MV	3 minimum
Calling party address	MV	3 minimum
Data	MV	$2-X^1$

[1] ITU-T states that the maximum length is for further study. ITU-T further notes that the transfer of up to 255 octets of user data is allowed when the SCCP called and calling party address do not include a global title. ANSI states that the maximum length is 251 octets.

SCCP Routing Control (SCRC)

SCRC performs the following three functions:

- Routes messages received from the MTP to appropriate local subsystem.

- Routes messages from local subsystems to other local subsystems.

- Routes messages from local subsystems to subsystems in remote nodes by utilizing MTP's transport services. The destination is specified in the called party (CdPA) address parameter, which is supplied by the subsystem. The address can contain a combination of point code, system number, and global title.

SCCP addressing capabilities are flexible in contrast to those of MTP 3. As a result, the addressing capabilities are somewhat complex, thereby allowing several different combinations of routing parameters.

SCCP provides a routing function that allows signaling messages to be routed to a signaling point based on dialed digits, for example. This capability is known as Global Title Translation (GTT), which translates what is known as a global title (for example, dialed digits for a toll free number) into a signaling point code and a subsystem number so that it can be processed at the correct application. The section on "Global Title Translation" explains global titles and GTT.

The following are different types of network addressing that SCCP supports:

- Point Code (PC) routing
- Subsystem Number (SSN) routing
- Global Title (GT) routing

The MTP layer can only use point code routing, which is described in Chapter 7. Figure 9-9 shows a summary of MTP point code routing. Using MTP point code routing, MSUs pass through the STPs until they reach the SP that has the correct DPC. The following sections describe the SSN and GT routing.

Figure 9-9 *Showing MTP Point Code Routing*

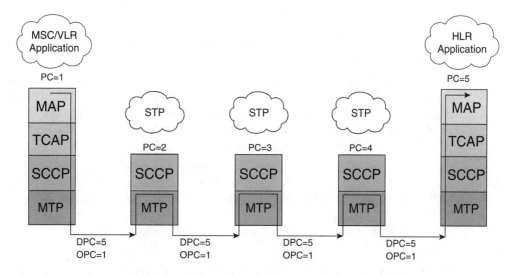

Subsystem Number (SSN) Routing

As previously mentioned, a subsystem is the name given to an application that uses SCCP; applications are predominantly database driven, except where ISUP is the subsystem (for a limited number of supplementary services), or where BSSAP uses SCCP (for radio-related signaling in GSM). As illustrated in Figure 9-10, a SSN is used to identify the SCCP user in much the same way as the service indicator identifies the MTP3 user (see Chapter 7).

Figure 9-10 *An SSN and DPC Are Required for the Final Delivery of an SCCP Message*

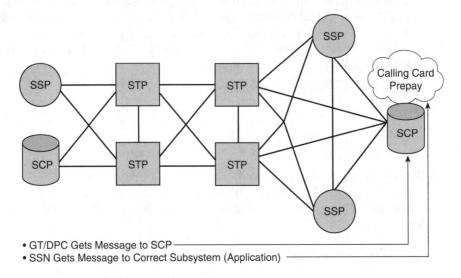

- GT/DPC Gets Message to SCP
- SSN Gets Message to Correct Subsystem (Application)

Figure 9-10 shows that a DPC and SSN are required in order to deliver a message to the correct application at the destination node.

It should be clear that noncircuit-related signaling (for example, database transactions to support IN/cellular, and so on) involve two distant applications (subsystems) exchanging information. The SSN is used to identify the application. Appendix L contains a trace that shows the decoding of a VLR calling an HLR (to perform a location update).

NOTE   Applications using TCAP rely on SCCP for message routing since TCAP itself has no routing capabilities. Therefore, each application is explicitly identified by an SSN at the SCCP level.

If SSN routing is used, the SSN is placed inside the CdPA parameter. The SCCP uses the SSN to send an SCCP message to a particular subsystem (application) at an SP. The SSN of the originating subsystem is also included in the Calling Party Address (CgPA) parameter to identify the subsystem that sent the SCCP message.

NOTE	SCCP's CgPA and CdPA parameters should not be confused with the Calling Party Number and Called Party Number parameters found in TUP/ISUP.

The SSN field is one octet in length and, therefore, has a capacity of 255 possible combinations.

Table 9-12 shows the SSN values that are specified by the ITU-T.

Table 9-12   *ITU-T Specified Subsystem Numbers [60]*

Bits **8 7 6 5 4 3 2 1**	**Subsystem**
0 0 0 0 0 0 0 0	SSN not known/not used
0 0 0 0 0 0 0 1	SCCP management
0 0 0 0 0 0 1 0	Reserved for ITU-T allocation
0 0 0 0 0 0 1 1	ISUP (ISDN user part)
0 0 0 0 0 1 0 0	OMAP (Operation, Maintenance, and Administration Part)
0 0 0 0 0 1 0 1	MAP (Mobile Application Part)
0 0 0 0 0 1 1 0	HLR (Home Location Register)
0 0 0 0 0 1 1 1	VLR (Visitor Location Register)
0 0 0 0 1 0 0 0	MSC (Mobile Switching Centre)
0 0 0 0 1 0 0 1	EIC (Equipment Identifier Centre)
0 0 0 0 1 0 1 0	AUC (Authentication Centre)
0 0 0 0 1 0 1 1	ISUP supplementary services[1]
0 0 0 0 1 1 0 0	Reserved for international use
0 0 0 0 1 1 0 1	Broadband ISDN edge-to-edge applications
0 0 0 0 1 1 1 0	TC test responder[1]
0 0 0 0 1 1 1 1 to 0 0 0 1 1 1 1 1	Reserved for international use
0 0 1 0 0 0 0 0 to 1 1 1 1 1 1 1 0	Reserved for national networks
1 1 1 1 1 1 1 1	Reserved for expansion of national and international SSN

[1]   ANSI [2] simply states this field value as reserved.

ITU-T network specific subsystem numbers should be assigned in descending order, starting with 11111110 (for example, BSSAP is allocated 11111110 within GSM).

In GSM, subsystem numbers can be used between Public Land Mobile Networks (PLMNs), in which case they are taken from the globally standardized range (1–31) or the part of the national network range (129–150) that is reserved for GSM use between PLMNs, or within a PLMN, in which case they are taken from the part of the national network range (32–128 and 151–254) that is not reserved for GSM use between PLMNs.

Table 9-13 lists the globally standardized subsystem numbers that have been allocated by 3GPP for use by GSM/GPRS/UMTS cellular networks [106].

Table 9-13   *3GPP Specified Subsystem Numbers [60]*

Bits	Subsystem
0000 0110	HLR
0000 0111	VLR
0000 1000	MSC
0000 1001	EIR
0000 1010	AuC
1111 1010	BSC
1111 1011	MSC
1111 1100	SMLC
1111 1101	BSS O&M
1111 1110	BSSAP
1000 1110	RANAP
1000 1111	RNSAP
1001 0001	GMLC
1001 0010	CAP
1001 0011	gsmSCF
1001 0100	SIWF
1001 0101	SGSN
1001 0110	GGSN

Additionally INAP is specified as 0000 1111 [106].

Table 9-14 shows some common subsystems that are used within North America.

Table 9-14   *Common North American Subsystem Numbers*

Bits	Subsystem
1111 1011	Custom Local Area Signaling Service (CLASS)
1111 1100	PVN (Private Virtual Network)
1111 1101 ACCS	Automatic Calling Card Service (ACCS)
1111 1110	E800 (Enhanced 800)

Global Title Routing

"A global title is an address, such as dialed-digits, which does not explicitly contain information that would allow routing in the SS7 network."

Source: ITU-T-T Q.714 Subclause 2.1 [61]

There are many examples of digit strings that are global titles: in fixed-line networks, toll free, premium rate, numbers ported under LNP, or in the case of GSM cellular networks, the Mobile Subscriber ISDN Number (MSISDN) and International Mobile Subscriber Identity (IMSI) of the cellular subscriber and each HLR and VLR.

A GT is a telephony address. As such, the GT address must be translated into an SS7 network address (DPC+SSN) before it can be finally delivered. The GT is placed in the global title address information (GTAI) parameter within the CgPA and CdPA fields.

Global title routing is often used in fixed-line networks for calling-card validation and such services as *telemarketing* numbers (like a toll-free or premium rate). It is used in cellular networks for exchanging messages when an HLR and VLR belong to different networks or when several signaling points separate them.

Global Title Translation

GTT is an incremental indirect routing method that is used to free originating signaling points from the burden of having to know every potential application destination (that is, PC+SSN). This section describes the GTT process and the parameters associated with GTT.

For example, calling-card queries (which are used to verify that a call can be properly billed to a calling card) must be routed to an SCP that is designated by the company that issued the calling card. Rather than maintaining a nationwide database of where such queries should be routed (based on the calling-card number), SSPs generate queries that are addressed to their local STPs, which use GTT, to select the correct destination to which the message should be routed. STPs must maintain a database that enables them to determine where a query should be routed. GTT centralizes SCCP routing information at designated nodes, generally an STP, although SSP or SCP nodes are normally capable of performing GTT.

Even the SP that has been requested by another SP to perform GTT does not have to know the exact final destination of a message. Instead, it can perform intermediate GTT, in which it uses its tables to locate another SP that might have the final address required in its routing tables. An SP that performs a final GTT provides both the PC and SSN needed to route the message to its final destination. Intermediate GTT further minimizes the need for STPs to maintain extensive information about nodes that are far removed from them. GTT also is used at the STP to share a load among mated SCPs in both normal and failure scenarios. In these instances, when messages arrive at an SP for final GTT and routing to destination SP, the STP that routes the message can select from among available redundant SPs (for example, two mated SCPs). It can select an SP on either a priority basis or to equalize the load across the available SPs (this is referred to as *loadsharing*).

As an example, GTT is performed to determine the SCP location to which queries should be sent for number translation services such as tollfree and LNP. If you dial 1-800-BUY-MORE in the U.S. (toll-free begins with 0800 in many countries, including Great Britain), a query is sent to an SCP to translate the toll-free number to a routing number. See Chapter 11 for a detailed explanation of how number translation services work.

When the SSP receives the tollfree or LNP number from the subscriber, it must determine the next hop destination to reach the SCP that provides the number translation service. In Figure 9-11, the SSP performs a GTT to determine that the next hop destination is the STP. The STP then performs the final GTT to route the message to the correct SCP. It is worth noting that when people in the SS7 field refer to "where the GTT is done", they are usually referring to the STP that provides the address of the final destination. In the previous example, GTT is actually done at the originating SSP in order to determine the next hop desination (the STP) towards the SCP and also at the STP to determine the final destination.

Figure 9-11 *Example of GTT*

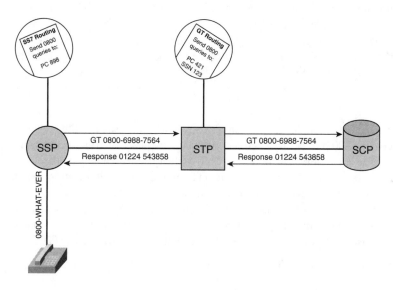

The SSP could always get the information from such a database (SCP) without using GTT if the DPC and SSN of the required toll free (or LNP) application were present in its routing tables. However, this would require maintaining a large number of routing entries at the SSP. New services (and applications) are frequently deployed into the SS7 network around the world. Some of the services might be proprietary and are, therefore, only accessible to the SSPs in the same proprietary network. Others are intended to be offered to other networks for a fee. If a service becomes universally available, it should not mean that every switch worldwide should be required to add the location (DPC) and application identifier (SSN) to its routing tables. Therefore, the GTT is used to centralize these routing functions.

SCCP routing (utilizing GTT) is an effective solution. The GTT information is placed at a limited number of network locations (such as STPs), and SSPs query these centralized locations without identifying from where the information is retrieved. When a switch requires a GT translation (that is, to address an application), it must only identify the nature of the translation it needs (for example, a toll-free number to E.164 "real" number), and send the request to a location that has GT routing tables to perform the translation. GTT is only performed on the number of digits required to identify where the SCCP message should be sent after translation. For example, in our toll-free illustration, GTT may only be performed on the three most significant digits (800) at the SSP to determine that all 800 numbers should be sent to a designated STP. At the STP, GTT could require translation of six digits (800-289) in order to determine the next STP for intermediate GTT or the final SCP destination. These decisions are made based on the administration of the network and agreements between network operators.

NOTE   It is important not to confuse directory number translation with GTT. When a query involving a number translation service is sent, GTT determines the SS7 address of the service (DPC + SSN) in order to deliver the message to the correct SP and subsystem. The service (such as toll-free) translates the number contained in the TCAP portion of the message, not the GT number in the SCCP portion of the message.

This allows a single entry in the SSP's routing table (such as the location of an STP) to provide 800 number translations. As stated previously in this section, with intermediate GTT, even the first location that receives the query (for DPC and/or SSN of destination application) does not have to maintain a routing table of all locations on the globe. Instead, it might have a table that indicates that all requests in several similar categories should be sent to one location, while requests in other categories can be sent somewhere else. These locations either directly identify the correct destination application (subsystem) or again, in the case of intermediate GTT, send it to another node for further GT routing analysis.

Figure 9-12 shows a further example using the GSM cellular network.

Figure 9-12 *GTT on a GSM Cellular Network*

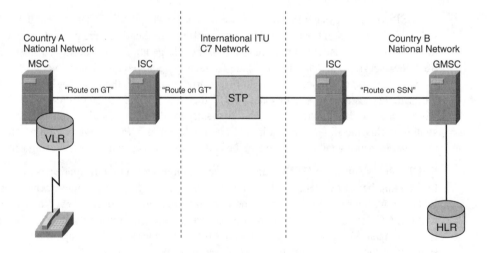

In Figure 9-12, a VLR in Country A originates a MAP *Update Location* message. The message contains the DPC of a Country A's International Switching Centre (ISC). The MSC/VLR contains the PC of the ISC that is provisioned in its routing tables. The message also contains the GT of the HLR (an E.164 number). The ISC at Country A changes the DPC to be an ISC of Country B. Again, this PC is already provisioned in its routing tables, and again, the GT of the HLR is present in the message. The ISC in Country B happens to have the data fill to translate the GT into a PC+SSN; therefore, it performs the GTT. Thus, the message is routed to the HLR via the GMSC using only the PC+SSN. GT translations are usually centralised at STPs to allow routing changes to be made easily.

Calling Party Address (CgPA) and Called Party Address (CdPA)

The CgPA contains information for identifying the originator of the SCCP message. The CdPA contains information to identify the SCCP message's intended destination. Figure 9-13 shows the placement of the CgPA/CdPA in the context of an MSU. Figure 9-14 shows the fields that are found within the CgPA/CdPA.

Figure 9-13 *Positioning of the CgPA and CdPA Fields in the Context of an MSU*

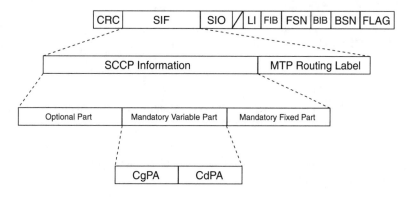

Address Indicator (AI)

The AI is the first field within CgPA/CdPA and is one octet in length. Its function is to indicate which information elements are present so that the address can be interpreted—in other words, it indicates the type of addressing information that is to be found in the address field so the receiving node knows how to interpret that data.

The Routing Indicator (RI) specifies whether GTT is required; it determines whether routing based on PC+SSN or GT. If routing is based on the GT, the GT in the address is used for routing. If routing is based on PC+SSN, the PC and SSN in the CdPA are used. The PC from the CdPA is then placed into the MTP3 routing label DPC before MTP routing takes place.

Figure 9-14 *The Subfields that Belong to Both the CgPA and CdPA Fields*

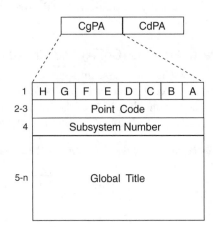

- **'A' Bit:** PC Indicator (1 = Included)
- **'B' Bit:** SSN Indicator (1 = Included)
- **C — F Bits:** GT Indicator
  (0000 = GT Not Included,
  0001 = GT Includes Nature of Address,
  0010 = GT Includes Translation Type,
  0011 = GT Includes Translation Type,
  Numbering Plan, and Encoding Scheme),
  0100 = GT Includes Translation Type,
  Numbering Plan, Encoding Scheme, and
  Nature of Address Indicator)
- **'G' Bit:** Routing Indicator (0 = Route on
  GT, 1 = Route on PC+SSN)
- **'H' Bit:** Reserved for National Use

The GT Indicator (GTI) specifies the GT format. In addition to those codes shown previously, 0101 to 0111 represent *spare international* use, and 1000 to 1110 represents *spare national* use.

The subsystem number is encoded "00000000" when the Subsystem Number is unknown (such as before GTT).

Figure 9-15 shows an example of SCCP routing using a GT.

There are four possible GT formats (bits C-F). '0100' is a common format that is used for international network applications, including INAP, which is discussed in Chapter 11, "Intelligent Networks (IN)," and MAP, which is discussed in Chapter 13, "GSM and ANSI-41 Mobile Application Part (MAP)." Figure 9-16 shows this common format.

We now examine the fields with the format '0100' that are found within a GT.

Translation Type (TT)

The Translation Type (TT) field indicates the type of translation. When it is not used, the TT is coded 00000000. A GTI of 0010 is for national use only; the translation types for GTI 0010 is a national decision; it can imply the encoding scheme and the numbering plan. The ITU-T has not specified the translation types for GTI 0011. Figure 9-17 shows the TT values [60].

Figure 9-15 *Example Routing Parameters and Values*

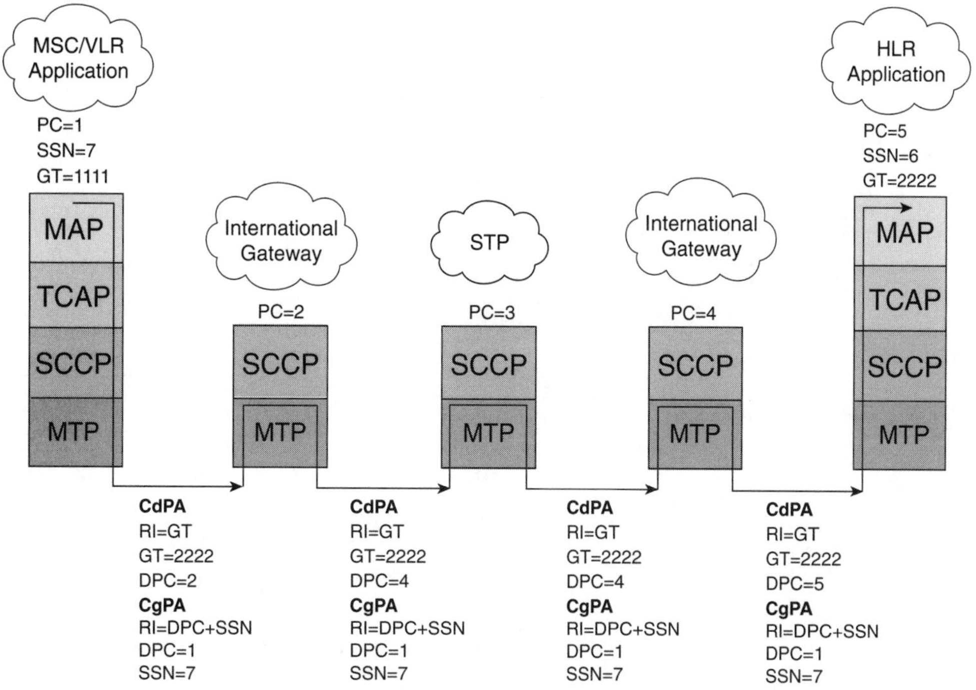

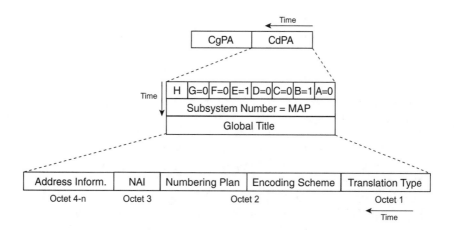

Figure 9-16 *GT Format 0100*

Figure 9-17 *Translation Type Values [60]*

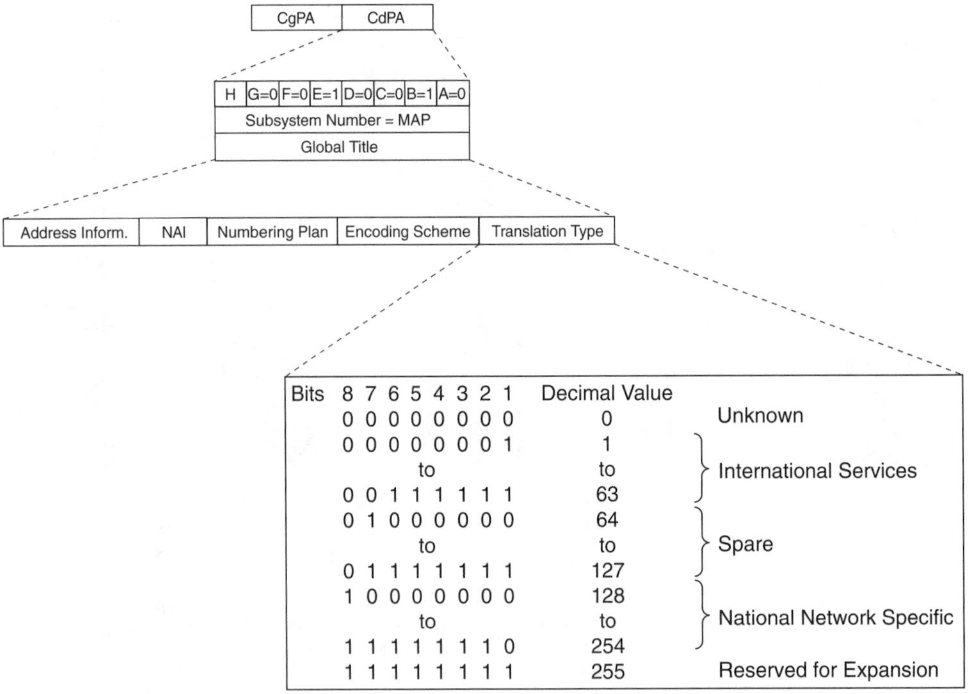

Encoding Scheme (ES)

The Encoding Scheme (ES) tells the receiving node how to translate the digits from binary code. Figure 9-18 shows the ES values [60].

Numbering Plan (NP)

The Number Plan (NP) field specifies the numbering plan that the address information follows. The E.164 standard for telephony has the format Country Code, National Destination Code, and Subscriber Number. The E.212 standard for the mobile station numbering plan has the format Mobile Country Code, Mobile Network Code, and Mobile Subscriber Identity Number (MSIN). The E.214 standard is a hybrid number with the Country Code and National Destination Code from E.164 and the MSIN from E.212. The E.214 format exists because international signaling networks require E.164 format. By replacing the leading digits of an E.212 number with the leading digits of an E.164 number, the existing translations can be used to route GTs. Figure 9-19 shows the NP values [60].

Figure 9-18 *Encoding Scheme Values [60]*

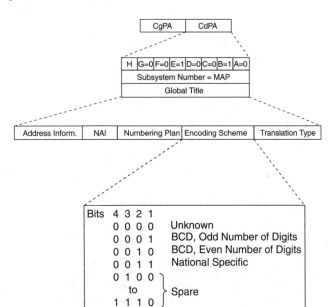

Nature of Address Indicator (NAI)

The Nature of Address Indicator (NAI) field defines the address range for a specific numbering plan. The exact meaning depends on the numbering plan, not on GTI values.

Figure 9-20 shows the NAI values [60].

Address Information (AI)

The AI contains the actual Global Title digits. These include enough of the most significant portion of the actual address digits to identify the destination node. For example, if a toll-free number of 800-123-4567 is dialed, the AI field might contain the digits 800 to identify an SCP to which the tollfree query should be sent. As shown in Figure 9-21, the address information is predominantly coded in Binary Coded Decimal (BCD) using four bits to code each digit.

Figure 9-19 *Numbering Plan (NP) Values [60]*

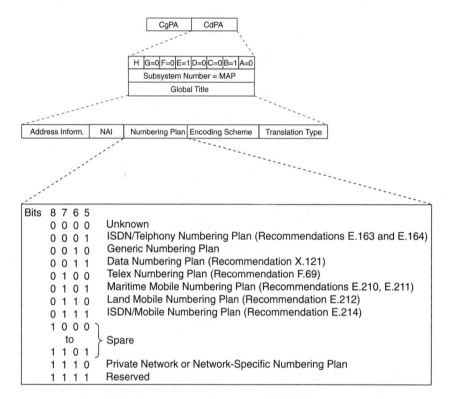

As an example of the parameters found for GT format "0100," we consider SCCP addressing for GSM-MAP messages (which is discussed in Chapter 13, "GSM and ANSI-41 Mobile Application Part [MAP]). For Inter-PLMN addressing, the CdPA/CgPA contains the following values: SSN Indicator = 1 (SSN included); GT Indicator = 0100, GT includes Translation Type, Numbering Plan, Encoding Scheme and Nature of Address Indicator; TT = 00000000 (not used), and Routing Indicator = 0 (routing on GT).

Figure 9-20 *The Nature of Address (NAI) Values [60]*

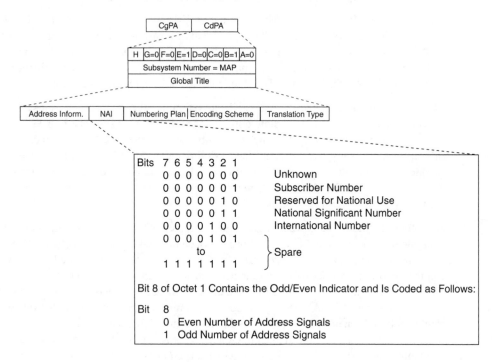

Figure 9-21 *BCD Encoding of Address Digits*

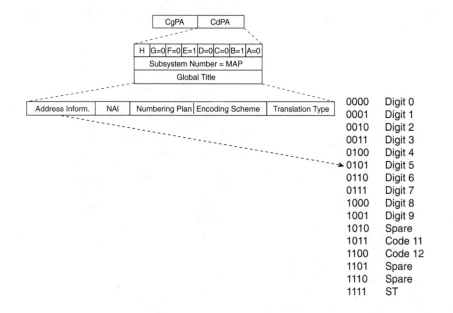

SCCP Management (SCMG)

SCMG manages the status of subsystems and SCCP-capable signaling points (SPs). It maintains the status of remote SCCP SPs and that of local subsystems. It interacts with the SCRC to ensure that SCCP traffic is not sent to inaccessible destinations; if they are available, they use alternative routes or alternative subsystems to provide SCCP traffic rerouting. In addition, SCMG throttles SCCP traffic in the event of network congestion.

SCMG uses the concept of a "concerned" subsystem or SP. A "concerned" subsystem or SP is marked as requiring immediate notification if the affected subsystem or SP status changes. An affected SP might not have any subsystems or SPs marked as "concerned"; in this case, when a subsystem fails or inaccessibility occurs at the affected SP, it does not broadcast the status change. If it has entities marked as "concerned," it will broadcast the SSP message so the SCMG at the "concerned" entities can react to circumvent routing to the unavailable SP or subsystem.

A response method is used when a message is received that is addressed to an unavailable subsystem from an SP/subsystem that has not been notified of the status change. Upon receiving such a message, the affected SP returns the SSP message. The notified SP/subsystem can then periodically check whether the affected subsystem is available by sending a SCMG Subsystem status Test (SST) to the affected SP. The affected SP returns an SCMG Subsystem Allowed (SSA) message if the subsystem is available again. An SP/subsystem might not have been notified of the status change because it was not on the "concerned" list, the SSA/SSP message sent from the affected SP was lost, or the affected SP was recovering from either an MTP or SCCP failure, in which case it does not make a broadcast upon recovery. Figure 9-22 presents an example of the response method.

Figure 9-22 *Possible Sequence of Messages Exchanged Between PC-Z and PC-Y When the Toll-Free Subsystem at PC-Z Becomes Unavailable*

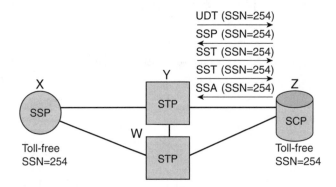

In Figure 9-22, the toll-free subsystem (SSN = 254) at SP-Z is down. When SP-Y tries to send connectionless data to the subsystem, SP-Z informs SP-Y that the subsystem is not available using the SSP message. SP-Y periodically checks whether the toll-free subsystem at SP-Z is back up again by using the SST message. On the second SST, the subsystem is available again and, as a result, SP-Z sends back a SSA message. It should be understood that other subsystems might exist at SP-Z and these might be functioning as normal, even though the toll free subsystem went down and later came back up again.

Upon receiving an SSP message, SP-Y updates its translation tables to select statically provisioned alternative routing to backup SPs and/or backup subsystems (if available).

Replicate Subsystems

Subsystems can be deployed in pairs; this is known as a replicate subsystem. Replicate subsystems are normally only used at an SCP pair and are connected to a common intermediate node (STP). Under normal conditions, SCCP traffic can be load-shared across the replicate subsystems. Optionally, one of the subsystems can be designated as primary and the other as backup. If the primary subsystem becomes prohibited, the backup subsystem services the SCCP messages that were originally destined for the primary subsystem.

SCMG messages are used to coordinate the activity of a replicated subsystem. When one subsystem that belongs to the pair wishes to go out of service, a Subsystem Out-of-service Request (SOR) is sent to the replicate's other subsystem. If the subsystem that receives the SOR determines that the replicate can be taken out of service without degrading SCCP performance, a Subsystem Out-of-service Grant (SOG) is sent in response. The determination of whether the SOG is sent is based on the traffic load and available resources.

The ANSI SCCP standards specify three optional messages [2] for providing SCCP traffic mix information when subsystems are deployed as primary/backup pairs:

- Subsystem Backup Routing (SBR)
- Subsystem Normal Routing (SNR)
- Subsystem Routing Test (SRT)

If a primary subsystem becomes prohibited, the intermediate node that is connected to the replicate pair sends an SBR message to the backup subsystem to inform the backup subsystem that it is receiving traffic that was originally destined for the primary subsystem. The SRT is periodically sent to verify the status of a subsystem that is marked as backup routed. When the primary subsystem becomes available again, the SNR message is sent to update the traffic mix information at the backup node. This allows the backup node to be aware that it is no longer serving traffic that is rerouted from the primary node.

Figure 9-23 shows an example of using a replicated subsystem with a designated primary and backup node. When subsystem 254 is being removed from service, an SOR message is sent from SCP A to SCP B. SCP B determines that it is acceptable for the replicate subsystem to be removed from service and returns a SOG. In this example, the optional SBR message indicating that backup traffic is being received is sent from STP C to SCP B.

Figure 9-23 *Replicate Subsystem Going Out of Service*

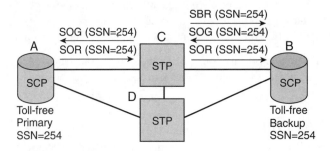

In Figure 9-24, subsystem 254 is returned to service at SCP A, and the optional SNR message is sent to SCP B to indicate that it is no longer receiving backup traffic.

Figure 9-24 *Replicate Subsystem Being Returned to Service*

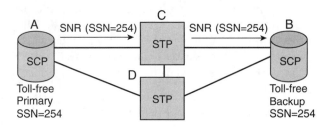

The messages used by SCMG are detailed in the following section.

SCMG Messages

SCMG messages are carried using the SCCP's connectionless service. When transferring SCMG messages, Class 0 is requested with no special option. The called and calling party address parameters that set the SSN to SCMG, and set the RI to route on SSN. SCMG messages are encapsulated in the data parameter of the UDT, XUDT, or LUDT message.

Table 9-15 shows the SCMG message types.

Table 9-15   *The Format Identifiers of ANSI and ITU-T SCCP Management Messages.*

Pseudonym/Message	Binary Code
Subsystem Allowed (SSA)	00000001
Subsystem Prohibited (SSP)	00000010
Subsystem Status Test (SST)	00000011
Subsystem Out-of-service request (SOR)	00000100
Subsystem Out-of-service Grant (SOG)	00000101
SCCP/Subsystem Congested (SSC)	00000110
Subsystem Backup Routing[1] (SBR)	11111101
Subsystem Normal Routing[1] (SNR)	11111110
Subsystem Routing Test[1] (SRT)	11111111

[1]   Found only in ANSI SCCP [2]

Appendix C includes a full description of these messages. It should be clear that these are independent from MTP3 signaling network management messages.

Signaling Point Status Management

Signaling point status management informs the other management functions of changes in other nodes. For point code failures, all functions that are associated with the failed node are marked as failed. Message routing programs broadcast messages to the rest of the network to inform the network of the failure.

Subsystem Status Management

Changes in the status of any of the local subsystems are reported to other SPs in the network. If the failure is at another node, this SCCP function informs the local subsystems about the problem.

Summary

The SCCP provides additional OSI network layer functionality and, with the MTP, provides an NSP. It uses the signaling network to transport noncircuit-related signaling, such as queries and responses between switches and telecommunications databases. SCCP provides two categories of service with two protocol classes in each. Classes 0 and 1 are within the connectionless category, and do not establish a virtual connection before transferring data. Classes 2 and 3 are within the connection-oriented category and establish a virtual (logical) connection before transferring data. SCCP provides flexible routing based on DPC, SSN, or GT, or a combination of all three. Global titles are an alias for a DPC and SSN and must be translated at nodes administered with the proper information (usually STPs). This process, which is known as GTT, frees originating nodes from having over-burdensome routing tables.

Transaction Capabilities Application Part (TCAP)

The *Transaction Capabilities Application Part (TCAP)* of the SS7 protocol allows services at network nodes to communicate with each other using an agreed-upon set of data elements. Prior to SS7, one of the problems with implementing switching services beyond the boundary of the local switch was the proprietary nature of the switches. The voice circuits also had very little bandwidth for signaling, so there was no room for transferring the necessary data associated with those services. Moving to a Common Channel Signaling (CCS) system with dedicated signaling bandwidth allows the transfer of a greater amount of service-related information. Coupling the standardization of data communication elements with the necessary bandwidth to transmit those elements creates the proper foundation for a rich service environment. To that end, TCAP provides a generic interface between services that is based on the concept of "components." Components comprise the instructions that service applications exchange at different nodes.

This chapter examines components and other details of the TCAP protocol, including the following:

- Overview of TCAP
- Message types
- Transactions
- Components
- Dialogue portion
- Message encoding
- Element structure
- Error handling
- ITU protocol message contents
- ANSI protocol message contents
- ANSI national operations

In trying to understand how TCAP works, the differences between ANSI TCAP (as presented in the ANSI T1.114) and ITU TCAP (as presented in the Q.700 series) are normalized as much as possible. While differences between the two certainly exist, a great deal of commonality also exists and often varies only in the naming of identifiers.

Overview

The following topics provide an overview of TCAP and how it is used to provide enhanced network services:

- Generic service interface
- Role of TCAP in call control
- TCAP within the SS7 protocol stack
- Transaction and component sublayers

Generic Service Interface

TCAP is designed to be generic to accommodate the needs of a wide variety of different services. This chapter focuses on understanding these generic mechanisms. Chapter 11, "Intelligent Networks (IN)," examines the prominent network services that use TCAP in an effort to understand how services use these generic mechanisms. Some common services that use TCAP include number translation services, such as Enhanced 800 Service (toll-free) and Local Number Portability (LNP). Other examples of TCAP users are Custom Local Area Signaling Services (CLASS), Mobile Wireless, and Advanced Intelligent Network (AIN) services. Figure 10-1 shows how TCAP uses standardized components as the basic building blocks for services across network nodes.

Figure 10-1 *Standardized Components Used to Create a Generic Interface*

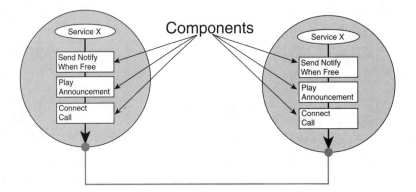

Most TCAP services can be viewed as a dialogue of questions and answers. A switch needs additional information that is associated with call processing, or with a particular service that causes it to send a TCAP query that requests the needed information. As shown in

Figure 10-2, the answer returns in a TCAP response, which provides the necessary information, and normal call processing or feature processing can resume. The query for information can be sent to a Service Control Point (SCP) or to another SSP, depending on the type of service and the information required. The SCP is an SS7-capable database that provides a centralized point of information retrieval. It typically handles number translation services, such as toll-free and LPN; however, SCPs are also used for a number of additional IN/AIN services.

Figure 10-2 *Simple Query and Response*

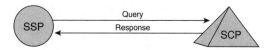

Role of TCAP in Call Control

TCAP is used to provide information to SSPs. This information is often used to enable successful call completion, but TCAP is not involved in the actual call-setup procedures. The protocol's circuit-related portion, such as ISUP and TUP, perform the call setup. This interaction between the service information provided by TCAP and the circuit-related protocol that performs the call setup occurs at the application level, not at the SS7 protocol layer. Within the SSP, the switching software that is responsible for call processing interacts with both the TCAP side of the SS7 stack and the call setup side of the stack (ISUP, TUP) to complete the call.

TCAP Within the SS7 Protocol Stack

As shown in Figure 10-3, TCAP is at level 4 of the SS7 protocol stack. It depends upon the SCCP's transport services because TCAP itself does not contain any transport information. First, SCCP must establish communication between services before TCAP data can be delivered to the application layer. Refer to Chapter 9, "Signaling Connection Control Part (SCCP)," for more information on SCCP's transport services. TCAP interfaces to the application layer protocols above it, such as the ITU Intelligent Network Application Part (INAP), ANSI AIN, and ANSI-41 Mobile Switching to provide service-related information in a generic format. The application layer that passes information down to be encapsulated within TCAP is known as a Transaction Capability User (TC-User). The terms application, service, and TC-User are used interchangeably.

Figure 10-3   *TCAP Within the SS7 Stack*

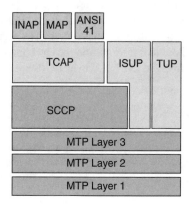

Transaction and Component Sublayers

The TCAP message is composed of two main sections: the transaction sublayer and the component sublayer. A transaction is a set of related TCAP messages that are exchanged between network nodes. The transaction portion identifies the messages that belong to the same transaction using a Transaction Identifier (TRID). The message's component portion contains the actual instructions, or "operations," that are being sent to the remote application. This chapter examines both areas in detail, along with the procedures surrounding their use.

Message Types

The TCAP *message type* (which is referred to as package type in ANSI) identifies the type of message being sent within the context of a transaction. Table 10-1 lists the seven package types for ANSI and Table 10-2 lists the five message types for ITU.

Table 10-1   *Package Types for ANSI*

ANSI Package Types	Hex Value	Description
Unidirectional	11100001	Sent in one direction and expects no reply.
Query with Permission	11100010	Initiates a transaction, giving the receiving node permission to end the transaction.
Query without Permission	11100011	Initiates a transaction but does not allow the receiving node to end the transaction.

Table 10-1   *Package Types for ANSI (Continued)*

ANSI Package Types	Hex Value	Description
Response	11100100	Ends a transaction.
Conversation with Permission	11100101	Continues a transaction, giving the receiving node permission to end the transaction.
Conversation without Permission	11100110	Continues a transaction, but does not allow the receiving node to end the transaction.
Abort	11110110	Sent to notify the destination node that an established transaction has been terminated without sending any further components that might be expected.

Table 10-2   *Message Types for ITU*

ITU Message Types	Hex Value	Description
Unidirectional	01100001	Sent in one direction and expects no reply.
Begin	01100010	Initiates a transaction.
(Reserved)	01100011	Not used.
End	01100100	Ends a transaction.
Continue	01100101	Continues an established transaction.
(Reserved)	01100110	Not used.
Abort	01100111	Sent to notify the destination node that an established transaction has been terminated without sending any further components that might be expected.

The message type also infers the stage of transaction processing. Figure 10-4 shows an example of an ITU conversation and an equivalent ANSI conversation. In ITU, a Begin message always starts a transaction, and an End message normally ends the transaction. (The "Transactions" section of this chapter discusses an exception to this rule.) The equivalent ANSI messages that begin and end transactions are Query (with or without permission) and Response, respectively. Conversation (ANSI) and Continue (ITU) messages indicate that further communication is required in an existing transaction.

Figure 10-4 *Examples of ITU and ANSI Message Flow*

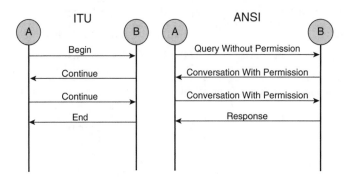

Transactions

The services that use TCAP vary in complexity. Some require a node to translate and receive only a single message. For example, a basic toll-free call typically works in this manner. Other services, such as Call Completion to a Busy Subscriber (CCBS), can exchange a number of messages between nodes.

A *transaction* is a set of related messages that are exchanged between application processes at two different nodes. At any time, a node can have many simultaneous transactions in progress and send and receive multiple TCAP messages. For example, several subscribers might invoke a CCBS during the same period of time.

NOTE   *CCBS* is a subscriber feature used for completing calls to a busy subscriber by monitoring the called party's line and completing a call attempt when the called party is free. TCAP messages are exchanged between the telephony switches of the calling and called parties to monitor the busy line and provide notification when it is free. The service is also popularly known as *Automatic Callback*.

When a node sends a message and expects a reply, the sending node establishes and maintains a Transaction ID. This allows an incoming message to be properly associated with previously sent messages.

Transaction IDs

Transactions always begin with an initiating TCAP message that contains an *Originating Transaction ID*. When the service has completed, the Transaction ID becomes available for use again by the application. Each transaction must have a unique Transaction ID for all outstanding transactions. When an ID is in use, it cannot be used again until the current transaction releases it. If the same ID belonged to two transactions, the system that received a message would not know the transaction to which it belonged. The ANSI Transaction ID is 4 octets in length, thereby allowing a total number of 2^{32} concurrent transactions to exist at a given time. The ITU Transaction ID is variable from 1 to 4 octets. Up to two Transaction IDs can be included in a TCAP message, an Originating Transaction ID, and a Responding Transaction ID (called a Destination Transaction ID in ITU). ANSI packages the Transaction IDs differently than ITU by nesting both IDs within a single Transaction ID Identifier. The following figure shows the Transaction ID section.

Figure 10-5 *Transaction ID Format*

ANSI Transaction ID Format

Transaction ID Identifier (10100111)
Length (0, 4 or 8)
Originating ID
Responding ID

ITU Transaction ID Format

Originating Transaction ID Tag (01001000)
Transaction ID Length
Transaction ID
Destination Transaction ID Tag (01001001)
Transaction ID Length
Transaction ID

Establishing Transaction IDs

The node that originates the transaction assigns an Originating Transaction ID, which the node sends to the destination in the first message, to establish the transaction. When the destination node receives a message, the application examines its contents and determines whether it should establish its own transaction.

When the destination node responds to the originating node, the message that is sent contains a Responding (or Destination) Transaction ID. The Responding Transaction ID is the same as the Originating Transaction ID that was received in the Begin/Query message. It can be thought of as a reflection of the Originating ID. The destination node examines the contents of the message to determine if it should establish a transaction with the originating node. If establishing a transaction is necessary, an Originating Transaction ID is assigned by the responding destination node and placed in an ANSI Conversation or ITU Continue message along with the Responding Transaction ID to be sent back to the transaction originator. In this situation, each node establishes a transaction from its own point of view. Depending on the message type, a TCAP message can contain zero, one, or two Transaction IDs. Tables 10-3 and 10-4 show the relationship between a message type and Transaction IDs for ITU and ANSI, respectively. For example, in Table 10-3, a Unidirectional message does not contain any Transaction IDs, while a Continue message contains two Transaction IDs.

Table 10-3   *ITU Message Transaction IDs*

ITU Message Type	Originating Transaction ID	Destination Transaction ID
Unidirectional	No	No
Begin	Yes	No
End	No	Yes
Continue	Yes	Yes
Abort	No	Yes

Table 10-4   *ANSI Message Transaction IDs*

ANSI Package Type	Originating Transaction ID	Responding Transaction ID
Unidirectional	No	No
Query with Permission	Yes	No
Query without Permission	Yes	No
Response	No	Yes
Conversation with Permission	Yes	Yes
Conversation without Permission	Yes	Yes
Abort	No	Yes

Releasing Transaction IDs

The communicating applications can end transactions in one of two ways: either with a terminating message or a prearranged end. The most common method is a terminating message—a Response package in ANSI and an End message in ITU. The prearranged transaction end is simply an agreement at the application layer that a transaction ends at a given point. Releasing the Transaction ID returns it to the available pool of IDs so that another transaction can use it.

Transaction Message Sequence

Applications do not always establish a transaction during TCAP communications. The Unidirectional message is used to communicate when no reply is expected, therefore, requiring no Transaction ID. All other messages require a Transaction ID.

Figure 10-6 shows an example of a transaction occurring between two SS7 nodes. A conversation is established between Node A and Node B. As mentioned previously, a Query or Begin message always initiates a transaction. Node A establishes a transaction with a

Transaction ID of 0. When the service logic at Node B processes the incoming message, it determines that it is necessary to establish a transaction from its own point of view. This is usually done to request additional information from the node that sent the message. In this example using the ANSI protocol, node B does not have a choice about engaging in a conversation because it has received a "Query without Permission" message. The message's "without Permission" designation is used to deny the receiving node the opportunity to end the transaction until it receives permission. In this example, Node B initiates a transaction with a Transaction ID of 1, thereby associating it with the received Transaction ID of 0.

Figure 10-6 *Transaction Example Using ANSI Protocol*

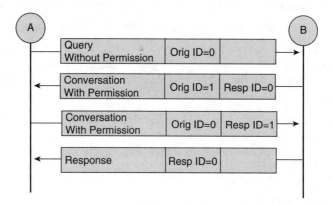

Figure 10-7 shows the same transaction using the ITU protocol. As shown by comparing the two examples, the two protocols are conceptually quite similar. Other than naming conventions and binary encoding, the primary difference is that the ITU message types do not explicitly state whether the receiving node must engage in a transaction from its perspective. This must be determined from the application logic.

Figure 10-7 *Transaction Example Using ITU Protocol*

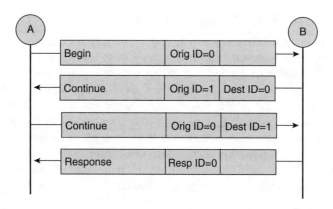

Components

Components are a means of invoking an operation at a remote node. A TCAP message can contain several components, thereby invoking several operations simultaneously. The TCAP component is based on the ITU X.410 specification for Remote Operations in Message Handling Systems. ITU X.229 has replaced this specification. The specification defines the following four Operational Protocol Data Units (OPDUs):

- **Invoke**—Requests an operation to be performed
- **Return Result**—Reports the successful completion of a requested operation
- **Return Error**—Reports the unsuccessful completion of a requested operation
- **Reject**—Reports a protocol violation, such as an incorrect or badly-formed OPDU

Each of the TCAP component types directly correlates to one of the previous OPDU types. The Invoke and Return Result component types are used for carrying out the normal operations between TCAP users. The Return Error and Reject component types are used for handling error conditions.

The contents of the Invoke and Return Result components include the following information:

- Component Type
- Component ID
- Operation Code (Invoke Component only)
- Parameters

The contents of the Return Error and Reject components are similar to the Invoke and Return Result components, except that the Operation Code used in an Invoke component is replaced by an Error/Problem code. The following sections discuss the contents of the components listed previously. The "Error Handling" section later in this chapter addresses the Return Error and Reject components.

Invoke and Return Result Components

Under normal circumstances, Invoke and Return Result Components are sent to carry out and verify operations between two communicating entities. For example, an SSP might "invoke" a number translation at an SCP, resulting in a new number being returned. A number of services, such as Toll-free, Premium Rate, and Local Number Portability, use TCAP to look up numbers in this manner. The application layer for these services and others use a standardized set of operations that is recognized by the network nodes involved in the communication. The information from the application layer is passed to the TCAP layer and encoded into components. Each Invoke Component is generally structured as an "instruction" and "data." The instructions are in the form of Operation Codes, which represent the operations that are being requested. The data is in the form of Parameters.

ITU Q.771 defines four classes of operations that determine how to handle Invoke replies. The TCAP message does not explicitly contain operation class information. Instead, it specifies the operation class using primitives between the application (TC-User) and the component sublayer.

NOTE   As used in this context, a primitive is a software indication that is used to pass information between software layers.

In other words, the indication of whether a reply is required and the tracking of whether that reply has been received are performed within the software. The main point is that operations can be handled differently, depending on the application logic. The four classes of operations are:

- **Class 1**—Success and failure are reported.
- **Class 2**—Only failure is reported.
- **Class 3**—Only success is reported.
- **Class 4**—Neither success nor failure is reported.

The application logic is also responsible for determining whether an operation is a success or a failure. Based on the operation's results, a reply might be required. If a reply is required, one of the following components is sent:

- **Return Result**—Indicates a successfully invoked operation
- **Return Error**—Indicates a problem
- **Reject**—Indicates an inability to carry out an operation

Here we focus only on the Return Result component; the "Error Handling" section discusses the Return Error and Reject components. The following are the two types of Return Result components:

- Return Result Last
- Return Result Not Last

The Return Result Last indicates that an operation's final result has been returned. The Return Result Not Last indicates that further results will be returned. This allows the result to be segmented across multiple components.

ANSI TCAP also allows the use of an Invoke to acknowledge a previous Invoke. Because ANSI allows an Invoke to be used in response to another Invoke where a Return Result would otherwise be used, the Invoke also has two types: *Invoke Last* and *Invoke Not Last*. There is only a single Invoke type in ITU networks, and it is the equivalent of the ANSI Invoke Last component type.

The details of segmenting results using the "Not Last" designation for both the Return Result and Invoke (ANSI Only) component types are more easily understood after a discussion of component IDs. We revisit this topic in a later section, after introducing correlation and linked-component IDs.

Component IDs

As mentioned previously, a message can contain several components. Each Invoke Component is coded with a numeric Invoke ID, which must be unique for each operation in progress because the ID is used to correlate the exchange of components for a particular operation. Just as a message can have several components, an operation can also have several parameters associated with it. Figure 10-8 shows an example of how Component IDs are used in an ANSI network message exchange. Node A sends a message to Node B that contains two Invoke Components indicating that two remote operations are being requested. Node B processes the incoming components, carries out the requested operations, and sends an Invoke Component and a Return Result Component back to Node A. The Invoke component contains two IDs: an Invoke ID and a Correlation ID (linked ID in ITU-T networks). As shown in this example, an Invoke ID can be used to respond to another Invoke ID, rather than using a Return Result. Node B is requesting an operation from Node A using Invoke ID 2 in response to the previously received Invoke, reflecting ID 1 in the Correlation ID. The Return Result Component in the message contains a Correlation ID of 0 to reflect the previous Invoke with a Component ID of 0 from Node A. Node A then replies to the Invoke ID 2 with a Return Result and also invokes another operation using Invoke ID 3 in the same Conversation message. Finally, Node B answers with a Return Result Not Last Component for Invoke ID 3, followed by a Return Result Last for the same Component ID. This completes the component exchange between the communicating nodes. Notice that for each Invoke, a reply was received using either another Invoke with a "Reflecting" ID (the correlation or linked ID) or a Return Result (Last) Component. The Correlation ID shown in the figure is used as the "Reflecting" ID in ANSI networks; for ITU networks, the Linked ID serves as the "Reflecting" ID.

Operation Codes

The *Operation Code* identifies the operation to be invoked at the node that receives the message. Operation Codes are context-dependent, meaning that they are understood only within the context of a particular service. For example, consider a caller who dials a toll-free number that is not supported in the region from which the caller is dialing. The SCP sends an Operation Code to the SSP for "Play an Announcement," instructing it to connect the subscriber to an announcement machine. The component that contains the "Play Announcement" Operation Code contains a parameter for identifying the proper announcement to be played. In this case, the caller hears an announcement that is similar to "The number you have dialed is not supported in your area."

Figure 10-8 *Component ID Association (ANSI Protocol)*

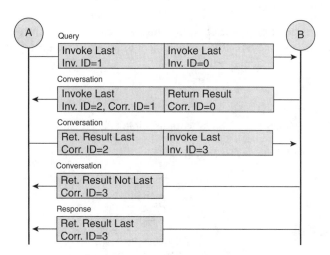

ANSI defines a number of national Operation Codes in the ANSI TCAP specifications. In ITU networks, these definitions are typically relegated to layers above the TCAP protocol, such as INAP. Examples of these can be found in Chapter 11.

Parameters

Components can have *parameters* associated with them. The parameters are the data that is necessary to carry out the operation requested by the component Operation Code. For example, a component containing a "Play Announcement" Operation Code also contains an announcement parameter. The announcement parameter typically provides the announcement ID so the correct recording is played to the listener. Just as a TCAP message can contain multiple components, a component can contain multiple parameters.

The ITU-T does not define any specific parameters. This responsibility is relegated to national or regional standards bodies, such as ANSI and ETSI. Parameters can be defined as part of the TCAP standards (for example, ANSI standards) or relegated to the definition of the protocol layers above TCAP, such as INAP (for example, ETSI standards). ANSI defines a number of national parameters in the ANSI T1.114 specification. Application processes can use these parameters directly.

Chapter 11, "Intelligent Networks" provides examples of TCAP parameters that are defined by protocols above the TCAP layer. The AIN and INAP parameters described here are used in TCAP messages for ANSI and ITU-T networks, respectively.

ANSI parameters are specified either as part of a set or a sequence. A parameter set is used when parameters are delivered with no particular order and can be processed in any order.

A parameter sequence specifies that the parameters should be processed in the order in which they are received.

ITU-T does not use parameter sequencing, so there is no designation of set or sequence. Parameters are handled in the same manner as an ANSI parameter set, with delivery occurring in no particular order.

ITU Parameters

Figure 10-9 shows a component with multiple ITU parameters.

Figure 10-9   *Component with Multiple ITU Parameters*

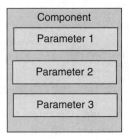

Dialogue Portion

The dialogue portion of the message is optional and is used to convey information about a dialogue between nodes at the component sublayer. It establishes a flow of information within a particular context for a transaction. Information, such as the protocol version and application context, is used to ensure that two nodes interpret the component sublayer's contents in the same manner using an agreed upon set of element definitions.

ITU Dialogue

There are two categories of dialogues: structured and unstructured. An unstructured dialogue is one in which no reply is expected. This type of dialogue uses a Unidirectional message type at the transaction layer. A structured dialogue requires a reply.

Within these two general categories of dialogues, dialogue-control Application Protocol Data Units (APDU) are used to convey dialogue information between TC-Users. The following are four types of APDU:

- Dialogue Request
- Dialogue Response
- Dialogue Abort
- Dialogue Unidirectional

Following is a description of each of these APDU and the information elements contained therein. The ITU unstructured dialogue uses the following dialogue-control APDU:

- **Unidirectional Dialogue**—The Unidirectional Dialogue consists of an Application Context Name and optional Protocol Version and User Information. It is used to convey dialogue information in one direction, for which no reply is expected.

The structured dialogue uses the following dialogue-control APDUs:

- **Dialogue Request**—The Dialogue Request consists of an Application Context Name and, optionally, Protocol Version and User Information. It is used to request dialogue information from another node, such as the context between the nodes (what set of operations will be included) and to distinguish that the correct protocol version is being used to interpret the information that is being sent.

- **Dialogue Response**—The Dialogue Response is sent as a reply to a Dialogue Request. In addition to the information elements of the Dialogue Request, it includes a Result field and a Result Source Diagnostic element. The result indicates whether the dialogue has been accepted. If a Rejection indication is returned, the dialogue does not continue. In cases where rejection occurs, the Result Diagnostic indicates why a dialogue is rejected.

As you can see from the descriptions, a number of the dialogue information elements are common across the dialogue APDU types. Following is a brief description of the dialogue information elements:

- **Application Context Name**—Identifies the application to which the dialogue components apply.

- **Protocol Version**—Indicates the version of the dialogue portion that can be supported. This helps ensure proper interpretation of the dialogue information between TC-Users when new versions of the dialogue portion are created.

- **User Information**—Information exchanged between TC-Users that is defined by and relevant only to the application. The contents of the user information element are not standardized.

- **Result**—Provides the initiating TC-User with the result of the request to establish a dialogue.

- **Result Source Diagnostic**—Identifies the source of the *Result* element and provides additional diagnostic information.

- **Abort Source**—Identifies the source of an abnormal dialogue release. The source might be the TC-User or the dialogue portion of the message.

- **Dialogue Abort**—The Dialogue Abort is used to terminate a dialogue before it would normally be terminated. The Dialogue Abort contains only an *Abort Source* and, optionally, *User Information*. The Abort Source is used to indicate where the Abort was initiated—from the user or the service provider.

ANSI Dialogue

The *ANSI Dialogue* can contain any of the following optional Dialogue elements. Note that the Application Context and Security can use either an integer for identification or an OID (Object Identifier). The OID is a common structure used for identifying objects in communications protocols by using a hierarchical tree notation such as "3.2.4."

- **Dialogue Portion Identifier**—This identifier indicates the beginning of the dialogue portion of the message. The following elements are included within this dialogue section.

- **Protocol Version**—Identifies the version of TCAP to be used in interpreting the message; for example, T1.114 version 1992 versus TCAP T1.114 version 1996.

- **Application Context Integer/Application Context OID**—Identifies the context in which to interpret the message. Since TCAP is generic and the operations must always be interpreted in the context of a particular service or set of services that use unique identifiers for each operation, this can be used to specify the context.

- **User Information–**—Provides additional information that is only relevant to the application, to assist the receiving TC-User (such as an application) in interpreting the received TCAP data. An example is including a version number for the application that uses the encapsulated TCAP components.

- **Security Context Integer/Security Context OID**—Used for establishing a secure dialog. The Security Context is used to determine how other security information, such as Confidentiality, should be interpreted.

- **Confidentiality Integer**—Used to specify how confidentiality is accomplished by providing encryption/decryption procedures. It contains the following optional fields. If neither of these optional fields is included, the confidentiality information is not used because no specification exists regarding how information should be protected or interpreted.

  - **Confidentiality Algorithm ID**—An integer or OID that identifies the algorithm to use for decoding encrypted data.

  - **Confidentiality Value**—Any information that can be encoded using Basic Encoding Rules (BER). The BER are the ITU X.690 ASN.1 (Abstract Syntax Notation) rules for encoding information into binary format for transmission.

Message Encoding

The TCAP data element encoding is based on the ITU X.680 and X.690 ASN.1 standards. Many of the SS7 standards reference the older versions of these documents (X.208 and X.209). The ASN.1 provides a means of describing complex data structures in a logical, readable text form and specifying encoding procedures for transmission in binary form.

The following example shows the ASN.1 definition for the ANSI TCAP package type and is taken directly from the ANSI T1.114 specification.

Example 10-1 *The ANSI Definition for the ANSI TCAP Package Type*

```
PackageType   ::= CHOICE { unidirectional   [PRIVATE 1]   IMPLICIT UniTransactionPDU
                     QueryWithPerm        [PRIVATE 2]   IMPLICIT Transaction PDU
                     queryWithoutPerm     [PRIVATE 3]   IMPLICIT Transaction PDU
                     response             [PRIVATE 4]   IMPLICIT Transaction PDU
              conversationWithPerm        [PRIVATE 5]   IMPLICIT Transaction PDU
          conversationWithoutPerm         [PRIVATE 6]   IMPLICIT Transaction PDU
                     abort                [PRIVATE 22] IMPLICIT Abort }
```

The data is described in a precise way using textual description. In this example, the package type is a choice of one of the designated types—unidirectional, queryWithPerm, and so forth. Each is coded as a "Private" Class (which we discuss shortly) and has a defined numeric identifier. Also, the choice of the package type implies whether it is a UniTransactionPDU, a Transaction PDU, or an Abort. While this is a simple example, ASN.1 is used to describe very complex nested structures. You can find complete TCAP definitions in ASN.1 format in both the ANSI T1.114 and the ITU Q.773 specifications.

Element Structure

From a structural point of view, a TCAP message is a collection of data elements. Each element takes the form of Identifier, Length, and Contents. The TCAP element is the basic building block for constructing a message.

Figure 10-10 *TCAP Element*

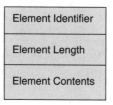

The TCAP element is constructed with a commonly used data encoding scheme, which is often referred to as TLV: Tag, Length, Value format. The identifier specifies the type of element so that the receiving node can interpret its contents correctly. The length is the number of bytes in the element contents, beginning with the first byte past the element length. The contents are the actual data payload being transmitted.

Element Identifier

The *Element Identifier* is one or more octets comprised of bit fields that creates the class, form, and tag. Tables 10-5 and 10-6 list the values for the class and form. Bit H is the most significant bit.

Table 10-5 *Class Values*

Class	Bit Value Bits (HG)	Definition
Universal	00	Universal
Application-wide	01	International TCAP
Context-specific	10	Context Specific
Private Use	11	National TCAP/Private TCAP

The class defines the identifier's scope or context. The universal class is used for identifiers that are defined in X.690 and do not depend on the application. Application-wide is used for international standardized TCAP. Context-specific identifiers are defined within the application for a limited context, such as a particular ASN.1 sequence. Private Use identifiers can be defined within a private network. These identifiers vary in scope and can represent elements within a national network, such as ANSI, or can be defined within a smaller private network. The tag bits (bits A-E) help to further determine whether the element is national or private. For more information, see "Identifier Tag" in this section.

Constructors and Primitives

The Form bit (Bit F) indicates whether the value is a primitive or constructor, as listed in Table 10-6. A primitive is simply an atomic value.

NOTE   An *atomic value* is one that cannot be broken down into further parts. Be careful not to confuse the term primitive, used here, with software primitives, used earlier in the chapter.

A constructor can contain one or more elements, thereby creating a nested structure. For example, a Component Tag is a constructor because a component is made up of several elements, such as the Invoke ID and Operation Code.

Table 10-6   *Form Bit*

Form	Bit F
Primitive	0
Constructor	1

Identifier Tag

Bits A-E of the element identifier uniquely identify the element within a given class. If all bits are set to 1, this is a special indicator, which specifies that the identifier is octet-extended. In this case, one or more octets follow with additional identifier bits. This format allows the protocol to scale in order to handle a potentially large number of identifiers. If Bit H in the extension octet is set to 1, the identifier is octet-extended to another octet. If it is set to 0, it indicates the identifier's last octet. In the following table, the identifier is extended to three octets using the extension mechanism. As previously noted, the identifier is further discriminated based on the tag bits. When coded as class Private Use, bits A-E are used for national TCAP. If bits A-E are all coded to 1, the G bit in the first extension octet (X13 in the example below) indicates whether it is private or national. The G bit is set to 0 for national or to 1 for private.

Table 10-7   *Class Encoding Mechanism*

H	G	F	E	D	C	B	A	
CLASS		0	1	1	1	1	1	First Octet
1	X13	X12	X11	X10	X9	X8	X7	Second Octet
0	X6	X5	X4	X3	X2	X1	X0	Third Octet

An example illustrates how class, form, and tag are used to create a TCAP element. Figure 10-11 shows an ITU Begin message type in its binary form as it is transmitted on the signaling link. Bit A represents the least significant bit. The ITU Q.773 specification defines the ASN.1 description in the following manner:

Example 10-2 *ASN.1 Definition for ITU Begin Message*

```
MessageType ::= Choice {unidirectional [APPLICATION 1] IMPLICIT Unidirectional,
                  Begin          [APPLICATION 2] IMPLICIT Begin,
```

The message type is defined with a class of Application-wide and a tag of 2. It is a constructor because the message is comprised of multiple elements.

Figure 10-11 *ITU Begin Message Type Encoding*

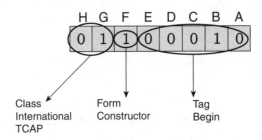

Class
International
TCAP

Form
Constructor

Tag
Begin

Length Identifier

The length field is also coded using an extension mechanism. If the length is 127 octets or less, Bit H is set to 0 and bits A-G contain the length. If the length is 128 or greater, Bit H is set to 1 and A-G contains the number of octets used to encode the Length field. The additional octets contain the actual length of the element contents. Table 10-8 shows an example using the extension mechanism to represent a length of 131 octets. The H bit is set in the first octet, and the value represented by bits A-G is 1; this means that one additional byte is used to represent the length. The second octet indicates that the element is 131 octets in length using standard binary representation.

Table 10-8 *Length Identifier Bits*

Length Identifier Bits								
H	G	F	E	D	C	B	A	
1	0	0	0	0	0	0	1	First Octet
1	0	0	0	0	0	1	1	Second Octet

Message Layout

Now that we have examined in detail how each of the TCAP data elements are constructed, let's take a look at how they are assimilated into a message. There are three distinct sections into which a message is divided: the transaction, dialogue, and component portions. The dialogue portion of the message is optional. Figure 10-12 shows the complete structure of a TCAP message within the context of its supporting SS7 levels.

Figure 10-12 *TCAP Message Structure*

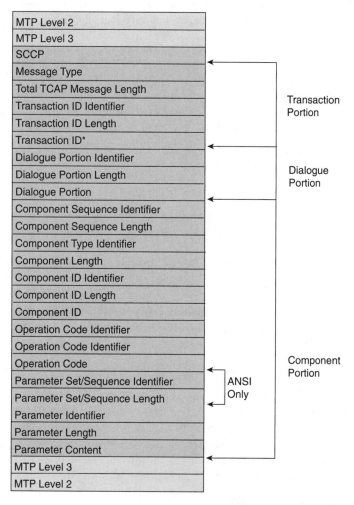

| MTP Level 2 |
| MTP Level 3 |
| SCCP |
| Message Type |
| Total TCAP Message Length |
| Transaction ID Identifier |
| Transaction ID Length |
| Transaction ID* |
| Dialogue Portion Identifier |
| Dialogue Portion Length |
| Dialogue Portion |
| Component Sequence Identifier |
| Component Sequence Length |
| Component Type Identifier |
| Component Length |
| Component ID Identifier |
| Component ID Length |
| Component ID |
| Operation Code Identifier |
| Operation Code Identifier |
| Operation Code |
| Parameter Set/Sequence Identifier |
| Parameter Set/Sequence Length |
| Parameter Identifier |
| Parameter Length |
| Parameter Content |
| MTP Level 3 |
| MTP Level 2 |

Transaction Portion

Dialogue Portion

Component Portion

ANSI Only

*0, 1, or 2 Transaction ID fields may be included, depending on message type.

From the message structure, you can see the TLV format that is repeated throughout, in the form of Identifier, Length, and Content. A single component is shown with a single parameter in its parameter set; however, multiple parameters could exist within the component. If multiple parameters are included, another parameter identifier would immediately follow the Parameter Content field of the previous parameter. The message could also contain multiple components, in which case the next component would follow the last parameter of the previous component. Only the maximum MTP message length limits the TCAP message length.

Error Handling

As with any other protocol, errors can occur during TCAP communications. TCAP errors fall into three general categories:

- Protocol Errors
- Application Errors
- End-user Errors

Protocol Errors

Protocol Errors are the result of TCAP messages being incorrectly formed, containing illegal values, or being received when not expected. For example, receiving an unrecognized message type or component type would constitute a protocol error. Another example of an error would be receiving a responding Transaction ID for a nonexistent transaction. While the actual value of the ID might be within the acceptable range of values, the lack of a transaction with which to associate the response causes a protocol error.

Errors at the Transaction Layer

Protocol Errors that occur at the transaction sublayer are reported to the remote node by sending an Abort message type with a P-Abort cause—in other words, a Protocol Abort. The Abort message is sent only when a transaction must be closed and a Transaction ID can be derived from the message in which the error occurred. Figure 10-13 shows an Abort message being sent for an open transaction in which a protocol error is detected.

Figure 10-13 *Protocol Error Causes an Abort*

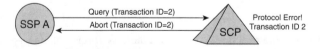

Because no Transaction ID is associated with a Unidirectional message, no Abort message would be sent if the message was received with an error. If a Query or Begin message is received and the Originating Transaction ID cannot be determined because of the message error, the message is simply discarded and an Abort message is not returned to the sender.

If the Transaction ID can be determined, the Abort message is sent to report the error. Without the Transaction ID, there is no way for the sending node to handle the error because it cannot make an association with the appropriate transaction.

Errors at the Component Layer

Protocol errors at the component sublayer are reported using a Reject Component. The errored component's Component ID is reflected in the Reject Component. A number of different errors can be detected and reported. For example, a duplicate Invoke ID error indicates that an Invoke ID has been received for an operation that is already in progress. This results in an ambiguous reference because both operations have the same ID. Another type of error is a component that is simply coded with an incorrect value, such as an unrecognized component type. Refer to the TCAP specifications for a complete list of errors that can be detected and reported.

Application Errors

Application Errors are anomalies within the application procedure. An example is an unexpected component sequence, in which the received components do not match what the application procedures expect. Another example is a missing customer record error, which is an error that is used to indicate that a database lookup failed to find the requested information. The application is responsible for determining what actions to take when errors of this type are encountered.

End-User Errors

The *End-User Error* is similar to the Application Error in that it is an anomaly of the application procedure. However, as indicated by the name, the anomaly is the result of some variance from the normal actions by the user. The user might take an action, such as abandoning the call prematurely, as shown in Figure 10-14; or the user might enter an unexpected response when connected to a digit collection unit and prompted for input, thereby causing the error.

Handling Application and End-User Errors

Both the Application Error and the End-User Error are reported using the *Return Error* component for component-related errors. Because the errors in these two categories are actually variations in the application's script or procedure flow, the application determines how they are handled. These errors also imply that no error exists at the actual TCAP layer because a protocol error would trigger prior to an error at the application level. The application can also send an Abort message type (U-Abort) to the other node to indicate that a *User Abort* has occurred for the transaction and that it should be closed.

Figure 10-14 *Error Caused by User Action*

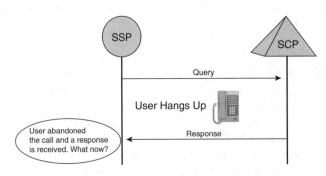

ITU Protocol Message Contents

The definition of each message type indicates a set of fields that comprise the message. While some fields are mandatory, others are optional. As specified by Q.773, the standard set of ITU messages includes:

- Unidirectional
- Begin
- End
- Continue
- Abort

The following sections describe these messages, the fields that are included in each one, and indicate which fields are mandatory or optional.

Unidirectional Message

The *Unidirectional Message* is sent when no reply is expected. Table 10-9 lists the message contents.

Table 10-9 *Unidirectional Message Fields*

Unidirectional Message Fields	Mandatory/Optional
Message Type Total Message Length	Mandatory
Dialogue Portion	Optional

Table 10-9   *Unidirectional Message Fields (Continued)*

Unidirectional Message Fields	Mandatory/Optional
Component Portion Tag Component Portion Length	Mandatory
One or More Components	Mandatory

Begin Message

The *Begin Message* is sent to initiate a transaction. Table 10-10 lists the message contents.

Table 10-10   *Begin Message Fields*

Begin Message Fields	Mandatory/Optional
Message Type Total Message Length	Mandatory
Originating Transaction ID Tag Transaction ID Length Transaction ID	Mandatory
Dialogue Portion	Optional
Component Portion Tag Component Portion Length	Optional[*]
One or More Components	Optional

[*]   The component Portion Tag is present only if the message contains components.

End Message

The *End Message* is sent to end a transaction. Table 10-11 lists the message contents.

Table 10-11   *End Message Fields*

End Message Fields	Mandatory/Optional
Message Type Total Message Length	Mandatory
Destination Transaction ID Tag Transaction ID Length Transaction ID	Mandatory

continues

Table 10-11   *End Message Fields (Continued)*

End Message Fields	Mandatory/Optional
Dialogue Portion	Optional
Component Portion Tag Component Portion Length	Optional[*]
One or More Components	Optional

[*]   The component Portion Tag is present only the message contains components.

Continue Message

The *Continue Message* is sent when a transaction has previously been established and additional information needs to be sent without ending the transaction. Table 10-12 lists the message contents.

Table 10-12   *Continue Message Fields*

Continue Message Fields	Mandatory/Optional
Message Type Total Message Length	Mandatory
Originating Transaction ID Tag Transaction ID Length Transaction ID	Mandatory
Destination Transaction ID Tag Transaction ID Length Transaction ID	Mandatory
Dialogue Portion	Optional
Component Portion Tag Component Portion Length	Optional[*]
One or More Components	Optional

[*]   The component Portion Tag is present only if the message contains components.

Abort Message

The *Abort Message* is sent to terminate a previously established transaction. Table 10-13 lists the message contents.

Table 10-13 *Abort Message Fields*

Abort Message Fields	Mandatory/Optional
Message Type Total Message Length	Mandatory
Destination Transaction ID Tag Transaction ID Length Transaction ID	Mandatory
P-Abort Cause Tag P-Abort Cause Length P-Abort Cause	Optional[*]
Dialogue Portion	Optional

[*]   P-Abort is present when the TC-User generates the Abort message.

ANSI Protocol Message Contents

The following sections describe the set of ANSI messages, the fields included in each, and specify the mandatory and optional fields for each message type. The message types specified by ANSI include:

- Unidirectional
- Query
- Conversation
- Response
- Protocol abort
- User abort
- Dialogue portion

In the messages, fields marked as "Mandatory*" must be present, but their contents can be empty.

Unidirectional Message

The *Unidirectional Message* is sent when no reply is expected. Table 10-14 lists the message contents.

Table 10-14   *Unidirectional Message Fields*

Unidirectional Message Fields	Mandatory/Optional
Package Type Identifier Total Message Length	Mandatory
Transaction ID Identifier Transaction ID Length (Set to 0)	Mandatory
Dialogue Portion	Optional
Component Sequence Identifier Component Sequence Length Components	Mandatory

Query With/Without Permission

The *Query Message* is used to initiate a transaction. There are two types of Query messages: *Query with Permission* and *Query without Permission*.

The Query with Permission message gives the receiving node permission to end the transaction at any time.

The Query without Permission message does not give the receiving node permission to end the transaction. After receiving this message, the transaction remains established until the originator ends it or sends a subsequent message giving the receiving node permission to end the transaction. Table 10-15 lists the message contents.

Table 10-15 *Query Message Fields*

Query With/Without Permission Message Fields	Mandatory/Optional
Package Type Identifier Total Message Length	Mandatory
Transaction ID Identifier Transaction ID Length Originating Transaction ID	Mandatory
Dialogue Portion	Optional
Component Sequence Identifier Component Sequence Length Components	Optional

Conversation With/Without Permission

The *Conversation Message* is used to exchange additional information for a previously established transaction. There are two types of Conversation Messages: *Conversation with Permission* and *Conversation without Permission Message*.

The Conversation with Permission Message gives the receiving node permission to end the transaction at any time.

The Conversation without Permission message does not give the receiving node permission to end the transaction. After receiving this message, the transaction remains established until the originator ends it or sends a subsequent message giving the receiving node permission to end the transaction. Table 10-16 lists the message contents.

Table 10-16 *Conversation Message Fields*

Conversation With/Without Permission Message Fields	Mandatory/Optional
Package Type Identifier Total Message Length	Mandatory
Transaction ID Identifier Transaction ID Length Originating Transaction ID Responding Transaction ID	Mandatory
Dialogue Portion	Optional
Component Sequence Identifier Component Sequence Length Components	Optional

Response Message

The *Response Message* is sent to end a transaction. Table 10-17 lists the message contents.

Table 10-17 *Response Message Fields*

Response Message Fields	Mandatory/Optional
Package Type Identifier Total Message Length	Mandatory
Transaction ID Identifier Transaction ID Length Responding Transaction ID	Mandatory

continues

Table 10-17 *Response Message Fields (Continued)*

Response Message Fields	Mandatory/Optional
Dialogue Portion	Optional
Component Sequence Identifier Component Sequence Length Components	Optional

Protocol Abort (P-Abort) Message

The *Protocol Abort (P-Abort) Message* is sent to terminate a previously established transaction. A P-Abort is initiated because of an error at the TCAP protocol layer. Table 10-18 lists the message contents.

Table 10-18 *Abort Message Fields*

Abort (P-Abort) Message Fields	Mandatory/Optional
Message Type Total Message Length	Mandatory
Transaction ID Identifier Transaction ID Length Transaction ID	Mandatory
P-Abort Cause Identifier P-Abort Cause Length P-Abort Cause	Mandatory

User Abort (U-Abort) Message

The *User Abort (U-Abort) Message* is sent to terminate a previously established transaction. A U-Abort is initiated at the Application Layer based on application logic. Table 10-19 lists the message contents.

Table 10-19 *User Abort Message Fields*

Abort (U-Abort) Message Fields	Mandatory/Optional
Message Type Total Message Length	Mandatory
Transaction ID Identifier Transaction ID Length Transaction ID	Mandatory

Table 10-19 *User Abort Message Fields (Continued)*

Abort (U-Abort) Message Fields	Mandatory/Optional
Dialogue Portion	Optional
U-Abort Information Identifier	Mandatory
U-Abort Information Length	
U-Abort Information	

ANSI National Operations

The *ANSI Operation Codes* are divided into an Operation Family and an Operation Specifier. Each specifier belongs to a family and must be interpreted in the context of that family. ANSI defines a base set of national operation codes and parameters. At the time of this writing, these codes and parameters continue to be used for IN services such as toll-free and LNP; however, specifications now exist to provide the AIN-equivalent functionality for these services. Table 10-21 lists the operation families with their associated specifiers and definitions.

Table 10-20 *ANSI Operation Codes*

Operation Family	Operation Specifier	Binary Value	Definition
Parameter		00000001	Indicates an operation to be performed on a parameter.
	Provide Value	00000001	Request to provide a value for this parameter.
	Set Value	00000010	Request to set the parameter's value.
Charging		00000010	Charging operations are related to how calls are billed.
	Bill Call	00000001	Indicates that a billing record should be made for this call.
Provide Instructions		00000011	Requests instructions according to the service script, which is the application logic that is used to implement a service and handle the incoming and outgoing TCAP message information.
	Start	00000001	Initiates the interpretation of the service script.
	Assist	00000010	Used to request instructions when assisting with a service request. This situation arises when a node does not have the necessary resources, such as an announcement or IVR system, to connect to the user and another node that has the proper resources is connected to "assist" with the transaction.

continues

Table 10-20 *ANSI Operation Codes (Continued)*

Operation Family	Operation Specifier	Binary Value	Definition
Connection Control		00000100	Used for specifying the handling of call connections.
	Connect	00000001	Indicates that a connection is to be made using the given called address.
	Temporary Connect	00000010	A connection is to be made using the given called address and will be followed by a Forward Disconnect. The Forward Disconnect releases the connection to the temporary resource.
	Disconnect	00000011	Used to terminate a connection.
	Forward Disconnect	00000100	This operation informs a node that might discontinue its Temporary Connect to another node.
Caller Interaction		00000101	This family is used for instructing a node about how to interact with a caller. This can include such operations as connecting the collector to an announcement or collecting digits from the user.
	Play Announcement	00000001	Indicates that an announcement should be played to the caller. An Announcement Identifier specifies which announcement should be played.
	Play Announcement and Collect Digits	00000010	This operation plays an announcement and then collects digits from the user. In this case, announcements typically provide the appropriate prompts to request information from the caller.
	Indicate Information Waiting	00000011	This operation specifies to another application process that information is waiting.
	Indicate Information Provided	00000100	Informs an application process that all information has been provided.
Send Notification		00000110	This family is used to request the notification of an event, such as a change of call state.
	When Party Free	00000001	The sender should be informed when the party is idle.
Network Management		00000111	This family is used for Network Management operations.
	Automatic Code Gap	00000001	Selective inhibiting of codes are initiated for a given period of time.

Table 10-20 *ANSI Operation Codes (Continued)*

Operation Family	Operation Specifier	Binary Value	Definition
Procedural Family		00001000	This family is used to indicate a particular procedure to be performed.
	Temporary Handover	00000001	Obsolete specifier that was formerly used in a Temporary Handover.
	Report Assist Termination	00000010	This operation indicates the end of an Assist.
	Security	00000011	This operation passes the Security Authorization, Integrity, Sequence Number and Time Stamp parameters for identification, authorization, and access control.
Operation Control		00001001	This family allows the subsequent control of operations that have been invoked.
	Cancel	00000001	This operation is used to cancel a previously invoked operation. For example, if a Send Notification has been invoked, this operation can be used to cancel this notification.
Report Event		00001010	This family is used to indicate that an event has occurred at a remote location.
	Voice Message Available	00000001	This operation is used to report that a voice message is available from a Voice Message Storage and Retrieval (VMSR) system.
	Voice Message Retrieved	00000010	This operation is used to indicate that the message available indicator for a VMSR subscriber should be removed.
Miscellaneous		11111110	A general Operation Family that does not fit in the other family categories.
	Queue Call	00000001	This operation is used to place a call in the call queue. Many voice features use various call queuing, such as multiple instances of Automatic Callback, Automatic Redial, and Automatic Call Distribution.
	Dequeue Call	00000010	This operation is used to remove a call from call queue.

ANSI Parameters

The following is a list of the national parameters defined for ANSI networks, the binary value of the parameter identifier, and a brief description of each. Because they are small values, the enumerations for the parameter indicator subfields are shown in decimal value for simplicity.

Time Stamp (00010111)—Defines the time that an event occurred in the form of YY/MM/DD/hh/mm, along with a time delta between local time and Greenwich Mean Time. The time delta provides a reference point for nodes in different time zones so timestamps can be compared meaningfully.

Automatic Code Gap Indicators (10000001)—Sent to control the number of operations being requested. This is typically used in overload situations where a large number of messages are being received for a specific range of number codes. It is sent for the following causes:

- **Vacant Code (01)**—Calls received for an unassigned number.
- **Out of Band (02)**—Calls received for a customer who has not subscribed.
- **Database Overload (03)**—The database is overloaded.
- **Destination Mass Calling (04)**—An excessive number of calls are being received for a destination.
- **Operational Support System Initiated (05)**—An OSS has initiated ACG OSS.

Additional fields identifying the duration for applying the control and the interval in seconds between controls are also sent as part of the parameter.

Standard Announcement (10000010)—Indicates one of the standard announcements, which include:

- **Out of Band (01)**—Customer is not subscribed to this zone or band.
- **Vacant Code (02)**—Unassigned number.
- **Disconnected Number (03)**—The called number has been disconnected.
- **Reorder (04)**—All trunks are busy. Uses the standard 120 IPM tone cadence.
- **Busy (05)**—The called number is busy. Uses the standard 60 IPM tone cadence.
- **No Circuit Available (06)**—No circuit is available for reaching the called number.
- **Reorder (07)**—A Reorder announcement is played instead of a Reorder tone.
- **Audible Ring (08)**—An indication that the called party is being alerted.

Customized Announcement (10000011)—Used to identify a customized announcement that is not part of the standard announcements. It includes an Announcement Set and an Announcement Identifier, both of which are user-defined.

Digits (10000100)—Used to provide digit information and includes the following information:

- **Type of Digits**—Identifies the type of digits, such as Called Party, Calling Party, LATA digits, and so forth.
- **Nature of Number**—Indicates whether digits are National or International and indicates the Presentation Restriction Indicator.

- **Encoding**—Indicates whether the digits are encoded using a Binary Coded Decimal or IA5 method.
- **Numbering Plan**—Indicates the numbering plan, such as ISDN or telephony.
- **Number of Digits**—The number of digits that are included.
- **Digits**—The actual digit string.

Standard User Error Code (10000101)—Provides the Error Identifier for User Errors. The errors can be:

- **Caller Abandon**—The caller hangs up before the TCAP transaction is complete.
- **Improper Caller Response**—The caller provides unexpected input during an operation involving caller interaction, such as when being prompted for digits by a voice menu system.

Problem Data (10000110)—Indicates the data that caused a problem in a TCAP transaction. The problem data element is contained within the parameter.

SCCP Calling Party Address (10000111)—Obsolete parameter that was previously used in a Temporary Handover.

Transaction ID (10001000)—Obsolete parameter that was previously used in a Temporary Handover.

Package Type (10001001)—Obsolete parameter that was previously used in a Temporary Handover.

Service Key (10001010)—The Service Key is an encapsulation parameter that is used for accessing a database record. Its contents consist of additional parameters that are used as the record's key.

Busy/Idle Status (10001011)—Indicates whether a line is busy or idle. The status field is set to one of the following:

- Busy (01)
- Idle (02)

Call Forwarding Status (10001100)—Indicates the availability and status of a line's Call Forwarding feature. The following Call Forwarding variants are indicated within the parameter:

- Selective Forwarding
- Call Forwarding Don't Answer
- Call Forwarding on Busy
- Call Forwarding Variable

Each variant's status is provided as a 2-bit field with one of the following values:

- Service Not Supported (0)
- Active (1)
- Not Active (2)

Originating Restrictions (10001101)—Identifies restrictions on a line's outgoing calls. For example, a business might restrict its employees from making long distance calls to outside parties. The Restrictions Identifier has one of the following values:

- **Denied Originating (0)**—No originating calls are permitted.

- **Fully Restricted Originating (1)**—Direct and indirect access to parties outside of a Business Group are blocked.

- **Semi-Restricted Originating (2)**—Direct access to parties outside of a Business Group are blocked, but the caller can still access outside parties through the attendant, call forwarding, call pick-up, three-way calling, call transfer, and conferencing.

- **Unrestricted Originating (3)**—No restrictions exist on the calls that might normally be originated.

Terminating Restrictions (10001110)—Identifies any restrictions on a line's incoming calls. An example would be a business that does not allow direct, incoming calls to an employee from outside of the company. The Terminating Restriction Identifier has one of the following values:

- **Denied Termination (0)**—No calls are permitted to be terminated.

- **Fully Restricted Terminating (1)**—Direct access from parties outside of a Business Group are blocked.

- **Semi-restricted Terminating (2)**—Direct access from parties outside of a Business Group are blocked, but calls from an attendant, call forwarded calls, call pick-up, three-way calling, call transfer, and conferencing are.

- **Unrestricted Terminating (3)**—No restrictions exist on calls that are terminated to the line.

- **Call Rejection Applies (4)**—An indication that the called party has requested to reject a call.

Directory Number to Line Service Type Mapping (10001111)—Indicates what type of line service type is associated with a Directory Number. The Identifier has one of the following values:

- **Individual (0)**—Single Party Service in which only one subscriber is associated with the line.

- **Coin (1)**—A pay station line.

- **Multi-line Hunt (2)**—Calls coming to a single DN are routed to one of multiple lines in a Hunt Group associated with the DN. This allows one number to be advertised with multiple agents handling calls to that number.

- **PBX (3)**—A Private Branch Exchange line.

- **Choke (4)**—A DN to which Network Management constraints are applied.

- **Series Completion (5)**—Calls to a busy line are routed to another DN in the same office.

- **Unassigned DN (6)**—The DN is valid, but not assigned or not subscribed to a customer.

- **Multi-Party (7)**—A line shared by two or more parties.

- **Non-Specific (8)**—A service type that does not fit into any of the above categories.

- **Temporarily Out of Service (9)**—A DN that is out of service temporarily.

Duration (10010000)—The Duration parameter provides timing information in the form of hours, minutes, and seconds to allow a service to specify a timer for an operation. For example, if a "Send Notification When Party Free" is issued, the duration indicates the period of time during which the line is monitored to detect an idle line.

Returned Data (10010001)—When a problem occurs with a parameter, this parameter can be used to return the actual data that caused the problem.

Bearer Capability Requested (10010010)—Indicates the Bearer Capabilities that are being requested. Bearer Capabilities describe the attributes of the physical medium that is being used. For example, the Information Transfer Capability category describes whether the information being transferred is speech, 3.1kHz audio, video, and so on. You can request the following bearer capabilities:

- Coding Standard
- Information Transfer Capability
- Transfer Mode
- Information Transfer Rate
- Structure
- Configuration
- Establishment
- Symmetry
- Information Transfer Rate
- Multiplier or Layer Identification
- Bearer Capability Multiplier/Protocol Identification

Bearer Capability Supported (10010011)—Indicates whether a requested Bearer Capability is supported. The Indicator has one of the following values:

- Bearer Capability is not supported (01)
- Bearer Capability is supported (02)
- Not authorized (03)
- Not presently available (04)
- Not implemented (05)

Reference ID (10010100)—Identifies the transaction between the database and an exchange during a service assist.

Business Group Parameter (10010101)—Contains the Multilocation Business Group (MBG) information that is associated with a number parameter. It is used to identify the MBG information that is associated with one of the following types of numbers:

- Calling Party Number
- Called Party Number
- Connected Party Number
- Redirecting Number
- Original Called Party Number

The Business Group Parameter contains the following information:

- **Attendant Status**—Identifies whether the number belongs to an attendant console.
- **Business Group Identifier Type**—Identifies whether the service associated with the Business Group is MBG or IWPN (Interworking with Private Networks).
- **Line Privileges Information Indicator**—Indicates whether the privileges associated with the line are fixed or customer defined.
- **Party Selector**—Indicates the number to which this Business Group information applies.
- **Business Group ID**—Identifies the Business Group to which the party belongs.
- **Sub-group ID**—Used to identify a customer-defined sub-group within the Business Group.
- **Line Privileges**—Used by the customer to define the line privileges associated with the line that the Party Selector specifies.

Signaling Networks Identifier (10010110)—Contains one or more SS7 Network Identifiers, which consist of the Point Code's Network and Cluster IDs.

Generic Name (10010111)—This parameter contains a name (such as the name displayed on Caller ID systems). It includes the following information:

* **Type of Name**—Indicates to which number the name belongs (for example, Calling Name or Redirecting Name)

* **Availability**—Indicates whether the name is available.

* **Presentation**—Indicates whether the name should be displayed.

Message Waiting Indicator Type (10011000)—A two-digit identifier that provides additional information about waiting messages. The identifier's definition is left up to the service provider and customer.

Look Ahead for Busy Response (10011001)—Indicates whether resources were found during the search for available circuits. Includes the following information:

* Location—Indicates the type of network in which the initiator resides.

* Acknowledgement Type—Indicates whether search and reservation of circuits were accepted.

Circuit Identification Code (10011010)—Contains a Circuit Identification Code (CIC), which is used in ISUP to identify a trunk circuit.

Precedence Identifier (10011011)—This parameter is used to identify service domain and preference information for an MLPP (Multi Level Precedence and Preemption) call. Military or government emergency services use the MLPP domain for prioritizing calls. The Precedence Identifier contains the following information:

* **Precedence Level**—Indicates the level of precedence.

* **Network Identity**—The Telephone Country Code, and possibly the Recognized Private Operating Agency (RPOA) or Network ID.

* **Service Domain**—The number allocated to a national MLPP service.

Call Reference (10011100)—Identifies a particular MLPP call that is independent from the physical circuit and contains the following information:

* **Call Identity**—An identification number that is assigned to the call.

* **Point Code**—The SS7 Point Code that is associated with the Call Identity.

Authorization (11011101)—Contains information for the sender's identification and authentication—for example, login ID, password, and so on.

Integrity (11011110)—Contains information that allows the destination SS7 node to determine whether the received message has been modified.

Sequence Number (01011111 00011111)—The Sequence Number is used to identify a particular message in a sequence of messages to verify proper message ordering.

Number of Messages (01011111 00100000)—Indicates the number of messages waiting in a voice mail storage and retrieval system.

Display Text (01011111 00100001)—Text information about messages that are waiting in a voice mail storage and retrieval system.

Key Exchange (01111111 00100010)—Contains information used for exchanging cryptographic keys.

Summary

TCAP provides a standard mechanism for telephony services to exchange information across the network. It is designed to be generic so it can interface with a variety of services.

TCAP resides at Level 4 of the SS7 protocol and depends on SCCP's transport services. It is comprised of a transaction sublayer and a component sublayer. The transaction sublayer correlates the exchange of associated messages, while the component sublayer handles the remote operation requests.

All information elements in the TCAP message are defined and encoded using the syntax and BER of ASN.1. The ITU Q.771—Q.775 series of specifications defines the TCAP protocol. Specifications such as the ETSI.300.374 INAP series build on the ITU Q Series Recommendations to provide additional information needed for implementing network services. The ANSI T1.114 defines the TCAP specifications for ANSI networks. ANSI defines a number of national operations and parameters on which basic services can be built. Similar to ITU, many specifications build upon the basic TCAP provisions as defined in T1.114. For example, the Telcordia GR-1298 and GR-1299 AIN specifications provide the North American equivalent of the ETSI INAP service framework for IN services.

TCAP traffic on telephony signaling networks has increased in recent years because of an increase in services such as LNP, Calling Name Delivery, and Short Messaging Service (SMS), which rely on TCAP communication. This upward trend is likely to continue as IN services are more widely deployed, thereby making TCAP an increasingly important component in the role of network services.

PART III

Service-oriented Protocols

Intelligent Networks (IN)

The Intelligent Network (IN) is an architecture that redistributes a portion of the call processing, that is traditionally performed by telephony switches, to other network nodes. This chapter explores how the IN moves service logic and service data out of the SSP, and the rationale behind it.

The complete set of IN capabilities has not been fully realized, but it continues to evolve and be implemented over time. It is a radical shift in architecture that requires coordinated changes by both vendors and service providers on a number of levels. Over approximately the last 20 years or so, standards have been published that define a common framework to enable its adoption. A variety of terms are used to describe the various stages of this evolution: IN, IN/1, AIN 0, AIN 1, AIN 0.1, AIN 0.2, IN CS-1, and IN CS-2. The list is only partially complete, and yet it represents a number of views of the Intelligent Network (IN) concept and its progression.

The Advanced Intelligent Network (AIN) is a term that Telcordia (formerly Bellcore) uses for North American IN standards that were released in the 1990s. This chapter presents the general concepts of the Intelligent Network (IN) and briefly examines the progression towards IN CS-2/AIN 0.2. The Intelligent Network Capability Set 2 (IN CS-2) is the set of standards published by ITU, while the Advanced Intelligent Network 0.2 (AIN 0.2) is the North American equivalent. Because it is the most recent specification that has a considerable amount of implementation at the time of this writing, the AIN 0.2 version of the IN is the primary focus of this chapter.

NOTE	The Telcordia AIN specifications dropped the use of the "0.2" version number from the specifications. These documents are simply referred to as the AIN specifications. Throughout this chapter, the term AIN 0.2 is retained. There are still AIN implementations that are only 0.1 compliant and the version number is useful to discriminate the functionality implemented by each version.

Because the terminology can become confusing, the term IN is used generically throughout this chapter to represent all versions of the Intelligent Network. The term AIN is used for the North American releases beyond IN/1. When a specific version is being referenced, the version number (such as AIN 0.2) is included. The call models within this chapter are based on the ITU IN standards, while most of the message examples are based on the North American AIN standards. This chapter includes an INAP section, which provides an example of how the European region uses INAP to provide IN capabilities.

The Intelligent Network

In its simplest form, a SSP communicating with a Service Control Point (SCP) to retrieve information about processing a phone call demonstrates an IN. This communication is triggered in different ways, but most often occurs in response to dialing phone numbers that have special significance—such as Service Access Codes (SAC), numbers that have been "ported" by the Local Number Portability (LNP) act, or numbers that have special services subscribed to them, such as the *O Called Party Busy* feature (described with trigger types in the "IN CS-2/AIN 0.2" section of this chapter). In the existing telephony network, this exchange of IN messages happens millions of times each day and is transparent to the phone user. Figure 11-1 shows a simple IN message exchange between an SSP and an SCP.

Figure 11-1 *Simple IN Service*

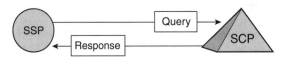

The communication between the SSP and the SCP takes place over the SS7 network using the TCAP layer of SS7. As the SSP handles calls, the SCP is queried for information about how to process the call. It does not happen for every call but only for those that require IN services, such as those mentioned previously. While a complete view of the IN architecture includes a number of other nodes with additional functions, these two nodes are at the core of IN processing. We begin with this minimal view to gain an understanding of how the IN model works and why it is needed.

Service Logic and Data

The introduction and proliferation of digital switches in the 1970s and 1980s enabled services to flourish. The computer-enabled network allowed software programs to process calls in a much more sophisticated manner than its electro mechanical predecessors. This led to a continual growth in features provided by digital switching exchanges. With the continual growth of features also came growth in software program complexity and the data maintained at each switch. These two areas are more formally defined as Service Logic and Service Data and are the central focus for the IN.

Service data is the information needed to process a call or a requested feature. Information such as the Line Class Code, Feature Codes, Called Party Number, Routing Number, and Carrier are examples of service data.

Service logic is the decision-making algorithms implemented in software that determine how a service is processed. The service logic acts on service data in making these decisions and directing call processing to create the proper connections, perform billing, provide interaction to the subscriber, and so forth.

Service Logic

Until IN was introduced, vendors completely implemented service logic. Service providers would submit requests for features to switch vendors. If the feature was accepted, the vendor would design and implement the feature in their switching software and eventually release it for general availability to the service providers. This process was usually quite long because of the stringent standards regarding telephony reliability. From the time the request was submitted to the time it was ready for deployment, it was common for an average feature to take two years or more because of the extensive design and testing involved. Of course the development cycle varied based on the complexity of the service. The importance of this issue increased even more when the introduction of competition created a need for faster service deployment in order to effectively compete in the market.

IN introduced the Service Creation Environment (SCE) to allow service providers to create their own service logic modules, thereby implementing the services they choose. This places the service provider in control of which services can be developed and how quickly they are deployed. It provides much greater flexibility, allowing customized services for specific markets to be readily created. The Service Logic Programs (SLP) created by the SCE are executed at the SCP, thereby moving a portion of the services execution environment out of the SSP. This helps to address the complexity of switching software by removing service code from an already complex environment for processing calls and switch-based features.

Service Data

Until IN capabilities were introduced in the 1980s, the service data for the PSTN resided within the telephone switches throughout the network. The expansion of telecom services and the resulting growth in the data maintained by each switching node created several issues with this architecture, including the following:

- Increased storage demands
- Maintaining synchronization of replicated data
- Administrative overhead

Service data used by services such as toll-free, premium rate, Automatic Calling Card Service and LNP change frequently, thereby causing increased overhead in maintaining service data. One of the benefits of the IN is centralizing service data in a small number of nodes. Each SSP obtains the information from a central location (SCP) when it is needed during a call's progression. This alleviates the overhead of administering data at each switching node and reduces the problem of data synchronization to a much smaller number of nodes.

Service Distribution and Centralization

The IN redistributes service data and service logic while centralizing them. As discussed, service data and logic previously existed in the telephone switch. Although the network contains many switches, each one can be considered a monolithic platform, because it contains all call-processing functions, service logic, and service data. IN redistributes the service data and logic to other platforms outside of the switch, leaving the switch to perform basic call processing.

The SCP and Adjunct are two new nodes that IN has introduced for hosting service data and logic. They both perform similar functions with the primary difference being scale and proximity. The SCP usually serves a large number of SSPs and maintains a large amount of data. It is typically implemented on larger-scale hardware to meet these needs. The Adjunct is a much smaller platform that normally serves one or possibly a few local offices and is often colocated with the switch. Adjuncts characteristically use generic hardware platforms, such as a network server or even personal computers equipped with an Ethernet interface card or SS7 interface cards. This chapter uses the SCP for most of the examples, although an Adjunct can often perform the same or similar functions. The SSP uses SS7 messages to query an SCP or Adjunct for service data and processing instructions. As shown in Figure 11-2, service logic in the SCP or Adjunct is applied to the incoming query to provide a response to the SSP with the requested information and further call processing instructions.

The amount of service logic supplied by the SCP has increased with each phase of the IN implementation. In the most recent phases, a call in a fully IN-capable switch can be primarily controlled from the SCP or Adjunct.

Figure 11-2 *IN Distribution of Service Logic and Service Data*

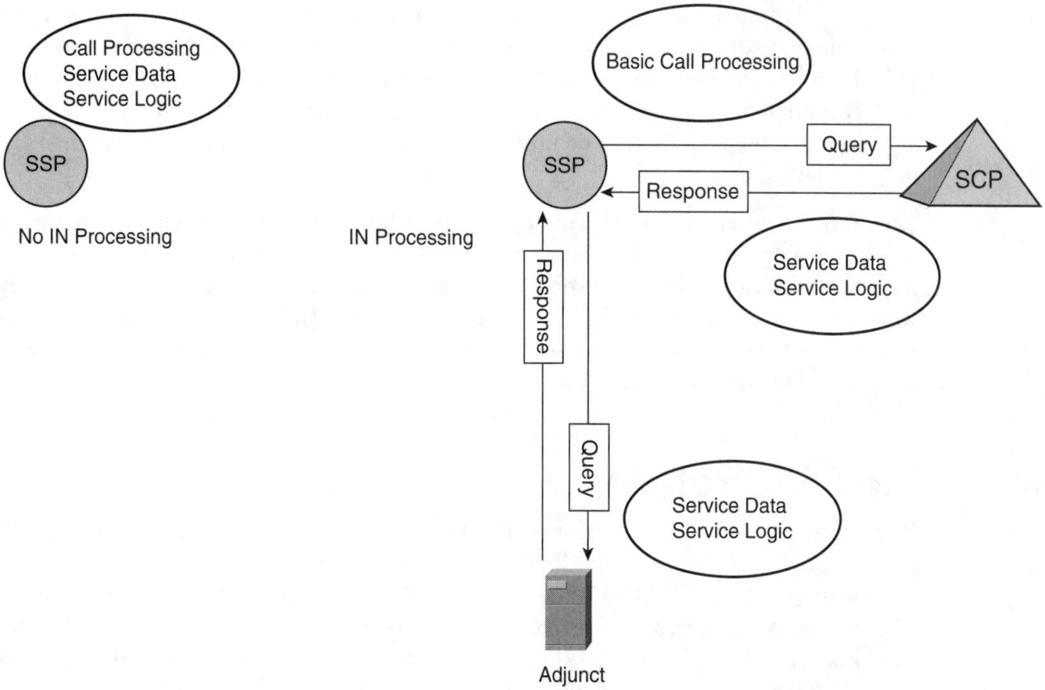

IN Services

There have been two primary drivers for IN services: regulatory mandates and revenue-generating features. Both toll-free number portability and LNP are examples of regulatory mandates that have greatly expanded the use of IN. The sections on "Intelligent Network Application Protocol (INAP)" and "Additional IN Service Examples" provide examples of these services. When faced with managing number portability issues where large amounts of service data must be maintained, the IN provides a logical solution. From a customer perspective, services like Automatic Flexible Routing (AFR), Time Of Day (TOD) Routing, and Private Virtual (PVN) Networking provide solutions for everyday business needs while generating revenue for service providers.

Since IN has been continually evolving, some services have been implemented using IN/1, and then later implemented using AIN. In fact, every service that has been implemented using IN/1 could be implemented using AIN. However, the decision does not only depend on technology. Usually there must be a business justification for upgrading a working service to use newer methodologies. The IN networks of today reflect a mix of IN/1 and

AIN services. Using the toll-free service within the United States as an example, Bellcore TR-NWT-533 describes toll-free service for IN/1, and GR-2892 describes toll-free service using AIN. Different messages are used in AIN than those of IN/1 so that the service implementations between the two are not compatible; however, the services themselves are functionally equivalent. For example, an IN/1 SCP does not understand AIN messages from an SSP. This is simply a result of the evolutionary nature of the IN. AIN 0.2 was developed to be compatible with AIN 0.1, so compatibility is not as much of a concern within the AIN incremental releases.

The services chosen as examples throughout this chapter are only a selected few of the IN services that are available. This is not intended to be a comprehensive list; rather, it is intended to provide examples of some of the more common services and to show how they work. The very nature of the AIN SCE is to allow service providers to craft their own services to meet their customers' needs. This means that a number of custom services likely exist in various service provider environments.

IN and the SS7 Protocol

With respect to SS7, the IN is an application that uses the SS7 protocol. It is not a part of the protocol, but is often associated with SS7 because it provides appropriate capabilities for enabling the IN architecture both at the protocol level and the network architecture level. The various IN versions are considered TCAP users functioning at level 4 of the SS7 protocol stack. As shown in Figure 11-3, the SSP and SCP or Adjunct exchange IN messages using the TCAP layer. Throughout Europe, the Intelligent Network Application Part (INAP), developed by the ETSI standards body, interfaces with ITU TCAP for delivering IN information between nodes. In North America, IN/1 and AIN, developed by Telcordia, interface with ANSI TCAP to deliver the equivalent information.

Figure 11-3 *INAP/AIN in Relation to the SS7 Protocol*

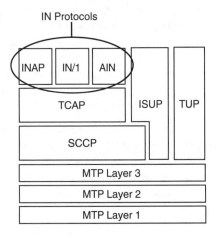

As with any SS7 application layer protocol, IN depends on the SS7 transport without explicit knowledge of all the underlying levels. It interfaces directly with TCAP to pass information in the form of components and parameters between nodes. IN capability is, of course, dependent upon correctly functioning SS7 transport layers.

Evolution of the Network

This section provides a synopsis of the various IN phases. As noted in the introduction, a number of stages have introduced additional capabilities. How they fit together into a coherent view of what currently comprises the IN can be difficult to understand. The focus here is more on the progression of the different phases and what each phase introduces, and less on the actual dates on which they were introduced. Figure 11-4 shows the progression.

Figure 11-4 *IN Evolutionary Progression*

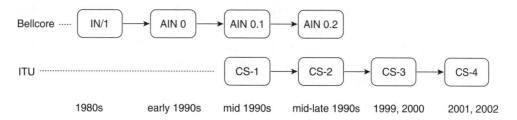

The IN began with IN/1, which Bellcore introduced in the 1980s. This brought the SSP to SCP communication exchange into existence. Following IN/1, Bellcore published a series of specifications under the new title, the AIN. This series of specifications included version numbers; each moved in increments towards a full realization of an IN-centric network in which the SCP had full control of service processing logic at each stage of call processing. This was known as AIN 1. The AIN series created a structured call model, which evolved from a simple model in AIN 0 to a much more complete representation in AIN 0.2.

When the AIN 0.1 specification was published, the ITU-T adopted the IN concept and created a set of standards known as the IN Capability Set 1 (CS-1). The capabilities of CS-1 aligned fairly well with the AIN 0.1 release. The idea was to publish a series of IN standards that described the set of capabilities added with each release as the IN continued to evolve, much in the same manner as the AIN incremental version numbers. The IN CS-2 was later published; it aligns with AIN 0.2 with minimal differences. More recent CS-3 and CS-4 editions have continued to expand the list of capabilities in the IN domain.

The following specification series defines the ITU IN recommendations. The "x" in the series number represents a number from 1 to 9 because each suite contains multiple documents.

- **Q.120x**—General Intelligent Network Principles
- **Q.121x**—Intelligent Network Capability Set 1
- **Q.122x**—Intelligent Network Capability Set 2
- **Q.123x**—Intelligent Network Capability Set 3
- **Q.124x**—Intelligent Network Capability Set 4
- **Q.1290**—Intelligent Network Glossary of terms

The following specifications define Telcordia AIN standards. The latter two documents define what most people in the industry refer to as the AIN 0.2 standards, even though the documents do not carry the version number in the name.

- TR-NWT-001284, Advanced Intelligent Network (AIN) 0.1 Switching Systems Generic Requirements
- TR-NWT-001285, Advanced Intelligent Network (AIN) 0.1 Switch-Service Control Point (SCP Application Protocol Interface Generic Requirements)
- GR-1298-CORE, AINGR: Switching Systems
- GR-1299-CORE, AINGR: Switch-service Control Point (SCP)/Adjunct

Figure 11-5 shows the hierarchal view of IN standards. The AIN standards developed by North America have been largely adopted and generalized for global use by the ITU. The ITU standards now represent the specifications from which national variants should be based. Beneath the ITU are the AIN standards for North America and Europe's INAP standards. At the call model level, the ITU and AIN standards are functionally very similar. However, the TCAP message encoding between AIN and ITU remain quite different. The ETSI INAP standards use the ITU encoding, while AIN uses the ANSI TCAP encoding.

Figure 11-5 *IN Standards Bodies*

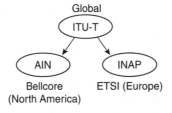

The existence of a standard does not always signify that its capabilities have been implemented and deployed. There has been a reasonably widespread deployment of IN/1, which has been superceded by the deployment of AIN 0.1 in many cases. AIN 0 saw very limited deployment because it was more of an interim step on the path to AIN 0.1. AIN 0.1 and CS-1 are deployed in many networks; there is a smaller deployment of AIN 0.2 and CS-2 in existence. Inside each of these releases is also a vendor implementation progression, particularly with the larger scope of capabilities in CS-1/AIN 0.1 and CS-2/AIN 0.2. Switching vendors has implemented the SSP software to support portions of the capability set over time and has responded to customer demands for the most important services. While the ultimate goal of service providers is to remove the dependence on switching vendors for services, the SSP software must be modified significantly to support the new processing logic.

Having established the reasons for the IN and the progression of the various phases, the following sections explore the major phases in more detail.

IN/1

Bellcore defined the first phase of the IN at the request of a few of the Regional Bell Operating Companies and began deployment during the 1980s. This phase primarily used the TCAP operation codes and parameters defined by the ANSI TCAP standard but also included some private Bellcore parameters. These message codes do not provide a context of the call processing sequence as do the messages that were encountered later in the AIN network. Each message is processed in an atomic manner based on the contents of the message, without explicit knowledge of what stage of call processing is occurring at the SSP. Later IN releases resolved this problem by adopting a formal call model with generic messages that are defined for each stage of call processing.

Initial Services

IN/1 was only used for a small number of services—primarily *number services*. Number services use the dialed number as a SAC for identifying a call that requires access to special services. The following are examples of the early services offered by IN/1.

- Enhanced 800 (E800)
- Automatic Calling Card Service (ACCS)
- Private Virtual Network (PVN)

Placing hooks in the call processing software to trigger queries to the SCP modified the SSP control logic. For example, during digit analysis or number translations, a check for the SAC would determine whether a query should be sent to the SCP.

IN/1 Toll-Free (E800) Example

The E800 toll-free service, as implemented in the United States, is chosen as an example to walk through an IN/1 message flow. There are several good reasons to use this as an example. It was among the first IN/1 services available, and it has an AIN version of the same service that provides for a comparison between them. The section "AIN Toll-Free Service Example" further discusses the toll-free services and describes it for the AIN architecture.

The 800 Portability Act of 1993 was a significant business driver for SS7 and, to a large degree, for IN deployment in North America. Before this act, LECs could route toll-free calls to the correct carrier based on the dialed number's NXX (where NXX represents the 3 most significant digits after 800). The 800 portability act allowed businesses to choose a different carrier for 800 service, while retaining the same toll-free number. This meant that switches could no longer statically route calls to a particular carrier based on the NXX codes. Instead, they first had to determine the carrier for the toll-free number and route to that carrier. The IN provided an efficient way of managing the dynamic service by having the SSP query an SCP to determine a call's carrier. The carrier could be changed at the SCP without having to update all of the network switches. The new IN-based version of toll-free service was called Enhanced 800 (E800). Figure 11-6 shows how the E800 service is implemented in the United States.

Figure 11-6 *IN/1 Toll-free Service*

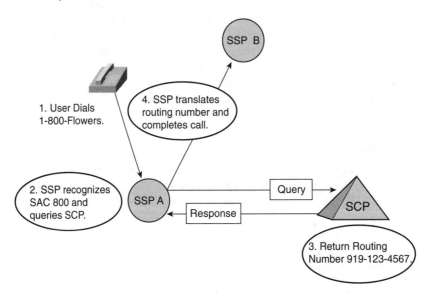

This example shows the simplest case. The SCP has determined that the LEC will handle the toll-free call. The SCP returns a special Carrier Code Identification along with the destination number in the Routing Number field for completing the call. However, if the

SCP had determined that another carrier were to handle the toll-free call, that carrier's Carrier Code would be returned with the original dialed number in the Routing Number field. Rather than routing the call based on the routing number, SSP A would then route the call to an SSP in the carrier's network based on the carrier code. The carrier would perform another query to determine the call's final routing number.

Because IN/1 does not define a formal call model, hooks are placed at some point in the call processing software to provide the necessary information for routing the call. As shown in Figure 11-7, when the 800 SAC is identified at SSP A during digit translation, a query is sent to the SCP. Note that the 800 number is a service-specific code that must be recognized by the SSP. This outlines one of the important differences between IN/1 and AIN. The AIN version discussed in "The Advanced Intelligent Network (AIN 0.*X*, IN CS-*X*)" section uses a generic trigger mechanism to identify service codes.

Figure 11-7 *IN/1 Trigger Mechanism*

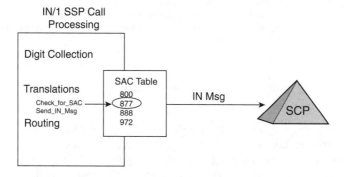

Example 11-1 shows the messages exchanged between the two nodes. These messages are representative of the requirements specified in Bellcore TR-NWT-000533, but they can vary depending on the particular call. Be aware that the entire TCAP messages are not shown—only the key components. The following are the key components of the query that are sent to the SSP.

Example 11-1 *SSP Query*

```
TCAP Component
        Operation Family: Provide Instructions
        Operation Specifier: Start
    Parameter: Service Key
            Parameter: Digits (Dialed)
            Parameter: Digits (Calling)
            Parameter: Digits (LATA)
            Parameter: Origination Station Type (Bellcore specific parm)
```

The query to the SCP does not contain any information that indicates the current Point-In-Call (PIC) processing at the SSP. This is another key difference between the service-specific interface of IN/1 and the service-independent interface in the later IN revisions.

The SCP applies its service logic based on the incoming message and sends a response to the SSP with instructions about how to direct the call. This is the point at which the SCP logic accesses the data associated with the toll-free number and determines such information as carrier code, routing number, and billing information to be returned to the SCP. The Response message includes the following key components and parameters.

Example 11-2 *SCP Response*

```
TCAP Component
        Operation Family: Connection Control
        Operation Specifier: Connect
      Parameter: Service Key
              Parameter: Digits (Carrier)
              Parameter: Digits (Routing Number)
              Parameter: Billing Indicator (Specific Billing data to collect)
              Parameter: Origination Station Type (ANI Information digits)
              Parameter: Digits (Billing)
```

When the SSP receives the Response message, it resumes call processing using the information the SCP returns to perform translations and route the call.

The Query and Response messages shown are for a simple, successful toll-free query. In some instances, additional TCAP components can be sent between the SSP and SCP. For example, the SCP can send Automatic Call Gapping (ACG) to request that calls be throttled. This instructs the SSP to skip some calls and can be particularly useful during high-volume calling. Another request that the SCP might make is for the SSP to send a notification when the call is disconnected. The SCP can include a *Send Notification/Termination* component in the message to the SSP for this purpose.

The toll-free service can also involve messages other than the ones shown. For example, if the toll-free number is being dialed from outside of a particular service band (the geographic area within which the toll-free number is valid), a message is sent to the caller with a TCAP operation of *Caller Interaction/Play Announcement*. These are just examples of common message exchanges for an IN/1 toll-free service in the U.S. network and do not include all possible variations. Errors, missing data records at the SSP, and other errata have their own defined set of interactions between the SSP and SCP and are handled in the toll-free specifications for the particular network being used.

The Advanced Intelligent Network (AIN 0.*X*, IN CS-*X*)

The term "Advanced Intelligent Network" can be misleading. People often consider AIN a separate entity from the IN. It is simply part of the evolution of the original IN concept. AIN is a term that is primarily used in North America to describe the evolution of the IN beyond the IN/1 phase. The AIN specifications introduced by Bellcore solidified and extended the concepts introduced by the early IN standards. AIN 0 was the first version released. However, it is only given a brief introduction here because AIN 0.1 and AIN 0.2 have made it obsolete. Both AIN 0.1, and 0.2 are incremental releases toward the IN concept documented in AIN 1. As explained earlier, beginning with AIN 0.1, the ITU IN and Bellcore AIN standards align fairly well; although ITU uses the term IN and Bellcore uses the term AIN, they both describe the same general architecture and call model. The following sections discuss IN CS-1 and AIN 0.1 as well as IN CS-2 and AIN 0.2 together. Message encodings remain incompatible because of the differences between ITU TCAP and ANSI TCAP. The examples use AIN messages with ANSI TCAP encodings.

Basic Call State Models (BCSM)

One of the key differences between IN/1 and the succeeding AIN/IN CS phases is the introduction of a formal call model. A *call model* is a definition of the call processing steps that are involved in making a call. During call processing in a switch, a call progresses through various stages, such as Digit Collection, Translations, and Routing. These stages existed before the introduction of the IN; however, there was no agreement between vendors on exactly what constituted each phase and what transitional events marked the entry and exit of each stage. Even within a vendor's implementation, the delineation of stages could be ambiguous. IN defines a Basic Call State Model (BCSM), which identifies the various states of call processing and the points at which IN processing can occur—known as Points In Call (PIC) and Detection Points (DP), respectively. This is essential for distributing service processing between the SSP and SCP because the SCP must identify the PIC processing that has been reached by SSPs from a number of different vendors. The SCP can determine the call-processing context based on messages sent from specific DP, thereby allowing it to apply its own logic in a more intelligent way.

Point in Call (PIC)

The BCSM assigns a formal name, known as a PIC, to each call processing state. Figure 11-8 illustrates the components that are used to define the BCSM. A set of entry events define the transitional actions that constitute entering into a PIC. Exit events mark the completion of processing by the current PIC. The entry and exit events provide a means of describing what constitutes being in a particular PIC because the exact point at which one stage has been processed completely and the next stage is beginning can be vague. The ITU and Bellcore standards specify the list of events that constitute each of these PICs. Within each PIC, the switch software performs call processing for that stage of the call. This is the same call processing that existed before the introduction of IN, except with a clear delineation between processing stages.

Detection Point (DP)

DPs between the various PICs represent points at which IN processing can occur. The DP detects that the call has reached a particular state, as indicated, by having exited the previous PIC and encountering the DP. IN processing can be invoked to communicate with the SCP to determine further information about the call or request instructions about how the call should be handled.

Figure 11-8 *Call Model Components*

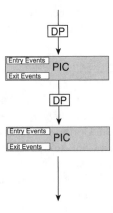

DP is a generic term that identifies the insertion point for IN processing. More specifically, each DP is either a Trigger Detection Point (TDP) or an Event Detection Point (EDP).

Trigger Detection Point (TDP)

The TDP is a point at which the SSP can set triggers that execute when the TDP is encountered. The trigger represents an invocation point for an IN service. Triggers are provisioned at the SSP based on what call-processing events need intervention from the SCP. When a trigger has been subscribed for a particular TDP and the TDP is encountered, the SSP software launches a query to the SCP. Triggers can be subscribed with different granularities, ranging from an individual subscriber line to the entire SSP. The following are the different levels for which triggers can apply.

- Individual line or Trunk Group
- Business or Centrex Group
- Office-wide (meaning they apply to an entire SSP)

Multiple triggers can be defined at a given TDP. The IN and AIN standards define the trigger types that can be encountered at each TDP. For example, the IN CS-2 defines the Off_Hook_Immediate trigger type at the Origination Attempt TDP. Section "IN CS-2/AIN 0.2" discusses the TDPs and specific triggers in detail.

Event Detection Point (EDP)

An EDP is a point at which the SCP "arms" an event at the SSP. The event is armed to request that the SCP be notified when the particular EDP is reached during call processing. The SCP can then determine how the call should be further directed. For example, the SCP might want to be notified before a user is connected to a "busy" treatment so that a call attempt can be made to another number without the phone user being aware that a busy signal has been encountered.

An EDP can be one of two types: an EDP-Request or an EDP-Notification. An EDP-R requests that the SSP stop call processing (except in the case of O_No_Answer and T_No_Answer DPs) and send an EDP-R message to the SCP. No further action is taken until a response is received. An EDP-N requests that the SSP send an EDP-Notification but continue call processing. The SCP does not respond to the notification. The SCP can use the notification for billing, statistics, or other purposes.

Figure 11-9 *Triggers Set by the SSP, Events Armed by the SCP*

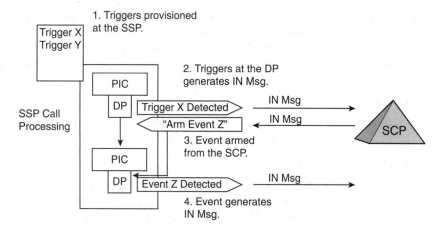

When the SCP has received a message from the SSP, TCAP can establish a transaction. This is known as having an open transaction in IN. It is only within the context of an open transaction that the SCP can arm events. The SSP always initiates the transaction, so the SCP must wait for a message from the SSP before arming an EDP. There is one exception to this rule. AIN 0.2 introduced the Create_Call message, which allows the SCP to initiate an IN message to the SSP without previous communication from the SSP. The function of the Create_Call message is to have the SSP initiate a call to a specified destination. The Create_Call message can include a request to arm events on the SSP.

IN CS-2 and AIN differ slightly in the way events are armed. Each EDP is treated separately for IN CS-2. In AIN, a single component can contain a list of events, called a Next Event List (NEL). IN CS-2/AIN 0.2 introduced EDPs; specific EDP types are discussed in more detail in the "Event Detection Point" section.

Trigger and Event Precedence

Because multiple triggers and events can exist at a single DP, it is necessary to establish precedence for the order in which processing should occur. The following lists the generally followed order in which triggers and events are processed, beginning with the highest precedence.

- Event Notifications
- Trigger Notifications
- Event Requests
- Triggers Requests

There are exceptions to the generalized precedence listed. For example, in AIN 0.2, if an AFR trigger and a Network Busy Event are armed at the same DP, the AFR trigger takes precedence because its purpose is to provide more route selections, and the Network Busy Event is intended to indicate that all routes have been exhausted. Triggers are assigned at a particular level or scope. The precedence of trigger processing at each level, beginning with the highest priority, includes the following:

- Individually subscribed triggers (triggers against an ISDN service profile have precedence over triggers subscribed against the line)
- Group triggers (for example, centrex groups)
- Office-wide triggers

Multiple triggers, such as multiple individually subscribed triggers on the same line, can also be subscribed within the same scope. An example that applies to trunks is the Collected Information TDP, in which Off_Hook_Delay, Channel_Setup_PRI, and Shared_Interoffice_Trunk triggers can be assigned. The complete set of precedence rules for triggers occurring at the same scope can be found in the AIN 0.2 specifications [120].

Escape Codes

At times it is desirable for a trigger to be bypassed for certain calls. Escape codes provide a means for a subscriber with the Off_Hook_Delay trigger to make certain calls without invoking the trigger. Although any valid code can usually be provisioned as an escape code, common examples include emergency (911) calls and 0 calls to an operator. In the case of emergency calls, if the SS7 routes from the SSP to the SCP are down and the SSP triggers on the emergency number, the caller would not be able to make an emergency call unless the trigger could be bypassed.

Originating and Terminating Call Models

From the perspective of an SSP, each phone call can be described as two separate call halves: an originating call half and a terminating call half. The originating call half is established whenever the SSP detects an incoming call. The terminating call half is established when the SSP is setting up the outgoing portion of the call. In Figure 11-10, a line originates a call to SSP A. The incoming call from the subscriber line represents the originating call half. The call proceeds through call processing and connects to a trunk. The terminating call half is represented by the trunk connected to SSP A. When the call comes into SSP B, the trunk represents the originating call half from the perspective of SSP B. The call proceeds through call processing and terminates to a subscriber line, representing the terminating call half.

Figure 11-10 *Originating and Terminating Call Halves*

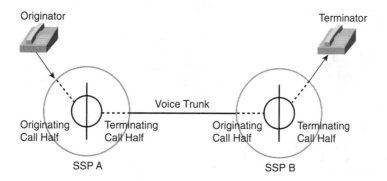

Beginning with IN CS-1/AIN 0.1, an IN BCSM model has been created for each call half.

- Originating Basic Call State Model (OBCSM)—Represents the originating call half.
- Terminating Basic Call State Model (TBCSM)—Represents the terminating call half.

This allows the originator or terminator who is involved in a call to be handled independently under the direction of the IN.

This section provides a general understanding of the IN/AIN call model and how it fits into the existing SSP call-processing domain. The later sections that cover IN CS-1/AIN 0.1 and IN CS-2/AIN 0.2 discuss the specifications of each model.

Network Architecture

A modern IN network consists of several components that work collectively to deliver services. Figure 11-11 shows a complete view of an IN network, with all elements in place to support the AIN and IN Capability Set.

Figure 11-11   *AIN Network Architecture*

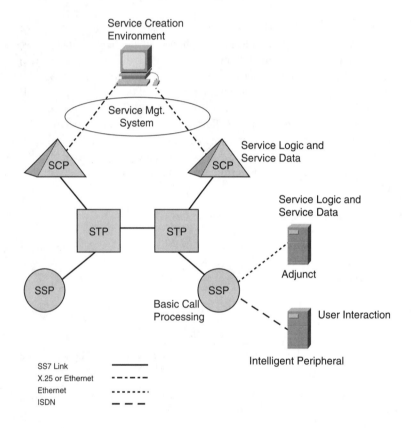

The architecture from a network point of view has remained constant from the initial concept released as IN/1. The evolutionary changes have been more focused at the processing within each node. It is important to understand that IN has not replaced the existing PSTN; rather, it has been overlaid onto it. The SSP represents the traditional PSTN switching exchange, but the software has been enhanced to support IN processing. The SCP, Adjunct, and IP are all additional nodes that were added to support the IN architecture.

Service Switching Point (SSP)

The SSP performs basic call processing and provides trigger and event detection points for IN processing. The primary change for enabling the SSP for IN is switching software that implements the IN call model and supporting logic for all of the triggers and events. Different switching vendors can have a limited IN implementation that only supports a portion of the call model. The SSP continues to handle the actual call connections and call state, as well as switch-based features. Currently, IN processing usually occurs at one or perhaps a few Detection Points so the SSP is still directing the majority of the call processing flow.

Service Control Point (SCP)

The SCP stores service data and executes service logic for incoming messages. The SCP acts on the information in the message to trigger the appropriate logic and retrieve the necessary data for service processing. It then responds with instructions to the SSP about how to proceed with the call, thereby providing the data that is necessary to continue call processing. The SCP can be specialized for a particular type of service, or it can implement multiple services.

Adjunct

The Adjunct performs similar functions to an SCP but resides locally with the SSP and is usually on a smaller scale. The Adjunct is often in the same building, but it can serve a few local offices. It handles TCAP queries locally, thereby saving on the expense of sending those queries to a remote SCP—particularly when the SCP belongs to another network provider who is charging for access. The connection between the Adjunct and the SSP is usually an Ethernet connection using the Internet Protocol; however, sometimes SS7 interface cards are used instead. The line between the SCP and Adjunct will continue to blur as the network evolves toward using the Internet Protocol for transporting TCAP data.

Intelligent Peripheral (IP)

The Intelligent Peripheral (IP) provides specialized functions for call processing, including speech recognition, prompting for user information, and playing custom announcements. Many services require interaction with the user and provide voice menu prompts in which the user makes choices and enters data through Dual-Tone Multifrequency (DTMF) tones on the phone keypad or by speaking to a Voice Recognition Unit. In the past, some of these functions have been performed using the SSP, but this occupies an expensive resource. Moving this function into an IP allows the IP to be shared between users and frees up dependency on SSP resources.

Service Management System (SMS)

Most of the IN services require the management of a significant amount of data. As with other IN nodes, multiple vendors exist that provide SMS solutions. The SMS generally consists of databases that can communicate with IN nodes to provide initial data loading and updates. The SMS systems often interface with other SMS systems to allow for hierarchical distribution of data throughout the network. While older SMS systems used X.25 to communicate with IN nodes, TCP/IP is now much more common.

Number services represent large portions of SMS data. LNP and toll-free numbers are examples; they require large amounts of storage with constantly changing data. The SMS provides the needed administration tools for managing these types of services.

Service Creation Environment (SCE)

The SCE allows service providers and third-party vendors to create IN services. The section titled "Service Creation Environment" describes the SCE in more detail.

ITU Intelligent Network Conceptual Model (INCM)

The ITU Intelligent Network Conceptual Model (INCM) divides the network into different "planes." Each plane shows a particular view of the components that make up the IN. The model is an abstract representation that provides a common framework for vendors and service providers, thereby giving IN architects and implementers a common terminology base for discussion and allowing the development of modular network components. The entities shown in Figure 11-12 are examples of how they fit into these planes.

Figure 11-12 *Intelligent Network Conceptual Model*

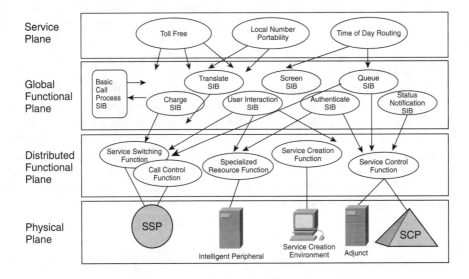

As shown in Figure 11-12, the INCM consists of four planes, or views. While the views create a way of looking at a set of entities from a particular viewpoint, these entities ultimately collapse to tangible software and hardware in order to carry out network service functions. For example, consider that an SSP is a physical switching exchange that contains hardware and software to perform Call Control Functions (CCFs) and Service Switching Functions (SSFs). The Service Switching software is ultimately comprised of collections of Service Independent Building Blocks (SIB) that perform the work of translations, billing, user interaction, and so on for all services supported by the SSP. In the same way, the SCP contains software that performs the Service Control Function (SCF). The SCF is also ultimately comprised of collections of SIBs for performing the work of translations, billing, user interaction, and so on for the services it supports. Following is a brief description of each plane.

- **Service Plane**—Represents a view of the network strictly from the view of the service. The underlying implementation is not visible from the service plane.

- **Global Functional Plane**—A view of the common building blocks across the network that comprise service functions and how they interact with Basic Call Processing. The SIB represents each functional building block of a service. A "Basic Call Processing" SIB exists to represent the interactions of those service-related SIBs with call processing. This interaction is more tangibly represented by the call models that are defined in the Distributed Functional Plane (DFP).

- **Distributed Functional Plane**—A view of the Functional Entities (FE) that compose the IN network structure. The DFP is where the collection of SIB implementations represent real actions in the course of processing actual service functions. The formal term used to describe these functions is Functional Entity Actions (FEA). For example, this plane describes BCSM within the CCF.

- **Physical Plane**—Represents the physical view of the equipment and protocols that implement the FE that are described in the DFP.

Correlating Distributed Functional Plane and Physical Plane

The ITU describes the concept of a DFP, which maps FEs onto the network. These FEs are a means of describing which nodes are responsible for particular functions: a "functional view" of the network. Table 11-1 shows the mapping of nodes to FE. Not surprisingly, the descriptions are quite similar to the previous node descriptions. Nevertheless, these FE terms are used throughout the ITU standards, so they are introduced here for familiarity.

This concludes the general introduction to the AIN/IN CS network. The following sections focus on the particular versions released in the IN evolution chain.

Table 11-1 *IN Physical Plane and Distributed Functional Plane*

Physical Plane	Distributed Functional Plane
SSP	**Call Control Function (CCF)**—Provides call processing and switch-based feature control. This includes the setup, maintenance, and takedown of calls in the switching matrix and the local features that are associated with those calls.
	Call Control Agent Function (CCAF)—Provides users with access to the network.
	Service Switching Function (SSF)—Provides cross-functional processing between the CCF and SCF, such as the detection of trigger points for IN processing.
SCP	**Service Control Function (SCF)**—Directs call processing based on Service Logic Programs.
	Service Data Function (SDF)—Provides service-related customer and network data for access by the SCF during the execution of service logic.
SMS	**Service Management Function (SMF)**—Manages the provisioning and deployment of IN services and service-related data.
	Service Management Access Function (SMAF)—Provides the interface for accessing the SMF.
SCE	**Service Creation Environment Function (SCEF)**—Provides for the creation and validation of new services. Generates the logic used by the SCF.
IP	**Specialized Resource Function (SRF)**—Provides resources for end-user interactions, such as recorded announcements and user input via keypads, voice recognition, and so forth.

AIN 0

AIN 0 was a short-lived interim phase for reaching AIN 0.1, so this chapter dedicates little attention to it. AIN 0 was the first IN release to establish a formal call model at the SSP. It was a simple model that used Trigger Checkpoints (TCPs) at the following call points:

- Off hook
- Digit Collection and Analysis
- Routing

This expanded the capabilities of AIN beyond simply doing number services and allowed new features like Automatic Flexible Routing (AFR), which is based on the routing checkpoint. AFR allows the SSP to query the SCP for new routes if all the routes identified by the local switch are busy. AIN 0.1 establishes and supercedes all of the capabilities of AIN 0.

IN CS-1/AIN 0.1

This version of the IN introduced a much richer call model than the interim AIN 0 release. The model is divided into an originating and terminating call model to provide a complete, but basic description of the call. The term Trigger Checkpoints was changed to Trigger Detection Points, and new PICs and DPs were added to the model.

The next two sections examine originating and terminating models, showing the PICs that define each call stage along with their associated DPs.

IN CS-1 OBCSM

Figure 11-13 shows the IN CS-1 PICs and DPs that are supported in this version for the originating call model. The AIN 0.1 version is similar.

Figure 11-13 *IN CS-1 OBCSM*

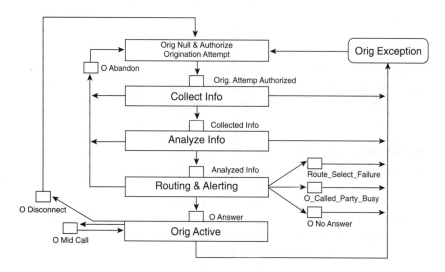

In IN CS-1, the Analyzed Info DP now provides the detection point for the number services that IN/1 originally supported. The Specific_Digit_String (SDS) is the trigger type now used at the DP to trigger a query for services like toll-free calling. In AIN 0.1, The Public Office Dial Plan (PODP) trigger is used for this trigger type. AIN 0.2 converges with the IN CS-2 to replace the PODP trigger with the SDS trigger type. Again, this is part of the continual evolution and standards convergence issues. This particular trigger type is mentioned for reader awareness because it is used in the popular number services and is commonly seen in IN networks.

IN CS-1 TBCSM

Figure 11-14 shows the terminating call model with its supported PICs and DPs.

Figure 11-14 *IN CS-1 TBCSM*

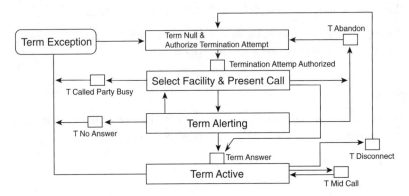

Several existing IN networks use the capabilities provided by the AIN 0.1 release. Because the capabilities of IN CS-1/AIN 0.1 are generally a subset of those that are supported in IN CS-2/AIN 0.2, they are explained in the "IN CS-2/AIN 0.2" section.

AIN Toll-Free Service Example

Section "IN/1" discussed the IN/1 version of the toll-free service. The same service is discussed here using AIN messaging instead of IN/1. For a review of how the E800 service works, refer to the example in the "IN/1" section. Because this example is shown using AIN 0.1, note that the PICs, DPs, and trigger type are slightly different than the IN CS-1 counterparts. This is a matter of semantics, and IN CS-1 provides the equivalent functions. Figure 11-15 shows the flow of events for the E800 service.

The same digit collection, translations, and routing software routines shown in the IN/1 example of the service still exist. The major difference with AIN is that they are now represented by discrete PICs. Rather than checking for a particular SAC, the SSP now reaches the Info_Analyzed DP and checks for any triggers that are applicable to the DP. As shown in Figure 11-16, the Called Party Number contains the leading "888" digit string, which has been provisioned as a PODP trigger (equivalent to the IN-CS1 SDS trigger) at the SSP that generates a query to the SCP.

Figure 11-15 *AIN 0.1 Toll-Free Service*

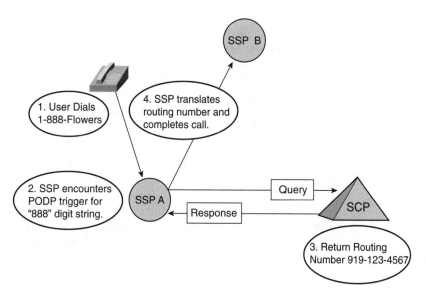

Figure 11-16 *AIN Toll-Free Trigger Processing*

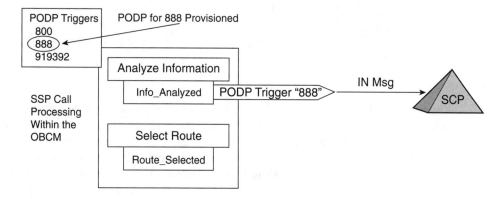

The query sent from the SSP is built using information that the SCP needs when processing the message. The query includes the following key components. Note that the entire TCAP messages are not shown—only the key components.

The SCP applies its service logic based on the incoming message and sends the SSP a response that includes instructions on how to direct the call. The key information the SCP provides is either the service provider's carrier code or a routing number if the LEC handles

Example 11-1 *SSP Query*

```
TCAP Component
        Operation Family: Request_Instructions
        Operation Specifier: Info_Analyzed
                Parameter: UserID
                Parameter: BearerCapabilityID
                Parameter: AINDigits (CalledPartyID)
                Parameter: AINDigits (LATA)
                Parameter: TriggerCriteriaType (indicates "npa" or "npaNXX")
                Parameter: AINDigits (ChargeNumber)
                Parameter: AINDigits (CallingPartyID)
                Parameter: ChargePartyStationType (ANI II)
                Parameter: PrimaryCarrier
```

the toll-free service. This decision is made during execution of the service logic at the SCP. When the SSP receives the Response message, it resumes call processing using the information returned by the SCP to perform translations and routing of the call.

Example 11-2 *SSP Response*

```
TCAP Component
        Operation Family: Connection Control
        Operation Specifier: Analyze_Route
                Parameter: ChargePartyStationType (ANI II)
                Parameter: AINDigits (CalledPartyID)
                Parameter: PrimaryCarrierID
                Parameter: AMALineNumber
                Parameter: AMASLPID
```

IN CS-2/AIN 0.2

The IN CS-2/AIN 0.2 represents the most recent version of IN that most switching vendors support to date. Of course, this is a moving target, and vendors might not fully comply with the full specifications of the release; therefore, it should be considered a generalization. As noted earlier, the 0.2 version number has actually been dropped from the specifications. The term IN CS-2 is used throughout this section to describe the call models, unless referencing something specific to AIN 0.2, because the two standards are aligned in a very similar manner.

The IN CS-2 call models provide a fairly comprehensive list of PICs to accurately describe call flow in the originating and terminating call halves. Although they are functionally the same, a comparison of the CS-2 and AIN call models shows that naming is often slightly different. The IN CS-2 call model is used here. Even the name of the model is slightly different, with AIN using the term *Basic Call Model* and ITU using *Basic Call State Model*. When discussing the call models, explanations are kept as common as possible—aside from the naming conventions.

Originating Basic Call State Model (BCSM)

Figure 11-17 shows the originating call model for IN CS-2. The call model supports several TDPs and EDPs. IN CS-2 is the first call model to support EDPs, thereby giving the SCP greater control of call processing at the SSP.

Figure 11-17 *IN CS2 Originating Basic State Call Model (BCSM)*

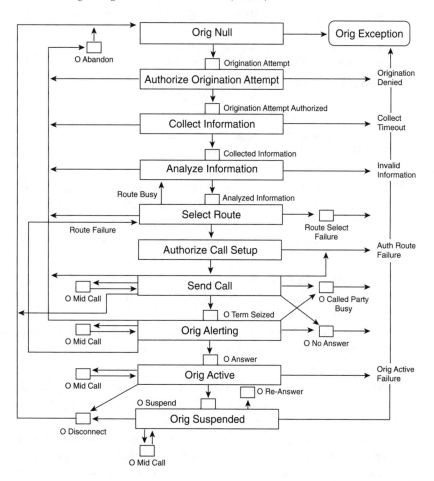

IN CS-2 OBCSM PICs

Here we examine each of the PICs and DPs of the originating call model to gain an understanding of each stage of call processing and the possible DPs where IN processing might occur. While studying the model, keep in mind that what the model describes is the flow of processing that occurs in modern digital switches for an individual call. Each of the PICs and their transition events represent processing that existed before IN was introduced. This model introduces a standard agreement of the functions represented at each stage (PIC) and defined points for the invocation of IN processing (DP).

- **Orig Null**—This PIC represents an idle interface (line or trunk), indicating that no call exists. For example, when a phone is on-hook and not in use, it is at the Orig Null PIC.

- **Authorize Origination Attempt**—Indicates that an origination is being attempted and that any needed authorization should be performed. The calling identity is checked against any line restrictions, bearer capability restrictions, service profile information, and so on to determine whether the origination should be permitted.

- **Collect Information**—Represents the collecting of digits from the originating party. The number of digits to collect might be done according to the dialing plan, or by specific provisioning data from the switch.

- **Analyze Information**—Analysis or translation of the collected digits according to the dial plan. The analysis determines the routing address and call type associated with the analyzed digits.

- **Select Route**—The routing address and call type are used to select a route for the call. For example, a trunk group or line DN might be identified to route the call.

- **Authorize Call Setup**—Validates the authority of the calling party to place the call to the selected route. For example, business group or toll restrictions on the calling line can prevent the call from being allowed to continue.

- **Send Call**—An indication requesting to set up the call is sent to the called party. For example, if the call is terminating to an SS7 trunk, an IAM is sent to the far end to set up the call.

- **Alerting**—The calling party receives audible ringback, waiting for the called party to answer. For example, when terminating to a trunk, the remote office might send ringback in-band over the trunk.

- **Active**—Answer is received and the connection between the originating and terminating parties is established. The two parties can now communicate. At this point, the call has exited the setup phase and is considered stable.

- **Suspended**—A suspend indication has been received from the terminating call half, providing notification that the terminating party has disconnected (gone on-hook). For example, the terminating party disconnects on an SS7 signaled interoffice call, and the originating switch receives an ISUP Suspend message.

- **Exception**—An exception condition, such as an error or other condition that is not associated with the normal flow of processing, has occurred.

IN CS-2 OBCSM TDPs and Trigger Types

The TDPs are closely associated with the PICs because they identify a transition point between the PICs at which IN processing can be invoked. For each TDP, a brief description is given of the transition point being signaled and the trigger types that might be encountered are listed. IN processing only acts on the TDPs if triggers for that particular TDP have been defined.

Origination Attempt

This TDP signals that the originator is attempting to originate a call. It is encountered when an off-hook is detected.

Triggers: Off_Hook_Immediate

Origination Attempt Authorized

This TDP signals that the originator has been authorized to attempt a call. Checks against bearer capability, line restrictions, group restrictions, and so on have been validated.

Triggers: Origination_Attempt_Authorized

Collected Information

AIN 0.2 labels this TDP "Info Collected." It signals that all of the digits have been collected. For example, if the originator is dialing from a line, the expected number of digits has been entered according to the dialing plan.

Triggers:

- Off_Hook_Delay
  - Channel_Setup_PRI
  - Shared_Interoffice_Trunk

Analyzed Information

AIN 0.2 labels this TDP as "Info Analyzed." It signals that the digits have been analyzed and all translations performed, thereby resulting in a routing address and Nature Of Address (for example, subscriber number and national number). Note that AIN 0.2 has replaced the PODP trigger type from AIN 0.1 with the ITU specified SDS trigger type.

Triggers:

- BRI_Feature_Activation_Indicator
- Public_Feature_Code
- Specific_Feature_Code
- Customized_Dialing_Plan
- Specific_Digit_String
- Emergency_Service (N11 in AIN 0.2)
- One_Plus_Prefix (AIN 0.2 only)
- Specified_Carrier (AIN 0.2 only)
  - International (AIN 0.2 only)
  - Operator_Services (AIN 0.2 only)
  - Network_Services (AIN 0.2 only)

Route Select Failure

AIN 0.2 labels this TDP as "Network Busy." It signals that a route could not be selected. The transition back to the Analyze Information PIC can be the result of an individual route being attempted unsuccessfully. A route list often contains a number of routes that might be attempted before routing is considered to have failed. This is particularly true when trunks are involved because different trunk groups are selected from a route list. Also note that AIN 0.2 includes a *Route Selected TDP*, which is not included in IN CS-2. This is one of the slight differences in the call model. The Route Selected TDP indicates that a route has been successfully selected for sending the call.

Triggers: Automatic Flexible Routing (AFR)

O Called Party Busy

This TDP signals to the originator that the terminating party is busy. For example, the call terminates to a line that is already involved in a call.

Triggers: O_Called_Party_Busy

O Term Seized

This TDP signals to the originator that the terminating party has accepted the call.

O Answer

This TDP signals that the originator has received an O Answer event from the terminating call model.

Triggers: *O_ Answer*

O No Answer

This TDP signals that the originator has not received an O Answer event before the *O No Answer* timer expired.

Triggers: *O_No_Answer*

O Suspend

This TDP signals that the originator has received a suspend indication from the terminating call model. The terminating call model sends the suspend in response to the terminator going on-hook.

O Re-Answer (IN CS-2 DP Only)

This TDP signals that a suspended call has resumed (the terminator has gone back off-hook on the call). This is equivalent to the Called Party Reconnected event in AIN 0.2; however, in AIN 0.2, no DP is supported when this event occurs.

O Midcall

This TDP signals that the originator has performed a hook flash or, in the case of an ISDN line, has sent a feature activator request.

Triggers:

- O_ Switch_Hook_Flash_Immediate
- O_Switch_Hook_Flash_Specified_Code

O Disconnect

This TDP signals that the originating or terminating party has disconnected from the call. When the call is active, this signal might be generated from the originating or terminating call model.

Triggers: O_ Disconnect

O Abandon

This TDP signals that the originating party has disconnected before the call has been answered. For example, this can occur from an originating line going on-hook, an ISDN set sending call clearing, or a REL message from an SS7 trunk occurring before receiving an answer from the terminating call model.

Terminating Basic Call State Model

The IN CS-2 TBCSM represents the stages of a call in the terminating call half. Figure 11-18 shows each of the PICs and TDPs that are supported by the CS-2 model.

Figure 11-18 *IN CS-2 Terminating Basic Call State Model*

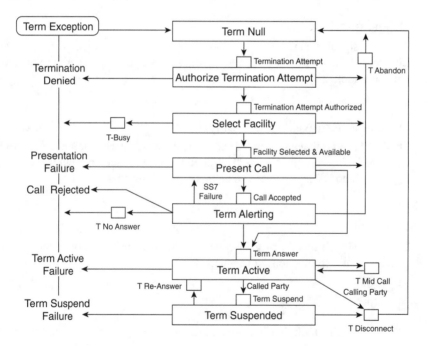

IN CS-2 TBCSM PICs

The following PICs are defined to support IN processing in the terminating call model:

- **Term Null**—This PIC indicates that no call exists.

- **Authorize Termination Attempt**—Determines whether a call has the authority to terminate on the selected interface (for example, DN and trunk group) based on business group restrictions, line restrictions, bearer capability, and so on.

- **Select Facility**—Determines the busy/idle status of the terminating access.

- **Present Call**—The terminating access is informed of an incoming call. For example, a line is seized and power ringing applied—or in the case of an SS7 trunk, an IAM is sent.

- **Term Alerting**—An indication is sent to the originating half of the BCSM that the terminating party is being alerted.

- **Term Active**—The call is answered and the connection is established in both directions. The call has exited the setup phase and is now stable.

- **Term Suspended**—The terminator has disconnected (gone on-hook). This occurs only for basic telephone service lines. It does not apply to ISDN or Electronic Key Telephone Set (EKTS)-terminating access types. Release Disconnect timing is started and the connection maintained. For SS7 signaled trunks, a Suspend message is sent in the backwards direction.

IN CS-2 TBCSM TDPs and Trigger Types

The following are the TDPs for the terminating call model. A brief description is given of the transition point being signaled for each TDP. After the descriptions, the trigger types that are applicable to each TDP are listed.

Termination Attempt

This TDP signals an incoming call attempt on the terminating call model.

Triggers: Termination_Attempt

Termination Attempt Authorized

AIN 0.2 labels this TDP as "Call Presented." It signals that the call has been authorized to route to the terminating access. Line or trunk group restrictions, business group restrictions, and bearer capability have all been validated.

Triggers: Termination_Attempt_Authorized

T Busy

This TDP signals that the terminating access is busy (in other words, it is not idle).

Triggers: T_Busy

Facility Selected and Available

This TDP Signals that the terminating access has been chosen and is available (in other words, it is not busy).

Triggers: Term_Resource_Available

Call Accepted

This TDP signals that the terminating interface has accepted the call and is about to be alerted.

T No Answer

This TDP signals that the terminator has not answered within the ring timeout period. The terminating switch starts the ring timer when alerting begins.

Triggers: T_No_Answer

T Answer

This TDP signals that the called party has answered.

Triggers: T_ Answer (not defined for AIN 0.2)

T Suspended

This TDP signals that the called party has disconnected, but the terminating call model is maintaining the connection.

T Disconnect

This TDP signals that a disconnect has been received from the originating or terminating party.

Triggers: T_Disconnect

T Midcall

This TDP signals that the terminating access has performed a flash hook or, in the case of an ISDN interface, sent a feature activator request.

Triggers: T_Switch_Hook_Flash_Immediate

T Re-Answer (IN CS-2 DP Only)

This TDP signals that the terminating access has resumed a previously suspended call (it has gone off-hook). This is equivalent to the *Called Party Reconnected* event in AIN 0.2, but in AIN 0.2, no DP is supported at the occurrence of this event.

T Abandon

This TDP signals that the originating party abandoned the call before it was set up.

AIN 0.2 Call Control Messages from the SCP

The SSP initiates IN processing. The following is a list of AIN 0.2 call control messages that the SCP can send in response to an SSP message. The SCP can also send several non-call related messages that are not included here. Reference the Bellcore GR-1298 for a complete list of messages.

- **Analyze_Route**—Requests that the SSP continue call processing using the information provided in the message. Examples of the data returned in this message include an address, route, billing, trunk group parameters, and carrier parameters.

- **Continue**—Requests that the SSP continue processing the call without any new information returned from the SCP.

- **Authorize_Termination**—Request for the SSP to continue processing at the Authorize_Termination PIC. This allows the SSP to verify the authority to route the call.

- **Forward_Call**—Request for the SSP to forward the call using the information provided in the message. The SSP creates a new originating call for the forwarding call leg and merges it back into the terminating call half.

- **Offer_Call**—This message is sent in response to the T_Busy message that instructs the SSP to offer the call to the called party. This allows a called party with Call Waiting to have the opportunity to accept the call.

- **Disconnect_Call**—Requests that the SSP disconnect the call.

- **Send_To_Resource**—Requests the SSP to route the call to a resource such as an IP. For example, the caller hears an announcement and inputs digits to be collected (for example, a pin code, menu choice, and so on).

- **Collect_Information**—Request for the SSP to return to the Collect Information PIC. This request can come at certain DPs after the Info Collected PIC has been passed in the progression of the call to send the call back to that point. It can be sent in response to the following SSP messages:
  - Info_Analyzed
  - O_Called_Party_Busy
  - O_No_Answer
  - O_Suspended
  - O_Disconnect

AIN 0.2 Time Of Day (TOD) Routing Example

This example demonstrates the use of AIN for TOD routing along with the O_Called_Party_Busy_Event. A fictitious company XYZ is using the TOD Routing service to route calls to their East Coast support center before 4:00 P.M. EST and to their West Coast support center after 4:00 P.M. EST. In addition, if a busy signal is encountered at the east coast center, an attempt is made to reach the west coast. This happens transparently for the customer; they simply dial a number and reach a technical support person.

In Figure 11-19, the subscriber dials the technical support number. SSP A encounters the SDS trigger at the Analyzed Information DP and matches the called number with a provisioned SDS. A query is sent to the SCP with an Info Analyzed component. The called number is coded into a TCAP parameter that belongs to this component, along with other necessary supporting parameters such as calling number, charge number, and so forth. The SCP receives the message and applies the appropriate service logic for the query, which includes a TOD routing decision. The SCP returns an Analyze Route message with a Called Party Number that is based on the current TOD. The Analyze Route is encoded into a TCAP component with an operation code of Analyze Route. In addition, the SCP includes a Request_Report_BCM_event component that contains a NEL. The NEL contains a list of the events that the SCP is requesting. In this case, only one event is being requested: the O Called Party Busy EDP-R. The OCPB event is now "armed," meaning that IN processing will be invoked when the event occurs. The SSP uses the Called Party Number that is returned in the Analyze Route message to continue call processing, going through normal translations and routing. When a termination attempt is made to the destination, the status of the Called Party Number is busy, which causes the SSP to encounter the OCPB DP. Because the OCPB EDP-R is armed, rather than providing a busy treatment to the originator, IN processing is invoked to send a notification to the SCP, thereby allowing it to intervene. The service logic at the SCP determines that another number has been provided if a busy status is encountered at the first number. The SCP responds with another Analyze Route message that contains the west coast center's Called Party Number. Call processing at the SSP resumes with translations and routing of the new number. The call is then completed successfully.

Figure 11-19 *Time of Day Routing with OCPB Event*

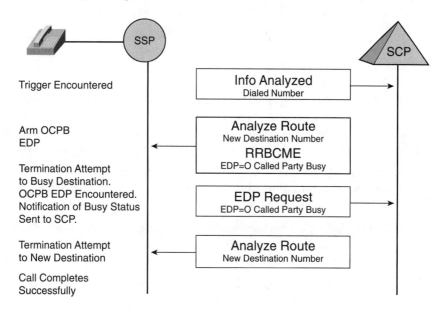

Additional IN Service Examples

Two additional services are presented here to reinforce how IN operates in a real network context. The LNP service represents a government mandated service need, while the PVN demonstrates a solution to a common business need. Both services can be implemented using any of the IN versions discussed in this chapter.

Local Number Portability (LNP)

The North American Local Number Portability Act of 1996 relies on IN technology to deliver number portability for subscriber numbers. Prior to LNP, blocks of phone numbers were associated to specific exchanges. Routing of interexchange calls was based on the NPA-NXX portion of the called number. The NPA identifies a particular geographic region, and the NXX identifies the particular exchange. The long-term goal of LNP is to associate the phone number with individual subscribers, effectively removing the network node association and allowing subscribers to keep their numbers. This means that, as users migrate throughout the network, a particular SSP will eventually handle many different

NPA-NXX combinations instead of just one or two. Number Portability is being rolled out in phases that are designated by three different types of portability:

- Service Provider Portability
- Service Portability
- Location Portability

Service Provider Portability is the first phase and is currently being implemented. It allows subscribers to choose a different service provider but remain within their local region. More specifically, they must remain within their present rate center, which is generally defined as a local geographic area of billing, such as a Local Access Transport Area (LATA).

Service Portability gives the subscriber the ability to change types of service while keeping their same phone number. For example, a basic telephone service subscriber can switch to ISDN service without changing numbers.

Location Portability allows subscribers to change geographical regions and take their phone numbers with them. At this point, phone numbers will not necessarily represent the geographical area in which they reside.

Because LNP is removing the association between subscriber numbers and network nodes, some means of associating a particular user with a point of network access is required. Each office now has a Location Routing Number (LRN) assigned to it that uses the same numbering scheme that existed before the introduction of LNP. The LRN uses the NPA-NXX-XXXX format to allow compatibility with the existing routing method that is used in the network. In essence, subscribers retain their numbers, while the exchange retains its primary identification number and creates a mapping between the two. This brings us to the point of IN's role in providing the LNP service. When the first subscriber within an NPA-NXX changes service providers, the entire NPA-NXX is considered "ported," which means that this particular NPA-NXX combination has become a portable number and no longer represents a specific exchange. Every call to that NPA-NXX must now determine the LRN of the number that is being called. Because all subscribers with that NPA-NXX no longer necessarily reside in the same exchange, the exchange must be determined before the call can be completed. This immediately creates two needs that are readily satisfied using IN:

- Trigger an LRN request for NPA-NXX codes that have been ported
- Maintain the relationship between subscriber number and LRN

The SSP maintains a list of ported NPA-NXX codes. When the call is being translated, the called number's NPA-NXX can be compared with the list of ported codes to determine whether a query should be sent to the SCP.

NOTE   At the point in time at which most numbers are ported within each network spanning a numbering plan, it will no longer be necessary to determine whether a query should be performed. Queries will then be performed for all calls. This decision point is generally governed by individual service providers. Until that point, each SSP must differentiate between the codes that have and have not been ported.

The SCP maintains the relationship of subscriber numbers to LRNs. It maps the Called Party Number sent in the query to an LRN and returns the LRN to the SSP. The SSP uses the LRN as the Called Party Number to route the call to the correct exchange and includes the real Called Party Number in the GAP parameter of the ISUP IAM so that the terminating switch can deliver the call to the subscriber. If the SCP determines that the number has not been ported, it simply returns the original Called Party Number, which the SSP uses to route the call. Figure 11-20 shows an example of a subscriber changing service providers, resulting in their DN being ported from SSP B to SSP A. SSP B is considered the donor switch because it is donating a number that once resided at that exchange. SSP A is considered the recipient switch because it is receiving a number that it did not previously have. When the subscriber at SSP C dials the 392-4000 number, SSP C performs a number translation and determines that 919-392 is open to portability. Because the number is portable and does not reside on the local switch, an IN query is sent to the SCP. The SCP returns the LRN of SSP A, which is now the home for the dialed number. The call is then routed from SSP C to SSP A using ISUP signaling. The original dialed number is placed in the ISUP GAP, and the LRN is placed in the Called Party Number (CDPN) field. For more information about how ISUP is used with LNP, refer to Chapter 8, "ISDN User Part (ISUP)."

The LNP service can be supported using IN/1, IN CS-1, or IN CS-2 call models. Using IN/1, the query sent to the SCP contains a "Provide Instructions/Start" component, while the response from the SCP contains a "Connection Control/Connect" component. In an AIN network, it is triggered at the SSP by the PODP (AIN 0.1) or SDS trigger at the Info_ Analyzed DP. The AIN response from the SCP is an Analyze_Route message. Because the query could be performed at different points in the network, the LNP standards identify the N-1 network as the node for sending the query. This is the last network to handle the call before the terminating local network.

Figure 11-20 *Local Number Portability Service*

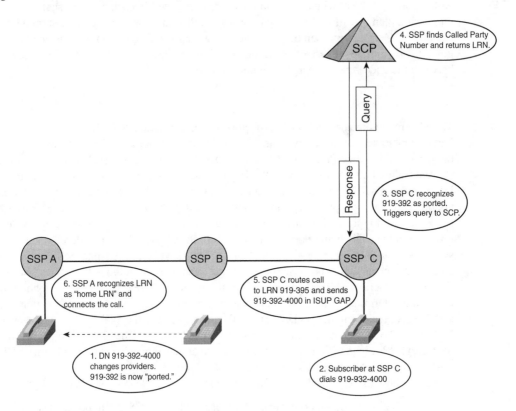

Private Virtual Network (PVN)

The PVN is a service that uses public network facilities to create a private network. An organization with geographically separate locations can share an abbreviated dialing plan using IN to translate the dialed numbers into network-routable addresses. From the user's perspective, it appears that they are on a private network. To determine the call's routing address, the SSP that serves the originating access queries an SCP using the called number, ANI, and other information. An IN response is returned to the SSP with the new routing address and call processing is resumed.

Figure 11-21 shows a company with three locations that are virtually networked over the PSTN. The company employees can use an abbreviated dialing plan to access other locations in the same manner as on-campus calls. The number the employee dials must be translated into an address that the PSTN can route. This happens transparently to the originator of the call, using the IN network to retrieve routing information. The call can then be completed across the PSTN to the San Jose location.

Figure 11-21 *Private Virtual Network Service*

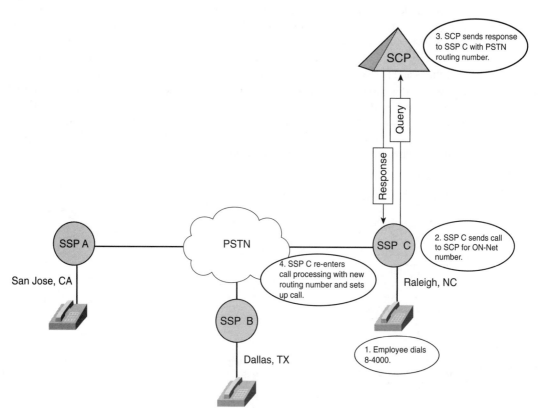

The PVN service can be supported using IN/1, IN CS-1, or IN CS-2 protocols. Using IN/1, the query sent to the SCP contains a "Provide Instructions/Start" component, while the response from the SCP contains a "Connection Control/Connect" component. In an AIN network, the PODP (AIN 0.1) triggers it at the SSP or the SDS triggers it at the Info_ Analyzed DP. The AIN response from the SCP is an Analyze_Route message.

Intelligent Network Application Protocol (INAP)

The ITU defines the INAP protocol, which is based on the same ITU capability sets and CS call models that are discussed in previous sections of this chapter. The ITU Q.12xx recommendation series defines this protocol. INAP is the protocol that is used for IN communication throughout Europe and in most places outside of North America. The ETSI 300 374 1-6 series of specifications refines the ITU documents for the use of INAP in the European region. Application processes use the INAP protocol to perform remote operations between network nodes, such as an SSP and SCP, in the same general manner as the AIN examples that were previously discussed. INAP uses ITU TCAP to deliver these remote operations, which are encapsulated within the TCAP component sublayer to peer application processes at the remote node. Like the various versions of AIN, INAP defines its own set of remote operations and parameters that are used at the component sublayer. While they provide similar functionality to those used by North American AIN, they are distinct in their definition and encoding. Table 11-2 shows the operation codes that are used between the SSF/CCF and SCF FEs for CS1 and CS2. These operations are invoked between the SSP and SCP network nodes. Recall from the earlier discussions about FEs that the SSF/CCF FEs reside within the SSP, while the SCF FE resides within the SCP (or adjunct processor).

Table 11-2   *SSF/SCF Operations for CS1 and CS2*

SSF/CCF—SCF Operation	CS1	CS2
ActivateServiceFiltering	✓	✓
ActivityTest	✓	✓
ApplyCharging	✓	✓
ApplyChargingReport	✓	✓
AssistRequestInstructions	✓	✓
CallGap	✓	✓
CallInformationReport	✓	✓
CallInformationRequest	✓	✓
Cancel	✓	✓
CollectInformation	✓	✓
Connect	✓	✓
ConnectToResource	✓	✓
Continue	✓	✓
ContinueWithArgument		✓
CreateCallSegmentAssociation		✓
DisconnectForwardConnection	✓	✓
DisconnectForwardConnectionWithArgument		✓
DisconnectLeg		✓

Table 11-2   *SSF/SCF Operations for CS1 and CS2 (Continued)*

SSF/CCF—SCF Operation	CS1	CS2
EntityReleased		✓
EstablishTemporaryConnection	✓	✓
EventNotificationCharging	✓	✓
EventReportBCSM	✓	✓
FurnishChargingInformation	✓	✓
InitialDP	✓	✓
InitiateCallAttempt	✓	✓
ManageTriggerData		✓
MergeCallSegments		✓
MoveCallSegments		✓
MoveLeg		✓
ReleaseCall	✓	✓
ReportUTSI		✓
RequestNotificationChargingEvent	✓	✓
RequestReportBCSMEvent	✓	✓
RequestReportUTSI		✓
ResetTimer	✓	✓
SendChargingInformation	✓	✓
SendSTUI		✓
ServiceFilteringResponse	✓	✓
SplitLeg		✓

Table 11-3 shows the operation codes that are used between the SCF and SRF FEs for CS1 and CS2. These operations are invoked between the SCP (or adjunct processor) and Intelligent Peripheral (IP) nodes, which hosts the SCF and SRF FEs, respectively. Note that these tables do not include all INAP operations. Additional operations for communication, such as SCF-SCF, exist; however, this section focuses only on those operations that are directly related to services at an SSP.

Table 11-3   *SCF—SRF Operations for CS1 and CS2*

SCF—SRF Operation	CS1	CS2
PlayAnnouncement	✓	✓
PromptAndCollectUserInformation	✓	✓
PromptAndReceiveMessage		✓
ScriptClose		✓
ScriptEvent		✓
ScriptInformation		✓
ScriptRun		✓
SpecializedResourceReport	✓	

Basic Toll-Free Example Using INAP

This example uses a few of the INAP operations from Table 11-2 to define a simple example to illustrate how INAP is used. Figure 11-22 shows the message flow for a basic toll-free service using INAP. The toll-free application at the SSP determines that communication with the SCP is necessary to retrieve information for the toll-free service.

A TCAP Begin message is sent to the SCP with an InitialDP operation code. The InitialDP operation indicates that a TDP has been encountered at the SSP, thereby requiring instructions from the SCP to complete the call. The only mandatory parameter for the InitialDP operation is the ServiceKey parameter, which selects the appropriate SLP or application for processing the operation at the SCP. The InitialDP component can include several optional parameters. Using our example in Figure 11-21, the CalledPartyNumber parameter is included to indicate the toll-free number. In this case, the CalledPartyNumber parameter is required to obtain a routable destination number from the SCP. The SCP translates the toll-free number to a routable number that is to be returned to the SSP.

The SCP responds with a TCAP End message that contains Apply Charging and Connect operation codes. The Apply Charging operation indicates that charging should be applied for the call and might contain a PartyToCharge parameter to indicate whether charges should be applied to the calling or called party. In the case of a toll-free or free phone call, charges are applied to the called party. The Connect operation contains the Destination-RoutingAddress parameter to specify the routable destination number for connecting the call. Depending on regulatory policies and agreements, information such as the Carrier parameter can be returned in the Connect component to specify a particular IXC-providing service for the freephone number.

Figure 11-22 *INAP Toll-Free Message Flow*

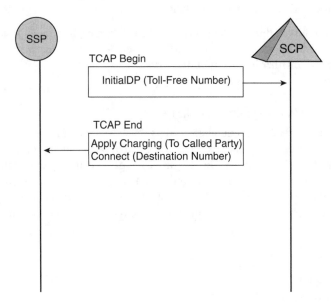

This example is a very simple version of a toll-free service. It could also include connections to an IP, along with many other variations in the message flow and parameters. The example has been kept simple to provide an understanding of what a simple INAP exchange looks like for a service and to avoid the varying nuances of how the service might be deployed.

As the figure shows, INAP provides operations that are similar to those of AIN at the component sublayer. However, the operations have been tailored to the needs of the European region, thus adhering to the ETSI specifications.

Service Creation Environment (SCE)

SCE provides a set of tools for creating the service logic that is executed at the SCP. This allows SPs to build and deploy their own services. Several SCEs are available, each differing in features and capabilities; however, they all share a common purpose of generating program code that can be executed by the SCP. Many SCEs provide a Graphical User Interface that allows software components to be joined together at a high level using visual tools to represent a service. Further modifications and customizations are applied by setting the properties that are associated with the high level objects and often by making software modifications at the software coding level. The program code is then generated for the service, which can be executed at an SCP.

The SCE refers to this program code as a SLP, while each of the high-level software components is referred to as a SIB. SLPs provide the "glue" logic and overall program flow to join SIBs together into meaningful services.

Service Independent Building Blocks (SIB)

The IN standards define a number of SIBs. Each SIB identifies a common telephony function that is used across services. Within each SIB, one or more operations take place to implement the SIB function. One of the SCE's goals is to implement the SIB, or the operations that comprise an SIB, and allow them to be joined together to create a service. SIBs are currently quite generic and lack ample detail, making them primarily useful only for high-level modeling of service functions. An example of some SIBs include:

- Charge
- Join
- Screen
- Translate
- User Interaction

These building blocks are easily recognizable as part of standard telephony call and feature processing. A complete list of SIBs can be found in the ITU IN specifications.

To explore a specific example, consider the User Interaction SIB. The two most common functions involving User Interaction are collecting information from the user and playing audible messages (or tones). Audible messages can be used for a number of different purposes, including the following:

- Prompts that request information from the user
- Messages that provide information to the user
- Branding or advertisement
- Voicemail
- Custom messages that are created by the service subscriber

Input is collected to make decisions about how a call should be directed and to determine the services the user needs. User input is usually provided in one of the following forms:

- DTMF digits using the phone keypad
- Voice Recognition
- Web interface (Internet telephony)

Figure 11-23 shows an exchange between the SSP and SCP that requires the user to enter information based on voice prompts. These actions are driven by the User Interaction SIB functions, which are implemented at the SCP as part of the service.

Figure 11-23 *Example of User Interaction*

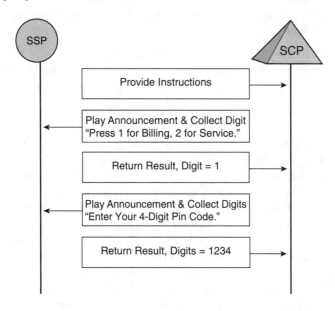

The operation within the User Interaction SIB that implements the collection of digits does not determine how the digits will be used. That would defeat the SIB's "independence" aspect.

As the network and services evolve, new means for interacting with the user will inevitably surface, thereby adding additional operations to the User Interaction SIB. Services that use new protocols, such as Wireless Access Protocol (WAP), have already changed User Interaction to some extent. However, the fundamental building block of this SIB will still be needed.

Service Logic Programs (SLP)

The SLP is the executable logic that results from the service creation process. Whether the service is constructed using graphical tools or programming libraries, the end result must be able to run on the SCP platform. The SCE allows subcomponents that make up an SIB to be joined together in a logical flow with decision branch points based on the results of the subcomponent operations. The result is a complete logic program that can be executed.

Before running it on an SCP platform, the SCE generally provides some level of simulation to determine how the service will function. Good simulators allow phone calls to be placed using resources such as recorded announcements and Voice Recognition Units, to provide a complete simulation of the service. When the service has been constructed using the SCE tools, code modules or program scripts that are eventually deployed to the SCP or Adjunct are generated. The code modules are triggered by incoming messages, which match a given criteria for the script, from the SSP.

The SLP processes the incoming messages from the SSP, accesses data that is stored at the SCP, and makes decisions about how to direct call processing at the SSP.

Summary

The Intelligent Network is a continually-evolving model for distributed service processing in the telecommunications network. The models that represent call processing provide a generic interface for distributed control, thereby allowing intelligence to move out of the SSP. The IN model also fits well into some next generation telecom architectures, such as those built on IP-based softswitches. There are standards for delivering TCAP over the IP transport, such as the Bellcore GDI interface, which allows IN services to continue to work with little or no modifications. Adjuncts already provide IP connections to IN SLPs, so the migration path to IP-based IN networks is occurring. A common theme among the proposed next-generation architectures is distribution of the functions performed by switching exchanges. The IN model fits into this structure by providing a generic framework for both extending the PSTN and allowing it to interwork with the new architectures.

Of course, there are other intelligent endpoint architectures that provide alternatives to the IN model, such as the Session Initiation Protocol (SIP). The point of this chapter is not to debate the merits of which architecture is best but to provide an understanding of the IN architecture, which so heavily depends on SS7 signaling to function.

CHAPTER 12

Cellular Networks

This chapter introduces Global System for Mobile communications (GSM), which is the most popular digital cellular network standard in terms of architecture, discusses interfaces and protocols, and concludes by presenting examples of mobility management and call processing in the network. The protocols that are found in GSM to perform these functions — namely, Base Station Subsystem Application Part (BSSAP) and Mobile Application Part (MAP) — are applications (subsystems) that utilize the underlying functionality of the SS7 protocols and network. This chapter aims to provide enough background on GSM cellular networks for you to understand the MAP that is used for mobility management and call processing within the GSM network, which is discussed in Chapter 13, "GSM and ANSI-41 Mobile Application Part (MAP)."

The European Telecommunication Standard Institute (ETSI) formulated GSM. Phase one of the GSM specifications was published in 1990, and the commercial operation using the 900 Mhz range began in 1991. The same year, a derivative of GSM, known as Digital Cellular System 1800 (DCS 1800), which translated GSM to the 1800 Mhz range, appeared. The United States adapted DCS 1800 into the 1900 Mhz range and called it Personal Communication System 1900 (PCS 1900). By 1993, 36 GSM networks existed in 22 countries [119].

Pre-GSM cellular networks are analog and vary from country to country — for example, the United States still uses Advanced/American Mobile Phone Service (AMPS), and the UK used Total Access Communication System (TACS). With these older analog standards, it was impossible to have one phone work in more than one country. In addition, because of the analog nature of the speech, quality could be relatively poor, and there were no provisions for supplementary services (such as call waiting). Although it is standardized in Europe, GSM is not just a European standard. At the time of this writing, there are more than 509 GSM networks (including DCS 1800 and PCS 1900) operating in 182 countries around the world, with 684.2 million subscribers [Source: GSM Association]. See Appendix I for a list of mobile networks by country.

GSM has been released in phases. The following are the features of these phases:

GSM Phase 1 (1992) Features

- Call Forwarding
- All Calls
- No Answer
- Engaged
- Unreachable
- Call Barring
- Outgoing—Bar certain outgoing calls
- Incoming—Bar certain incoming calls
- Global roaming——If you visit any other country or parts in an existing country with GSM, your cellular phone remains connected without having to change your number or perform any action.

GSM Phase 2 (1995) Features

- **Short Message Service (SMS)**—Allows you to send and receive text messages.
- **Multiparty Calling**—Talk to five other parties and yourself at the same time.
- **Call Holding**—Place a call on hold.
- **Calling Line Identity Service**—This facility allows you to see the incoming caller's telephone number on your handset before answering.
- **Advice of Charge**—Allows you to keep track of call costs.
- **Cell Broadcast**—Allows you to subscribe to local news channels.
- **Mobile Terminating Fax**—Another number you are issued that can receive faxes.
- **Call Waiting**—Notifies you of another call while you are on a call.
- **Mobile Data Services**—Allows handsets to communicate with computers.
- **Mobile Fax Service**—Allows handsets to send, retrieve, and receive faxes.

GSM Phase 2 + (1996) Features

- Upgrades and improvements to existing services; the majority of the upgrade concerns data transmission, including bearer services and packet switched data at 64 kbps and above
- DECT access to GSM
- PMR/Public Access Mobile Radio (PAMR)-like capabilities to GSM in the local loop

- SIM enhancements
- Premium rate services
- Virtual Private Networks Packet Radio

Unlike Europe (and most of the world), which only pursued GSM for digital cellular networks, North America has pursued a mix of TDMA (IS-54, IS-136), CDMA, and GSM. At the time of this writing, TDMA and CDMA have been more widely deployed in North America than GSM. However, this situation is rapidly beginning to reverse with GSM continually gaining ground.

One benefit of 3G technology is that it unifies these diverse cellular standards. Although three different air interface modes exist—wideband CDMA, CDMA 2000, and the Universal Wireless Communication (UWC-136) interfaces—each should be able to work over both current GSM network architectures.

Network Architecture

GSM architecture can be divided into three broad functional areas: the Base Station Subsystem (BSS), the Network and Switching Subsystems (NSS), and the Operations Support Subsystem (OSS). Each of the subsystems is comprised of functional entities that communicate through various interfaces using specified protocols. The "Interfaces and Protocols" section of this chapter overviews the interfaces and SS7/C7 protocols that are used in the NSS and BSS.

Figure 12-1 shows a general GSM architecture to illustrate the scope and the entities that comprise the three subsystems.

The BSS is comprised of the Base Transceiver Station (BTS) and the Base Station Controller (BSC). The BSS provides transmission paths between the Mobile Stations (MSs) and the NSS, and manages the transmission paths. The NSS is the brain of the entire GSM network and is comprised of the Mobile Switching Center (MSC) and four intelligent network nodes known as the Home Location Register (HLR), Visitor Location Register (VLR), Equipment Identity Register (EIR), and the Authentication Center (AuC). The OSS consists of Operation and Maintenance Centers (OMCs) that are used for remote and centralized operation, administration, and maintenance (OAM) tasks. The OSS provides means for a service provider to control and manage the network. The OSS is usually proprietary in nature and does not have standardized interfaces (using SS7 is irrelevant). Therefore, it is not considered. The BSS is the radio part, and this book does not detail radio related signaling. Therefore, the focus is on the NSS where the MAP protocol is used.

Figure 12-1 *General GSM Architecture, Including the Three Main Separations in the Network*

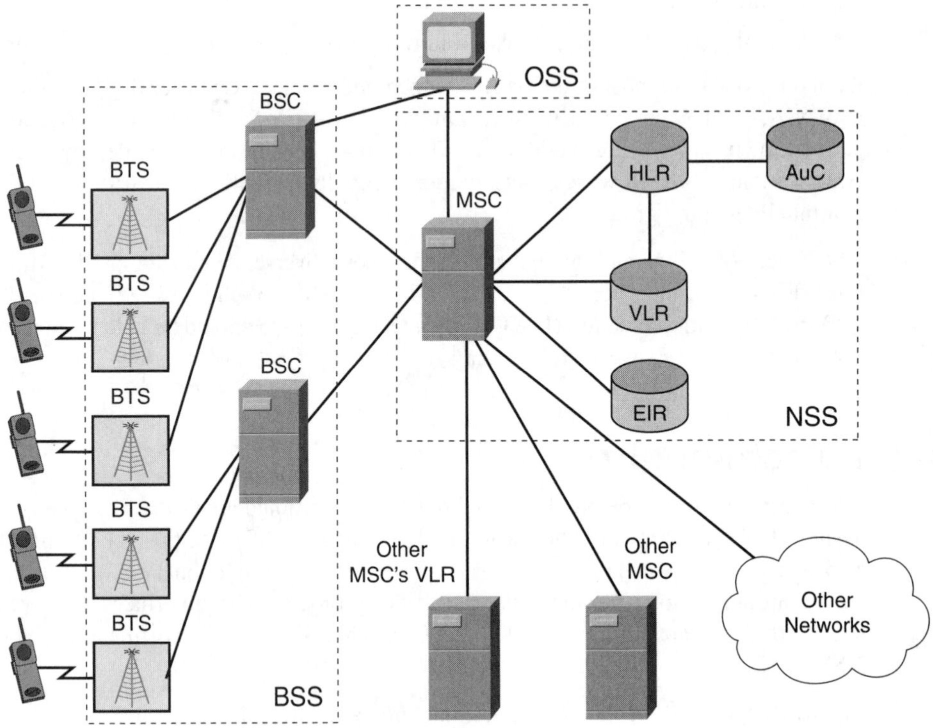

GSM utilizes a cellular structure. Each cell is hexagonal in shape so that the cells fit together tightly. Each cell is assigned a frequency range. The size of the cell is relatively small so the scarce frequencies can be reused in other cells. Each cell contains a base station, and a lot of planning goes into ensuring that base stations from different cells do not interfere with each other. One disadvantage of small cells is that the number of required base stations increases the infrastructure costs. The primary difference between GSM 900 and the GSM 1800/1900 systems is the air interface. In addition to using another frequency band, they both use a microcellular structure. As shown in Figure 12-2, this permits frequency reuse at closer distances, thereby enabling increases in subscriber density. The disadvantage is the higher attenuation of the air interface because of the higher frequency.

One interesting point is that cell sizes vary because each cell can only serve a finite number of subscribers—typically 600 to 800. This means that cells become smaller for higher population density areas.

Figure 12-2 *Frequency Reuse and Cellular Structure*

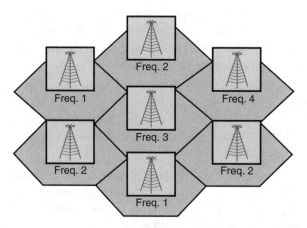

If a mobile moves from one cell to another during an active call, it should be clear that the call must be handed over to the new cell; this should be done in a fully transparent fashion to the subscriber. This process is known as a *handover*. The Mobile Switching Centre (MSC) monitors the strength of the incoming signal from the cellular phone (known as *MS*). When the signal power drops below a certain level, it indicates that the user might have entered another cell or is at the edge of the current cell. The MSC then checks to see if another cell is receiving a stronger cell. If it is, the call is transferred to that cell.

The approximate location of an MS, even if idle, has to be tracked to allow incoming calls to be delivered.

NOTE   Handovers and location tracking involve extensive and complex SS7/C7 signaling. In a cellular network, most signaling relates to the support of roaming functionality. Only a fraction of the signaling relates to call control.

The architecture that is presented in this section is not meant to be all-inclusive. Rather, its purpose is to provide the reader with the basic knowledge to comprehend SS7/C7 protocols that relate to cellular networks. When "GSM" is stated, it includes DCS, PCS, and GPRS networks. The rest of this section discusses the function of the components that comprise the NSS and BSS, along with the cellular phone itself and the identifiers associated with it.

Mobile Station (MS)

GSM refers to the cellular handsets as MS. PCMIA cards are also available for laptops to allow data transfer over the GSM network, without the need for a voice-centric handset. The MS consists of the physical equipment that the subscriber uses to access a PLMN and a removable smart card, known as the SIM, to identify the subscriber.

GSM was unique to use the SIM card to break the subscriber ID apart from the equipment ID. The SIM card is fully portable between *Mobile Equipment* (ME) units. This allows many features that we take for granted, such as being able to swap MS simply by swapping our SIM card over. All functionality continues seamlessly, including billing, and the telephone number remains the same.

An MS has several associated identities, including the International Mobile Equipment Identity (IMEI), the International Mobile Subscriber Identity (IMSI), the Temporary Mobile Subscriber Identity (TMSI), and the Mobile Station ISDN (MSISDN) number. The following sections examine each of these identities, in turn, so that signaling sequences in which they are involved make sense.

IMEI

Each ME has a unique number, known as the IMEI, stored on it permanently. The IMEI is not only a serial number; it also indicates the manufacturer, the country in which it was produced, and the type approval. It is assigned at the factory.

GSM 03.03 specifies the IMEI, which is also defined by the 3GPP TS 23.003 [106]. The IMEI is used so actions can be taken against stolen equipment or to reject equipment that it cannot accept for technical and/or safety reasons. The IMEI allows tracing and prevention of fraudulent use and, in some circumstances, special network handling of specific MS types. Figure 12-3 shows the structure of the IMEI.

Figure 12-3 *IMEI Structure*

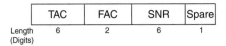

	TAC	FAC	SNR	Spare
Length (Digits)	6	2	6	1

In the figure, the Type Approval Code (TAC) identifies the country in which the phone's type approval was sought, and its approval number. The first two digits of the TAC represent the country of approval. The Final Assembly Code (FAC) identifies the facility where the phone was assembled. Table 12-1 shows the codes that are currently in effect. The Serial

Number (SNR) is an individual serial number that uniquely identifies each MS (within each TAC and FAC).

Table 12-1   *Final Assembly Codes*

Code	Facility
01, 02	AEG
07, 40	Motorola
10, 20	Nokia
30	Ericsson
40, 41, 44	Siemens
47	Option International
50	Bosch
51	Sony
51	Siemens
51	Ericsson
60	Alcatel
70	Sagem
75	Dancall
80	Philips
85	Panasonic

The IMEI is used for several fundamental network operations, such as when an MS is switched on; the IMEI number is transmitted and checked against a black/gray list. Operations that involve the IMEI are further discussed in later sections of this chapter.

In addition to current BCD coding, 3GPP is currently proposing to change the IMEI message structure to allow the use of hexadecimal coding. This would allow the production of 16.7 million mobile terminals with one TAC+FAC combination.

To display the IMEI on most MSs, enter ***#06#** on the keypad. This is useful for insurance purposes and allows the device to be blocked from network access, should it be stolen (network permitting).

IMSI

Each subscriber is assigned a unique number, which is known as the IMSI. The IMSI is the only absolute identity a subscriber has within GSM, and as such, it is stored on the SIM. The SIM is a credit size, or quarter-credit card size smart card that contains the subscriber's subscription details and grants the subscriber service when placed into a piece of ME. Among other purposes, it is used for subscriber billing, identification, and authentication when roaming.

The IMSI is specified in GSM 03.03, by 3GPP in TS 23.003, and the ITU in E.212. Figure 12-4 shows an IMSI's format.

Figure 12-4 *IMEI Structure*

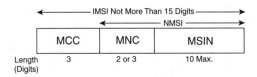

In Figure 12-4, the Mobile Country Code (MCC) identifies the mobile subscriber's country of domicile. The Mobile Network Code (MNC) identifies the subscriber's home GSM PLMN.

The Mobile Station Identification Number (MSIN) identifies the mobile subscriber. The National Mobile Station Identity (NMSI) is the name given to MNC+MSIN fields.

The MCN's administration is the National Regulatory Authority's (NRAs) responsibility— for example, OFTEL in the UK or Telcordia in the USA—while network operators are usually responsible for the MSIN's arrangement and administration following the MNC assigned by the respective NRA. Appendix I contains a list of MCCs and MNCs.

TMSI

A TMSI is an alias used by the VLR (and the SGSN in GPRS enabled networks) to protect subscriber confidentiality. Please see section VLR for a description of the VLR. It is temporarily used as a substitute for the IMSI to limit the number of times the IMSI is broadcast over the air interface because intruders could use the IMSI to identify a GSM subscriber. TMSI is issued during the *location update* procedure. The VLR and SGSNs must be capable of correlating an allocated TMSI with the MS's IMSI to which it is allocated. The VLR assigns the TMSI to an MS during the subscriber's initial transaction with an MSC (for example, location updating). Because the TMSI has only local significance (within an area controlled by VLR), each network administrator can choose its structure to suit his needs. To avoid double allocation under failure/recovery conditions, it is generally considered good practice to make part of the TMSI related to time.

The TMSI is defined in 3GPP TS 23.003 [106].

MSISDN

MSISDN is the number the calling party dials to reach the called party—in other words, it is the mobile subscriber's directory number. This parameter refers to one of the ISDN numbers that is assigned to a mobile subscriber in accordance with ITU Recommendation E.213. A subscriber might have more than one MISDN on their SIM; examples include an MISDN for voice and an MISDN for fax. You can find additional MISDN details in GSM 03.02 and GSM 03.12. Figure 12-5 shows the format of an MSISDN.

Figure 12-5 *MSISDN (E.164) Structure*

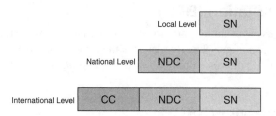

In Figure 12-5, the National Destination Code (NDC) identifies the numbering area with a country and/or network/services. Country Code (CC) identifies a specific country, countries in an integrated NP, or a specific geographic area. Subscriber Number (SN) identifies a subscriber in a network or numbering area.

MSRN

The Mobile Station Roaming Number (MSRN) is solely used to route an incoming call. It is a temporary identifier that is used to route a call from the gateway MSC to the serving MSC/VLR.

The serving MSC/VLR is the MSC/VLR for the area where the subscriber currently roams. The VLR assigns an MSRN when it receives a request for routing information from the HLR. When the call has been cleared down, the MSRN is released back to the VLR.

Additional details about the MSRN can be found in GSM 03.03.

Subscriber Identity Module (SIM)

SIM cards are like credit cards and identify the user to the GSM network. They can be used with any GSM handset to provide phone access, ensure delivery of appropriate services to that user, and automatically bill the subscriber's network usage back to the home network.

As previously stated, GSM distinguishes between the subscriber and the MS. The SIM determines the subscriber's cellular number, thus permitting the subscriber to use other equipment (change MS) while maintaining one number and one bill. The SIM is a chip that is embedded in a card approximately the size of a credit card, or around a quarter of the size (the former tends to be outdated).

The SIM is the component that communicates directly with the VLR and indirectly with the HLR. These two critical networks components will be described later in this chapter.

Base Transceiver Station (BTS)

The base transceiver stations provide the connectively between the cellular network and the MS via the Airinterface. The BTS houses the radio transceivers that define a cell and handles the radio interface protocols with the mobile station.

Base Station Controller (BSC)

A number of BTSs are connected to the BSC on an interface that is known as the Abis interface.

It manages the radio interface channels, such as setup, release, frequency hopping, and handovers.

Mobile Switching Centre (MSC)

The MSC is the network subsystem's central component. Because a large number of BSCs are connected to an MSC, an MSC is effectively a regular ISDN switch that connects to the BSCs via the A-interface. The MSC provides routing of incoming and outgoing calls and assigns user channels on the A-interface.

It acts like a normal switching node of the PSTN or ISDN and provides all the necessary functionality for handling a mobile station, including registration, authentication, location updating, inter-MSC handovers, and call routing to a roaming subscriber.

The MSC also provides the connection to the public fixed networks.

Together with the MSC, the HLR and VLR provide GSM call routing and roaming capabilities.

Home Location Register (HLR)

The HLR can be regarded as a huge database that contains the information for hundreds of thousands of subscribers. Every PLMN has at least one HLR. While there is logically one HLR per GSM network, it might be implemented as a distributed database.

The HLR contains all administrative data that is related to each subscriber, who is registered in the corresponding GSM network, along with his current location. The location of each mobile station that belongs to the HLR is stored in order to be able to route calls to the mobile subscribers served by that HLR. The location information is simply the VLR address that currently serves the subscriber. An HLR does not have direct control of MSCs.

Two numbers that are attached to each mobile subscription and stored in the HLR include the IMSI and the MSISDN. The HLR also stores additional information, including the location information (VLR), supplementary services, basic service subscription information, and service restrictions (such as roaming permission). GSM 03.08 details the subscriber data's organization.

Visitor Location Register (VLR)

Like the HLR, the VLR contains subscriber data. However, it only contains a subset (selected administrative information) of the data that is necessary for call control and provision of the subscribed services for each mobile that is currently located in the geographical area controlled by the VLR. The VLR data is only temporarily stored while the subscriber is in the area that is served by a particular VLR. A VLR is responsible for one or several MSC areas. When a subscriber roams into a new MSC area, a location updating procedure is applied. When the subscriber roams out of the area that is served by the VLR, the HLR requests that it remove the subscriber-related data.

Although the VLR can be implemented as an independent unit, to date, all manufacturers of switching equipment implement the VLR with the MSC so the geographical area controlled by the MSC corresponds to that which is controlled by the VLR. The proximity of the VLR information to the MSC speeds up access to information that the MSC requires during a call.

Equipment Identity Register (EIR)

The EIR is a database that contains a list of all valid mobile equipment on the network. Each MS is identified by its IMEI. An IMEI is marked as invalid if it has been reported stolen or is not type approved.

The EIR contains a list of stolen MSs. Because the subscriber identity can simply be changed by inserting a new SIM, the theft of GSM MSs is attractive. The EIR allows a call bar to be placed on stolen MSs. This is possible because each MS has a unique IMEI.

Authentication Center (AuC)

The AuC is a protected database that stores a copy of the secret key that is stored in the subscriber's SIM card and is used for authentication and ciphering on the radio channel.

Serving GPRS Support Node (SGSN)

A SGSN is responsible for delivering data packets from and to the mobile stations within its geographical service area. Its tasks include packet routing and transfer, mobility management (attach/detach and location management), logical link management, and authentication and charging functions. The location register of the SGSN stores location information (such as current cell and current VLR) and user profiles (such as IMSI and address(es) used in the packet data network) of all GPRS users who are registered with this SGSN.

The SGSN delivers packets to mobile stations within its service area. SGSNs detect subscribers in their service area, query HLRs to obtain subscriber profiles, and maintain a record of their location.

Gateway GPRS Support Node (GGSN)

GGSNs maintain routing information that is necessary to tunnel the Protocol Data Units (PDUs) to the SGSNs that service specific mobile stations. Other functions include network and subscriber screening and address mapping.

Interfaces and Protocols

The previous section introduced GSM network architecture, and this section introduces the SS7/C7 protocols that are used. It also discusses interfaces, because different protocols are used on different interfaces. The SS7/C7 protocols MTP, SCCP, TUP, ISUP are protocols that were used before digital wireless networks were available. The final part of this section introduces SS7/C7 protocols that were specifically developed for GSM.

Table 12-2 summarizes the interfaces and protocols that are used in GSM.

In terms of the physical layer, the air interface (MS-BTS) uses RF radio transmission. The A-bis interface (BTS-BSC) uses 64 kbps over whatever medium is most convenient for installation: wire, optical, or microwave. All other interfaces in the GSM system use SS7/C7s MTP1 at the physical layer.

The data link layer that is used at the air interface (MS-BTS) is LAP-Dm; LAP-D is the data link layer that is used at the A-bis interface (BTS-BSC). All other interfaces in the GSM system use SS7/C7s MTP2 at the data link layer.

The air interface (MS-BTS) and the Abis interface (BTS-BSC) do not have a network layer. All other interfaces in the GSM system use SS7/C7s MTP3 and SCCP at the network layer.

The transport, session, and presentation layers are not used in SS7/C7 — these functions are grouped together at the application layer, which is known as Level 4 in SS7/C7. GSM interfaces to fixed-line networks using ISUP or TUP (TUP is never used in North America).

Table 12-2   *GSM Interfaces and Protocols*

Interface	Between	Description
U$_m$	MS-BSS	The air interface is used for exchanges between a MS and a BSS. LAPDm, a modified version of the ISDN LAPD, is used for signaling.
Abis	BSC-BTS	This is a BSS internal interface that links the BSC and a BTS; it has not been standardized. The Abis interface allows control of radio equipment and radio frequency allocation in the BTS.
A	BSS-MSC	The A interface is between the BSS and the MSC. It manages the allocation of suitable radio resources to the MSs and mobility management. It uses the BSSAP protocols (BSSMAP and DTAP).
B	MSC-VLR	The B interface handles signaling between the MSC and the VLR. It uses the MAP/B protocol. Most MSCs are associated with a VLR, making the B interface "internal." Whenever the MSC needs to access data regarding an MS that is located in its area, it interrogates the VLR using the MAP/B protocol over the B interface.
C	GMSC-HLR or SMSG-HLR	The C interface is between the HLR and a GMSC or a SMSC. Each call that originates outside of GSM (such as an MS terminating call from the PSTN) must go through a gateway to obtain the routing information that is required to complete the call, and the MAP/C protocol over the C interface is used for this purpose. Also, the MSC can optionally forward billing information to the HLR after call clearing.
D	HLR-VLR	The D interface is between the HLR and VLR, and uses the MAP/D protocol to exchange data related to the location of the MS and subsets of subscriber data.
E	MSC-MSC	The E interface connects MSCs. The E interface exchanges data that is related to handover between the anchor and relay MSCs using the MAP/E protocol. The E interface can also be used to connect the GMSC to an SMSC.
F	MSC-EIR	The F interface connects the MSC to the EIR and uses the MAP/F protocol to verify the status of the IMEI that the MSC has retrieved from the MS.
G	VLR-VLR	The G interface interconnects two VLRs of different MSCs and uses the MAP/G protocol to transfer subscriber information—for example, during a location update procedure.

continues

Table 12-2 *GSM Interfaces and Protocols (Continued)*

Interface	Between	Description
H	MSC-SMSG	The H interface is located between the MSC and the SMSG and uses the MAP/H protocol to support the transfer of short messages. Again, GSM as well as ANSI-41 is unknown, but H in ANSI-41 is used for HLR–AC interface.
I	MSC-MS	The I interface is the interface between the MSC and the MS. Messages exchanged over the I interface are transparently relayed through the BSS.

Figure 12-6 shows the SS7 protocols that operate at each interface.

Figure 12-6 *Protocols Operating at Each Interface*

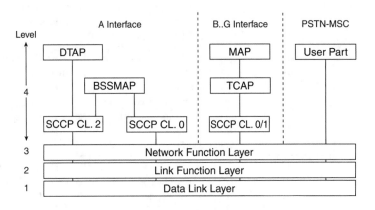

All of the interfaces around the MSC use SS7/C7-based protocols. The B, C, D, F, and G interfaces are referred to as MAP interfaces. These either connect the MSC to registers or connect registers to other registers. The E interface supports the MAP protocol and calls setup protocols (ISUP/ TUP). This interface connects one MSC to another MSC within the same network or to another network's MSC.

By this point, you can gather that different functional entities (e.g. HLR, MSC, and so on) run the required and therefore differing stack of SS7/C7 protocols. In relation to the following diagram, remember that the MSC runs MAP-MSC, and that MAP-VLR and the HLR run MAP-HLR.

Figure 12-7 *Protocols Required for Functional Entities*

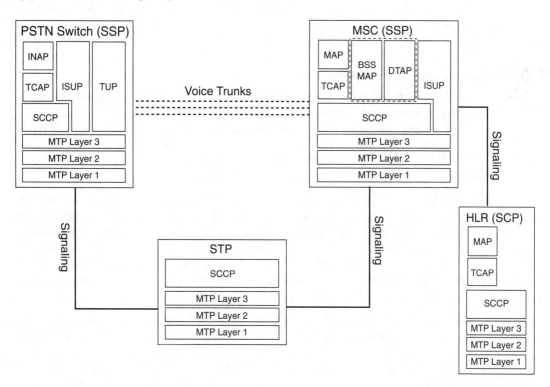

BSSAP (DTAP/BSSMAP)

On the A interface, an application part known as the BSSAP is used. BSSAP can be further separated into the base station subsystem management application part (BSSMAP) and the direct transfer application part (DTAP).

Neither the BTS nor the BSC interpret CM and MM messages. They are simply exchanged with the MSC or the MS using the DTAP protocol on the A interface. RR messages are sent between the BSC and MSC using the BSSAP.

BSSAP includes all messages exchanged between the BSC and the MSC that the BSC actually processes—examples include PAGING, HND_CMD, and the RESET message. More generally, BSSAP comprises all messages that are exchanged as RR messages between MSC and BSC, and messages that are used for call-control tasks between the BSC and the MSC.

The DTAP comprises all messages that the subsystem of the NSS and the MS exchange. DTAP transports messages between the MS and the MSC, in which the BSC has just the relaying function.

Mobile Application Part (MAP)

The MAP is an extension of the SS7/C7 protocols that are added to support cellular networks. It defines the operations between the MSC, the HLR, the VLR, the EIR, and the fixed-line network. It comes in two incompatible variants: GSM-MAP and ANSI-41 MAP. While GSM-MAP only supports GSM, ANSI-41 supports AMPS, NAMPS, D-AMPS/TDMA, CDMA (cdma One and cdma 2000), and GSM. GSM-MAP is the international version, while ANSI-41 is the North American version.

The MAP is used to define the operations between the network components (such as MSC, BTS, BSC, HLR, VLR, EIR, MS, and SGSN/GGSN in GPRS). This involves the transfer of information between the components using noncircuit-related signaling. MAP signaling enables location updating, handover, roaming functionality, authentication, incoming call routing, and SMS. MAP specifies a set of services and the information flows between GSM components to implement these services. MAP can be considered an extension of the SS7/ C7 protocol suite created specifically for GSM and ANSI-41 networks.

MAP uses TCAP over SCCP and MTP. TCAP correlates between individual operations. The TCAP transaction sublayer manages transactions on an end-to-end basis. The TCAP component sublayer correlates commands and responses within a dialog. Chapter 10, "Transaction Capabilities Application Part (TCAP)," describes TCAP in more detail.

MAP protocols are designated MAP/B–MAP/H, according to the interface on which the protocol functions. For example, the MAP signaling between the GMSC and the HLR is MAP/F.

Figure 12-8 shows the specific MAP-n protocols. The PCS 1900 specifications use the same MAP interfaces, but PCS 1900 also defines MAP-H.

MAP allows implementation of functions such as location updating/roaming, SMS delivery, handover, authentication, and incoming call routing information. The MAP protocol uses the TCAP protocol to transfer real-time information (between NSS components).

- MAP provides the functionality to route calls to and from the mobile subscribers—it has the mechanisms necessary for transferring information relating to subscribers roaming between network entities in the PLMN.
- The U.S. version is known as ANSI-41-MAP (standardized by EIA/TIA).
- The international version is known as GSM-MAP (standardized by ITU/ETSI).

MAP only makes use of the connectionless classes (0 or 1) of the SCCP.

Figure 12-8 *MAP-n Protocols*

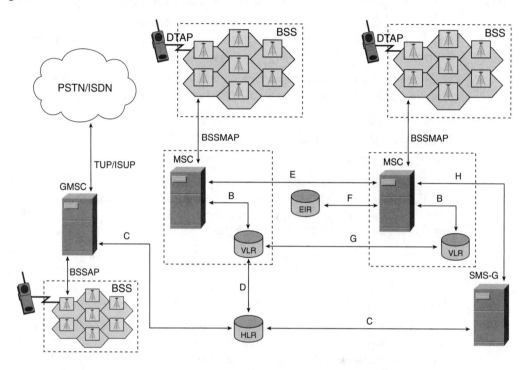

Table 12-4 shows the SCCP Subsystem Numbers (SSNs) that are specified for MAP.

Table 12-3 *SSNs Used by MAP*

SCCP Subsystem Numbers	Use
0 0 0 0 0 1 0 1	For the entire MAP (reserved for possible future use)
0 0 0 0 0 1 1 0	HLR
0 0 0 0 0 1 1 1	VLR
0 0 0 0 1 0 0 0	MSC
0 0 0 0 1 0 0 1	EIR
0 0 0 0 1 0 1 0	Allocated for evolution (possible Authentication centre)

Mobility Management and Call Processing

This section provides an introductory overview of mobility management (i.e., allowing a subscriber to roam) and call processing (the setting up and clearing down of calls) in GSM networks.

Mobility management entails keeping track of the MS while it is on the move. The mobility management procedures vary across three distinct scenarios, namely:

- MS is turned off
- MS is turned on but is idle
- MS has an active call

In the first scenario, when it cannot be reached by the network because it does not respond to the paging message, the MS is considered to be in the turned-off state. In this scenario, the MS obviously fails to provide any updates in relation to changes in Location Area (LA), if any exist. In this state, the MS is considered detached from the system (IMSI detached).

In the second scenario, the MS is in the ready state to make or receive calls. The system considers it attached (IMSI attached), and it can be successfully paged. While on the move, the MS must inform the system about any changes in LA; this is known as location updating.

In the third scenario, the system has active radio channels that are allowed to the MS for conversation/data flow. The MS is required to change to new radio channels if the quality of current channels drops below a certain level; this is known as handover. The MSC (sometimes BSC) makes the decision to handover an analysis of information that is obtained real-time from the MS and BTS.

All operations revolve around the three scenarios presented above. The rest of this chapter examines these operations in more detail, beginning with simple operations: paging, IMSI detach/attach. Following, more complex operations are presented, such as location update, call handover, mobile terminated call, mobile originated call, and mobile-to-mobile call.

Location Update

Location updating is the mechanism that is used to determine the location of an MS in the idle state. The MS initiates location updating, which can occur when:

- The MS is first switched on
- The MS moves within the same VLR area, but to a new LA
- The MS moves to a new VLR area
- A location updated timer expires

Mobile Terminated Call (MTC)

In the case of an MTC, a subscriber from within the PSTN dials the mobile subscriber's MSISDN. This generates an ISUP IAM message (it also could potentially be TUP as Level 4) that contains the MSISDN as the called party number. The ISDN (i.e., PSTN) routes the call to the GMSC in the PLMN, based on the information contained in the MSISDN (national destination code and the country code).

The GMSC then identifies the subscriber's HLR based upon the MSISDN and invokes the MAP/C operation *Send Routing Information (SRI)* towards the HLR to locate the MS. The SRI contains the MSISDN. The HLR uses the MSISDN to obtain the IMSI.

Because of past location updates, the HLR already knows the VLR that currently serves the subscriber. The HLR queries the VLR using the MAP/D operation Provide Roaming Number (PRN) to obtain the MSRN. The PRN contains the subscriber's IMSI.

The VLR assigns a temporary number known as the *mobile station roaming number* (MSRN), which is selected from a pool, and sends the MSRN back in an MAP/D *MSRN Acknowledgement* to the HLR.

The HLR then passes the MSRN back to the GMSC in a MAP/C Routing Information Acknowledgement message. To the PSTN, the MSRN appears as a dialable number.

Since the GMSC now knows the MSC in which the MS is currently located, it generates an IAM with the MSRN as the called party number. When the MSC receives the IAM, it recognizes the MSRN and knows the IMSI for which the MSRN was allocated. The MSC then returns the MSRN to the pool for future use on another call.

The MSC sends the VLR a MAP/B Send Information message requesting information, including the called MS's capabilities, services subscribed to, and so on. If the called MS is authorized and capable of taking the call, the VLR sends a MAP/B Complete Call message back to the MSC.

The MSC uses the LAI and TMSI received in the Complete Call message to route a BSSMAP Page message to all BSS cells in the LA.

Air interface signaling is outside the scope of this book.

Figure 12-9 shows the sequence of events involved in placing an MTC.

Figure 12-9 *Placing an MTC*

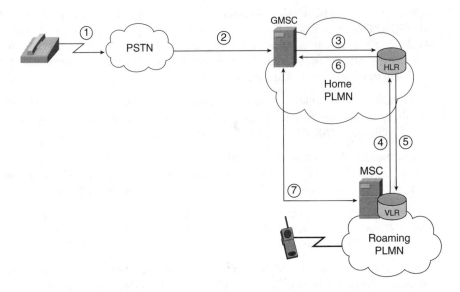

In Figure 12-9, the sequence of events involved in placing an MTC is as follows:

1 The calling subscriber uses the MSISDN to dial the mobile subscriber.

2 The MSISDN causes the call to be routed to the mobile network gateway MSC (GMSC).

3 The GMSC uses information in the called number digits to locate the mobile subscriber's HLR.

4 The HLR has already been informed about the location (VLR address) for the mobile subscriber; it requests a temporary routing number to allow the call to be routed to the correct MSC.

5 The MSC/VLR responds with a temporary routing number that is only valid for the duration of this call.

6 The routing number is returned to the GMSC.

7 The call is made using ISUP (or TUP) signaling between the GMSC and the visited MSC.

If the calling subscriber were in the same PLMN as the called party (internal MS-to-MS call), steps 2 and 3 would not be required.

Chapter 13 describes GSM-MAP operations in more detail. Appendix F, "GSM and ANSI MAP Operations," provides a list of GSM-MAP operations.

Summary

Cellular networks have undergone a rapid development phase since their initial introduction in the early 1980s. Modern cellular networks are digital and use SS7 for communication between network entities. GSM is the most popular digital cellular standard. GSM management call control, subscriber mobility, and text messaging (SMS) use a SS7 subsystem known as MAP. MAP provides operations for tracking the subscriber's location to deliver a call, signal the subscriber's intention to place a call, and deliver text messages between handsets. Operations and maintenance staff also use it to change the subscriber's profile—to add or revoke services.

GSM and ANSI-41 Mobile Application Part (MAP)

In fixed-line networks, the subscriber's location is static and specified according to the numbering scheme used in the network.

In cellular telephony systems, the subscriber's location can change drastically without the system being aware—for example, the subscriber might switch his cell phone off just before boarding a plane, and then switch it back on in a new country. For incoming calls to mobile subscribers, there is no direct relationship between the subscriber's location and the cell phone number. Because the location and other information must be derived real-time before a call can be delivered to a cell phone, such mobile terminating calls require the performance of a large amount of initial noncircuit-related signaling.

In contrast, mobile-originated calls (outgoing calls) place far less initial signaling overhead because the radio system to which the subscriber is connected knows the subscriber's location. Furthermore, because a subscriber is on the move, the base transceiver system (BTS), the base station controller (BSC), and even the mobile switching centre (MSC) can change. These changes require a lot of noncircuit-related signaling, particularly if the subscriber is currently engaged in a call—the subscriber should not be aware that such handovers between cellular network equipment takes place.

Retrieving the subscriber's profile is also a straightforward task for fixed-line networks because it resides at the subscriber's local exchange. In cellular networks, the ultimate exchange (MSC) to which the mobile subscriber is connected changes because the subscriber is mobile, and it would be completely unmanageable to place the subscriber's profile (which might change) at every MSC throughout the world.

It is primarily for these reasons that cellular networks contain two databases, known as the *Home Location Register (HLR)* and the *Visitor Location Register (VLR)*, in addition to the cellular-specific switch known as the MSC. For a description of the nodes used in a Global System for Mobile communications (GSM) network, see Chapter 12, "Cellular Networks."

Mobile application part (MAP) is the protocol that is used to allow the GSM network nodes within the Network Switching Subsystem (NSS) to communicate with each other to provide services, such as roaming capability, text messaging (SMS), and subscriber authentication. MAP provides an application layer on which to build the services that support a GSM network. This application layer provides a standardized set of operations. MAP is transported and encapsulated with the SS7 protocols MTP, SCCP, and TCAP.

This chapter specifies the MAP operations (or messages) that are used in GSM Phase 2. A small number of operations have been added to support General Packet Radio Service (GPRS) and 3rd Generation (3G) Universal Mobile Telecommunications System (UMTS), but they are beyond the scope of this book.

See Appendix F, "GSM and ANSI MAP Operations," for a list of the MAP operations used in GSM.

MAP Operations

MAP Phase 2 operations can be divided into the following main categories, which are addressed in this chapter:

- Mobility Management
- Operation and Maintenance
- Call Handling
- Supplementary Services
- Short Message Service

The chapter ends with a summary of GSM and ANSI MAP operations.

Mobility Management

Mobility management operations can be divided into the following categories:

- Location Management
- Paging and Search
- Access Management
- Handover
- Authentication Management
- Security Management
- IMEI Management
- Subscriber Management
- Identity Management
- Fault Recovery

The following section examines the MAP operations that are used in each of these categories, excluding Paging and Search, Access Management, Security Management and Identity Management because these categories were removed at Phase 2.

Location Management

To minimize transactions with the HLR, it only contains location information about the MSC/VLR to which the subscriber is attached. The VLR contains more detailed location information, such as the location area in which the subscriber is actually roaming. See Chapter 12, "Cellular Networks," for more information about location areas. As a result, the VLR requires that its location information be updated each time the subscriber changes location area. The HLR only requires its location information to be updated if the subscriber changes VLR.

Location management operations include the following:

- updateLocation
- cancelLocation
- sendIdentification
- purgeMS

updateLocation

This message is used to inform the HLR when an MS (in the idle state) has successfully performed a location update in a new VLR area. In this way, the HLR maintains the location of the MS (VLR area only). In Appendix L, "Tektronix Supporting Traffic," Figure 13-3 contains a trace that shows an HLR's decode calling a VLR (to perform cancel location). In Figure 13-1, the MS has roamed from a VLR area that is controlled by VLR-A to an area that is controlled by VLR-B. Note that the purgeMS operation is optional in a location update procedure.

Figure 13-1 *Showing the MAP Operation Sequences Involved in a Location Update*

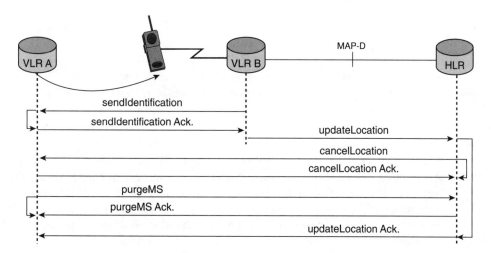

cancelLocation

The cancelLocation operation is used to delete a subscriber's profile from the previous VLR, following registration with a new VLR—in other words, following an updateLocation. When the HLR receives an updateLocation from a VLR other than the one that is currently stored in its tables, it sends a cancelLocation to the old VLR. The cancelLocation includes the International Mobile Subscriber Identity (IMSI) and the Local Mobile Subscriber Identity (LMSI) to identify the subscriber whose profile should be deleted as parameters. For details of the IMSI and LMSI see Chapter 12, "Cellular Networks." In Appendix L, "Tektronix Supporting Traffic," Example L-3 contains a trace that shows an HLR's decode calling a VLR (to perform cancel location).

Operators can also use the operation to impose roaming restrictions following a change in the subscriber's subscription. It is also used as part of the process of completely canceling a subscriber's subscription. When the HLR receives a request from the Operation and Maintenance Center (OMC) to delete the subscriber, the HLR deletes the subscriber's data and sends a cancelLocation to the VLR that serves the subscriber. Figure 13-2 shows a subscriber's subscription being cancelled, thereby disabling their service.

Figure 13-2 *MAP Operation Sequences in Which a Subscriber's Service is Disabled*

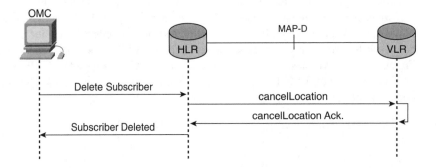

In addition, a cancelLocation operation is sent from the HLR to the VLR if the authentication algorithm or authentication key of the subscriber is modified.

sendIdentification

When the MS changes to a new VLR area, the new VLR queries the old VLR using a sendIdentification operation to obtain authentication information. The sendIdentification operation sends the TMSI as its argument, and the result contains the IMSI and other authentication information (RAND, SRES, and optionally KC). If it is unable to obtain this information, it can retrieve the information from the HLR via a sendAuthenticationInfo operation.

purgeMS

This message is sent if an MS has been inactive (no call or location update performed) for an extended period of time. The VLR sends this message to the HLR to indicate that it has deleted its data for that particular MS. The HLR should set a flag to indicate that the MS should be treated as not reached; as a result, the HLR no longer attempts to reach the MS in the case of a mobile terminated call or a mobile terminated short message.

Handover

Handover between MSCs is known as inter-MSC handover: basic inter-MSC handover and subsequent inter-MSC handover. A basic inter-MSC handover is where the call is handed from the controlling MSC (MSC-A) to another MSC (MSC-B). A subsequent inter-MSC handover is an additional inter-MSC handover during a call. After a call has been handed over from MSC-A to MSC-B, another handover takes place, either to a new MSC (MSC-C) or back to the original MSC (MSC-A).

The following sections describe these MAP handover operations:

- prepareHandover
- sendEndSignal
- processAccessSignalling
- forwardAccessSignalling
- prepareSubsequentHandover

prepareHandover

The prepareHandover message is used to carry a request and response between the two MSCs at the start of a basic inter-MSC handover (MSC-A to MSC-B). It is used to exchange BSSAP messages, such as HAN_REQ and HAN_ACK, for this purpose. It is the decision of MSC-A to hand over to another MSC. The prepareHandover message does not contain subscriber information—only information that is necessary for MSC-B to allocate the necessary radio resources and possibly some optional information, such as an IMSI.

sendEndSignal

Following a successful inter-MSC handover (from MSC-A to MSC-B in the case of a basic handover), MSC-B sends a sendEndSignal message to MSC-A to allow it to release its radio resources. If the call was originally established with MSC-A, it keeps control of the call and is known as the *anchor* MSC following the handover. As a result, MSC-B does not receive information about the release of the call. To solve this problem, MSC-A sends a sendEndSignal to MSC-B to inform it that it can release its own radio resources.

Figure 13-3 *MAP Operation Sequences in a Handover*

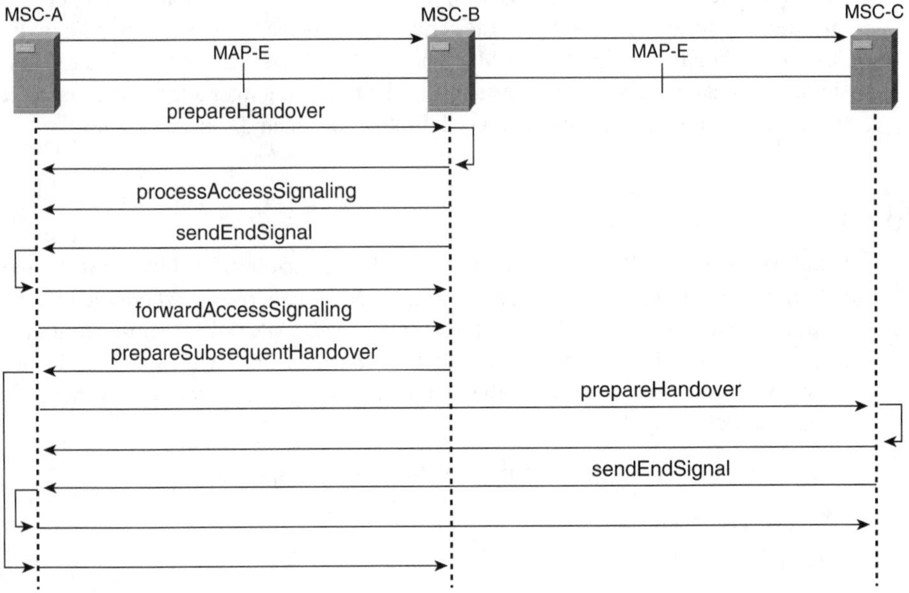

processAccessSignaling

The messages processAccessSignaling and forwardAccessSignaling are used to pass BSSAP messages between the MS and the anchor MSC transparently and between the anchor MSC and the MS, respectively. As stated previously, MSC-A keeps control of the call after a successful inter-MSC handover from MSC-A to MSC-B. The BSSAP messages travel from the MS to MSC-A via MSC-B. The message processAccessSignaling carries data from the MS to MSC-A and is sent from MSC-B to MSC-A. The message forwardAccessSignaling is the reverse; it carries data from MSC-A to the MS via MSC-B, as shown in Figure 13-3.

forwardAccessSignaling

See processAccessSignaling. If call control information is required to be passed to the serving MSC (MSC-B), the anchor (controlling MSC, MSC-A) sends the information using a forwardAccessSignaling message.

Figure 13-4 *Direction of processAccessSignaling and forwardAccessSignaling*

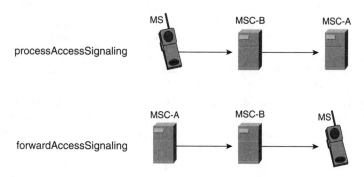

prepareSubsequentHandover

If another inter-MSC is required (back to MSC-A or to another MSC, C), then MSC-B sends this message to MSC-A. It contains the information required for MSC-A to send a prepareHandover message to MSC-C. Refer to Figure 13-3.

Authentication Management

MAP operation sendIdentificationInfo is the only operation in Phase 2 that falls under the category of authentication management. See sendIdentification for a description of this operation.

IMEI Management

The only MAP operation in the IMEIs management category is checkIMEI, which is used to check whether a piece of mobile equipment is on a black, gray, or white list. To perform an IMEI check, the serving MSC requests that the MS provide its IMEI. On receiving the IMEI from the MS, the MSC sends the IMEI to the EIR in a MAP checkIMEI operation. The EIR checks the status of the IMEI and sends the result back to the MSC. The equipment status can be white listed, gray listed, blacklisted, or unknown.

Blacklisted equipment is equipment that has been reported stolen and is, therefore, not granted permission to use the network (barred). If the status indicates that the equipment is blacklisted, an alarm might be generated on the operation and maintenance interface; this is network operator-dependent. The network operator can use the gray listed equipment list to block a certain model of equipment (or even a particular software version) from using his network if, for example, a certain handset type has proven to act erroneously on the network. Gray listed equipment cannot be barred; instead, it can be chosen to track the equipment for observation purposes. The white list contains all the equipment identities that are permitted for use and to which service should therefore be granted.

Criminals have been able to change mobile handsets' IMEI fairly easily using a data cable (to connect it to a PC) and specialist software. Because of this and the abundance and the high price of mobile handsets, theft has hit epidemic levels in many parts of the world. Recently, the United Kingdom passed legislation known as the Mobile Telephones (Reprogramming) Act making it illegal to reprogram the IMEI, and manufacturers were pressed (with limited success) to make the IMEI tamper-proof. In addition, the operators and the GSM association set up a nationwide EIR, known simply as the Central Equipment Identity Register (CEIR) so that stolen mobile equipment could be reported as easily as a stolen credit card. Before CEIR, if the equipment had been blacklisted with one operator, in most cases you could simply put in an SIM card for another operator because the operators failed to pool information.

Subscriber Management

An HLR uses subscriber management procedures to update a VLR with specific subscriber data when the subscriber's profile is modified. A subscriber's profile can be modified, because the operator has changed the subscription of the subscriber's basic services or one or more supplementary services. A subscriber's profile might also be modified, because the subscriber himself has activated or deactivated one or more supplementary services.

Subscriber management uses the insertSubscriberData and deleteSubscriberData operations.

insertSubscriberData

The HLR uses the insertSubscriberData operation to provide the VLR with the current subscriber profile—for example, during a location update or restore data procedure. It is also used if the operator (via the OMC) or the subscriber himself modifies the data—for example, barring all or certain types of calls. The operation insertSubscriberData is sent as many times as necessary to transfer the subscriber data from the HLR to the VLR.

deleteSubscriberData

The HLR uses the deleteSubscriberData operation to inform the VLR that a service has been removed from the subscriber profile. The subscriber might have subscribed to a number of services, such as international roaming. The operator can use this operation to revoke such subscriptions.

Fault Recovery

The fault recovery procedures ensure that the subscriber data in the VLR becomes consistent with the subscriber data that is stored in the HLR for a particular MS, and that the MS location information in the HLR and VLR is accurate following a location register fault.

3GPP TS 23.007 gives the detailed specification of fault recovery procedures of location registers.

The fault recovery procedures use the following three MAP operations:

- reset
- forwardCheckSsIndication
- restoreData

reset

The HLR that returns to service following an outage sends this operation to all VLRs in which that HLR's MSs are registered according to any available data following the outage.

forwardCheckSsIndication

This operation is optionally sent to all MSs following an HLR outage. The MSs are requested to synchronize their supplementary service data with that which is held in the HLR.

restoreData

When a VLR receives a provideRoamingNumber request from the HLR for either an IMSI that is unknown to the VLR or an IMSI in which the VLR entry is unreliable because of an HLR outage, the VLR sends a restoreData message to the HLR to synchronize the data.

Operation and Maintenance

Operation and maintenance can be divided into the following categories:

- Subscriber Tracing
- Miscellaneous

The following sections review the MAP operations that are used in each of these categories.

Subscriber Tracing

Subscriber tracing has two operations: activateTraceMode and deactivateTraceMode.

activateTraceMode

The HLR uses activateTraceMode to activate trace (subscriber tracking) mode for a particular subscriber (IMSI); the OSS requests activateTraceMode. The VLR waits for that particular MS to become active, at which time it sends a request to its MSC to trace the MS.

Figure 13-5 *MAP Operation Sequence to Initiate and Terminate Subscriber Tracing*

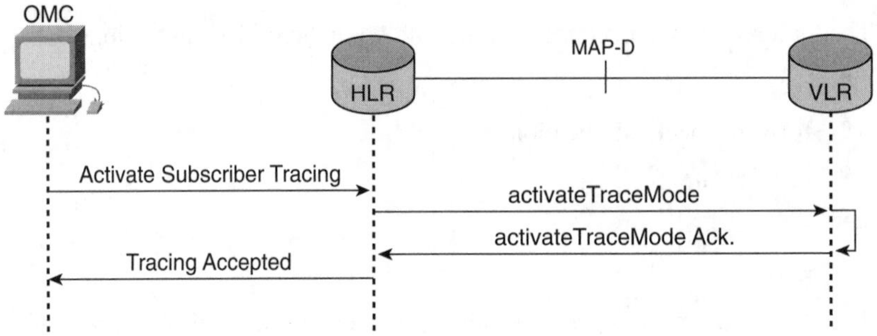

deactivateTraceMode

Upon receiving this message, the HLR turns off the trace mode and sends the message to the VLR, which also disables trace mode for that particular subscriber. See activateTraceMode.

Miscellaneous

The only operation in the Miscellaneous subcategory is sendIMSI.

Following the OMC's request to the VLR to identify a subscriber based on his Mobile Subscriber ISDN Number (MSISDN), the VLR and HLR exchange sendIMSI messages. If the MSISDN cannot be identified, an unknown subscriber indication is passed to the VLR. Otherwise, the IMSI is obtained from the HLR and returned to the VLR.

Figure 13-6 *MAP Operation Sequence When an Operations and Management Center (OMC) Requests Subscriber Identity*

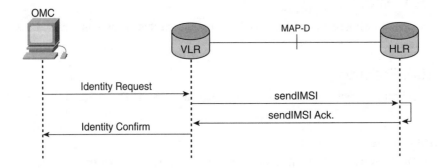

Call Handling

The call handling procedures primarily retrieve routing information to allow mobile terminating calls to succeed. When a mobile originating or a mobile terminating call has reached the destination MSC, no further MAP procedures are required.

Other procedures performed by MAP's call handling routines include the restoration of call control to the Gateway Mobile Switching Center (GMSC) if the call is to be forwarded. In addition, the call handling routing processes the notification that the remote user is free for the supplementary service message call completion to busy subscribers (CCBS).

Call handling does not have subcategories of operations; it simply has the following two operations:

- sendRoutingInfo
- provideRoamingNumber

In the case of an MTC, a subscriber from within the PSTN/ISDN dials the mobile subscriber's MSISDN, thereby generating an ISUP IAM message (alternatively, TUP could be used) that contains the MSISDN as the called party number. Based on the information contained in the MSISDN (national destination code and the country code), the PSTN/ISDN routes the call to the GMSC in the PLMN.

The GMSC then identifies the subscriber's HLR based on the MSISDN, and invokes the MAP operation sendRoutingInformation with the MSISDN as a parameter towards the HLR to find out where the MS is presently located.

Because of past location updates, the HLR already knows the VLR that currently serves the subscriber. To obtain a mobile station roaming number (MSRN), the HLR queries the VLR using the operation provideRoamingNumber with the IMSI as a parameter. The VLR assigns an MSRN from a pool of available numbers and sends the MSRN back to the HLR in an acknowledgement.

Because the GMSC now knows the MSC in which the MS is currently located, it generates an IAM with the MSRN as the called party number. When the MSC receives the IAM, it recognizes the MSRN and knows the IMSI for which the MSRN was allocated. The MSRN is then returned to the pool for use on a future call.

Figure 13-7 shows how the routing information is obtained to route the call from the calling parties exchange to the called parties exchange (serving MSC).

Figure 13-7 *MAP Operations When the GMSC Requests a Routing Number for the MSC When the Subscriber is Roaming*

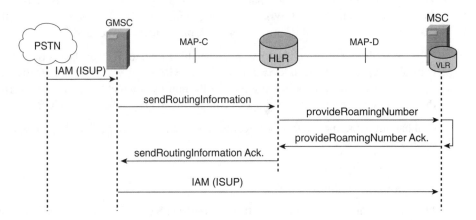

The BSSAP PAGE message is used for contacting all BSS cells in the location area (LA) when searching for the MS. The radio-related signaling is outside the scope of this book; however, this book does reference radio-related messages that are required for understanding NSS signaling. When the MS responds with a DTAP ALERT message, the serving MSC sends an ISUP ACM back to the GMSC, which forwards it to the calling subscriber's PSTN/ISDN switch. When the called subscriber accepts the call, the MS sends a DTAP CON message to the serving MSC that, in turn, sends an ISUP ANM message back to the calling party's PSTN/ISDN switch through the GMSC.

When one party hangs up, the switches exchange the usual series of ISUP REL messages, followed by an RLC message. If the fixed-line PSTN/ISDN subscriber hung up first, the MSC sends a BSSAP DISC message to the MS when it receives the REL message; the MS should respond with a DTAP REL message. When the serving MSC receives the expected DTAP REL in return, it should finally release the connection by sending a DTAP REL_COM to the MS and an IAM REL through the GMSC back to the calling party's PSTN/ISDN switch. If the PLMN subscriber hung up first, the MS sends a DTAP DISC message to the serving MSC, which then initiates the ISUP REL and sends a DTAP REL back to the MS. The MS should respond with a DTAP REL_COM to confirm the release; this response allows the serving MSC to send an ISUP RLC back through the network to the calling party's PSTN/ISDN switch, thereby releasing the connection.

sendRoutingInfo (SRI)

In the case of a mobile terminating call, the GMSC sends this message to the called party's HLR to obtain routing information, such as the MSRN. Upon receiving the message, the HLR sends a provideRoamingNumber request to the VLR where the subscriber is currently roaming.

provideRoamingNumber (PRN)

The VLR uses this message to provide routing information (MSRN) to the HLR in the case of a mobile terminating call, which is sent to the GMSC. See Figure 13-7 and the description of sendRoutingInfo for more information.

In Appendix L, Example L-4 shows a trace that depicts an HLR decode calling a VLR to request an MSRN using the provideRoamingNumber operation. Also in Appendix L, Example L-5 shows how a trace illustrates a VLR's decode calling an HLR to return an MSRN that uses the provideRoamingNumber operation.

Supplementary Services

Supplementary services includes the following operations:

- registerSS
- eraseSS
- activateSS
- deactivateSS
- interrogateSS
- registerPassword
- getPassword

In addition to these supplementary services, the following operations are considered unstructured supplementary services:

- processUnstructuredSS-Request
- unstructuredSS-Request
- unstructuredSS-Notify

The following section introduces the unstructured supplementary services (USSs) concept and discusses operations.

Unstructured Supplementary Services (USSs)

GSM 02.04 defines supplementary services. In addition to supplementary services, GSM has defined the concept of USSs. USSs allow PLMN operators to define operator-specific supplementary services and to deliver them to market quickly. The final three operations listed at the beginning of this chapter are used in USS implementation. USS allows the MS (subscriber) and the PLMN operator-defined application to communicate in a way that is transparent to the MS and intermediate network entities.

The communication is carried out using Unstructured supplementary service data (USSD) data packets, which have a length of 80 octets (91 ASCII characters coded, using seven bits) and are carried within the MAP operation. USSD uses the dialogue facility (which is connection oriented) of TCAP and is specified in GSM 02.90 (USSD Stage 1) and GSM 03.90 (USSD Stage 2). Unlike SMS, which is based on a store and forward mechanism, USSD is session oriented and, therefore, has a faster turnaround and response time than SMS, which is particularly beneficial for interactive applications. USSD can carry out the same two-way transaction up to seven times more quickly than SMS can.

The wireless application protocol (WAP) supports USSD as a bearer; the mobile chatting service relies on USSD transport for the text, and most, if not all, prepay roaming solutions are implemented using USSD. With such prepay applications, the subscriber indicates to the network from a menu on the MS the desire to place a roaming call. The serving MSC connects to the subscriber's HLR, which sends the request to a USSD gateway, which, in turn, sends the request to a prepay application server. The server checks the balance and then issues call handling instructions back to the MSC in the visited network. USS is still likely to find applications even in 3G networks.

Operations

The following bullets describe the operations for supplementary services and unstructured supplementary services:

- registerSS

The registerSS operation is used to register a supplementary service for a particular subscriber. The supplementary service (such as call forwarding) is often automatically activated at the same time.

- eraseSS

EraseSS is used to delete a supplementary service that was entered for a particular subscriber using registerSS.

- activateSS

ActivateSS is used to activate a supplementary service for a particular subscriber. Example supplementary services include CLIP/CLIR.

- deactivateSS

This operation switches off a supplementary service for a particular subscriber; it is the reverse of activateSS.

- interrogateSS

InterogateSS allows the state of a single supplementary service to be queried for a particular subscriber in the HLR.

- registerPassword

This operation is used to create or change a password for a supplementary service. When the HLR receives this message, it responds with a getPassword message to request the old password, the new password, and a verification of the new password. If the old password is entered incorrectly three consecutive times, this operation is blocked.

- getPassword

The HLR sends this message if the subscriber wants to change his current password or modify or activate a supplementary service. See also registerPassword. This operation is blocked if the old password is entered incorrectly three consecutive times.

- processUnstructuredSS-Request

This message is used to provide a means to support non-GSM standardized supplementary services. Both the MS and the addressed NSS network entity use it, only if the MS initiated the transaction.

- unstructuredSS-Request

Same as processUnstructuredSS-Request, except that both the MS and the addressed NSS network entity use it, only if the NSS entity initiated the transaction.

Short Message Service (SMS)

SMS provides paging functionality for alphanumeric messages of up to 160 characters to be exchanged with other GSM users. The network itself can also generate messages and broadcast to multiple MSs or to a specific MS. For example, a welcome message can be sent to a subscriber when he or she roams onto a new network; in addition, it can provide useful information, such as how to retrieve voicemail. The SMS service also transfers ring tones and logos to the MS.

The SMS slightly blurs the image of the user traffic being separate from signaling because, in a sense, the messages are user traffic; they are for human processing (written and read), rather than for communication between network entities.

The SMS does not have subcategories. It has the following operations:

- forwardSM
- sendRoutingInfoForSM
- reportSMDeliveryStatus
- readyForSM
- alertServiceCentre
- informServiceCentre

The following sections examine each of these.

forwardSM

Both the mobile originating (MO-SMS) and mobile terminating SMS (MT-SMS) procedures use the forwardSM operation to carry text messages between the MSC where the subscriber roams and the SMS-IWMSC or the SMS-GMSC, respectively. Figure 13-8 shows the MO-SMS procedure.

Figure 13-8 *MAP Operations Involved in Sending an SMS from MS to the SMS-SC*

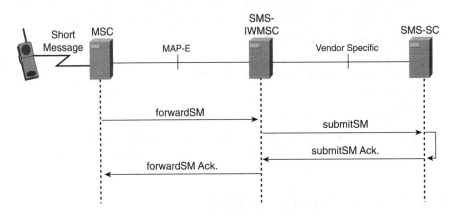

In Appendix L, Example L-6 contains a trace that shows the decode of a MAP operation forwardSM, including its SMS text.

sendRoutingInfoForSM

The SMS-GMSC uses this message during an MT-SMS to deliver an SMS to the MSC in whose area the subscriber is currently roaming. The message contains the subscriber's MSISDN, and the result contains the destination MSC's ISDN number. SCCP then uses this ISDN number to deliver the SMS using a forwardSM message. Figure 13-9 shows the MT-SMS procedure.

In Appendix L, Example L-2 shows a trace showing a VLR's decode calling an HLR (to perform a location update).

Figure 13-9   *MAP Operations Involved in Sending an SMS from the SMS-SC to the MS*

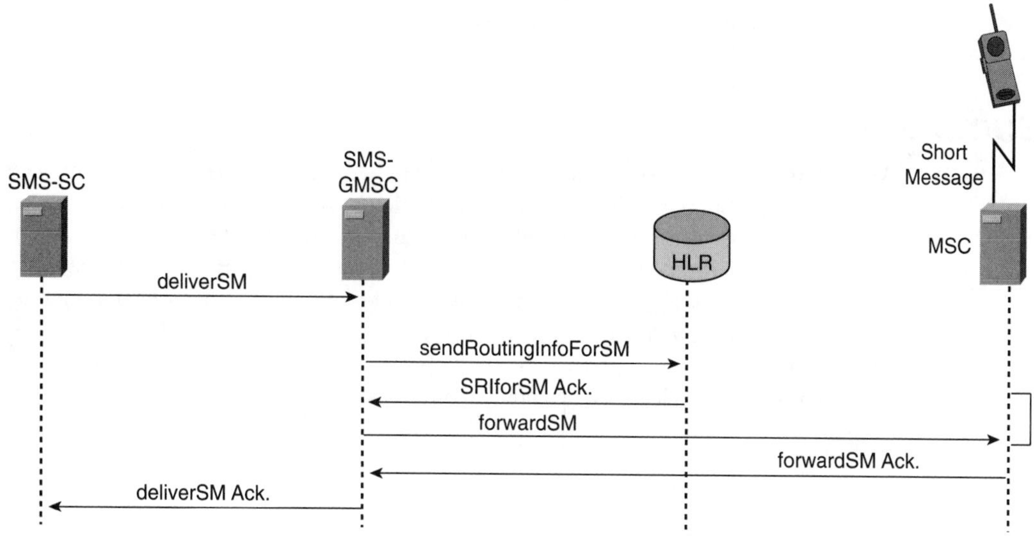

reportSMDeliveryStatus

If the SMS-SC cannot deliver the MT-SMS to the MS (because the subscriber is not reachable, for example), then the SMS-SC returns a negative result to the SMS-GMSC. Upon receiving this result, the SMS-GMSC sends a reportSMDeliveryStatus to the HLR, which, in turn, sets a message waiting flag in the appropriate subscriber data. The HLR also sends an alertServiceCentre message to the SMS-IWMSC to inform it about the negative SM delivery and waits until the subscriber can be reached. When the VLR (also aware of SM delivery failure) detects that the subscriber is again reachable, it sends a readforSM message to the HLR. The HLR, in turn, sends an alertServiceCentre message to the SMS-IWMSC, which informs the SMS-SC. The delivery process then begins again with a forwardSM message.

NOTE   The previous section also pertains to the readyForSM and alertServiceCentre.

informServiceCentre

If a sendRoutingInfoForSM is received for a subscriber that is currently unavailable, the HLR sends this message to the SMS-GMSC.

Summary

MAP primary use is to allow calls to be delivered to mobile subscribers. Unlike with fixed-line networks, the subscriber's location cannot be determined from the numbering scheme that is used in the network. Therefore, the subscriber's location must be known in real-time so a call can be connected to the nearest switch to the mobile subscriber. MAP keeps track of a mobile subscriber and provides other functionality, including allowing mobile subscribers to send alphanumeric two-way text between handsets; this is known as SMS. MAP also provides mobile operator's with the functionality to manage a subscriber's subscription so that services can be added and removed in real-time.

SS7/C7 Over IP

CHAPTER 14

SS7 in the Converged World

The "Converged World" of Next Generation Networks (NGNs) brings with it the promise of voice, video, and data over a single broadband network. This transition from the traditional circuit-switched networks to packet-switched networks has been underway for many years, and Voice over IP (VoIP) is now leading the transition. The immediate benefits of NGNs are decreased cost of infrastructure and improved ease of management. Longer-term benefits include the ability to rapidly deploy new services.

This chapter introduces the next generation architecture and presents a detailed discussion of the Signaling Transport (SigTran) protocols between the Media Gateway Controller (MGC) and the Signaling Gateway (SG). It also discusses the Transport Adaptation Layer Interface (TALI) and briefly covers an early Cisco SS7 over IP solution. Finally, it looks at the role of SS7 in decentralized VoIP signaling protocols such as Session Initiation Protocol (SIP) [124] and H.323 [125].

Next Generation Architecture

One NGN architecture for VoIP with centralized call processing decomposes the functional elements of a traditional circuit switch into specialized components with open interfaces. Following are the key logical elements of this reconstruction are the following:

- The MG handles the media, or bearer, interface. It converts media from the format used in one network to the format required in another network. For example, it can terminate the TDM trunks from the PSTN, packetize and optionally compress the audio signals, and then deliver the packets to the IP network using the Real Time Protocol (RTP) [120].

- The MGC (also known as a Call Agent) contains the call processing. In addition, it manages the resources of the MGs that it controls. The MGC controls the MG using a control protocol to set up the RTP connections and control the analog or TDM endpoint in the MG.

- The SG sits at the edge of an IP network and terminates circuit-switched network signaling, such as SS7 or ISDN, from the circuit-switched network. It transports, or backhauls, this signaling to the MGC or other IP-based application endpoint.

Figure 14-1 shows an example of these logical elements and their connections.

Figure 14-1 *NGNs—Sample Architecture*

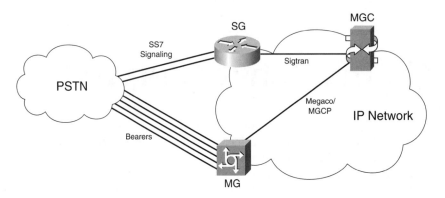

As Figure 14-1 shows, the evolution of specialized components provided open interfaces between these logical elements. The Internet Engineering Task Forces (IETF) created two working groups to address these open interfaces at the same time that ITU-T SG16 began to study the MGC to MG interface. Thus, the definition of the bearer control protocol between the MG and the MGC became a joint effort by the IETF MeGaCo (MGC) Working Group and the ITU-T SG16. The output from these groups is known as the Megaco [RFC 3015] [121] protocol in the IETF, and the H.248 [122] protocol in the ITU-T.

Also worth mentioning is a precursor to Megaco protocol: the Media Gateway Control Protocol (MGCP) [RFC 3435] [123].

NOTE   MGCP was originally published in RFC 2705, which has now been replaced by RFC 3435.

MGCP can also be used as a control protocol between an MGC MGCU (TG) and an MG. While MGCP is defined by an Informational (versus standards track) RFC, it is commonly used in many products today because the specification was available before Megaco and H.248 were finished. Both MGCP and Megaco/H.248 assume that the call control intelligence is outside the MGs and that the MGC handles it.

Closely related to the MGCP protocol are the PacketCable protocols, Network-Based Call Signaling (NCS) and PSTN Gateway Call Signaling Protocol (TGCP). These protocols provide functionality similar to MGCP for cable-based networks.

The IETF SigTran Working Group focused on the SG to MGC open interface. The Working Group produced a set of standard protocols to address the needs and requirements of this interface.

SigTran

There has been interest in interworking SS7 and IP for quite some time. However, the initial solutions were proprietary. This began to change in the late 1990s, when an effort to standardize Switched Circuit Network (SCN) signaling (SS7) over IP transport began in the IETF.

The IETF SigTran Working Group was founded after a Birds of a Feather (BOF) session, which was held at the Chicago 1998 IETF meeting, to discuss transport of telephony signaling over packet networks. The result of the BOF was the creation of the SigTran Working Group to do the following:

- Define architectural and performance requirements for transporting SCN signaling over IP.

- Evaluate existing transport protocols, and, if necessary, define a new transport protocol to meet the needs and requirements of transporting SCN signaling.

- Define methods of encapsulating the various SCN signaling protocols.

The SigTran Working Group first met at the Orlando 1998 IETF meeting.

The SigTran Working Group defined the framework architecture and performance requirements in RFC 2719 [126]. The framework included the concept of reconstructing the traditional circuit switch into MGC, MG, and SG elements, thereby separating the signaling and the media control plane.

The framework document identified three necessary components for the SigTran protocol stack:

- A set of adaptation layers that support the primitives of SCN telephony signaling protocols

- A common signaling transport protocol that meets the requirements of transporting telephony signaling

- IP [127] network protocol

Figure 14-2 shows the three layers of the protocol stack.

Further functional requirements were defined for the transport protocol and adaptation layers. The transport had to be independent of the telephony protocol it carried, and, more importantly, had to meet the stringent timing and reliability requirements of that telephony protocol.

Figure 14-2 *SigTran Protocol Layers*

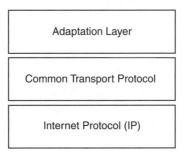

The Working Group began evaluating the two commonly used transport protocols, User Datagram Protocol (UDP) [128] and Transport Control Protocol (TCP) [129], against these requirements. UDP was quickly ruled out because it did not meet the basic requirements for reliable, in-order transport. While TCP met the basic requirements, it was found to have several limitations. A team of engineers from Telcordia (formerly Bellcore) completed an analysis of TCP against SS7's performance and reliability requirements. Their analysis was documented in an IETF draft [130], which introduced the following limitations of TCP:

- **Head-of-line blocking**—Because TCP delivery is strictly sequential, a single packet loss can cause subsequent packets to also be delayed. The analysis showed that a 1% packet loss would cause 9% of the packets being delayed greater than the one-way delay time.

- **Timer granularity**—While this is not a limitation of the TCP protocol, it is a limitation of most implementations of TCP. The retransmission timer is often large (typically one second) and is not tunable.

The Working Group noted additional TCP limitations, including the following:

- A lack of built-in support for multihoming. This support is necessary for meeting reliability requirements, such as five 9s and no single point of failure.

- Also, because of a timer granularity issue and the lack of a built-in heartbeat mechanism, it takes a long time to detect failure (such as a network failure) in a TCP connection.

Because of the deficiencies of UDP and TCP, a new transport protocol, Stream Control Transmission Protocol (SCTP) [131], was developed for transporting SCN signaling. Note that SCTP is a generic transport that can be used for other applications equally well.

Stream Control Transmission Protocol (SCTP)

The SigTran Working Group presented several proposals for a new transport protocol. One proposal was Multinetwork Datagram Transmission Protocol (MDTP), which became the foundation for SCTP. RFCNext Generation Network2960 defines SCTP, which has been updated with RFC 3309 [132] to replace the checksum mechanism with a 32-bit CRC mechanism. Further, there is an SCTP Implementers Guide [133] that contains corrections and clarifications to RFC 2960.

SCTP provides the following features:

- Acknowledged error-free, nonduplicated transfer of user data
- Data segmentation to conform to path MTU size (dynamically assigned)
- Ordered (sequential) delivery of user messages on a per "stream" basis
- Option for unordered delivery of user messages
- Network-level fault tolerance through the support of multihoming
- Explicit indications of application protocol in the user message
- Congestion avoidance behavior, similar to TCP
- Bundling and fragmenting of user data
- Protection against blind denial of service and blind masquerade attacks
- Graceful termination of association
- Heartbeat mechanism, which provides continuous monitoring of reachability

SCTP is a connection-oriented protocol. Each end of the connection is a SCTP endpoint. An endpoint is defined by the SCTP transport address, which consists of one or more IP addresses and an SCTP port. The two endpoints pass state information in an initialization procedure to create an SCTP association. After the association has been created, user data can be passed. Figure 14-3 provides an example of two SCTP endpoints in an association.

Figure 14-3 *SCTP Endpoints in an Association*

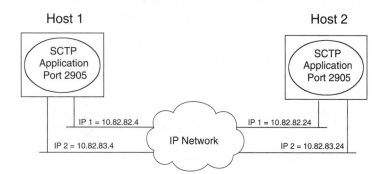

In Figure 14-3, Host A has endpoint [10.82.82.4, 10.82.83.4 : 2905] and Host B has endpoint [10.82.82.24, 10.82.83.24 : 2905]. The association is the combination of the two endpoints.

The following sections discuss how SCTP addresses the deficiencies of TCP that are related to meeting the requirements for delivering telephony signaling over IP. For additional details about the internals of SCTP, the *Stream Control Transmission Protocol, A Reference Guide*, by Randall Stewart and Qiaobing Xie, is a good resource.

Head-of-Line Blocking

SCTP uses streams as a means of decreasing the impact of head-of-line blocking. In SCTP, a stream is a unidirectional channel within an association. Streams provide the ability to send separate sequences of ordered messages that are independent of one another.

Figure 14-4 provides an example of head-of-line blocking with TCP. When packet 2 is dropped, packets 3 to 5 cannot be delivered to the application because TCP provides in-order delivery.

Figure 14-4 *Example of Head-of-Line Blocking in TCP*

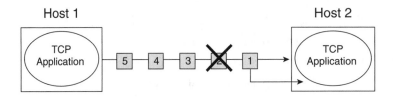

SCTP provides the ability to have multiple streams within an association. Each stream provides reliable delivery of ordered messages that are independent of other streams. Figure 14-5 shows an example of how SCTP can help resolve head-of-line blocking. In this example, packet 2 is dropped again. However, because packets 3, 4, and 5 belong to a different stream, they can be delivered to the application without delay.

Figure 14-5 *Use of Streams in SCTP to Avoid Head-of-Line Blocking*

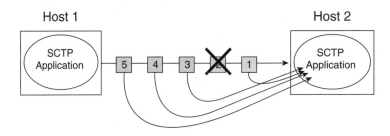

Failure Detection

Quick failure detection and recovery is important for meeting the performance and reliability requirements that are specified for transporting SCN signaling. For a multihomed host, two types of failures can occur:

- One or more destination addresses in the peer endpoint become unavailable or unreachable.
- The peer endpoint becomes unavailable or unreachable.

A destination address can become unreachable for one of several reasons. First, there could be a failure in the network path to the destination address, or a failure in the Network Interface Card (NIC) that supports the destination address. Likewise, a peer endpoint can become unavailable for several reasons. By definition, the peer endpoint is unavailable or unreachable if all of its destination addresses are unavailable or unreachable. SCTP provides two mechanisms for detecting failures:

1 Use of the Path.Max.Retrans threshold, which is the maximum number of consecutive retransmission that are allowed for a path.

2 Use of the heartbeat mechanism.

When an endpoint sends a data message to a particular destination address, an acknowledgement is expected in return. If the acknowledgement has not been received when the retransmission timer expires, SCTP increases an error counter for that destination address and then retransmits the data message to the same destination or to another destination address, if one is available. The destination address is considered unreachable if the error counter reaches a defined threshold (Path.Max.Retrans).

The other mechanism for detecting failures is a heartbeat mechanism. This mechanism is useful for monitoring idle destination addresses, such as a destination address that has not received a data within the heartbeat period. The heartbeat is sent periodically, based on a configured heartbeat timer. If a heartbeat response is not received, the same error counter is increased. Again, when the error counter reaches a defined threshold (Path.Max.Retrans), the destination address is considered unavailable or unreachable.

To determine the availability of the peer endpoint, an error counter is kept for the peer endpoint. This error counter represents the number of consecutive times the retransmission timer has expired. It is also increased each time a heartbeat is not acknowledged. When this error counter reaches a defined threshold (Association.Max.Retrans), the peer endpoint is considered unavailable or unreachable.

SCTP enables faster failure detection by encouraging implementations to support tunable parameters. As noted, TCP is limited in this respect because most implementations do not allow the application to tune key TCP parameters. SCTP encourages an implementation to support tunable parameters through the definition of the upper-layer interface to the application. In RFC 2960, Section 10 contains an example that describes the upper-layer interface definition. One function in this definition, SETPROTOCOLPARAMETERS(), provides a means setoff-setting parameters such as minRTO, maxRTO, and maxPathRetrans. More importantly, the SCTP sockets Application Programmer Interface (API) [134] defines a socket option (SCTP_RTOINFO) for setting key parameters.

Multihoming and Failure Recovery

Multihoming provides a means for path level redundancy. This feature enables SCTP endpoints to support multiple transport addresses. Each transport address is equivalent to a different path for sending and receiving data through the network. Figure 14-6 shows an example of multihoming.

Figure 14-6 *Multihoming Support in SCTP*

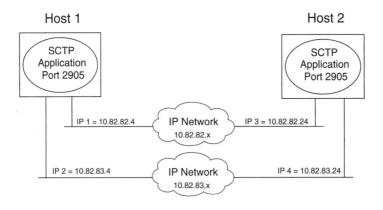

In the case of multihoming, one network path is selected as the primary path. Data is transmitted on the primary path while that path is available. If a packet gets dropped—for instance, because of a failure in the path—the retransmission should be sent on the alternate path. Figure 14-7 provides an example based on the diagram in Figure 14-6, with the primary path between IP1 and IP3 (the 10.82.82.x network) and the alternate path between IP2 and IP4 (the 10.82.83.x network). In this example, the packet with Transmission Sequence Number (TSN) 1 is retransmitted on the alternate path.

Retransmitting on the alternate path decreases failure recovery time. Further, if the primary path fails, the alternate path is automatically selected as the primary path. The path failure recovery mechanism is completely transparent to the application that uses SCTP.

Figure 14-7 *Failure Recovery Example*

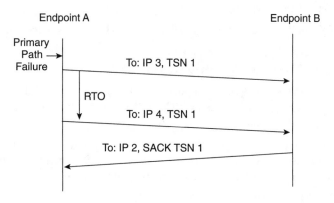

Proposed Additions

The IETF Transport Working Group proposes two promising additions to the SCTP protocol:

- Dynamic Address Reconfiguration [135]
- Partial Reliability [136]

The first proposal is to allow for IP address information reconfiguration on an existing association. This feature can be useful for hardware that provides for hot swap of an Ethernet card, for example. A new Ethernet card could be added and the Ethernet card's IP address could then be added to the association without requiring system downtime.

The second proposal allows for partially reliable transport on a per message basis. In other words, the application can determine how a message should be treated if it needs to be retransmitted. For instance, the application can decide that a message is stale and no longer useful if it has not been delivered for two seconds. SCTP then moves past that message and stops retransmitting it.

User Adaptation (UA) Layers

The User Adaptation (UA) layers encapsulate different SCN signaling protocols for transport over an IP network using SCTP. While each UA layer is unique in terms of the encapsulation because of the differences of the signaling protocols themselves, following are some common features among all UA layers:

- Support for seamless operation of the UA layer peers over an IP network.
- Support for the primitive interface boundary of the SCN lower layer, which the UA layer replaces. For example, M2UA supports the primitive interface boundary that MTP Level 2 supports.

- Support for the management of SCTP associations.

- Support for asynchronous reporting of status changes to layer management.

The SigTran Working Group has defined several UA layers, which include the following:

- The MTP Level 2 User Adaptation (M2UA) layer is defined for the transport of MTP Level 3 messages between a SG and a MGC or IP database.

- The MTP Level 3 User Adaptation (M3UA) layer is defined for the transport of SS7 User Part messages (such as ISUP, SCCP, and TUP) between an SS7 SG and a MGC or other IP Signaling Point (IPSP).

- The SCCP User Adaptation (SUA) layer is defined for the transport of SCCP User Part messages (such as TCAP and RANAP) from an SS7 SG to an IP-based signaling node or database, or between two endpoints in the same IP network.

- The MTP Level 2 Peer Adaptation (M2PA) layer is defined for the transport of MTP Level 3 data messages over SCTP. M2PA effectively replaces MTP Level 2. It provides the ability to create an IP-based SS7 link.

- The ISDN User Adaptation (IUA) layer is defined for the transport of Q.931 between an ISDN SG and a MGC. IUA supports both Primary Rate Access and Basic Rate Access lines.

Each of these adaptation layers will be discussed in detail, with the exception of IUA because it is beyond the scope of this book. Other proposed adaptation layers (such as DPNSS/DASS2 DUA [144] UA and V5.2 V52UA [145] UA) are being worked on in the SigTran Working Group; however, like IUA, those adaptation layers are beyond the scope of an SS7 discussion.

When these adaptation layers were being developed, it became evident that some terminology and functionality were common, with the exception of M2PA. There was an effort to keep the UA documents synchronized with common text for these terms and functional discussions.

UA Common Terminology

The UAs introduce some new terminology that did not exist in the SS7 world. Some of these terms are common across all of the SS7 UAs; therefore, it is worth discussing them before starting with the adaptation layers. Following are the definitions of these terms, provided by RFC 3332 [137]:

- **Application Server (AS)**—A logical entity that serves a specific Routing Key. An example of an Application Server is a virtual switch element that handles all call processing for a unique range of PSTN trunks, identified by an SS7 SIO/DPC/OPC/CIC_range. Another example is a virtual database element, handling all HLR transactions for a particular SS7 DPC/OPC/SCCP_SSN combination. The AS contains a set of one or more unique ASPs, of which one or more is normally actively processing traffic. Note that there is a 1:1 relationship between an AS and a Routing Key.

- **Application Server Process (ASP)**—A process instance of an Application Server. An ASP serves as an active or backup process of an Application Server (for example, part of a distributed virtual switch or database). Examples of ASPs are processes (or process instances) of MGCs, IP SCPs, or IP HLRs. An ASP contains an SCTP endpoint and can be configured to process signaling traffic within more than one Application Server.

- **Signaling Gateway Process (SGP)**—A process instance of a SG. It serves as an active, backup, load-sharing, or broadcast process of a SG.

- **Signaling Gateway (SG)**—An SG is a signaling agent that receives/sends SCN native signaling at the edge of the IP network. An SG appears to the SS7 network as an SS7 Signaling Point. An SG contains a set of one or more unique SG Processes, of which one or more is normally actively processing traffic. Where an SG contains more than one SGP, the SG is a logical entity, and the contained SGPs are assumed to be coordinated into a single management view to the SS7 network and the supported Application Servers.

- **IP Server Process (IPSP)**—A process instance of an IP-based application. An IPSP is essentially the same as an ASP, except that it uses M3UA in a point-to-point fashion. Conceptually, an IPSP does not use the services of a SG node.

Figure 14-8 puts these terms into context. In this diagram, the SG consists of two SGP. Each SGP is a separate hardware platform. The SGPs share a point code. The MGC supports the Application Server, which is a logical entity. For example, the Application Server is commonly provisioned as a point code and service indicator (SI) for M3UA. For more information, see the Application Servers section.

Finally, the ASP runs on the MGC platform that handles the UA protocol stack. In this diagram, the MGC consists of two hosts, each of which has an ASP. Therefore, the AS consists of ASP1 and ASP2. Depending on the MGC redundancy model (Active-Standby, Load Share, or Broadcast), one or more of the ASPs are Active (or able to send and receive user data) for the AS at any given time.

In addition to the common terminology, the text related to how the SG and SGPs manage the AS and ASP states is common in all of the UA layers (again, with the exception of M2PA).

Figure 14-8 *UA Terminology Example*

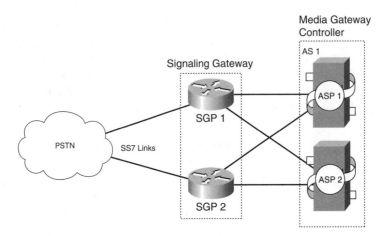

Routing Keys and Interface Identifiers

The SG must be capable of distributing incoming SS7 data messages to the appropriate Application Server. For M3UA and SUA, the SG performs this routing based on statically or dynamically defined Routing Keys. From RFC 3332, a Routing Key is defined as:

A Routing Key describes a set of SS7 parameters and parameter values that uniquely define the range of signaling traffic to be handled by a particular Application Server. Parameters within the Routing Key cannot extend across more than a single Signaling Point Management Cluster.

The Routing Key has a one-to-one relationship with an Application Server. Further, it is uniquely identified by a 32-bit value, called a *Routing Context*.

The Routing Key is used to distribute messages from the SS7 network to a specific Application Server. According to SigTran, this key can be any combination of the following SS7 routing information:

- Network Indicator (NI)
- Service Indicator (SI)
- Destination Point Code (DPC)
- Originating Point Code (OPC)
- Subsystem number (SSN)

Refer to Chapter 7, "Message Transfer Part 3 (MTP3)," for more information on NI, SI, OPC and DPC. Refer to Chapter 9, "Signaling Connection Control Part (SCCP)," for more information on SSN.

A SG does not have to support all of these parameters.

Figure 14-9 provides an example of how a SG might be provisioned with Routing Key, Routing Context, Application Server, and ASP information. This diagram contains a mated pair of SGs that also act as STPs. Each SG has the same Application Server database. When a SG receives a message, it tries to match that message against its database. In the example, a message arrives for DPC 1.1.1 at SG2. This message matches Application Server CHICAGO, so it is sent to ASP ASP1.

NOTE   The SGs in this diagram are labeled ITP. The ITP, or IP Transfer Point, is a Cisco SG product offering. For more information, please refer to the following Web site:

http://www.cisco.com/en/US/products/sw/wirelssw/ps1862/index.html

---

Figure 14-9 *Routing Key Example*

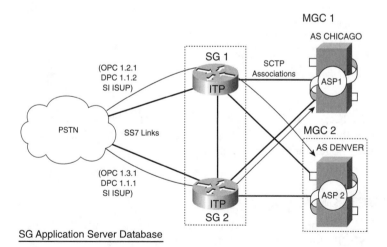

SG Application Server Database

Application Server: CHICAGO
  Routing Key: DPC 1.1.1, SI ISUP, Routing Context = 4
  Application Server Process: ASP 1

Application Server: DENVER
  Routing Key: DPC 1.1.2, SI ISUP, Routing Context = 5
  Application Server Process: ASP 2

For M2UA and IUA, the SG uses an Interface Identifier value to determine the distribution of incoming messages. The Interface Identifier is unique between the SG and the ASP. Unlike Routing Keys, there can be a many-to-one relationship between Interface Identifiers and Application Servers. In other words, an Application Server can contain more than one Interface Identifiers. Also, Interface Identifiers can be a 32-bit integer value or an ASCII string.

To give meaning to the Interface Identifier, one suggestion is to use the physical slot and port the SG's information to create the 32-bit value or ASCII string. Figure 14-10 provides an example of how Interface Identifiers would be configured on the SG. Note that the MGC must have the same Interface Identifiers provisioned. In this example, AS CANTON contains four Interface Identifiers, with each one mapped to a SS7 link.

Figure 14-10 *Interface Identifier Example*

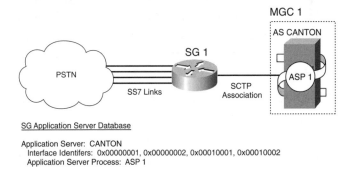

SG Application Server Database

Application Server: CANTON
  Interface Identifers: 0x00000001, 0x00000002, 0x00010001, 0x00010002
Application Server Process: ASP 1

Finally, because M2PA is a peer-to-peer arrangement between two IP-based SS7 Signaling Points, there is no need for message distribution or routing. Therefore, there is not a concept of Routing Key or Interface Identifier.

MTP Level 3 UA (M3UA)

M3UA [137] provides for the transport of MTP Level 3-user part signaling (such as ISUP and SCCP) over IP using SCTP. RFC 3332 defines and supplements it with an Implementers Guide [138]. M3UA provides for seamless operation between the user part peers by fully supporting the MTP Level 3 upper-layer primitives. M3UA can be used between an SG and an MGC or IP-resident database, or between two IPSP.

The most common use for M3UA is between a SG and a MGC or IP-resident databases (such as SCPs). The SG receives SS7 signaling over standard SS7 links. It terminates MTP

Levels 1 to 3 and provides message distribution, or routing, of the user part messages that is destined for MGCs or IP-resident databases. The MGCs can send to other MGCs via the SG.

Figure 14-11 shows the protocol stacks at each network element for using M3UA between a SG and a MGC. The SEP, or SEP, is a node in the SS7 network. The NIF, or Nodal Interworking Function, provides for the interworking of SS7 and IP. RFC 3332 does not define the functionality of the NIF because it was considered out of scope.

Figure 14-11 *Use of M3UA Between a SG and a MGC*

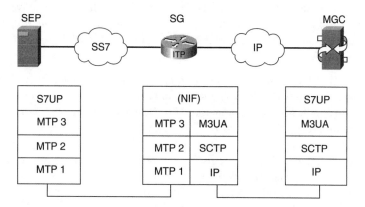

The M3UA on the MGC or IP-resident database supports the MTP Level upper-layer primitives so the user parts are unaware that MTP is terminated on the SG. The MTP service primitives [49] consist of the following:

- MTP Transfer request and indication
- MTP Pause indication
- MTP Resume indication
- MTP Status indication

The MTP Transfer primitive is used to pass user data. MTP Pause indicates that an Affected Point Code is Unavailable, and MTP Resume indicates that an Affected Point Code is Available. MTP Status provides congestion and User Part Availability information on an Affected Point Code. Later, in the Messages and Formats description of M3UA messages, it will be clear how these primitives are supported.

The M3UA layer on the SGP must maintain the state of all the configured ASPs and ASes. M3UA at the ASP must maintain the state of all configured SGPs and SGs.

The M3UA layer on the SG supports message distribution of incoming messages from the SS7 and IP-based sources. The distribution is based on matching the incoming message against the Routing Keys. When a Routing Key is selected, the Application Server state is checked to see if it is active. An Active Application Server has at least one ASP that is ready to receive data messages. If the Application Server is active, the message is forwarded to the appropriate ASP(s) that support the AS.

To determine the appropriate ASP, the SG must take into account the AS's traffic mode. There are three possible traffic modes: Override, Load Share, and Broadcast. Override traffic mode is basically an Active-Standby arrangement in which one ASP is active for receiving data messages and one or more ASPs are Standby. In this case, the SGP sends to the active ASP. In Load Share mode, one or more ASPs can be active. The SGP load shares across the active ASPs using an implementation-specific algorithm. Finally, in Broadcast mode, one or more ASPs can be active, and the SGP sends the data message to each active ASP.

The M3UA layer on the ASP must also make decisions about the distribution of outgoing messages. To do so, the M3UA layer maintains the availability and congestion state of the routes to remote SS7 destinations. An *M3UA route* refers to a path through an SG to an SS7 destination. If an SS7 destination is available through more than one route (more than one SG), the M3UA layer must perform some additional functions. In addition to keeping the state of each route, M3UA must also derive the overall state from the individual route states. The derived state is provided to the upper layer. Also, if each individual route is available, the M3UA should load balance across the available routes. Further, if the SG consists of more than one SGP, M3UA should load share across the available SGPs.

The M3UA layer at the SGP and ASP must maintain the state of each SCTP association. M3UA uses a client-server model with the ASP defaulting to the client and SG as the server. However, both SG and ASP should be able to be provisioned as the client or server. The client side of the relationship is responsible for establishing the association.

During the establishment of the association, several inbound and outbound streams are negotiated between the SCTP peers. The M3UA layer at both the SGP and ASP can assign data traffic to individual streams based on some parameter that ensures proper sequencing of messages, such as SLS.

M3UA has an Internet Assigned Numbers Authority (IANA) registered port number of 2905. It also has an IANA registered SCTP payload protocol identifier value of 3.

Messages and Formats

All of the UA layers use the same common header format. The common header includes the version, message type, message class, and message length. Figure 14-12 shows the format of the common message header.

Figure 14-12 *UA Common Message Header*

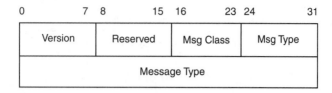

The RFC provides the list of currently defined message classes and types. Several values are reserved for future extensions. IANA provides a registry of these extensions at the following Web site:

http://www.iana.org/assignments/sigtran-adapt

Table 14-1 lists the M3UA message classes and types.

Table 14-1 *M3UA Message Classes and Types*

Msg Class Value	Message Class and Type Names	Msg Type Value
0	Management (MGMT) messages	
	Error message	0
	Notify message	1
1	Transfer messages	
	Protocol Data	1
2	SS7 Signaling Network Management (SSNM) messages	
	Destination Unavailable (DUNA)	1
	Destination Available (DAVA)	2
	Destination State Audit (DAUD)	3
	Signaling Congestion (SCON)	4
	Destination User Part Unavailable (DUPU)	5
	Destination Restricted	6

continues

Table 14-1 *M3UA Message Classes and Types (Continued)*

Msg Class Value	Message Class and Type Names	Msg Type Value
3	ASP State Maintenance (ASPSM) messages	
	ASP Up	1
	ASP Down	2
	Heartbeat	3
	ASP Up Acknowledge	4
	ASP Down Acknowledge	5
	Heartbeat Acknowledge	6
4	ASP Traffic Maintenance (ASPTM) messages	
	ASP Active	1
	ASP Inactive	2
	ASP Active Acknowledge	3
	ASP Inactive Acknowledge	4
9	Routing Key Management (RKM) messages	
	Registration Request	1
	Registration Response	2
	Deregistration Request	3
	Deregistration Response	4

In addition, all UA Layers use the Tag, Length, Value (TLV) format for all parameters in a message. Figure 14-13 shows the TLV format.

Figure 14-13 *TLV Format*

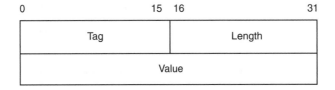

Transfer Messages

There is only one transfer message: the Payload Data message type.

The Payload message type maps directly to the MTP Transfer primitive. It contains the OPC, DPC, Service Indicator Octet (SIO), SLS, and ISUP information. In addition, it can contain a Routing Context, Network Appearance, and/or Correlation Identifier.

The Routing Context associates the message with a configured Routing Key, or Application Server. It must be present if the SCTP association supports more than one Application Server.

The Network Appearance provides the SS7 network context for the point codes in the message. It is useful in the situation in which a SG is connected to more than one SS7 network and the traffic associated with these different networks is sent to the ASP over a single SCTP association. An example is the case of an SG in multiple national networks. The same Signaling Point Code value can be reused within these different national networks, and Network Appearance is needed to provide uniqueness. The Network Appearance might be necessary to indicate the format of the OPC and DPC.

The Correlation Identifier provides a unique identifier for the message that the sending M3UA assigns.

SS7 Signaling Network Management (SSNM) Messages

The SSNM messages map to the other MTP primitives: MTP Pause, MTP Resume, and MTP Status. In addition, there is support for the ASP to audit the state of an SS7 destination.

The Routing Context and Network Appearance parameters are optional in these messages just as they are in the Protocol Data message. The same rules apply.

The following are SSNM messages:

- **Destination Unavailable (DUNA)**—The DUNA message maps to the MTP Pause primitive. The SGP sends it to all concerned ASPs to indicate that one or more SS7 destinations are unreachable. The message can be generated from an SS7 network event if an ASP sends a message to an unavailable SS7 destination or when the ASP audits the SS7 destination. The DUNA contains the Affected Point Code parameter, which allocates 24 bits for the point code and 8 bits for a mask field. Figure 14-14 shows the Affected Point Code parameter.

Figure 14-14 *Affected Point Code Parameter*

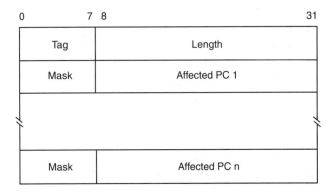

The mask field indicates a number of bits in the point code value that are wild-carded. For example, ANSI networks use the mask field to indicate that all point codes in a cluster are unavailable by setting the mask field to a value of 8.

The DUNA can also contain a Network Appearance, Routing Context, and/or Info String parameters. Again, the Routing Context must be sent if the SCTP association supports more than one Application Server. The Routing Context parameter contains all of the Routing Contexts that apply to concerned traffic flows that are affected by the state change of the SS7 destination.

- **Destination Available (DAVA)**—The DAVA message maps to the MTP Resume primitive. An SGP sends it to all concerned ASPs to indicate that one or more SS7 destinations are reachable. The message can be generated from an SS7 network event, or when the ASP audits the SS7 destination. It contains the same parameters as the DUNA.

- **Destination State Audit (DAUD)**—The DAUD message does not map to an MTP primitive. It is sent by the ASP to audit SS7 destinations that are of interest. The parameters in the message are identical to those in the DUNA.

- **Signaling Congestion (SCON)**—The SCON message maps to the MTP Status primitive. The SGP sends it to all concerned ASPs when the SG determines or is notified that the congestion state of an SS7 destination has changed, or in response to an ASP's Protocol Data or DAUD message. Like the DUNA and DAVA, it contains the Affected Point Code, Routing Context, Network Appearance, and Info String parameters. In addition, it includes optional Concerned Point Code and Congestion Indication parameters.

- **Destination User Part Unavailable (DUPU)**—The DUPU message maps to the MTP Status primitive. The SGP sends it to concerned ASPs to indicate the availability of a user part. It contains the same parameters as the DUNA message, and a User/Cause parameter that provides the user part that is affected and the unavailability cause.

- **Destination Restricted (DRST)**——The SGP sends the DRST message to concerned ASPs to indicate that the SG has determined that one or more SS7 destinations are restricted from that SG's point of view. It is also sent in response to a DAUD, if appropriate. It contains the same parameters as the DUNA message.

ASPSM and ASPTM Messages

Together, the ASPSM and ASPTM messages provide a means of controlling the state of the ASP. Further, the state of the ASP feeds into the state machine of each AS it serves. Therefore, these messages also provide a means of controlling the state of the AS.

As the RFC suggested, an ASP can have one of three states: ASP-Down, ASP-Inactive, or ASP-Active. ASP-Down indicates that the ASP is unavailable. ASP-Inactive indicates that the ASP is available but is not yet ready to send or receive data traffic. Finally, ASP-Active indicates that the ASP is available and desires to send and receive data traffic.

The RFC also suggests the following AS states: AS-Down, AS-Inactive, AS-Pending, and AS-Active. The AS-Down state indicates that all ASPs in the AS are in the ASP down state. The AS-Inactive state indicates that at least one ASP in the AS is in the ASP-Inactive state, and that no ASPs in the AS are in the ASP active state. The AS-Active state indicates that at least one ASP in the AS is in the ASP-Active state. The AS-Pending state is a transitory state; it is entered when the last active ASP transitions to ASP inactive or ASP-Down. It provides a means for the AS to recover without losing any messages if another ASP quickly becomes active.

Further, to provide an additional reliability measure, an optional heartbeat mechanism ensures that the M3UA peers are still available. Either side can initiate a heartbeat message, and the other side must respond with a heartbeat acknowledgement.

Following are ASPSM messages:

- **ASP Up message**—The ASP Up message is used to transition from ASP down to ASP-INACTIVE.

- **ASP Up Acknowledge message**—The ASP Up Acknowledge message is sent in response to an ASP Up message. The ASP does not consider itself in the ASP inactive state until the acknowledgement is received.

- **ASP Down message**—The ASP Down message is used to transition to ASP down from any other state.

- **ASP Down Acknowledge message**—The ASP Down Acknowledge message is sent in response to an ASP Down message. The SGP can also asynchronously send this message if, for instance, the SGP is going out of service. The ASP transitions to ASP down when it receives this message.

- **Heartbeat message**—The Heartbeat message is used to query if the peer is still available.

- **Heartbeat Acknowledge message**—The Heartbeat Acknowledge message is sent in response to the Heartbeat message.

The following are ASPTM messages:

- **ASP Active message**—The ASP Active message is used to transition from ASP inactive to ASP active.

- **ASP Active Acknowledge message**—The ASP Active Acknowledge message is sent in response to an ASP Active message. The ASP does not consider itself in the ASP active state until the acknowledgement is received.

- **ASP Inactive message**—The ASP Inactive message is used to transition from ASP active to ASP inactive.

- **ASP Inactive Acknowledge message**—The ASP Inactive Acknowledge message is sent in response to an ASP Inactive message. This message can also be sent asynchronously by the SGP if, for instance, an Application Server is taken out of service. The ASP transitions to ASP inactive when it receives this message.

Management (MGMT) Messages

There are two MGMT messages: Notify and Error.

The Error message provides a means of notifying the peer of an error event associated with a received message. There are a few errors worth noting because they can indicate a configuration error between the peers: "Invalid Routing Context," "Invalid Network Appearance" and "No Configured AS for ASP" errors.

The Notify message is used to notify appropriate ASPs in the ASP inactive state of Application Server state changes. It can also indicate a lack of resources for load share or that an alternate ASP has become active for an Application Server(s). Finally, it can be used to indicate an ASP failure.

Routing Key Management (RKM) Messages

As noted, Routing Keys can be statically or dynamically provisioned. The means for static provisioning is outside the scope of M3UA, but it could include a Command Line Interface (CLI) or network management system.

The RKM messages provide a means for dynamic provisioning of Routing Keys from an ASP to an SGP or between two IPSPs. These messages and procedures are optional so they do not have to be implemented by a SG or MGC:

- **Registration Request and Response messages**—The Registration Request message is used to register a Routing Key with the SGP or peer IPSP. The Registration Response is used to provide a response (success or failure) to the registration. Included in the response is the Routing Context assigned to the Routing Key.

- **Deregistration Request and Response messages**—The Deregistration Request message is used to deregister a Routing Key with the SGP or peer IPSP. It must contain the Routing Context provided in the Registration Response message. The Deregistration Response is used to respond (success or failure) to the deregistration.

SS7/C7 Variant Specifics

Mostly, M3UA is independent of the SS7/C7 variant that it is transporting. However, there are parameters that depend on the variant.

The most obvious are the point code parameters: OPC, DPC, Affected Point Code, and Concerned Point Code. Typically both the SGP and the ASP are configured to know which SS7 variant is being supported. Therefore, there is no need to pass the variant information in the messages with these parameters. If more than one variant is supported on a single SCTP association between the SGP and the ASP, either the Routing Context or Network Appearance parameter value must indicate the SS7 variant.

The Congestion Indication parameter in the SCON message is also treated differently based on the SS7/CS7 variant. This parameter contains the congestion threshold, except when the MTP congestion method does not support multiple levels. In that case, the SCON message does not include this parameter.

Message Flow Example

Figure 14-15 shows a simple message flow example between an SGP and an ASP. The ASP wants to become active for the Application Server associated with Routing Context 2 so it sends the appropriate ASPSM and ASPTM messages. At point (a), the ASP is ready to send and receive Protocol Data messages.

Figure 14-15 *M3UA Message Flow Example*

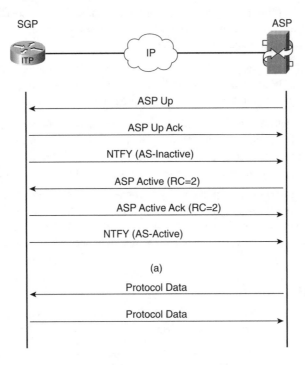

SCCP User Adaptation (SUA)

SUA provides for the transport of SCCP user signaling (TCAP and RANAP) over IP using SCTP. In effect, it duplicates SCCP's services by providing support for the reliable transfer of SCCP user messages, including support for both connectionless (Class 0 and 1) and connection-oriented (Class 2 and 3) services. SUA also provides SCCP management services to manage the status of remote destinations and SCCP subsystems. In addition, in some configurations, SUA also provides address mapping and routing functionality. SUA is currently defined by an Internet Draft (ID) [139] and is in the process of becoming an RFC.

SUA can be used between an SG and an IP-based SEP or between two IP Signaling Points (IPSP). Figure 14-16 shows an example of SUA transporting signaling information between an SG and an IP-based SEP. SUAP refers to any SCCP user, such as MAP over TCAP.

Figure 14-16 *Use of SUA Between a SG and an IP-Based SEP*

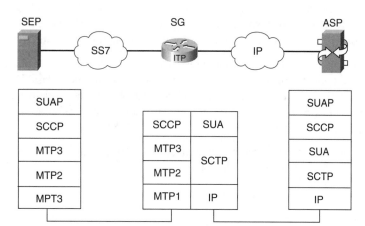

With SUA, an SG can act as an endpoint or a relay node. For the endpoint configuration, the point code and SSN of the SCCP user on the IP-based SEP are considered to be on the SG. Therefore, from the SS7 point of view, the SCCP user on the IP-based Signaling Point is on the SG. When the SG receives an incoming message from the SS7 network, it might have to perform Global Title Translation (GTT) on the message to determine its destination.

When the SG acts as a relay node, the SG must perform an address translation before it can determine the destination of incoming messages. This translation can be modeled on an SCCP GTT or based on hostname, IP address, or other information in the Called Party Address (CdPA). Thus, the determination of the IP-based SEP is based on the global title or other CdPA information in the SUA message. A hop counter is used to avoid looping (refer to Chapter 9, "Signaling Connection Control Part (SCCP)," for more information).

The SUA layer on the ASP must also make decisions about the distribution of outgoing messages. To make this decision, the SUA layer considers the following information:

- Provisioning information
- Information in the outgoing message (such as destination and SCCP subsystem)
- Availability of SGP
- Source local reference or sequence parameter
- Other, such as Routing Context information

The ASP sends responses to the SGP from which it received the message.

The SUA layer at the SGP and ASP must maintain the state of each SCTP association. SUA uses a client-server model with the ASP defaulting to the client and SG as the server. However, both SG and ASP should be able to be provisioned as the client or server. The client side of the relationship is responsible for establishing the association.

Several inbound and outbound streams are negotiated during the association establishment. The assignment of data traffic to streams depends on the protocol class. There is no restriction on Class 0 traffic. For Class 1 traffic, SUA must ensure ordered delivery by basing the stream selection on the sequence number. The source local reference is used to select the stream number for Classes 2 and 3.

SUA has an IANA registered port number of 14001. It also has an IANA registered SCTP payload protocol identifier value of 4.

Messages and Formats

The common message header and TLV format for parameters, defined previously for M3UA, apply equally for SUA.

Table 14-2 lists the message classes and message types for SUA.

Table 14-2 *SUA Message Classes and Types*

Msg Class Value	Message Class and Type Names	Msg Type Value
0	Management (MGMT) messages	
	Error message	0
	Notify message	1
2	SS7 Signaling Network Management (SSNM) messages	
	Destination Unavailable (DUNA)	1
	Destination Available (DAVA)	2
	Destination State Audit (DAUD)	3
	Signaling Congestion (SCON)	4
	Destination User Part Unavailable (DUPU)	5
	Destination Restricted	6

Table 14-2   *SUA Message Classes and Types (Continued)*

Msg Class Value	Message Class and Type Names	Msg Type Value
3	ASP State Maintenance (ASPSM) messages	
	ASP Up	1
	ASP Down	2
	Heartbeat	3
	ASP Up Acknowledge	4
	ASP Down Acknowledge	5
	Heartbeat Acknowledge	6
4	ASP Traffic Maintenance (ASPTM) messages	
	ASP Active	1
	ASP Inactive	2
	ASP Active Acknowledge	3
	ASP Inactive Acknowledge	4
7	Connectionless (CL) Messages	
	Connectionless Data Transfer (CLDT)	1
	Connectionless Data Response (CLDR)	2
8	Connection-oriented (CO) messages	
	Connection Request (CORE)	1
	Connection Acknowledge (COAK)	2
	Connection Refused (COREF)	3
	Release Request (RELRE)	4
	Release Complete (RELCO)	5
	Reset Confirm (RESCO)	6
	Reset Request (RESRE)	7
	Connection-oriented Data Transfer (CODT)	8
	Connection-oriented Data Acknowledge (CODA)	9
	Connection-oriented Error (COERR)	10
	Inactivity Test (COIT)	11

continues

Table 14-2 *SUA Message Classes and Types (Continued)*

Msg Class Value	Message Class and Type Names	Msg Type Value
9	Routing Key Management (RKM) messages	
	Registration Request	1
	Registration Response	2
	Deregistration Request	3
	Deregistration Response	4

Connectionless Messages

The Connectionless messages are used for protocol Class 0 and Class 1 traffic. There are two connectionless messages: CLDT and CLDR.

The *Connectionless Data Transfer message* corresponds to the SCCP unitdata (UDT), extended unitdata (XUDT), and long unitdata (LUDT) messages. It is used to transfer data between SUA peers for Class 0 and Class 1 traffic.

The *Connectionless Data Response message* corresponds to the SCCP unitdata service (UDTS), extended unitdata service (XUDTS), and long unitdata service (LUDTS) messages. It is sent in response to the CLDT, to report errors in the CLDT message if the return option was set.

Connection-Oriented Messages

The Connection-oriented messages are used for protocol Class 2 and Class 3 traffic.

- **Connection Request (CORE)**—The Connection Request is used to request that a connection be established between two endpoints. This message corresponds to the SCCP Connection Request (CR) message.

- **Connection Acknowledgement (COAK)**—The Connection Acknowledgement is used to send a positive acknowledgement to the Connection Request. This message corresponds to the SCCP Connection Confirm (CC) message.

- **Connection Refusal (COREF)**—The Connection Refusal is used to refuse a Connection Request. This message corresponds to the SCCP Connection Refusal (CREF) message.

- **Connection-oriented Data Transfer (CODT)**—The Connection-oriented Data Transfer message is used to send data messages on an established connection. It corresponds to the SCCP Data Form 1 (DT1), Data Form 2 (DT2), and Expedited Data (ED) messages.

- **Connection-oriented Data Acknowledge (CODA)**—The peer endpoint uses the Connection-oriented Data Acknowledge message to acknowledge receipt of the data. It is only used for protocol Class 3 messages. It corresponds to the SCCP Data Acknowledgement (AK) message.

- **Release Request (RELRE)**—The Release Request message is used to request the release of an established connection. This message corresponds to the SCCP Connection Released (RLSD) message.

- **Release Complete (RELCO)**—The Release Complete message is used to acknowledge the release of an established connection. All resources that are associated with the connection should be freed. This message corresponds to the SCCP Release Complete (RLC) message.

- **Reset Request (RESRE)**—The Reset Request message is used to request the source and destination sequence numbers that are associated with the established connection being reinitialized. This message corresponds to the SCCP Reset Request (RSR) message.

- **Connection-oriented Error (COERR)**—The Connection-oriented Error message is used to indicate that there was an error in a protocol data unit. This message corresponds to the SCCP Protocol Data Unit Error (ERR) message.

- **Connection-oriented Inactivity Test (COIT)**—The Connection-oriented Inactivity Test message is used to acknowledge the release of an established connection. All resources that are associated with the connection should be freed. This message corresponds to the SCCP Inactivity Test (IT) message.

MGMT Messages

SUA supports the same MGMT messages as M3UA but also provides SCCP subsystem state information. The DUNA, DAVA, DRST, SCON, and DAUD messages can optionally contain the SubSystem Number (SSN). In addition, the DUNA, DAVA, DRST, and SCON messages can optionally contain the Subsystem Multiplicity Indicator (SMI) parameter.

ASPSM and ASPTM Messages

For more information about ASPSM and ASPTM messages, see the description in section, "MTP Level 3 User Adaptation (M3UA)."

RKM Messages

SUA supports the same RKM messages as M3UA, but the Routing Key parameter is different in that it contains options for source and destination address and address ranges.

Message Flow Example

Figure 14-17 shows an example of connectionless and connection-oriented data transfer. This diagram assumes that the Application Server is already active.

For the connection-oriented data transfer, the connection must be established first and can be removed when it is no longer needed.

Figure 14-17 *SUA Message Flow Example*

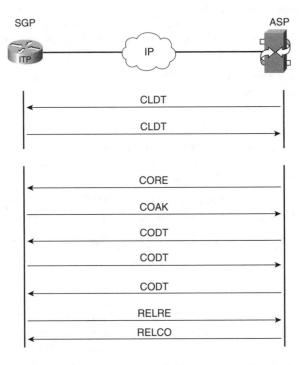

MTP Level 2 User Adaptation (M2UA)

The M2UA protocol defines the layer split between MTP Level 2 and MTP Level 3. M2UA is defined by RFC 3331 [140]. The M2UA protocol can be used between a SG, which is called a Signaling Link Terminal (SLT), and an MGC.

The SG would terminate standard SS7 links using MTP Level 1 and MTP Level 2 to provide reliable transport of MTP Level 3 messages to the SEP or STP. The SG also provides reliable transfer of MTP Level 2 primitives over IP, using SCTP as the transport protocol.

Figure 14-18 shows an example of an SG to the MGC application of M2UA. The SEP is a SEP in the SS7 network. Just as it does for M3UA, NIF stands for Nodal Interworking Function. It is the software in the SG that provides the SS7 to IP network interworking.

Figure 14-18 *Example of M2UA Between SG and MGC*

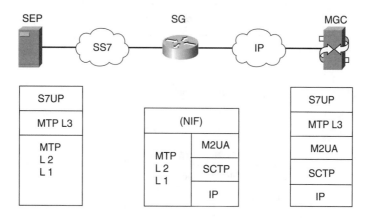

Although not discussed, M2UA can be used between two SGs, but not in a peer-to-peer arrangement. One SG would terminate the SS7 links and backhaul the MTP Level 3 messages to the other SG, which would terminate MTP Level 3.

As noted, the M2UA layer supports the MTP Level 2 to MTP Level 3 primitive boundary, including support for link alignment, message retrieval during link changeover, remote and local processor outage, and link congestion notifications.

Messages and Formats

M2UA uses the common header and TLV format for parameters that were defined in the M3UA section. In addition, M2UA introduces an M2UA specific header that is required because an Application Server can support more than one Interface Identifier.

Figure 14-19 shows the M2UA specific header, which is placed between the common message header and message-specific parameters. Note that it follows the TLV format. The Interface Identifier can be an integer-based or text-based (ASCII) value. If it is integer-based, the length is always equal to eight. If it is text-based, the length is based on the length of the ASCII string, up to a maximum of 255 octets.

Figure 14-19 *M2UA Specific Message Header*

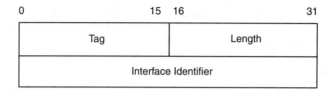

Table 14-3 lists the message classes and message types for M2UA.

Table 14-3 *M2UA Message Classes and Types*

Msg Class Value	Message Class and Type Names	Msg Type Value
0	Management (MGMT) messages	
	Error message	0
	Notify message	1
3	ASP State Maintenance (ASPSM) messages	
	ASP Up	1
	ASP Down	2
	Heartbeat	3
	ASP Up Acknowledge	4
	ASP Down Acknowledge	5
	Heartbeat Acknowledge	6
4	ASP Traffic Maintenance (ASPTM) messages	
	ASP Active	1
	ASP Inactive	2
	ASP Active Acknowledge	3
	ASP Inactive Acknowledge	4

Table 14-3   *M2UA Message Classes and Types (Continued)*

Msg Class Value	Message Class and Type Names	Msg Type Value
6	MTP2 User Adaptation (MAUP) messages	
	Data	1
	Establish Request	2
	Establish Confirm	3
	Release Request	4
	Release Confirm	5
	Release Indication	6
	State Request	7
	State Confirm	8
	State Indication	9
	Data Retrieval Request	10
	Data Retrieval Confirm	11
	Data Retrieval Indication	12
	Data Retrieval Complete Indication	13
	Congestion Indication	14
	Data Acknowledge	15
10	Interface Identifier Management (IIM) messages	
	Registration Request	1
	Registration Response	2
	Deregistration Request	3
	Deregistration Response	4

MTP2 User Adaptation (MAUP) Messages

The MAUP messages support the interface boundary to MTP Level 3.

The Data message is an MAUP message that contains MTP Level 3 protocol data, beginning with SIO—except in the case of the Japanese TTC [153] variant. For the TTC variant, the protocol data begins with the Length Indicator (LI) because its first two bits are used for priority information.

The Data message can contain an optional Correlation Identifier that is generated by the sender. This parameter is included to request an acknowledgement that the M2UA peer has received the protocol data.

The following is a list of MAUP messages:

- **Data Acknowledge**

  The Data Acknowledge message confirms the receipt of the Data message that is specified by the Correlation Identifier.

- **Establish Request and Confirm**

  The ASP sends an Establish Request message to request the alignment of an SS7 link. The mode of the alignment defaults to Normal and can be changed with the State Request message. When the link is aligned, the SGP sends an Establish Confirm message.

- **Release Request, Indication, and Confirm**

  The ASP sends a Release Request message to request that an SS7 link be taken out of service. When the SS7 link transitions to out of service, the SGP sends a Release Confirm message. If the SS7 link transitions to out of service asynchronously (the SEP takes the link out of service), the SGP sends a Release Indication message to notify the ASP.

- **State Request, Indication, and Confirm**

  The ASP sends a State Request message to request an action, such as setting link alignment state to emergency, clearing congestion, or flushing buffers for the specified SS7 link. The SGP sends the State Confirm message to confirm receipt of the State Request. The SGP sends the State Indication message to indicate a local or remote process state change for the specified SS7 link.

- **Congestion Indication**

  The SGP sends the Congestion Indication to the ASP when there has been a change in the congestion or discard status of the specified SS7 link. The message accommodates those MTP variants that support multiple congestion levels.

- **Retrieval Request, Indication, Complete Indication, and Confirm**

  These messages are used for the link changeover procedure. The ASP starts the procedure by using the Retrieval Request message to request the BSN for the failed SS7 link. The SGP responds with the Retrieval Confirm message. If there are any user data messages to retrieve, the MTP Level 3 on the ASP can choose to retrieve them. Again, the Retrieval Request message is used for this purpose. The SGP sends the user data messages in the Retrieval and Retrieval Complete Indication messages.

MGMT Messages

The messages are the same as those described under M3UA. However, there are some errors that are specific to M2UA. The "Invalid Interface Identifier" error might indicate a misconfiguration between the SGP and ASP.

ASPSM and ASPTM Messages

As with the MGMT messages, the ASPSM and ASPTM messages are the same as those described under M3UA. However, instead of Routing Context, Interface Identifier is an optional field in the ASPTM messages.

Interface Identifier Management (IIM) Messages

The IIM messages provide a means of supporting the MTP Level 3 procedures for automatic allocation of Signaling Terminals and Signaling Data Links. The Registration Request requests that an Interface Identifier be assigned to a Signaling Data Terminal and Signaling Data Link Identifier pair. The Registration Response provides a result (success or fail) for the registration and, if successful, the assigned Interface Identifier. The ASP can deregister the Interface Identifier (in other words, give it back to the pool) using the Deregistration Request message. The SGP confirms this request using the Deregistration Response message.

SS7 Variant Specifics

Like the other UAs, M2UA provides support for all SS7 variants. There is one parameter that is specific to the Japanese TTC [153] variant. A TTC-specific Protocol Data parameter provides the means of carrying priority information. This Protocol Data parameter differs from the generic Protocol Data parameter by starting with the Length Indicator (the Japanese TTC variant uses the spare bits of this octet for priority information), rather than the SIO. The Congestion Indication message also accommodates MTP variants that support multiple congestion levels.

Message Flow Examples

Figure 14-20 shows a message flow example for an SGP that supports an Application Server containing IIDs 1 and 2. The ASP brings the Application Server to the AS-ACTIVE state by sending the appropriate ASPSM and ASPTM messages. It then decides to align the first SS7 link (identified by IID 1) in-service using emergency alignment. Then, it requests to align the second SS7 link (identified by IID 2) using normal (the default) alignment.

Figure 14-20 *M2UA Message Flow Example*

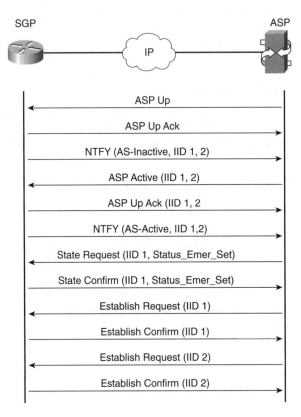

MTP Level 2 Peer Adaptation (M2PA)

Similar to the M2UA layer, the MTP Level 2 Peer Adaptation (M2PA) layer transports SS7 MTP Level 2 user (MTP Level 3) signaling messages over IP using SCTP. However, in addition, M2PA supports full MTP Level 3 message handling and network management between two SS7 nodes that communicate over an IP network. An ID [141] defines an M2PA, which is in the process of becoming an RFC.

M2PA supports the following features:

- Seamless operation of MTP Level 3 protocol peers over an IP network
- Support for the MTP Level 2 to MTP Level 3 primitive boundary
- Support for the management of SCTP associations as IP links
- Support for reporting asynchronous status changes to layer management

M2PA can be used between a SG and a MGC, between a SG and an IPSP, and between two IPSPs. In any scenario, both sides of the M2PA protocol must be assigned an SS7 point code. Two IPSPs can use M2PA IP links and standard SS7 links simultaneously to send and receive MTP Level 3 messages.

Figure 14-21 shows an SG to MGC application of M2PA.

Figure 14-21 *Example of M2PA Used Between a SG and a MGC*

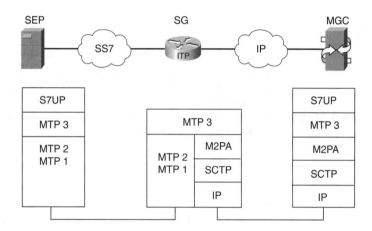

M2PA can also be used between two SGs. This configuration would be useful for long-haul SS7 link replacement. Figure 14-22 shows an example of such a configuration.

Figure 14-22 *Example of M2PA Used Between Two SGs*

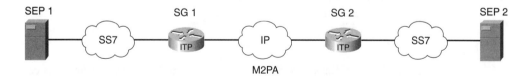

M2PA and M2UA Comparison

M2PA and M2UA are similar in that they both support the MTP Level 2 primitive boundary to MTP Level 3, and they both transport MTP Level 3 data messages. However, they also have some significant differences.

The differences arise from the treatment of the MTP Level 2 primitive boundary interface. M2UA "backhauls," or transports, the boundary primitives by way of M2UA messages between the M2UA peers. M2PA processes the boundary primitives, in effect replacing MTP Level 2 without necessarily repeating all of the MTP Level 2 functionality. Therefore, M2PA provides an IP-based SS7 link. This requires that the M2PA SG is an SS7 node with a point code. The M2UA SG does not have such a requirement; rather, it shares the MGC or IPSP's point code.

M2PA Differences from Other UAs

M2PA does share the same common message header with the other UA layers, but it is different in many ways. Because M2PA is a peer-to-peer with a single "IP link" that is defined by a single association, there is no need for Routing Keys or Interface Identifiers. Further, M2PA does not support the concepts of Application Servers, ASPs, or SGP. M2PA's redundancy model is based on SS7. The peer-to-peer connection based on a SCTP association supports a single SS7-based IP-link. SS7 link sets support redundancy.

Messages and Formats

As noted, M2PA does support the common message header. In addition, M2PA has a M2PA specific header that is used with each message. Figure 14-23 shows the M2PA specific header.

Figure 14-23 *M2PA Specific Message Header*

0 7	8 31
Unused	BSN
Unused	FSN

As with MTP Level 2, Backward Sequence Number (BSN) is the Forward Sequence Number (FSN) that was last received from the peer. FSN is the sequence number of the user data message being sent.

Table 14-4 lists the message classes and message types for M2PA.

Table 14-4   *M2PA Message Classes and Types*

Msg Class Value	Message Class and Type Names	Msg Type Value
11	M2PA messages	
	User Data	1
	Link Status	2

MTP2 Peer Adaptation Messages

The following are M2PA messages:

- **User Data**—The User Data message carries the MTP Level 3 Payload's SIO and Signaling Information Field (SIF). It also contains a LI field to support the Japanese TTC variant that requires two bits in the LI field to be used for priority. However, the LI field is not used for any other purpose (such as to indicate message length) and is set to zero.

- **Link Status**—The Link Status message is similar to the Link Signal Status Unit (LSSU) in MTP Level 2. It is used to indicate the state of the "IP link." The possible states are: Alignment, Proving Normal, Proving Emergency, Ready, Processor Outage, Process Recovered, Busy, Busy Ended, and Out of Service. The Proving message can contain optional filler to enable the SCTP send window size to be increased (in other words, to move beyond the SCTP slow start threshold) before the "IP link" is aligned.

Message Flow Example

Figure 14-24 shows a message flow example for aligning a link by using normal proving between two SGs supporting M2PA. In this diagram, the timer information is only shown for SG1. When alignment is complete, the M2PA peers inform their respective MTP Level 3 stacks that the link is in-service; MTP Level 3 messages can then be sent across the "IP link."

Figure 14-24 *M2PA Message Flow Example*

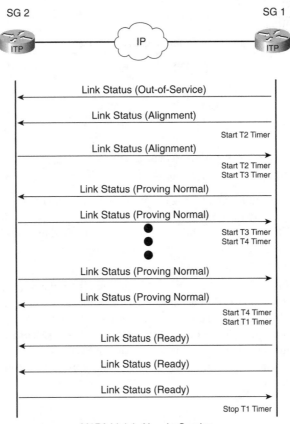

SG 2

SG 1

IP

Link Status (Out-of-Service)

Link Status (Alignment)

Start T2 Timer

Link Status (Alignment)

Start T2 Timer
Start T3 Timer

Link Status (Proving Normal)

Link Status (Proving Normal)

Start T3 Timer
Start T4 Timer

Link Status (Proving Normal)

Link Status (Proving Normal)

Start T4 Timer
Start T1 Timer

Link Status (Ready)

Link Status (Ready)

Link Status (Ready)

Stop T1 Timer

M2PA Link is Now In-Service
MTP Level 3 May Begin Sending Data Messages.

ISDN User Adaptation (IUA)

In addition to addressing SS7 over IP, the SigTran group also addressed the backhaul of ISDN over an IP network. RFC 3057 [142] defined the IUA, which is supplemented by an Implementer's Guide [143] that seamlessly supports the Q.921 user (Q.931 and QSIG). It also supports both ISDN Primary Rate Access (PRA) and Basic Rate Access (BRA) as well as Facility Associated Signaling (FAS), Non-Facility Associated Signaling (NFAS), and NFAS with backup D channel. Further, extensions to IUA are defined for DPNSS/DASS2 [144], V5.2 [145], and GR 303 [146] that will most likely become RFCs in the future.

Figure 14-25 shows an example of the use of IUA. The MG has a SG component embedded in it that terminates the ISDN Layer 2 protocol and SigTran protocol stack.

Figure 14-25 *IUA Example*

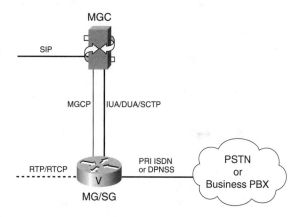

Transport Adaptation Layer Interface (TALI)

There is one proprietary solution that is worth mentioning briefly. Tekelec developed the TALI, which is defined by an Informational RFC 3094 [147]. TALI provides much of the same functionality as M3UA and SUA. However, unlike the SigTran UA layers, TALI uses TCP for its transport layer.

Early Cisco SS7/IP Solution

Cisco was working on a SLT device before the SS7/IP IETF standardization efforts began. The Cisco SLT is a modular access router (Cisco 2611 or 2651) that terminates SS7 signaling links and backhauls MTP Level 3 and above to a PGW 2200 (formerly SC 2200 and VSC 3000) MGC. Figure 14-26 shows an example configuration of two Cisco SLTs providing SS7 termination and backhaul for the Cisco PGW 2200 Softswitch.

NOTE   For additional information about Cisco Softswitch products, including the PGW2200 and BTS10200, visit the following Web site:

http://www.cisco.com/en/US/products/sw/voicesw/index.html.

Figure 14-26 *Cisco SLT Example*

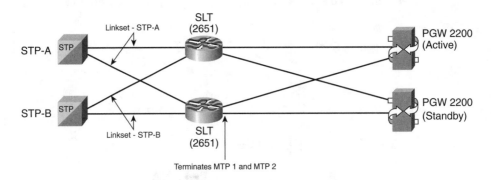

The SLT supports either SS7 A-link or F-link configurations. As noted previously, some SS7 links are deployed with bearer channels that are provisioned on the time slots that are not used by signaling channels. The SLT supports a drop-and-insert feature, which allows the signaling channels to be groomed from the facility. The bearer channels are hair pinnned on the interface card that is to be sent to a MG. Figure 14-27 shows an example of the drop-and-insert feature.

Figure 14-27 *Example of SLT Drop-and-Insert Feature*

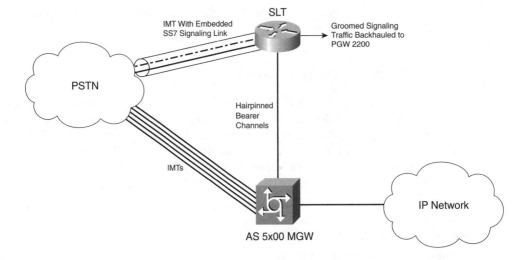

Each 2611 SLT can terminate up to two SS7 links, and the 2651 SLT can terminate up to four links. Both have support for ANSI, ITU, TTC, and NTT variants. Several physical layer interfaces are supported on the SLT, including V.35, T1, and E1.

The SLT function can also be integrated into the MG, as is done on some of the Cisco universal gateways. The following Web site contains more information about the Cisco SLT:

http://www.cisco.com/en/US/products/hw/vcallcon/ps2152/products_data_sheet09186a0080091b58.html

To deliver the backhauled messages to the PGW2200 reliably, the SLT makes use of Reliable UDP (RUDP) and Session Manager (SM) protocols. A generic backhaul protocol layer is used to provide adaptation between MTP Level 2 and MTP Level 3. Figure 14-28 shows the protocol stacks used by the SLT and PGW2200.

Figure 14-28 *Cisco SLT Protocol Stack*

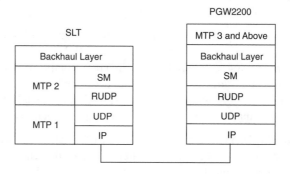

RUDP is a simple packet-based transport protocol that is based on Reliable Data Protocol (RFC 1151 [148] and RFC 908 [149]). RUDP has the following features:

- Connection-oriented
- Guarantees packet delivery with retransmission
- Maintains session connectivity using keepalive messages
- Provides notification of session failure

The SLT maintains up to two RUDP sessions to each PGW2200 host. The use of two sessions provides for additional reliability because they provide for two different network paths between the SLT and the PGW2200.

The SM layer manages the RUDP sessions under control of the PGW2200. A single RUDP session is used to pass messages between the SLT and PGW2200 based on RUDP session availability and the PGW2200 hosts' Active/Standby state. The Active PGW2200 selects one or two possible RUDP sessions and indicates its selection to the SLT via the SM protocol.

The generic backhaul protocol layer is very similar to M2UA; it provides the same basic functionality for backhauling MTP Level 3 and above over IP to the PGW2200.

SS7 and SIP/H.323 Interworking

The ITU-T originally developed the H.323 [125] for multimedia over Local Area Networks (LANs). It is not a single protocol; rather, it is a vertically-integrated suite of protocols that define the components and signaling. Though it was originally used for video-conferencing, H.323 was enhanced to better support VoIP with the Version 2 release. It is currently the most widely-deployed VoIP solution today.

One of the main complaints about H.323 is its complexity. With H.323, many messages must be passed to set up even a basic voice call. SIP [124], is considered a simpler, more flexible alternative to H.323. SIP is a signaling protocol that handles the setup, modification and teardown of multimedia sessions. It was developed in the IETF as a signaling protocol for establishing sessions in an IP network. A session can be a simple two-way telephone call or a multimedia conference. SIP is becoming a popular favorite as the future of VoIP.

So, how does SigTran play a role in H.323 and SIP? SigTran can provide PSTN connectivity to H.323 and SIP networks. A PSTN Gateway application can be used to fulfill this need. The PSTN Gateway sits on the edge of the circuit-switched and packet-switched networks and provides SIP or H.323 interworking to SS7 in the PSTN. Figure 14-29 shows an example of an SIP PSTN Gateway application. In this example, the MGC connects to the SGs using SigTran.

Figure 14-30 shows a similar example of an H.323 PSTN Gateway application.

Another interesting application is the PSTN transit application, in which calls originate and terminate on TDM interfaces and then transit a voice packet network (such as SIP or H.323). Service providers can use this application to offload their tandem and transit Class 4 and Class 3 switches. This application creates the need for an ISUP transparency. SIP-T [150] (SIP for Telephones) provides a framework for the integration of the PSTN with SIP. Figure 14-31 shows an example of using SIP-T for a PSTN transit application.

Figure 14-29 *SIP-PSTN Gateway Application*

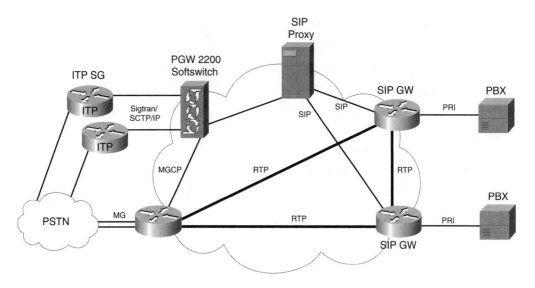

Figure 14-30 *H.323-PSTN Gateway Application*

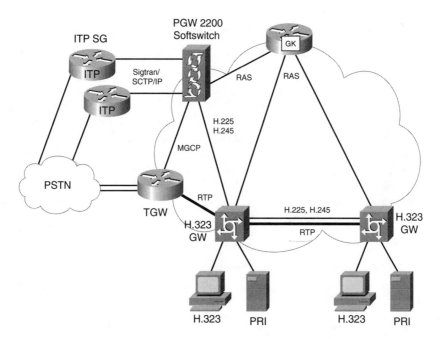

Figure 14-31 *SIP Transit Application*

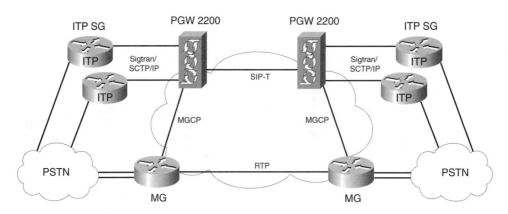

SIP-T meets the SS7 to SIP interworking requirements by providing the following functions:

- A standard way of mapping ISUP information into the SIP header for calls that originate in the PSTN. This function ensures that the SIP contains sufficient information to route calls (for example, in the case where routing depends on some ISUP information).

- Use of the SIP INFO [151] Method to transfer mid-call ISUP signaling messages.

- A means for MIME [152] encapsulation of the ISUP signaling information in the SIP body provides for ISUP transparency.

When the MGC receives an ISUP message, the appropriate ISUP parameters are translated to the SIP header fields and the ISUP message is encapsulated in a MIME attachment, which intermediate SIP entities treat as an opaque object. If the SIP message terminates the call, it ignores the ISUP attachment because it has no need for it. However, if the call terminates on the PSTN, the encapsulated ISUP message is examined and used to generate the outgoing ISUP message. The version parameter included in the MIME media type information indicates the encapsulated ISUP message's ISUP variant. If there are different ISUP variants on the origination and termination side, it is up to the terminating MGC to perform ISUP translation between the variants.

Summary

This chapter focused on the key SigTran protocols and their role in a next-generation architecture of voice products. The SigTran work grew from a desire to decompose a traditional circuit switch into specialized components. It focused on the following two areas:

- A transport protocol that is suitable for meeting the requirements of carrying telecommunication protocols, especially SS7, over a packet network.

- The creation of adaptation layers that support the primitives of SCN telephony signaling protocols.

SCTP was developed as the new generic transport protocol. It provides performance and reliability benefits for telephony signaling transport over the UDP and TCP transport protocols.

The common elements of the adaptation layers were introduced and described in some detail, as were the following key adaptation layers:

- **M3UA**—Provides for the transport of MTP Level 3 user part signaling (for example, ISUP and SCCP).

- **SUA**—Provides for the transport of SCCP user signaling (for example, TCAP).

- **M2UA**—Provides for the transport of MTP Level 2 user signaling (for example, MTP Level 3).

- **M2PA**—Provides a means of creating an IP SS7 link by replicating MTP Level 2 and supporting the MTP Level 2 primitive boundary to MTP Level 3.

- **IUA**—Provides for the transport of Q.921 user signaling (for example, Q.931).

In addition, two protocols related to SigTran were introduced: TALI and the early Cisco backhaul protocol stack. Finally, some examples of SS7 to SIP and H.323 interworking were provided to provide a context for how SigTran protocols can be used with other VoIP protocols.

PART **V**

Supplementary Topics

SS7 Security and Monitoring

Signaling System No. 7 (SS7) is a castle in terms of security, although the castle walls are increasingly coming under attack. The main forces acting on the protocol to wear down its defenses are market liberalization and ever-increasing convergence.

When SS7 was designed and initially deployed, comparatively few telephone companies with well-defined network boundaries existed. That environment no longer exists because of market liberalization; there are more telephony providers than could have been imagined when SS7 was first drawn up.

The convergence of SS7 with next generation architectures such as IP networks has created the need for additional security enforcement. SS7 has relied on an isolated signaling network for much of its' security and the interconnection with IP networks and interworking with other packet protocols changes this paradigm.

The lack of security inherent in the SS7 protocol is likely to be increasingly exposed in line with communications convergence and with the ever-increasing number of operator interconnects.

At present, traditional SS7 has no security mechanisms to ensure that a sender is who he says he is, nor is there cryptographic protection against alteration of messages. Securing traditional SS7 currently focuses on screening incoming traffic and monitoring for unusual traffic. This chapter examines each of these security measures.

Traffic Screening

This section provides a practical overview of SS7 traffic screening. Traffic screening is normally applied at Signal Transfer Points (STPs) because these are normally the gateways between operator networks. Network operators are responsible for ensuring the security of their own SS7 networks to defend against any unwarranted incoming traffic. At present, SS7 traffic can be altered, injected, or deleted after physical access to the signaling links is gained.

STPs normally have extensive screening functionality. Typically, the screening rules are specified on a per-linkset basis. Usually the STP can support something in the range of a few thousand conditional statements that can be applied to each linkset. Screening usually adds only a couple milliseconds to cross STP transmission time.

STP gateway screening is typically applied to provide access-control mechanisms to nonhome SS7 networks (interconnects). Figure 15-1 illustrates this concept.

Figure 15-1   *STPs May Be Used to Filter Incoming SS7 Messages*

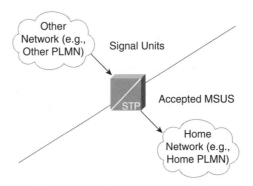

Before an incoming Message Signal Unit (MSU) is accepted, it should pass a series of filtering rules that ensure conformance to the specified criteria. If an MSU does not pass the test, it should be discarded. This operation is known as message screening. Screening normally is applied only to the incoming internetwork SS7 MSUs. Screening procedures normally are not applied to outgoing or intranetwork MSUs. Internetwork MSUs are of high importance because they constitute the traffic coming in from other operators via interconnects. Screening is normally applied at the Message Transfer Part (MTP) 3 and Signaling Connection Control Part (SCCP) protocols layers. MTP screening is applied before any Global Title Translation (GTT). Normally there are pre-GTT and post-GTT SCCP screening rules.

The following typical MTP basic screening rules can be combined to build more complex screening functionality:

- Allow specified Originating Point Code (OPC)
- Block specified OPC
- Allow specified Destination Point Code (DPC)
- Block specified DPC

- Permitted Service Information Octet (SIO) values include priority values as per the Service Indicator (SI) subfield, network values as per the Network Indicator (NI) subfield, and the User Part values as per the Subservice field (SSF)

- Allow certain MTP3 H0/H1 values (signaling network management messages)

The following typical pre-GTT SCCP screening rules can be combined to build more complex screening functionality:

- Calling Party Address (CgPA) parameters such as point code allowed, subsystem number allowed, SCCP message type allowed, routing indicator allowed, and translation type allowed

The following typical post-GTT SCCP screening rules can be combined to build more complex screening functionality:

- Called Party Address (CdPA) parameters such as point code allowed, subsystem number allowed, and SCCP management messages allowed

The next sections look at the protocol issues you should keep in mind when planning to implement screening rules.

Screening Considerations

The following sections discuss areas of concern surrounding the various protocols in a core SS7 stack. In general, signaling related to the control and management of the whole network is somewhat more of a target for fraud than, say, signaling relating to one call only.

MTP

The lower levels of MTP (MTP1 and MTP2) are involved in the reliable transfer of SUs on only a link-by-link basis, rather than on an end-to-end basis. Therefore, screening is not provided at these layers, and monitoring systems may take many measurements relating to MTP2 performance instead. MTP screening is provided for MTP3, because it provides the routing of MSUs through the SS7 network and as such, contains information related to the network topology, such as routing tables. The information relating to network topology can change dynamically by the network management functions of MTP3. Therefore, MTP3 network management messages need to be both screened and monitored, because they can access and modify the network's routing information.

SCCP

As with MTP3, SCCP carries messages arriving from both Level 4 and self-generated SCCP network management messages. SCCP management informs other nodes of application status, such as whether a particular application is working.

MTP3: Management Messages

These messages are generated by the MTP3 level to maintain the signaling service and to restore normal signaling conditions in the case of failure, either in signaling links or signaling points. MTP3 is explained in Chapter 7, "Message Transfer Part 3 (MTP3)."

MTP3 messages carrying relevant information that can affect the network if abused and can be split into two categories:

- Messages communicating unavailability (such as COO, COA, ECO, ECA, TFP, TFR, and TFC)

- Messages communicating availability (such as CBD and TFA)

A higher degree of risk is associated with the first category, because they diminish available resources. As such, care should be given to the screening of such messages. For example, the Transfer Restricted (TFR) message is involved in routing reconfiguration and traffic diversion. Therefore, a degree of risk is involved in receiving or sending this message if it is propagated unintentionally or with malicious intent. Unintentional transmission is likely to be caused by software or configuration errors. Malicious intent is because someone with physical access (an insider) sends the message intentionally with the use of a protocol analyzer, for example.

Table 15-1 lists the main MTP3 messages that should be screened.

Table 15-1   *MTP3 Messages to Be Screened*

Message	Parameter	Reason for Screening
MSU (in case of an STP)	OPC	Verifies that the originating node is known (is present in the routing tables). This provides a degree of protection against unauthorized access to the network.
	DPC	Verifies that the message is destined for a valid node (a node to which the originating point is allowed to route).
Changeover, Changeback, and Emergency Changeover	OPC	Verifies that the message is received from an adjacent node that is allowed to send this message type.
	DPC	Verifies that the message is destined for itself.
Transfer Prohibited Transfer Restricted	OPC	Verifies that the message is received from a node allowed to send these types of messages.
Management Inhibiting	OPC	Verifies that the message is received from an adjacent node allowed to send this type of message.

Table 15-1   *MTP3 Messages to Be Screened (Continued)*

Message	Parameter	Reason for Screening
Transfer Control	OPC	Verifies that the message is received from a node allowed to send this type of message. The operator should choose the allowed node list according to their network topology and routing.
	DPC	Verifies that the message is destined for a node to which the originating node can route traffic.

It should be verified that all messages' MSUs are received on a valid linkset—that is, the originating point is allowed to use that particular linkset.

The primary MTP3 parameters that should be screened are the originating and destination point code. These are described next.

Originating Point Code

This parameter is the address of the originating node and forms part of the routing label. The OPC should be verified, as well as the rights that the node sending the message can route via the STP. This can be done by checking that the node is present in routing tables. Note that no mechanisms prove that the node is the one claimed. Instead, the OPC simply acts as a check that the node at least claims to be the correct node.

Destination Point Code

This parameter is the address of the destination node, and it forms part of the routing label. The DPC should be analyzed to verify the following:

- MSUs coming from an external node are addressed to a node inside your own network (to keep the STP from being used as a transit node of unwarranted traffic).

- MTP3 management messages coming from an external node are addressed only to the STP and not to a node inside your own network. (Management messages should involve interconnecting only nodes at the interface with other networks, not other parts of the signaling network itself.)

SCCP

This section describes typical SCCP screening considerations. SCCP is explained in Chapter 9, "Signaling Connection Control Part (SCCP)."

SCCP User Messages

These messages come from above SCCP via Transaction Capabilities Application Part (TCAP) and are related to the applications running on TCAP (for example, intelligent network services, mobility services, and value-added services). These messages typically use GTT functionality. Some STPs offer the functionality to screen so that only permitted nodes may request translations, the translations themselves are valid, and the translations themselves are permitted.

Management Messages

Management messages are generated by the SCCP level to maintain network performance by rerouting or throttling traffic in the event of failure or congestion.

The messages that can reroute the traffic constitute the means by which the integrity of the signaling network at SCCP level can be penetrated and endangered. These messages are discussed in the following sections.

Subsystem Prohibited (SSP)

A Subsystem Prohibited (SSP) message is sent to concerned destinations to inform SCCP Management (SCMG) at those destinations of the failure of a subsystem. The receiving end of an SSP message updates its translation tables; therefore, traffic could be rerouted to a backup subsystem if available. If not, an SCCP user might no longer be able to offer a particular service. It is imperative that verification takes place to ensure that this message is received from a permitted node. The only means of verification is to check the OPC from which the message is received.

Subsystem Allowed (SSA)

A Subsystem Allowed (SSA) message is sent to concerned destinations to inform them that a subsystem that was formerly prohibited is now allowed or that an SCCP that was formerly unavailable is now available. The node receiving the SSA, therefore, updates its translation tables. Because the message indicates availability, less risk is associated with it.

Subsystem Status Test (SST)

The Subsystem Status Test (SST) message is sent to verify the status of a subsystem that is marked prohibited or the status of an SCCP marked unavailable. The receiving node checks the status of the named subsystem. If the subsystem is allowed, an SSA message is sent in response. If the subsystem is prohibited, no reply is sent.

The originating node should be verified by checking the OPC to make sure that it has the necessary rights.

Parameters

To provide screening, you do not need to read every field comprising a message. Instead, you read only the fields (parameters) that can cause a security threat. The parameters that contain the message's origin and destination and those used in GTT have particular security importance.

Table 15-2 lists the main SCCP messages that should be screened.

Table 15-2 *SCCP Messages to Be Screened*

Message	Parameter	Reason for Screening
UDT and XUDT	Calling Party Address	Verifies that the message is received from a specified remote subsystem (such as a specified combination of SSN+SPC).
	Called Party Address	For routing on SSN, verifies that the message is destined for a local subsystem.
		For routing on GT, verifies that the message uses a valid translation table (such as a table allowed for the origin).
	Results of the translation	Verifies that the new values of DPC and SSN match values allowed by the originating node.
SSP and SSA	Calling Party Address	Verifies that the message is received from a specified remote subsystem (such as a specified combination of SSN+SPC).
	Called Party Address	Verifies that the message is destined for the management of SCCP (SSN = 1).
	Affected point code	Verifies that the affected node is inside the originating network.
	Affected subsystem number	Verifies that the affected subsystem is known.
SST	Calling Party Address	Verifies that the message is received from a valid remote subsystem (such as a valid SSN+SPC).
	Called Party Address	Verifies that the message is destined for the management of SCCP (SSN=1).

Traffic Monitoring

Monitoring signaling traffic is the simplest method of revealing accidental (because of misconfiguration, for example) or intentional abuse of the SS7 network. Because signaling is the nervous system of the telecommunications network, it should be clear that if the SS7 network goes down, so does the entire telecommunications network it supports. Intentional or other acts that cause impairments in signaling performance can cause all kinds of critical failure scenarios, including incorrect billing, lack of cellular roaming functionality, failure of Short Messaging Service (SMS) transfer, unexpected cutoff during calls, poor line quality, poor cellular handovers, nonrecognition of prepay credits, multiple tries to set up calls, ghost calls, and the inability to contact other subscribers on certain other networks.

The SS7 network's quality of service (QoS) directly relates to the lack of QoS to subscribers. Thus, it is vital to monitor the SS7 network sufficiently to ensure that impairments, whatever their origin, are realized as soon as possible. Monitoring is specified in ITU-T recommendation Q.752 [71]. Further useful ITU-T references are provided in Q.753 [72].

Monitoring entails measuring the traffic in terms of messages, octets, or more detailed information, such as counts of certain message types or GTTs requested. Monitoring can be applied to any set of links, but it is considered essential at links that interconnect with other networks (for example, those crossing an STP or certain switches). In fact, monitoring systems tend to connect with a multiple number of links throughout the SS7 network, in effect, producing an overlay monitoring network. The monitoring points simply consist of line cards that are tapped onto the links to unobtrusively gather and process real-time data. The information obtained from the multiple points is then aggregated and analyzed at a central point (common computing platform). The processing platform is likely to vary in power and complexity, depending on the scale of the purchase. Higher-end systems provide intelligent fraud and security monitoring, and lower-end systems simply provide statistics and alerts when performance thresholds are crossed.

The values measured are compared to a predetermined threshold for "regular traffic." When a value exceeds the predetermined threshold, an alarm normally is generated, and a notification might be sent to maintenance personnel. In this way, SS7 network monitoring helps the network operator detect security breaches. Some examples of high-level measurements are Answer Seizure Ratio (ASR), Network Efficiency Ratio (NER), and Number of Short Calls (NOSK). ASR is normal call clearing divided by all other scenarios. NER is normal call clearing, plus busy, divided by all other call-clearing scenarios. NOSK is simply the number of calls with a hold time less than a prespecified value. To reflect a high QoS, a high NER and ASR are desired as well as a low NOSK.

SS7 monitoring systems are changing to reflect the convergence taking place. Many can show the portions of the call connected via SS7, and other portions of the call connected via other means, such as Session Initiation Protocol (SIP).

As convergence takes hold, a call has the possibility of traversing multiple protocols, such as SIGTRAN, SIP, H.323, TALI, MGCP, MEGACO, and SCTP. Monitoring systems that support converged environments allow the operator to perform a call trace that captures the entire call. SIGTRAN is explained in Chapter 14, " SS7 in the Converged World."

It should also be mentioned that monitoring the signaling network has other advantages in addition to being a tool to tighten up network security:

- **Customer satisfaction**—Historically, information was collected at the switches, and operators tended to rely on subscriber complaints to know that something was wrong. QoS can be measured in real time via statistics such as, call completion rates, transaction success rates, database transaction analysis, telemarketing call completion (toll free, for example), and customer-specific performance analysis. The captured data is stored in a central database and, therefore, can be used for later evaluation—for example, by network planning.

- **Billing verification**

- **Business-related opportunities**—Data mining for marketing data, producing statistics such as how many calls are placed to and from competitors.

- **Enforcing interconnect agreements**—Ensure correct revenue returns and validate revenue claims from other operators. Reciprocal compensation is steeply rising in complexity.

Presently, the most common security breach relates to fraud. The monitoring system may be connected to a fraud detection application. Customer profiles are created based on the subscriber's typical calling patterns and can detect roaming fraud, two calls from the "same" mobile (for example, SIM cloning), subscription fraud, and so on. The real-time nature of monitoring allows active suspicious calls to be released before additional operator revenue is lost.

Monitoring systems should be capable of most of the measurements defined in ITU-T recommendation Q.752 [71]. The rest of this section lists the bulk of these measurements for each level in the SS7 protocol stack.

Q.752 Monitoring Measurements

The number of measurements defined in Recommendation Q.752 [71] is very large. They are presented in the following sections. Note that most of the measurements are not obligatory, and that many are not permanent but are on activation only after crossing a predefined threshold. The obligatory measurements form the minimum set that should be used on the international network.

MTP: Link Failures

Measurements:

- Abnormal Forward Indicator Bit Received (FIBR)/Backward Sequence Number Received (BSNR)

- Excessive delay of acknowledgment

- Excessive error rate
- Excessive duration of congestion
- Signaling link restoration

MTP: Surveillance

Measurements:

- Local automatic changeover
- Local automatic changeback
- Start of remote processor outage
- Stop of remote processor outage
- SL congestion indications
- Number of congestion events resulting in loss of MSUs
- Start of linkset failure
- Stop of linkset failure
- Initiation of Broadcast TFP because of failure of measured linkset
- Initiation of Broadcast TFA for recovery of measured linkset
- Start of unavailability for a routeset to a given destination
- Stop of unavailability for a routeset to a given destination
- Adjacent signaling point inaccessible
- Stop of adjacent signaling point inaccessible
- Start and end of local inhibition
- Start and end of remote inhibition

Additional measurement may be provided to the user for determining the network's integrity.

Measurements:

- Local management inhibit
- Local management uninhibit
- Duration of local busy
- Number of SIF and SIO octets received
- Duration of adjacent signaling point inaccessible

MTP: Detection of Routing and Distribution Table Errors

Measurements

- Duration of unavailability of signaling linkset
- Start of linkset failure
- Stop of linkset failure
- Initiation of Broadcast TFP because of failure of measured linkset
- Initiation of Broadcast TFA for recovery of measured linkset
- Unavailability of route set to a given destination or set of destinations
- Duration of unavailability in measurement
- Start of unavailability in measurement
- Stop of unavailability in measurement
- Adjacent SP inaccessible
- Duration of adjacent SP inaccessible
- Stop of adjacent SP inaccessible
- Number of MSUs discarded because of a routing data error
- User Part Unavailable MSUs transmitted and received

MTP: Detection of Increases in Link SU Error Rates

Measurements:

- Number of SIF and SIO octets transmitted
- Number of SIF and SIO octets received
- Number of SUs in error (monitors incoming performance)
- Number of negative acknowledgments (NACKS) received (monitors outgoing performance)
- Duration of link in the in-service state
- Duration of link unavailability (any reason)

MTP: Detection of Marginal Link Faults

Measurements:

- SL alignment or proving failure (this activity is concerned with detecting routing instabilities caused by marginal link faults)
- Local automatic changeover

- Local automatic changeback
- SL congestion indications
- Cumulative duration of SL congestions
- Number of congestion events resulting in loss of MSUs

MTP: Link, Linkset, Signaling Point, and Route Set Utilization

Measurements by link:

- Duration of link in the in-service state
- Duration of SL unavailability (for any reason)
- Duration of SL unavailability because of remote processor outage
- Duration of local busy
- Number of SIF and SIO octets transmitted
- Number of octets retransmitted
- Number of message signal units transmitted
- Number of SIF and SIO octets received
- Number of message signal units received
- SL congestion indications
- Cumulative duration of SL congestions
- MSUs discarded because of SL congestion
- Number of congestion events resulting in loss of MSUs

Measurements by linkset:

- Duration of unavailability of signaling linkset

Measurements by signaling point:

- Number of SIF and SIO octets received:
  - With given OPC or set of OPCs
  - With given OPC or set of OPCs and SI or set of SIs
- Number of SIF and SIO octets transmitted:
  - With given DPC or set of DPCs
  - With given DPC or set of DPCs and SI or set of SIs

- Number of SIF and SIO octets handled:
  - With given SI or set of SIs
  - With given OPC or set of OPCs, DPC or set of DPCs, and SI or set of SIs
- Number of MSUs handled with given OPC set, DPC set, and SI set

Measurements by signaling route set:

- Unavailability of route set to a given destination or set of destinations
- Duration of unavailability in measurement 4.9
- Duration of adjacent signaling point inaccessible
- MSUs discarded because of routing data error
- User Part Unavailability MSUs sent and received
- Transfer Controlled MSU received

MTP: Component Reliability and Maintainability Studies

These studies are aimed at calculating the Mean Time Between Failures (MTBF) and Mean Time To Repair (MTTR) for each type of component in the SS7 network.

Measurements:

- Number of link failures:
  - All reasons
  - Abnormal FIBR/BSNR
  - Excessive delay of acknowledgment
  - Excessive error rate
  - Excessive duration of congestion
  - Duration of SL inhibition because of local management actions
  - Duration of SL inhibition because of remote management actions
  - Duration of SL unavailability because of link failure
  - Duration of SL unavailability because of remote processor outage
  - Start of remote processor outage
  - Stop of remote processor outage
  - Local management inhibit
  - Local management uninhibit

SCCP: Routing Failures

Measurements:

- Routing failure because of:
  - No translation for address of such nature
  - No translation for this specific address
  - Network failure (point code unavailable)
  - Network congestion
  - Subsystem failure (unavailable)
  - Subsystem congestion
  - Unequipped user (subsystem)
  - Reason unknown
  - Syntax error detected

In addition, the following measurements can be used as a consistency check or a network protection mechanism:

- Hop counter violation (indicates a possible SCCP circular route)
- UDTS messages sent
- XUDTS messages sent
- LUDTS messages sent
- UDTS messages received
- XUDTS messages received
- LUDTS messages received

SCCP unavailability and congestion:

Local SCCP unavailable because of

- Failure
- Maintenance made busy
- Congestion

A remote SCCP measurement is

- SCCP/subsystem congestion message received

SCCP: Configuration Management

Measurements:

- Subsystem out-of-service grant message received
- Subsystem out-of-service request denied

SCCP: Utilization Performance

Measurements:

SCCP traffic received:

- UDTS messages
- UDT messages
- XUDT messages
- XUDTS messages
- LUDT messages
- LUDTS messages
- DT1 messages/SSN
- DT2 messages/SSN
- ED messages/SSN
- Total messages (connectionless classes 0 and 1 only) per SSN

SCCP traffic sent:

- UDTS messages
- UDT messages
- XUDT messages
- LUDT messages
- XUDTS messages
- LUDTS messages
- DT1 messages/SSN
- DT2 messages/SSN
- ED messages/SSN
- Total messages (connectionless classes 0 and 1 only) per SSN

General:

- Total messages handled (from local or remote subsystems)
- Total messages intended for local subsystems
- Total messages requiring global title translation
- Total messages sent to a backup subsystem

SCCP: Quality of Service

The SCCP quality of service can be estimated using the following measurements:

Connectionless outgoing traffic:

- UDT messages sent
- XUDT messages sent
- LUDT messages sent
- UDTS messages received
- XUDTS messages received
- LUDTS messages received

Connectionless incoming traffic:

- UDT messages received
- XUDT messages received
- LUDT messages received
- UDTS messages sent
- XUDTS messages sent
- LUDTS messages sent

Connection-oriented establishments:

- Outgoing:
  - CR messages sent
  - CREF messages received
- Incoming:
  - CR messages received
  - CREF messages sent

Connection-oriented syntax/protocol errors:

- RSR messages sent/received
- ERR messages sent/received

Congestion:

- SCCP/subsystem congestion
- SSC messages received

ISUP: Availability/Unavailability

Measurements:

- Start of ISDN-UP unavailable because of failure
- Start of ISDN-UP unavailable because of maintenance
- Start of ISDN-UP unavailable because of congestion
- Stop of ISDN-UP unavailable (all reasons)
- Total duration of ISDN-UP unavailable (all reasons)
- Stop of local ISDN-UP congestion
- Duration of local ISDN-UP congestion
- Start of remote ISDN-UP unavailable
- Stop of remote ISDN-UP unavailable
- Duration of remote ISDN-UP unavailable
- Start of remote ISDN-UP congestion
- Stop of remote ISDN-UP congestion
- Duration of remote ISDN-UP congestion

ISUP: Errors

Measurements:

- Missing blocking acknowledgment in CGBA message for blocking request in previous CGB message
- Missing unblocking acknowledgment in CGUA message for unblocking request in previous CGU message
- Abnormal blocking acknowledgment in CGBA message with respect to previous CGB message
- Abnormal unblocking acknowledgment in CGUA message with respect to previous CGU message
- Unexpected CGBA message received with an abnormal blocking acknowledgment
- Unexpected CGUA message received with an abnormal unblocking acknowledgment
- Unexpected BLA message received with an abnormal blocking acknowledgment

- Unexpected UBA message received with an abnormal unblocking acknowledgment
- No RLC message received for a previously sent RSC message within timer T17
- No GRA message received for a previously sent GRS message within timer T23
- No BLA message received for a previously sent BLO message within timer T13
- No UBA message received for a previously sent UBL message within timer T15
- No CGBA message received for a previously sent CGB message within timer T19
- No CGUA message received for a previously sent CGU message within timer T21
- Message format error
- Unexpected message received
- Released because of unrecognized information
- RLC not received for a previously sent REL message within timer T5
- Inability to release a circuit
- Abnormal release condition
- Circuit blocked because of excessive errors detected by CRC failure

ISUP: Performance

Measurements:

- Total ISDN-UP messages sent
- Total ISDN-UP messages received

TCAP Fault Management

- Protocol error detected in transaction portion
- Protocol error detected in component portion
- TC user generated problems

TCAP Performance

Measurements:

- Total number of TC messages sent by the node (by message type)
- Total number of TC messages received by the node (by message type)
- Total number of components sent by the node
- Total number of components received by the node
- Number of new transactions during an interval

- Mean number of open transactions during an interval
- Cumulative mean duration of transactions
- Maximum number of open transactions during an interval

Summary

SS7 was designed without integral security in mind. Its design is based on the use of dedicated physical facilities, making it difficult to compromise externally. In addition, at the time of design, fewer network operators existed, and the number of interconnections was limited. With the increasing convergence in communications, SS7 is no longer as isolated as it once was. To minimize the risks, screening may be implemented and monitoring systems put in place. Screening lets you establish rules governing whether to receive SS7 packets based on sender, destination, service requested, and so on. Monitoring systems allow operators to diagnose and resolve network failures, whether because of security lapses or otherwise.

CHAPTER 16

SS7 Testing

When a new implementation of C7 is introduced into a network, it must be conformance tested against the appropriate standard to ensure that it functions correctly. This is known as *validation* testing. Validation testing is performed before the implementation is put into a live network.

After validation testing has been successfully completed, the implementation can be deployed into the live network, where more testing will be performed. Testing at this stage is known as *compatibility* testing. Compatibility testing ensures that the implementation can interwork properly with the other signaling points that are already in the network; it might also be referred to as *interoperability* testing. The validation phase is performed against an offline implementation and is used for protocol verification, whereas compatibility testing is performed against an online implementation and is used to verify the proper interworking of two or more protocol implementations.

The ITU-T has produced framework test specifications covering both validation and compatibility for MTP2, MTP3, TUP, ISUP, ISUP Supplementary Services, SCCP, and TCAP. The test specifications are contained in Recommendations Q.781 to Q.787, respectively. While all tests are validation tests, a subset is also marked as compatibility tests:

- Q.781 [87] covers MTP2 [50]
- Q.782 [88] covers MTP3 [51]
- Q.783 [89] covers TUP [64]
- Q.784.1 [90] covers ISUP [75–78, 80–81]
- Q.785 [91] covers ISUP Supplementary Services [69]
- Q.786 [92] covers SCCP [58–63]
- Q.787 [93] covers TCAP [82–86]

Test Specifications for SIGTRAN (see Chapter 14, "SS7 in the Converged World") are just becoming available at the time of this writing. The following are available as drafts from the IETF:

- MTP2—User Peer-to-Peer Adaptation Layer (M2PA) Test Specification
- MTP2—User Adaptation Layer (M2UA) Test Specification
- MTP3—User Adaptation Layer (M3UA) Test Specification

A prerequisite for testing a given protocol layer is that the underlying layers have been implemented correctly; that is, they have already passed validation and compatibility testing. The tests intend to test the given protocol's key functionality under normal and abnormal conditions; testing all work under all abnormal conditions is impossible and impractical because of the nearly endless number of tests that would be required.

The tests do not have to be performed sequentially; however, on the whole it is generally more convenient to follow the test list in order. For some parts of the test specification it might be easier to order by pre-test conditions because the end of a test might be the pre-test condition of another test.

The chapter begins with an overview of the types of equipment that are available for SS7 testing and discusses how to use the appropriate ITU-T test specification to produce the required test specification. The rest of the chapter provides examples with full explanations for common tests (as specified by the ITU-T) for validation and compatibility of MTP2 to show the breadth of testing against a particular layer. Finally, a few examples for MTP3, ISUP, Supplementary Services, and TCAP are shown.

Test Equipment

SS7 testing equipment can be used for a several purposes, including the following:

- System and conformance tests
- Functional testing from development to operation
- Integration/testing of new products
- Network entity emulation, such as Mobile Switching Center (MSC)
- Monitoring networks for error detection and analysis in the field
- Functional testing to reproduce error scenarios

The functionality of SS7 test equipment can be split into three categories: monitoring, simulation, and emulation. Test equipment tends to come as monitor only, with monitor and simulation, or with all three broad features of monitoring, simulation, and emulation.

Monitoring entails the decoding and filtering of SS7 traffic, which results in a determined subset being presented to the user in a readable format. The user is presented with the message names according to protocol level, along with parameters (further nesting might be present) and values. Monitoring can be considered akin to a "record button" that can display the traffic afterwards.

Simulation is the ability to generate desired traffic. For example traffic already caught using the monitoring function could be "played back" using the simulation function. Often when an SS7 implementation—be it a national ISUP or another part of the stack, such as a national INAP—is written following the appropriate specification(s), it tends to be problematic. This usually arises from undocumented implementation issues and specification ambiguity, including differing developer interpretations. If you can obtain traffic of the protocol you are implementing, captured from the live network via a tester's monitor functionality, you can use simulation functionality to test your implementation against real network traffic. This can save a lot of time when the product is connected to the live network for compatibility testing.

Creating test traffic in this fashion is both faster and more accurate than coding test traffic by hand entering hex. Simulation can be considered analogous to a "play button."

Emulation can be the most advanced area of functionality. It gives the test instrument the ability to pretend that it is another network entity—such as a signaling gateway (SG) or a mobile switching center (MSC). For example, if you wish to perform conformance and interoperability testing of a Base Station Controller (BSC) and a Base Transceiver Station (BTS) but the MSC is not in place, you would ordinarily be stuck until the MSC was in place. However, with emulation functionality you can substitute a tester for the missing MSC. The instrument works like a fully compliant and functioning MSC and interacts with the network and even imitates erroneous behavior, if desired. Before installation of the real MSC begins, a set of acceptance test cases could be agreed upon with the vendor and you should be armed with the knowledge that the BTS and BSC are operating correctly. The responsibility spotlight is put onto the MSC vendor to prove that their equipment is functioning correctly.

NOTE   Some analyzers that do not have the emulation function call the simulation function by the name of "emulation." Be aware of this when considering what test equipment is required for a particular application.

The modern trend in test equipment is to provide it in a portable form, with multiprotocol capability. These test instruments not only work with the SS7 set of protocols, but also with other established and emerging protocols, such as those being used in GSM/PCS, GPRS, UMTS, cdma2000, and VoIP networks. For example, a current product could offer monitoring, simulation, and emulation of M3UA and SCTP (SIGTRAN), emulation of IPv6, a conformance test suite for AAL2 Layer 3, a conformance test suite for MTP3b (Q.2210), monitoring and simulation of IU UP (TS25.415), monitoring and simulation of RANAP

(TS25.413), in addition to providing monitoring, and simulation and emulation of C7 protocols in a single package aimed at UMTS operators.

A fundamental yet often overlooked point is ensuring that the instrument can support all the physical interface connections that might be required—let alone issues of protocol support. For example, to fully test a UMTS network, the following physical interface connections might be required:

- 2x E1 ATM
- 2x OC-3 ATM
- 2x E1
- 1x Fast Ethernet

When you are satisfied that the instrument can meet the requirements of the network(s) in which it is to operate at the physical level, work up the stack to ensure that it supports all appropriate protocols. The instrument should also able to evolve along with the standards it supports so it does not quickly become obsolete.

Test Specification Creation

The test specifications produced by the ITU-T are unlikely to be run exactly as is. Remember that the ITU-T C7 specifications are tailored to each country's needs—the SS7 specifications provide national options and national coding space for the purpose of nationalization. For additional details, see Chapter 2, "Standards."

The ITU-T test specification must be modified to reflect the national specification against which it is to be tested. If we use UK ISUP as an example, the ITU-T specifies ISUP in recommendations Q.761–Q.764 [75–78, 80]. The *British Standards Institute (BSI)* specify the UK nationalized version in PNO-ISC #007 [41]. If we were to test UK ISUP, we would have to modify the ITU-T ISUP test specification [90] to reflect UK ISUP [41]. This is not a daunting task. Remember that national SS7 specifications are simply exception documents against ITU-T recommendations that, in addition, state what national messages and parameters have been selected for use, and what additional messages, parameters, and values have been added (if any) into the coding space that the ITU-T set aside for the process of nationalization. Where regional specifications exist, the national specifications are, instead, likely to be exception documents against the regional specifications. For example, UK ISUP is an exception document against the ETSI specifications. But the regional specifications themselves are exception documents (plus clarifications) against the ITU-T recommendations.

NOTE   North America, Japan, and China use regional specifications that do not adhere to the ITU-T recommendation framework.

A copy of the tests laid out by the ITU-T ISUP test specification should be taken as the basis for producing a UK ISUP test specification. It should then be modified largely in terms of deleting the tests that are not required and adding some additional tests; the national specification is unlikely to have selected all messages offered by the ITU-T recommendation and, in addition, might have coded some extra messages and parameters. This process is simply one of pulling the ITU-T ISUP specification in line with the national variant.

Following are some example modifications:

- In relation to exceptions to Q.761 (ISUP functional description), Table 1.1 in UK ISUP [41] states that the UK has elected not to use multirate connection types (that is 128, 384, 1536 and 1920Kbps bearer rates, which are achieved by stacking up a number of 64 Kbps circuits). The six ISUP tests 7.3.1 through 7.3.6 involve testing multirate connection types and can therefore be removed.

- In relation to exceptions to Q.762 (ISUP general functions and signals), no UK-specific signaling messages have been defined; therefore, no new tests are required to check the validation and interoperability of new messages. But 11 UK-specific signaling parameters have been defined—for example, *National Forward Call Indicators* (UK-specific information sent in the forward direction relating to characteristics of the call). Therefore, up to 11 new tests should be created to ensure that these parameters are being handled correctly.

- In relation to exceptions to Q.763 (formats and codes), the UK has elected not to use the following message types: *Forward Transfer (FOT)*, *Continuity (COT)*, and *Continuity Check Request (CCR)*. FOT is tested in tests 6.4.1 through 6.4.4 [90], COT in tests 6.1.1 through 6.1.5 [90] and CCR in tests 1.4.1 through 1.4.5 [90]. These fourteen tests can therefore be removed.

A national test specification might be available; if so, it can be obtained from the national incumbent or the national standards body. But it is still recommended that one is self-produced because it familiarizes the person(s) performing the testing with the tests and the national variant. In addition, the protocol test equipment manufacturer is likely to be able to provide Q.78x conformance testing scripts—that is, the tests that are configured almost ready to run. However, it should be clear that these must also be brought into line with the national specification; this can effectively be done in parallel with the test-specification production.

When the relevant ITU-T test specification and protocol tester Q.78x scripts (if available) have been "nationalized," the next and final stage is to modify them to reflect the actual solution/product under test, thereby producing a product/solution specific C7 test specification. For example, if we were testing a method of terminating ISP traffic, then the signaling portion of that solution is only going to receive calls (terminate incoming ISP traffic); therefore, none of the tests that necessitate any forward setup messages are required. This means that many of the tests should be removed, such as all those tests that expect the *device under test (DUT)* to generate an ISUP Initial Address Message (IAM)—for example, tests 2.3.x [90].

MTP 2 Testing

The MTP 2 test specification is found in ITU Q.781 [87]. The purpose of the tests is to ensure complete validation and compatibility of an SP's MTP 2 protocol according to ITU Q.703 [51]. See Chapter 6, "Message Transfer Part 2 (MTP2)," for a description of the MTP2 protocol.

The tests are split up by functional area into ten categories.

Table 16-1 shows the test categories and the tests that they contain.

Table 16-1 *Test Categories and Numbers Found in Q.781*

Category	Test Number(s)	Total
Link state control—expected signal units/orders	1.1–1.35	35
Link state control—unexpected signal units/orders	2.1–2.8	8
Transmission failure	3.1–3.8	8
Processor outage control	4.1–4.3	3
SU delimitation, alignment, error detection, and correction	5.1–5.5	5
SUERM check	6.1–6.4	4
AERM check	7.1–7.4	4
Transmission and reception control (basic)	8.1–8.13	13
Transmission and reception control (PCR)	9.1–9.13	13
Congestion control	10.1–10.4	4

Totals   97

The remainder of this section explains fourteen of these tests, covering at least one from each category. The tests explained include: 1.1, 1.5, 1.22, 1.28, 2.7, 3.1, 3.2, 4.1, 5.1, 6.1, 7.1, 8.3, 9.3, and 10.1. These numbers refer to the test numbers that are allocated in Q.781. Many of the tests that are not used as examples are variations of the example tests given; therefore, taking at least one test out of each category gives the reader a good understanding of the test methods.

Test Configuration

A single link is used for MTP2 tests. Figure 16-1 shows a single link between SP A and SP B. SP A is the device under test DUT, while SP B is the Tester.

Figure 16-1 *Test Configuration Used for MTP2 Testing*

Example 1: Initialization (Power-up), Test 1.1

This test ensures that the DUT enters the correct state upon power up and that it is used for both validation and compatibility testing purposes. It consists of two parts: part (a) and part (b). Part (b) is the same test repeated in the reverse direction.

Part (a)

Before beginning this test, switch the DUT off and the tester on. This results in status indication out of service (SIOS) periodically being sent in only one direction, from the tester to the DUT.

The test begins when you power up the DUT. The DUT should periodically send LSSUs with the SIOS in the direction SP A to SP B. The FIB and the BIB should each be initialized to 1, and the FSN and BSN should both be set to 127. Figure 16-2 shows the expected message sequence for this test.

Figure 16-2 *Expected Message Sequence for Test 1.1 (a)*

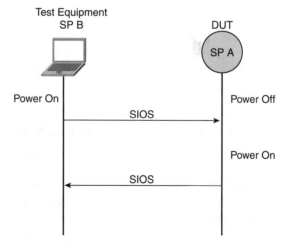

If the DUT sends an LSSU with the SIOS and the fields FIB, BIB, FSN, BSN are initialized correctly, then test 1.1(a) should be considered passed.

Part (b)

Switch the DUT on and the tester off before beginning this test. This results in SIOS periodically being sent in only one direction, from the DUT to the Tester.

The test begins when you power up the Tester. The Tester should periodically send LSSUs with the SIOS in the direction SP B to SP A. The FIB and the BIB should both be set to 1, and the FSN and BSN should both be set to 127. Figure 16-3 shows the expected message sequence for this test.

Figure 16-3 *Expected Message Sequence*

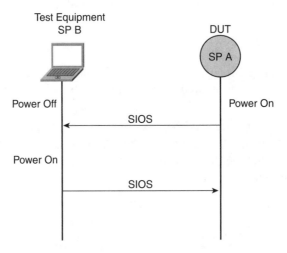

If the fields FIB, BIB, FSN, and BSN have been received correctly, then test 1.1(b) should be considered passed.

Example 2: Normal Alignment—Correct Procedure (FISU), Test 1.5

This test ensures that the DUT can perform the normal alignment procedure, and that the "in-service" state can be maintained once it has been achieved. It consists of two parts, part (a) and part (b), which is the same test except that it uses two octet LSSUs. Part (a) is used for both validation and compatibility testing purposes, while part (b) is used for validation testing purposes only.

Part (a)

The link should be put in the "out-of-service" state before commencing this test.

As shown in Figure 16-4, the test begins when you start the alignment procedure at the DUT. The normal alignment procedure should follow; DUT should cease to send SIOS and start sending SIO. Upon receiving SIO back from the Tester, it should request normal alignment by sending SIN. Upon receiving SIN back from the Tester, the "in-service" state should be entered. FISUs should flow in both directions, and the DUT should remain in the "in-service" state.

Figure 16-4 *Expected Message Sequence for Test 1.5*

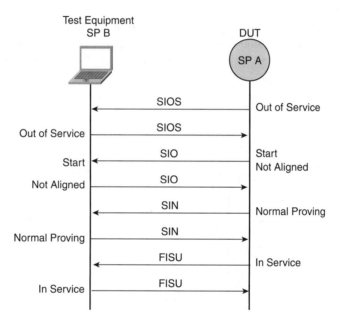

Consider the test passed if the DUT achieves link alignment, enters the "in-service" state, and remains in the "in-service" state after FISUs have been exchanged.

Part (b)

Part (b) is exactly the same as part (a), except that the Tester should send the LSSUs with a length of two octets rather than one.

Example 3: Individual End Sets Emergency, Test 1.22

This test ensures that the DUT performs emergency alignment when requested by the other side even when it perceives a normal condition, but that the other side request emergency alignment. It is used for validation testing purposes only.

You should put the link in the "out-of-service" state before commencing this test.

The test begins when you start the alignment procedure at the Tester. The Tester should request emergency alignment by sending LSSUs with emergency alignment indication (SIEs). The DUT should be set to "perceive" normal alignment conditions, and should thus cease to send SIOS, send back SIO, and then start sending LSSUs with normal alignment indication (SINs).

Even though the DUT "perceives" that normal alignment should be carried, it should carry out the alignment within the emergency proving period because it has received a request from the other side for emergency alignment. Figure 16-5 shows the expected message sequence for this test.

Figure 16-5 *Expected Message Sequence for Test 1.22*

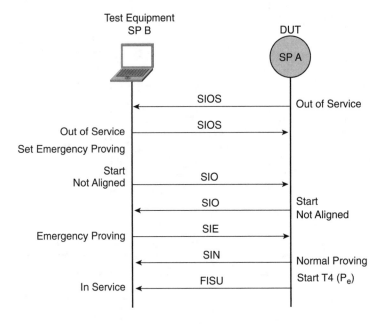

P_e is the emergency proving period, which can by measured by subtracting the time stamp of the SIN from the time stamp for the FISU. Consider the test passed if the alignment occurs within the emergency proving period.

Example 4: SIO Received During Link In-Service, Test 1.28

This test ensures that the DUT can deactivate a link from the "in-service" state. It is only used for validation testing purposes.

The link should be put in the in-service state before commencing this test.

The test begins by sending an LSSU with the SIO from the Tester to the DUT. The DUT should then place the link in the out-of-service state returning an LSSU with SIOS. It should also indicate "out-of-service" to MTP3 with reason "Received SIO." Figure 16-6 shows the expected message sequence for this test.

Figure 16-6   *Expected Message Sequence for Test 1.28*

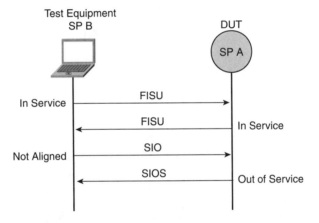

Consider the test passed if the DUT responds to the SIO reception by returning SIOS.

Example 5: Unexpected Signal Units/Orders in "In-Service" State, Test 2.7

This test ensures that the DUT ignores a corrupt LSSU receipt and unexpected requests from MTP3. The test is used for validation testing purposes only.

The link should be put in the in-service state before commencing this test; if it is already in service, it should be put out of service, and then put back to the in-service state.

The test begins by sending an LSSU with a corrupt status, or a status for which there is no meaning (such as 00000110) to the DUT. A sequence of unexpected MTP3 commands should be issued at the DUT. These commands are as follows:

- –command "Set Emergency"
- –command "Clear Emergency"
- –command "Clear Local Processor Outage" (LPO)
- –command "Start"

Figure 16-7 shows the expected message sequence for this test.

Figure 16-7 *Expected Message Sequence for Test 2.7*

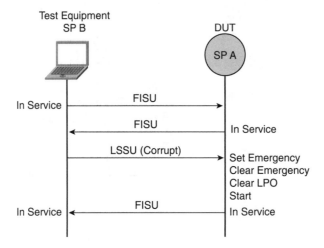

Consider the test passed if the DUT ignores the corrupt LSSU status indication, and the unexpected MTP3 commands.

Example 6: Link Aligned Ready (Break Tx Path), Test 3.1

This test ensures that the DUT responds correctly to a transmission failure that SUERM detects by placing the link out of service when in the Aligned Ready state. The test is used for validation testing purposes only.

Put the link in the out-of-service state before commencing this test.

The test begins when you initiate normal alignment at the DUT. The Tx path should be broken after alignment is achieved.

Figure 16-8 shows the expected message sequence for this test.

Figure 16-8 *Expected Message Sequence for Test 3.1*

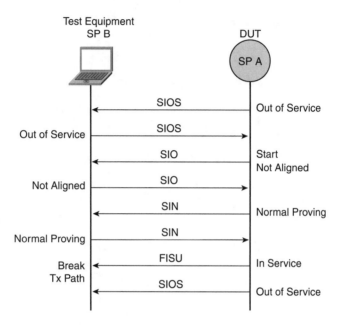

Consider the test passed if the DUT places the link out of service by sending SIOS, sends "out-of-service" to the local MTP3 with reason "Excessive error rate SUERM," and remains in the "out-of-service" state.

Example 7: Link Aligned Ready (Corrupt FIBs—Basic), Test 3.2

This test ensures that the DUT puts the link out of service after receiving two consecutive corrupt FIBs, while in the Aligned Ready state. It is used for validation testing purposes only.

Put the link in the Aligned Ready state before commencing this test.

The test begins by sending an FISU with an inverted FIB from the Tester to the DUT. Another consecutive FISU should be sent with the FIB still inverted. According to the MTP2 specification, if any two out of three FIBs that were received consecutively (MSUs or FISUs only) indicate the start of a retransmission when no negative acknowledgment has been sent, then MTP3 should informed that the link is faulty with reason "Abnormal FIB Received." For more information, see Q.703 Clause 5.3.2.

Figure 16-9 shows the expected message sequence for this test.

Figure 16-9 *Expected Message Sequence for Test 3.2*

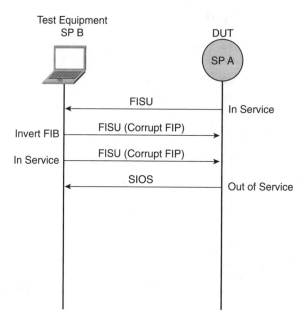

Consider the test passed if the DUT places the link out of service by sending SIOS, sends "out of service" to the local MTP3 with reason "Abnormal FIB Received," and remains in the "out-of-service" state.

Example 8: Set and Clear LPO While Link In-Service, Test 4.1

This test ensures that the DUT performs correctly when a *local processor outage (LPO)* is set and then recovered from while the link is in service. It is used for validation testing purposes only.

The link should be put in the "in-service" state before commencing this test.

The test begins by sending two normal MSUs from the DUT to the Tester. An LPO condition should then be set at the DUT. While in an LPO state, the DUT should discard all received SUs. To verify that the DUT buffer is clearing properly, the Tester should send at least one MSU and one FISU to the DUT. Then the LPO state should be cleared at the DUT. The DUT should resume sending FSUs as normal and should be given at least one MSU to send after LPO clears. Clause 12 Q.703 [51] describes the LPO condition.

Figure 16-10 shows the expected message sequence for this test.

Figure 16-10 *Expected Message Sequence for Test 4.1*

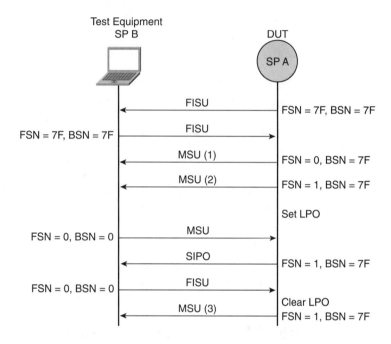

Consider the test passed if the DUT sends SIPO, discards the received MSU and sends no further status messages after clear LPU is issued.

Example 9: SU Delimitation, Alignment, Error Detection, and Correction, Test 5.1

This test ensures that the DUT detects seven or more consecutive "1's" as an error, realizes that SU alignment has been lost, regains SU alignment, and subsequently behaves as though unaffected. It is used for validation testing purposes only.

The link should be put in the "in-service" state before commencing this test.

The test begins by sending the DUT a corrupt MSU that contains seven or more consecutive "1's." The DUT should then go into "octet counting" by discarding all SUs until a correct SU is received, thereby ending the "octet counting" mode and remaining in the "In-Service" state. Q.703 clause 4.1.4 describes the "octet counting" mode.

Figure 16-11 shows the expected message sequence for this test.

Figure 16-11 *Expected Message Sequence for Test 5.1*

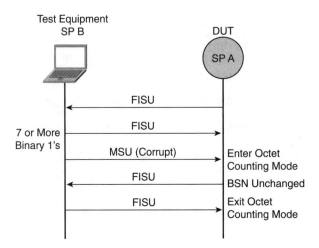

Consider the test passed if the BSN in the FISU that was sent immediately after the corrupt MSU was received remains unchanged (meaning that the corrupt MSU was discarded).

Example 10: Error Rate of 1 in 256—Link Remains In-Service, Test 6.1

This test ensures that the DUT has implemented the threshold to correctly increment the SUERM counter. It is used for validation testing purposes only.

The link should be put in the "in-service" state before commencing this test.

The test is performed by sending the DUT one corrupt FISU in every 256 FISUs, and sending enough blocks of 256 SUs to cause the SUERM to close the link if it has been increased. As long as no more than one corrupt SU is detected in 256 SUs, the link should remain in-service because the SUERM counter should not be increased.

Recall from Chapter 6 that the SUERM is an up/down counter that is weighted such that for every 256 SUs received correctly, it decreases by one; for each corrupt SU, it increases by one; and if it reaches the threshold value 64 (this value is for 64 Kbps links only), it should inform MTP3, which commands it to put the link out of service by sending SIOS. Q.703 clause 10.2 [51] describes the SUERM.

Figure 16-12 shows this test's expected message sequence.

Figure 16-12 *Expected Message Sequence for Test 6.1*

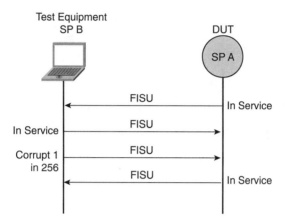

Consider the test passed if the link remains in the "in-service" state.

Example 11, Test 7.1

This test ensures that the DUT has implemented the AERM threshold correctly. It is used for validation testing purposes only.

The link should be put in the "out-of-service" state before commencing this test.

The test is performed by sending the DUT up to three corrupt (bad CRC) LSSUs during the proving period. Three corrupt LSSUs should be sent.

Recall from Chapter 6 that the AERM is a counter that is used during the proving of a link. It is zeroed at the start of proving, incremented for each corrupt LSSU received, and proving should be abandoned if it reaches the value 4 (for normal proving, or 1 for emergency proving). Q.703 clause 10.3 [51] describes the AERM.

Figure 16-13 shows the expected message sequence for this test.

Figure 16-13 *Expected Message Sequence for Test 7.1*

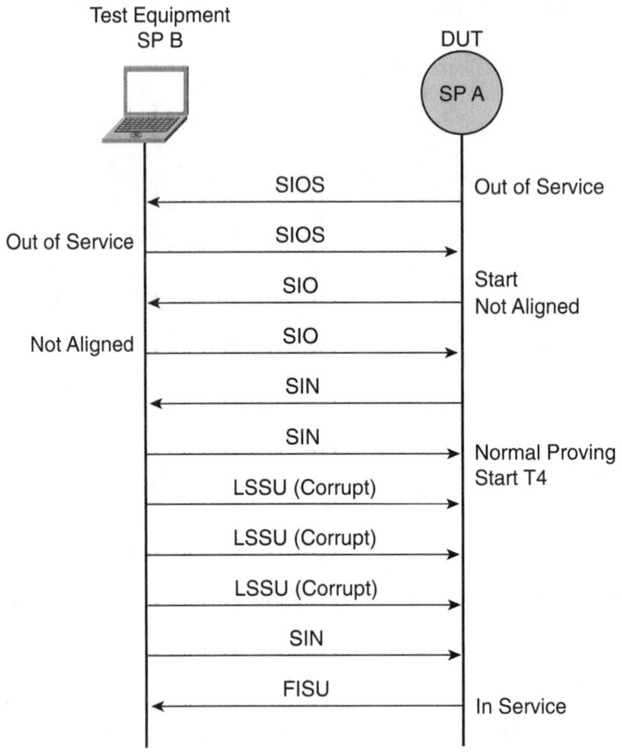

Consider the test passed if the proving period continues and the link aligns successfully.

Example 12: Check RTB Full, Test 8.3

This test ensures that the DUT buffers MSUs when no acknowledgments are received. It is used for validation testing purposes only.

The link should be put in the "in-service" state before commencing this test.

The test is performed by sending the 100 DUT MSUs per second and, in order to fill the retransmission buffer (RTB), not providing any acknowledgments until T7 is on the threshold of timing out. The number of MSUs to send is not specified, but 128 is enough. The acknowledgment that is sent on the verge of T7's expiration should negatively acknowledge all messages received, thereby requesting the DUT to send all messages in its RTB.

Timer T7 "excessive delay of acknowledgment" is used to detect when an unreasonably long period has elapsed while waiting for a positive or negative acknowledgment after sending an MSU. When T7 expires, link failure is assumed and it is reported to MTP3. This is the reason that MSUs should be generated at a rate of at least 100 per second to fill the RTB before T7 expires. Q.703 clause 5.3 [51] describes retransmission, including T7.

Figure 16-14 shows the expected message sequence for this test.

Figure 16-14 *Expected Message Sequence for Test 8.3*

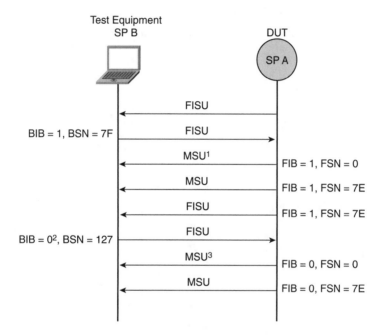

^{1} Fill the RTB
^{2} Negatively acknowledge all 127 messages in the RTB
^{3} Retransmit all messages in the RTB

Consider the test passed if the DUT retransmits the RTB's complete contents.

Example 13: Forced Retransmission with the Value N_1, Test 9.3

This test ensures that N_1 detects the "RTB full" and that forced retransmission occurs as a result. It is used for validation testing purposes only.

Before beginning this test, the link should be put in the "in-service" state and set to use the preventive cyclic retransmission (PCR) method of error correction at both sides of the link.

The test is performed by sending the DUT 128 MSUs at the rate of 100 per second. To fill the RTB, the Tester should not provide a positive acknowledgment until timer T7 is on the threshold of timing out. The acknowledgment that is sent on the verge of expiration of T7 should be a positive acknowledgment of message 0, thereby requesting that the DUT send all messages in its RTB. See Example 12 for more information about T7. Q.703 clause 6.4 [51] describes forced transmission.

Recall from Chapter 6 that PCR does not use negative acknowledgments. Note that N_1 is the maximum number of MSUs that are available for retransmission—usually 127. Q.703 clause 10.3 [51] describes N_1.

Figure 16-15 shows the expected message sequence for this test.

Figure 16-15 *Expected Message Sequence for Test 9.3*

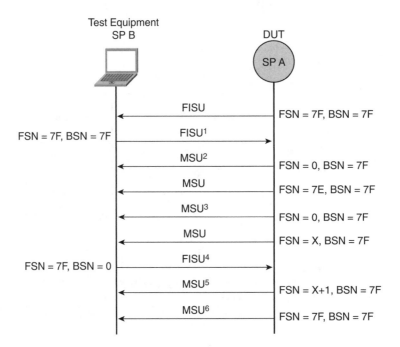

[1] Clears the RTB
[2] 127 new MSUs sent
[3] Forced retransmission as RTB is full
[4] Prevent T7 expiring
[5] Continue forced retransmission until RTB is empty
[6] New MSU—signifies that forced retransmission was ended

Consider the test passed if the DUT performs forced retransmission of all MSUs in the RTB and then ends forced retransmission after the last MSU in RTB has been sent.

Example 14: Congestion Abatement, Test 10.1

This test ensures that the congestion abatement procedure has been implemented properly. It is used for validation testing purposes only.

The link should be put in the "in-service" state before commencing this test.

The test is performed by setting a MTP2 congested state at the DUT. The DUT should then send SIBs at intervals of Timer T5 "sending SIB" until congestion abates. Next, the congestion should be cleared, resulting in the DUT ceasing to send SIB and sending FISUs instead.

Q.703 clause 9.3 [51] describes the sending of SIB. It is interesting to note that the mechanism for detecting congestion is implementation-dependent and is not specified.

Figure 16-16 shows the expected message sequence for this test.

Figure 16-16 *Expected Message Sequence for Test 10.1*

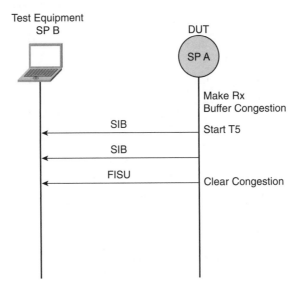

Consider the test passed if the DUT sends SIBs when there is congestion at intervals of T5, and returns to a normal state when congestion is cleared.

MTP 3 Testing

The MTP 3 test specification is found in ITU Q.782 [88]. The purpose of the tests is to ensure complete validation and compatibility of an SP's MTP 3 protocol according to ITU Q.704 [53]. See Chapter 7, "Message Transfer Part 3 (MTP3)," for a description of the MTP 3 protocol.

The tests are split up by functional area into thirteen categories. Table 16-2 shows the test categories and the tests that they contain.

Table 16-2   *Test Categories and Test Numbers found in Q.782*

Category	Test Number(s)	Total
Signaling link management	1.1–1.3	3
Signaling message handling	2.1–2.3, 2.4.1–2.4.2, 2.5.1–2.5.4, 2.6.1–2.6.3, 2.7	13
Changeover	3.1–3.21	21
Changeback	4.1–4.11	11
Forced rerouting	5	1
Controlled rerouting	6	1
Management inhibiting	7.1.1–7.1.2, 7.2.1–7.2.4, 7.3.1–7.3.2, 7.4, 7.5, 7.6.1–7.6.2, 7.7–7.9, 7.10.1–7.10.2, 7.11–7.16, 7.17.1–7.17.4	28
Signaling traffic flow control	8.1–8.4	4
Signaling route management	9.1.1–9.1.2, 9.2.1–9.2.2, 9.3, 9.4.1–9.4.2, 9.5.1–9.5.2, 9.6, 9.7	11
Signaling point restart	10.1.1–10.1.1, 10.2.1–10.2.1, 10.3–10.6, 10.7.1–10.7.2	11
Traffic test	11	1
Signaling link test	12.1–12.6	6
Invalid messages	13.1–13.12	12

Totals   *123*

The remainder of this section explains three of these tests: 1.1, 2.41, and 2.61. These numbers refer to the test numbers allocated in Q.782.

Test Configuration

Four test configurations (named A, B, C, and D) are used for MTP3 testing. Only configuration A is used for the three tests presented in this section. Figure 16-17 shows configuration A.

Figure 16-17 *Configuration A*

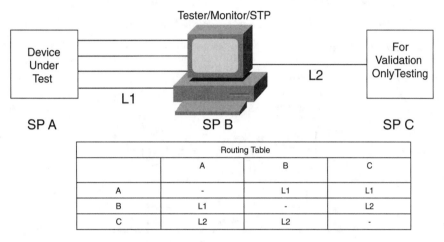

Key:
L1 = Link Set 1
L2 = Link Set 2

Links are identified as follows: "number of linkset"—"number of link in the linkset" (1–1 means link 1 of the linkset 1). This identification is independent of SLC that is attributed to these links. When the number of the link is X, the concerned message can use any link in the linkset.

Example 1: First Signaling Link Activation, Test 1.1

This test checks that a link can be activated properly. It is used for both validation and compatibility testing purposes.

The link should be deactivated before commencing this test.

Signaling link activation is the process of making a link ready to carry signaling traffic. If the initial alignment procedure (MTP2) is successful, a signaling link test that utilizing MTP3 SLTM and SLTA messages is started. If this test is successful, the link becomes ready to convey traffic.

Chapter 7 describes the sending of SLTM/SLTA. Additional details can be found in ITU Q.707 [56].

The test is performed by activating the link. MTP2 should bring the link into service via the alignment procedure. Next, MTP3 should use the SLTM/SLTA mechanism to make sure that the MTP3 peers can communicate. The DUT should reply to the SLTM with a SLTA.

The test pattern received in the SLTA should match the one that is sent in the SLTM. Next, some variable length MSUs should be sent to and from the DUT.

The test should be repeated with different SLC values.

Figure 16-18 shows the expected message sequence for this test.

Figure 16-18 *Expected Message Sequence for Test 1.1*

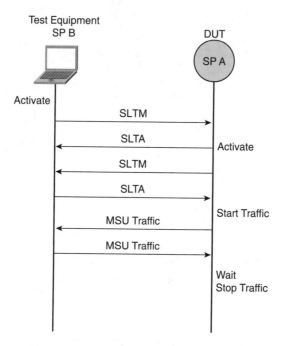

Consider the test passed if all messages are correctly received (no loss of messages, no duplication, and no mis-sequencing).

Example 2: Load Sharing within a Linkset (All Links Available), Test 2.4.1

This test checks that DUT performs load sharing when all links are available.

The linkset should be activated before commencing this test.

The test is performed by sending traffic from the DUT to SP B (and SP C for validation testing) on all SLS.

When two or more links are used between two points, the load-sharing function should distribute traffic among them.

Figure 16-19 shows the expected message sequence for this test.

Figure 16-19 *Expected Message Sequence for Test 2.4.1*

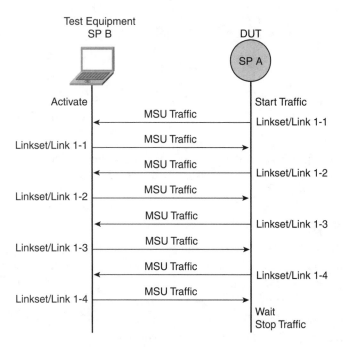

Consider the test passed if all messages are correctly received (no loss of messages, no duplication, and no mis-sequencing) and the messages were transmitted on the correct link, according to the SLS field.

Example 3: Inaccessible Destination—Due to a Linkset Failure, Test 2.6.1

This test verifies that the DUT performs message handling correctly when a linkset failure makes a destination inaccessible.

A linkset should be activated with only a single link available before commencing this test.

The test is performed by sending traffic from the DUT to SP B (and SP C for validation testing) on all SLS. Linkset L1 should then be deactivated.

Figure 16-20 shows the expected message sequence for this test.

Figure 16-20 *Expected Message Sequence for Test 2.6.1*

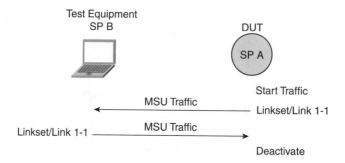

Consider the test passed if SP B and C become unavailable and messages stored or received after the unavailability of the linkset are discarded.

ISUP Testing

The ISUP test specification is found in ITU Q.784.1 [90]. The purpose of the tests is to ensure complete validation and compatibility of an SP's ISUP protocol for basic call control according to ITU Q.704 [75–78, 80–81]. See Chapter 8, "ISDN User Part (ISUP)," for a description of the ISUP protocol.

The tests are split into six major categories according to functional area. Table 16-3 shows the test categories and the tests that they contain.

Table 16-3 *Test Categories and Test Numbers in Q.784.1*

Category	Test Number(s)	Total
Circuit supervision and signaling supervision		
Circuit supervision	1.1	1
Reset of circuits	1.2.1–1.2.7	7
Circuit group blocking/unblocking	1.3.1.1–1.3.1.2, 1.3.2.1–1.3.2.5	7
Continuity check procedure	1.4.1–1.4.6	6
Receipt of unreasonable signaling information messages	1.5.1–1.5.3	3
Receipt of unknown signaling information	1.6.1, 1.6.1.1–1.6.1.2, 1.6.2.1–1.6.2.2, 1.6.3.1–1.6.3.2	6
Receipt of unknown signaling information (compatibility procedure)	1.7.1.1–1.7.1.7, 1.7.2.1–1.7.2.10, 1.7.3.1–1.7.3.2	19

Table 16-3   *Test Categories and Test Numbers in Q.784.1 (Continued)*

Category	Test Number(s)	Total
Normal call setup—ordinary speech calls		
Both-way circuit selection	2.1.1–2.1.2	2
Called address sending	2.2.1–2.2.2	2
Successful call setup	2.3.1–2.3.6	6
Propagation delay determination procedure	2.4.1–2.4.5	5
Normal call release	3.1–3.8	8
Unsuccessful call setup	4.1	1
Abnormal situations during a call	5.1	1
Timers	5.2.1–5.2.11	11
Reset of circuits during a call	5.3.1–5.3.2	2
Special call setup		
Continuity check call	6.1–6.1.5	5
Automatic repeat attempt	6.2.1–6.2.5	5
Dual seizure	6.3.1	1
Semi-automatic operation	6.4.1–6.4.4	4
Simple segmentation	6.5.1–6.5.5	5
Signaling procedures for connection type with Fallback capability	6.6.1–6.6.4	4
Bearer services		
64 kbit(s) unrestricted	7.1.1–7.1.3	3
3.1 kHz audio	7.2.1	1
Multirate connection types	7.3.1–7.3.6	6
Congestion control and user flow control		
Automatic congestion control	8.1.1, 8.1.2	2
ISDN user part availability control	8.2.1–8.2.3	3
Echo control procedure		
Echo control procedure according to Q.767	9.1.1–9.1.2, 9.2	2

Totals   128

The remainder of this section explains three of these tests: 1.4.1, 2.2.2, and 5.2.3. These numbers refer to the test numbers allocated in Q.784.1.

Test Configuration

Only a single test configuration is used. The test configuration consists of SP A and SP B. SP A is the device under test (DUT), while SP B is the Tester or an SP whose ISUP protocol has been verified. Links and bearers are provided between the two SPs.

Example 1: CCR Received—Successful, Test 1.4.1

This test verifies that the DUT performs the continuity check procedure correctly. It is used for both validation and compatibility testing purposes.

The circuit should be in the idle condition before commencing the test.

The test is performed by sending a *continuity check request (CCR)* message from the Tester to the DUT. Associated timers are not verified as part of this test.

Unlike *channel associated signaling (CAS)*, SS7/C7 does not pass over a bearer—therefore, no inherent circuit testing is present. It is for this reason that a continuity test can be performed to check a circuit before placing a call over it. For more details on the continuity-check procedures, see Q.764 [78] Clause 2.1.8 and Chapter 8.

Figure 16-21 below shows the expected message sequence for this test.

Figure 16-21 *Expected Message Sequence for Test 1.4.1*

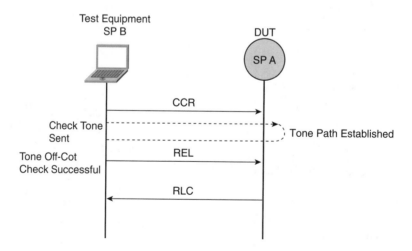

Consider the test passed if the DUT successfully performs a continuity test (routes the tone back to SP B) and the circuit is still in the idle state at the end of the test.

Example 2: Overlap Operation (with SAM), Test 2.2.2

This test verifies that the DUT can set up a call using overlap address signaling. It is used for both validation and compatibility testing purposes.

The circuit should be in the idle condition, and both SPs should be configured for overlap operation before commencing the test. The IAM should not contain enough digits to complete the call, thereby ensuring that at least one Subsequent Address Message (SAM) is sent.

The test is performed by initiating an overlap call setup (IAM plus one or more SAMs) from the DUT; following communications establishment, the circuit should then be released.

Overlap signaling entails sending the called party number in installments. See Q.764 [78] Clause 2.1.2 and Chapter 8 for additional details.

Figure 16-22 *Message Sequence for Test 2.2.2*

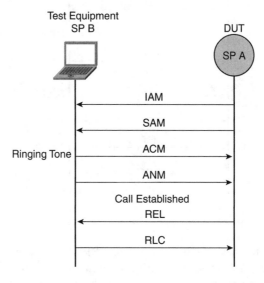

Consider the test passed if the DUT successfully establishes and releases the call.

Example 3: Timers T1 and T5—Failure to Receive a RLC, Test 5.2.3

This test checks that the DUT performs appropriate actions at the expiration of timers T1 and T5. It is used for validation testing purposes only.

The circuit should be in the idle condition before commencing the test.

The test is performed by setting up a call and then only partially clearing it down. When the DUT indicates that it has released the call, the Tester should be programmed not to respond with a *release complete message (RLC)* message. The value of timers T1 and T5 should be measured.

See Q.764 [78] Clause 2.9.6 for more on the use of T1 and T5 on failure to receive RLC.

Figure 16-23 shows the message sequence for this test.

Figure 16-23   *Expected Message Sequence for Test 5.2.3*

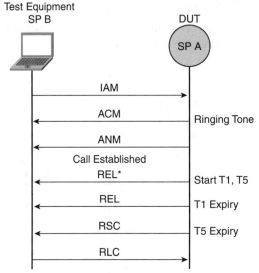

*REL is retransmitted during T5 interval and T1 is restarted

Consider the test passed if the DUT sends a REL message upon T1's expiration, sends a *reset circuit (RSC)* message upon T5's expiration, alerts the "maintenance system" (on many "soft" implementations this could just be the sending of an alarm to a log file), and removes the circuit from service.

ISUP Supplementary Services Testing

The ISUP supplementary test specification is found in ITU Q.785 [91]. The purpose of the tests is to ensure validation and compatibility of an SP's *user-to-user signaling (UUS)*, *closed user group (CUG)*, *calling line identification (CLI)*, and *connected line identification (COL)* supplementary services according to ITU Q.730 [69]—to a reasonable, but not exhaustive degree. Tests for the other supplementary services have not been specified.

The tests are split into four categories according to supplementary service. Table 16-4 shows the test categories and the tests therein.

Table 16-4   *Test Categories and Test Numbers in Q.785*

Category	Test Number(s)	Total
User-to-User Signaling (UUS)—implicit request	1.1.1.1.1–1.1.1.1.2, 1.1.1.2.1–1.1.1.2.2, 1.1.1.3.1–1.1.1.3.2	6
Closed User Group (CUG)—decentralized	2.1.1–2.1.8	9
Calling Line Identification (CLI)	3.1.1–3.1.2, 3.2.1–3.2.2, 3.3.1–3.3.2, 3.4.1–3.4.2, 3.5.1–3.5.2, 3.6.1–3.6.4, 3.7.1–3.7.2	16
Connected Line Identification (COL)	6.1.1–6.1.2, 6.2.1–6.2.2, 6.3.1–6.3.2, 6.4.1–6.4.2, 6.5.1–6.5.2, 6.6.1 – 6.6.2, 6.7.1–6.7.2, 6.8.1	15

Totals   46

The remainder of this section provides an explanation of three of these tests: 2.1.1, 3.1.1, and 6.1.1. These numbers refer to the test numbers allocated in Q.785.

Test Configuration

Only a single test configuration is used: the same one that is used in ISUP basic call control testing. The test configuration consists of SP A and SP B. SP A is the device under test DUT, while SP B is the Tester or an SP whose ISUP protocol has been verified. Links and bearers are provided between the two SPs. The test specification makes use of stimulus in relation to creating certain conditions.

Example 1: CUG Call with Outgoing Access Allowed and Sent, Test 2.1.1

This test is to check that the DUT can correctly send the parameters that are necessary for a CUG call with outgoing access allowed. It is used for both validation and compatibility testing purposes.

The DUT should generate an IAM that contains the optional *CUG interlock code* parameter set to "interlock code included" and the *forward call indicators* parameter with the *CUG call indicator* set to "CUG call, outgoing access allowed." It is up to the person(s) carrying out the testing how "invoke" should be used. A call should be established even if SP B is not connected to a network that supports the CUG service.

Figure 16-24 shows the expected message sequence for this test.

Figure 16-24 *Expected Message Sequence for Test 2.1.1*

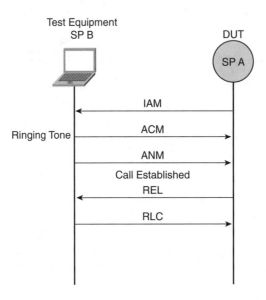

Consider the test passed if the IAM contains the *CUG interlock code* parameter and *forward call indicators* with the contents specified previously, and if the call is successfully set up and cleared.

Example 2: CLIP—Network Provided and Sent, Test 3.1.1

This test is to verify that the DUT can correctly send an IAM with *calling line identification presentation (CLIP)* set in the *calling party number* parameter. It is used for both validation and compatibility testing purposes.

The DUT should generate an IAM that contains the optional *calling party number* parameter, with the fields *presentation restriction indicator* set to 00 (presentation allowed) and screening indicator set to 11 (network provided).

Consider the test passed if the received IAM contains the *calling party number* parameter with the contents specified previously, and the call is successfully set up and cleared.

Example 2: COL—Requested and Sent, Test 6.1.1

This test is to check that the DUT can correctly send an IAM with a request for COL. It is used for both validation and compatibility testing purposes.

The DUT should generate an IAM containing the optional *forward call indicators* parameter with the field *connected line identification indicator* set to 1 (requested). It is up to the person(s) carrying out the testing to decide how to provoke such an IAM.

Consider the test passed if the IAM contains the *forward call indicators* parameter with the contents specified above, and the call is successfully setup and cleared.

SCCP Testing

The SCCP test specification is found in ITU Q.786 [92]. The purpose of the tests is to ensure validation and compatibility of an SP's SCCP connectionless protocol according to ITU Q.711–716 [58–63], with a degree of confidence. There are no tests covering management, segmentation, or connection-oriented procedures—these are listed in the specification for further study. This test specification can be considered inadequate for many purposes, leading some European operators to write their own in-house test specifications completely from scratch.

The tests are split up into three categories. Table 16-5 shows the test categories and the tests that they contain.

Table 16-5   *Test Categories and Test Numbers in Q.786*

Category	Test Number(s)	Total
Messages from SCCP users		
Route not on GT	1.1.1.1.1.1–1.1.1.1.1.2, 1.1.1.1.2–1.1.1.1.6	7
Route on GT	1.1.1.2.1.1–1.1.1.2.1.2, 1.1.1.2.2–1.1.1.2.3, 1.1.1.2.4.1–1.1.1.2.4.2, 1.1.1.2.5–1.1.1.2.9	11
Messages from MTP		
Route on GT	1.1.2.1.1–1.1.2.1.9	9
Route not on GT	1.1.2.2.1.1–1.1.2.2.1.2, 1.1.2.2.2–1.1.2.2.3	4
Data transfer		
Data transfer with sequential delivery capability	1.2.1.1–1.2.1.2	2
Data transfer with syntax error	1.2.2	1

continues

Table 16-5   *Test Categories and Test Numbers in Q.786 (Continued)*

Category	Test Number(s)	Total
Message return	1.2.3	1
UDTS deliverable	1.2.3.1.1–1.2.3.1.2	2
UDTS undeliverable	1.2.3.2.1	1

Totals   38

The remainder of this section explains three of these tests: 1.1.1.1.1 , 1.1.1.1.6, and 1.1.2.2.1.2. These numbers refer to the test numbers allocated in Q.786.

Test Configuration

Two test configurations(named 1 and 2) are used for SCCP testing. For the three tests presented in this section, only configuration 1 is used. Figure 16-25 shows configuration 1.

Figure 16-25   *The Test Configuration 1, Used for SCCP Testing*

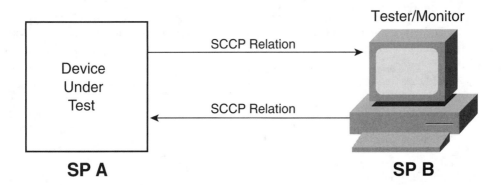

Example 1: Local DPC and SSN Included, DPC and SSN Available, GT and SSN Included and Sent, Test 1.1.1.1.1.1

This test is to check that the DUT SCCP can deliver user data to the correct SCCP user at the DUT when routing is not on Global Title (GT). It is used for validation testing purposes only.

An SSN should be made available at the DUT.

The DUT should request delivery of user data to a DUT SCCP user with a DPC and SSN of the DUT in the request.

Figure 16-26 shows the primitive sequence for this test.

Figure 16-26 *Expected Message Sequence for Test 1.1.1.1.1.1*

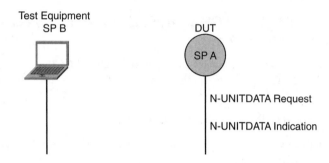

Consider the test passed if the DUT does not send a message to SPB B and the data is correctly delivered to the SCCP user at the DUT.

Example 2: Remote DPC and SSN Included, DPC and/or SSN Unavailable—Return Option Not Set, Test 1.1.1.1.6

This test checks that the DUT does not return user data sent from the DUT SCCP user when the return option is not set (and the route is not on GT). It is used for validation testing purposes only.

The SCCP routing control data should be set such that the DPC of SP B is unavailable and/or SSN at SP B is unavailable.

The DUT SCCP user should request delivery of user data to the remote DPC and the SSN at SP B.

Figure 16-27 shows the primitive sequence for this test.

Figure 16-27 *Expected Message Sequence for Test 1.1.1.1.6*

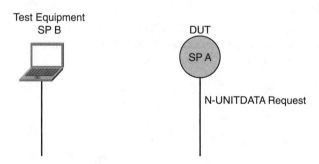

Consider the test passed if the DUT does not send a message to SPB B, and if the data is not returned to the SCCP user at the DUT.

Example 3: Local DPC and SSN, and SSN Available GT Not Included, SSN Included, Test 1.1.2.2.1.2

This test is to check that the user data sent to the DUT SCCP user can be delivered to the correct DUT SCCP user when routing is not on GT. It is used for validation testing purposes only.

An SSN should be made available at the DUT.

The Tester should generate a *Unitdata (UDT)* message toward the DUT that is addressed with the SSN, no GT, and route on DPC+SSN.

Figure 16-28 shows the primitive sequence for this test.

Figure 16-28 *Expected Message Sequence for Test 1.1.2.2.1.2*

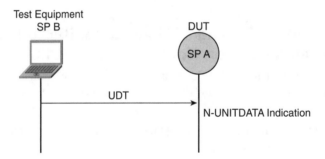

Consider the test passed if the DUT does not send an error message to SPB B and the data is delivered to the correct SCCP user at the DUT.

TCAP Testing

The TCAP specification is found in ITU Q.787 [93]. The purpose of the tests is to ensure validation and compatibility of an SP's TCAP protocol according to ITU Q.771–775 [82–86], to a reasonable but not exhaustive degree.

The tests are split into the TC *Transaction sublayer (TSL)* test specification and the TC *Component sublayer (CSL)* test specification. These test categories along with the tests that they contain are shown below in Tables 16-6 and 16-7.

Table 16-6   *Transaction Sublayer Test Categories and Test Numbers Found in Q.787*

Category	Test Number(s)	Total
Valid function		
Unstructured dialogue	1.1.1.1–1.1.1.2	2
Structured dialogue	1.1.2.1.1.1–1.1.2.1.2, 1.1.2.1.2.1–1.1.2.1.2.2, 1.1.2.2.1.1.1–1.1.2.2.1.1.3, 1.1.2.2.1.2.1–1.1.2.2.1.2.3, 1.1.2.2.2.1.1–1.1.2.2.2.1.3, 1.1.2.2.2.2.1–1.1.2.2.2.2.3, 1.1.2.3–1.1.2.5	25
Encoding and value variations	1.1.3.1.1.1.1–1.1.3.1.1.1.2, 1.1.3.1.1.2.1, 1.1.3.1.1.3, 1.1.3.2.1.1–1.1.3.2.1.2	6
Syntactically invalid behavior		
Invalid values for information elements	1.2.1.1.1–1.2.1.1.2, 1.2.1.2.1, 1.2.1.3.1, 1.2.1.4.1, 1.2.1.5.1–1.2.1.5.2	7
Invalid structure	1.2.2.1.1, 1.2.2.2.1–1.2.2.2.2, 1.2.2.3.1–1.2.2.3.5, 1.2.2.4.1–1.2.2.4.2, 1.2.2.5.1, 1.2.2.6.1, 1.2.2.7.1–1.2.2.7.3, 1.2.3.1.1, 1.2.3.2.1	17
Inopportune messages	1.3.1.1, 1.3.2.1, 1.3.3.1	3
Multiple transaction encoding	1.4.1.1–1.4.1.2, 1.4.2.1–1.4.2.2	4

Totals 64

Table 16-7   *Component Sublayer Tests*

Category	Test Number(s)	Total
Valid function		
Invoke component, unlinked operations	2.1.1.1.1–2.1.1.1.5, 2.1.1.2.1–2.1.1.2.2, 2.1.1.3.1–2.1.1.3.2, 2.1.1.4.1	10
Invoke component, linked operations	2.1.2.1.1–2.1.2.1.4, 2.1.2.2.1–2.1.2.2.2,	6
Remote reject	2.1.3.1.1–2.1.3.1.4, 2.1.3.2.1 –2.1.3.2.3, 2.1.3.3.1–2.1.3.3.4	11
Reception of component leading to TC-User reject	2.1.4.1.1–2.1.4.1.4, 2.1.4.2.1, 2.1.4.3.1–2.1.4.3.3,	8
Segmentation for return result	2.1.5.1.1–2.1.5.1.2, 2.1.5.2.1	3

continues

Table 16-7 *Component Sublayer Tests (Continued)*

Category	Test Number(s)	Total
User cancel	2.1.6	1
Encoding variations	2.1.7.1–2.1.7.3, 2.1.7.4.1.1–2.1.7.4.1.2, 2.1.7.4.2	6
Multiple components grouping	2.1.8.1–2.1.8.3	3
Dialogue portion	2.1.9.1.1–2.1.9.1.3, 2.1.9.2.1–2.1.9.2.2, 2.1.9.3, 2.1.9.4, 2.1.9.5.1–2.1.9.5.4, 2.1.9.6, 2.1.9.7.1–2.1.9.7.4	16
Syntactically invalid behaviour		
Invalid values for information elements	2.2.1.1–2.2.1.2	2
Invalid structure	2.2.2.1.1, 2.2.2.1.2, 2.2.2.2.1–2.2.2.2.3, 2.2.2.3.1, 2.2.2.3.2, 2.2.2.4.1, 2.2.2.4.2, 2.2.2.5.1–2.2.2.5.8	17
Invalid encoding for invoke component	2.2.3.1–2.2.3.3	3
Inopportune behaviour		
Inopportune invoke component	2.3.1.1	1
Unrecognized invoke ID	2.3.2.1–2.3.2.4	4
Unexpected components	2.3.3.1–2.3.3.6	6
Dialogue portion, unexpected APDUs	2.3.4.1–2.3.4.8	8

Totals 105

The remainder of this section explains three of these tests: 1.1.2.1.1 (1), 1.2.3.3 (1), and 2.3.2.4 (1). These numbers refer to the test numbers allocated in Q.787.

Test Configuration

A single test configuration is used for TCAP testing. This configuration is the same one configuration 1 used in SCCP testing.

Example 1: Clearing Before Subsequent Message; Valid Clearing from Initiating Side; Prearranged Ending, Test 1.1.2.1.1 (1)

This test verifies that the DUT is able to correctly send a *begin* message and then terminate the transaction locally using the "prearranged end" method. It is used for both validation and compatibility testing purposes.

The DUT should send a *begin* message to the Tester; however, so that the Tester does not have a chance to reply, *TR-END request* primitive (prearranged) destined for the TSL at the DUT should follow immediately.

Figure 16-29 shows the expected primitive and message sequence for this test.

Figure 16-29 *Expected Message Sequence for Test 1.1.2.1.1 (1)*

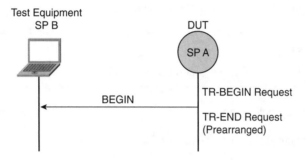

The transaction ID should be released at SP A. Consider the test passed if the DUT sends the *begin* message, but does not send an *end* message.

Example 2: First Continue Message; OTID Absent, Test 1.2.2.3 (1)

This test is to check that the DUT discards a corrupt *continue* message. It is used for validation testing purposes only.

Both SP A (DUT TSL) and SP B (Tester TSL) should be in the idle state before testing commences.

The DUT should send a *begin* message to the Tester, and the Tester should respond with a corrupt *continue* message. The *continue* should have a syntax error and an OTID that is not deliverable. Figure 16-30 shows the expected primitive and message sequence for this test.

Figure 16-30 *Expected Message Sequence for Test 1.2.2.3 (1)*

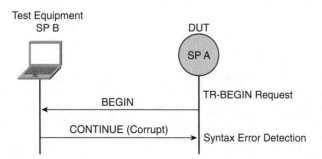

Consider the test passed if the DUT sends the *begin* message, does not inform the TR-User of the *continue*, and does not respond to the *continue*.

Example 3: Inopportune Reject Component, Test 2.3.2.4 (1)

This test is to check that the DUT does not affect any active invocation(s) if it receives a Reject component with an Invoke ID that does not correspond to any active invocation. It is used for validation testing purposes only.

Both SP A (DUT TSL) and SP B (Tester TSL) should be in the idle state before testing commences.

The DUT should initiate an operation invocation (send an Invoke component Class 1 or 2) to the Tester, which should respond with a Reject component that has an invalid Invoke ID.

Figure 16-31 below shows the expected primitive and message sequence for this test.

Figure 16-31 *Expected Message Sequence for Test 2.3.2.4 (1)*

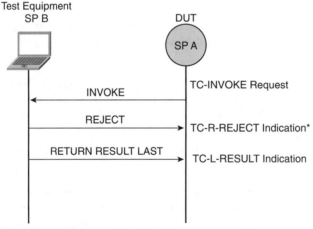

*Usage-implementation dependent

Summary

New SS7 implementations must be tested for both validation and compatibility. Validation is performed before the implementation is connected to a live network and is used to check that the implementation functions correctly; that is, it conforms to the appropriate protocol standards. Compatibility testing is executed after the implementation has passed the validation phase of testing. Compatibility seeks to check interoperability and requires the implementation to be connected to the live network. The ITU-T has specified test documents, which cover both validation and compatibility testing for the core SS7 protocols. These documents should be tailored to suit the implementation under test — specifically, the implemented protocol variants and the nature of the solution itself. This is achieved by aligning the ITU-T test specifications to the national (or regional) variant specifications and the nature of the implementation itself. For example, particular country (or regional) variants might not use particular messages so that any tests relating to these messages can be removed; in addition, where a variant adds messages or parameters, tests should be added to check these areas. Where a particular solution under test does not have an area of functionality (for example, it can only terminate calls), tests surrounding the areas of functionality that do not require implementation can be removed (for example, the ability to originate calls). Each of the core SS7 protocols (MTP 2, MTP 3, ISUP, ISUP supplementary services, SCCP, and TCAP) has a corresponding ITU-T test specification. These specifications aim to broadly test the main functional areas of each protocol. The IETF is currently working on similar test specifications, which are to be used for the SigTran protocol suite.

PART VI

Appendixes

MTP Messages (ANSI/ETSI/ITU)

The table in this appendix summarizes Message Transfer Part (MTP) messages and the purpose of each. The signaling network management (SNM) procedures of MTP3 generate MTP messages. For an introduction to MTP3, refer to Chapter 7, "Message Transfer Part 3 (MTP3)."

NOTE   Messages in Table A-1 are marked as (ITU) or (ANSI) when they have the same encoding and meaning but different naming conventions.

Table A-1   *MTP Message Explanation and Codings*

H1/H0 Code	MESSAGE NAME	PURPOSE
0 0 0 1 0 0 0 1	**COO** Changeover Order	Indicates that traffic is being changed over from a primary link to an alternate link.
0 0 1 0 0 0 0 1	**COA** Changeover Acknowledgement	Acknowledgement sent in response to a COO.
0 1 0 1 0 0 0 1	**CBD** Changeback Declaration	Indicates that traffic is being changed back to a primary link from an alternate link.
0 1 1 0 0 0 0 1	**CBA** Changeback Acknowledgement	Acknowledgement sent in response to a CBD.
0 0 0 1 0 0 1 0	**ECO** Emergency Changeover Order	Indicates that traffic is being changed over from a primary link to an alternative link. This differs from a COO in that the last accepted FSN cannot be determined, resulting in possible message loss.
0 0 1 0 0 0 1 0	**ECA** Emergency Changeover Acknowledgement	Acknowledgement sent in response to an ECO.

continues

Table A-1 *MTP Message Explanation and Codings (Continued)*

H1/H0 Code	MESSAGE NAME	PURPOSE
0 0 0 1 0 0 1 1	**RCT** Routeset Congestion Test	Sent after receiving a TFC in order to test whether a routeset is at the congestion level specified by the priority of the RCT message.
0 0 1 0 0 0 1 1	**TFC** Transfer Controlled	Indicates routeset congestion for a destination. The level of congestion is indicated in the message to prevent messages of a lower priority from being sent.
0 0 0 1 0 1 0 0	**TFP** Transfer Prohibited	Sent by an STP to indicate that messages to a particular destination must be sent via another route because of a total loss of routing capability to that destination.
0 0 1 0 0 1 0 0	**TCP** Transfer Cluster Prohibited (A)	Sent by an STP to indicate that messages to a particular cluster must be sent via another route because of a total loss of routing capability to that cluster.
0 0 1 1 0 1 0 0	**TFR** Transfer Restricted	Sent by an STP to indicate that messages to a particular destination should be sent via another route, if possible, because of diminished routing capability to that destination.
0 1 0 0 0 1 0 0	**TCR** Transfer Cluster Restricted (A)	Sent by an STP to indicate that messages to a particular cluster should be sent via another route, if possible, because of diminished routing capability to that cluster.
0 1 0 1 0 1 0 0	**TFA** Transfer Allowed	Sent by an STP to indicate that messages to a particular destination can be routed normally.
0 1 1 0 0 1 0 0	**TCA** Transfer Cluster Allowed (A)	Sent by an STP to indicate that messages to a particular cluster can be routed normally.
0 0 0 1 0 1 0 1	**RST (ITU)** **RSP (ANSI)** Routeset Prohibited Test	Sent periodically after receiving a TFP to test whether the routeset state is still prohibited.
0 0 1 0 0 1 0 1	**RSR** Routeset Restricted Test	Sent periodically after receiving a TFR to test whether the routeset state is still restricted.
0 0 1 1 0 1 0 1	**RCP (A)** Routeset Cluster Prohibited Test	Sent periodically after receiving a TCP to test whether the routeset state for a cluster is still prohibited.

Table A-1   *MTP Message Explanation and Codings (Continued)*

H1/H0 Code	MESSAGE NAME	PURPOSE
0 1 0 0 0 1 0 1	**RCR (A)** Routeset Cluster Restricted Test	Sent periodically after receiving a TCR to test whether the routeset state for a cluster is still restricted.
0 0 0 1 0 1 1 0	**LIN** Link Inhibit	A request to place a link in the inhibited state. An inhibited link cannot transmit user traffic from level 4.
0 0 1 0 0 1 1 0	**LUN** Link Uninhibit	A request to uninhibit a link that has been placed in the inhibited state.
0 0 1 1 0 1 1 0	**LIA** Link Inhibit Acknowledge	Acknowledgement sent in response to a LIN, allowing a link to be inhibited.
0 1 0 0 0 1 1 0	**LUA** Link Uninhibit Acknowledgement	Acknowledgment sent in response to a LUN.
0 1 0 1 0 1 1 0	**LID** Link Inhibit Denied	Sent in response to an LIN, denying the request to inhibit a link.
0 1 1 0 0 1 1 0	**LFU** Link Forced Uninhibit	Sent to request that a previously inhibited link be uninhibited. Used when the inhibited link is the only available route to a destination.
0 1 1 1 0 1 1 0	**LLT (ITU)** **LLI (ANSI)** Link Local Inhibit Test	Sent for a link in the locally inhibited state to test that the far-end link state is marked as remotely inhibited.
1 0 0 0 0 1 1 0	**LRT (ITU)** **LRI (ANSI)** Link Remote Inhibit Test	Sent for a link in the remote inhibited state to test that the far-end link state is marked as locally inhibited.
0 0 0 1 0 1 1 1	**TRA** Traffic Restart Allowed	Sent as part of the MTP restart procedure to indicate that traffic may be restarted.
0 0 1 0 0 1 1 1	**TRW** Traffic Restart Waiting (A)	Sent as part of the MTP restart procedure to indicate that the sending of traffic should be delayed because of an MTP restart in progress.
0 0 0 1 1 0 0 0	**DLC** Data Link Connection *	No specification.

continues

Table A-1 *MTP Message Explanation and Codings (Continued)*

H1/H0 Code	MESSAGE NAME	PURPOSE
0 0 1 0 1 0 0 0	**CSS** Connection Successful*	No specification.
0 0 1 1 1 0 0 0	**CNS** Connection Not Successful*	No specification.
0 1 0 0 1 0 0 0	**CNP** Connection Not Possible*	No specification.
0 0 0 1 1 0 1 0	**UPU** User Part Unavailable	Sent to the originating signaling point when MTP cannot deliver a message to an MTP3 User.

KEY:

(A)   Messages supported in ANSI only (ANSI T1.111-2000). All others supported by ANSI and ITU (Q.704–1996).

*   These messages are defined by the ITU and ANSI standards, but no specifications are stated as to their use. The authors are not aware of their actual use in existing networks.

Note: ETSI MTP [9] uses exactly the same message set and codings as ITU-T.

ISUP Messages (ANSI/UK/ETSI/ITU-T)

The table in this appendix summarizes ISDN User Part (ISUP) messages and the purpose of each. For an introduction to ISUP, refer to Chapter 8, "ISDN User Part (ISUP)."

Table B-1 *ISUP Messages*

Message/Code	Full Message Name	Purpose
ACM 0 0 0 0 0 1 1 0	Address Complete	Sent in the backward direction, indicating that all address signals have been received and that the call set-up is progressing.
ANM 0 0 0 0 1 0 0 1	Answer	Sent in the backward direction to indicate that the called party has answered the call. May be used to trigger billing and measurements of call duration.
APM (NI99)(I) 0 1 0 0 0 0 0 1	Application Transport	Sent in either direction to convey application information using the Application Transport Mechanism.
BLO 0 0 0 1 0 0 1 1	Blocking	Sent to the exchange at the far end to block call originations for the specified circuit.
BLA 0 0 0 1 0 1 0 1	Blocking Acknowledgement	Sent in response to a BLO message, indicating that the identified circuit has been blocked to outgoing traffic.
CPG 0 0 1 0 1 1 0 0	Call Progress	Sent in either direction, indicating that an event has occurred in the progress of a call.
CGB 0 0 0 1 1 0 0 0	Circuit Group Blocking	Sent to the exchange at the far end to block call originations for a specified group of contiguous circuits.

continues

Table B-1   *ISUP Messages (Continued)*

Message/Code	Full Message Name	Purpose
CGBA 0 0 0 1 1 0 1 0	Circuit Group Blocking Acknowledgement	Sent in response to a CGB, indicating that the identified group of circuits has been blocked to outgoing traffic.
CQM (N) (NS67) 0 0 1 0 1 0 1 0	Circuit Group Query [Circuit Query Message (ANSI)]	Sent on a routine or demand basis to request the exchange at the other end of a group of circuits for the state of the circuits within the specified range.
CQR (N) (NS67) 0 0 1 0 1 0 1 1	Circuit Group Query Response [Circuit Query Response Message (ANSI)]	Sent in response to a CQM, indicating the state of the previously identified group of circuits.
GRS 0 0 0 1 0 1 1 1	Circuit Group Reset	Sent to align the state of a group of circuits with the state of those circuits as perceived by the exchange after releasing any calls in progress, and after removing any blocked condition from that group of circuits. Message is sent when an exchange does not know the particular state of a group of circuits, because of memory problems, for example.
GRA 0 0 1 0 1 0 0 1	Circuit Group Reset Acknowledgement	Sent in response to a GRS message to indicate that the group of circuits has been realigned.
CGU 0 0 0 1 1 0 0 1	Circuit Group Unblocking	Sent to the exchange at the far end to remove the blocked condition for a specified group of circuits, allowing call originations to occur.
CGUA 0 0 0 1 1 0 1 1	Circuit Group Unblocking Acknowledgement	Sent in response to a CGU, indicating that the identified group of circuits is now unblocked.
CRM (A) 1 1 1 0 1 0 1 0	Circuit Reservation Message	Sent in the forward direction only when interworking with exchange access multi-frequency signaling to reserve a circuit and initiate any required continuity checks.
CRA (A) 1 1 1 0 1 0 0 1	Circuit Reservation Acknowledgement	Sent in the backward direction in response to a CRM, indicating that the circuit has been reserved for an outgoing call.

Table B-1   *ISUP Messages (Continued)*

Message/Code	Full Message Name	Purpose
CVR (A) 1 1 1 0 1 0 1 1	Circuit Validation Response	Sent in response to a CVT to convey translation information for the indicated circuit.
CVT (A) 1 1 1 0 1 1 0 0	Circuit Validation Test	Sent on a routine or demand basis to request translation information for the identified circuit.
CRG (N) (I) (NS67) 0 0 1 1 0 0 0 1	Charge Information	Information sent in either direction for accounting and/or call-charging purposes.
CFN (NS67) 0 0 1 0 1 1 1 1	Confusion	Sent in response to any message (other than a confusion message) to indicate that all or part of a received message was unrecognized.
CON (I) 0 0 0 0 0 1 1 1	Connect	Sent in the backward direction, indicating that all of the address signals required for routing the call to the called party have been received, and that the call has been answered.
COT (NUK) 0 0 0 0 0 1 0 1	Continuity	Sent in the forward direction to indicate the result of the completed continuity test.
CCR (NUK) 0 0 0 1 0 0 0 1	Continuity Check Request	Sent to request a continuity check on the identified circuit (requests the exchange at the circuit to attach continuity checking equipment).
EXM (A) 1 1 1 0 1 1 0 1	Exit Message	Sent in the backward direction from an outgoing gateway exchange to indicate that the call has successfully progressed to the adjacent network (Intranetwork use only).
FAC (NS67) 0 0 1 1 0 0 1 1	Facility	Sent in either direction at any phase of a call to request an action at another exchange. Also used to carry the results, error, or rejection of a previously requested action.
FAA (I) (NS67) 0 0 1 0 0 0 0 0	Facility Accepted	Sent in response to a facility request message, indicating that the requested facility has been invoked.

continues

Table B-1   *ISUP Messages (Continued)*

Message/Code	Full Message Name	Purpose
FAJ (I) (NS67) 00100001	Facility Reject	Sent in response to a facility request message (FAR) to indicate that the facility request has been rejected.
FAR (I) (NS67) 00011111	Facility Request	Sent from one exchange to another to request activation of a facility.
FOT (NUK) 00001000	Forward Transfer	Sent in the forward direction on semi-automatic calls when the operator wants an operator at a distant exchange to help.
IDR (I) (NS67) 00110110	Identification Request	Sent in the backward direction to request an action regarding the malicious call identification supplementary service.
IDS (I) (NS67) 00110111	Identification Response	Sent in response to the IDR message.
INF (N) (NS67) 00000100	Information	Sent to convey additional call-related information that may have been requested in the INR message.
INR (N) (NS67) 00000011	Information Request	Sent by an exchange to request additional call-related information.
IAM 00000001	Initial Address	Sent in the forward direction to initiate seizure of an outgoing circuit and to transmit number and other information related to the routing and the handling of a call.
LPA (N) (NS67) 00100100	Loop Back Acknowledgement	Sent as a response to a CCR to indicate that the requested loop back has been connected (or transceiver in the case of a 2-wire connection).
LOP (I) (NI97) 01000000	Loop Prevention	Sent to convey information required by the ECT (explicit call transfer) supplementary service.
NRM (I) (NS67) (NUK) 00110010	Network Resource Management	Sent in order to modify network resources associated with a certain call, and sent along an established path in any direction in any phase of the call.

Table B-1 *ISUP Messages (Continued)*

Message/Code	Full Message Name	Purpose
OLM (N) (I) (NS67) 0 0 1 1 0 0 0 0	Overload	Sent in the backward direction on non-priority calls in response to an initial address message (IAM) to invoke temporary trunk blocking of the concerned circuit when the exchange generating the message is subject to load control.
PAM (N) (NS67) 0 0 1 0 1 0 0 0	Pass-Along	Sent in either direction to transfer information between two signaling points along the same signaling path as that used to establish a physical connection.
PRI (I) (NS67) (NI99) 0 1 0 0 0 0 1 0	Prerelease Information	Sent with a release message (REL) in cases where the inclusion of the information in the REL would cause compatibility problems with ISUP 1992 and subsequent versions.
REL 0 0 0 0 1 1 0 0	Release	Sent in either direction, indicating that the circuit identified in the message is being released.
RLC 0 0 0 1 0 0 0 0	Release Complete	Sent in either direction as a response to a REL or reset circuit (RSC) message to indicate that the circuit has been brought into the idle state.
RSC 0 0 0 1 0 0 1 0	Reset Circuit	Sent when an exchange does not know the state of a particular circuit and wants to release any call in progress, remove any remotely blocked state, and align states.
RES 0 0 0 0 1 1 1 0	Resume	Sent in either direction to indicate reconnection after being suspended (for example, reanswer from an interworking node, or in the case of a non-ISDN, the called party has gone off hook within a certain time after going onhook during the call's active phase).
SGM (I) (NS67) 0 0 1 1 1 0 0 0	Segmentation	Sent in either direction to convey an additional segment of an over-length message.
SAM (I) 0 0 0 0 0 0 1 0	Subsequent Address	May be sent in the forward direction following an IAM to convey additional information about the called party number.

continues

Table B-1 *ISUP Messages (Continued)*

Message/Code	Full Message Name	Purpose
SDN (N) (I) (NS67) (NI99) 0 1 0 0 0 0 1 1	Subsequent Directory Number	May be sent in the forward direction following an IAM to convey additional information about the called party number when the called party number information in the IAM was contained in the Called Directory Number parameter. Typically used in certain number portability scenarios.
SUS 0 0 0 0 1 1 0 1	Suspend	Sent in the backward direction to indicate that the called party has been temporarily disconnected (for example, a clear back from an interworking exchange, or in case a non-ISDN called party has gone on hook during a call's active state).
UBL 0 0 0 1 0 1 0 0	Unblocking	Sent to cancel the blocked condition of a circuit caused by a previously sent BLO message.
UBA 0 0 0 1 0 1 1 0	Unblocking Acknowledgement	Sent in response to a UBL, indicating that the identified circuit is now unblocked.
UCIC (N) (NS67) 0 0 1 0 1 1 1 0	Unequipped CIC	Sent from one exchange to another when it receives a message that contains an unequipped circuit identification code.
UPA (I) (NS67) 0 0 1 1 0 1 0 1	User Part Available	Sent in either direction as a response to a user part's test message to indicate that the user part is available.
UPT (I) (NS67) 0 0 1 1 0 1 0 0	User Part Test	Sent in either direction to test the status of a user part that is marked as unavailable for a signaling point.
USR (I) (NS67) 0 0 1 0 1 1 0 1	User-to-User Information	Used for transport of user-to-user signaling, independent of call-control messages.

KEY:

Note that the absence of a symbol beside a message indicates that the message exists in ITU-T ISUP [75–78], ETSI ISUP [18] and in ANSI ISUP [2].

- (A)—Messages supported in ANSI ISUP [2]only

- (I)—Messages not supported in ANSI ISUP [2]

- (N)—Messages designated by the ITU-T for national use

- (NUK)—Messages not supported by UK ISUP [41]

- (NS67)—Messages not supported in ITU-T international ISUP

- Q.767 [81] (NI99)—Messages new in ITU-T ISUP 1999

- (NI97)—Messages new in ITU ISUP 1997

SCCP Messages (ANSI/ETSI/ITU-T)

The table in this appendix summarizes Signaling Connection Control Part (SCCP) messages and the purpose of each. For an introduction to SCCP, refer to Chapter 9, "Signaling Connection Control Part (SCCP)."

Table C-1 *SCCP Messages*

MESSAGE/ CODE	FULL MESSAGE NAME	PURPOSE
CR 00000001	Connection Request	Sent by SCCP to another SCCP peer to request a setup of a logical signaling connection between them so that data transfer can take place in a connection-orientated fashion.
CC 00000010	Connection Confirm	Sent in response to a CR message to indicate that the node has performed the setup of the requested logical signaling connection.
CREF 00000011	Connection Refused	Sent by the destination or an intermediate SCCP node in response to a CR message to indicate a refusal to set up a logical signaling connection.
AK (NE) 00001000	Data Acknowledgment	May be sent when using protocol class 3 to control the window flow.
DT1 00000110	Data Form 1	Sent by either end of a logical signaling connection to pass SCCP user data transparently between two SCCP nodes. DT1 is only used in protocol class 2.
DT2 (NE) 00000111	Data Form 2	Sent by either end of a logical signaling connection to pass SCCP user data transparently between two SCCP nodes. DT2 is only used in protocol class 3.

continues

Table C-1   *SCCP Messages (Continued)*

MESSAGE/ CODE	FULL MESSAGE NAME	PURPOSE
ED (NE) 00001011	Expedited Data	Performs the same function as the DT2 message, but includes the capability to bypass the flow control mechanism and is, therefore, only used in protocol class 3.
EA (NE) 00001100	Expedited Data Acknowledgment	Used to acknowledge an ED message. Each ED message must be acknowledged before another is sent.
XUDT 00010001	Extended Unitdata	Used by SCCP to transmit data with optional parameters, using connectionless classes 0 and 1.
XUDTS 00010010	Extended Unitdata Service	Sent back in response to a XUDT message if the XUDT message cannot be delivered to its destination. Only used when the optional field in XUDT is set to "return on error." Protocol class indeterminate due to absence of protocol class parameter.
IT 00010000	Inactivity Test	May be sent periodically by either end of a logical signaling connection to make sure the logical signaling connection is active and to audit the consistency of connection data at both ends. Used in connection-orientated classes 2 and 3.
LUDT 00010011	Long Unitdata	Used by SCCP to transmit data with optional parameters, using connectionless 0 and 1. If ATM is the underlying network, it allows sending of Network Service Data Unit (NSDU) sizes up to 3952 octets without segmentation.
LUDTS 00010100	Long Unitdata Service	Sent back in response to a LUDT message if the LUDT message cannot be delivered to its destination. Only used when the optional field in LUDT is set to "return on error." Protocol class indeterminate due to absence of protocol class parameter.
ERR 00001111	Protocol Data Unit Error	Sent on detection of any protocol errors. Used during the data transfer phase in connection-orientated classes 2 and 3.

Table C-1   *SCCP Messages (Continued)*

MESSAGE/ CODE	FULL MESSAGE NAME	PURPOSE
RLC 0 0 0 0 0 1 0 1	Release Complete	Sent in response to the Released (RLSD) message to indicate that the RLSD message was received and that the necessary procedures have been performed. Used during connection release phase in connection-orientated classes 2 and 3.
RLSD 0 0 0 0 0 1 0 0	Released	Sent to indicate that the sending SCCP wishes to release a logical signaling connection and that the associated resources have been brought into the disconnect pending condition. Also indicates that the receiving node should release the logical signaling connection and its associated resources. Used during connection release phase in connection-orientated classes 2 and 3.
RSC (NE) 0 0 0 0 1 1 1 0	Reset Confirm	Sent in response to a Reset Request (RSR) message to indicate that RSR has been received and that the necessary procedure has been performed. Used during the data transfer phase in connection-orientated class 3.
RSR (NE) 0 0 0 0 1 1 0 1	Reset Request	Sent to indicate that the sending SCCP wishes to initiate a reset procedure (re-initialization of sequence numbers) with the receiving SCCP. Used during the data transfer phase in protocol class 3.
SBR (M)(A) 1 1 1 1 1 1 0 1	Subsystem Backup Routing	Optional message sent before rerouting traffic to the backup subsystem. Provides more connectivity information so the end node can determine the traffic mix received for a subsystem.

continues

Table C-1   *SCCP Messages (Continued)*

MESSAGE/ CODE	FULL MESSAGE NAME	PURPOSE
SNR (M)(A) 1 1 1 1 1 1 1 0	Subsystem Normal Routing	Optional message sent prior to rerouting traffic to the primary subsystem, to the backup of the subsystem that is now allowed. Allows the end node to update the traffic mix information that the subsystem is receiving.
SRT (A) 1 1 1 1 1 1 1 1	Subsystem Routing Status Test	Optional message sent to verify the routing status of a subsystem marked as under backup routing.
SSA (M) 0 0 0 0 0 0 0 1	Subsystem Allowed	Used by SCCP subsystem management (SCMG) to inform SCMG at concerned destinations that a formerly prohibited subsystem (such as VLR/HLR) is now available, or that a previously unavailable SCCP is now available. As a result, the node receiving the SSA updates its translation tables.
SSP (M) 0 0 0 0 0 0 1 0	Subsystem Prohibited	Used by SCCP subsystem management (SCMG) to inform SCMG at concerned destinations that a subsystem (such as VLR/HLR) has failed. The receiving end of an SSP message updates its translation tables; as a result, traffic could be re-routed to a backup subsystem, if available.
SST (M) 0 0 0 0 0 0 1 1	Subsystem Status Test	Used by SCCP subsystem management (SCMG) to verify the status of a subsystem marked prohibited or the status of an SCCP marked unavailable. The receiving node checks the status of the named subsystem and, if the subsystem is allowed, sends an SSA message in response. If the subsystem is prohibited, no reply is sent.
SOR (M) 0 0 0 0 0 1 0 0	Subsystem Out-of-Service Request	Used by SCCP subsystem management (SCMG) to allow subsystems to go out-of-service without degrading performance of the network.

Table C-1   *SCCP Messages (Continued)*

MESSAGE/ CODE	FULL MESSAGE NAME	PURPOSE
SOG (M) 00000101	Subsystem Out-of-service-grant	Used by SCCP subsystem management (SCMG) in response to a Subsystem Out-of-Service Request (SOR) message to the requesting SCCP if both the requested SCCP and the backup of the affected subsystem agree to the request.
SSC (M)(I) 00000010	SCCP/subsystem-congested	Sent when an SCCP node experiences congestion.
UDT 00001001	Unitdata	Used by SCCP to transmit data, using connectionless classes 0 and 1.
UDTS 00001010	Unitdata Service	Sent in response to a UDT message if the UDT message cannot be delivered to its destination. Only used when the optional field in UDT is set to "return on error." Used in connectionless protocol classes 0 and 1.

KEY: (A)—Messages supported in ANSI SCCP only [2].

(I)—Messages supported in ITU-T SCCP only [60].

(NE)—Messages not supported in ETSI SCCP [10].

(M)—SCCP subsystem management (SCMG). These are transmitted within the data parameter a UDT, XUDT or LUDT message.

TCAP Messages and Components

The tables in this appendix summarize Transaction Capabilities Application Part (TCAP) messages and components, and explain the purpose of each. For an introduction to TCAP, refer to Chapter 10, "Transaction Capabilities Application Part (TCAP)."

Table D-1 shows the TCAP messages used in ITU-T networks.

Table D-1 *ITU TCAP Message Reference*

Binary Code	Message Name	Purpose
0 1 1 0 0 0 0 1	Unidirectional	Used to send components to another TCAP user without establishing a transaction. No Transaction ID is allocated. No response is expected when this message is received.
0 1 1 0 0 0 1 0	Begin	Initiates a transaction. The transaction ID is allocated and included in all messages that are associated with the transaction. A TCAP user can respond with an End or Continue message.
0 1 1 0 0 1 0 0	End	Ends an existing transaction. The Transaction ID is released when this message is received.
0 1 1 0 0 1 0 1	Continue	Sent when a transaction has been established and further information exchange is needed. A Transaction ID is allocated and used in all messages associated with the transaction. The Continue message includes both an Origination Transaction ID and a Destination Transaction ID. A TCAP user can respond with an End or Continue message.
0 1 1 0 0 1 1 1	Abort	Indicates that an abnormal condition has occurred. The transaction is ended and all associated Transaction IDs are released. The abort might be initiated by the TCAP user (U-Abort) or the protocol itself (P-Abort).

Table D-2 shows the TCAP messages used in ANSI networks.

Table D-2   *TCAP Message Reference (ANSI)*

Binary Code	Message Name	Purpose
1 1 1 0 0 0 0 1	Unidirectional	Used to send components to another TCAP user without establishing a transaction. No Transaction ID is allocated. No response is expected when this message is received.
1 1 1 0 0 0 1 0	Query With Permission	Initiates a transaction and allows the receiving TCAP user to end the transaction. A Transaction ID is allocated and included in all messages associated with the transaction. The normal response from a TCAP user is a Conversation or Response message.
1 1 1 0 0 0 1 1	Query Without Permission	Initiates a transaction but does not allow the receiving TCAP user to end the transaction. A Transaction ID is allocated and included in all messages associated with the transaction. The normal response from a TCAP user is a Conversation message.
1 1 1 0 0 1 0 0	Response	Ends an existing transaction. The Transaction ID is released when this message is received.
1 1 1 0 0 1 0 1	Conversation With Permission	Sent when a transaction has been established and further information exchange is needed. The receiving TCAP user is allowed to end the transaction. A Transaction ID is allocated when the first Conversation message is sent and is used in subsequent messages associated with the transaction. The Conversation With Permission message includes both an Origination Transaction ID and a Destination Transaction ID. The normal response from a TCAP user is a Conversation or Response message.
1 1 1 0 0 1 1 0	Conversation Without Permission	Sent when a transaction has been established and further exchange of information is needed. The receiving TCAP user is not allowed to end the transaction. A Transaction ID is allocated when the first Conversation message is sent and is used in subsequent messages associated with the transaction. The Conversation With Permission message includes both an Origination Transaction ID and a Destination Transaction ID. The normal response from a TCAP user is a Conversation message.
1 1 1 1 0 1 1 0	Abort	Indicates that an abnormal condition has occurred. The transaction is ended and all associated Transaction IDs are released. The abort might be initiated by the TCAP user (U-Abort) or the protocol itself (P-Abort).

Table D-3 shows the TCAP components used in ITU and ANSI networks.

Table D-3   *TCAP Component Type Reference (ITU/ANSI)*

ITU Binary Code	ANSI Binary Code	Component Type	Purpose
1 0 1 0 0 0 0 1	1 1 1 0 1 0 0 1	Invoke	Invokes an operation at a remote node. This is a request to have an action, such as translating a number or creating a connection performed.
1 0 1 0 0 0 1 0	1 1 1 0 1 01 0	Return Result (Last)	Returns the result of a successfully invoked operation. No subsequent components are to be sent.
1 0 1 0 0 0 1 1	1 1 1 0 1 0 1 1	Return Error	Indicates that an error has occurred at the application or user level.
1 0 1 0 0 1 0 0	1 1 1 0 1 1 0 0	Reject	Indicates that an error has occurred at the protocol level.
	1 1 1 0 1 1 0 1	Invoke (Not Last)	Invokes an operation at a remote node. Further responding components are expected. Applies only to ANSI Networks.
1 0 1 0 0 1 1 1	1 1 1 0 1 1 1 0	Return Result (Not Last)	Returns the result of a successfully invoked operation. Subsequent components are sent.

ITU-T Q.931 Messages

The table in this appendix summarizes Q.931 messages and the purpose of each. Q.931 is the layer 3 protocol of the subscriber signaling system used for ISDN and is known as Digital Subscriber Signaling System No. 1 (DSS 1). It employs a message set that is made for interworking with SS7's ISDN User Part (ISUP). As such, the message set maps to the ISUP message set.

Table E-1   *Q.931 Messages*

Binary Code	Message Name	Purpose
Call Establishment Messages		
0 0 0 0 0 0 0 1	Alerting	Direction: Called User → Network and Network→ Calling User

The called user is being alerted; that is, "the 'B' party's phone is ringing." |
| 0 0 0 0 0 0 1 0 | Call Proceeding | Direction: Called User → Network or Network → Calling User

Call establishment is taking place and, as such, no more call establishment signaling is accepted. |
| 0 0 0 0 0 1 1 1 | Connect | Direction: Called User → Network and Network→ Calling User

The 'B' party has accepted the call; that is, has "answered the phone." |

continues

Table E-1 *Q.931 Messages (Continued)*

Binary Code	Message Name	Purpose
0 0 0 0 1 1 1 1	Connect Acknowledge	Direction: Network → Called user or Calling User→ Network Message sent to indicate that the called user has been awarded the call. If sent to the network by the calling user, the message allows symmetrical call-control procedures.
0 0 0 0 0 0 1 1	Progress	Direction: User→ Network or Network-> User Sent to indicate the progress of a call in the event of interworking or in relation to the provision of in-band information/patterns (for example, announcements).
0 0 0 0 0 1 0 1	Setup	Direction: Calling user→ Network and Network→ Called User Initial message sent to initiate a call.
0 0 0 0 1 1 0 1	Setup Acknowledge	Direction: Called user→ Network or Network-> Calling User Indicates that call establishment is underway, but additional information might be requested.
	Call Information Phase Messages	
0 0 1 0 0 1 1 0	Resume	Direction: User→ Network Sent request to resume a previously suspended call.
0 0 1 0 1 1 1 0	Resume Acknowledge	Direction: Network→ User Indicates to the user that the request to resume a suspended call has been completed.
0 0 1 0 0 0 1 0	Resume Reject	Direction: Network→ User Indicates to the user that a failure occurred while trying to resume a suspended call.

Table E-1 *Q.931 Messages (Continued)*

Binary Code	Message Name	Purpose
0 0 1 0 0 1 0 1	Suspend	Direction: User→ Network Sent to request that a call be suspended.
0 0 1 0 1 1 0 1	Suspend Acknowledge	Direction: Network→ User Informs the user that a request to suspend a call has been completed.
0 0 1 0 0 0 0 1	Suspend Reject	Direction: Network→ User Informs the user that a request to suspend a call cannot be completed.
0 0 1 0 0 0 0 0	User Information	Direction: User→ Network and Network→ User Sent to transfer information to the remote user.
	Call Clearing Messages	
0 1 0 0 0 1 0 1	Disconnect	Direction: User→ Network or Network→ User When sent by the network, indicates that the connection has been cleared end-to-end. When sent from user to network, it is used to request tear down of an end-to-end connection.
0 1 0 0 1 1 0 1	Release	Direction: User→ Network or Network→ User Indicates that the channel has been disconnected by the equipment sending the message, and that it intends to release the channel along with the call reference. As a result, the receiving equipment should release the channel and call references after sending a RELEASE COMPLETE.
0 1 0 1 1 0 1 0	Release Complete	Direction: User→ Network or Network→ User Sent to indicate that the equipment sending the message has released the channel and the call reference. The channel is ready for reuse and the receiving equipment shall release the call reference.

continues

Table E-1   *Q.931 Messages (Continued)*

Binary Code	Message Name	Purpose
0 1 0 0 0 1 1 0	Restart	Direction: User→ Network or Network→ User Sent to request that the recipient restarts (returns to idle) the indicated channels or interfaces.
0 1 0 0 1 1 1 0	Restart Acknowledge	Direction: User→ Network or Network→ User Sent to acknowledge a RESTART message and to indicate that the requested restart has been completed.
	Miscellaneous Messages	
0 1 1 1 1 0 0 1	Congestion Control	Direction: Network→ User or User→ Network Sent to indicate the beginning or ending of flow control on the transmission of USER INFORMATION messages.
0 1 1 1 1 0 1 1	Information	Direction: User - > Network or Network→ User Provides additional information in the case of overlap signaling for call establishment, for example, or for other miscellaneous call-related information.
0 1 1 0 1 1 1 0	Notify	Direction: User→ Network or Network→ User Indicates information relating to the call, such as when a user has suspended a call.
0 1 1 1 1 1 0 1	Status	Direction: Network→ User or User→ Network Indicates the current call state in terms of Q.931 state machine and is sent in response to a Status Enquiry message. Is also used to report certain error conditions at any time during a call.
0 1 1 1 0 1 0 1	Status Enquiry	Direction: User→ Network or Network→ User Requests a STATUS message, the sending of which is mandatory.
0 1 1 0 0 0 0 0	Segment	Used for segmented messages.

GSM and ANSI MAP Operations

Table F-1 lists the operations used in GSM/GPRS/UMTS networks, as specified by 3GPP [115] and their respective codes. The North American GSM/GPRS/UMTS T1 MAP standard [117] contains exactly the same operations as [115].

GSM MAP Operations

Table F-1   *GSM MAP Operations*

Operation	Binary Code
Location Registration Operations	
UpdateLocation	0 0 0 0 0 0 1 0
CancelLocation	0 0 0 0 0 0 1 1
PurgeMS	0 1 0 0 0 0 1 1
SendIdentification	0 0 1 1 0 1 1 1
GPRS Location Registration Operations	
UpdateGprsLocation [3G]	0 0 0 1 0 1 1 1
Subscriber Information Enquiry Operations	
ProvideSubscriberInfo [3G]	0 1 0 0 0 1 1 0
Any Time Information Enquiry Operations	
AnyTimeInterrogation [3G]	0 1 0 0 0 1 1 1
Any Time Information Handling Operations	
AnyTimeSubscriptionInterrogation [3G]	0 0 1 1 1 1 1 0
AnyTimeModification [3G]	0 1 0 0 0 0 0 1
Subscriber Data Modification Notification Operations	
NoteSubscriberDataModified [3G]	0 0 0 0 0 1 0 1

continues

Table F-1 *GSM MAP Operations (Continued)*

Operation	Binary Code
Handover Operations	
PerformHandover [P1]	0 0 0 1 1 1 0 0
PrepareHandover	0 1 0 0 0 1 0 0
SendEndSignal	0 0 0 1 1 1 0 1
ProcessAccessSignaling	0 0 1 0 0 0 1 0
ForwardAccessSignaling	0 0 1 0 0 0 1 0
PerformSubsequentHandover [P1]	0 0 0 1 1 1 1 0
PrepareSubsequentHandover	0 1 0 0 0 1 0 1
Authentication Management Operations	
SendAuthenticationInfo	0 0 1 1 1 0 0 0
AuthenticationFailureReport [3G]	0 0 0 0 1 1 1 1
IMEI Management Operations	
CheckIMEI	0 0 1 0 1 0 1 1
Subscriber Management Operations	
SendParameters [P1O]	0 0 0 0 1 0 0 1
InsertSubscriberData	0 0 0 0 0 1 1 1
DeleteSubscriberData	0 0 0 0 1 0 0 0
Fault Recovery Management Operations	
Reset	0 0 1 0 0 1 0 1
ForwardChecksIndication	0 0 1 0 0 1 1 0
RestoreData	0 0 1 1 1 0 0 1
GPRS Location Information Retrieval Operations	
SendRoutingInfoForGprs [3G]	0 0 0 1 1 0 0 0
Failure Reporting Operations	
FailureReport [3G]	0 0 0 1 1 0 0 1
GPRS Notification Operations	
NoteMsPresentForGprs [3G]	0 0 0 1 1 0 1 0
Mobility Management Operations	
NoteMmEvent [3G]	0 1 0 1 1 0 0 1

Table F-1   *GSM MAP Operations (Continued)*

Operation	Binary Code
Operation and Maintenance Operations	
ActivateTraceMode	0 0 1 1 0 0 1 0
DeactivateTraceMode	0 0 1 1 0 0 1 1
TraceSubscriberActivity [P1O]	0 1 0 1 0 0 1 0
NoteInternalHandover [P1O]	0 0 1 1 0 1 0 1
SendIMSI	0 0 1 1 1 0 1 0
Call Handling Operations	
SendRoutingInfo	0 0 0 1 0 1 1 0
ProvideRoamingNumber	0 0 0 0 0 1 0 0
ResumeCallHandling [3G]	0 0 0 0 0 1 1 0
ProvideSIWFSNumber [3G]	0 0 0 1 1 1 1 1
Siwfs-SignallingModify [3G]	0 0 1 0 0 0 0 0
SetReportingState [3G]	0 1 0 0 1 0 0 1
StatusReport [3G]	0 1 0 0 1 0 1 0
RemoteUserFree [3G]	0 1 0 0 1 0 1 1
Ist-Alert [3G]	0 1 0 1 0 1 1 1
Ist-Command [3G]	0 1 0 1 1 0 0 0
Supplementary Service Operations	
RegisterSS	0 0 0 0 1 0 1 0
EraseSS	0 0 0 0 1 0 1 1
ActivateSS	0 0 0 0 1 1 0 0
DeactivateSS	0 0 0 0 1 1 0 1
InterrogateSS	0 0 0 0 1 1 1 0
ProcessUnstructuredSsData	0 0 0 1 1 0 0 1
ProcessUnstructuredSsRequest	0 0 1 1 1 0 1 1
UnstructuredSsRequest	0 0 1 1 1 1 0 0
UnstructuredSsNotify	0 0 1 1 1 1 0 1
RegisterPassword	0 0 0 1 0 0 0 1
GetPassword	0 0 0 1 0 0 1 0

continues

Table F-1 *GSM MAP Operations (Continued)*

Operation	Binary Code
Supplementary Service Operations (Continued)	
BeginSubscriberActivity [P1O]	0 1 0 1 0 1 0 0
SsInvocationNotification [3G]	0 1 0 0 1 0 0 0
RegisterCcEntry [3G]	0 1 0 0 1 1 0 0
EraseCcEntry [3G]	0 1 0 0 1 1 0 1
Short Message Service Operations	
SendRoutingInfoForSM	0 0 1 0 1 1 0 1
ForwardSM MoForwardSM [3G]	0 0 1 0 1 1 1 0
MtForwardSM [3G]	0 0 1 0 1 1 0 0
ReportSmDeliveryStatus	0 0 1 0 1 1 1 1
NoteSubscriberPresent [P1O]	0 1 0 0 1 0 0 0
AlertServiceCentreWithoutResult [P1O]	0 1 0 0 1 0 0 1
AlertServiceCentre	0 1 0 0 0 0 0 0
InformServiceCentre	0 0 1 1 1 1 1 1
ReadyForSM	0 1 0 0 0 0 1 0
Group Call Operations	
PrepareGroupCall [3G]	0 0 1 0 0 1 1 1
SendGroupCallEndSignal [3G]	0 0 1 0 1 0 0 0
ProcessGroupCallSignaling [3G]	0 0 1 0 1 0 0 1
ForwardGroupCallSignaling [3G]	0 0 1 0 1 0 1 0
Location Service Operations	
SendRoutingInfoForLCS [3G]	0 1 0 1 0 1 0 1
ProvideSubscriberLocation [3G]	0 1 0 1 0 0 1 1
SubscriberLocationReport [3G]	0 1 0 1 0 1 1 0

Table F-1   *GSM MAP Operations (Continued)*

Operation	Binary Code
Secure Transport Operations	
SecureTransportClass1 [3G]	0 1 0 0 1 1 1 0
SecureTransportClass2 [3G]	0 1 0 0 1 1 1 1
SecureTransportClass3 [3G]	0 1 0 1 0 0 0 0
SecureTransportClass4 [3G]	0 1 0 1 0 0 0 1

Key:

P1O = Specified for use in MAP Phase 1 only (no longer published).

3G = Found in 3GPP R6 MAP Phase 3 specification [115], but not in ETSI MAP Phase 2 [116].

ANSI-41 MAP Operations

Table F-2 details the ANSI-41D MAP operations [1] and their respective codes. Unlike GSM MAP operations, they are not precategorized into sections.

Table F-2   *ANSI-41 MAP Operations*

ANSI-41 MAP Operations	Op Code
HandoffMeasurementRequest	0 0 0 0 0 0 0 1
FacilitiesDirective	0 0 0 0 0 0 1 0
MobileOnChannel	0 0 0 0 0 0 1 1
HandoffBack	0 0 0 0 0 1 0 0
FacilitiesRelease	0 0 0 0 0 1 0 1
QualificationRequest	0 0 0 0 0 1 1 0
QualificationDirective	0 0 0 0 0 1 1 1
Blocking	0 0 0 0 1 0 0 0
Unblocking	0 0 0 0 1 0 0 1
ResetCircuit	0 0 0 0 1 0 1 0
TrunkTest	0 0 0 0 1 0 1 1
TrunkTestDisconnect	0 0 0 0 1 1 0 0

continues

Table F-2 *ANSI-41 MAP Operations (Continued)*

ANSI-41 MAP Operations	Op Code
RegistrationNotification	0 0 0 0 1 1 0 1
RegistrationCancellation	0 0 0 0 1 1 1 0
LocationRequest	0 0 0 0 1 1 1 1
RoutingRequest	0 0 0 1 0 0 0 0
FeatureRequest	0 0 0 1 0 0 0 1
UnreliableRoamerDataDirective	0 0 0 1 0 1 0 0
MSInactive	0 0 0 1 0 1 1 0
TransferToNumberRequest	0 0 0 1 0 1 1 1
RedirectionRequest	0 0 0 1 1 0 0 0
HandoffToThird	0 0 0 1 1 0 0 1
FlashRequest	0 0 0 1 1 0 1 0
AuthenticationDirective	0 0 0 1 1 0 1 1
AuthenticationRequest	0 0 0 1 1 1 0 0
BaseStationChallenge	0 0 0 1 1 1 0 1
AuthenticationFailureReport	0 0 0 1 1 1 1 0
CountRequest	0 0 0 1 1 1 1 1
InterSystemPage	0 0 1 0 0 0 0 0
UnsolicitedResponse	0 0 1 0 0 0 0 1
BulkDeregistration	0 0 1 0 0 0 1 0
HandoffMeasurementRequest2	0 0 1 0 0 0 1 1
FacilitiesDirective2	0 0 1 0 0 1 0 0
HandoffBack2	0 0 1 0 0 1 0 1
HandoffToThird2	0 0 1 0 0 1 1 0
AuthenticationDirectiveForward	0 0 1 0 0 1 1 1
AuthenticationStatusReport	0 0 1 0 1 0 0 0
InformationDirective	0 0 1 0 1 0 1 0
InformationForward	0 0 1 0 1 0 1 1
InterSystemAnswer	0 0 1 0 1 1 0 0
InterSystemPage2	0 0 1 0 1 1 0 1
InterSystemSetup	0 0 1 0 1 1 1 0

Table F-2   *ANSI-41 MAP Operations (Continued)*

ANSI-41 MAP Operations	Op Code
OriginationRequest	0 0 1 0 1 1 1 1
RandomVariableRequest	0 0 1 1 0 0 0 0
RedirectionDirective	0 0 1 1 0 0 0 1
RemoteUserInteractionDirective	0 0 1 1 0 0 1 0
SMSDeliveryBackward	0 0 1 1 0 0 1 1
SMSDeliveryForward	0 0 1 1 0 1 0 0
SMSDeliveryPointToPoint	0 0 1 1 0 1 0 1
SMSNotification	0 0 1 1 0 1 1 0
SMSRequest	0 0 1 1 0 1 1 1

MTP Timers in ITU-T/ETSI/ANSI Applications

This appendix defines all MTP timers used in ITU-T, ETSI, and ANSI specifications. ITU-T timer values are specified in ITU-T Q.704 [53]. ETSI timer values are specified in ETSI EN 300 008-1 [9]. ANSI timer values are specified in T1.111-2001 [1].

Message Transfer Part 2 Timers

Table G-1 lists the Message Transfer Part 2 (MTP2) timers.

Table G-1   *MTP2 Timers*

Timer	Use	Range
T1	Timer "aligned/ready"	40–50 s (ITU-T 64 kbps)
		12.9–16 s (ANSI 56/64 kbps)
		170 s (ANSI 1.5 mbps)
T2	Timer "not aligned"	5–50 (low) s (ITU-T 64 kbps)
		70–150 (high) s (ITU-T 64 kbps)
		25–350 s, 300 s nominal (ITU-T 1.5/2 Mbps)
		5–14 (low) s, nominal 11.5 s (ANSI 56/64 kbps)
		16–30 (high) s, nominal 23 s (ANSI 56/64 kbps)
T3	Timer "aligned"	1–2 s (ITU-T 64 kbps)
		5–14 s, nominal 11.5 s (ANSI 56/64 kbps)
T4n	Normal proving period timer	7.5–9.5 s, nominal 8.2 s (ITU-T 64 kbps)
		3–70 s, nominal 30 s (ITU-T 1.5/2 Mbps)
		2.3 s ±10% (ANSI 56/64 kbps)
		30 s ±10% (ANSI 1.5 Mbps)
T4e	Emergency proving period timer	400–600 ms, nominal 500 ms (ITU-T 64 kbps, 1.5/2 Mbps)
		0.6 s ±10% (ANSI 56/64 kbps)
		5 s ±10% (ANSI 1.5 Mbps)

continues

Table G-1   *MTP2 Timers (Continued)*

Timer	Use	Range
T5	Timer "sending SIB"	80–120 ms
T6	Timer "remote congestion"	3–6 s (ITU-T 64 kbps) 1–6 s (ANSI 56/64 kbps, 1.5 Mbps)
T7	Timer "excessive delay of acknowledgement"	0.5–2 s (ITU-T 64 kbps, ANSI 56/64 kbps) 0.5–2 s, for PCR 0.8–2 s (ITU-T 64 kbps) 0.5–2 s, for PCR 0.8–2 s (ANSI 56/64 kbps, 1.5 Mbps)
T8	Timer "errored interval monitor"	100 ms (ANSI 1.5 Mbps)

Note: ETSI [9] timers are identical to ITU-T timers.

Message Transfer Part 3 Timers

Tables G-2 and G-3 define the Message Transfer Part 3 (MTP3) timer values for ITU and ANSI networks, respectively. Timers T1 through T17 are defined the same for both ITU and ANSI. However, the subsequent timer values are defined differently.

The values in parentheses are applicable where routes with long propagation delays—such as routes including satellite sections—are used.

ITU timer values are defined in ITU-T Q.704 [53]. ANSI T1.111-2001 [1] and Telcordia GR-246-Core (formerly Bellcore TR-NWT-000246) [114] specify timers that are applicable to the U.S. network.

Whereas 56 kbps and 64 kbps links are assumed for ANSI, 64 kbps links are assumed for ITU-T.

Table G-2   *MTP3 Timers for ITU Networks*

Timer	Use	Range
T1	Delay to avoid missequencing on changeover	500 (800)–1200 ms
T2	Waiting for changeover acknowledgment	700 (1400)–2000 ms
T3	Time-controlled diversion delay—avoid missequencing on changeback	500 (800)–1200 ms
T4	Waiting for changeback acknowledgment (first attempt)	500 (800)–1200 ms
T5	Waiting for changeback acknowledgment (second attempt)	500 (800)–1200 ms

Table G-2   *MTP3 Timers for ITU Networks (Continued)*

Timer	Use	Range
T6	Delay to avoid message missequencing on controlled rerouting	500 (800)–1200 ms
T7	Waiting for signaling data link connection acknowledgment	1–2 s
T8	Transfer prohibited inhibition timer	800–1200 ms
T9	Not used	Not used
T10	Waiting to repeat signaling route-set test message	30–60 s
T11	Transfer restricted timer	30–90 s
T12	Waiting for uninhibit acknowledgment	800–1500 ms
T13	Waiting for force uninhibit	800–1500 ms
T14	Waiting for inhibition acknowledgment	2–3 s
T15	Waiting to start signaling route-set congestion test	2–3 s
T16	Waiting for route-set congestion status update	1.4–2 s
T17	Delay to avoid oscillation of initial alignment failure and link restart	800–1500 ms
T18	Within an SP with MTP restart for supervision of links, link set activation and routing data updating	The value is implementation- and network-dependent (ITU-T); criteria to choose T18 can be found in § 9.2 of Q.704
T19	Supervision timer during MTP restart to avoid possible ping-pong of TFP, TFR, and TRA messages	67–69 s
T20	Overall MTP restart timer at the SP whose MTP is restarting	59–61 s 90–120 s
T21	Overall MTP restart timer at an SP adjacent—one whose MTP is restarting	63–65 s
T22	Local inhibit test timer	3–6 minutes (provisional value)
T23	Remote inhibit test timer	3–6 minutes (provisional value)
T24	Stabilization timer after removal of local processor outage (national option)	500 ms (provisional value)

Table G-3   *MTP3 Timers for ANSI Networks*

Timer	Use	Range
T1	Delay to avoid missequencing on changeover	500 (800)–1200 ms
T2	Waiting for changeover acknowledgment	700 (1400)–2000 ms
T3	Time-controlled diversion delay—avoid missequencing on changeback	500 (800)–1200 ms
T4	Waiting for changeback acknowledgment (first attempt)	500 (800)–1200 ms
T5	Waiting for changeback acknowledgment (second attempt)	500 (800)–1200 ms
T6	Delay to avoid message missequencing on controlled rerouting	500 (800)–1200 ms
T7	Waiting for signaling data link connection acknowledgment	1–2 s
T8	Transfer prohibited inhibition timer	800–1200 ms
T9	Not used	Not used
T10	Waiting to repeat signaling route; set test message	30–60 s
T11	Transfer restricted timer	30–90 s
T12	Waiting for uninhibit acknowledgment	800–1500 ms
T13	Waiting for force uninhibit	800–1500 ms
T14	Waiting for inhibition acknowledgment	2–3 s
T15	Waiting to start signaling route-set congestion test	2–3 s
T16	Waiting for route-set congestion status update	1.4–2 s
T17	Delay to avoid oscillation of initial alignment failure and link restart	800–1500 ms
T18	Repeat TFR once by response method	2–20 s
T19	Failed link craft referral timer	480–600 s
T20	Waiting—repeat local inhibit test	90–120 s
T21	Waiting—repeat remote inhibit test; repeat local inhibit test	90–120 s
T22	Timer used at a restarting SP; waiting for signaling links to become available	Network-dependent
T23	Timer used at a restarting SP; waiting to receive all traffic restart allowed message after starting T22	Network-dependent

Table G-3   *MTP3 Timers for ANSI Networks (Continued)*

Timer	Use	Range
T24	Timer used at a restarting STP; waiting to broadcast all traffic restart allowed messages after starting T23	Network-dependent
T25	Timer at adjacent SP to restarting SP; waiting for traffic restart message	30–35 s
T26	Timer at restarting SP; waiting to repeat traffic restart waiting message	12–15 s
T27	Minimum duration of unavailability for full restart	2(3)–5 s
T28	Timer at adjacent SP to restarting SP; waiting for traffic restart waiting message	3–35 s
T29	Timer started when TRA is sent in response to unexpected TRA or TRW	60–65 s
T30	Timer to limit sending of TFPs and TFRs in response to unexpected TRA or TRW	30–35 s

ISUP Timers for ANSI/ETSI/ITU-T Applications

This appendix lists all ISUP timers. The timer values are specified in ITU-T Q.764 [78]. ETSI ISUP timers [18] are identical to ITU-T timers.

Timers applicable to the US network are specified in ANSI T1.113-2000 [3].

Table H-1 *ISUP Timers Specified in ANSI, ETSI and ITU-T*

Timer	Duration Before Time-Out	Starts	Normal Termination	Action at Time-Out
T1	15–60 sec (ITU) 4–15 sec (ANSI)	When Release Message is sent	Upon receipt of Release Complete Message	Retransmit Release Message and start timer T1
T2 (ITU-T ONLY)	3 min	When controlling exchange receives Suspend (User) Message	Upon receipt of Resume (User) Message, at controlling exchange	Initiate release procedure
T3 (ITU-T ONLY)	2 min	Upon receipt of Overload Message	Upon expiry	Initiate release procedure
T4 (ITU-T ONLY)	5–15 min	Upon receipt of MTP-STATUS primitive with the cause "inaccessible remote user" or at receipt of MTP-RESUME primitive[1]	Upon expiry, or at receipt of User Part Available Message (or any other)	Send User Part Test Message and start T4
T5	5–15 min (ITU) 1 min (ANSI)	When initial Release Message is sent	Upon receipt of Release Complete Message	Send Reset Circuit Message, alert maintenance personnel, and remove the Circuit from service, stop T1, and start T17

continues

Table H-1   *ISUP Timers Specified in ANSI, ETSI and ITU-T (Continued)*

Timer	Duration Before Time-Out	Starts	Normal Termination	Action at Time-Out
T6	10–32 sec, with preference for 30 sec (specified in Rec. Q.118 [113])	When controlling exchange receives suspend (network)	Upon receipt of Resume (Network) Message or Release Message	Initiate release procedure
T7	20–30 sec	When the latest Address Message is sent	When the condition for normal release of address and routing information is met (receipt of ACM and CON Messages)	Release all equipment and connection (send Release Message)
T8	10–15 sec	Upon receipt of Initial Address Message requiring continuity check on this circuit, or indicating that continuity check has been performed on a previous circuit	Upon receipt of Continuity Message	Release all equipment and connection into the network (send Release Message)
T9	1.5–3 min (Specified in Q.118 [113])	When national controlling (ITU ONLY) or outgoing international exchange receives ACM (ANSI and ITU)	Upon receipt of Answer Message	Release connection and send Release Message
T10 (ITU-T ONLY)	4–6 sec	Upon receipt of last digit in interworking situations	Upon receipt of fresh information	Send Address Complete Message
T11	15–20 sec	Upon receipt of the latest address message (i.e., IAM) in interworking situations	When Address Complete Message is sent	Send Address Complete Message
T12	15–60 sec (ITU) 4–15 sec (ANSI)	When Blocking Message is sent	Upon receipt of Blocking Acknowledgement Message	Retransmit Blocking Message and restart T12

Table H-1   *ISUP Timers Specified in ANSI, ETSI and ITU-T (Continued)*

Timer	Duration Before Time-Out	Starts	Normal Termination	Action at Time-Out
T13	5–15 min (ITU) 1 min (ANSI)	When initial Block-ing Message is sent	Upon receipt of Blocking Acknowledgment	Retransmit Blocking Message and alert maintenance personnel, start T13, and stop T12
T14	15–60 sec (ITU) 4-15 sec (ANSI)	When Unblocking Message is sent	Upon receipt of Unblocking Acknowledgment	Retransmit Unblocking Message and start T14
T15	5–15 min (ITU) 1 min (ANSI)	When initial Unblocking Message is sent	Upon receipt of Unblocking Acknowledgment Message	Retransmit Unblocking Message, alert maintenance personnel, start T15, and stop T14
T16	15–60 sec (ITU) 4-15 sec (ANSI)	When Reset Circuit Message is sent not due to expiry of T5	Upon receipt of the Acknowledgment (RLC Message)	Retransmit Reset Circuit Message and start T16
T17	5–15 min (ITU) 1 min (ANSI)	When initial Reset Circuit Message is sent	At the receipt of the Acknowledgment (RLC Message)	Alert maintenance personnel, retransmit Reset Circuit Message, start T17, and stop T16
T18	15–60 sec (ITU) 4–15 sec (ANSI)	When Circuit Group Blocking Message is sent	At receipt of Circuit Group Blocking Acknowledgment	Retransmit Circuit Group Blocking Message and start T18
T19	5–15 min (ITU) 1 min (ANSI)	When initial Circuit Group Blocking Message is sent	Upon receipt of Circuit Group Blocking Acknowledgment	Retransmit Circuit Group Blocking Message, alert maintenance personnel, start T19, and stop T18
T20	15–60 sec (ITU) 4–15 sec (ANSI)	When Circuit Group Unblocking Message is sent	Upon receipt of Circuit Group Unblocking Acknowledgment	Retransmit Circuit Group Unblocking Message and start T20

continues

Table H-1   *ISUP Timers Specified in ANSI, ETSI and ITU-T (Continued)*

Timer	Duration Before Time-Out	Starts	Normal Termination	Action at Time-Out
T21	5–15 min (ITU) 1 min (ANSI)	When initial Circuit Group Unblocking Message is sent	Upon receipt of Circuit Group Unblocking Acknowledgment	Retransmit Circuit Group Unblocking Message, alert maintenance personnel, start T21, and stop T20
T22	15–60 sec (ITU) 4–15 (ANSI)	When Circuit group Reset Message is sent	Upon receipt of the Acknowledgment	Retransmit Circuit Group Reset Message and start T22
T23	5–15 min (ITU) 1 min (ANSI)	When initial Circuit Group Reset Message is sent	Upon receipt of the Acknowledgment	Alert maintenance personnel and start T23; retransmit Circuit Group Reset Message, and stop T22
T24	< 2 sec	When check tone is sent	Upon receipt of the backward check tone	Send Continuity Message indicating failure, and (ITU-T ONLY) a) Start T25 if continuity check was asked in IAM and make automatic repeat attempt, or b) Start T24 if continuity check was asked in CCR (ANSI ONLY) c) Start T25 and make automatic repeat attempt (if applicable)
T25	1–10 sec	When initial continuity check failure is detected	Upon expiry	Send Continuity Check Request Message and repeat continuity check
T26	1–3 min	When second or subsequent continuity check failure is detected	When continuity is detected	Send Continuity Check Request Message and repeat continuity check (starting T26)

Table H-1   *ISUP Timers Specified in ANSI, ETSI and ITU-T (Continued)*

Timer	Duration Before Time-Out	Starts	Normal Termination	Action at Time-Out
T27	4 min (ITU-T) >3 min (ANSI)	Upon receipt of continuity check failure	Upon receipt of Continuity Check Request Message	Send Reset Circuit Message, start T16 and T17
T28	10 sec	When a Circuit Query Message is sent	Upon receipt of Circuit Query Response Message	Alert maintenance
T29 (ITU-T ONLY)	300–600 ms	Congestion indication received when T29 not running	–	New congestion indication will be taken into account
T30 (ITU-T ONLY)	5–10 sec	Congestion indication received when T29 not running	–	Restore traffic by one step if not yet at full load, and start T30
T31	> 6 min	Release of ISDN user part end-to-end signaling connection, based on connection oriented SCCP	Upon expiry	Call reference reusable
T32	3–5 sec	When response to request of end-to-end connection establishment is sent	Upon receipt of first End-to-end Message from the remote end	End-to-end Message allowed to be sent
T33	12–15 sec	When Information Request Message is sent	Upon receipt of an Information Message	Release call and alert maintenance personnel
T34 (ITU-T)	2–4 sec	When indication of a Segmented Message is received on an IAM, ACM, CPG, ANM or CON Message	At receipt of a Segmentation Message	Proceed with call

continues

Table H-1 *ISUP Timers Specified in ANSI, ETSI and ITU-T (Continued)*

Timer	Duration Before Time-Out	Starts	Normal Termination	Action at Time-Out
T34 (ANSI)	10–15 sec	When Loop-Back Acknowledgment Message is sent in response to receipt of Continuity Check Request Message	Upon receipt of Continuity or Release Message	Release all equipment, send Reset Circuit Message, and start T16 and T17
T35 (ITU-T)	15–20 sec	Upon receipt of the latest digit (< or >ST) and before the minimum or fixed number of digits have been received	Upon receipt of ST, or when the minimum or fixed number of digits have been received	Send Release Message (cause 28)
T36 (ITU-T)	10–15 sec	When transit or incoming international exchange receives Continuity Check Request Message	Upon receipt of Continuity or Release Message	Release all equipment, send Reset Circuit Message, start T16 and T17
T36 (ANSI)	2–4 sec	When a message is received indicating that another segment follows	Upon receipt of a Segmentation Message	Proceed with call processing
T37 (ITU-T) —reserved for ISUP '92	2–4 sec			
T37 (ANSI)	30 sec	When ISUP availability test is started	Upon receipt of a message from the affected ISUP	Proceed with call processing
T38 (ITU-T)	Interval Specified in Rec. Q.118 [113]	When the incoming international exchange sends a Suspend (network) Message to the preceding exchange	Upon receipt of Resume (Network) or Release Message	Send Release Message (cause 102)
T39 (ITU-T ONLY)	4–15 sec interval specified in Rec. Q. 731-7 §7.9	When a MCID request is sent	Upon receipt of a MCID response	Call continues

Table H-1   *ISUP Timers Specified in ANSI, ETSI and ITU-T (Continued)*

Timer	Duration Before Time-Out	Starts	Normal Termination	Action at Time-Out
$T_{ACC,r}$ (ANSI ONLY)	5 sec	Upon receipt of ACC indicator	Upon expiry	Remove ACC controls in the exchange
T_{CCR} (ANSI ONLY)	2 sec	When Continuity Check Request Message is sent	Upon receipt of Loop-Back Acknowledgment Message	Disconnect transceiver, send Reset Circuit Message, and start T16 and T17
$T_{CCR,r}$ (ANSI ONLY)	20 sec	Upon receipt of initial Continuity Message, indicating failure	Upon receipt of Continuity Check Request Message	Send Reset Circuit Message and start T16 and T17
T_{CGB} (ANSI ONLY)	5 sec	Upon receipt of Circuit Group Blocking Message	Upon receipt of Circuit Group Blocking or Circuit Group Unblocking Message	Accept subsequent Circuit Group Blocking Message as a new message
T_{CRA} (ANSI ONLY)	20 sec	When Circuit Reservation Acknowledgment Message is sent	Upon receipt of Initial Address Message or Release Message	Initiate release procedure
T_{CRM} (ANSI ONLY)	3–4 sec	When Circuit Reservation Message is sent	Upon receipt of Circuit Reservation Acknowledgment Message	Initiate release procedure
T_{CVT} (ANSI ONLY)	10 sec	When Circuit Validation Test Message is sent	Upon receipt of Circuit Validation Response Message	Retransmit Circuit Validation Test Message and restart T_{CVT}; alert maintenance personnel at second expiry
$T_{EXM,d}$ (ANSI ONLY)	Network Dependent	When Initial Address Message is sent to succeeding network	Upon expiry	Send Exit Message to proceeding exchange
T_{GRS} (ANSI ONLY)	5 sec	Upon receipt of Circuit Group Reset Message	Upon receipt of Circuit Group Reset Message	Accept subsequent Circuit Group Reset Message as new message
T_{HGA} (ANSI ONLY)	0–5 min	Carrier loss	Carrier restoral	Alert maintenance personnel

continues

Table H-1   *ISUP Timers Specified in ANSI, ETSI and ITU-T (Continued)*

Timer	Duration Before Time-Out	Starts	Normal Termination	Action at Time-Out
T_{SCGA} (ANSI ONLY)	0–2 min	Upon failure of initial Demand Continuity Check in SCGA group	Upon success of initial Demand Continuity Check in SCGA group	Alert maintenance personnel
$T_{SCGA,d}$ (ANSI ONLY)	5–120 sec	Upon failure of initial Demand Continuity Check in SCGA group	Upon expiry	Initiate Demand Continuity Check on another circuit in failed group

[1.]   Extra condition for ETSI only [18]

min = minute(s)

sec = seconds(s)

ms = millisecond(s)

GSM Mobile Country Codes (MCC) and Mobile Network Codes (MNC)

MCC	Country	MNC
0XX	Reserved	
1XX	Reserved	
202	Greece	001—Cosmote
		005—Vodafone-Panafon
		009—Q-Telecom
		010—Telestet
204	Netherlands	004—Vodafone Libertel
		008—KPN Telecom
		012—02
		016—BEN
		020—Dutchtone
206	Belgium	001—Proximus
		010—Mobistar
		020—BASE
208	France	001—Orange F
		010—SFR
		020—Bouygues Telecom
212	Monaco	TBA—Monaco Telecom
213	Andorra	003—MobilAnd
214	Spain	001—Vodafone
		003—Amena
		004—Xfera
		007—Movistar

continues

MCC	Country	MNC
216	Hungary	001 — Pannon GSM
		030 — Westel Mobile Co.
		070 — Vodafone
218	Bosnia and Herzegovina	003 — Eronet Mobile
		005 — Mobilna Srpske
		090 — GSMBIH
219	Croatia	001 — Cronet
		010 — VIPnet
220	Yugoslavia	001 — MOBTEL
		002 — ProMonte GSM
		003 — Mobilna Telefonija Srbije
		004 — Monet
222	Italy	001 — Telecom Italia Mobile
		010 — Vodafone Omnitel
		088 — WIND
		098 — Blu SpA
		TBA — H3G[†]
		TBA — IPSE 2000 S.p.A[†]
225	Vatican City State	
226	Romania	001 — Connex
		003 — Cosmorom
		010 — Orange
228	Switzerland	001 — Swiss
		002 — Sunrise
		003 — Orange
230	Czech Republic	001 — T-Mobile
		002 — EuroTel
		003 — Oskar Mobil
231	Slovak Republic	001 — Orange
		002 — EuroTel

MCC	Country	MNC
232	Austria	001—A1
		003—T-Mobile
		005—One
		007—Tele.ring
		010—Hutchison 3G
234	United Kingdom of Great Britain and Northern Ireland	002—O2 UK
		010—O2 UK
		011—O2 (UK)
		012—Railtrack Plc
		015—Vodafone
		020—3
		030—T-Mobile
		031—T-Mobile
		032—T-Mobile
		033—Orange
		34—Orange
		50—Jersey Telecoms
		55—Guernsey Telecoms
		58—Manx Telecom
		75—Earthadvice
		91—Vodafone
		94—3
		95—Railtrack Plc
235	United Kingdom of Great Britain and Northern Ireland	
238	Denmark	001—TDK-MOBIL
		002—SONOFON
		020—TELIA
		030—Orange

continues

MCC	Country	MNC
240	Sweden	001—Telia Mobile
		002—3
		007—COMVIQ
		008—Vodafone
242	Norway	001—Telenor
		002—NetCom
244	Finland	003—Telia
		005—Radiolinja Origo
		009—Finnet
		012—Suomen 2G Oy
		014—Alands Mobiltelefon Ab
		091—Sonera
		TBA—Suomen Kolmegee Oy[†]
246	Lithuania	001—OMNITEL
		002—Bite GSM
		003—TELE2
247	Latvia	001—LMT GSM
		002—TELE2
248	Estonia	001—EMT GSM
		002—Radiolinja Eesti
		003—TELE2
250	Russian Federation	001—Mobile Telesystems
		001—SANTEL
		001—Tambov RUS
		002—Megafon
		002—MegaFon Moscow
		003—NCC
		004—SIBCHALLENGE
		005—Mobile Comms Systems
		005—SCS-900

MCC	Country	MNC
250	Russian Federation	005 — Tomsk Cellular Communication
		005 — Yeniseitelecom
		007 — BM Telecom
		007 — Smarts
		010 — Don Telecom
		011 — Orensot
		012 — Far Eastern Cellular Systems
		012 — Sakhalin GSM
		012 — Sibintertelecom
		012 — Ulan-Ude Cellular Network
		013 — Kuban-GSM
		016 — NTC
		017 — Ermak RMS
		019 — INDIGO
		020 — TELE2
		028 — Extel
		039 — JSC Uralsvyazinform
		039 — SUCT
		039 — Uraltel
		044 — North-Caucasian GSM
		092 — Primtelefone
		093 — Telecom XXI JSC
		099 — Bee Line GSM
		TBA — BaykalWestCom[†]
		TBA — ECC[†]
		TBA — Gorizont-RT[†]
		TBA — KEDR RMS[†]
		TBA — MegaFon[†]
		TBA — Zao Mobicom-Kavzaz Joint Stock Company[†]

continues

MCC	Country	MNC
255	Ukraine	001—UMC
		002—WellCOM
		003—Kyivstar
		005—Golden Telecom GSM
257	Belarus	001—VELCOM
259	Moldova	001—VOXTEL
		002—Moldcell
260	Poland	001—PLUS GSM
		002—ERA GSM
		003—IDEA
262	Germany	001—T-D1
		002—D2 vodafone
		003—E-Plus
		007—O2
		013—Mobilcom Multimedia
		014—Group 3G UMTS
266	Gibraltar	001—Gibtel GSM
268	Portugal	001—VODAFONE
		003—OPTIMUS
		006—TMN
		TBA—ONI WAY Infocomunicacoes[†]
270	Luxembourg	001—LUXGSM
		077—TANGO
272	Ireland	001—Vodafone
		002—O2
		003—METEOR
274	Iceland	001—Landssiminn
		002—TAL hf
		003—Islandssimi GSM ehf
		004—Viking Wireless
		TBA—Hallo![†]

MCC	Country	MNC
276	Albania	001 — AMC
		002 — VODAFONE
278	Malta	001 — Vodafone Malta — GSM 900
		021 — Go Mobile
280	Cyprus	001 — CYTA
282	Georgia	001 — Geocell
		002 — Magti GSM
		TBA — Ibercom[†]
283	Armenia	001 — ARMGSM
284	Bulgaria	001 — M-TEL GSM BG
		005 — GloBul
286	Turkey	001 — Turkcell
		002 — TELSIM GSM
		003 — ARIA
		004 — AYCELL
288	Faroe Islands	001 — Faroese Telecom
		002 — KALL-GSM
290	Greenland	001 — Tele Greenland
292	San Marino	
293	Slovenia	040 — SI.MOBIL
		041 — MOBITEL
		070 — VEGA
294	The Former Yugoslav Republic of Macedonia	001 — MobiMak
		002 — MTS A.D
295	Liechtenstein	001 — Telecom FL AG
		002 — EuroPlatform
		005 — FL1
		077 — Tele 2 AG
302	Canada	370 — Microcell Connexions Inc
		720 — Rogers Wireless

continues

MCC	Country	MNC
308	Saint Pierre and Miquelon	
310	Papua New Guinea	001—Cellnet
310	United States of America	011—Wireless 2000 Telephone Co.
		016—VOICESTREAM
		020—VOICESTREAM
		021—VOICESTREAM
		022—VOICESTREAM
		023—VOICESTREAM
		024—VOICESTREAM
		025—VOICESTREAM
		026—VOICESTREAM
		027—VOICESTREAM
		031—VOICESTREAM
		038—AT&T Wireless
		058—PCS One Inc
		064—Airadigm Communications
		066—VOICESTREAM
		068—NPI Wireless
		077—Iowa Wireless Services LP
		080—VOICESTREAM
		150—Cingular Wireless
		170—Cingular Wireless
		270—Powertel
		340—Westlink Communications
		460—TMP Corp
		530—West Virginia Wireless
		560—Dobson
		630—Choice Wireless L.C.
		660—Eliska Wireless
		690—Conestoga
		740—WTC

MCC	Country	MNC
310	United States of America	790—PinPoint Wireless
		TBA—AirlinkPCS[†]
		TBA—Cincinnati Bell Wireless[†]
		TBA—Epic Touch Co.[†]
		TBA—MBO Wireless, Inc[†]
		TBA—Oklahoma Western Telephone Company[†]
		TBA—Panhandle Telecommunications System Inc[†]
		TBA—Quantum Communications Group Inc[†]
		TBA—SunCom AT&T—Atlanta[†]
		TBA—SunCom AT&T—GSM 1900—Charlotte-Greensboro-Greenvill[†]
		TBA—SunCom AT&T—Knoxville[†]
		TBA—SunCom AT&T—Richmond-Norfolk[†]
		TBA—SunCom AT&T—Washington-Baltimore[†]
311	United States of America	
312	United States of America	
313	United States of America	
314	United States of America	
315	United States of America	
316	United States of America	
330	Puerto Rico	
332	United States Virgin Islands	TBA—OPM Auction Co.[†]
334	Mexico	020—TELCEL GSM
338	Jamaica	005—Digicel
340	Martinique (French Department of)	
340	French West Indies	001—ORANGE CARAIBE
		003—Saint Martin et Saint Barthelemy Tel Cell SARL
		020—Bouygues Telecom Caraibe
342	Barbados	-
344	Antigua and Barbuda	030—APUA PCS

continues

MCC	Country	MNC
346	Cayman Islands	
348	British Virgin Islands	
350	Bermuda	001—Telecom Bermuda
		002—BTC MOBILITY LTD
352	Grenada	TBA—Grenada Wireless Ventures Ltd[†]
354	Montserrat	
356	Saint Kitts and Nevis	
358	Saint Lucia	
360	Saint Vincent and the Grenadines	
362	Netherlands Antilles	051—Telcell N.V.
		069—CT GSM
		091—UTS Wireless Curacao
363	Aruba	001—SETAR GSM
		TBA—SETAR GSM[†]
364	Bahamas	039—Bahamas Telecommunications Company
365	Anguilla	
366	Dominica	
368	Cuba	001—C_Com
370	Dominican Republic	001—Orange
372	Haiti	
374	Trinidad and Tobago	012—TSTT
376	Turks and Caicos Islands	
400	Azerbaijani Republic	001—AZERCELL GSM
		002—Bakcell
401	Kazakstan	001—K-MOBILE
		002—K'cell
404	India	001—Aircel Digilink India Limited—Haryana
		002—AirTel—Punjab
		003—AirTel—Himachal Pradesh
		005—CELFORCE

MCC	Country	MNC
404	India	009—Reliance Telecom
		010—AirTel—Delhi
		011—Essar Cellphone (Delhi)
		012—Escotel Haryana
		013—BSSL—Andhra Pradesh
		014—SPICE—Punjab
		015—Aircel Digilink India Limited—UP East
		018—Reliance Telecom
		019—Escotel Kerala
		020—Orange
		021—BPL—Mobile—Mumbai
		022—IDEA—Maharashtra Circle
		024—IDEA—Andhra Pradesh Circle
		027—BPL Mobile—Maharshtra/Goa
		030—Command
		031—AIRTEL
		036—Reliance Telecom
		040—AIRTEL—City of Madras
		041—RPG Cellular
		042—AIRCEL
		043—BPL Mobile—Tamil Nadu/Pondicherry
		044—Spice—Karnataka
		045—Airtel—Karnataka
		046—BPL Mobile—Kerala
		049—Airtel—Andhra Pradesh
		050—Reliance Telecom
		052—Reliance Telecom
		056—Escotel UP(W)
		060—Aircel Digilink India—Rajasthan
		067—Reliance Telecom Private

continues

MCC	Country	MNC
404	India	068—Mahanagar Telephone Nigam—Delhi
		069—Mahanagar Telephone Nigam—Mumbai
		070—Oasis Cellular
		078—IDEA—Gujarat Circle
		085—Reliance Telecom
		086—BSSL—Karnataka
		090—AirTel—Maharashtra
		092—AirTel—Mumbai Metro
		093—AirTel—Madhya Pradesh
		094—AirTel—Tamilnadu
		095—AirTel—Kerala
		096—AirTel—Haryana
		097—AirTel—Uttar Pradesh
		098—AirTel—Gujarat
		TBA—B MOBILE[†]
		TBA—BSSL—Chennai[†]
		TBA—IDEA—Delhi Circle[†]
		TBA—IDEA—Madhya Pradesh[†]
		TBA—USHAFONE (INA USHA)[†]
410	Pakistan	001—Mobilink
		003—Ufone
412	Afghanistan	001—Afghan Wireless Communication Company
413	Sri Lanka	002—DIALOG GSM[†]
		003—Celltel Infiniti
		TBA—Lanka Cellular Services (Pte)
414	Myanmar	001—MPT GSM Network
415	Lebanon	001—CELLIS
		003—LIBANCELL
416	Jordan	001—Fastlink
		077—MobileCom

MCC	Country	MNC
417	Syria	001 — SYRIATEL
		002 — 94
		009 — MOBILE SYRIA
418	Iraq	
419	Kuwait	002 — MTCNet
		003 — Wataniya Telecom
420	Saudi Arabia	001 — Saudi Telecom
421	Yemen	001 — Yemen Mobile Phone Company
		002 — SPACETEL
422	Oman	002 — GTO
424	United Arab Emirates	002 — ETISALAT
425	Israel	001 — Orange
		002 — Cellcom
		002 — Cellcom
425	Palestinian Authority	005 — JAWWAL
426	Bahrain	001 — BHR MOBILE PLUS
427	Qatar	001 — QATARNET
428	Mongolia	099 — MobiCom
429	Nepal	001 — Nepal Mobile
430	United Arab Emirates b	
431	United Arab Emirates	
432	Iran	011 — TCI
		014 — Payam Kish
434	Uzbekistan	001 — Buztel
		002 — Uzmacom
		004 — Daewoo Unitel
		005 — Coscom
		007 — Uzdunrobita GSM
436	Tajikistan	003 — Mobile Lines of Tajikistan
437	Kyrgyz Republic	001 — BITEL GSM

continues

MCC	Country	MNC
438	Turkmenistan	001—BCTI
440	Japan	TBA—J-PHONE[†]
441	Japan	TBA—NTT DoCoMo, Inc[†]
450	Korea	
452	Vietnam	001—MOBIFONE
		002—Vinaphone
454	Hong Kong, China	003—Hutchison 3G
		004—Orange
		006—SMARTONE
		010—New World Mobility
		012—PEOPLES
		016—SUNDAY
		TBA—CSL GSM 900/1800[†]
455	Macao, China	001—TELEMOVEL+
		003—Hutchison
		TBA—SMC [†]
456	Cambodia	001—MobiTel
		002—SAMART
		018—Cambodia Shinawatra
457	Lao People's Democratic Republic	001—Lao
		002—ETL Mobile
		008—Millicom Lao
460	China	001—CU-GSM
		TBA—China Mobile[†]
461	China	
466	Satellite	068—ACeS Taiwan
466	Taiwan, China	001—Far EasTone GSM 900/1800
		088—KG Telecom
		092—Chunghwa GSM
		093—MobiTai
		097—TWNGSM
		099—TransAsia

MCC	Country	MNC
467	Korea	
470	Bangladesh	001—GrameenPhone
		002—AKTEL
		019—Mobile 2000
472	Maldives	001—DhiMobile GSM 900
502	Malaysia	012—Maxis Mobile
		013—TMTOUCH
		016—DiGi
		017—TIMECel
		019—CELCOM
505	Australia	001—Telstra MobileNet
		002—OPTUS
		003—VODAFONE
		006—Hutchison
510	Indonesia	001—SATELINDO
		008—Lippo Telecom
		010—TELKOMSEL
		011—Excelcom
		021—INDOSAT-M3
		TBA—TELKOMobile[†]
510	Satellite	TBA—ACeS[†]
515	Philippines	001—ISLACOM
		002—Globe Telecom
		003—Smart Gold GSM
		005—DIGITEL
515	Satellite	011—ACeS
520	Satellite	020—ACeS
520	Thailand	001—AIS GSM
		015—ACT Mobile
		018—DTAC
		023—GSM 1800
		099—TA Orange Co

continues

MCC	Country	MNC
525	Singapore	001—SingTel
		002—SingTel
		003—MOBILEONE
		005—StarHub
528	Brunei Darussalam	011—DSTCom
530	New Zealand	001—VODAFONE
534	Northern Mariana Islands	
535	Guam	
536	Nauru	
537	Papua New Guinea	
539	Tonga	001—U-CALL
		TBA—Shoreline Communications[†]
540	Solomon Islands	
541	Satellite	TBA—ACeS International Limited (AIL)[†]
541	Vanuatu	001—SMILE
542	Fiji	001—Vodafone
543	Wallis and Futuna	
544	American Samoa	011—Blue Sky
545	Kiribati	
546	New Caledonia	001—Mobilis
547	French Polynesia	020—VINI
548	Cook Islands	
549	Samoa	
550	Micronesia, The Federated States of	001—FSM
602	Egypt	001—ECMS
		002—Vodafone
603	Algeria	001—AMN
		002—Djezzy
604	Morocco	001—IAM
		TBA—Meditel[†]

MCC	Country	MNC
605	Tunisia	002—TUNTEL
606	Libya	TBA—ORBIT[†]
607	Gambia	001—Gamcell
		002—AFRICELL
608	Senegal	001—ALIZE
		002—Sentel GSM
609	Mauritania	TBA—MATTEL[†]
		TBA—MAURITEL[†]
610	Mali	001—Malitel
611	Guinea	001—Mobilis Guinee
		002—Lagui
		TBA—Celtel Guinee SA[†]
		TBA—Telecel Guinee SARL[†]
612	Côte d'Ivoire	001—CORA de COMSTAR
		003—Orange CI
		005—Telecel
613	Burkina Faso	002—Celtel Burkina Faso
		003—Telecel Faso
		TBA—ONATEL[†]
614	Niger	002—Celtel Niger
615	Togo	001—TOGOCEL
		TBA—Telecel Togo[†]
616	Benin	001—LIBERCOM
		002—TELECEL BENIN
		003—BeninCell
617	Mauritius	001—Cellplus Mobile Comms
		010—Emtel
618	Liberia	001—Lonestar Cell

continues

MCC	Country	MNC
619	Sierra Leone	TBA—Celtel[†]
		TBA—Lintel[†]
		TBA—Millicom Sierra Leone[†]
620	Ghana	001—SPACEFON
		002—Ghana Telecom Mobile
		003—MOBITEL
621	Nigeria	020—Econet Wireless
		030—MTN Nigeria Communications
		040—NITEL GSM
622	Chad	001—CELTEL
		002—Libertis
623	Central African Republic	TBA—Centrafrique Telecom Plus[†]
		TBA—Telecel Centrafrique[†]
624	Cameroon	001—MTN
		002—Orange
625	Cape Verde	001—CVMOVEL
626	Sao Tome and Principe	001—CSTmovel
627	Equatorial Guinea	TBA—ECUATOR[†]
628	Gabon Republic	001—LIBERTIS
		002—Telecel Gabon
		003—Celtel Gabon
629	Congo	001—CelTel Congo
		010—Libertis Telecom
630	Democratic Republic of the Congo	001—CONGO-GSM
		002—Celtel
		004—CELLCO
		089—OASIS
		TBA—Intercel[†]
		TBA—Supercell Sprl[†]
631	Angola	002—UNITEL
632	Guinea-Bissau	

MCC	Country	MNC
633	Seychelles	001—Cable & Wireless
		010—AIRTEL
634	Sudan	001—MobiTel
635	Rwanda, Republic of	010—Rwandacell
636	Ethiopia	001—ETMTN
637	Somali Democratic Republic	001—BARAKAAT
		010—Nationlink
		082—Telsom Mobile
638	Djibouti	
639	Kenya	002—SAFARICOM
		003—Kencell
640	Tanzania	001—TRITEL
		002—Mobitel
		003—ZANTEL
		004—Vodacom
		005—Celtel Tanzania
641	Uganda	001—CelTel Cellular
		010—MTN-Uganda
		011—UTL Mobile Network
642	Burundi	001—Spacetel
		002—SAFARIS
		TBA—Telecel[†]
643	Mozambique	001—Mcel
645	Zambia	001—CELTEL
		002—Telecel Zambia
646	Madagascar	001—Madacom
		002—ANTARIS
647	Reunion	002—Outremer Telecom
		010—SRR
		TBA—Orange Reunion[†]

continues

MCC	Country	MNC
648	Zimbabwe	001—NETONE
		003—Telecel
		004—Econet
649	Namibia	001—MTC
650	Malawi	001—Callpoint 900
		010—CelTel
651	Lesotho	001—Vodacom Lesotho (Pty)
		002—Econet Ezi-Cel
652	Botswana	001—MASCOM
		002—Vista Cellular
653	Swaziland	010—Swazi MTN
654	Comoros	
655	South Africa	001—Vodacom
		007—Cell C (Pty)
		010—MTN
657	Eritrea	
702	Belize	067—Belize Telecommunications
704	Guatemala	
706	El Salvador	001—CTE Telecom Personal
		002—DIGICEL
708	Honduras	
710	Nicaragua	TBA—ENITEL[†]
712	Costa Rica	001—I.C.E.
714	Panama	TBA—Cable & Wireless[†]
716	Peru	010—TIM Peru
722	Argentine Republic	007—UNIFON
		034—Telecom Personal
		035—PORT-HABLE
724	Brazil	031—Oi
		TBA—TIM[†]

MCC	Country	MNC
730	Chile	001—Entel PCS
		010—Entel PCS
732	Colombia	
734	Venezuela	001—Infonet
		002—DIGITEL
		003—DIGICEL
736	Bolivia	001—Nuevatel PCS
		002—Entel
738	Guyana	
740	Ecuador	
742	French Guiana	
744	Paraguay	001—VOX
		002—Hutchison Telecommunications
746	Suriname	001—ICMS
		002—TELESUR
748	Uruguay	
8XX	Reserved	
901	Global Mobile Satellite System	001—ICO Global
		002—NetSystem International
		002—Iridium
		004—GlobalStar
		005—Thuraya RMSS Network
		006—Constellation System

TBA = To Be Assigned

[†] = Forthcoming 3G Network

ITU and ANSI Protocol Comparison

This appendix highlights some of the key differences between the ITU-T C7 and ANSI SS7 protocols.

ITU-T protocols are used on the international plane; every country that wishes to connect to the International C7 network worldwide strictly adheres to these protocols. The comparison presented here is between the North American ANSI protocols (national plane) and the ITU-T recommendations that are to be adapted for use on the national plane. Apart from North America, China and Japan made some modifications outside of the ITU national recommendation framework; however, we do not discuss these here.

Message Transfer Part 3

ANSI [1] uses 24-bit Point Codes (PCs) for addressing, while ITU [52] uses 14 bits. This is a result of the greater number of nodes needing to be addressed within North America. China also uses 24-bit PCs to ease numbering strain.

ANSI uses an 8-bit SLS (formerly 5-bit—it actually still supports both), while ITU uses 4 bits and its corresponding load-sharing mechanism is different. (See Chapter 7, "Message Transfer Part 3 (MTP3)" for more information.)

There are some differences in terms of the Service Indicator (part of the SIO) values. Spare and reserved fields differ slightly, and ANSI [1] uses the SI value 2 (Signaling network management messages' special messages).

ANSI assigns message priorities to manage congestion, while ITU does not. ANSI network congestion is measured in four levels: 0 (lowest) through 3 (highest). Each network message is assigned a congestion priority code (level). As the congestion level increases, lower priority messages are not allowed to be sent.

ISDN User Part

ANSI ISUP [3] is based on the ITU ISUP [75–78] recommendations and adheres to the signaling procedures, parameters, and message types without great exceptions. Therefore, it can be considered a nationalized ISUP. As expected, many of the timers have different values; some timers belong in ITU only, and some belong in ANSI only. ANSI does not specify many ITU messages/parameters and many additional messages/parameters that have been added. The ITU and ANSI Timers are listed in Appendix H, "ISUP Timers for ANSI/ETSI/ITU-T Applications." The ITU and ANSI messages are listed in Appendix B, "ISUP Messages (ANSI/UK/ETSI/ITU-T)."

Signaling Connection User Part

ITU [58–63] and ANSI [2] have identical message sets.

ITU SCCP has an *Importance* parameter in the Connection Request, Connection Confirm, Connection Refused, and Released messages, and ANSI does not.

ANSI and ITU state different lengths for the *Calling Party Address* and the *Data* parameters that are used inside Unitdata and Unitdata Service messages.

The specified subsystem numbers (SSNs) are the same, except ANSI specifies SSN 11, 13, and 14 as "Reserved," and ITU specifies them as *ISDN supplementary services*, *broadband ISDN edge-to-edge applications*, and *TC test responder*, respectively.

SCCP management differs between ANSI and ITU in terms of the number of messages available. ITU provides six SCCP management messages, while ANSI provides a total of nine. For more details see Chapter 9, "Signaling Connection Control Part SCCP."

Transaction Capabilities User Part

Variations are much greater at the TCAP level; the variations are so great above TCAP that a comparison could only be made in general terms.

While ITU [82–86] uses the term "message types," ANSI [3] uses the term "package types." ANSI TCAP has seven messages, as opposed to ITU-T TCAP's five. ITU-T TCAP does not have the concept of permission.

Table J-1 shows the comparable messages used in the two protocols.

Table J-1   *ANSI and ITU TCAP Messages*

ANSI "Package Types"	ITU-T "Message Types"
Unidirectional	Unidirectional
Query with Permission	Begin
Query without Permission	
Response	End
Conversation with Permission	Continue
Conversation without Permission	
Abort	Abort

APPENDIX **K**

SS7 Standards

This appendix presents a list of the SS7 standards, including where to obtain them. Only the protocol definition documents are referenced where appropriate. In addition to protocol definition documents, there are a number of supporting documents for most of the protocols listed. A significant number of the supporting documents can be found in the References.

ITU-T Recommendations

Table K-1 shows the International Telecommunications Union (ITU-T) protocol specification documents.

Table K-1   *ITU-T Protocol Specification Documents*

Protocol	Documents
MTP2	Q.703
MTP3	Q.704
MTP3b	Q.2210
TUP	Q.721 to Q.724
ISUP	Q.761 to Q.764
BISUP	Q.2761 to Q.2764
International ISUP	Q.767
SCCP	Q.711 to Q.714
TCAP	Q.771 to Q.774
INAP CS-1	Q.1218
INAP CS-2	Q.1228
INAP CS-3	Q.1238.1 to Q.1238.7
INAP CS-4	Q.1248.1 to Q.1248.7
BICC CS-1	Q.1901
BICC CS-2	Q.1902.1 to Q.1902.6, Q.1930, Q.1950, Q.1970, Q.1990

To obtain a copy of a standard, contact the International Telecommunications Union (ITU) at the following address:

ITU
Sales and Marketing Division
Place des Nations
CH-1211 Geneva 20
Switzerland
Telephone: +41 22 730 61 41 (English)
Telephone: +41 22 730 61 42 (French)
Telephone: +41 22 730 61 43 (Spanish)
Telex: 421 000 uit ch
Fax: +41 22 730 51 94
Email: sales@itu.int
URL: *http://www.itu.int/publications/*

ETSI Publications

Table K-2 shows the European Telecommunications Standards Institute (ETSI) protocol specification documents.

Table K-2   *ETSI Protocol Specification Documents*

Protocol	Documents
MTP	EN 300 008-1
MTP3b	ETSI EN 301 004-1
TUP+	ETR 256
ISUP	EN 300 356-1
ISUP SS	EN 300 356-2 to EN 300 356-12, EN 300 356-14 to EN 300 356-22
SCCP	ETS 300 009-1
TCAP	ETS 300 134, ETS 300 287-1
MAP	ETS 300 599
CAP	TS 101 046
DTAP	ETS 300 940
BSSMAP	ETS 300 590

To obtain a standard, contact the European Telecommunications Standards Institute (ETSI) at the following address:

ETSI Publications Office
Bolte Postal 152
06921 Sophia-Antipolis Cedex
France
Tel: +33 (0) 4 92 94 42 00
Fax: +33 (0) 4 93 65 47 16
URL: *http://www.etsi.org*

3GPP Publications

Table K-3 shows the 3rd Generation Partnership Project (3GPP™) protocol specification documents.

Table K-3   *3GPP Specification Documents*

Protocol	Documents
MAP	29.002
CAP	29.078
DTAP	4.08
BSSMAP	9.08
RANAP	29.108

To obtain a standard, contact the 3GPP at the following address:

ETSI
Mobile Competence Centre
650, route des Lucioles
06921 Sophia-Antipolis Cedex
France
Email: 3gppcontact@etsi.org
URL: *http://www.3gpp.org/specs/specs.htm*

ANSI Standards

Table K-4 shows the American National Standards Institute (ANSI) protocol specification documents.

Table K-4   *ANSI Protocol Specification Documents*

Protocol	Documents
MTP	T1.111
SCCP	T1.112
ISUP	T1.113
TCAP	T1.114

To obtain a standard, contact the American National Standards Institute (ANSI) at the following address:

ANSI
25 West 43rd Street,
4th Floor
New York, NY 10036
United States of America
Tel: +1 212 642 4900
Fax: +1 212 398 0023
Email: info@ansi.org

URL: *http://www.ansi.org*

Telcordia Standards

The following are the Telcordia protocol specification documents for AIN:

* GR-246
* GR-1298
* GR-1299

To obtain a standard, contact Telcordia at the following address:

Telcordia Technologies, Inc. (Direct Sales)
8 Corporate Place, PYA 3A-184
Piscataway, NJ 08854-4156
United States of America
Tel: +1 800 521 2673 (US and Canada)
Tel: +1 732 699 5800 (Outside of North America)
Email: telecom-info@telcordia.com
URL: *http://www.telcordia.com*

BSI and BTNR standards

Table K-6 shows the British Standards Institute (BSI) and British Telecom Network Requirements (BTNR) protocol specification documents. The BSI documents supercede the BTNR documents.

Table K-5   *British Standards Institute (BSI) and British Telecom Network Requirements (BTNR) Protocol Specification Documents*

Protocol	BSI Documents	BNTR Documents
MTP	SPEC 005	146
IUP	SPEC 006	5167
ISUP	SPEC 007	5167
SCCP	SPEC 003	145
TCAP	SPEC 004	140

To obtain a standard, contact the British Standards Institute (BSI) at the following address:

BSI
389 Chiswick High Road
London
W4 4AL
United Kingdom
Tel: +44 (0) 20 8996 9000
Fax: +44 (0)20 8996 7001
Email: cservices@bsi-global.com
URL: *http://www.bsi-global.com*

IETF Documents

Table K-7 shows the Internet Engineering Task Force (IETF) protocol specification documents.

Table K-6   *IETF Specification Documents*

Protocol	IETF Documents
SCTP	RFC2960, RFC3309
M2UA	RFC3331
M3UA	RFC3332
IUA	RFC3057

To obtain a standard, contact the Internet Engineering Task Force (IETF) at the following URL:

URL: *http://www.ietf.org*

Test Documents

Table K-8 shows protocol test specification documents that the ITU-T and ETSI have made available. Please see Chapter 16, "SS7 Testing," for more information on the test specifications.

Table K-7 *Protocol Test Specification Documents*

Protocol	ITU-T Documents	ETSI Documents
MTP2	Q.781	ETS 300 336
MTP3	Q.782	ETS 300 336
TUP	Q.783	-
ISUP	Q.784.1 to Q.784.3	EN 300 356-33
ISUP SS	Q.785	EN 300 356-33
SCCP	Q.786	ETS 300 009-3
TCAP	Q.787	ETS 300 344

Tektronix Supporting Traffic

Example L-1 shows the Message Transfer Part 2 (MTP2) exchange of Link Status Signal Units (LSSUs) that is used to bring a link into alignment, and prove it before using it for the first time or following recovery. For more information, refer to Chapter 6, "Message Transfer Part 2 (MTP2)."

Example L-1 *A Trace File of a Link Alignment (Captured on Tektronix K1297)*

```
+--------------------+------------------------+--------------+------------+
¦Long Time           ¦From                    ¦2. Prot       ¦2. MSG      ¦
+--------------------+------------------------+--------------+------------+
¦11:02:14,125,970    ¦1:B (Tx):16             ¦MTP-L2        ¦LSSU-SIOS   ¦
¦11:02:14,126,618    ¦1:A (Rx):16             ¦MTP-L2        ¦LSSU-SIOS   ¦
¦11:02:14,126,981    ¦1:B (Tx):16             ¦MTP-L2        ¦LSSU-SIO    ¦
¦11:02:14,128,477    ¦1:A (Rx):16             ¦MTP-L2        ¦LSSU-SIO    ¦
¦11:02:28,530,771    ¦1:A (Rx):16             ¦MTP-L2        ¦LSSU-SIO    ¦
¦11:02:28,531,557    ¦1:A (Rx):16             ¦MTP-L2        ¦LSSU-SIO    ¦
¦11:02:28,532,943    ¦1:A (Tx):16             ¦MTP-L2        ¦LSSU-SIOS   ¦
¦11:02:28,533,316    ¦1:B (Rx):16             ¦MTP-L2        ¦LSSU-SIOS   ¦
¦11:02:28,533,822    ¦1:A (Tx):16             ¦MTP-L2        ¦LSSU-SIN    ¦
¦11:02:28,535,127    ¦1:B (Rx):16             ¦MTP-L2        ¦LSSU-SIN    ¦
¦11:02:28,536,134    ¦1:B (Rx):16             ¦MTP-L2        ¦LSSU-SIN    ¦
¦11:02:28,538,793    ¦1:B (Tx):16             ¦MTP-L2        ¦LSSU-SIN    ¦
¦11:02:28,540,793    ¦1:A (Rx):16             ¦MTP-L2        ¦LSSU-SIN    ¦
¦11:02:29,083,821    ¦1:B (Rx):16             ¦MTP-L2        ¦LSSU-SIN    ¦
¦11:02:29,084,078    ¦1:A (Rx):16             ¦MTP-L2        ¦LSSU-SIN    ¦
¦11:02:29,086,544    ¦1:B (Tx):16             ¦MTP-L2        ¦FISU        ¦
¦11:02:29,087,064    ¦1:A (Tx):16             ¦MTP-L2        ¦FISU        ¦
```

Example L-2 shows a global system for mobile communication (GSM) Mobile Application Part (MAP) operation updateLocation being sent from a Visitor Location Register (VLR) to a Home Location Register (HLR) to inform it that the mobile subscriber has roamed into a new VLR area. The example shows the other protocols layers, which show how MAP is encapsulated inside Transaction Capabilities Part (TCAP); TCAP, in itself, is encapsulated inside of Signaling Connection Control Part (SCCP). SCCP, in turn, is encapsulated inside MTP. For more information, see Chapter 13, "GSM and ANSI-41 Mobile Application Part (MAP)."

Example L-2 *A Trace of the MAP Operation updateLocation Being Sent from a VLR to a HLR (Captured on Tektronix K1297)*

```
+----------+--------------------------------------+------------------------------------+
¦BITMASK   ¦ID Name                               ¦Comment or Value                    ¦
+----------+--------------------------------------+------------------------------------+
¦07:10:47 AM,077,259  C7HLR2-MSC1-2-10-0-2 -..  MTP-L2  MSU  SCCP  UDT  MAP  BEG        ¦
¦MTP Level 2 (MTP-L2)  MSU (= Message Signal Unit)                                      ¦
¦Message Signal Unit                                                                    ¦
¦-0110010 ¦Backward Sequence Number               ¦50                                    ¦
¦1------- ¦Backward Indicator Bit                 ¦1                                     ¦
¦-1111010 ¦Forward Sequence Number                ¦122                                   ¦
¦0------- ¦Forward Indicator Bit                  ¦0                                     ¦
¦--111111 ¦Length Indicator                       ¦63                                    ¦
¦00------ ¦Spare                                  ¦0                                     ¦
¦----0011 ¦Service Indicator                      ¦SCCP                                  ¦
¦--00---- ¦Sub-Service: Priority                  ¦Spare/priority 0 (U.S.A. only)        ¦
¦10------ ¦Sub-Service: Network Ind               ¦National message                      ¦
¦**b14*** ¦Destination Point Code                 ¦11-2-16-3                             ¦
¦**b14*** ¦Originating Point Code                 ¦11-3-00-2                             ¦
¦CCITT Blue Book SCCP (SCCP)  UDT (= Unitdata)                                          ¦
¦Unitdata                                                                               ¦
¦1001---- ¦Signalling Link Selection              ¦9                                     ¦
¦00001001 ¦SCCP Message Type                      ¦9                                     ¦
¦----0000 ¦Protocol Class                         ¦Class 0                               ¦
¦0000---- ¦Message Handling                       ¦No special options                    ¦
¦00000011 ¦Pointer to parameter                   ¦3                                     ¦
¦00000101 ¦Pointer to parameter                   ¦5                                     ¦
¦00001001 ¦Pointer to parameter                   ¦9                                     ¦
¦Called address parameter                                                               ¦
¦00000010 ¦Parameter Length                       ¦2                                     ¦
¦-------0 ¦Point Code Indicator                   ¦PC absent                             ¦
¦------1- ¦Subsystem No. Indicator                ¦SSN present                           ¦
¦--0000-- ¦Global Title Indicator                 ¦No global title included              ¦
¦-1------ ¦Routing Indicator                      ¦Route on DPC + Subsystem No.          ¦
¦0------- ¦For national use                       ¦0                                     ¦
¦00000110 ¦Subsystem number                       ¦HLR                                   ¦
¦Calling address parameter                                                              ¦
¦00000100 ¦Parameter Length                       ¦4                                     ¦
¦-------1 ¦Point Code Indicator                   ¦PC present                            ¦
¦------1- ¦Subsystem No. Indicator                ¦SSN present                           ¦
¦--0000-- ¦Global Title Indicator                 ¦No global title included              ¦
¦-1------ ¦Routing Indicator                      ¦Route on DPC + Subsystem No.          ¦
¦0------- ¦For national use                       ¦0                                     ¦
¦**b14*** ¦Calling Party SPC                      ¦11-3-00-2                             ¦
¦00------ ¦Spare                                  ¦0                                     ¦
¦00000111 ¦Subsystem number                       ¦VLR                                   ¦
¦Data parameter                                                                         ¦
¦01010110 ¦Parameter length                       ¦86                                    ¦
¦**B86*** ¦Data                                   ¦62 55 48 04 fa 87 3a 1e 6b 1a 28...  ¦
¦GSM 09.02 Rev 3.8.0 (MAP)  BEG (= Begin)                                               ¦
¦Begin                                                                                  ¦
¦01100010 ¦Tag                                    ¦(APPL C [2])                          ¦
```

Example L-2 *A Trace of the MAP Operation updateLocation Being Sent from a VLR to a HLR (Captured on Tektronix K1297) (Continued)*

```
¦01010100 ¦Length                          ¦84
¦1 Origination Transaction ID
¦01001000 ¦Tag                             ¦(APPL P [8])
¦00000100 ¦Length                          ¦4
¦***B4*** ¦Orig Trans ID                   ¦4203166238
¦2 User Abort Information
¦01101011 ¦Tag                             ¦(APPL C [11])
¦00011010 ¦Length                          ¦26
¦2.1 External
¦00101000 ¦Tag                             ¦(UNIV C External)
¦00011000 ¦Length                          ¦24
¦**B24*** ¦Contents                        ¦06 06 00 11 86 05 01 01 01 a0 0d...
¦3 Component Portion
¦01101100 ¦Tag                             ¦(APPL C [12])
¦00110000 ¦Length                          ¦48
¦3.1 Invoke
¦10100001 ¦Tag                             ¦(CONT C [1])
¦00101110 ¦Length                          ¦46
¦3.1.1 Invoke ID
¦00000010 ¦Tag                             ¦(UNIV P Integer)
¦00000001 ¦Length                          ¦1
¦00000001 ¦Invoke ID value                 ¦1
¦3.1.2 Local Operation
¦00000010 ¦Tag                             ¦(UNIV P Integer)
¦00000001 ¦Length                          ¦1
¦00000010 ¦Operation Code                  ¦Update Location
¦3.1.3 Parameter Sequence
¦00110000 ¦Tag                             ¦(UNIV C Sequence (of))
¦00100110 ¦Length                          ¦38
¦3.1.3.1 IMSI
¦00000100 ¦Tag                             ¦(UNIV P OctetString)
¦00001000 ¦Length                          ¦8
¦**b60*** ¦MCC + MNC + MSIN                ¦'505029000011031'
¦1111---- ¦Filler                          ¦15
¦3.1.3.2 Msc Number
¦10000001 ¦Tag                             ¦(CONT P [1])
¦00000110 ¦Length                          ¦6
¦1------- ¦Extension Indicator             ¦No Extension
¦-001---- ¦Nature of Address               ¦International number
¦----0001 ¦Numbering Plan Indicator        ¦ISDN Telephony No plan (E.164)
¦**b36*** ¦MSC Address Signals             ¦'6129802011'
¦1111---- ¦Filler                          ¦15
¦3.1.3.3 VLR Number
¦00000100 ¦Tag                             ¦(UNIV P OctetString)
¦00000110 ¦Length                          ¦6
¦1------- ¦Extension Indicator             ¦No Extension
¦-001---- ¦Nature of Address               ¦International number
¦----0001 ¦Numbering Plan Indicator        ¦ISDN Telephony No plan (E.164)
```

continues

Example L-2 *A Trace of the MAP Operation updateLocation Being Sent from a VLR to a HLR (Captured on Tektronix K1297) (Continued)*

```
|**b36*** |VLR Address Signals                          |'6129802011'              |
|1111---- |Filler                                       |15                        |
|3.1.3.4 LMs ID                                                                    |
|10001010 |Tag                                          |(CONT P [10])             |
|00000100 |Length                                       |4                         |
|***B4*** |LMS ID                                       |00 01 6c 04               |
```

Example L-3 shows a GSM MAP operation cancelLocation being sent from an HLR to a VLR so the VLR can release resources and data related to a particular subscriber because they have moved into a new VLR area. The example shows all protocol layers. For more information, see Chapter 13, "GSM and ANSI-41 Mobile Application Part (MAP)."

Example L-3 *A Trace of the MAP Operation cancelLocation Being Sent from an HLR to a VLR (Captured on Tektronix K1297)*

```
+---------+-------------------------------------------+------------------------------------+
|BITMASK  |ID Name                                    |Comment or Value                    |
+---------+-------------------------------------------+------------------------------------+
|19:03:40 PM,129,265  C7HLR2-MSC2-2-4-1-2 - RX  MTP-L2  MSU  SCCP  UDT  MAP  BEG           |
|MTP Level 2 (MTP-L2)  MSU (= Message Signal Unit)                                         |
|Message Signal Unit                                                                       |
|-1101110 |Backward Sequence Number                   |110                                 |
|1------- |Backward Indicator Bit                     |1                                   |
|-1000011 |Forward Sequence Number                    |67                                  |
|0------- |Forward Indicator Bit                      |0                                   |
|--111111 |Length Indicator                           |63                                  |
|00------ |Spare                                      |0                                   |
|----0011 |Service Indicator                          |SCCP                                |
|--00---- |Sub-Service: Priority                      |Spare/priority 0 (U.S.A. only)      |
|10------ |Sub-Service: Network Ind                   |National message                    |
|**b14*** |Destination Point Code                     |10-1-14-5                           |
|**b14*** |Originating Point Code                     |10-1-13-4                           |
|CCITT Blue Book SCCP (SCCP)  UDT (= Unitdata)                                             |
|Unitdata                                                                                  |
|0101---- |Signalling Link Selection                  |5                                   |
|00001001 |SCCP Message Type                          |9                                   |
|----0000 |Protocol Class                             |Class 0                             |
|0000---- |Message Handling                           |No special options                  |
|00000011 |Pointer to parameter                       |3                                   |
|00000101 |Pointer to parameter                       |5                                   |
|00001001 |Pointer to parameter                       |9                                   |
|Called address parameter                                                                  |
|00000010 |Parameter Length                           |2                                   |
|-------0 |Point Code Indicator                       |PC absent                           |
|------1- |Subsystem No. Indicator                    |SSN present                         |
|--0000-- |Global Title Indicator                     |No global title included            |
|-1------ |Routing Indicator                          |Route on DPC + Subsystem No.        |
|0------- |For national use                           |0                                   |
```

Example L-3 *A Trace of the MAP Operation cancelLocation Being Sent from an HLR to a VLR (Captured on Tektronix K1297) (Continued)*

```
¦00000111 ¦Subsystem number                    ¦VLR                                    ¦
¦Calling address parameter                                                             ¦
¦00000100 ¦Parameter Length                     ¦4                                      ¦
¦------1 ¦Point Code Indicator                 ¦PC present                             ¦
¦------1- ¦Subsystem No. Indicator              ¦SSN present                            ¦
¦--0000-- ¦Global Title Indicator               ¦No global title included               ¦
¦-1------ ¦Routing Indicator                    ¦Route on DPC + Subsystem No.           ¦
¦0------- ¦For national use                     ¦0                                      ¦
¦**b14*** ¦Calling Party SPC                    ¦10-1-13-4                              ¦
¦00------ ¦Spare                                ¦0                                      ¦
¦00000110 ¦Subsystem number                     ¦HLR                                    ¦
¦Data parameter                                                                        ¦
¦01000000 ¦Parameter length                     ¦64                                     ¦
¦**B64*** ¦Data                                 ¦61 3f 48 04 7a 31 32 cb 6b 1a 28... ¦
¦GSM 09.02 Rev 3.8.0 (MAP)  BEG (= Begin)                                              ¦
¦Begin                                                                                 ¦
¦01100010 ¦Tag                                  ¦(APPL C [2])                           ¦
¦00111110 ¦Length                               ¦62                                     ¦
¦1 Origination Transaction ID                                                          ¦
¦01001000 ¦Tag                                  ¦(APPL P [8])                           ¦
¦00000100 ¦Length                               ¦4                                      ¦
¦***B4*** ¦Orig Trans ID                        ¦2050044619                             ¦
¦2 User Abort Information                                                              ¦
¦01101011 ¦Tag                                  ¦(APPL C [11])                          ¦
¦00011010 ¦Length                               ¦26                                     ¦
¦2.1 External                                                                          ¦
¦00101000 ¦Tag                                  ¦(UNIV C External)                      ¦
¦00011000 ¦Length                               ¦24                                     ¦
¦**B24*** ¦Contents                             ¦06 07 00 11 86 05 02 01 01 a0 0d... ¦
¦3 Component Portion                                                                   ¦
¦01101100 ¦Tag                                  ¦(APPL C [12])                          ¦
¦00011010 ¦Length                               ¦26                                     ¦
¦3.1 Invoke                                                                            ¦
¦10100001 ¦Tag                                  ¦(CONT C [1])                           ¦
¦00011000 ¦Length                               ¦24                                     ¦
¦3.1.1 Invoke ID                                                                       ¦
¦00000010 ¦Tag                                  ¦(UNIV P Integer)                       ¦
¦00000001 ¦Length                               ¦1                                      ¦
¦00000001 ¦Invoke ID value                      ¦1                                      ¦
¦3.1.2 Local Operation                                                                 ¦
¦00000010 ¦Tag                                  ¦(UNIV P Integer)                       ¦
¦00000001 ¦Length                               ¦1                                      ¦
¦00000011 ¦Operation Code                       ¦Cancel Location                        ¦
¦3.1.3 Parameter Sequence                                                              ¦
¦00110000 ¦Tag                                  ¦(UNIV C Sequence (of))                 ¦
¦00010000 ¦Length                               ¦16                                     ¦
¦3.1.3.1 IMSI                                                                          ¦
¦00000100 ¦Tag                                  ¦(UNIV P OctetString)                   ¦
¦00001000 ¦Length                               ¦8                                      ¦
```

continues

Example L-3   *A Trace of the MAP Operation cancelLocation Being Sent from an HLR to a VLR (Captured on Tektronix K1297) (Continued)*

```
|**b60***  |MCC + MNC + MSIN              |'219019000011031'                    |
|1111----  |Filler                       |15                                   |
|3.1.3.2 LMs ID                                                                |
|00000100  |Tag                          |(UNIV P OctetString)                 |
|00000100  |Length                       |4                                    |
|***B4***  |LMS ID                       |00 00 12 71                          |
```

Example L-4 shows a GSM MAP operation provideRoamingNumber being sent from an HLR to a VLR to obtain a Mobile Station Routing Number (MSRN) so that a mobile terminating call can be delivered. The example shows all protocol layers. For more information, see Chapter 13, "GSM and ANSI-41 Mobile Application Part (MAP)."

Example L-4   *A Trace of the MAP Operation provideRoamingNumber that is Being Sent from an HLR to a VLR to request the MSRN (Captured on Tektronix K1297)*

```
+----------+---------------------------------------------+--------------------------------------+
|BITMASK   |ID Name                                      |Comment or Value                      |
+----------+---------------------------------------------+--------------------------------------+
|10:10:37 PM,351,042  C7HLR2-MSC2-1-5-1-3 - RX  MTP-L2  MSU  SCCP  UDT  MAP  BEG                 |
|MTP Level 2 (MTP-L2)  MSU (= Message Signal Unit)                                               |
|Message Signal Unit                                                                             |
|-1000101  |Backward Sequence Number                     |69                                    |
|1-------  |Backward Indicator Bit                       |1                                     |
|-0001010  |Forward Sequence Number                      |10                                    |
|0-------  |Forward Indicator Bit                        |0                                     |
|--111111  |Length Indicator                             |63                                    |
|00------  |Spare                                        |0                                     |
|----0011  |Service Indicator                            |SCCP                                  |
|--00----  |Sub-Service: Priority                        |Spare/priority 0 (U.S.A. only)        |
|10------  |Sub-Service: Network Ind                     |National message                      |
|**b14***  |Destination Point Code                       |12-2-12-3                             |
|**b14***  |Originating Point Code                       |12-2-12-2                             |
|CCITT Blue Book SCCP (SCCP)  UDT (= Unitdata)                                                   |
|Unitdata                                                                                        |
|1111----  |Signalling Link Selection                    |15                                    |
|00001001  |SCCP Message Type                            |9                                     |
|----0000  |Protocol Class                               |Class 0                               |
|1000----  |Message Handling                             |Return message on error               |
|00000011  |Pointer to parameter                         |3                                     |
|00001110  |Pointer to parameter                         |14                                    |
|00010111  |Pointer to parameter                         |23                                    |
|Called address parameter                                                                        |
|00001011  |Parameter Length                             |11                                    |
|-------0  |Point Code Indicator                         |PC absent                             |
|------1-  |Subsystem No. Indicator                      |SSN present                           |
|--0100--  |Global Title Indicator                       |Has transln,n-plan,code,natur         |
|-0------  |Routing Indicator                            |Route on Global Title                 |
|0-------  |For national use                             |0                                     |
|00000111  |Subsystem number                             |VLR                                   |
```

Example L-4 *A Trace of the MAP Operation provideRoamingNumber that is Being Sent from an HLR to a VLR to request the MSRN (Captured on Tektronix K1297) (Continued)*

```
00000000 |Translation Type                 |Not used
----0001 |Encoding Scheme                  |BCD, odd number of digits
0001---- |Numbering Plan                   |ISDN/Telephony (E.164/E.163)
-0000100 |Nat. of Address Indicator        |International number
0------- |Spare                            |0
**b44*** |Called Address Signals           |'25510121110'
0000---- |Filler                           |0
|Calling address parameter
00001001 |Parameter Length                 |9
-------0 |Point Code Indicator             |PC absent
------1- |Subsystem No. Indicator          |SSN present
--0100-- |Global Title Indicator           |Has transln,n-plan,code,natur
-0------ |Routing Indicator                |Route on Global Title
0------- |For national use                 |0
00000110 |Subsystem number                 |HLR
00000000 |Translation Type                 |Not used
----0001 |Encoding Scheme                  |BCD, odd number of digits
0001---- |Numbering Plan                   |ISDN/Telephony (E.164/E.163)
-0000100 |Nature of Address Indicator      |International number
0------- |Spare                            |0
**b28*** |Calling Address Signals          |'3879812'
0000---- |Filler                           |0
|Data parameter
01001100 |Parameter length                 |76
**B76*** |Data                             |62 4b 48 04 7a 2a cc cb 6b 1a 27...
|GSM 09.02 Rev 3.8.0 (MAP)  BEG (= Begin)
|Begin
01100010 |Tag                              |(APPL C [2])
01001010 |Length                           |74
|1 Origination Transaction ID
01001000 |Tag                              |(APPL P [8])
00000100 |Length                           |4
***B4*** |Orig Trans ID                    |2049625291
|2 User Abort Information
01101011 |Tag                              |(APPL C [11])
00011010 |Length                           |26
|2.1 External
00101000 |Tag                              |(UNIV C External)
00011000 |Length                           |24
**B24*** |Contents                         |06 06 00 11 86 05 01 01 01 a0 0e...
|3 Component Portion
01101100 |Tag                              |(APPL C [12])
00100110 |Length                           |38
|3.1 Invoke
10100001 |Tag                              |(CONT C [1])
00100100 |Length                           |36
|3.1.1 Invoke ID
00000010 |Tag                              |(UNIV P Integer)
00000001 |Length                           |1
```

continues

Example L-4   *A Trace of the MAP Operation provideRoamingNumber that is Being Sent from an HLR to a VLR to request the MSRN (Captured on Tektronix K1297) (Continued)*

```
¦00000001 ¦Invoke ID value                       ¦1                                        ¦
¦3.1.2 Local Operation                                                                      ¦
¦00000010 ¦Tag                                   ¦(UNIV P Integer)                         ¦
¦00000001 ¦Length                                ¦1                                        ¦
¦00000100 ¦Operation Code                        ¦Provide Roaming Number                   ¦
¦3.1.3 Parameter Sequence                                                                   ¦
¦00110000 ¦Tag                                   ¦(UNIV C Sequence (of))                   ¦
¦00011100 ¦Length                                ¦28                                       ¦
¦3.1.3.1 IMSI                                                                                ¦
¦10000000 ¦Tag                                   ¦(CONT P [0])                             ¦
¦00001000 ¦Length                                ¦8                                        ¦
¦**b60*** ¦MCC + MNC + MSIN                      ¦'640211600028829'                        ¦
¦1111---- ¦Filler                                ¦15                                       ¦
¦3.1.3.2 Msc Number                                                                          ¦
¦10000001 ¦Tag                                   ¦(CONT P [1])                             ¦
¦00000111 ¦Length                                ¦7                                        ¦
¦1------- ¦Extension Indicator                   ¦No Extension                             ¦
¦-001---- ¦Nature of Address                     ¦International number                      ¦
¦----0001 ¦Numbering Plan Indicator              ¦ISDN Telephony No plan (E.164)           ¦
¦**b44*** ¦MSC Address Signals                   ¦'25510121110'                            ¦
¦1111---- ¦Filler                                ¦15                                       ¦
¦3.1.3.3 MSIsdn                                                                              ¦
¦10000010 ¦Tag                                   ¦(CONT P [2])                             ¦
¦00000111 ¦Length                                ¦7                                        ¦
¦1------- ¦Extension Indicator                   ¦No Extension                             ¦
¦-001---- ¦Nature of Address                     ¦International number                      ¦
¦----0001 ¦Numbering Plan Indicator              ¦ISDN Telephony No plan (E.164)           ¦
¦***B6*** ¦MS ISDN Address Signals               ¦'255981628820'                           ¦
```

Example L-5 shows the result (the roaming number) of a GSM MAP operation provideRoamingNumber being returned from the VLR to the HLR, which (not shown) returns it to the Gateway Mobile Switching Center (MSC), thereby allowing an incoming mobile terminating call to be routed. All protocol layers are shown. For more information, see Chapter 13.

Example L-5   *A Trace of the MAP Operation provideRoamingNumber Result (MSRN Returned in Response) Being Sent from the HLR to the VLR (Captured on Tektronix K1297)*

```
+---------+------------------------------------------------+------------------------------------+
¦BITMASK  ¦ID Name                                         ¦Comment or Value                    ¦
+---------+------------------------------------------------+------------------------------------+
¦10:30:47 AM,033,754  C7HLR2-MSC2-1-2-1-0 - TX  MTP-L2  MSU  SCCP  UDT  MAP  END               ¦
¦MTP Level 2 (MTP-L2)  MSU (= Message Signal Unit)                                              ¦
¦Message Signal Unit                                                                            ¦
¦-1011010 ¦Backward Sequence Number                        ¦90                                  ¦
¦0------- ¦Backward Indicator Bit                          ¦0                                   ¦
¦-1011001 ¦Forward Sequence Number                         ¦89                                  ¦
¦0------- ¦Forward Indicator Bit                           ¦0                                   ¦
```

Example L-5 *A Trace of the MAP Operation provideRoamingNumber Result (MSRN Returned in Response)*
Being Sent from the HLR to the VLR (Captured on Tektronix K1297) (Continued)

```
¦--111111 ¦Length Indicator              ¦63
¦00------ ¦Spare                         ¦0
¦----0011 ¦Service Indicator             ¦SCCP
¦--00---- ¦Sub-Service: Priority         ¦Spare/priority 0 (U.S.A. only)
¦10------ ¦Sub-Service: Network Ind      ¦National message
¦**b14*** ¦Destination Point Code        ¦12-2-12-2
¦**b14*** ¦Originating Point Code        ¦12-2-15-1
¦CCITT Blue Book SCCP (SCCP)  UDT (= Unitdata)
¦Unitdata
¦0010---- ¦Signalling Link Selection     ¦2
¦00001001 ¦SCCP Message Type             ¦9
¦----0000 ¦Protocol Class                ¦Class 0
¦0000---- ¦Message Handling              ¦No special options
¦00000011 ¦Pointer to parameter          ¦3
¦00000101 ¦Pointer to parameter          ¦5
¦00001001 ¦Pointer to parameter          ¦9
¦Called address parameter
¦00000010 ¦Parameter Length              ¦2
¦-------0 ¦Point Code Indicator          ¦PC absent
¦------1- ¦Subsystem No. Indicator       ¦SSN present
¦--0000-- ¦Global Title Indicator        ¦No global title included
¦-1------ ¦Routing Indicator             ¦Route on DPC + Subsystem No.
¦0------- ¦For national use              ¦0
¦00000110 ¦Subsystem number              ¦HLR
¦Calling address parameter
¦00000100 ¦Parameter Length              ¦4
¦-------1 ¦Point Code Indicator          ¦PC present
¦------1- ¦Subsystem No. Indicator       ¦SSN present
¦--0000-- ¦Global Title Indicator        ¦No global title included
¦-1------ ¦Routing Indicator             ¦Route on DPC + Subsystem No.
¦0------- ¦For national use              ¦0
¦**b14*** ¦Calling Party SPC             ¦12-2-15-1
¦00------ ¦Spare                         ¦0
¦00000111 ¦Subsystem number              ¦VLR
¦Data parameter
¦01000111 ¦Parameter length              ¦71
¦**B71*** ¦Data                          ¦64 45 49 04 7a 31 24 cb 6b 26 28...
¦GSM 09.02 Rev 3.8.0 (MAP)  END (= End)
¦End
¦01100100 ¦Tag                           ¦(APPL C [4])
¦01000101 ¦Length                        ¦69
¦1 Destination Transaction ID
¦01001001 ¦Tag                           ¦(APPL P [9])
¦00000100 ¦Length                        ¦4
¦***B4*** ¦Dest Trans ID                 ¦2050041035
¦2 User Abort Information
¦01101011 ¦Tag                           ¦(APPL C [11])
¦00100110 ¦Length                        ¦38
¦2.1 External
```

continues

Example L-5   *A Trace of the MAP Operation provideRoamingNumber Result (MSRN Returned in Response)*
Being Sent from the HLR to the VLR (Captured on Tektronix K1297) (Continued)

```
¦00101000 ¦Tag                           ¦(UNIV C External)                   ¦
¦00100100 ¦Length                        ¦36                                  ¦
¦**B36*** ¦Contents                      ¦06 07 00 11 86 05 01 01 01 a0 19... ¦
¦3 Component Portion                                                          ¦
¦01101100 ¦Tag                           ¦(APPL C [12])                       ¦
¦00010101 ¦Length                        ¦21                                  ¦
¦3.1 Return Result Last                                                       ¦
¦10100010 ¦Tag                           ¦(CONT C [2])                        ¦
¦00010011 ¦Length                        ¦19                                  ¦
¦3.1.1 Invoke ID                                                              ¦
¦00000010 ¦Tag                           ¦(UNIV P Integer)                    ¦
¦00000001 ¦Length                        ¦1                                   ¦
¦00000001 ¦Invoke ID value               ¦1                                   ¦
¦3.1.2 Return Result Sequence                                                 ¦
¦00110000 ¦Tag                           ¦(UNIV C Sequence (of))              ¦
¦00001110 ¦Length                        ¦14                                  ¦
¦3.1.2.1 Local Operation                                                      ¦
¦00000010 ¦Tag                           ¦(UNIV P Integer)                    ¦
¦00000001 ¦Length                        ¦1                                   ¦
¦00000100 ¦Operation Code                ¦Provide Roaming Number              ¦
¦3.1.2.2 Parameter Sequence                                                   ¦
¦00110000 ¦Tag                           ¦(UNIV C Sequence (of))              ¦
¦00001001 ¦Length                        ¦9                                   ¦
¦3.1.2.2.1 Roaming Number                                                     ¦
¦00000100 ¦Tag                           ¦(UNIV P OctetString)                ¦
¦00000111 ¦Length                        ¦7                                   ¦
¦1------- ¦Extension Indicator           ¦No Extension                        ¦
¦-001---- ¦Nature of Address             ¦International number                 ¦
¦----0001 ¦Numbering Plan Indicator      ¦ISDN Telephony No plan (E.164)      ¦
¦**b44*** ¦Roaming Address Signals       ¦'445980091600'                      ¦
¦1111---- ¦Filler                        ¦15                                  ¦
```

Example L-6 shows a GSM MAP operation forwardSM, including the short message
(SMS) it contains. The example only shows the TCAP/MAP layers. For more information,
see Chapter 13.

Example L-6   *Trace of the MAP Operation forwardSM, Including the SMS Message it Contains. Only the*
TCAP/MAP layers are Shown (Captured on Tektronix K1297)

```
+---------+-----------------------------------------+-----------------------------------------+
¦BITMASK  ¦ID Name                                  ¦Comment or Value                         ¦
+---------+-----------------------------------------+-----------------------------------------+
¦2.1.2 Local Operation                                                                        ¦
¦00000010 ¦Tag                                      ¦(UNIV P Integer)                         ¦
¦00000001 ¦Length                                   ¦1                                        ¦
¦00101110 ¦Operation Code                           ¦Forward short message                    ¦
¦2.1.3 Parameter Sequence                                                                     ¦
¦00110000 ¦Tag                                      ¦(UNIV C Sequence (of))                   ¦
```

Example L-6 *Trace of the MAP Operation forwardSM, Including the SMS Message it Contains. Only the TCAP/MAP layers are Shown (Captured on Tektronix K1297) (Continued)*

```
|00110011 |Length                              |51
|2.1.3.1 Service Centre Address
|10000100 |Tag                                 |(CONT P [4])
|00000110 |Length                              |6
|1------- |Extension Indicator                 |No Extension
|-001---- |Nature of Address                   |International number
|----0001 |Numbering Plan Indicator            |ISDN Telephony No plan (E.164)
|**b36*** |SCA Address Signals                 |'353980500'
|1111---- |Filler                              |15
|2.1.3.2 MSIsdn
|10000010 |Tag                                 |(CONT P [2])
|00000111 |Length                              |7
|1------- |Extension Indicator                 |No Extension
|-001---- |Nature of Address                   |International number
|----0001 |Numbering Plan Indicator            |ISDN Telephony No plan (E.164)
|**b44*** |MS ISDN Address Signals             |'35398239945'
|1111---- |Filler                              |15
|2.1.3.3 SM-RP-UI
|00000100 |Tag                                 |(UNIV P OctetString)
|00100000 |Length                              |32
|**B32*** |SM-RP-UI                            |91 01 0b 91 83 95 78 80 44 f7 00...
|GSM 03.40 3.5.0 (SMTP)  SMSB (= SMS-SUBMIT)
|SMS-SUBMIT
|-------1 |Message type indicator              |1
|-----00- |Spare                               |0
|---10--- |Validity Period format              |TP-VP present, integer
|100----- |Spare                               |- unknown / undefined -
|Message Reference
|00000001 |TP-Message Reference                |1
|Destination Address
|00001011 |Address Length                      |11
|----0001 |Number plan                         |ISDN/telephony numbering plan
|-001---- |Type of number                      |International number
|1------- |Extension bit                       |No Extension
|**b44*** |Destination Address                 |'35398708446'
|1111---- |Filler                              |15
|Protocol Identifier
|---00000 |SM-AL protocol                      |0
|--0----- |Telematic interworking              |No interwork, SME-to-SME prot
|00------ |Spare                               |0
|Data Coding Scheme
|00000000 |TP-Data-Coding Scheme               |0
|Validity Period
|10101101 |Validity Period                     |173
|TP-User-Data
|00010100 |User Data Length                    |21
|**B18*** |User Data                           |"up town, see you soon!"
```

Example L-7 shows an ISUP (ITU Whitebook) call being set up and then released. The call setup uses en bloc signaling, and a total of five messages are exchanged to establish and then release the call. The example shows all protocol layers. For more information, see Chapter 8, "ISDN User Part (ISUP)."

Example L-7   *A Trace of Five ISUP Messages Used to Set Up and Clear a Call Down (Captured on Tektronix K1297)*

```
+---------+----------------------------------------------+----------------------------------------+
¦BITMASK  ¦ID Name                                       ¦Comment or Value                        ¦
+---------+----------------------------------------------+----------------------------------------+
¦2:18:21 PM  1:A (Rx):16  199  300  MTP-L2  MSU  ISUP  IAM  00414736323458  00416859474732        ¦
¦MTP Level 2 (MTP-L2)  MSU (= Message Signal Unit)                                                ¦
¦Message Signal Unit                                                                              ¦
¦-1100100 ¦Backward Sequence Number                      ¦110                                     ¦
¦1------- ¦Backward Indicator Bit                        ¦1                                       ¦
¦-0100010 ¦Forward Sequence Number                       ¦24                                      ¦
¦1------- ¦Forward Indicator Bit                         ¦1                                       ¦
¦--100101 ¦Length Indicator                              ¦37                                      ¦
¦00------ ¦Spare                                         ¦0                                       ¦
¦----0101 ¦Service Indicator                             ¦ISDN User Part                          ¦
¦--00---- ¦Sub-Service: Priority                         ¦Spare/priority 0 (U.S.A. only)          ¦
¦10------ ¦Sub-Service: Network Ind                      ¦National message                        ¦
¦**b14*** ¦Destination Point Code                        ¦101                                     ¦
¦**b14*** ¦Originating Point Code                        ¦200                                     ¦
¦163 TR75 ISDN User Part (04.98) DBP (ISUP)  IAM (= Initial Address)                              ¦
¦Initial Address                                                                                  ¦
¦1000---- ¦Signalling Link Selection                     ¦8                                       ¦
¦**b12*** ¦Circuit Ident Code                            ¦004-20                                  ¦
¦0000---- ¦Spare                                         ¦0                                       ¦
¦00000001 ¦Message Type                                  ¦1                                       ¦
¦------00 ¦Satellite indicator                           ¦No satellite circuit in the connecti¦
¦----00-- ¦Continuity Check Ind.                         ¦Cont check not required                 ¦
¦---0---- ¦Echo Control Device Ind                       ¦O/G half echo dev not included          ¦
¦000----- ¦Spare                                         ¦0                                       ¦
¦-------0 ¦Nat./Internat. Indicator                      ¦Treat as a national call                ¦
¦-----00- ¦End-to-End Method Ind                         ¦No end-to-end method available          ¦
¦----0--- ¦Interworking Indicator                        ¦No interworking encountered             ¦
¦---0---- ¦Spare                                         ¦0                                       ¦
¦--1----- ¦ISDN-UP Indicator                             ¦ISDN-UP used all the way                ¦
¦01------ ¦ISDN-UP Preference Ind                        ¦ISDN-UP not required all way            ¦
¦-------0 ¦ISDN Access Indicator                         ¦Originating access non-ISDN             ¦
¦-----00- ¦SCCP Method Indicator                         ¦No indication                           ¦
¦00000--- ¦Spare                                         ¦0                                       ¦
¦00001010 ¦Calling Party's Category                      ¦Ordinary calling subscriber            ¦
¦00000011 ¦Transmission Medium Ind                       ¦3,1 kHz audio                           ¦
¦00000010 ¦Pointer to parameter                          ¦2                                       ¦
¦00001100 ¦Pointer to parameter                          ¦12                                      ¦
¦Called Party Number                                                                              ¦
¦00001010 ¦Parameter Length                              ¦10                                      ¦
¦-0000100 ¦Nature of Address                             ¦International number                    ¦
¦1------- ¦Odd/Even Indicator                            ¦Odd nmb of address signals              ¦
```

Example L-7   *A Trace of Five ISUP Messages Used to Set Up and Clear a Call Down*
(Captured on Tektronix K1297) (Continued)

```
¦----0000 ¦Spare                          ¦0
¦-001---- ¦Numbering Plan Indicator       ¦ISDN numbering plan (E.164)
¦0------- ¦Internal Network No. Ind       ¦Routing to INN allowed
¦**b60*** ¦Called Address Signals         ¦00416859474732f
¦0000---- ¦Filler                         ¦0
¦Calling Party Number
¦00001010 ¦Parameter name                 ¦Calling Party Number
¦00001000 ¦Parameter Length               ¦8
¦-0000100 ¦Nature of Address              ¦International number
¦1------- ¦Odd/Even Indicator             ¦Odd nmb of address signals
¦------11 ¦Screening Indicator            ¦Network provided
¦----00-- ¦Presentation restr. Ind        ¦Presentation allowed
¦-001---- ¦Numbering Plan Indicator       ¦ISDN numbering plan (E.164)
¦0------- ¦Number Incomplete Ind          ¦Number complete
¦**b44*** ¦Calling Address Signals        ¦00414736323458
¦0000---- ¦Filler                         ¦0
¦End of optional parameters
¦00000000 ¦Parameter name                 ¦End of Optional Params
+---------+------------------------------------------------+---------------------------------+
¦BITMASK  ¦ID Name                        ¦Comment or Value
+---------+------------------------------------------------+---------------------------------+
¦2:18:22 PM  1:B (Rx):16  200  101  MTP-L2  MSU  ISUP  ACM
¦MTP Level 2 (MTP-L2)  MSU (= Message Signal Unit)
¦Message Signal Unit
¦-0100010 ¦Backward Sequence Number       ¦24
¦1------- ¦Backward Indicator Bit         ¦1
¦-1100101 ¦Forward Sequence Number        ¦111
¦1------- ¦Forward Indicator Bit          ¦1
¦--001111 ¦Length Indicator               ¦15
¦00------ ¦Spare                          ¦0
¦----0101 ¦Service Indicator              ¦ISDN User Part
¦--00---- ¦Sub-Service: Priority          ¦Spare/priority 0 (U.S.A. only)
¦10------ ¦Sub-Service: Network Ind       ¦National message
¦**b14*** ¦Destination Point Code         ¦200
¦**b14*** ¦Originating Point Code         ¦101
¦163 TR75 ISDN User Part (04.98) DBP (ISUP)  ACM (= Address Complete)
¦Address Complete
¦1000---- ¦Signalling Link Selection      ¦8
¦**b12*** ¦Circuit Ident Code             ¦004-20
¦0000---- ¦Spare                          ¦0
¦00000110 ¦Message Type                   ¦6
¦------10 ¦Charge Indicator               ¦Charge
¦----01-- ¦Called Party's Status Ind      ¦Subscriber free
¦--01---- ¦Called Party's Category Ind    ¦Ordinary subscriber
¦00------ ¦End-to-End Method Ind          ¦No end-to-end method available
¦-------0 ¦Interworking Indicator         ¦No interworking encountered
¦------0- ¦Spare                          ¦0
¦-----1-- ¦ISDN UP Indicator              ¦ISDN UP used all the way
¦----0--- ¦Spare                          ¦0
```

continues

Example L-7 *A Trace of Five ISUP Messages Used to Set Up and Clear a Call Down*
          (Captured on Tektronix K1297) (Continued)

```
|---0---- |ISDN Access Indicator              |Terminating access non-ISDN    |
|--0----- |Echo Control Device Ind            |Inc half echo ctrl dev not incl|
|00------ |SCCP Method Indicator              |No indication                  |
|00000001 |Pointer to parameter               |1                              |
|Opt. Backward Call Indicators                                                |
|00101001 |Parameter name                     |Opt. Backward Call Ind         |
|00000001 |Parameter Length                   |1                              |
|-------1 |In-Band Info Ind                   |In-band info available         |
|------0- |Call Diversion Ind                 |No Indication                  |
|-----0-- |Simple segmentation ind.           |No add. info.                  |
|00000--- |Spare                              |0                              |
|End of optional parameters                                                   |
|00000000 |Parameter name                     |End of Optional Params         |
+---------+------------------------------------+------------------------------+
|BITMASK  |ID Name                            |Comment or Value               |
+---------+------------------------------------+------------------------------+
|2:18:29 PM  1:B (Rx):16  200  101  MTP-L2  MSU  ISUP  ANM                     |
|MTP Level 2 (MTP-L2)  MSU (= Message Signal Unit)                            |
|Message Signal Unit                                                          |
|-0100010 |Backward Sequence Number           |24                             |
|1------- |Backward Indicator Bit             |1                              |
|-1100110 |Forward Sequence Number            |112                            |
|1------- |Forward Indicator Bit              |1                              |
|--010010 |Length Indicator                   |18                             |
|00------ |Spare                              |0                              |
|----0101 |Service Indicator                  |ISDN User Part                 |
|--00---- |Sub-Service: Priority              |Spare/priority 0 (U.S.A. only) |
|10------ |Sub-Service: Network Ind           |National message               |
|**b14*** |Destination Point Code             |200                            |
|**b14*** |Originating Point Code             |101                            |
|163 TR75 ISDN User Part (04.98) DBP (ISUP)  ANM (= Answer)                    |
|Answer                                                                       |
|1000---- |Signaling Link Selection           |8                              |
|**b12*** |Circuit Ident Code                 |004-20                         |
|0000---- |Spare                              |0                              |
|00001001 |Message Type                       |9                              |
|00000001 |Pointer to parameter               |1                              |
|Call History Information                                                     |
|00101101 |Parameter Name                     |Call history info              |
|00000010 |Parameter Length                   |2                              |
|***B2*** |Call history information           |0                              |
|Parameter compatibility Info                                                 |
|00111001 |Parameter Name                     |Parameter compatibility        |
|00000010 |Parameter Length                   |2                              |
|00101101 |1. upgraded parameter              |45                             |
|-------0 |Transit interm. exchange           |Transit interpretation         |
|------0- |PCOMPI Release call ind.           |Do not release call            |
|-----0-- |Send notification ind              |Do not send notification       |
|----0--- |Discard message ind                |Do not discard message         |
|---0---- |Discard parameter ind              |Do not discard parameter       |
|-10----- |Pass on not possible ind           |Discard parameter              |
```

Example L-7 *A Trace of Five ISUP Messages Used to Set Up and Clear a Call Down*
             (Captured on Tektronix K1297) (Continued)

```
¦1------- ¦Extension Indicator                            ¦Last octet                         ¦
¦End of optional parameters                                                                  ¦
¦00000000 ¦Parameter name                                 ¦End of Optional Params             ¦
+---------+------------------------------------------------+-----------------------------------+
¦BITMASK  ¦ID Name                                         ¦Comment or Value                   ¦
+---------+------------------------------------------------+-----------------------------------+
¦2:22:04 PM  1:A (Rx):16  101  200  MTP-L2  MSU  ISUP  REL      Normal clearing               ¦
¦MTP Level 2 (MTP-L2)  MSU (= Message Signal Unit)                                           ¦
¦Message Signal Unit                                                                         ¦
¦-1100110 ¦Backward Sequence Number                        ¦112                                ¦
¦1------- ¦Backward Indicator Bit                          ¦1                                  ¦
¦-0100011 ¦Forward Sequence Number                         ¦25                                 ¦
¦1------- ¦Forward Indicator Bit                           ¦1                                  ¦
¦--001101 ¦Length Indicator                                ¦13                                 ¦
¦00------ ¦Spare                                           ¦0                                  ¦
¦----0101 ¦Service Indicator                               ¦ISDN User Part                     ¦
¦--00---- ¦Sub-Service: Priority                           ¦Spare/priority 0 (U.S.A. only)     ¦
¦10------ ¦Sub-Service: Network Ind                        ¦National message                   ¦
¦**b14*** ¦Destination Point Code                          ¦101                                ¦
¦**b14*** ¦Originating Point Code                          ¦200                                ¦
¦163 TR75 ISDN User Part (04.98) DBP (ISUP)  REL (= Release)                                 ¦
¦Release                                                                                     ¦
¦1000---- ¦Signalling Link Selection                       ¦8                                  ¦
¦**b12*** ¦Circuit Ident Code                              ¦004-20                             ¦
¦0000---- ¦Spare                                           ¦0                                  ¦
¦00001100 ¦Message Type                                    ¦12                                 ¦
¦00000010 ¦Pointer to parameter                            ¦2                                  ¦
¦00000000 ¦Pointer to parameter                            ¦0                                  ¦
¦Cause Indicators                                                                            ¦
¦00000010 ¦Parameter Length                                ¦2                                  ¦
¦----0000 ¦Location                                        ¦User                               ¦
¦---0---- ¦Spare                                           ¦0                                  ¦
¦-00----- ¦Coding Standard                                 ¦CCITT standard                     ¦
¦1------- ¦Extension Indicator 1                           ¦Last octet                         ¦
¦-0010000 ¦Cause Value                                     ¦Normal clearing                    ¦
¦1------- ¦Extension Indicator 2                           ¦Last octet                         ¦
+---------+------------------------------------------------+-----------------------------------+
¦BITMASK  ¦ID Name                                         ¦Comment or Value                   ¦
+---------+------------------------------------------------+-----------------------------------+
¦2:22:04 PM  1:B (Rx):16  200  101  MTP-L2  MSU  ISUP  RLC                                   ¦
¦MTP Level 2 (MTP-L2)  MSU (= Message Signal Unit)                                           ¦
¦Message Signal Unit                                                                         ¦
¦-0100011 ¦Backward Sequence Number                        ¦25                                 ¦
¦1------- ¦Backward Indicator Bit                          ¦1                                  ¦
¦-1100111 ¦Forward Sequence Number                         ¦113                                ¦
¦1------- ¦Forward Indicator Bit                           ¦1                                  ¦
¦--001001 ¦Length Indicator                                ¦9                                  ¦
¦00------ ¦Spare                                           ¦0                                  ¦
¦----0101 ¦Service Indicator                               ¦ISDN User Part                     ¦
```

continues

Example L-7   *A Trace of Five ISUP Messages Used to Set Up and Clear a Call Down*
               (Captured on Tektronix K1297) (Continued)

```
|--00----  |Sub-Service: Priority                     |Spare/priority 0 (U.S.A. only)  |
|10------  |Sub-Service: Network Ind                  |National message                |
|**b14***  |Destination Point Code                    |200                             |
|**b14***  |Originating Point Code                    |101                             |
|163 TR75 ISDN User Part (04.98) DBP (ISUP)  RLC (= Release Complete)                   |
|Release Complete                                                                        |
|1000----  |Signalling Link Selection                 |8                               |
|**b12***  |Circuit Ident Code                        |004-20                          |
|0000----  |Spare                                     |0                               |
|00010000  |Message Type                              |16                              |
|00000000  |Pointer to parameter                      |0                               |
```

Example L-8 shows a switch returning the result of a continuity test. The example shows
protocol layers. For more information, see Chapter 8, "ISDN User Part (ISUP)."

Example L-8   *A Trace of the Result of an ISUP Continuity Test (COT) Message*
               (Captured on Tektronix K1297)

```
+----------+------------------------------------------+------------------------------------+
|BITMASK   |ID Name                                   |Comment or Value                    |
+----------+------------------------------------------+------------------------------------+
|03:46:53,585,393  [1] B (Rx):1:-:56  MTP-L2  MSU  ISUP  COT                               |
|MTP Level 2 (MTP-L2)  MSU (= Message Signal Unit)                                         |
|Message Signal Unit                                                                       |
|-1011010  |Backward Sequence Number                  |90                                  |
|1-------  |Backward Indicator Bit                    |1                                   |
|-0100011  |Forward Sequence Number                   |35                                  |
|1-------  |Forward Indicator Bit                     |1                                   |
|--001100  |Length Indicator                          |12                                  |
|00------  |Spare                                     |0                                   |
|----0101  |Service Indicator                         |ISDN User Part                      |
|--10----  |Sub-Service: Priority                     |priority 2 (U.S.A. only)            |
|10------  |Sub-Service: Network Ind                  |National message                    |
|***B3***  |Destination Point Code                    |150-002-003                         |
|***B3***  |Originating Point Code                    |150-002-001                         |
|Bellcore GR-246-CORE ISDN User Part, 1997 (ISUP)  COT (= Continuity)                      |
|Continuity                                                                                |
|00000100  |Signalling Link Selection                 |4                                   |
|**b14***  |Circuit Ident Code                        |2                                   |
|00------  |Spare                                     |0                                   |
|00000101  |Message Type                              |5                                   |
|-------1  |Continuity indicator                      |Continuity check successful         |
|0000000-  |Spare                                     |0                                   |
```

Example L-9 shows MTP3 of two signaling points exchanging Signaling Link Test Message (SLTM) and Signaling Link Test Acknowledgement (SLTA) messages. The example shows all protocol layers. For more information, see Chapter 7, "Message Transfer Part 3 (MTP3)."

Example L-9 *Trace of MTP3 of Two Signaling Points Exchanging Signaling Link Test Message (SLTM) and Signaling Link Test Acknowledgement (SLTA) Messages (Captured on Tektronix K1297)*

```
+---------+----------------------------------------------+------------------------------------+
|BITMASK  |ID Name                                       |Comment or Value                    |
+---------+----------------------------------------------+------------------------------------+
|03:46:24,907,807  [1] A (Rx):1:-:56  MTP-L2  MSU  T+MS  SLTM                                  |
|MTP Level 2 (MTP-L2)  MSU (= Message Signal Unit)                                             |
|Message Signal Unit                                                                           |
|-0011100 |Backward Sequence Number                      |28                                  |
|1------- |Backward Indicator Bit                        |1                                   |
|-1010001 |Forward Sequence Number                       |81                                  |
|1------- |Forward Indicator Bit                         |1                                   |
|--001100 |Length Indicator                              |12                                  |
|00------ |Spare                                         |0                                   |
|----0010 |Service Indicator                             |Sig netwk test&maint spec msg       |
|--11---- |Sub-Service: Priority                         |priority 3 (U.S.A. only)            |
|10------ |Sub-Service: Network Ind                      |National message                    |
|***B3*** |Destination Point Code                        |150-002-001                         |
|***B3*** |Originating Point Code                        |150-003-000                         |
|Bellcore T1.111 MTP Testing+Maintenance (T+MS)  SLTM (= Signalling link Test Message)         |
|Signalling link Test Message                                                                  |
|00000000 |Signalling Link Selection                     |0                                   |
|----0001 |Heading code 0                                |1                                   |
|0001---- |Heading code 1                                |1                                   |
|----0000 |Signalling Link Code                          |0                                   |
|0010---- |Length Indicator                              |2                                   |
|***B2*** |Test Pattern                                  |05 ba                               |
+---------+----------------------------------------------+------------------------------------+
|BITMASK  |ID Name                                       |Comment or Value                    |
+---------+----------------------------------------------+------------------------------------+
|03:46:24,917,719  [1] B (Rx):1:-:56  MTP-L2  MSU  T+MS  SLTA                                  |
|MTP Level 2 (MTP-L2)  MSU (= Message Signal Unit)                                             |
|Message Signal Unit                                                                           |
|-1010001 |Backward Sequence Number                      |81                                  |
|1------- |Backward Indicator Bit                        |1                                   |
|-0011101 |Forward Sequence Number                       |29                                  |
|1------- |Forward Indicator Bit                         |1                                   |
|--001100 |Length Indicator                              |12                                  |
|00------ |Spare                                         |0                                   |
|----0010 |Service Indicator                             |Sig netwk test&maint spec msg       |
|--11---- |Sub-Service: Priority                         |priority 3 (U.S.A. only)            |
|10------ |Sub-Service: Network Ind                      |National message                    |
|***B3*** |Destination Point Code                        |150-003-000                         |
|***B3*** |Originating Point Code                        |150-002-001                         |
```

continues

Example L-9   *Trace of MTP3 of Two Signaling Points Exchanging Signaling Link Test Message (SLTM) and Signaling Link Test Acknowledgement (SLTA) Messages (Captured on Tektronix K1297) (Continued)*

```
¦Bellcore T1.111 MTP Testing+Maintenance (T+MS)  SLTA (= Signalling link Test Ack mess)  ¦
¦Signalling link Test Ack mess                                                           ¦
¦00000000 ¦Signalling Link Selection                      ¦0                             ¦
¦----0001 ¦Heading code 0                                 ¦1                             ¦
¦0010---- ¦Heading code 1                                 ¦2                             ¦
¦----0000 ¦Signalling Link Code                           ¦0                             ¦
¦0010---- ¦Length Indicator                               ¦2                             ¦
¦***B2*** ¦Test Pattern                                   ¦05 ba                         ¦
```

Example L-10 shows a trace of an ISUP suspend (SUS) message, which is used to allow a subscriber to put a handset down and pick another one up without loosing the call. The example shows all protocol layers. For more information, see Chapter 8, "ISDN User Part (ISUP)."

Example L-10 *A Trace of an ISUP Suspend (SUS) Message (Captured on Tektronix K1297)*

```
+---------+-----------------------------------------+----------------------------------+
¦BITMASK  ¦ID Name                                  ¦Comment or Value                  ¦
+---------+-----------------------------------------+----------------------------------+
¦03:46:56,293,447  [1] A (Rx):1:-:56  MTP-L2  MSU  ISUP  SUS                            ¦
¦MTP Level 2 (MTP-L2)  MSU (= Message Signal Unit)                                      ¦
¦Message Signal Unit                                                                    ¦
¦-0100011 ¦Backward Sequence Number                 ¦35                                ¦
¦1------- ¦Backward Indicator Bit                   ¦1                                 ¦
¦-1011100 ¦Forward Sequence Number                  ¦92                                ¦
¦1------- ¦Forward Indicator Bit                    ¦1                                 ¦
¦--001101 ¦Length Indicator                         ¦13                                ¦
¦00------ ¦Spare                                    ¦0                                 ¦
¦----0101 ¦Service Indicator                        ¦ISDN User Part                    ¦
¦--01---- ¦Sub-Service: Priority                    ¦priority 1 (U.S.A. only)          ¦
¦10------ ¦Sub-Service: Network Ind                 ¦National message                  ¦
¦***B3*** ¦Destination Point Code                   ¦150-002-001                       ¦
¦***B3*** ¦Originating Point Code                   ¦150-002-002                       ¦
¦Bellcore GR-246-CORE ISDN User Part, 1997 (ISUP)  SUS (= Suspend)                      ¦
¦Suspend                                                                                ¦
¦00010100 ¦Signalling Link Selection                ¦20                                ¦
¦**b14*** ¦Circuit Ident Code                       ¦3                                 ¦
¦00------ ¦Spare                                    ¦0                                 ¦
¦00001101 ¦Message Type                             ¦13                                ¦
¦-------1 ¦Network indicated ind                    ¦Network initiated                 ¦
¦0000000- ¦Spare                                    ¦0                                 ¦
¦00000000 ¦Pointer to parameter                     ¦0                                 ¦
```

Example L-11 shows a trace of an AIN CLASS provideValue message, which is used to indicate that the values of the Parameters identified in the Parameter Set are to be provided. The example shows all protocol layers. For more information, see Chapter 11, "Intelligent Networks."

Example L-11 *A Trace of an AIN CLASS provideValue Message (Captured on Tektronix K1297)*

```
+---------+---------------------------------------------+--------------------------------------------+
¦BITMASK  ¦ID Name                                      ¦Comment or Value                            ¦
+---------+---------------------------------------------+--------------------------------------------+
¦04:57:48,076,989 [1] C (Rx):1:-:56  MTP-L2  MSU  SCCP  UDT  TCAP  QRYP                               ¦
¦MTP Level 2 (MTP-L2)  MSU (= Message Signal Unit)                                                   ¦
¦Message Signal Unit                                                                                 ¦
¦-1001010 ¦Backward Sequence Number                     ¦74                                          ¦
¦1------- ¦Backward Indicator Bit                       ¦1                                           ¦
¦-1100110 ¦Forward Sequence Number                      ¦102                                         ¦
¦1------- ¦Forward Indicator Bit                        ¦1                                           ¦
¦--111111 ¦Length Indicator                             ¦63                                          ¦
¦00------ ¦Spare                                        ¦0                                           ¦
¦----0011 ¦Service Indicator                            ¦SCCP                                        ¦
¦--01---- ¦Sub-Service: Priority                        ¦priority 1 (U.S.A. only)                    ¦
¦10------ ¦Sub-Service: Network Ind                     ¦National message                            ¦
¦***B3*** ¦Destination Point Code                       ¦150-005-001                                 ¦
¦***B3*** ¦Originating Point Code                       ¦150-002-001                                 ¦
¦Bellcore SCCP T1.112 GR-246-CORE, issue 2, 12/1997 (SCCP)  UDT (= Unitdata)                         ¦
¦Unitdata                                                                                            ¦
¦00010101 ¦Signaling Link Selection                     ¦21                                          ¦
¦00001001 ¦SCCP Message Type                            ¦9                                           ¦
¦----0000 ¦Protocol Class                               ¦Class 0                                     ¦
¦1000---- ¦Message Handling                             ¦Return message on error                     ¦
¦00000011 ¦Pointer to parameter                         ¦3                                           ¦
¦00001001 ¦Pointer to parameter                         ¦9                                           ¦
¦00001110 ¦Pointer to parameter                         ¦14                                          ¦
¦Called address parameter                                                                            ¦
¦00000110 ¦Parameter Length                             ¦6                                           ¦
¦-------1 ¦Subsystem No. Indicator                      ¦SSN present                                 ¦
¦------0- ¦Point Code Indicator                         ¦PC absent                                   ¦
¦--0010-- ¦Global Title Indicator                       ¦Has translation type                        ¦
¦-0------ ¦Routing Indicator                            ¦Route on Global Title                       ¦
¦1------- ¦For national use                             ¦National address                            ¦
¦00000000 ¦Subsystem number                             ¦SSN not known/not used                      ¦
¦11111011 ¦Translation Type                             ¦CLASS                                       ¦
¦***B3*** ¦Called Address Signals                       ¦'312344'                                    ¦
¦Calling address parameter                                                                           ¦
¦00000101 ¦Parameter Length                             ¦5                                           ¦
¦-------1 ¦Subsystem No. Indicator                      ¦SSN present                                 ¦
¦------1- ¦Point Code Indicator                         ¦PC present                                  ¦
¦--0000-- ¦Global Title Indicator                       ¦No global title included                    ¦
¦-1------ ¦Routing Indicator                            ¦Route on DPC + Subsystem No.                ¦
¦1------- ¦For national use                             ¦National address                            ¦
¦11111011 ¦Subsystem number                             ¦CLASS                                       ¦
¦***B3*** ¦Calling Party SPC                            ¦150-002-001                                 ¦
¦Data parameter                                                                                      ¦
¦01011000 ¦Parameter length                             ¦88                                          ¦
¦**B88*** ¦Data                                         ¦e2 56 c7 04 00 00 a7 00 e8 4e e9...         ¦
¦TCAP + BELLCORE TR-NWT-000246 Issue 3, 1993 (TCAP)  QRYP (= Query With Perm)                        ¦
¦Query With Perm                                                                                     ¦
```

continues

Example L-11 *A Trace of an AIN CLASS provideValue Message (Captured on Tektronix K1297) (Continued)*

¦11100010	¦Tag	¦(PRIV C [2])	
¦01010110	¦Length	¦86	
¦1 Transaction ID			
¦11000111	¦Tag	¦(PRIV P [7])	
¦00000100	¦Length	¦4	
¦***B4***	¦Originating ID	¦00 00 a7 00	
¦2 Component Sequence			
¦11101000	¦Tag	¦(PRIV C [8])	
¦01001110	¦Length	¦78	
¦2.1 Invoke			
¦11101001	¦Tag	¦(PRIV C [9])	
¦00100001	¦Length	¦33	
¦2.1.1 Component ID			
¦11001111	¦Tag	¦(PRIV P [15])	
¦00000001	¦Length	¦1	
¦00000000	¦Component ID value	¦0	
¦2.1.2 National Operation			
¦11010000	¦Tag	¦(PRIV P [16])	
¦00000010	¦Length	¦2	
¦1-------	¦Reply Required	¦Yes	
¦-1111110	¦Operation Family	¦Miscellaneous	
¦00000001	¦Operation Specifier	¦Queue Call	
¦2.1.3 Parameter Set			
¦11110010	¦Tag	¦(PRIV C [18])	
¦00011000	¦Length	¦24	
¦2.1.3.1 Service Key			
¦10101010	¦Tag	¦(CONT C [10])	
¦00010110	¦Length	¦22	
¦2.1.3.1.1 Digits			
¦10000100	¦Tag	¦(CONT P [4])	
¦00001001	¦Length	¦9	
¦00000110	¦Type of Digits	¦Destination Number	
¦000000--	¦Spare	¦0	
¦------0-	¦Presentation Restriction	¦No	
¦-------0	¦Inter/national	¦National	
¦0010----	¦Numbering Plan	¦Telephony CCITT Rec E.163	
¦----0001	¦Encoding	¦BCD	
¦00001010	¦Number of Digits	¦10	
¦***B5***	¦Digits	¦'3123441962'	
¦2.1.3.1.2 Digits			
¦10000100	¦Tag	¦(CONT P [4])	
¦00001001	¦Length	¦9	
¦00001011	¦Type of Digits	¦Calling Directory Number	
¦000000--	¦Spare	¦0	
¦------0-	¦Presentation Restriction	¦No	
¦-------0	¦Inter/national	¦National	
¦0010----	¦Numbering Plan	¦Telephony CCITT Rec E.163	
¦----0001	¦Encoding	¦BCD	
¦00001010	¦Number of Digits	¦10	
¦***B5***	¦Digits	¦'3129935018'	
¦2.2 Invoke			
¦11101001	¦Tag	¦(PRIV C [9])	

Example L-11 *A Trace of an AIN CLASS provideValue Message (Captured on Tektronix K1297) (Continued)*

```
¦00101001 ¦Length                         ¦41
¦2.2.1 Component ID
¦11001111 ¦Tag                            ¦(PRIV P [15])
¦00000001 ¦Length                         ¦1
¦00000001 ¦Component ID value             ¦1
¦2.2.2 National Operation
¦11010000 ¦Tag                            ¦(PRIV P [16])
¦00000010 ¦Length                         ¦2
¦1------- ¦Reply Required                 ¦Yes
¦-0000001 ¦Operation Family               ¦Parameter
¦00000001 ¦Operation Specifier            ¦Provide Value
¦2.2.3 Parameter Set
¦11110010 ¦Tag                            ¦(PRIV C [18])
¦00100000 ¦Length                         ¦32
¦2.2.3.1 Service Key
¦10101010 ¦Tag                            ¦(CONT C [10])
¦00010110 ¦Length                         ¦22
¦2.2.3.1.1 Digits
¦10000100 ¦Tag                            ¦(CONT P [4])
¦00001001 ¦Length                         ¦9
¦00000110 ¦Type of Digits                 ¦Destination Number
¦000000-- ¦Spare                          ¦0
¦------0- ¦Presentation Restriction       ¦No
¦-------0 ¦Inter/national                 ¦National
¦0010---- ¦Numbering Plan                 ¦Telephony CCITT Rec E.163
¦----0001 ¦Encoding                       ¦BCD
¦00001010 ¦Number of Digits               ¦10
¦***B5*** ¦Digits                         ¦'3123441962'
¦2.2.3.1.2 Digits
¦10000100 ¦Tag                            ¦(CONT P [4])
¦00001001 ¦Length                         ¦9
¦00001011 ¦Type of Digits                 ¦Calling Directory Number
¦000000-- ¦Spare                          ¦0
¦------0- ¦Presentation Restriction       ¦No
¦-------0 ¦Inter/national                 ¦National
¦0010---- ¦Numbering Plan                 ¦Telephony CCITT Rec E.163
¦----0001 ¦Encoding                       ¦BCD
¦00001010 ¦Number of Digits               ¦10
¦***B5*** ¦Digits                         ¦'3129935018'
¦2.2.3.2 Busy/Idle Status
¦10001011 ¦Tag                            ¦(CONT P [11])
¦00000000 ¦Length                         ¦0
¦2.2.3.3 Call Forwarding Status
¦10001100 ¦Tag                            ¦(CONT P [12])
¦00000000 ¦Length                         ¦0
¦2.2.3.4 Terminating Restrictions
¦10001110 ¦Tag                            ¦(CONT P [14])
¦00000000 ¦Length                         ¦0
¦2.2.3.5 DN to Ln Service Type Mapping
¦10001111 ¦Tag                            ¦(CONT P [15])
¦00000000 ¦Length                         ¦0
```

Example L-12 shows a trace of an INAP requestReportBCSmEvent, which is an Intelligent Network (IN) request sent from a Service Control Point (SCP) to a switch to request notification when a specified event in the Basic Call Model (BCM) occurs. The example shows all protocol layers. For more information, see Chapter 11, "Intelligent Networks."

Example L-12 *A Trace of an INAP requestReportBCSmEvent (Captured on Tektronix K1297)*

```
+---------+-----------------------------------------+----------------------------------------+
¦BITMASK  ¦ID Name                                  ¦Comment or Value                        ¦
+---------+-----------------------------------------+----------------------------------------+
¦11:30:17 AM  1:A (Rx):2  400  0  MTP-L2  MSU  SCCP  UDT  INAP  CON  Disconnect Forward C   ¦
¦MTP Level 2 (MTP-L2)  MSU (= Message Signal Unit)                                          ¦
¦Message Signal Unit                                                                        ¦
¦-0111001 ¦Backward Sequence Number                 ¦60                                      ¦
¦1------- ¦Backward Indicator Bit                   ¦1                                       ¦
¦-0000000 ¦Forward Sequence Number                  ¦0                                       ¦
¦1------- ¦Forward Indicator Bit                    ¦1                                       ¦
¦--111111 ¦Length Indicator                         ¦60                                      ¦
¦00------ ¦Spare                                    ¦0                                       ¦
¦----0011 ¦Service Indicator                        ¦SCCP                                    ¦
¦--00---- ¦Sub-Service: Priority                    ¦Spare/priority 0 (U.S.A. only)          ¦
¦10------ ¦Sub-Service: Network Ind                 ¦National message                        ¦
¦**b14*** ¦Destination Point Code                   ¦0                                       ¦
¦**b14*** ¦Originating Point Code                   ¦400                                     ¦
¦ITU-T White Book SCCP (SCCP)  UDT (= Unitdata)                                             ¦
¦Unitdata                                                                                   ¦
¦0101---- ¦Signalling Link Selection                ¦5                                       ¦
¦00001001 ¦SCCP Message Type                        ¦9                                       ¦
¦----0001 ¦Protocol Class                           ¦Class 1                                 ¦
¦0000---- ¦Message Handling                         ¦No special options                      ¦
¦00000011 ¦Pointer to parameter                     ¦3                                       ¦
¦00000111 ¦Pointer to parameter                     ¦7                                       ¦
¦00001011 ¦Pointer to parameter                     ¦11                                      ¦
¦Called address parameter                                                                   ¦
¦00000100 ¦Parameter Length                         ¦4                                       ¦
¦-------1 ¦Point Code Indicator                     ¦PC present                              ¦
¦------1- ¦Subsystem No. Indicator                  ¦SSN present                             ¦
¦--0000-- ¦Global Title Indicator                   ¦No global title included                ¦
¦-1------ ¦Routing Indicator                        ¦Route on DPC + Subsystem No.            ¦
¦0------- ¦For national use                         ¦0                                       ¦
¦**b14*** ¦Called Party SPC                         ¦0                                       ¦
¦00------ ¦Spare                                    ¦0                                       ¦
¦11111011 ¦Subsystem number                         ¦MSC                                     ¦
¦Calling address parameter                                                                  ¦
¦00000100 ¦Parameter Length                         ¦4                                       ¦
¦-------1 ¦Point Code Indicator                     ¦PC present                              ¦
¦------1- ¦Subsystem No. Indicator                  ¦SSN present                             ¦
¦--0000-- ¦Global Title Indicator                   ¦No global title included                ¦
¦-1------ ¦Routing Indicator                        ¦Route on DPC + Subsystem No.            ¦
¦0------- ¦For national use                         ¦0                                       ¦
¦**b14*** ¦Calling Party SPC                        ¦400                                     ¦
¦00------ ¦Spare                                    ¦0                                       ¦
¦11111100 ¦Subsystem number                         ¦SMLC                                    ¦
```

Example L-12 *A Trace of an INAP requestReportBCSmEvent (Captured on Tektronix K1297) (Continued)*

```
¦Data parameter
¦11000001 ¦Parameter length                    ¦193
¦**B193** ¦Data                                 ¦65 81 be 48 03 86 00 fb 49 03 ea 00
¦Ericsson INAP CS1+ (INAP)  CON (= Continue)
¦Continue
¦01100101 ¦Tag                                  ¦(APPL C [5])
¦***B2*** ¦Length                               ¦190
¦1 Origination Transaction ID
¦01001000 ¦Tag                                  ¦(APPL P [8])
¦00000011 ¦Length                               ¦3
¦***B3*** ¦Orig Trans ID                        ¦8782075
¦2 Destination Transaction ID
¦01001001 ¦Tag                                  ¦(APPL P [9])
¦00000011 ¦Length                               ¦3
¦***B3*** ¦Dest Trans ID                        ¦15335678
¦3 Component Portion
¦01101100 ¦Tag                                  ¦(APPL C [12])
¦***B2*** ¦Length                               ¦177
¦3.1 Invoke
¦10100001 ¦Tag                                  ¦(CONT C [1])
¦00000110 ¦Length                               ¦6
¦3.1.1 Invoke ID
¦00000010 ¦Tag                                  ¦(UNIV P Integer)
¦00000001 ¦Length                               ¦1
¦00000100 ¦Invoke ID value                      ¦4
¦3.1.2 Local Operation
¦00000010 ¦Tag                                  ¦(UNIV P Integer)
¦00000001 ¦Length                               ¦1
¦00010010 ¦Operation Code                       ¦Disconnect Forward Connection
¦3.2 Invoke
¦10100001 ¦Tag                                  ¦(CONT C [1])
¦00101100 ¦Length                               ¦44
¦3.2.1 Invoke ID
¦00000010 ¦Tag                                  ¦(UNIV P Integer)
¦00000001 ¦Length                               ¦1
¦00000101 ¦Invoke ID value                      ¦5
¦3.2.2 Local Operation
¦00000010 ¦Tag                                  ¦(UNIV P Integer)
¦00000001 ¦Length                               ¦1
¦00101110 ¦Operation Code                       ¦Send Charging Information
¦3.2.3 Parameter Sequence
¦00110000 ¦Tag                                  ¦(UNIV C Sequence (of))
¦00100100 ¦Length                               ¦36
¦3.2.3.1 S CI Bill Charg Characts
¦10100000 ¦Tag                                  ¦(CONT C [0])
¦00011101 ¦Length                               ¦29
¦3.2.3.1.1 Charging Information
¦10100000 ¦Tag                                  ¦(CONT C [0])
¦00011011 ¦Length                               ¦27
¦3.2.3.1.1.1 Charge Message
```

continues

Example L-12 *A Trace of an INAP requestReportBCSmEvent (Captured on Tektronix K1297) (Continued)*

```
|10100001 |Tag                                    |(CONT C [1])
|00011001 |Length                                 |25
|3.2.3.1.1.1.1 Event Type Charging
|10000001 |Tag                                    |(CONT P [1])
|00000001 |Length                                 |1
|00000001 |Event Type Charging                    |Tariff Information
|3.2.3.1.1.1.2 Event Specific Info Charg
|10100010 |Tag                                    |(CONT C [2])
|00010100 |Length                                 |20
|3.2.3.1.1.1.2.1 Tariff Information
|10100000 |Tag                                    |(CONT C [0])
|00010010 |Length                                 |18
|3.2.3.1.1.1.2.1.1 Number Of Start Pulses
|10000000 |Tag                                    |(CONT P [0])
|00000001 |Length                                 |1
|00000001 |Number Of Start Pulses                 |1
|3.2.3.1.1.1.2.1.2 Start Interval
|10000001 |Tag                                    |(CONT P [1])
|00000001 |Length                                 |1
|00000001 |Start Interval                         |1
|3.2.3.1.1.1.2.1.3 Start Interval Accuracy
|10000010 |Tag                                    |(CONT P [2])
|00000001 |Length                                 |1
|00000011 |Start Interval Accuracy                |Seconds
|3.2.3.1.1.1.2.1.4 Number Of Periodic Pulses
|10000011 |Tag                                    |(CONT P [3])
|00000001 |Length                                 |1
|00000001 |Number Of Periodic Pulses              |1
|3.2.3.1.1.1.2.1.5 Periodic Interval
|10000100 |Tag                                    |(CONT P [4])
|00000001 |Length                                 |1
|00000001 |Periodic Interval                      |1
|3.2.3.1.1.1.2.1.6 Periodic Interval Accuracy
|10000101 |Tag                                    |(CONT P [5])
|00000001 |Length                                 |1
|00000011 |Periodic Interval Accuracy             |Seconds
|3.2.3.2 Leg Id Constr
|10100001 |Tag                                    |(CONT C [1])
|00000011 |Length                                 |3
|3.2.3.2.1 Sending Side Id
|10000000 |Tag                                    |(CONT P [0])
|00000001 |Length                                 |1
|00000001 |Sending Side Id                        |1
|3.3 Invoke
|10100001 |Tag                                    |(CONT C [1])
|01001011 |Length                                 |75
|3.3.1 Invoke ID
|00000010 |Tag                                    |(UNIV P Integer)
|00000001 |Length                                 |1
|00000111 |Invoke ID value                        |7
|3.3.2 Local Operation
|00000010 |Tag                                    |(UNIV P Integer)
```

Example L-12 *A Trace of an INAP requestReportBCSmEvent (Captured on Tektronix K1297) (Continued)*

```
¦00000001 ¦Length                               ¦1
¦00010111 ¦Operation Code                       ¦Request Report BCSMEvent
¦3.3.3 Parameter Sequence
¦00110000 ¦Tag                                  ¦(UNIV C Sequence (of))
¦01000011 ¦Length                               ¦67
¦3.3.3.1 BCSM Events
¦10100000 ¦Tag                                  ¦(CONT C [0])
¦01000001 ¦Length                               ¦65
¦3.3.3.1.1 Bcsmevent
¦00110000 ¦Tag                                  ¦(UNIV C Sequence (of))
¦00001011 ¦Length                               ¦11
¦3.3.3.1.1.1 Event Type BCSM
¦10000000 ¦Tag                                  ¦(CONT P [0])
¦00000001 ¦Length                               ¦1
¦11111110 ¦Event Type BCSM                      ¦O Called Party Not Reachable
¦3.3.3.1.1.2 Monitor Mode
¦10000001 ¦Tag                                  ¦(CONT P [1])
¦00000001 ¦Length                               ¦1
¦00000000 ¦Monitor Mode                         ¦Interrupted
¦3.3.3.1.1.3 Leg Id Constr
¦10100010 ¦Tag                                  ¦(CONT C [2])
¦00000011 ¦Length                               ¦3
¦3.3.3.1.1.3.1 Sending Side Id
¦10000000 ¦Tag                                  ¦(CONT P [0])
¦00000001 ¦Length                               ¦1
¦00000010 ¦Sending Side Id                      ¦2
¦3.3.3.1.2 Bcsmevent
¦00110000 ¦Tag                                  ¦(UNIV C Sequence (of))
¦00001011 ¦Length                               ¦11
¦3.3.3.1.2.1 Event Type BCSM
¦10000000 ¦Tag                                  ¦(CONT P [0])
¦00000001 ¦Length                               ¦1
¦00000101 ¦Event Type BCSM                      ¦O Called Party Busy
¦3.3.3.1.2.2 Monitor Mode
¦10000001 ¦Tag                                  ¦(CONT P [1])
¦00000001 ¦Length                               ¦1
¦00000000 ¦Monitor Mode                         ¦Interrupted
¦3.3.3.1.2.3 Leg Id Constr
¦10100010 ¦Tag                                  ¦(CONT C [2])
¦00000011 ¦Length                               ¦3
¦3.3.3.1.2.3.1 Sending Side Id
¦10000000 ¦Tag                                  ¦(CONT P [0])
¦00000001 ¦Length                               ¦1
¦00000010 ¦Sending Side Id                      ¦2
¦3.3.3.1.3 Bcsmevent
¦00110000 ¦Tag                                  ¦(UNIV C Sequence (of))
¦00001011 ¦Length                               ¦11
¦3.3.3.1.3.1 Event Type BCSM
¦10000000 ¦Tag                                  ¦(CONT P [0])
¦00000001 ¦Length                               ¦1
```

continues

Example L-12 *A Trace of an INAP requestReportBCSmEvent (Captured on Tektronix K1297) (Continued)*

```
|00000100 |Event Type BCSM                    |Route Select Failure
|3.3.3.1.3.2 Monitor Mode
|10000001 |Tag                                |(CONT P [1])
|00000001 |Length                             |1
|00000000 |Monitor Mode                       |Interrupted
|3.3.3.1.3.3 Leg Id Constr
|10100010 |Tag                                |(CONT C [2])
|00000011 |Length                             |3
|3.3.3.1.3.3.1 Sending Side Id
|10000000 |Tag                                |(CONT P [0])
|00000001 |Length                             |1
|00000010 |Sending Side Id                    |2
|3.3.3.1.4 Bcsmevent
|00110000 |Tag                                |(UNIV C Sequence (of))
|00001011 |Length                             |11
|3.3.3.1.4.1 Event Type BCSM
|10000000 |Tag                                |(CONT P [0])
|00000001 |Length                             |1
|00000110 |Event Type BCSM                    |O No Answer
|3.3.3.1.4.2 Monitor Mode
|10000001 |Tag                                |(CONT P [1])
|00000001 |Length                             |1
|00000000 |Monitor Mode                       |Interrupted
|3.3.3.1.4.3 Leg Id Constr
|10100010 |Tag                                |(CONT C [2])
|00000011 |Length                             |3
|3.3.3.1.4.3.1 Sending Side Id
|10000000 |Tag                                |(CONT P [0])
|00000001 |Length                             |1
|00000010 |Sending Side Id                    |2
|3.3.3.1.5 Bcsmevent
|00110000 |Tag                                |(UNIV C Sequence (of))
|00001011 |Length                             |11
|3.3.3.1.5.1 Event Type BCSM
|10000000 |Tag                                |(CONT P [0])
|00000001 |Length                             |1
|00000111 |Event Type BCSM                    |O Answer
|3.3.3.1.5.2 Monitor Mode
|10000001 |Tag                                |(CONT P [1])
|00000001 |Length                             |1
|00000000 |Monitor Mode                       |Interrupted
|3.3.3.1.5.3 Leg Id Constr
|10100010 |Tag                                |(CONT C [2])
|00000011 |Length                             |3
|3.3.3.1.5.3.1 Sending Side Id
|10000000 |Tag                                |(CONT P [0])
|00000001 |Length                             |1
|00000010 |Sending Side Id                    |2
|3.4 Invoke
|10100001 |Tag                                |(CONT C [1])
|00010111 |Length                             |23
|3.4.1 Invoke ID
```

Example L-12 *A Trace of an INAP requestReportBCSmEvent (Captured on Tektronix K1297) (Continued)*

```
│00000010 │Tag                          │(UNIV P Integer)
│00000001 │Length                       │1
│00001000 │Invoke ID value              │8
│3.4.2 Local Operation
│00000010 │Tag                          │(UNIV P Integer)
│00000001 │Length                       │1
│00010111 │Operation Code               │Request Report BCSMEvent
│3.4.3 Parameter Sequence
│00110000 │Tag                          │(UNIV C Sequence (of))
│00001111 │Length                       │15
│3.4.3.1 BCSM Events
│10100000 │Tag                          │(CONT C [0])
│00001101 │Length                       │13
│3.4.3.1.1 Bcsmevent
│00110000 │Tag                          │(UNIV C Sequence (of))
│00001011 │Length                       │11
│3.4.3.1.1.1 Event Type BCSM
│10000000 │Tag                          │(CONT P [0])
│00000001 │Length                       │1
│00001010 │Event Type BCSM              │O Abandon
│3.4.3.1.1.2 Monitor Mode
│10000001 │Tag                          │(CONT P [1])
│00000001 │Length                       │1
│00000000 │Monitor Mode                 │Interrupted
│3.4.3.1.1.3 Leg Id Constr
│10100010 │Tag                          │(CONT C [2])
│00000011 │Length                       │3
│3.4.3.1.1.3.1 Sending Side Id
│10000000 │Tag                          │(CONT P [0])
│00000001 │Length                       │1
│00000001 │Sending Side Id              │1
│3.5 Invoke
│10100001 │Tag                          │(CONT C [1])
│00010011 │Length                       │19
│3.5.1 Invoke ID
│00000010 │Tag                          │(UNIV P Integer)
│00000001 │Length                       │1
│00000110 │Invoke ID value              │6
│3.5.2 Local Operation
│00000010 │Tag                          │(UNIV P Integer)
│00000001 │Length                       │1
│00010100 │Operation Code               │Connect
│3.5.3 Parameter Sequence
│00110000 │Tag                          │(UNIV C Sequence (of))
│00001011 │Length                       │11
│3.5.3.1 Destination Routing Address
│10100000 │Tag                          │(CONT C [0])
│00001001 │Length                       │9
│3.5.3.1.1 Called Party Number
│00000100 │Tag                          │(UNIV P OctetString)
```

continues

Example L-12 *A Trace of an INAP requestReportBCSmEvent (Captured on Tektronix K1297) (Continued)*

```
00000111  Length                        7
0-------  Odd/Even Indicator            Even number of address signals
-0000011  Nature of Address             National (significant) number
0-------  Internal Network No. Ind      Routing to INN allowed
-001----  Numbering Plan Indicator      ISDN Nr.plan (E.164)
----0000  Spare                         0
***B5***  Called Address Signals        5342542365
```

Cause Values

Table M-1 lists the ITU-T cause values. Table M-2 lists additional cause values that are specific to ANSI networks. The cause value, which is included as a field in each ISUP REL message, indicates the reason a call was released. Bits 1 through 4 indicate the value within each cause class, while bits 5 through 7 indicate the class.

Table M-1 *ITU-T Cause Values*

Cause Values	Definition
	Normal Class
0 0 0 0 0 0 1	Unallocated (unassigned) number
0 0 0 0 0 1 0	No route to specified transit network
0 0 0 0 0 1 1	No route to destination
0 0 0 0 1 0 0	Send special information tone
0 0 0 0 1 0 1	Misdialed trunk prefix
0 0 0 0 1 1 0	Channel unacceptable
0 0 0 0 1 1 1	Call awarded and being delivered in an established channel
0 0 0 1 0 0 0	Preemption
0 0 0 1 0 0 1	Preemption—circuit reserved for reuse
0 0 0 1 1 1 0	Query On Release (QOR)—ported number
0 0 1 0 0 0 0	Normal clearing
0 0 1 0 0 0 1	User busy
0 0 1 0 0 1 0	No user responding
0 0 1 0 0 1 1	No answer from user (user alerted)
0 0 1 0 1 0 0	Subscriber absent

continues

Table M-1 *ITU-T Cause Values (Continued)*

Cause Values	Definition
0 0 1 0 1 0 1	Call rejected
0 0 1 0 1 1 0	Number changed
0 0 1 0 1 1 1	Redirection to new destination
0 0 1 1 0 0 0	Call rejected because of a feature at the destination
0 0 1 1 0 0 1	Exchange routing error
0 0 1 1 0 1 0	Nonselected user clearing
0 0 1 1 0 1 1	Destination out of order
0 0 1 1 1 0 0	Invalid number format (address incomplete)
0 0 1 1 1 0 1	Facility rejected
0 0 1 1 1 1 0	Response to Status Enquiry
0 0 1 1 1 1 1	Normal, unspecified
	Resource Unavailable Class
0 1 0 0 0 1 0	No circuit/channel available
0 1 0 0 1 1 0	Network out of order
0 1 0 0 1 1 1	Permanent frame mode connection out of service
0 1 0 1 0 0 0	Permanent frame mode connection operational
0 1 0 1 0 0 1	Temporary failure
0 1 0 1 0 1 0	Switching equipment congestion
0 1 0 1 0 1 1	Access information discarded
0 1 0 1 1 0 0	Requested circuit/channel not available
0 1 0 1 1 1 0	Precedence call blocked
0 1 0 1 1 1 1	Resource unavailable, unspecified
	Service or Option Unavailable Class
0 1 1 0 0 0 1	Quality of service unavailable
0 1 1 0 0 1 0	Requested facility not subscribed
0 1 1 0 1 0 1	Outgoing calls barred within Closed User Group
0 1 1 0 1 1 1	Incoming calls barred within Closed User Group
0 1 1 1 0 0 1	Bearer capability not authorized
0 1 1 1 0 1 0	Bearer capability not presently available

Table M-1   *ITU-T Cause Values (Continued)*

Cause Values	Definition
0 1 1 1 1 1 0	Inconsistency in designated outgoing access information and subscriber class
0 1 1 1 1 1 1	Service or option unavailable, unspecified
	Service or Option Not Implemented Class
1 0 0 0 0 0 1	Bearer capability not implemented
1 0 0 0 0 1 0	Channel type not implemented
1 0 0 0 1 0 1	Requested facility not implemented
1 0 0 0 1 1 0	Only restricted digital information bearer capability is available
1 0 0 1 1 1 1	Service or option not implemented, unspecified
	Invalid Message Class
1 0 1 0 0 0 1	Invalid call reference value
1 0 1 0 0 1 0	Identified channel does not exist
1 0 1 0 0 1 1	A suspended call exists but this call identity does not
1 0 1 0 1 0 0	Call identity in use
1 0 1 0 1 0 1	No call suspended
1 0 1 0 1 1 0	Call that has the requested call identity has been cleared
1 0 1 0 1 1 1	User not member of Closed User Group
1 0 1 1 0 0 0	Incompatible destination
1 0 1 1 0 1 0	Nonexisting Closed User Group
1 0 1 1 0 1 1	Invalid transit network selection
1 0 1 1 1 1 1	Invalid message, unspecified
	Protocol Error Class
1 1 0 0 0 0 0	Mandatory information element is missing
1 1 0 0 0 0 1	Message type nonexistent or not implemented
1 1 0 0 0 1 0	Message not compatible with call state, or message type nonexistent or not implemented
1 1 0 0 0 1 1	Information element/parameter nonexistent or not implemented
1 1 0 0 1 0 0	Invalid information element contents
1 1 0 0 1 0 1	Message not compatible with call state

continues

Table M-1   *ITU-T Cause Values (Continued)*

Cause Values	Definition
1 1 0 0 1 1 0	Recovery on timer expiry
1 1 0 0 1 1 1	Parameter nonexistent or not implemented, passed on
1 1 0 1 1 1 0	Message with unrecognized parameter, discarded
1 1 0 1 1 1 1	Protocol error, unspecified
	Interworking Class
1 1 1 1 1 1 1	Interworking, unspecified

Table M-2   *ANSI-Specific Cause Values*

Cause Value	Definition
	Normal Class
0 0 1 0 1 1 1	Unallocated destination number
0 0 1 1 0 0 0	Unknown business group
0 0 1 1 0 0 1	Exchange routing error
0 0 1 1 0 1 0	Misrouted call to a ported number
0 0 1 1 0 1 1	Number portability Query On Release number not found
	Resource Unavailable Class
0 1 0 1 1 0 1	Preemption
0 1 0 1 1 1 0	Precedence Call blocked
	Service or Option not available
0 1 1 0 0 1 1	Call type incompatible with service requested
0 1 1 0 1 1 0	Call blocked because of group restrictions

ACRONYMS

0–9

1G — 1st Generation (Mobile Wireless)

2G — 2nd Generation (Mobile Wireless)

2.5G — 2nd and a half Generation (Mobile Wireless)

3G — 3rd Generation (Mobile Wireless)

3GPP — 3rd Generation Partnership Project

3GPP2 — 3rd Generation Partnership Project 2

A

A — Interface between BSS and GSM-NSS

A-link — Access Link

AAL — ATM Adaptation layerL

AAL2 — ATM Adaptation Layer Type 2

AAL5 — ATM Adaptation Layer Type 5

A$_{bis}$ — Interface between BTS and BSC

AC — Authentication Center

ACD — Automatic Call Distribution

ACK — Acknowledgement

ACQ — All Call Query

AERM — Alignment Error Rate Monitor

AIN — Advanced Intelligent Network

ANI — Automatic Number Identification

AMPS — Advanced/American Mobile Phone Service

ANSI — American National Standards Institute

APDU — Application Protocol Data Unit

ASE — Application Service Element (Intelligent Network)

ASN.1 — Abstract Syntax Notation One

ASP — Application Service Part

ATM — Asynchronous Transfer Mode

AuC — Authentication Center

AUTOVON — Automatic Voice Network

B

B-ISDN — Broadband ISDN

BCF — Base Station Control Function

BEC — Basic Error Correction

BER — Basic Encoding Rules

BCF — Bearer Control Function

BCSM — Basic Call State Model (Intelligent Network)

BICC — Bearer Independent Call Control

BCD — Binary Coded Decimal

BHCA — Busy Hour Call Attempt(s)

BINAP — Broadband IN Application Protocol

B-ISDN — Broadband ISDN

B-ISUP—Broadband ISDN User Part

B link—Bridge Link

BISDN—Broadband ISDN

BISUP—Broadband ISUP

BOC—Bell Operating Company

BRI—Basic Rate Interface

BS—Base Station

BSC—Base Station Controller

BSDB—Business Service Database

BSS—Base Station Subsystem

BSSGP—Base Station Subsystem GPRS Protocol

BSSAP—Base Station System Application Part

BSSMAP—Base Station Subsystem Mobile Application Part

BSSOMAP—Base Station System Operation and Maintenance Application Part

BTS—Base Transceiver Station

C

C7—CCITT Signaling System 7

CAS—Channel-Associated Signaling

CAMEL—Customised Application for Mobile Network Enhanced Logic

CAP—CAMEL Application Part

CC—Country Code

CCBS—Completion of Calls to Busy Subscriber

C link—Cross-Link

CCF—Connection Control Function (Intelligent Network)

CCAF—Call Control Agent Function (Intelligent Network)

CCITT—Comité Consultatif International Télégraphique et Téléphonique (The International Telegraph and Telephone Consultative Committee)

CCS—Common Channel Signaling

CCS7—Common Channel Signaling System No. 7

CDMA—Code Division Multiple Access

CDR—Call Detail Record

CDR—Charging Data Record

CEPT—Conférence des Administrations Européennes des Postes et Telecommunications

CFB—Call Forwarding Busy

CFNRc—Call Forwarding on Mobile Subscriber Not Reachable Supplementary Service

CFNRy—Call Forwarding on No Reply Supplementary Service

CIC—Circuit Identification Code

CLASS—Custom Local Area Signaling Service

CLEC—Competitive Local Exchange Carrier

CLI—Calling Line Identification

CLIP—Calling Line Identification Presentation

CLIR—Calling Line Identification Restriction

CUG—Closed User Group

COLI—Connected Line Identity

COLP—Connected Line Identification Presentation

COLR—Connected Line Identification Restriction

CNAM—Calling Name

CNAP—Calling Name Presentation

CPE—Customer Premises Equipment

CPL—Call Processing Language

CPS—Calls Per Second

CPU—Central Processor Unit

CRC—Cyclic Redundancy Check

CS—Capability Set

CS—Circuit Switched

CS-x—Capability Set x

CSD—Circuit Switched Data

CSE—Camel Service Environment

CTI—Computer Telephony Integration

CUG—Closed User Group

CW—Call Waiting

D

DAC—Digital-to-Analog Converter

DCE—Data Communications Equipment

DCS1800—Digital Communications Systems at 1800 MHz

DDI—Direct Dial-In

DFP—Distributed Functional Plane (Intelligent Network)

D Link—Diagonal Link

DP—Detection Point

DPC—Destination Point Code

DPNSS—Digital Private Network Signaling System

DTAP—Direct Transfer Application Part

DTE—Data Terminal Equipment

DTMF—Dual-Tone Multiple Frequency

DUP—Data User Part

DUT—Device Under Test

DS0—Digital Signal Level 0 (64Kbits/sec)

DS1—Digital Signal Level 1 (1.544Mbits/sec)

DSS 1—Digital Subscriber Signaling System 1

DTMF—Dial Tone Multi-Frequency

E

E911—Enhanced 911

E-1—European Digital Signal Level 1 (2.048Mbits/sec)

E-GGSN—Enhanced GGSN

E-HLR—Enhanced HLR

EAEO—Equal Access End Office

EDGE—Enhanced Data rates for GSM Evolution

EGPRS—Enhanced General Packet Radio System

EIA—Electronic Industries Association

EIR—Equipment Identity Register

E Link—Extended Link

EDP—Event Detection Point (Intelligent Network)

EKTS—Electronic Key Telephone Set

EMS—Enhanced Messaging Service

EO—End Office

ETR—ETSI Technical Report

ETSI—European Telecommunications Standards Institute

F

FAX—Facsimile

FCC—Federal Communications Commission

FDDI—Fibre Distributed Data Interface

FEA—Functional Entity Actions (Intelligent Network)

FIB—Forward Indicator Bit

FISU—Fill-In Signal Unit

FE—Functional Entity

FPLMTS—Future Public Land Mobile Telecommunications System

G

G_b—Interface between BSS and SGSN

G_c—Interface between GGSN and HLR

G_d—Interface between SGSN and GMSC

G_i—Interface between GGSN and external PDN

G_f—Interface between SGSN and EIR

G_n—Interface between SGSN and GGSN

G_p—Interface between SGSN and GGSN of external PLMN

G_r—Interface between SGSN and HLR

G_s—Interface between SGSN and VMSC/VLR

GR—Generic Requirement

GFP—Global Functional Plane (Intelligent Network)

GGSN—Gateway GPRS Support Node

GMSC—Gateway Mobile Switching Center

GMLC—Gateway Mobile Location Centre

GPRS—General Packet Radio Service

GPS—Global Positioning System

GSL—Global Service Logic

GSM—Global System for Mobile communications

gsmSCF—GSM Service Control Function

GSN—GPRS Support Node

GTP—GPRS Tunneling Protocol

GT—Global Title

GTT—Global Title Translation

H

HANDO—Handover

HE—Home Environment

HHO—Hard Handover

HLR—Home Location Register

HLSIB—High-Level SIB

HSCSD—High-Speed Circuit Switched Data

HPLMN—Home Public Land Mobile Network

I

ICW—Internet Call Waiting

IEEE—Institute of Electronic and Electrical Engineers

IETF—Internet Engineering Task Force

ILEC—Incumbent Local Exchange Carrier

IMEI—International Mobile Equipment Identity

IMSI—International Mobile Subscriber Identity

IMT—Inter-Machine Trunk

IMT-2000—International Mobile Telephony 2000

IN—Intelligent Network

INAP—IN Application Protocol

INCM—IN Conceptual Model

IP—Intelligent Peripheral

IP—Internet Protocol

IPv4—Internet Protocol version 4

IPv6—Internet Protocol version 6

ISP—Internet Service Provider

ISDN—Integrated Service Digital Network

ISO—International Standards Organizations

ISP—Internet Service Provider

ISUP—ISDN User Part

IS-41—Interim Standard-41

ITU—International Telecommunications Union

ITU-TS—ITU Telecommunications Sector

IUT—Implementation Under Test

IXC—Inter Exchange Carrier

J - K - L

JAIN—Java APIs for Integrated Networks (Intelligent Network)

Kbps—Kilobits per second

L1—Level 1 (physical layer)

L2—Level 2 (data link layer)

L2ML—Level 2 Management Link

LAPD—Link Access Procedure on the D Channel

LAPB—Link Access Protocol Balanced

LAPDm—Link Access Protocol on the Dm channel

LATA—Local Access Transport Area

LE—Local Exchange

LEC—Local Exchange Carrier

LI—Length Indicator

LIDB—Line Information Database

LLI—Logical Link Identifier

LMSI—Local Mobile Subscriber Identity

LNP—Local Number Portability

LRN—Location Routing Number

LSB—Least Significant Bit

LSSU—Link Status Signal Unit

M

MAP—Mobile Application Part

Mbps—Megabits per second

MCC—Mobile Country Code

MCI—Malicious Call Identification Supplementary Service

MCID—Malicious Call Identification

MDF—Main Distribution Frame

MEGACO—Media Gateway Control

MF—Multi-Frequency

MG—Media Gateway

MGC—Media Gateway Controller

MGCP—Media Gateway Control Protocol

MGCF—Media Gateway Control Function

MIN—Mobile Identification Number

MGW—Media Gateway

MLPP—Multi-Level Precedence and Pre-emption

MM—Mobility Management

MMI—Man-Machine Interface

MNC—Mobile Network Code

MNP—Mobile Number Portability

MS—Mobile Station

MSB—Most Significant Bit

MSC—Mobile Switching Center

MS-ISDN—Mobile Station ISDN Number (also known as Mobile Subscriber ISDN Number)

MSP—Multiple Subscriber Profile

MSRN—Mobile Station Roaming Number

MSRN—Mobile Station Roaming Number

MSU—Message Signal Unit

MTC—Mobile Terminating Call

MTP—Message Transfer Part

MTP3b—Message Transfer Part 3 Broadband

N

NAI—Network Access Identifier

NBAP—Node B Application Part

NE—Network Element

NEL—Next Event List (Intelligent Network)

NSS—Network Switching Subsystem

NISDN—Narrowband ISDN

NP—Number Portability

NP—Numbering Plan

NPA—Numbering Plan Area

NSP—Network Services Part

NSDU—Network Service Data Unit

NSS—Network Sub-System

NUP—National User Part (SS7)

O

O&M—Operations and Maintenance

OAMP—Operations, Administration, Maintenance, and Provisioning

OLO—Other Licensed Operator

OMAP—Operations, Maintenance, and Administration Part

O_BCSM—Originating Basic Call State Model (Intelligent Network)

OMC—Operation and Maintenance Center

OPC—Originating Point Code

OSA—Open Service Architecture

OSI—Open System Interconnection

ONO—Other Network Operator

P

P-TMSI—Packet TMSI

PABX—Private Automatic Branch eXchange

PBX—Private Branch eXchange

PC—Point Code

PCM—Pulse Code Modulation

PCR—Preventive Cyclic Retransmission

PCS—Personal Communication Systems

PCU—Packet Control Unit

PDN—Public Data Network

PDH—Plesiochronous Digital Hierarchy

PDU—Protocol Data Unit

PICS—Protocol Implementation Conformance Statement

PIXIT—Protocol Implementation eXtra Information for Testing

PE—Physical Entity

PIC—Point in Call (Intelligent Network)

PIN—Personal Identification Number

PIXT—Protocol Implementation eXtra information for Testing

PINT—PSTN and Internet Interworking

PLMN—Public Land Mobile Network

PNP—Private Numbering Plan

PNO—Public Network Operator

POI—Point of Interconnection

POP—Point of Presence

PP—Physical Plane (Intelligent Network)

PRI—Primary Rate Interface

PSPDN—Packet Switched Public Data Network

PSTN—Public Switched Telephone Network

PTT—Post, Telephone, and Telegraph

PVC—Permanent Virtual Circuit

PVN—Private Virtual Network

Q - R

QoR—Query on Release

QoS—Quality of Service

R-SGW—Roaming Signaling Gateway

RADIUS—Remote Authentication Dial-Up Service

RF—Radio Frequency

RFC—Request for Comments

RAN—Radio Access Network

RANAP—Radio Access Network Application Part

RBOC—Regional Bell Operating Company

RFC—Request for Comment

RNSAP—Radio Network Subsystem Application Part

ROSE—Remote Operations Service Element

RTP—Release to Pivot

S

SAAL—Signaling ATM Adaptation Layer

SACF—Single Association Control Function

SACF—Service Access Control Function (in IMT-2000)

SAP—Service Access Point

SAPI—Service Access Point Identifier

SC—Service Centre (used for SMS)

SCCP—Signaling Connection Control Part

SCE—Service Creation Environment (Intelligent Network)

SCLC—SCCP Connectionless Control

SCMG—SCCP Management

SCOC—SCCP Connection-Oriented Control

SCEF—Service Creation Environment Function (Intelligent Network)

SCF—Service Control Function (Intelligent Network)

SCF—Service Capability Feature (VHE/OSA context)

SCP—Service Control Point

SCTP—Stream Control Transmission Protocol

SCRC—SCCP Routing Control

SDLC—Signaling Data Link Connection

SDF—Service Data Function (Intelligent Network)

SDL—Service Description Language (Intelligent Network)

SDU—Service Data Unit (Intelligent Network)

SF—Service Feature (Intelligent Network)

SF—Service Factory (TINA)

SG—Signaling Gateway

SGCP—Simple Gateway Control Protocol

SGSN—Serving GPRS Support Node

SMS—Short Message Service

SIB—Service Independent Building Block (Intelligent Network)

SIF—Signaling Information Field

SigTran—Signaling Transport

SIM—GSM Subscriber Identity Module

SIP—Session Initiation Protocol

SIP-T—Session Initiation Protocol for Telephones

SIWF—Shared Interworking Function

SLC—Signaling Link Code

SLP—Service Logic Program (Intelligent Network)

SLS—Signaling Link Selection

SM—Short Message

SMLC—Serving Mobile Location Center

SM-SC—Short Message Service Center

SMS-GMSC—Short Message Service Gateway MSC

SMS-IWMSC—Short Message Service Interworking MSC

SMF—Service Management Function (Intelligent Network)

SMAF—Service Management Access Function (Intelligent Network)

SMS—Short Message Service

SNM—Signaling Network Management

SONET—Synchronous Optical Network

SP—Signaling Point

SP—Service Plane (Intelligent Network)

SPC—Stored Program Control

SPC—Signaling Point Code

SPMO—Service Provider Managed Object

SRF—Specialized Resource Function (Intelligent Network)

SS—Supplementary Service

SS7—Signaling System No. 7

SSF—Service Switching Function (Intelligent Network)

SSN—Subsystem Number

SSP—Service Switching Point

SST—Subsystem Status Test

STP—Signaling Transfer Point

SUERM—Signal Unit Error Rate Monitor

SUT—System Under Test

T

T1—Transmission Carrier 1

TACS—Total Access Communication System

TCP—Transmission Control Protocol

TAPI—Telephony Application Programming Interface

T_BCSM—Terminating Basic Call State Model (Intelligent Network)

TC—Transaction Capabilities

TCAP—Transaction Capabilities Application Part

TDD—Time Division Duplex

TDM—Time Division Multiplexing

TDMA—Time Division Multiple Access

TDP—Trigger Detection Point (Intelligent Network)

TIA—Telecommunication Industry Association

TR—Technical Reference

TRAU—Transcoder and Rate Adaptor Unit

TINA—Telecommunication Information Networking Architecture

TMSI—Temporary Mobile Subscriber Identity

TTCN—Tree and Tabular Combined Notation

TUP—Telephony User Part

U - V - W

UDP—User Datagram Protocol

UE—User Equipment

Um—Air interface

UTRAN—UMTS Terrestrial Radio Access Network

UMTS—Universal Mobile Telecommunications System

UNI—User-to-Network Interface

UPA—User Part Available

UTRA—Universal Terrestrial Radio Access

UTRAN—Universal Terrestrial Radio Access Network

VC—Virtual Circuit

VLR—Visitor Location Register

VHE—Virtual Home Environment

VoIP—Voice over IP

VPN—Virtual Private Network

WATS—Wide-Area Telephone Service

W-CDMA—Wideband CDMA, Wideband Code Division Multiple Access

WiFi—Wireless Fidelity

WIN—Wireless Intelligent Network

WLAN—Wireless LAN

REFERENCES

1 ANSI T1.111-2001 Signaling System No. 7, Message Transfer Part.

2 ANSI T1.112-2001 Signaling System No. 7, Signaling Connection Control Part.

3 ANSI T1.113-2000 Signaling System No. 7, ISDN User Part.

4 ANSI T1.114-2000 Signaling System No. 7 (SS7)—Transaction Capability Application Part (TCAP).

5 ANSI T1.116-2000 Signaling System No. 7 (SS7) Operations, Maintenance, and Administrative Part (OMAP) (Revision and Consolidation of ANSI T1.115-1990).

6 ETSI ETR 256 ed.1 (1996–03) Integrated Services Digital Network (ISDN); Signalling System No. 7; Telephone User Part "Plus" (TUP+) [CEPT Recommendation T/S 43-02 E (1988)].

7 ETSI ETS 300 134 ed.1 (1992–12) Integrated Services Digital Network (ISDN); Signalling System No. 7; Transaction Capabilities Application Part (TCAP).

8 ETSI ETS 300 287 ed.1 (1993–10) Integrated Services Digital Network (ISDN); Signalling System No. 7; Transaction Capabilities Application Part (TCAP) version 2.

9 ETSI EN 300 008-1 V1.3.1 (2000–09) Integrated Services Digital Network (ISDN); Signalling System No. 7; Message Transfer Part (MTP) to support international interconnection; Part 1: Protocol specification [ITU-T Recommendations Q.701, Q.702, Q.703, Q.704, Q.705, Q.706, Q.707, and Q.708 modified].

10 ETSI ETS 300 009-1 ed.3 (1996–09) Integrated Services Digital Network (ISDN); Signalling System No. 7; Signalling Connection Control Part (SCCP) (connectionless and connection-oriented class 2) to support international interconnection; Part 1: Protocol specification [ITU-T Recommendations Q.711 to Q.714 and Q.716 (1993), modified].

11 ETSI ETS 300 008-2 ed.1 (1997–09) Integrated Services Digital Network (ISDN); Signalling System No. 7; Message Transfer Part (MTP) to support international interconnection; Part 2: Protocol Implementation Conformance Statement (PICS) proforma specification.

12 ETSI ETS 300 343 ed.1 (1994–07) Integrated Services Digital Network (ISDN); Signalling System No. 7; ISDN User Part (ISUP) version 1; Test specification.

13 ETSI EN 301 004-1 V1.1.3 (1998–02) Broadband Integrated Services Digital Network (B-ISDN); Signalling System No. 7; Message Transfer Part (MTP) level 3 functions and messages to support international interconnection; Part 1: Protocol specification [ITU-T Recommendation Q.2210 (1996), modified].

14 ETSI EN 301 004-2 V1.1.2 (2000–01) Broadband Integrated Services Digital Network (B-ISDN); Signalling System No. 7; Message Transfer Part (MTP) level 3 functions and messages to support international interconnection; Part 2: Protocol Implementation Conformance Statement (PICS) proforma specification.

15 ETSI EN 301 008 V1.1.2 (1998–05) Integrated Services Digital Network (ISDN); Signalling System No. 7; Signalling Connection Control Part (SCCP); Interoperability test specification.

16 ETSI ETS 300 599 ed.9 (2000–12) Digital cellular telecommunications system (Phase 2); Mobile Application Part (MAP) specification (GSM 09.02 version 4.19.1).

17 ETSI ETS 300 344 ed.1 (1994–08) Integrated Services Digital Network (ISDN); Signalling System No. 7; Transaction Capabilities Application Part (TCAP); Test specification.

18 ETSI EN 300 356-1 (2001–07) Integrated Services Digital Network (ISDN); Signalling System No. 7; ISDN User Part (ISUP) version 3 for the international interface; Part 1: Basic Services.

19 ETSI EN 300 356-2 (2001–07) Integrated Services Digital Network (ISDN); Signalling System No. 7; ISDN User Part (ISUP) version 3 for the international interface; Part 2: ISDN supplementary services.

20 ETSI EN 300 356-3 (2001–07) Integrated Services Digital Network (ISDN); Signalling System No. 7; ISDN User Part (ISUP) version 3 for the international interface; Part 3: Calling Line Identification Presentation (CLIP) supplementary service.

21 ETSI EN 300 356-4 (2001–07) Integrated Services Digital Network (ISDN); Signalling System No. 7; ISDN User Part (ISUP) version 3 for the international interface; Part 4: Calling Line Identification Restriction (CLIR) supplementary service.

22 ETSI EN 300 356-5 (2001–07) Integrated Services Digital Network (ISDN); Signalling System No. 7; ISDN User Part (ISUP) version 3 for the international interface; Part 5: Connected Line Identification Presentation (COLP) supplementary service.

23 ETSI EN 300 356-6 (2001–07) Integrated Services Digital Network (ISDN); Signalling System No. 7; ISDN User Part (ISUP) version 3 for the international interface; Part 6: Connected Line Identification Restriction (COLR) supplementary service.

24 ETSI EN 300 356-7 (2001–07) Integrated Services Digital Network (ISDN); Signalling System No. 7; ISDN User Part (ISUP) version 3 for the international interface; Part 7: Terminal Portability (TP) supplementary service.

25 ETSI EN 300 356-8 (2001–07) Integrated Services Digital Network (ISDN); Signalling System No. 7; ISDN User Part (ISUP) version 3 for the international interface; Part 8: User-to-User Signalling (UUS) supplementary service.

26 ETSI EN 300 356-9 (2001–07) Integrated Services Digital Network (ISDN); Signalling System No. 7; ISDN User Part (ISUP) version 3 for the international interface; Part 9: Closed User Group (CUG) supplementary service.

27 ETSI EN 300 356-10 (2001–07) Integrated Services Digital Network (ISDN); Signalling System No. 7; ISDN User Part (ISUP) version 3 for the international interface; Part 10: Subaddressing (SUB) supplementary service.

28 ETSI EN 300 356-11 (2001–07) Integrated Services Digital Network (ISDN); Signalling System No. 7; ISDN User Part (ISUP) version 4 for the international interface; Part 11: Malicious Call Identification (MCID) supplementary service.

29 ETSI EN 300 356-12 (2001–07) Integrated Services Digital Network (ISDN); Signalling System No. 7; ISDN User Part (ISUP) version 4 for the international interface; Part 12: Conference call, add-on (CONF) supplementary service.

30 ETSI EN 300 356-14 (2001–07) Integrated Services Digital Network (ISDN); Signalling System No. 7; ISDN User Part (ISUP) version 4 for the international interface; Part 14: Explicit Call Transfer (ECT) supplementary service.

31 ETSI EN 300 356-15 (2001–07) Integrated Services Digital Network (ISDN); Signalling System No. 7; ISDN User (ISUP) version 4 for the international interface; Part 15: Diversion supplementary services.

32 ETSI EN 300 356-16 (2001–07) Integrated Services Digital Network (ISDN); Signalling System No. 7; ISDN User Part (ISUP) version 4 for the international interface; Part 16: Call Hold (HOLD) supplementary service.

33 ETSI EN 300 356-17 (2001–07) Integrated Services Digital Network (ISDN); Signalling System No. 7; ISDN User Part (ISUP) version 4 for the international interface; Part 17: Call Waiting (CW) supplementary service.

34 ETSI EN 300 356-18 (2001–07) Integrated Services Digital Network (ISDN); Signalling System No. 7; ISDN User Part (ISUP) version 4 for the international interface; Part 18: Completion of Calls to Busy Subscriber (CCBS) supplementary service.

35 ETSI EN 300 356-19 (2001–07) Integrated Services Digital Network (ISDN); Signalling System No. 7; ISDN User Part (ISUP) version 4 for the international interface; Part 19: Three-party (3PTY) supplementary service.

36 BSI PD 6646:1999 PNO-ISC specification number 001. Use of Signalling System No. 7 Point Codes for Network Interconnect in the UK.

37 BSI PD 6638:2000 PNO-ISC specification number 003. C7 Interconnect Signalling Connection Control Part (SCCP).

38 BSI PD 6650:1999 PNO-ISC specification number 004. C7 Interconnect Transaction Capabilities (TC).

39 BSI PD 6639:2001 PNO-ISC specification number 005 C7. Interconnect Message Transfer Part (MTP).

40 BSI PD 6645:2000 PNO-ISC specification number 006. Interconnect User Part (IUP).

41 BSI PD 6623:2000 PNO-ISC specification number 007. ISDN User Part (ISUP).

42 BSI PD 6651:1999 IUP-ISUP Interworking.

43 BSI PD 6659:2000 PNO-ISC information document number 004. Proprietary Extensions to C7 Interconnect User Part (IUP).

44 BSI PD 6627:2001 PNO-ISC Information document number 007. UK Interconnect User of SCCP and MTP.

45 ITU-T Rec. E.164 (5/97) The international public telecommunication numbering plan.

46 ITU-T Rec. Q.7 (11/88) Signalling Systems to Be Used for International Automatic and Semi-Automatic Telephone Working.

47 ITU-T Rec. Q.9 (11/88) Vocabulary of Switching and Signalling Terms.

48 ITU-T Rec. Q.23 (11/88) Technical Features of Push-Button Telephone Sets.

49 ITU-T Rec. Q.701 (03/93) Functional Description of the Message Transfer Part (MTP) of Signalling System No. 7.

50 ITU-T Rec. Q.702 (11/88) Signalling Data Link.

51 ITU-T Rec. Q.703 (07/96) Signalling Link.

52 ITU-T Implementors' Guide (03/99) for Recommendation Q.703 (07/96).

53 ITU-T Rec. Q.704 (07/96) Signalling Network Functions and Messages.

54 ITU –T Implementors' Guide (03/99) for Recommendation Q.704 (07/96).

55 ITU-T Rec. Q.706 (03/93) Message Transfer Part Signalling Performance.

56 ITU-T Rec. Q.707, Testing and Maintenance.

57 ITU-T Rec. Q.708 (03/99) Assignment Procedures for International Signalling Point Codes.

58 ITU-T Rec. Q.711 (03/01) Functional Description of the Signalling Connection Control Part.

59 ITU-T REC. Q.712 (07/96) Definition and Function of Signalling Connection Control Part Messages.

60 ITU-T REC. Q.713 (03/01) Signalling Connection Control Part Formats and Codes.

61 ITU-T Recommendation Q.714 (05/01) Signalling Connection Control Part Procedures.

62 ITU-T Recommendation Q.715 (07/96) Signalling Connection Control Part User Guide.

63 ITU-T Rec. Q.716 (03/93) Signalling System No. 7—Signalling Connection Control Part (SCCP) Performance.

64 ITU-T Rec. Q.721 (11/88) Functional Description of the Signalling System No. 7 Telephone User Part (TUP).

65 ITU-T Rec. Q.722 General Function of Telephone Messages and Signals.

66 ITU-T Rec. Q.723 (11/88) Formats and Codes.

67 ITU-T Rec. Q.724 (11/88) Signalling Procedures.

68 ITU-T Rec. Q.725 (03/93) Signalling System No. 7—Signalling Performance in the Teletelephone Application.

69 ITU-T Rec. Q730 (12/99) ISDN User Part Supplementary Services.

70 ITU-T Rec. Q.750 (06/97) Overview of Signalling System No. 7 Management.

71 ITU-T Rec. Q.752 (06/97) Monitoring and Measurements for Signalling System No. 7 Networks.

72 ITU-T Rec. Q.753 (06/97) Signalling System No. 7 Management Functions MRVT, SRVT and CVT and Definition of the OMASE-USER.

73 ITU-T Rec. Q.754 (06/97) Signalling System No. 7 Management Application Service Element (ASE) Definitions.

74 ITU-T Rec. Q.756 (06/97) Guidebook to Operations, Maintenance and Administration Part [OMAP].

75 ITU-T Rec. Q.761 (12/99) Signalling system No. 7—ISDN User Part Functional Description.

76 ITU-T Rec. Q.762 (12/99) Signalling System No. 7—ISDN User Part General Functions of Messages and Signals.

77 ITU-T Rec. Q.763 (12/99) Signalling system No. 7—ISDN User Part Formats and Codes.

78 ITU-T Rec. Q.764 (12/99) Signalling System No. 7—ISDN User Part Signalling Procedures.

79 ITU-T Rec. Q.765 (05/98) Signalling System No. 7—Application Transport Mechanism.

80 ITU-T Rec. Q.766 (03/93) Performance Objectives in the Integrated Services Digital Network.

81 CCITT Rec. Q.767 Application of the ISDN User Part of CCITT Signalling System No. 7 for International ISDN Interconnections.

82 ITU-T Rec. Q.771 (06/97) Functional Description of Transaction Capabilities.

83 ITU-T Rec. Q.772 (06/97) Transaction Capabilities Information Element Definitions.

84 ITU-T Rec. Q.773 (06/97) Transaction Capabilities Formats and Encoding.

85 ITU-T Rec. Q.774 (06/97) Transaction Capabilities Procedures.

86 ITU-T Rec. Q.775 (06/97) Guidelines for Using Transaction Capabilities.

87 ITU-T Rec. Q.781 (04/02) MTP Level 2 Test Specification.

88 ITU-T Rec. Q.782 (04/02) MTP Level 3 Test Specification.

89 ITU-T Rec. Q.783 (11/88) TUP Test Specification.

90 ITU-T Rec. Q.784.1 (07/96) ISUP Basic Call Test Specification: Validation and Compatibility for ISUP'92 and Q.767 Protocols.

91 CCITT Rec. (09/91) Q.785 ISUP Protocol Test Specification for Supplementary Services.

92 ITU-T Rec. Q.786 (03/93) SCCP Test Specification.

93 ITU-T Rec. Q.787 (09/97) Transaction Capabilities [TC] Test Specification.

94 ITU-T Recommendation Q.1290 (1995) Glossary of terms used in the definition of intelligent networks.

95 ITU-T Recommendation Q.1400 (1993) Architecture framework for the development of signalling and OA&M protocols using OSI concepts.

96 ITU-T Rec. Q.1901 (06/00) Bearer independent call control protocol.

97 ITU-T Rec. Q.2140 (02/95) B-ISDN ATM Adaptation Layer—Service Specific Coordination Function for Signalling at the Network Node Interface (SSCF at NNI).

98 ITU-T Rec. Q.2210 (07/96) Message Transfer Part Level 3 Functions and Messages Using the Services of ITU-T Recommendation Q.2140.

99 CCITT Recommendation X.650 (1992) Open Systems Interconnections (OSI)— Reference model for naming and addressing.

100 ITU-T Recommendation X.200 (1994) Information technology—Open Systems Interconnection—Basic reference model: The basic model.

101 ITU-T Recommendation X.213 (1995) Information technology—Open Systems Interconnection—Network service definition.

102 Van Bosse, J.G., *Signaling in Telecommunications Networks*. New York, New York; Wiley and Sons, 1998..

103 Manterfield, R. *Telecommunications Signalling*. New York, New York; IEEE Publishing, 1999.

104 Rosenbaum, R. "Secrets of the Little Blue Box. "*Esquire*," October 1971.

105 3G TS 22.016: "International Mobile station Equipment Identities (IMEI)."

106 3G TS 23.003: "Numbering, addressing, and identification."

107 GSM 02.16: "Digital cellular telecommunications system (Phase 2+); International Mobile station Equipment Identities (IMEI)."

108 Long, J. "Crackdown on Telemarketers Equals Risk, Opportunity for Telcos." *Phone+*, December 2, 2002.

109 "SS7 Makes the Switch to Regular Cable," Communication News Online Edition, 10/2000, http://www.comnews.com.

110 Hatfield, S. "American Idolatry," The Guardian, XXNEED DATEXXXX.

111 ITU-T Recommendation Q.700 (03/1993) Introduction to CCITT Signalling System No. 7.

112 ANSI T1.110-1999 Signaling System No. 7, general information.

113 ITU-T Recommendation Q.118 (09/97) Abnormal conditions—Special release arrangements.

114 Telcordia GR-246-CORE (12/02) Specification of Signalling System No 7.

115 ITU-T Recommendation E.733 (11/98) Methods for Dimensioning Resources in Signalling System No. 7 networks.

116 3GPP Mobile Application Part (MAP) Specification; (Release 5). TS 29.002 V5.1.0 (2002–03).

117 ETSI Digital Cellular Telecommunications System (Phase 2); Mobile Application Part (MAP) specification (GSM 09.02 version 4.19). ETS 300-599.

118   T1 Mobile Application Part (MAP) Specification. T1.3GPP.29.120V310.

119 Déchaux, C. and Scheller, R. "What Are GSM and DCS." *Electrical Communication*, 2nd Quarter, 1993.

120 Schulzrinne, H. et. al. "RTP: A Transport Protocol for Real-Time Applications," RFC1889.

121 Cuervo F., et. al. "Megaco Protocol Version 1.0", RFC3015.

122 ITU-T Recommendataion H.248 (05/2002), Gateway Control Protocol: Version 2.

123 Arango, M. et. al. "Media Gateway Control Protocol (MGCP) Version 1.0," RFC2705, 10/1999.

124 Rosenberg, J. et. al. "SIP: Session Initiation Protocol", RFC3261, 6/2002.

125 ITU-T Recommendation H.323 (11/2000), Packet-Based Multimedia Communication Systems.

126 Ong, L. et al. "Framework Architecture for Signaling Transport," RFC2791, 7/2000.

127 Postel, J. "Internet Protocol", RFC791, 9/1981.

128 Postel, J. "User Datagram Protocol," RFC768, 9/1980.

129 Postel, J. "Transmission Control Protocol," RFC793, 9/1981.

130 Seth, T. et. al. "Performance Requirements for Signaling in Internet Telephony", IETF (work in progress).

131 Stewart, R. et. al. "Stream Control Transmission Protocol," RFC2790, 3/2000.

132 Stone, J. et. al. "Stream Control Transmission Protocol (SCTP) Checksum Change," RFC3309, 9/2000.

133 Stewart, R. et. al. "Stream Control Transmission Protocol (SCTP) Implementers Guide," IETF (work in progress).

134 Stewart, R. et. al. "Sockets API Extensions for Stream Control Transmission Protocol (SCTP)," IETF (work in progress).

135 Stewart, R. et. al. "Stream Control Transmission Protocol (SCTP) Dynamic Address Reconfiguration," IETF (work in progress).

136 Stewart, R. et. al. "SCTP Partial Reliability," IETF (work in progress).

137 Sidebottom, G. et. al. "Signaling System 7 (SS7) Message Transfer Part 3 (MTP3)—User Adaptation Layer," RFC3332, 9/2002.

138 Balbas-Pastor, J. and Morneault, K. "M3UA Implementers Guide," IETF (work in progress).

139 Loughney, J. et. al. "Signalling Connection Control Part User Adaptation Layer (SUA)," IETF (work in progress).

140 Morneault, K. et. al. "Signaling System 7 (SS7) Message Transfer Part 2 (MTP2)—User Adaptation Layer," RFC3331, 9/2002.

141 George, T. et. al. "SS7 MTP2-User Peer-to-Peer Adaptation Layer," IETF (work in progress).

142 Morneault, K. et. al. "ISDN Q.921-User Adaptation Layer," RFC3057, 2/2001.

143 Morneault, K. et. al. "IUA (RFC 3057) Implementers Guide," IETF (work in progress).

144 Mukundan, R. et. al. "DPNSS/DASS 2 Extensions to the IUA Protocol," IETF (work in progress).

145 Weilandt, E. et. al. "V5.2-User Adaptation Layer (V5UA)," IETF (work in progress).

146 Mukundan, R. and Morneault, K. "GR-303 Extensions to the IUA Protocol," IETF (work in progress).

147 Sprague, D. et. al. "Tekelec's Transport Adapter Layer Interface," RFC3094, 4/2001.

148 Partridge, C. et. al. "Version 2 of the Reliable Data Protocol (RDP)," RFC1151, 4/1990.

149 Velten, D. et. al. "Reliable Data Protocol," RFC908, 7/1984.

150 Vemuri, A. and Peterson, J. "Session Initiation Protocol for Telephones (SIP-T): Context and Architectures," RFC3372, 9/2002.

151 Donovan, S. "The SIP INFO Method," RFC2976, 9/2002.

152 Zimmerer, E. et al. "MIME Media Types for ISUP and QSIG Objects," RFC3204, 12/2001.

153 TTC recommendation JT-Q704 (04/92), Message Transfer Part Signalling Network Functions.

INDEX

Numerics

A

N

V

W-X-Y-Z

Cisco Press

Learning is serious business.

Invest wisely.

Cisco Press

CISCO CERTIFICATION SELF-STUDY
#1 BEST-SELLING TITLES FROM CCNA® TO CCIE®

Look for Cisco Press Certification Self-Study resources at your favorite bookseller

Learn the test topics with **Self-Study Guides**

Gain hands-on experience with **Practical Studies** books

Prepare for the exam with **Exam Certification Guides**

Practice testing skills and build confidence with **Flash Cards and Exam Practice Packs**

Visit **www.ciscopress.com/series** to learn more about the Certification Self-Study product family and associated series.

Learning is serious business.
Invest wisely.

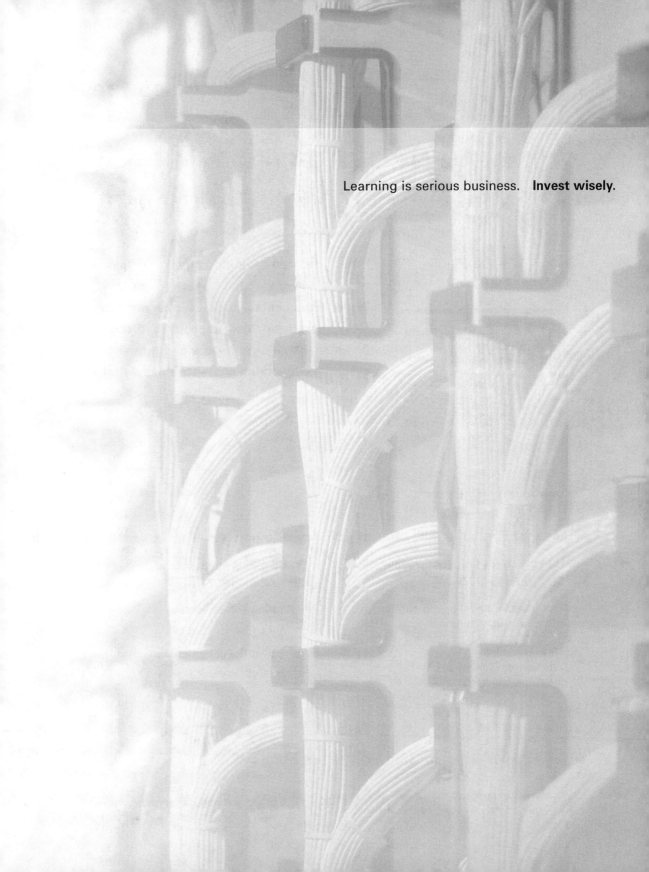

Learning is serious business.   **Invest wisely.**

DISCUSS

NETWORKING PRODUCTS AND TECHNOLOGIES WITH CISCO EXPERTS AND NETWORKING PROFESSIONALS WORLDWIDE

VISIT NETWORKING PROFESSIONALS
A CISCO ONLINE COMMUNITY
WWW.CISCO.COM/GO/DISCUSS

CISCO SYSTEMS

THIS IS THE POWER OF THE NETWORK. now.

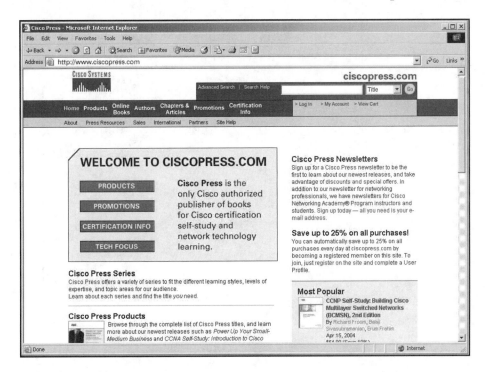
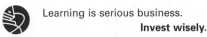

ciscopress.com

SEARCH THOUSANDS OF BOOKS FROM LEADING PUBLISHERS

Safari® Bookshelf is a searchable electronic reference library for IT professionals that features more than 2,000 titles from technical publishers, including Cisco Press.

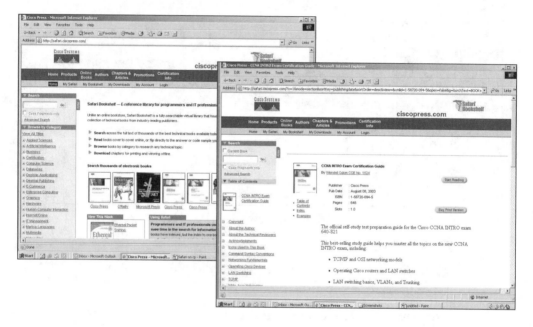

With Safari Bookshelf you can

- **Search** the full text of thousands of technical books, including more than 70 Cisco Press titles from authors such as Wendell Odom, Jeff Doyle, Bill Parkhurst, Sam Halabi, and Karl Solie.

- **Read** the books on My Bookshelf from cover to cover, or just flip to the information you need.

- **Browse** books by category to research any technical topic.

- **Download** chapters for printing and viewing offline.

With a customized library, you'll have access to your books when and where you need them—and all you need is a user name and password.

TRY SAFARI BOOKSHELF FREE FOR 14 DAYS!

You can sign up to get a 10-slot Bookshelf free for the first 14 days.
Visit **http://safari.ciscopress.com** to register.

Cisco Press

Learning is serious business.

Invest wisely.

Stay updated in a fast changing market.

Tektronix provides telecom professionals with FREE wireless protocol information.

Tektronix has shaped tomorrow for over 50 years. We provide signaling test and monitoring equipment to the world's leading equipment manufacturers and service providers.
Get the latest at www.tektronix.com/wp.

– Design, deployment and monitoring solutions

– Wireless technology and test information

– Register to view instructional web seminars

– Subscribe to our free quarterly technology newsletters

Tektronix®

Enabling Innovation